# Royalty for Commoners

# Royalty
## *for*
# *Commoners*

The Complete Known Lineage of John of Gaunt,
Son of Edward III, King of England,
and Queen Philippa

Roderick W. Stuart

*Fourth Edition*

First Edition, 1988
Second Edition, 1992
Revised Second Edition, 1995
Third Edition, 1998
Fourth Edition, 2002
Second printing of the Fourth Edition, 2006
Published by Genealogical Publishing Co., Inc.
3600 Clipper Mill Rd., Suite 260
Baltimore, Maryland 21211
Library of Congress Catalogue Card Number 2001135382
International Standard Book Number 0-8063-1687-X
*Made in the United States of America*

# Contents

# Preface

*Royalty for Commoners,* in print since 1988, has been the only work in any language comprising the complete known genealogy of John of Gaunt, son of King Edward III and Queen Philippa of England.

The importance of this work is that for the past fourteen years any commoner who can connect his or her family lineage to that of John of Gaunt (or, of course, his siblings) can share the same basic royal heritage as the most noble knight—the complete heritage—not just the Plantagenet ascent. This is the only lineage through which a commoner can enter the domain of European royalty, though one might enter the lineage at any number of points. Even Queen Elizabeth (by no means a commoner!) has this descent.

*Royalty for Commoners,* a work in progress for over thirty years, has tried to overcome the criticisms of similar works preceding it. There are more than 6,300 names, with some duplication, in the direct line, listed in the General Index. People living today can, we know, extend the lineage so that family genealogies of some Americans and Europeans can run to five or six digits, with numerous researchers easily reaching the 30,000 mark. The author's American heritage adds more than 1,500 names in the direct line and connects with John of Gaunt in several places.

The General Index to this edition includes every name in the book along with the names of spouses where known. While it is not perfect, it is more useful than the indices of most major genealogical works in print. The Title Index, for the first time, includes minor titles (such as Sire).

The more than 930 books and periodicals listed in the Bibliography, and directly used in support of the work, comprise, for the most part, the writings of the greatest scholars in all countries and all periods. The older works stem from the Middle Ages and earlier, to the latest writings of the past few years.

More than a thousand additional works were consulted but usually they only reinforced the works listed in the Bibliography.

One final statement: the author didn't do it alone and I owe thanks to many people who made suggestions of importance.

The publication of this work has been a fulfilling experience. It is hoped that the reader will find it just as rewarding.

Roderick W. Stuart
1550 Rimpau Avenue, No. 55
Corona, CA 92881-3234

# Important Notes on Using This Book

## GENEALOGY SECTION

1. Abbreviations are standard: b. = birth; d. = death; md = married; c = about (c1350 = about 1350); liv = known to have been living in those years but probably not his entire life span; occ = "occurs" indicating that information about the person occurs in contemporary sources such as birth, death, marriage and land records. Since these records were generated during the person's lifetime, they lend credibility to the entries.

2. The generation numbering system is arbitrary. Generation 1 would be a middle-aged person living near the end of the twentieth century. By starting with someone living today, and working backwards into the past, the numbering system cannot be disturbed by adding or deleting names as new information comes to light. John of Gaunt appears as Generation 21. Most middle-aged persons living today will be 20 generations away from John of Gaunt and can connect their own lineage at this point. There are other systems: von Redlich, in his *Pedigrees of Some of the Emperor Charlemagne's Descendants,* uses no numbering system at all. The Seventh Edition of Weis' *Ancestral Roots of Certain American Colonists* numbers from the oldest generation to the youngest. Just the opposite of my system.

3. Lines, of which there are 475, are arbitrary divisions of John of Gaunt's ancestry. They were developed by extending the lines as they appear on standard 31-name pedigree charts until they either terminate or begin a new family (often that of a person's spouse). Some lines could be combined but this would only create another arbitrary division. The lines appear in no particular order, but are carefully cross-referenced so the lack of order is unimportant.

4. Sources (formerly "References" and "Authorities") are placed at the end of each line. Sources cited appear to me to be the best of the many works available to me. Many sources have been changed from the earlier editions in order to cite newer and more accurate works, or to drop works that were more accessible in earlier years when I lived in Massachusetts. They are coded to save space. Refer to the Bibliography section (below) for interpretation of the coding system.

5. Numbers in parentheses, such as "(2-32)" are finding aids and indicate the line number and generation number of the entry. To find (2-32), the number assigned to Geoffrey, Count in the Gatinais, merely turn to Line 2, Generation 32 of the Genealogy section of the book.

ix

## BIBLIOGRAPHY SECTION

1. Sources (references, authorities) follow each individual line. For brevity, the entries are coded. In this Fourth Edition, some entries note the particular generation covered by the source. For example, in Line 3, ES VI 1978 covers only Generation 30-34. Renn, H 1941 covers the entire line. Refer to the first two paragraphs of the Bibliography for a complete explanation of the coding system.

2. The Bibliography includes only works actually cited in the Genealogy section of the book. Numerous other sources were consulted but their inclusion in the bibliography was unwarranted. Sources cited in the earlier editions are usually correct and were seldom dropped because they were faulty.

## GENERAL INDEX

1. Since a large proportion of people named in this book have no surnames, the Index is alphabetical by first name. Because a surname would be useless without a first name, this should be no inconvenience. John of Gaunt is alphabetized as "John of Gaunt" rather than, for instance, "Gaunt, John of."

2. The General Index covers all of the names in the book that can be identified. Sometimes there is more than one entry for a name.

3. Index numbers refer to Lines not Pages.

4. Names of people sometimes have several variants. I have tried to use the names as they generally appear in books and periodicals. These variants are neither right nor wrong. They are merely different. For instance, Maud and Matilda are usually (but not always) interchangeable. Variants include Mathilda, Matilde, Mechtild and Mechtilde. When you use the Index, look up variants if you can't find the name for which you are searching. Knowing what a person was called in his lifetime, or the way he signed his name on documents, is helpful.

5. The person numbering system (Henry I, Henry II, Henry III) is a minor problem and I use numbers as they appear in the works cited. A person might be one number for a certain title and another number for another title (The Emperor of the West, Frederick III was, as King of Germany, Frederick I). I settled for what seemed reasonable. Many title numbers were assigned after the fact by historians and were never used by the persons themselves. Rarely did the first person using a name call himself "the First." The first Queen Elizabeth was never called Elizabeth I until the current Queen Elizabeth called herself Elizabeth II. Also, genealogists assign numbers in parentheses (II) to help sort out people who are unnumbered.

*Royalty for Commoners*

# Genealogy

## LINE 1

25. **Henry III** (2-25), King of England, md **Eleanor of Provence** (54-25).

24. **Edward I**, Duke of Aquitaine, 1272; King of England, 1272–1307, called "Longshanks;" b. 17 June 1239, Westminster, London, England; d. 8 July 1307, Burgh-on-Sands, Cumberland; crowned 19 Aug 1272; bur Westminster Abbey; md (1) 18 Oct 1254, Burgos, Spain, **Eleanor of Castile** (52-24) (mother of Gen. 23 below); d. 29 Nov 1290; bur Westminster Abbey. Their tombs can be viewed today. He md (2) 10 Sept 1299, Marguerite of France, Princess of France.

23. **Edward II**, King of England, 1307–1327; first English Prince of Wales, 1301; b. 25 Apr 1284, Caernarvon Castle, Caernarvon, Wales; murdered 21 Sept 1327, Berkeley Castle, near Gloucester; bur Gloucester Cathedral where his tomb may be viewed today; md 25 Jan 1308, Boulogne, Pas-de-Calais, France, **Isabella** (51-23), Princess of France.

22. **Edward III**, King of England, 1327–1377; b. 13 Nov 1312, Windsor Castle, Berkshire, England; d. 21 June 1377; bur Westminster Abbey, London, where his tomb may be viewed today with that of his wife; md 24 Jan 1328, York, **Philippa of Hainault** (50-22).

21. **John of Gaunt**, Prince of England, Duke of Lancaster, Earl of Richmond, Titular King of Castile and Leon, Knight of the Garter; b. March 1340, Bavon Abbey, Ghent, Flanders; d. 3 Feb 1399; md (1) 19 May 1359, Blanche of Lancaster; md (2) June 1371, Constance, dau of Pedro "the Cruel," King of Castile; md (3) 13 Jan 1396, his longtime mistress, **Katherine Roet**, widow of Sir Hugh Swynford; Katherine was b. 1350; d. 10 May 1403; bur Lincoln Cathedral; her father was Sir **Paon** (Payne) **Roet**, Guienne King of Arms; a Gascon; her sister Philippa md Geoffrey Chaucer, the poet.

Sources: Armitage-Smith, S. 1914; Baildon, W. 1926; Banfield, A. 1990; Barrow, C. 1995: Bevan, B. 1992; Brady, R. 1998; Brooke, C. 1969; Cokayne, G. 1959, II:153; V:320, 736 and chart; VII:415; ES, II 1984, 83–84 (Gen. 21-25); Goodman, A. 1992; Lee, M. 1995; Moriarty, G.1985, 2 (Gen. 21-25); Parsons, J. 1990; Prestwich, M. 1981; Stone, D. 1995.

46. **N.N.** (perhaps Bodilon), an Austrasian, Neustrian or Burgundian nobleman, said to descend from St. **Liutwin** (330-34) Count and Bishop of Treves. **N.N.** md **Sigrada** (Sigree) (236-44).

45. **Guerin** (Warin, Warinus), Count of Poitiers; d. 677; md **Kunza** (Gunza) (358-45), b. 596; d. 690; dau of St. **Clodoule**, Bishop of Metz; whose parents were **St. Arnulf** (171-46), Bishop of Metz, and **Dode** (Clothilde, Oda).

44. **Lambert of Hesbaye** (352-44), occ in Hesbaye, 706-725.

43. **Robert**, Count of Hesbaye; b. c700; liv 750; md **Williswinda**, dau **Alleaume**.

42. **Guerin** (same as 101-41, 345-44), Count in the Thurgovie, 754-772; d. 20 May 772; md **Adelindis**.

41. **Bouchard** "the Constable," Minur Dominicur in Corsica.

40. **Aubri** "the Burgundian," Count of Fezensac.

39. **Bouchard**, Prefect of the Royal Hunt.

38. **N.N.** (perhaps Geoffrey).

37. **Aubri** "Dux," Vicomte d'Orleans; living in 886 when he witnessed the charter of Odo, Abbot of St. Martin.

36. **Geoffrey**, Vicomte d'Orleans, Count in the Gatinais; occ 933-942; witnessed the charter of Hugh the Great of France, 939.

35. **Aubri**, Count in the Gatinais, Vicomte d'Orleans; occ 957-966.

34. **Geoffrey**, Count in the Gatinais; occ 975-987.

33. **Aubri**, Count in the Gatinais; occ 990.

32. **Geoffrey** "Ferreol," Count in the Gatinais and Château-Landon; liv 990; md **Beatrice of Macon** (92-32).

31. **Geoffrey II** "Ferreol," C of Château-Landon, Count in the Gatinais; b. c1004; d. 1043/1046; md 1035, **Ermengarde of Anjou** (91-31).

30. **Fulk IV** "Rechin," Count of Anjou; chronicler of the counts of Anjou; b. 1043; d. 14 Apr 1109; md (5) c1090, **Bertrade de Montfort** (90-28).

29. **Fulk V** "le Jeune" (the younger), Count of Anjou, King of Jerusalem, 1131; Crusader; b. 1092; d. 10 Nov 1143 at Acre; bur Church of the Holy Sepulcher, Jerusalem; md (1) c1108, **Erembourge** (313-29) (mother of Gen. 28), heiress of Maine; md (2) 2 June 1129, **Melisende de Rethel**, d. 11 Sept 1161, dau of **Baldwin II** (145-30), King of Jerusalem.

28. **Geoffrey V Plantagenet**, Duke of Normandy, Count of Anjou; b. 24 Nov 1113, Anjou, France; d. Château Eure-et-Loire, France; md 22 May 1127, **Matilda** (89-28), Princess of England and Empress of Germany.

27. **Henry II** "Curt Mantel," Duke of Normandy, Count of Maine and Anjou, King of England, 1154-1189; b. 5 Mar 1133, le Mans, Sarthe, France; d. 6 July 1189, Chinon, Indre-et-Loire, France; bur at Fontevrault; md 18 May 1152, Bordeaux, Gironde, France, **Eleanor of Aquitaine** (88-29).

26. **John** "Lackland," King of England, 1199–1216; b. 24 Dec 1167, Beaumont Palace, Oxford, England; d. 19 Oct 1216, Newark, Nottingham; bur Worcester Cathedral; md (1) 29 Aug 1189, Isabella of Gloucester (divorced); md (2) 24 Aug 1200, Bordeaux, Gironde, France, **Isabella of Angoulême** (87-26).

25. **Henry III** (1-25), King of England, 1216–1272; b. 1 Oct 1207, Winchester, Hampshire; d. 16 Nov 1272, Westminster, London; bur Westminster Abbey, where his altar-tomb and that of his wife may be seen today; md 14 Jan 1236, Canterbury, **Eleanor of Provence** (1-25, 54-25).

Sources: Archern, K. 1973; Brook, C. 1969; Cokayne, G. 1959, V:736; VI :appendix D, 214; Conder, C. 1978; ES, II 1984:82–83 (Gen. 25–31); Lee, M. 1995; Mackensie, A. 1937; Mayer, H. 1978; Moriarty, G.1985, 1–2 (Gen. 25–46); Munro, D. 1935; Prawler, J. 1952; Prawler, J. 1972; Prawler, J. 1980; Riley-Smith, J. 1973; Settipani, C. 1997b; Turner, R. 1994.

## LINE 3

34. **Siegfried** (316-36, 353-36), Count of Luxemburg and in the Moselgau, md **Hedwig**, a Saxon, perhaps dau of **Eberhard IV** (33-35,202-37), Count in Alsace, and **Luitgarde of Trier.**

33. **Frederick**, Count in the Moselgau, Seigneur of Gleiberg; d. 6 Oct 1019; md after 985, **N.N. von Gleiberg**, dau of **Heribert** (351-36), Count in the Wetterau, and **Ermentrude of Avalgau.**

32. **Giselbert I** (391-32), Count of Luxemburg, Salm and Longwy; b. c1005; d. 14 Aug 1059.

31. **Conrad I**, Count of Luxemburg, advocate of St. Maximin in Malmedy; b. c1040; d. 8 Aug 1086 returning from a pilgrimage to Jerusalem; md c1070, **Clemence of Poitou** (same as 119-31), heiress of Longwy and Blieskastel; b. 1060; d. after 1129; dau of **Count William V.**

30. **Ermesinde of Luxemburg**, heiress of Luxemburg and Longwy; b. c1075; d. 1141; md (2) **Godfrey** (Geoffrey) (126-30), Count of Dagsburg and Namur.

Sources: ES, VI 1978:128 (Gen. 30–34); Moriarty, G.1985, 22 (Gen. 32–34); 36, 128, 129 (Gen. 32–34); Renn, H. 1941; Vannerus, J. 1946, vol. 25, pt. 2 (1946/7), 801–858.

## LINE 4

33. **Landry**, Seigneur de Baugency; liv c1000, (perhaps father of Gen. 32 says Turton, W. 1984, 175.

32. **Lancelin I** (313-32), Seigneur de Baugency in the Orleannaise; d. 1051/1060. *NOTE: Turton, W. 1984 makes **Paula du Maine** (357-31) the wife of Lancelin I, whereas she is actually his daughter-in-law, the wife of his son, **Jean** (313-31). Her ancestry is carried in Line 357.*

31. **Lancelin II**, Seigneur de Baugency, d. 1098; md **Alberga.**

30. **Raoul** (Réné) I, Seigneur de Baugency; d. 1130; md **Mathilda de Vermandois; b.** c1080; dau of **Hugh Magnus de Crepi** (143-30), Count of Vermandois, and **Adelaide de Vermandois** (239-30).

29. **Agnes de Baugency**, b. c1108; md 1132, **Engelram II** (37-29), Sire de Coucy, etc.

Sources: Blass, R. 1939, II:239, 247, 252; Brandenburg, E. 1935, VII 1979: 80 (Gen. 30–31); ES XIII 1990:45 (Gen. 29-32); Latouche, R. 1959b; Moriarty, G.1985, 197 (Gen. 29–31); Winkhaus, E. 1953.

## LINE 5

32. **Guy I de Montlhery** (145-31,241-32), Seigneur de Montlhery; md **Hodierne de Gometz** (145,31,241-32).

31. **Guy II** "the Red," Sire de Montlhery, Count of Rochefort-en-Yvelines, Lord of Chateaufort, Seneschal of France, Seigneur of Fornay and Gomez; d. 1108; md **Adelaide de Crecy**, heiress of Crecy, d. after 1104.

30. **Melisende de Crecy**, d. after 1147; md **Thomas de Coucy** (37-30), Sire de Coucy and Merle, Count of Amiens.

Sources: Blass, R. 1939, II:241, 244, 255; Bournazel, 32+, 46; ES III 1989:624 (Gen. 31, 32); ES, VII 1979:80 (Gen. 30–31); Moriarty, G.1985, 63 (Gen. 31–32); Moutie, A. 1960's; Newman, W. 1971, 189; Turton, W. 1984; Winkhaus, E. 1953.

## LINE 6

34. **Giselbert** (145-32,170-33), Count of Roucy; md **N.N. de Poitiers**.

33. **Lietaud [1]**, Seigneur de Marle, c1000.

32. **Lietaud [II]**, Seigneur de Marle.

31. **Adele** (Ada) **de Roucy**, heiress of Marle, md **Engelram de Coucy** (37-31), Seigneur de Boves and de Coucy, Count of Amiens.

Sources: Blass, R. 1939, II:246; Brandenburg, E. 1935; Chaume.0, I:465n2, 533; ES, VII 1979:80 (Gen. 31–32); Florival, R. 1907, 175–182 (Gen. 31–34); Moranville, 83:1–42 (Gen. 31–34); Moriarty, G.1985, 50 (Gen. 31–34).

## LINE 7

34. **Henry von Schweinfurt**, Margrave in the Nordgau (47-35,270-35), md **Gerberga of Henneburg** (102-35, 307-32).

33. **Otto III von Schweinfurt**, Duke of Swabia, md **Ermengarde**, dau of **Odalrico Manfredo II** ( 32-31, 47-34,93-33, 315-34), and **Bertha of Este** (93-33).

32. **Gisela von Schweinfurt**, heiress of the lordship of Plassenburg; d. 2 Feb 1100; md **Berthold III**, Count of Andechs, d. 1098; son of **Berthold II** (64-33), Count in the Upper Isar, and wife **N.N. von Hohenwart**.

31. **Berthold IV**, Count of Diessen, Strain and Plassenburg. He called

4

himself the ruler of the Castle of Andechs on Ammersea; established the family seat at Andechs, 1127; b. 1096/1098; d. 27 June 1151; md **Sophia of Istria** (10-31), heiress of the dukedom of Meran.

    30. **Berthold V**, Count of Andechs, Innsbruch and Wolfratschausen; Margrave of Istria; b. 1122/23; d. c1188; bur at Diessen; md (her 1st), 1152, **Hedwig von Formbach-Putten** (9-30), heiress of the lordship of Newburg; d. 16 July 1174.

    29. **Berthold VI**, Crusader, Count of Andechs, Margrave of Istria; Duke of Croatia, Dalmatia, and of the Coast Meran (not the Tyrol town); b. c1152; d. 12 Aug 1204; md 1170, **Agnes von Groitzsch-Rochlitz** (8-29).

    28. **Gertrude von Meran**, d. 8 Sept 1213; md (1) before 1203, **Andrew II** (51-27), King of Hungary, 1205–1235.

    Sources: ES I.1 1997; ES, II 1984: 155 (Gen. 28–29); II 1984:99 (Gen. 30); I 1980:36 (Gen. 31–33); Isenburg, W. 1953, Part i, table 82; Moriarty, G.1985, 198 (Gen. 28–32); 57, 163 (Gen. 32–33).

## LINE 8

    33. **Dietrich II von Wettin** (210-35), Count of Brehna; md c1016, **Mathilda von Meissen** (212-35).

    32. **Thiemo I**, Count of Brehna, Wettin and of Kostritz; co-founder of Naumburg Cathedral; d. c1091; bur at Naumburg; md **Ida von Northeim**, dau of **Otto I von Northeim** (26-31) and **Richenza of Swabia** (26-31), dau of **Otto**, Duke of Swabia.

    31. **Konrad** "the Great," Count of Brehna and Camburg, Margrave of Meissen and Lausitz, Count in the Groitsch-Rochlitz; divided his lands in 1156 among his five sons and became a monk in the monastery of Petersburg near Halle; b. 1098; d. 5 Feb 1157 at Petersburg monastery, Halle; md before 1119, **Luitgard von Ravenstein**; d. 19 June 1145 in the monastery of Gerbstedt; dau of **Albert von Ravenstein**, Count of Ravenstein.

    30. **Dedo V** "the Strong," Count in the Groitzsch-Rochlitz and of Eilenburg, Margrave of Niederlausitz; heir to the Castle of Groitzsch; b. 1142; d. 16 Aug 1190; md before 1160, **Mathilde von Heinsberg** (11-30).

    29. **Agnes von Groitzsch-Rochlitz**, d. 25 Mar 1195; md **Berthold VI** (7-29), Count of Andechs, etc.

    Sources: Blass, R. 1939, II:292, 293; Brandenburg, E. 1935; Dungern, O. von 1931; ES I 1980::41 (Gen. 29–33); ES VIII 1980:132 (Gen. 32); Isenburg, W. 1953; Moriarty, G.1985, 179, 202, 203 (Gen. 29–32); 95–97 (Gen. 32–33); Winkhaus, E. 1953, E. 1953.

## LINE 9

    34. **Thiemo I (Dietmar)** (41-34), Count in Schweinachgau, advocate of Monastery of St. Emmerson, 1009-1049; d. 2 Mar c1050.

33. **Thiemo** (Dietmar) II, Count in the Quinziggau; b. c1015; killed in Bohemia, 28 Aug 1040.

32. **Ecbert I**, Count in the Quinziggau; d. (prob 24 Aug) 1109; md **Mathilda von Lamback-Puttin**, heiress of Lambeck-Puttin and the countship on the Inn; d. c1106; dau of **Godfrey** (13-32), Count of Puttin and Margrave of the Carinthian Mark.

31. **Eckbert II**, Count of Formbach-Puttin and Newburg; d. before 1140; md before 1134, **Wilibirg von Steirermark** (12-31).

30. **Hedwig von Formbach-Puttin**, heiress of the lordship of Newburg; d. 16 July 1174; md 1152, **Berthold V** (7-30), Count of Andechs, Diessen, etc.

Sources: Bernardi, W. 1874, 810–811; Blass, R. 1939, II:290–293; Brandenburg, E. 1935; ES XVI:37; Isaenburg, W. 1932; Meyer, T. 1933; Moriarty, G.1985, 199 (Gen. 30–33); Trotter, K. 1933, 31; Winkhaus, E. 1953.

## LINE 10

33. **Udalrich I** (281-30), Margrave of Carniola and Istria; md **Sophia**, Princess of Hungary; dau of **Bela I** (51-33), King of Hungary, and **Rixa** (75-33), Princess of Poland.

32. **Poppo II**, Margrave of Istria; d. c1095; md **Richilda** (Richgard) (mother of Gen. 31), dau of **Engelbert I von Sponheim** (228-32), Count in the Levanthal and Ortemburg; who md **Hedwig**, dau of **Bernard von Flinsbach** and wife **Cecilia**.

31. **Sophia of Istria**, heiress of the dukedom of Meran; d. 6 Sept 1128; md (his 1st) **Berthold IV** (7-31), Count of Diessen.

Sources: Blass, R. 1939, II:283, 293; Brandenburg, E. 1935; ES, I 1980:36 (31–32); Isenburg, W. 1953, pt. i, table 8, 26a; Meyer, T. 1933; Moriarty, G.1985, 140, 169 (Gen. 33); 120, 188, 198 (Gen. 31, 32); Winkhaus, E. 1953, 423.

## LINE 11

34. **Gerard Flamens** (119-33), Count of Teisterbant.

33. **Dietrich Flamens** (119-32), Count in the Velue; d. 1082.

32. **Goswin I**, Lord of Heinsberg; b. c1060; d. 1 Apr 1128; md c1085/90, **Oda von Walbeck** (15-32), who as a widow founded, c1140, the monastery of Heinsberg.

31. **Goswin II**, Lord of Heinsberg, advocate of Maersen, Count of Heinsberg and Falkenburg; b. 1090/1100; d. c1168; md **Aleidis von Sommerschenburg** (14-31).

30. **Mathilde von Heinsberg**, d. 10 Jan 1189; md before 1160, **Dedo V** (8-30), Count of Groitzsch-Rochlitz, etc.

Sources: ES, I 1980:41 (30–31); ES VII 1979:134 (32); ES XVIII 1998; Hoffman, W. 1950; Moriarty, G.1985, 203 (Gen. 30–32); 127 (Gen. 32–

33); Winkhaus, E. 1950.

## LINE 12

39. **Aubert**, Count of Bavaria.
38. **Ottokar I** (48-38), Count in Carinthia; d. Aug 907; md **N.N.**, dau of **Aribo** (48-39), Count in the Traungau.
37. **Ottokar II**, Count in the Chiemgau, liv 923.
36. **Ottokar III**, Count in the Chiemgau, liv 951–976; d. soon after 976; md **N.N.**, prob a sister of **Arnold I**, Count in the Traungau, (13-34).
35. **Arnulf**, Count in the Chiemgau, liv 980.
34. **Ottokar V**, Count in the Chiemgau and advocate of Traunkirchen; d. c1020; md **N.N. von Wels-Lambach**, dau of **Arnold II**, Count of Wels-Lambach and in the Chiemgau, 1056.
33. **Ottokar VI**, Count in the Chiemgau, d. Rome, 1075; md (2) **Wilibirg von Eppenstein** (229-33).
32. **Ottokar VII**, Count in the Chiemgau, and as Ottokar IV, Margrave of Styria; d. 28 Nov 1122; md before 1082, **Elizabeth of Austria**, d. 16 Oct 1107/1114; dau of **Leopold II** (279-32), Margrave of Austria, who md **Ida of Cham** (279-32).
31. **Wilibirg von Steirermark**, d. 18 Jan (1145); md **Eckbert II** (9-31), Count of Formbach-Puttin.

Sources: Blass, R. 1939, II:293; Brandenburg, E. 1935; Chaume, M. 1977, I:112 and 112n, 528–529, 551n; ES 1984, III:27 (Gen. 31–37); Isenburg, W. 1953, table 183 (Gen. 31–41); Moriarty, G.1985, 200–201 (Gen. 31–41); Winkhaus, E. 1953 (Gen. 31–38).

## LINE 13

37. **Meginhard I** (same as 41-37), Count in the Traungau in upper Austria, liv 30 March 930.
36. **Meginhard II**, Count in the Traungau, liv 955–963.
35. **Meginhard III**, Count in the Trungau; liv 947-985/91.
34. **Arnold I**, Count in the Traungau and in the Rotagau; d. 1 Mar c1020.
33. **Arnold II**, Count in Upper Austria, Margrave of Carinthian Mark; founded the monastery of Lambach; d. 3 Mar 1050; bur at the monastery of Lambach; md before 1 May 1025, **Reginlint**, dau of **Godfrey** (104-35), Count of Verdun, and **Mathilda**.
32. **Godfrey**, Count in the Ennsthal and of Putten, Margrave of the Carinthian Mark; murdered 8 Feb 1050.
31. **Mathilda von Lambach-Puttin** md **Eckbert I** (9-32), Count of Formbach-Puttin.

Sources: Blass, R. 1939, II:293; Isenburg, W. 1953; Meyer, T. 1933; Moriarty, G.1985, 199–200 (Gen. 31–36); Winkhaus, E. 1953.

## LINE 14

34. **Lothar V**, Count of Walbach, son of **Lothar IV**, (15-35), Count of Walbach, or his brother, **N.N.**

33. **Adalbert von Sommerschenburg**, called "Seneko," Count in the Nordthuringgau and Oerlingen; md 1059, **Oda of Goseck** (17-33).

32. **Frederick I**, Count of Sommerschenburg, Pfalzgrave of Saxony; liv 1088; d. 1120; md (her 2nd) after 1090 (c1091/94), **Adelaide von Laufen** (16-32).

31. **Aleidis von Sommerschenburg**, b. c1095/1100; d. before 1180; md **Goswin II** (11-31), Count of Heinsberg and Falkenburg.

Sources; Brandenburg, E. 1935; Diederich, A. 1967 (Gen. 31–34); Moriarty, G.1985, 203–205 (32–34); Schlagenhauf, P. 1967, 27+ (Gen. 31–34); Schwarzmaier, H. 1983 (Gen. 31–34); Trautz, F. 1953, 81–84; Winkhaus, E. 1953,168, 185.

## LINE 15

39. **Lothar**, Count of Stade, slain 2 Feb. 880, Ebstorf; md **Oda of Saxony** (301-38); d. after 874.

38. **Lothar I**, Count of Walbech and Stade, slain 5 Sept 929, at Lenzen, in conflict with the Wends.

37. **Lothar II** (301-37), Count of Walbech and Stade; established the monastery of Walbech, on the Upper Allord; b. 5 Sept 929; md **Mathilda von Arneburg** (271-37).

36. **Lothar III**, Margrave of Nordmark, Count in the Derlingau and Nordthuringgau; d. 25 Jan 1003; md (1) 979, **Godila von Rothenburg**, d. 1015; dau of **Werner**, Count of Rothenburg.

35. **Lothar IV**, Count of Walback, and in the Harzgau, Nordthuringgau and Derlingau; fell in battle, 1033, at Werbin; md **N.N.**, b. c966; d. before 1015; dau of a Count **Bernard.**

34. **Lothar V**, Count of North Thuringia, 1049-1063.

33. **Siegfried II von Walbeck**, Count in Nordthuringgau and in the Derlingau; d. after 1107.

32. **Oda von Walbeck**, as a widow, founded, c1140, the monastery of Heinsburg; d. 1152; md c1085/90, **Goswin I** (11-32), Lord of Heinsburg.

Sources: Bode, G. 1937; Brandenburg, E. 1935; ES, VIII 1980:134 (32–37); Moriarty, G.1985, 203–204 (32–35); 57 (35–38); Winkhaus, E. 1953.

## LINE 16

34 **Poppo I von Weimar** (281-31), Count in the Lobdengau, liv 1065/1067.

33. **Henry**, Count of Laufen, md 1050, **Ida von Werl** (19-33).

32. **Adelaide von Laufen** md (2) **Frederick I** (14-32), Count of Sommerschenburg, Pfalzgrave of Saxony; d. 1120.

Sources: Diederich, A. 1967, 226 (Gen. 32–35); ES I.1 1997; ES, XI

8

1986:119a (Gen. 32–35); Jackman, D. 1997; Moriarty, G.1985, 204 (Gen. 32–33); Schlagenhauf, P. 1967, 27+ (Gen. 32–35); Schwarzmeier, H. 1983, 183–191 (Gen. 32–35); Trautz, F. 1953, 81–84 (Gen. 32–35).

## LINE 17

36. **Dedi** (210-38), Count in the Hessegau; md **N.N.**, dau of **Frederick II**, Count in the Herzgau.

35. **Berkhard of Wettin**, slain 13 July 982 at Calabria, Italy, in the war of Otto V with the Arabs.

34. **Frederick I of Goseck**, Lord of Goseck, Count in the Northern Hessegau; inherited from his childless nephew, Siegfrid, in 1038, the countship of Merseburg and the pfalzgraveship of Saxony; liv 992; d. before 1042; md **Agnes von Weimar**, dau of **William II von Weimar** (281-32), Duke of Thuringia; d. 1003.

33. **Oda of Goseck**, d. c1088; md 1059, **Adalbert von Sommerschenburg** (14-33), Count in the Nordthuringgau.

Sources: Blass, R. 1939, II:293; Bode, G. 1937; Brandenburg, E. 1935; Moriarty, G.1985, 204–205 (Gen. 33–35); 95 (Gen. 35, 36); Winkhaus, E. 1953.

## LINE 18

35. **Eberhard III** (98-33), Count in the Thurgau.

34. **Manegold I** (351-36), Count in the Thurgau, advocate of Einsiedeln; b. 935/40; d. 28 May 991.

33. **Eberhard IV**, Count in the Thurgau; b. 960/970; d. c8 Feb 1041; md (2) c1009, **Hedwig.**

32. **Eberhard V** "the Blessed," Count of Nellenburg, Count in the Zurichgau; founded the monastery of Allerheiligau and that of Schwabenheim, near Kreuzmark; b. c1010; d. a monk, 25 Mar 1075, in the monastery of Schaffhausen; md **Ida von Alshausen** (of Welf ancestry), bur, a recluse, in the convent of St. Agnes., dau of **Wolfrad of Altshausen** (18A-33).

31. **N. N. von Nellenburg** md **Adalbert** (364-31), Lord of Burgeln.

Sources: ES I.1 1997; ES XII: 32, 77C; Jackman, D. 1990; Jackman, D. 1997; Kruger, E. 1899; Moriarty, G.1985, 206 (Gen. 31–35); Winkhaus, E. 1953, 411.

## LINE 18A

37. **Huchbald**, d. c909 at Wittislingen; md **Dietrich**, d. after 923.

36. **Liutgard** md **Peiere**, d. 973.

35. **Manegold** (?), liv 973.

34. **Bertha**, d. 22 Dec 1032, md **Wolfrad**, Count, d. 4 Mar 1010.

33. **Wolfrad of Altshausen**, d. c8 Apr 1065; md 1009, **Hiltrud**, b. 991/992; d, 9 Jan 1052; dau of **Peregrin** and **Bertha**.

9

**32. Ida von Altshausen** (18-32); md **Eberhard V.**

Sources: ES I.1 (1997; ES XII: 32, 77c.

## LINE 19

37. **Bernard I von Werl**, Count in Westphalia; d. before 992; md Princess **Gerberge**, b.965/6; d. 1017; widow of Hermann II, Duke of Swabia; dau of **Conrad I** "the Peaceful" (175-34), King of both Burgundies, and **Matilda** (230-35), Princess of France.
36. **Hermann II von Werl**, Count of Werl and in the Locktrapgau; advocate of Werden and ruler of lands near Arnsburg, 997–1024.
35. **Henry II von Werl**, advocate of Werden and of Paderborn; liv 1016–1051.
34. **Bernard III von Werl**, Count of Westphalia; b. 982/986; d. 1063.
33. **Ida von Werl**, b. c1030; md 1050, **Henry** (16-33), Count of Laufen.

Sources: Diederich, A. 1967, 226; ES, XI 1986:119a (Gen. 33–34); Moriarty, G.1985, 205 (Gen. 33–37); Schlagenhauf, P. 1967, 27+; Schwarzmaier; Trautz, F. 1953, 81–84; Winkhaus, E. 1953.

## LINE 20

39. **Gutiar** (same as 21-39) md **Elvira.**
38. **Osorio Gutierrez.**
37. **Gutierre Osoriz**, Count of Galicia, d. c941; md **Ildonca Gutierrez** (21-37), d. 942.
36. **Adosinda Gutierrez**, md 925, **Ramiro II** (223-38,276-36), King of Leon.

Sources: Arteta, A. 1952; Candeira, A. 1950; ES, II 1984:50 (36–37); Levi, E. 1950; Moriarty, G.1985, 223 (36–39); Salazar, J. de 1984; Saly, E. 1946; Saly, E. 1949; Urbal, J. 1945;

## LINE 21

39. **Gutiar** (same as 20-39) md **Elvira.**
38. **Hermenegildo Gutierrez** (227-36,276-37), of Portugal, md **Hermesinde Gatonez**, dau of **Gaton**, Count of Viero, who md **Egilona.**
37. **Ildonca Gutierrez** md **Gutierre Osoriz** (20-37).

Sources: Abadel, L. 1912; Mateos, R. 1984; Moriarty, G.1985, 223 (Gen. 37–39); Salazar, J. de 1984.

## LINE 22

36. **Wulfrun**, taken prisoner at Farnworth, 943.
35. **Wulfric**, Earldorman in Mercia; founded Burton Abbey; ruled as High Reeve in Northern Mercia; he d. c1002, testate (made a will), giving his lands to his brother Alfhelm, his son Wulfeah and his dau Eadgyth.
34. **Eadgyth** md **Morcar**, High Reeve of Northumbria.
33. **Ealdgyth** md **Edmund** "Ironside" (233-34), King of England.

10

Sources: Moriarty, G.1985, 31, (Gen. 34-36); Robertson, E. 1872, 185–186; Searle, W. 1899; Smith, H. 1953, 466.

## LINE 23

30. **Siegbert I**, Count in the Saargau. *NOTE: Siegbert II, formerly thought to be Frederick's father, is now known to have been his brother.*
29. **Frederick I**, Count of Saarbrucken; d. 1135; md **Gisela of Lorraine**, dau of **Dietrich I** (158-31), Duke of Upper Lorraine; and **Hedwig von Formbach** (41-32).
28. **Simon I**, Count of Saarbrucken; b. c1120; d. 23 June 1181/1182; md **Mathilda von Sponheim** (365-28).
27. **Sophia von Saarbrucken**; b. 1150; liv 1150–1215; md **Henry III** (71-27), Duke of Limburg, etc.

Sources: Blass, R. 1939, II:267, 273; ES, VI 1978:26 (Gen. 27–28); VI 1978:152 (Gen. 27–30); ES XVIII 1997:147; Hoppstadter, K. 1977, II:279–296 (1977) (Gen. 27–30); Kaul, T. 1970, 222–292; Moller.S, table xvi; Moriarty, 192 (27-30).

## LINE 24

36. **Conan I** (334-35), Duke of Brittany, md **Ermengarde of Anjou** (167-34).
35. **Geoffrey**, Duke of Brittany, b. c980; d. 20 Nov 1008; md 996/999, **Hawise of Normandy**, dau of **Richard I** (89-33, 166-33), Duke of Normandy, and **Gunnor de Crepon** (89-33).
34. **Alan III**, Duke of Brittany, b. c997; d. 1 Oct 1040; md 1018, **Bertha of Blois**, d. 11/13 Apr 1085; dau of **Odo II** (Eudes II) (133-33), Count of Blois and Champagne, and **Ermengarde of Auvergne** (127-33).

Sources: Cokayne, G. 1959 X:779 et seq.; ES, II 1984:75 (Gen. 34–36); Saillot, J. 1980, (Gen. 34–36), 284; Stokvis, A. 1966, II:77 (1966) (Gen. 34–36).

## LINE 25

42. **Lothar I** (263-40,302-40), Emperor of the West, md **Ermengarde of Orleans** (302-40).
41. **Louis II**, Emperor of the West; d. 12 Aug 875; md 851, **Engelberge**, d.896/901; dau of **Erchanger I**, Count of Alsace; liv 811-841; son of **N.N.** and **Rotrudis**.
40. **Ermengard** (Trungard, Irmingardis), b. 852/855; d. 896; md 876, **Boso II** (343-39), Count of Vienne, 870; King of Lower Burgundy); d. 897.
39. **Louis III Beronides** "the Blind," King of Provence and Italy, Emperor of the West, 901-905; b. c883; d. 5 June 928, Arles; blinded, 905; md (1) c900, **Anna of Byzantium** (253-38).
38. **Charles Constantine** (see also 333-36, 375-34), Count of Vienne;

b. c901; d. after Jan. 962; md **Teutberge de Troyes**, d. after 960; dau of **Garnier** (Warinus) (173-37), Vicomte of Troyes, and **Teutberga** (174-37).

37. **Richard** (see also 196-36), Prince of Provence, d. after Jan 962; md **N.N.**

Sources: Allen, J. 1985; Chaume, M. 1977, I:254n2, 416n2, 539, 544, 545; ES, II 1984:189 (Gen. 37–41); I 1980:95 (Gen. 42); Hartwell, R. 1991 (Gen. 37-39): Isenburg, W. 1953; Knetsch, C. 1931; Mantayer.M, 50–119 and 307–326; Moriarty, G.1985, 259–260 (Gen. 37–42); Settipani, C. 1991 (Gen. 37-39); Settipani, C. 1993: 269, 299, and Notes; Settipani, C. 1997.

## LINE 26

33. **Siegfried**, Count in the Rittegau and Northeim; d. 1004; md (1) 980, **Mathilda** (mother of Gen. 32); md (2) Ethelinde, liv 1002.

32. **Benno** (Bernard) **von Northeim**, Count in the Rittegau and the Morungagau; d. 1047/1049; prob md **Eilika**.

31. **Otto I von Northeim** (237-34), Count in the Rittegau; advocate of the Abbey of Cowey; made Duke of Bavaria in 1061, by Empress Agnes; removed 1070; went with the Emperor Henry II to Italy; fought the Hungarians; revolted and deprived of Bavaria; led the Saxon revolt against Henry IV and supported the anti-kings; d. 11 Jan 1083; md after 1050, **Richenza of Swabia**, d. 1083; dau of **Otto**, Duke of Swabia, and **N.N.**, a dau of **Egisheim**, (whose parents were **Hugh VI Von Egisheim** (33-33), Count in the Nordgau and of Egisheim, and wife **Heilwig von Dagsburg**).

30. **Ida von Northeim** md **Thiemo I** (8-32), Count of Brehna and Kostritz.

Sources: Barraclough, G. 1966; Blass, R. 1939, II:290; Brandenburg, E. 1935; ES, VIII 1980:132 (Gen. 30–33); Isenburg, W. 1932; Kimpen, E. 1933; Moriarty, G.1985, 179 (Gen. 31–33); Winkhaus, E. 1953.

## LINE 27

41. **Ezerd.**

40. **Dietrich.**

39. **Berhard.**

38. **Benno.**

37. **Dietrich**, (210-36), Lord of the Haldensleben, Count of the Saxon Nordmark, of North Thuringia, and in the Durlingau; Margrave of the Nordmark; liv 953–985; d. 19 Dec 985, Magdenburg.

36. **Bernard I** (34-34), Margrave of the Saxon Nordmark, Count in North Thuringia; enemy of the deposed Margrave, Werner von Waldbach; prob md **N.N.**, dau of **St. Vladimir I Swjatoslawitsch** (143-33), Grand Prince of Kiev, and **N.N.**, wife #6, a Bulgarian.

35. **Bernard II**, Lord of Haldensleben, Margrave of the Saxon

Nordmark; d. 1045; md **N.N. von Orlamunda**, dau of **William III,** Count of Weimar and in the Eichsfeld, Burgrave of Meissen; d. 16 Apr 1039; and **Oda von der Ostmark** (211-34); granddau of **William II von Weimar** (281-32).

    34. **Konrad** "of the Nordmark," Count of Haldensleben; d. before 1056.

    33. **Gertrude,** heiress of Haldensleben; d. 21 Feb 1116; md **Frederick** (41-33), Count of Formbach; she md (2) **Ordulf** (41-33), Duke of Saxony; b. c1020; d. 28 Mar 1072; son of **Bernard II** (312-34), Duke of Saxony.

    Sources: Bernardi, W. 1874; Blass, R. 1939, II:290; Curschmann, F. 1921, 27; Isenburg, W. 1953; Jackman, D. 1997; Moriarty, G.1985, 172–173 (Gen. 33–35); 97–98 (Gen. 35–41); Winkhaus, E. 1953.

## LINE 28

    38. **Harold I** "Haarfager" (thick hair) (204-37), first overking of Norway; b. 860; d. c936; md (3) **Schwanhild** (44-38).

    37. **Bijorn** "Kyobmand" (the merchant), Under-king of Vestfold; murdered c927 by his brother, Eric "Bloodaxe," at Salheim.

    36. **Gudrod Bjornsson,** Under-king of Vestfold; murdered c955; md **Cacilie.**

    35. **Harald Granske** "Greenlander," made Under-king of Vigulmark, Vestfold and Agde by Harald "Bluetooth," c960; b. c952; murdered c995, by Sigrid Starraade; md **Astrid,** dau of **Gudbrand Kule** of Upland, and wife **Ulfrida.**

    34. **St. Olaf Haraldsson** first Christian King of Norway, fought against the Danes in England; b. posthumously, c995; slain in battle, 29 July 1030, at Stiklestadt in conflict with King Knut of Denmark and England; bur at Droutheim; md Feb. 1019, Princess **Astrid,** dau of **Olaf III** (240-33), King of Sweden, and (1) **Endia,** dau of a Wendish magnate.

    33. **Ulfhild** (Wulhilda) **of Norway,** b. c1023; d. 24 May 1071; md (2) Nov 1042, **Ordulf** (father of Gen. 32), Duke of Saxony, 1059; fought along with his brother-in-law, Magnus I of Norway, against the Wends; b. c1020; d. 28 Mar 1072; Ordulf md (2) **Gertrude von Haldensleben** (27-33); Ulfhild md (1) **Frederick** (41-33), Count of Formbach. Ordulf was son of **Bernard II** (312-34), Duke of Saxony, and **Elica von Schweinfurt** (270-34).

    32. **Magnus** (281-30), Duke of Saxony; enemy of the Emperor Henry IV; b. c1045; d. 23 Aug 1106; bur at Artlemburg; md (2) c1071, **Sophia,** Princess of Hungary, d. 18 June 1095; widow of Udalrich, Count of Istria (d. 1070); dau of **Bela I** (51-33), King of Hungary, and **Rixa** (75-33), Princess of Poland.

    31. **Ulfhild** (Wulfhilda) **of Saxony,** b. c1071, Altdorf; d. 29 Dec 1126, Altdorf; md 1095/1100, **Henry I** "the Black" (43-31), Duke of Bavaria.

    Sources: Blass, R. 1939, II:296 (Gen. 31–33); ES, II 1984:105 (Gen. 36-38); ES, II 1984:109 (33-36); Howarth, H. 1920, IX; Isenburg, W. 1953

(1953); Moriarty, G.1985, 169–171 (Gen. 31–38).

## LINE 29

40. **Konrad I** (300-40), Count in the Argengau and Linzgau, Count of Auxerre; md **Adelaide of Tours**, dau of **Hugh** "le Méfiant" (300-40, 302-40), Count of Tours, and wife **Aba** (Bava).

39. **Welf I**, Count in the Argengau and the Linzgau; adherent of Charles "the Bald;" d. by 876; md **Heilwig**.

38. **Eticho**, Count in the Breisgau and Ammergau; founded the monastery at Ettal in the Ammergau, and d. a monk there, c910; md **Judith of Wessex**, dau of **Aethelwulf** (233-40), King of England, and **Osburh**.

37. **Henry**, Count of Altdorf, Count in the Ammergau; founded the monastery at Altdorf; b. c883; d. after 934; md **Beata** (Atha) **von Hohenwarth**; d. a widow, after 975, at Hohenwarth-on-the-Paar; dau of **Ratpot I**.

36. **Rudolph I**, Count of Altdorf, b. c905/910; liv 950; md, perhaps, **Siburgis**.

35. **Rudolph II**, Count of the Swabian Altdorf; b. c927; d. 985/990; md **Itha** (Ita) **von Oeningen**, dau of **Kuno** (33-33), Count of Oeningen, d. c1020; and **Richilde**, dau of **Liudolf** (321-35), Duke of Swabia, and **Ita of Swabia** (321A-35).

34. **Welf II**, Count of Altdorf, Count in the Lechrain; adherent of Bishop Werner of Strasburg and of Duke Ernst of Swabia, 1020; founded the monastery of Ravensburg; b. c965; d. 10 Mar 1030 at Altdorf; md c1015, **Ermentrude** (Irmtrude) **of Luxemburg**, b. c1000; d. 21 Aug 1057, Altemunster; dau of **Frederick I** (353-35), Count of Luxemburg; Count in the Moselgau, and **Ermentrude von Gleiberg** (351-35), heiress of Gleiberg.

33. **Kunigunde** (Kuniza) **of Altdorf**, heiress (from her brother) of Altdorf; b. c1020; d. after 1055; bur 1060 in her husband's foundation in Vangadicendis, Italy; md c1035, **Alberto Azzo II** (43-33), Marchese d'Este.

Sources: Blass, R. 1939, II:296; Brandenburg, E. 1935; ES I 1980: 57 (Gen. 33–40); ES III 1989; Kruger, E. 1899, tables XI and XII; Moriarty, G.1985, 168 (Gen. 33–39); 33 (Gen. 39–40); Settipani, C.1993:286; Winkhaus, E. 1953.

## LINE 30

33. **Hugh VI von Egisheim** (26-31,33-33), Count of Lower Alsace; d. 1049; md 990/995, **Heilwig von Dagsburg** (33-33,149-32), b. c970/975.

32. **Hugh VII**, Count of Dagsburg, d. 1046/1049; md **Matilda**.

31. **Henry I von Egisheim**, Count of Egisheim and Dagsburg, d. 28 June 1065; md **N.N. von Moha**, dau and heiress of **Albert**, Lord of Moha, 1031–1040.

14

30. **Adalbert II von Egisheim**, Count of Egisheim and Dagsburg-Moha; d. 24 Aug 1098; md (his 2nd, her 1st) 1092/1095, **Ermesinde of Luxemburg** (3-30,126-30), heiress of the countship of Luxemburg and Longwy; b. c1075; d. 1141; she md (2) c1101, **Godfrey** (126–30), Count of Namur. Ermesinde's parents were **Conrad I** (119-31), Count of Luxemburg, and **Clemence of Poitou** (3-31).

29. **Mathilda**, heiress of Dagsburg-Moha and Egisheim; b. c1095/1100; d. after 1135; md 1120, **Folmar** (45-29), Count of Metz and Homburg.

Sources: ES, VI 1978:160 (Gen. 29–33); Moller, W. 1950, table XXIX; Parisse, M. 1976; Vanderkindere, L. 1902; Winkhaus, E. 1953.

## LINE 31

39. **Adalbert I** (93-39), Count of Lucca, Margrave of Tuscany, md **Rothieda** (Rohaut) **of Spoleto**.

38. **Adalbert II**, Margrave of Tuscany, d. 17 Aug 915; md c895, **Bertha**, Princess of Lorraine (263-38), widow of **Thibaud** (174-38), Count of Arles.

37. **Lambert of Spoleto**, Margrave of Tuscany, d. c932; blinded and exiled by his half-brother, **Hugh of Provence**, (186-38), King of Italy.

36. **Giovanni**, Count of Laurino, md **Gaitelgrima**, dau of **Atenolfo**, Count of Teano, who was son of **Atenolfo II**, Prince of Benevento and Capua (d. 940).

35. **Giovanni II**, Prince of Salerno, d. 999; md **Sikelgaita** (297-35), heiress of Salerno.

Sources: Blass, R. 1939, Table 3, p. 249; Carruti, D. 1889; Carruti, D. 1884b; Curchmann, F. 1921; Evans, C. 1976; Kruger, E. 1899, p. 153; Moriarty, G.1985, 71 (Gen. 35–37); 61 (Gen. 38–39).

## LINE 32

35. **Wickmann**, Count of Engern; d. in battle 21 Apr 944; md **Frederunda**, dau of **Dietrich** (65-41,338-37), Count of Saxony, and **Reginhilde von Friesland**, dau of **Godefrid** (217-38), King of Haithabu.

34. **Eckbert** "der Einaugige" (the one-eyed), Count in the Ambergau, Lord of Alaburg; liv 952; d. 5 Apr 994.

33. **Bruno von Braunschweig**, the first proved ancestor of the early counts of Brunswick; Count in the Derlingau and in Middle Friesland; built the town of Brunswick; b. c960; d. c1003; md (1) after 1000, **Gisele of Swabia** (199-34) (mother of Gen. 32); b. 11 Nov 985; d. 14 Feb 1043; she md (3) **Conrad II** (359-34). Salic Emperor of the West.

32. **Ludolf von Braunschweig**, Count in the Derlingau; Margrave of West Friesland; d. 23 Apr 1038; md before 1036, **Gertrude von Egisheim** (33-32).

31. **Eckbert I von Braunschweig** (318-35), Margrave of Middle Friesland and Meissen, Count in the Darlingau; adherent of Henry IV who

made him Margrave of Meissen; b. c1036; d. 11 Jan 1068; md **Ermengarde,** dau of **Odelerico Manfredo II** (7-33,93-33,315-34), and **Bertha of Este** (93-33).

Sources: Bottger, F. 1965; Brandenburg, E. 1935, Hofmeister, A. 1920, 33; Isenburg, W. 1953, pt. i, table 42; Moriarty, G.1985, 180 (Gen. 31–35); Rollnow, H. 1930; Winkhaus, E. 1953.

## LINE 33

35. **Eberhard IV** (3-34,202-37), Count in the Nordgau, (md) **Luitgarde of Trier** (202-37), dau of **Wigeric** (104-37, 319-37), Count in the Triergau.

34. **Hugh V** (246-33), Count in the Nordgau; liv 951; d. before 986; md **Berlinda** (33A-34).

33. **Hugh VI** (175-32), Count of Egisheim and in the Nordgau; d. 1049; md 990/995, **Heilwig von Dagsburg** (149-32), heiress of Dagsburg; b. c970/975; d. 1046; dau of **Ludwig,** Count of Dagsburg; founder of the monastery at St. Quirin; and **Judith of Ohningen,** whose parents were **Kuno** (381-33), Count of Ohningen, and **Richilde** (321-34), Princess of Germany.

32. **Gertrude von Egisheim,** d. 21 July 1077; md before 1036, **Ludwig von Braunschweig** (32-32), Count in the Derlingau.

Sources: Blass, R. 1939, II:274; ES, VI 1978:160 (Gen. 32–35); Parisse, M. 1976 (Gen. 32–35); Wilsdorf, C. 1964, 1–33; (Gen. 32–35).

## LINE 33A

40. **Hildegarde** (171-41), md **Charlemagne** (171-41), Emp of the West.

39. **Louis I,** Emperor of the West, 814-840; md **Ermengarde.**

38. **Louis,** King of Bavaria, 805-867; md **Emma.**

37. **Carloman,** King of Bavaria and Italy, 887-880.

36. **Arnulf,** Holy Roman Emperor, 867-899

35. **Glismode.**

34. **Berlinda** md **Hugh V,** Count in the Nordgau (33-34).

Sources: ES I.1 1997; ES VI 1978; Parisse, M. 1976; Wilsdorf, C. 1964.

## LINE 34

36. **Bouchard,** liv 909, prob father of Gen. 35.

35. **Bouchard de Bray-sur-Seine,** Seigneur de Montmorency; liv 959; md **Hildegarde de Chartres Blois,** b after 940.

34. **Bouchard,** Seigneur de Montmorency; knight; liv 958-975; md **Hildegarde.**

33. **Bouchard I** "the Bearded," Seigneur de Montmorency; d. 1012; md **Hildegarde,** Dame de Chateau-Bassett, 1009-1012;

32. **Bouchard II,** Seigneur de Montmorency (1022-1024); Seigneur de Chateau-Bassett, 1028-1031; md **Adeliza of Clermont.**

31. **Herve,** Seigneur de Montmorency; royal cup bearer of France, 1074;

d. 1110; md 1087/1100, **Agnes**, d. 1124.

    **30. Bouchard III**, Seigneur de Montmorency, de Marle, and d'Herouville, 1096/1124; md (1) **Agnes de Beaumont** (274-30) (mother of Gen. 29); md (2) before 1005, Judith.

    **29. Adelaide** (Adaline, Helvide) **de Montmorency**, md **Gui**, Seigneur de Guise, d. after 1141; son of **Godfrey**, Seigneur de Guise, and **Ada**, d. after 1121; Adelaide bur at the monastery of Lescies.

    **28. Bernard**, Seigneur de Guise, liv 1185; md before 1150, **Adelaide** (Alix).

    **27. Adele** (Adelphie) **de Guise**, heiress of the seigneuries of Guise and Lesquilles; b. c1155, of Guise, Aisne, France; md **Jacques d'Avesnes** (50-27), Seigneur d'Avesnes, etc.

    Sources: Chenaye, F. 1964; Bulletin 1957, 96:37; Dek, A. 1955; ES, III 1984:50 (Gen. 27–28); XIV: 1991:116; Moriarty, G.1985, 176–177 (Gen. 27–33); Vanderkindere, L. 1904; Winkhaus, E. 1953.

## LINE 35

    **41. Ramiro I** (276-40), King of the Asturias, md (2) **Paterna of Castile**.

    **40. Rodrigo** (287-38), Count of Castile, d. 4/5 Oct 873.

    **39. Diego Rodriguez Porcelos**, Count of Castile, d. 885.

    **38. Gutina of Castile**, md **Fernando Nunez**, of Castrosiero (285-38).

    Sources: ES, II 1984:49 (Gen. 38–41); Mateos, R. 1984 (Gen. 38–41); Salazar, J. de 1984 (Gen. 38–41).

## LINE 36

    **29. Renaud I** (149-29), Count of Bar-le-Duc, md **Gisela de Vaudemont** (246-29).

    **28. Renaud II**, Count of Bar-le-Duc; b. c1115; 25 July 1170; md 1155, **Agnes of Blois**, heiress of the countship of Ligny; b. c1138; d. 7 Aug 1207; dau of **Thibaud IV** (81-29), Count of Champagne, and **Mathilda von Sponheim** (228-30).

    **27. Theobald I**, Count of Briey, Bar-le-Duc and Luxemburg; went on a Crusade against the Albigensians, 1196; b. c1160; d. 13 Feb 1214; bur at St. Michael; md (3) **Ermensinde**, of Bar-sur-Seine (383-27) (mother of Gen. 26); d. c1211.

    **26. Henry II**, Count of Luxemburg, Namur and Bar-le-Duc; Crusader; b. 1190; d. 13 Nov 1239, at Gaza in Palestine; md 1219, **Philippa de Dreux** (37-26), Dame de Coucy; b. 1192; d. 17 Mar 1242.

    **25. Mathilde** (Margaret) **de Bar-le-Duc**, d. 23 Nov 1275; md 4 June 1240; **Henry III** (71-25), Count of Luxemburg and of Arlon.

    Sources: Blass, R. 1939, II:272; Brandenburg, E. 1935; ES, I 1980:6 (25–26); Isenburg, W. 1953; Merz, W. 1914; Moriarty, G.1985, 194 (25–29); Weiss, S. 1910; Winkhaus, E. 1953.

33. **Hugh**, Seigneur de Boves, near Amiens.

32. **Dreux de Boves**, Seigneur de Boves and de Coucy; liv 1042–1069; md **Adele de Coucy**, dau of **Aubri**, Seigneur de Coucy, near Soissons; and **Adele**, whose parents were **Leon de Coucy**, Seigneur de Coucy, who fell 15 Nov 1037 at the Battle of Bar-le-Duc, and **Mathilda**.

31. **Engelram** (Enguerrand) **de Coucy**, Seigneur de Boves and de Coucy; Count of Amiens; b. c1042, Coucy, Ardennes, France; d.1116; md (1) (her 1st), **Adela de Roucy** (6-31) (mother of Gen. 30), heiress of Marle; md (2) Sibylle de Porcean, dau of Roger de Porcean.

30. **Thomas de Coucy**, Sire de Coucy and Marle; Count of Amiens; Crusader; went on the 1st Crusade; b. c1073, Coucy, Ardennes, France; d.1130; md (3) **Melisende de Crecy** (5-30).

29. **Engelram** (Enguerrand) **II**, Sire de Coucy, Marle, and le Fere; Crusader; d. 1148 on the 2nd Crusade, somewhere in the East, very likely in or near Damascus; bur at Nazareth (modern Israel); md 1132, **Agnes de Beaugency** (4-29).

28. **Raoul I de Coucy**, Sire de Coucy and Marle; adherent of Philip Augustus; Crusader; b. c1135; fell Nov 1191, at Acre, in the Holy Land, on the 3rd Crusade; bur at Foisny; md (1) before 1164, **Agnes of Hainault**; b. c1142; d. 1168/1173; dau of **Baldwin IV** (73-29), Count of Hainault, and **Alice de Namur** (126-29).

27. **Yolande de Coucy**, b. c1168; d. 18 Mar 1222; bur Braine St. Ived; md 1184, **Robert II** (124-29), Count of Dreux and Braine.

26. **Philippa de Dreux**, Dame de Coucy, a widow in 1240; md **Henry II** (36-26, 383-26), Count of Bar-le-Duc.

Sources: Agiles, R. 1968; Blass, R. 1939, II:239, 243; Brandenburg, E. 1935; Clairvaux, B. 1963; Constable, G. 1953; Eggenburger, D. 1985, 111–112; ES, VII 1979:80 (Gen. 26–33); Flahiff, G. 1947; Foucher, 1971; Krey, A. [n.d.]; Morenas, J. 1934; Moriarty, G.1985, 194–196 (Gen. 26–33); Tardif V. 1918 (Gen. 26–33); Iyre, W. 1943.

31. **Florenz I** (311-33), Count of West Friesland; md **Gertrude of Saxony** (312-33).

30. **Dietrich** (Dirk) **V**, Count of West Friesland, 1061; expelled 1071 and restored 1076; d. 17 June 1091; md before 26 July 1083 (or c1080), **Ulfhilde**, d. by 26 July 1083.

29. **Florenz II** "the Fat," Count of Holland, 1101; b. c1080/84; d. 2 Mar 1121; md c1113, **Gertrude** (Petronel) **of Alsace** (390-30), d. 23 May 1144; dau of **Dietrich II of Alsace** (158-31), Duke of Upper Lorraine; and **Gertrude** (205-31), heiress of Flanders.

Sources: Brandenburg, E. 1935, Dek, A. 1955; Moriarty, G.1985, 178

18

(Gen. 29–30); 55 (Gen. 30–31); Vanderkindere, L. 1902; Winkhaus, E. 1953.

## LINE 40

37. **Sieghard**, a count of Gibiet, near Salzburg, and Reichenhall; b. c890/900; d. after 9 June 959, perhaps father of Gen. 36.

36. **Sieghard** (Sizzo), a count; b. c930; d. after 9 Aug 987; md **N.N.** from near Teisendorf.

35. **(Walther?)**, Count in the Filsgau.

34. **Frederick of Buren**, Pfalzgrave in Swabia; b. c960/965; d. after summer of 1027; md c987 (prob later), **N.N.** (perhaps Kunigunde) **of Ohningen**; b. c980; d. after c1005; dau of **Kuno of Ohningen** (29-35) and **Richilde** (321-34).

33. **Frederick von Buren**, Pfalzgrave in Swabia; Count in Riesgau; b.c998; d. 1070/1075; md c1015/20, **N.N.** (perhaps Adelheid) of Filsgau, b. c995; d. shortly after 1020/1025.

32. **Frederick von Buren**, Count in the Riesgau; Lord of Buren (northwest of Hohenstaufen); b. c1020; d. c1053; md (3) c1042, **Hildegarde von Bar-Mousson** of Swabia; b. c1028; d. 1094; dau of **Otto**, Duke of Swabia, and **N.N.** a dau of **Hugh VI** (33-33), Count of Egisheim and in Lower Alsace, and wife **Hedwig von Dagsburg**.

31. **Frederick I**, Count von Hohenstaufen, Duke of Swabia and Alsace; built the castle at Hohenstaufen; founded the monastery of Lorch; b. c1050; d. 20 Jan 1105; bur at Lorch; md 1089, **Agnes of Franconia** (359-31); b. 1072/3; d. 24 Sept 1143; bur at Kloster Neuburg; she md (2) **Leopold III** (279-31), Margrave of Austria.

30. **Frederick II von Hohenstaufen**, Duke of Swabia; b. 1090; d. 4/6 Apr 1147; bur at St. Walpurgia in Alsace; md 1121, **Judith of Bavaria** (43-30); b. c1100; d. 22 Feb c1130/1135.

29. **Frederick III Barbarosa**, Duke of Swabia; King of Germany, 9 Mar 1158; Emperor of the West, 8 June 1155; Emperor of Germany as Frederick I; b. 1122; Crusader; drowned 10 June 1190 at Saleph in Silicia on 3rd Crusade; bur at Tyre; md 10/16 June 1156, **Beatrice of Burgundy** (of Macon) (41-29, 125-29).

Sources:; Barraclough, G. 1966; Blass, R. 1939, II:294; Buhler, H. 1984; Chaume, M. 1977, I:542, 551–552; ES, I 1980:5 (Gen. 29–32); Flahiff, G. 1947; Hlawitschka, E. 1987; Isenburg, W. 1953; Jackman, D. 1990; Jackman, D. 1997; Moriarty, G.1985, 166, 167 (Gen. 29–33); Moriarty, G. 1945; Stimmel, R. 1978, 109–120 (Gen. 29–37); Tyre, W. 1943.

## LINE 41

37. **Meginhard I** (same as 13-37), Count in the Traungau in Upper Austria; liv 930.

36. **Ulrich** (Udalrich) **I**, Count in Schweinachgau, liv 947-970; md

**Kunigunde** (41A-36).

35. **Berthold I**, Count in the Lurngau; md 980, **Himiltrude** "Mater Familias," c1020.

34. **Thiemo (Dietmar)**, Count in the Quinziggau; liv 1025–1040; advocate of the monastery of St. Emeram.

33. **Frederick**, Count of Formbach; b. c1020; slain 1059; bur at Formbach; angered the Emperor by his marriage with **Gertrude** (27-33), the great Saxon heiress, whom he wed secretly; heiress of Haldensleben; d. 21 Feb 1116; She md (2) after 1059, **Ordulf**, Duke of Saxony, b. c1020; d. 28 Mar 1072; son of **Bernard II** (312-34), Duke of Saxony.

32. **Hedwig von Formbach**, b. 1058; d. 1095–1100; md (his 1st) 1075, **Dietrich I of Alsace** (158-31), Duke of Upper Lorraine; d. 23 Jan 1115; bur at Chetenois (father of Gen. 31); she md (1) Gebhard, Count of Supplinburg in the Herzgau; slain 9 May 1075. Dietrich I md (2) c1100, **Gertrude** (205-31), heiress of Flanders.

31. **Simon I of Alsace**, Duke of Upper Lorraine, Lord of Bitsch; founded the Abbey at Sturzelbronn, 1135; b. c1076; d. 13 Jan 1138; md **Adelaide of Lorraine**, d. c1158, a nun, at Tart; perhaps dau of **Baldwin II** (73-31), Count of Hainault.

30. **Agatha of Alsace**, md 1130, **Reynold** (Renaud), Count of Macon and Burgundy; b. c1090; d. 22 Jan 1148; son of **Stephen** (187-31), Count of Vienne; and **Beatrice** (187-31).

29. **Beatrice of Burgundy** (of Macon), heiress of West Burgundy; b. c1145; d. 15 Nov 1184; md 10/16 June 1156, Wurzburg, **Frederick III** (I) **Barbarosa** (40-29, 125-29), Emperor of the West, etc.

Sources: Blass, R. 1939, II:290, 294; Brandenburg, E. 1935; Curschmann, F. 1921, 27; ES, I 1980:5,9; VI 1978:129 (Gen. 30–32); ES XVI:37Meyer, T. 1935, 33 (corrections); Moriarty, G.1985, 130 (Gen. 31–32); 172, 173 (Gen. 32–37).

## LINE 41A

38. **Luitpold**, Count in Karinthia, Margrave in Nordgau, d. 4 July 907; md **Kunigunde** (270-38), dau of **Berthold**, Count in Swabia. She also md **Konrad I**, Duke of the Franks, King of Germany, who d. 913.

37. **Berthold**, Duke of Bavaria in Karinthia, Count in Engadin in the Vintschgau, 927-427; d. 23 Feb 947; md **Biletrud** (Wialdrut), liv 976; dau of **Burkhard II** and **Reginlink of Swabia**. (See also 345-38).

36. **Kunigunde** md Ulrich (Udalrich) I (41-36).

Sources: ES I 1980:5,9; Jackman, D. 1990:105; Jackman, D. 1997: 41,70.

## LINE 42

32. **Alexios I Komnenos** (111-32), Emperor (Basilius) of the East, 1081–1118; b. c1048; d. 15 Aug 1118; md 1078, **Eirene Doukaina** (215-32).

31. **Isaakios Komnenos**, sebastokrator, 1129–1143; b. after 16 Jan 1093; d. after 1152; md after 20 July 1104, **Irene,** dau of **Volodar,** Prince of Przemysl.

30. **Andronikos I Komnenos,** Emperor of the East, 1183–1185; b. c1123; murdered, Constantinople, 12 Sept 1185; md (1) prob a sister of the pansebastos Georgios Palaiologos; md (2) Agnes (Anna) of France, b. 1171, d. c1240; dau of Louis VII, King of France. Concubines, by whom there are many children, are: (1) **Philippa of Antioch,** d. 1178, dau of **Raymond of Poitiers** (usually said to be mother of Gen. 29); (2) Eudokia Komnena (Gabraina), dau of the sebastokrator Andronikos Komnenos; (3) **Theodora Kalusine Komnena** (mother of Gen. 29 says ES II 1984:175) dau of the sebastokrator **Isaakios Komnenes.**

29. **Eirene Komnena** md **Isaakios II Angelos** (215-29), Emperor of the East *(NOTE: ES II 1984:175 says md Summer of 1183, Alexios Komnenos, Emperor of the East, 1185–1186, d. in a monastery, 1188).*

*NOTE: There is some confusion among authorities as to the parentage of Gen. 29, and of her husband(s). The similarity of names in these Byzantine families is a contributing factor.*

Sources: Allen, J. 1985; Buckler, G. 1929; ES, II 1984:175 (Gen. 29-32); Hanowelt, E. 1982; Isenburg, W. 1932; Moriarty, G.1985; 174 (Gen. 29-32); Polemis, D. 1986; Prosop. 1981; Winkhaus, E. 1953; Wise, L. 1967, 343.

## LINE 43

35. **Humbert** (93-34), Count of Genoa and Tortone, md **Railinda** (93-34).

34. **Alberto Azzo I,** Marchese in Liguria; established the family at Este in the Veronese; opponent of the Emperor Henry II; captured in flight on the Englesbrucke, and d. a captive in Germany; b. c970; d. c1029; md before 996, **Adela,** liv 996–1012; she "lived under the Salic law" (was a pagan).

33. **Alberto Azzo II,** Marchese d'Este and of the Lombards; sent by the Pope on a mission to the Hungarians; b. 997; d. 20 Aug 1097, "aged 100 years;" md c1035, **Kunigunde of Altdorf** (29-33).

32. **Welf IV,** Duke of Bavaria; a Crusader; b. 1037; d. 9 Nov 1101, Cyprus, on a Crusade; md (3, her 2nd) c1071, **Judith of Flanders,** b. 1033; d. 5 Mar 1094; bur at Weingarten; widow of Earl Tostig of Northumberland, d. 1066; son of Godwin, Earl of Essex; She was dau of **Baldwin IV de Lille** (141-33), Count of Flanders, and (2) **Judith** (Elena) **of Normandy,** dau of **Richard II** (89-32), Duke of Normandy, and **Judith of Brittany** (167-33).

31. **Henry I** "the Black," Duke of Bavaria; became a lay brother of his foundation at Weingarten, and was bur there; b. 1074; d. 13 Dec 1126, Ravensburg; md 1095/1100, **Ulfhild** (Wulfhilda) **of Saxony** (28-31).

21

30. **Judith of Bavaria,** b. c1100; d. 22 Feb 1130/1135; md c1121, **Frederick II of Hohenstaufen** (40-30), Duke of Swabia.

Sources: Agiles, R. a968; Barraclough, G. 1966; Blass, R. 1939, II:296; Brandenburg, E. 1935; Chaume, M. 1977, I:542, 551-552; ES I:5 (Gen. 30–31); I:58 (Gen. 31–33); II:190 (Gen. 35); Foucher, 1971; Krey, A., n.d.; Moriarty, G. 1945; Moriarty, G. 1947; Moriarty, G.1985, 166–167 (30–34); 62 (Gen. 34–35); Wise, L. 1967, 343.

## LINE 44

41. **Halfdan** "the Old."
40. **Ivar Oplaendinge,** Jarl of Uplanders of Norway; fl. c800; md **N.N. of Throndheim** (386-40).
39. **Eystein Ivarsson,** Jarl of Hedemarken (of the Uplands), c830; md **Aseda Rognvaldsdotter** (166-37).
38. **Schwanhilde** md (his 3rd) **Harold** "Haarfager" (Thick Hair) (28-38, 204-37), Overking of Norway.

Sources: Blass, R. 1939, II:251, 252; Brandenburg, E. 1935; Cokayne, G. 1959, X, app A, p.3; ES, II:105 (Gen. 39); Howarth, H. 1920, IX; Moriarty, G.1985, 10 (Gen. 38–41); Motey, V de 1920; Onslow, Earl of 1945.

## LINE 45

36. **Folmar,** a count, advocate of Worms, liv 920–930; md **Richilde.**
35. **Folmar,** a count, of Luneville and Amance, liv 933–980.
34. **Folmar** (337-36), Count of Metz and in the Bleisgau, Lord of Luneville, Blieskastel, and Saarburg; d. 995/996; md **Bertha,** a widow in 996; sister of Berenger, Abp of Trier.
33. **Folmar,** Count in the Bliesgau and of Metz; Lord of Amance and Luneville; d. before 1029; md **Gerberge,** dau of **Godfrey** "the Captive" (104-35), Count of Verdun, who md **Mathilda of Saxony.**
32. **Gottfried,** Count of Metz; liv 1032; d. 1075; md **Judith.**
31. **Folmar** (same as 278-32), Count of Metz; advocate of St. Stephen; liv 1055; d. 1087; md **Judith.**
30. **Folmar,** Count of Metz and Homburg; advocate of Longueville; d. 25 June 1111, a monk, in his foundation, the monastery of Rixheim; md **Swanhilde,** d. by 1075.
29. **Folmar,** Count of Metz and Homburg; founder and advocate of the Abbey of Beaupre; liv 1111; d. 1142; md 1120, **Mathilda** (30-29), heiress of Egisheim and Dagsburg-Moka; b. c1095/1100; d. after 1135.
28. **Agnes von Metz,** d. after 1175; md **Louis I** (320-28), Count of Loos and Rieneck.

Sources: ES, VI 1978:156 (Gen. 28–36); ES XIII 1997:152; Moller, W. 1950; Moriarty, G.1985, 189–191 (Gen. 28–36); Vanderkindere, L. 1902, II:425 (Gen. 28–36).

## LINE 46

33. Count **Meginhard**, liv 987.

32. **Arnold von Gilching**, advocate of Benediktbeuren; liv 1000–1027; md (1) Adelaide; md (2) **Ermengarde** (mother of Gen. 31).

31. **Ermengarde von Gilching** md (her 2nd) **Frederick II von Diessen** (49-34, 388-34), Count of Diessen, advocate of Regensburg Cathedral; liv 1035; d. c1075; bur at St. Blasien, son of **Frederick I** (64-34), Count in the Upper Isar, and Hemma.

30. **Haziga** (Hadagunda) **von Diessen** (279-32), d. c1104; md his 2nd, her 3rd) **Otto I von Scheyern** (307-30), Count in the Middle Paar. She also md Herman von Kastl (d. 1056) and **Hermann IV** (63-34, 279-30), d. 1038.

Sources: Dek, A. 1955, 52; ES, I 1980:23 (Gen. 30–31); I 1980:36 (Gen. 30–32); Moriarty, G.1985, 187 (Gen. 30–33); Tyroller, F. 1951; Winkhaus, E. 1953.

## LINE 47

35. **Henry von Schweinfurt** (270-35), Margrave in the Nordgau, md **Gerberge of Henneburg** (102-35).

34. **Otto III von Schweinfurt**, Duke of Swabia, 1048; Margrave in the Nordgau, 1034; b. c1000; d. 28 Sept 1057; md (2) 1036, **Ermengarde**; d. 21 Jan 1078, dau of **Odalrico Manfredo II** (7-37,93-33,315-34), Marchese de Torino-Albenza, and **Bertha of Este** (93-33).

33. **Judith von Schweinfurt**, d. 1094/1104; md after 1055, **Boto von Botenstein** (48-33).

Sources: Barraclough, G. 1966; Blass, R. 1939, II:268, 283; ES, III 1984:26 (Gen. 33); Isenburg, W. 1953; Moriarty, G.1985, 163 (Gen. 33–34); 57 (Gen. 34–35); Tyroller, F. 1951; Winkhaus, E. 1953, 31–33.

## LINE 48

39. **Aribo**, Margrave in the Donaugrafschaften; Count in the Traungau; d. after 909; md **N.N.**, perhaps sister of Archbishop Pilgrim of Salzburg, 907–923.

38. **Ottokar I** (12-38), Count in Carinthia, d. Aug 907.

37. **Arpo**, founded Goss-Schladnitz, 904; md **N.N. von Chadalhoch**, countess in Albgau and Aargau, d. after 903.

36. **Chadalhoch,** Count in Isengau; d. 976.

35. **Aribo I**, Pfalzgrave of Bavaria; liv 940; d. 13 Nov 1000; md (2) **Adela**, d. after 1020; dau **Hartwig I**, Pfalzgrave of Bavaria. Adela, as a widow, md **Engelbert III** (110-36), Count in the Chiemgau.

34. **Hartwig II**, Pfalzgrave in Bavaria, 1020; d. 24 Nov 1027; bur at Seeon; md c1024, **Frideruna** (136-34), dau of **Retig II**.

33. **Boto von Botenstein (62-32),** "the Bold," founded the monastery of Theres on his lands north of the Danube; enfieffed in Bavaria as adher-

ent of the Bavarian dukes; fought the Hungarians who captured him; gave his name to Botenstein Castle in Frankish Switzerland; b. c1027/8 (posthumously); d. 1 Mar 1104; md (his 2nd, her 1st), after 1055, **Judith von Schweinfurt** (47-33).

32. **Adelaide von Botenstein**, d. after 13 Aug 1106; md **Henry I** (62-32), Count of Arlon, etc.

Sources: Brandenburg, E. 1935; Buhler, H. 1984; ES, III 1984:26 (Gen. 32–39); Moriarty, G.1985, 162 (Gen. 32–35); 201 (Gen. 35–39); Winkhaus, E. 1953.

## LINE 49

37. **Poppo I von Rota**, liv 960.

36. **Poppo II von Rot**, perhaps a Count in the Isengau.

35. **Poppo III von Rot**, Count of Rot and in the Isengau, c1010; md **Hazaga of Karnten**.

34. **Kuno von Rot**, Pfalzgrave of Bavaria; founder of Rot monastery; liv 1055; d. 1086; md after 1050, **Uta von Diessen** who d. 1086; widow of Abalrech von Formbach; dau of **Frederick II von Diessen** (46-31, 388-34), Count of Diessen and **Ermengarde von Gilching** (46-31, 388-34).

33. **Irmgard** (Ermengard) **von Rot** md **Gebhard II** (63-32), Count of Sulzbach.

Sources: Blass, R. 1939, II:277; ES, I 1980:38 (Gen. 33–34); Heinrich, G. 1872; Isenburg, W. 1932; Jackman, D. 1990; Moriarty, G.1985 (Gen. 33–37); Winkhaus, E. 1953.

## LINE 50

31. **Fasted I d'Oisy**, advocate of Doornick, d. after 1092; md **Ada d'Avesnes**, dau of **Wedric**, Lord of Avesnes, son of **Wedric I** and his wife, **N.N. of Chievres**.

30. **Fasted II d'Oisy**, advocate of Doornick; d. after 1111; md **Richilde**.

29. **Walter I d'Oisy**, Lord of Avesnes and Leuze; md **Ada of Mortagne**, dau **Everard I Radulf** (50A-29), Burggrave of Doornick, Duke of Montagne.

28. **Nicholas d'Avesnes**, Lord d'Avesnes, Leuze and Conde; d. 1169/71; md before 1150, **Mathilda de la Roche**, dau **Henry I**, Lord de la Roche (of the House of Namur), advocate of Stablo, who was son of **Henry**, Seigneur de la Roche; and wife **Mathilde of Limburg** (387-29).

27. **Jacques d'Avesnes**, Seigneur d'Avesnes, Leuze, Conde and Guise; Constable of Flanders; Crusader; b. c1150; fell in the battle of Arsouf, Palestine, 7 Sept 1191, on the 3rd Crusade; In this battle, about ten miles from Joffa, the Crusaders, under Richard the Lion-Hearted, confronted Saladin's Turkish forces. The undisciplined knights charged prematurely and instead of a great victory, the enemy forces escaped into the woods; md **Adele de Guise** (34-27), b. c1155; heiress of the seigneuries of Guise

24

(in Aisne, France) and Lesquilles.

26. **Bouchard d'Avesnes**, Seigneur d'Avesnes and d'Etroen; Canon of St. Pierre de Lille; Archdeacon of Laon; held the Doctor Juris degree; at first a cleric but returned to the lay world, 1205; Knighted 1239; b. c1180; d. 1244, Etraeungt, Nord, France; bur in the Abbey of Clairefontaine; md (1) before 23 July 1212 (divorced 1221), **Margaret** (73-26), heiress of Hainault, 1244; and Flanders; b. 2 June 1202, Constantinople; d. 10 Feb 1280.

25. **Jean I d'Avesnes**, Seigneur d'Avesnes, Seneschal of Frederick II, Seigneur d' Etroen, Count of Hainault, Holland and Flanders; as the child of a cleric, declared a bastard by the Pope, 1236, 1244; legitimatized by the Emperor Frederick II, 1244; b. 1 May 1218, Etraeungt, Nord, France; d. 24 Dec 1257; bur Valenciennes; md 9 Oct 1246, **Adelaide** (Alhildis) **of Holland** (72-25, 120-25).

24. **Jean II d'Avesnes**, Count of Hainault, 1299; and Holland; b. 1247, Brabant, Holland; d. 22 Aug 1304; md 1270, **Philippa of Luxemburg** (71-24).

23. **William III d'Avesnes**, Count of Hainault and Holland; b. c1286, Hainault, Belgium; d. 7 June 1337, Valenciennes; md 19 May 1305, **Jeanne de Valois** (70-23).

22. **Philippa of Hainault**, b. 24 June 1311, Hainault, Belgium; d. 15 Aug 1369, Windsor Castle, Berkshire, England; bur Westminster Abbey; md **Edward III** (1-22), King of England, 1327–1377.

Sources; Barrow, C. 1995; Chenaye, F. 1964; Dek, A. 1955; ES, II 1984:14 (Gen. 22–26); III 1984:50 (Gen. 25–31); Flahiff, G. 1947; Moriarty, G.1985, 175–176 (Gen. 22–31); Rubincam, M. 1949 (Gen. 22–25); Tyre, W. 1943; Von Redlich, M. 1941, 267–268; Waugh, S. 1991; Winkhaus, E. 1953.

## LINE 50A

32. **Ingelbert I** "the Illustrious."
31. **Ingelbert II**, of Peteghem, 1002-1037; d. 1058; md **Glismode**.
30. **Alared I**, of Peteghem, liv 1034/37.
29. **Everard I Radulf** (50-29), Burggrave of Doornick and Duke of Mortagne.

Source: ES VII 1979: 88.

## LINE 51

41. **Venedobel**, a Magyar leader.
40. **Emse** (fem) md **Ogyek**, a Magyar leader in Asia, c819.
39. **Almos** "Chosen as best of 7 Magyar nomad princes to be chief and to have the honor of being sacrificed before they set out for Europe;" d.895.
38. **Arpad**, Prince of the Magyars, 886; Duke of Hungary; Led emi-

gration from Dnieper steppes in 889 to conquer Hungary and Transylvania by 895; d. 907.

37. **Zoltan,** Duke of Hungary, Magyar leader in the invasion of western and southern Europe; defeated by the Saxons, 933, near Merseburg while invading Germany; b. c896; d. 949; md N.N., a Khazar princess, dau of **Mariot** (Maroth), Prince of Bikar Khazars, Khagan of Jewish Khazars between the rivers Theiss and Szamos.

36. **Taksony,** Great Prince of Hungary, whose army was defeated by Otto the Great, 955; b. c931; d. c970; md 947, **N.N.,** a Kumanian.

35. **Michael,** Magyar prince, Kuman of Samogy, Regent of Poland; d. c976/978; md **Adelaide of Poland,** d. after 997; dau of **Mieszko I.**

34. **Ladislas I** (also called Vasul and Basil) "the Blind" (same as 225-35); Prince of Hungary, 1038-1040; d. c1040; He was a pagan Magyar prince, imprisoned and blinded by Stephen I, before 1038, and his sons were exiled to Poland. He md **Premylslava** of Kiev, Ukraine, Russia, b. c980, d. 1018, dau of St. **Vladimir I** (143-33), Great Prince of Novgorod, and wife **Rognieda** of Polotsk.

33. **Bela I,** King of Hungary, 1060–1063, Lord of one-third of Hungary, 1048; d. 1063; md c1040, **Rixa** (28-32; 75-33), Princess of Poland.

32. **Geza** (Geysa) **I,** proclaimed King of Hungary, 1074, by popular demand, but he never ruled; b. c1044; d. 24 Apr 1077; md (2) 1065, **N.N. Synadena,** d. after 1077; dau **Theodulos Synadenos** and **N.N. Botaneiata,** dau of **Michael Botaneiates** who was son of **Nikephoros Botaneiates,** strategos of Thessalonica, liv in 1016.

31. **Almos,** Duke of Croatia, Duke of Hungary, 1102; He was created King of Croatia, 1090, by St. Ladislas, King of Hungary, who then merged Croatia with Hungary; b. 1068; d. 1129; md (2) 21 Aug 1104, **Predslawa Swjatopolkowna** of Novgorod, dau of **Swjatopolk II,** Prince of Novgorod; b. 1050.

30. **Bela II** "the Blind" (blinded 1113); King of Hungary, 1131–1141; b. c1109; d. 13 Feb 1141; md 28 Apr 1127, **Helena of Serbia,** b. after 1109; d. after 1146; dau **Uros I,** Zupan (Prince) of Serbia; b. 1080; d. after 1130; md **Anna Diogenissa,** dau of **Konstantios Diogenes;** b. c1050; d. 1074; who md **Theodora Komnena,** b. c1053; dau of **Iohannes** (John) **Komnenos** (111-33) and **Anna Delassena.** The father of Uros I was **Vukan,** Zupan (Prince) of Raska.

29. **Geza** (Geysa) **II,** King of Hungary, 1141; b. c1130; d. 3 May 1162; md 1146, **Euphrosyne Mstislawna** (240-28).

28. **Bela III,** King of Hungary, 1173; b. c1148; d. 23 Apr 1196; md 1172, **Agnes** (Anne) **de Chatillon-sur-Loing** (80-28).

27. **Andrew** (Andreas) **II,** King of Hungary, 1205–1235; King of Galicia; b. 1176; d. 21 Sept 1235; md (2) 1215, **Yolande de Courtenay** (78-28, 79-26) (mother of Gen. 26); he also md **Gertrude von Meran** (7-28, 78-28).

26. **Yolande,** Princess of Hungary; b. 1213; d. 12 Oct 1251, Huesca,

Spain; md 8 Sept 1235, Barcelona, **James I** "the Conqueror," King of Aragon; historian of Aragon; b. 1 Feb 1207, Montpellier; d. 25 July 1276, Valencia; bur at Cabret; son of **Pedro II**, King of Aragon and (3) **Marie de Montpellier** (150-27).

25. **Isabella of Aragon**, b. 1243 or 1247; d. 28 Jan 1271, Clermont, Auvergne, France; md 28 May 1262, **Philip III** (70-25), King of France, 1270–1285.

24. **Philip IV** "the Fair," King of France, 1285–1314; b. 1268, Fontainbleau, France; d. 29 Nov 1314, Fontainebleau; bur St. Denis; md 16 Aug 1284, Paris, France, Princess **Jeanne of Navarre** (81-24).

23. **Isabella**, Princess of France; b. 1292; d. 27 Aug 1357, Roseing; bur Church of the Grey Friars, London; md 25 Jan 1308, Boulogne, **Edward II** (1-23), King of England.

Sources: Chaume, M. 1977, I:542, 551-552; ES, II 1984:12 (Gen. 23–25); II 1984:153–155 (Gen. 26–39); Fine, J. 1983, 32; Moncreiffe, I. 1982, 83 (Gen. 27–39); Moriarty, G 1945; Moriarty, G. 1947; Moriarty, G.1985, 116 (Gen. 23–25); 131 (Gen. 25–26); 143 (Gen. 26–32); 86 (Gen. 33–35); 31–32 (Gen. 35–41; Von Redlich, M. 1942, 96:138–143; Winkhaus, E. 1953.

## LINE 52

28. **Alfonso VII** (83-29, 86-29), King of Castile and Leon; md **Berengaria of Barcelona** (86-29).

27. **Fernando II**, King of Leon, 1157–1188; King of Galicia and Extremadura, 1157; b. 1137; d. 22 Jan 1188, Benavente, Italy; md (1) 1164, (divorced 1175), **Urraca** (85-27) (mother of Gen. 26), Princess of Portugal. He md (2) Aug 1179, Teresa Fernandez de Traba, d. 7 Feb 1180, Leon, dau of Fernando Perez de Traba and Sancha Gonzalez (not the Infanta Teresa of Portugal, as often stated); md (3) May 1187, Urraca Lopez de Haro, d. 1223, Vilena, dau of Lope Diaz V de Haro, Lord of Vizcaya and Najera, and wife Aldonza Ruiz. Fernando II was the first king to use the royal symbol of the lion in a truly heraldic form.

26. **Alfonso IX** "el Barboro," King of Leon, 1188–1229; b. 15 Aug 1171, Zamora, Leon, Spain; d. 24 Sept 1230, Villanueva de Sarria; md Dec 1197, Valladolid, Spain, **Berengaria of Castile** (83-26), heiress of Castile.

25. **Fernando III** "the Saint," King of Castile, Toledo and Extremadura, 1217–1252; and Leon, Galicia and Cordoba, 1236–1252; Canonized by Pope Clement X, 1671; b. July/Aug 1201, Castile, Spain; d. 30 May 1252, Seville; md 1237, Burgos, Spain, **Jeanne de Dammartin** (82-25) (mother of Gen. 24), Countess of Ponthieu.

24. **Eleanor of Castile**, Queen of England, Princess of Castile and Leon, Countess of Ponthieu; b. 1240, Castile, Spain; d. 28 Nov 1290, Hardeby (Herby), Nottinghamshire, England; bur Westminster Abbey; md 18 Oct

1254, Burgos, Spain, **Edward I** (1-24), King of England.

Sources: Banfield, A. 1990; Brandenburg, E. 1935; Cokayne, G. 1959, II:59 note G (Gen. 24–26); X:18; ES, II 1984:62–63 (Gen. 24–28); Evans, C. 1932 (Gen. 24–26); Isenburg, W. 1953; Martindale, J. 1992; Moriarty, G.1985, 108–109 (Gen. 24–28); Parsons, J. 1984; Parsons, J. 1989; Turner, R. 1988; Vajay, S de 1989, 374, 381 (Gen. 24-27).

## LINE 54

39. **Bellon** (same as 284-41 and 291-40), Count of Carcassonne, liv 812.

38. **Sunifred**, Count of Urgel, Barcelona, Gerona and Osona; Margrave of Gothie; d. after 847; md **Ermesende**. He was of Visagothic descent.

37 **Wilfred I (329-36)** "el Velloso," Count of Besalu, Gerona, Osona, Urgel and Cardena; d. c21 Aug 897; md 877, **Winilda** (Guinidilda), dau of **Baldwin I** (235-38), Count of Flanders, and **Judith** (250-38), Princess of France.

36. **Sunifred**, Count of Besalu; d. 15 Oct 950, as a monk; md 920/925, **Adelaide de Toulouse**; d. between 12 Nov and 27 Dec 954; dau of **Armengol de Toulouse**, Count of Rouergue, d. 937; and **Adelaide of Toulouse**; granddau of **Eudes**, Count of Toulouse and Rouergue; and **Garsinde de Albi**.

35. **Borrel II**, Marquis of Barcelona, Count of Gerona and Odona, vassal of the Emirs of Cordoba; liv 948; d. 30 Sept 992; md 968, **Luitgarde de Toulouse**, d. after 977; dau **Raimond III** (Raymond Pons) (329-35), Count of Toulouse, and **Gersende of Gascony** (329-35).

34. **Raymond Borrel I**, Count of Barcelona, Gerona and Osona; b. 972; d. 25 Feb 1018; md 990/991, **Ermesinde de Carcassonne** (291-34).

33. **Raymond** (Ramon) **Berenger I** "al Cuerva," Marquis of Barcelona, Count of Barcelona; b. 1005; d. 26 May 1035; bur at Santa Marie de Ripoll; md 1021, **Sancha Sanchez** (mother of Gen. 32), d. 26 June 1026; bur Santa Marie de Ripoll; dau **Sancho Garcia** (285-34), Count of Castile, who md Urraca Salvadores; md (his 3rd, her 3rd) , **Gisela of Lluca** (85-30)

32. **Raymond Berenger I** "el Viejo," Count of Barcelona, Gerona, Osona, Carcassonne and Rasez; b. 1023; d. 26 May 1076, Barcelona; md (his 3, her 3) 1053, **Almode de la Haute Marche**, murdered 1071/1075; dau **Bernard I** (327-33), Count de la Haute Marche and Perigord, d. 1047; and **Amelia** (327-33). *NOTE: It is strange that Raymond Berenger I isn't known as Raymond Berenger II, the change of titles notwithstanding.*

31. **Raymond Berenger II** "Cabeza de Estope," Count of Barcelona, Gerona, Osona, Carcassonne and Rasez; b. c1055; murdered 5 Dec 1082 by his half-brother; md 1078, **Mathilda of Apulia** (296-31) (mother of Gen. 30), b. c1058; d. 1111/1112; she md (2) 1085, Amalric II, Viscount of Narbonne, who d. in the East on a Crusade in 1105.

28

30. **Raymond Berenger III (86-29)** "el Grande," Marquis of Barcelona, Count of Provence; b. 11 Nov 1080; d. 19 Aug 1131; md (her 3rd) 3 Feb 1112, **Dulce di Gievaudun** (257-30), heiress of Provence-Arles; b. c1095.

29. **Raymond Berenger IV**, Marquis and Count of Barcelona; b. c1113; d. 6 Aug 1162, San Dalmacio, near Turin; md 11 Aug 1137, **Petronilla of Aragon** (95-29).

28. **Alfonso II**, King of Aragon, 1162–1195; Marquis and Count of Barcelona, Tortosa and Lerida; Count of Tarragona, Gerona and Cerdagne, 1162; Marquis of Provence, 1166; b. 1/25 Mar 1157, Villa Mayor del Valle, Spain; d. 25 Apr 1196, Perpignan; bur Monastery of Nuestra Senora, Poblet; md (2) 18 Jan 1174, Zaragoza, Spain, **Sancha** (Sanchia) (94-28), Princess of Castile and Leon.

27. **Alfonso of Aragon**, Prince of Aragon, Count of Provence; b. 1180; d. Feb 1209, Palermo, Sicily; md 1193, **Gersinde of Sabran** (Gersinda II) (116-27). She was heiress and regent (1213–1217) of Provence and Forcalquier; d. after 1222; was a nun in 1222.

26. **Raymond Berenger V** (164-27), Count of Provence and Forcalquier; b. 1198, France; d. 19 Aug 1245, at Aix, France; md Dec 1220, Dez, **Beatrice of Savoy** (93-26).

25. **Eleanor of Provence**, Queen of England; b. c1223, Aix-en-Provence, France; d. 25 June 1291, Amesbury, England; md 14 Jan 1236, Canterbury, Kent, **Henry III** (1-25), King of England, 1216–1272.

Sources: Bard, R. 1982; Bisson, T 1991; Brandenburg, E. 1935; Cokayne, G. 1959, IV:321; V:736; ES, II 1984:70 (25, 26); II:68–69 (Gen. 29–39); Evans, C. 1976; Mateos, R. 1984; Moriarty, G.1985, 67–68 (25–38); Salazar, J. de 1984; Winkhaus, E. 1953.

## LINE 55

38. **Garcia III Sanchez** (223-39), King of Navarre; b. 913; d. 970; md **Andregota Sanchez** (292-39).

37. **Urraca Garcia of Navarre**, md (2) 960/962, **Fernan Gonzalez** (285-36), Count of Castile, Leon, and Lara.

36. **Pedro Fernandez**, a count.

35. **Salvador Perez** (also called Pedro Fernandez).

34. **Urraca Salvadores**, d. 20 May 1025; md 994, **Sancho Garcia** (54-33,285-34), Count of Castile; d. 5 Feb 1017.

Sources: Bard, R 1982; ES, II 1984:51 (Gen. 34–38); Mateos, R. 1984 (Gen. 35–38); Salazar, J. 1983, 326 note 2; Salazar, J. de 1984 (Gen. 35–38).

## LINE 55A

31. **Archambaud I**, Seigneur de St. Geran, fl. 1111-c1150.

30. **William I**, Seigneur de St. Geran and de Montculon after the death of his uncle, William de Barbo.

29. **William II,** Seigneur de St. Geran and de Montculon, 1174-1197.

28. **Archambaud V,** Seigneur de Montculon in the Bourbonaise, 12 Oct 1203. *NOTE: Some researchers doubt that this is the father of Gen. 27.*

27. **Beatrice de Montculon,** occ 1212, 1216; md **Archambaud IX de Bourbon.**

26. **Marguerite de Bourbon** (84-26) md **Theobald IV,** King of Navarre, etc. (81-26).

Sources: Anselme, A. 1890; Blass, R. 1939, 244; Brandenburg, E. 1935; Coiffies, D. 1816; Isenburg, W. 1953; Jubainville, M, 1869, I:318; II:491-492; Watson, G. XI:41; Winkhaus, E. 1953.

## LINE 56

33. **Hugh de Creil** (de Mouchy) (344-29), Seigneur de Creil and Mouchy, Count of Clermont; md **Margaret de Roucy,** dau of **Hildouin III** (66-34, 266-31), Count of Montdidier, Seigneur de Rameru; and **Alice de Roucy** (170-31).

32. **Richilde de Creil** md **Dreux II,** Seigneur de Mouchy and de Mello; son of **Dreux I,** Seigneur de Mello.

31. **Dreux III,** Seigneur de Mouchy, md **Edith,** widow of Gerard de Gournay, Seigneur of Gourney-en-Brai; dau of **William de Warenne** (135-30), Earl of Surrey; d. 1088; and **Gundred,** sister of Gerbod, Earl of Chester, a Fleming.

30. **Dreux IV,** Seigneur de Mouchy; md **Adelaide.**

29. **Ermengarde de Mouchy** md **William I** (84-29), Seigneur de Dampierre. She md (2) Dreux de Mello, Constable of France.

Sources: Brandenburg, E. 1935; Mesmay, J. de 1963, III:2227+; Moriarty, G.1985, 151 (Gen. 29–32); 269 (Gen. 32–33); Winkhaus, E. 1953.

## LINE 57

33. **Gui de Montlhery** (5-32; 241-32), Seigneur de Montlhery, md **Hodierne de Gometz** (241-32).

32. **Milon** (Milo) **I** "the Grand," Seigneur de Montlhery, Bray, Chevreuse and la Ferte; Vicomte de Troyes; Crusader; captured at Roma, 1102, while on the 1st Crusade; b. c1035; d. 1118; md c1070, **Lithuaise 188-32),** heiress of the Vicomte de Troyes; Dame de Bray; dau of **William d'Eu** (222-33), Count of Eu and Troyes, and **Aelis** (188-33), heiress of Troyes and Soissons.

31. **Elizabeth** (Isabel) **de Montlhery** md **Thibaut de Dampierre-sur-l'Aube** (84-31), Seigneur de Dampierre.

Sources: Blass, R. 1939, II:244, 255; Bournazel, E.1975, 32+, 46; Brandenburg, E. 1935; ES, III 1989:624 (Gen. 31–33); Moriarty, G.1985, 149–150, (Gen. 31–32); 63 (Gen. 32–33); Winkhaus, E. 1953.

## LINE 58

35. **Frederick I** (353-35), Count in the Moselgau; md **N.N.**(perhaps Ermentrude) **von Gleiberg** (351-35), heiress of Gleiberg.

34. **Frederick II**, Duke of Lower Lorraine, Count in the Moselgau, Lord of Saarbrucken, advocate of St. Ablo and Malmedy, Margrave of Antwerp, and by exchange, Lord of Roca; b. c1005; d. 18 May 1065; md **Gerberge**, d. before 1049, dau of **Eustace I** (242-34), Count of Boulogne, and **Mathilda of Louvain** (121-34).

33. **Jutta of Luxemburg**, heiress of Limburg-Maas; b. c1040; md 1060/61, **Waleran** (Udo) **II** (62-33), Count of Arlon, etc.

Sources: Agiles, R. 1968; Blass, R. 1939, II:268, 271; Brandenburg, E. 1935; ES, VI 1978:26 (Gen. 33–34); VI 1978:128 (Gen. 35); Foucher, 1971; Krey, A. n.d.; Moriarty, G.1985, 159, 161 (Gen. 33–34); 247–248 (Gen. 34–35); Winkhaus, E. 1953.

## LINE 59

37. **Nievelong**.

36. **Aimard**, Sire de Sauvigny, held lands in the Bourbonnais and was advanced by Charles "the Simple;" Founded the Benedictine monastery at Sauvigny, and buried there; liv 915; d. before 953/954; md **Ermengarde**, d. 953/954.

35. **Aymon I**, Sire de Bourbon, d. after 954; md **Aldesinde**.

34. **Archambaud I**, Sire de Bourbon; liv 954–994; md **Rothilde**.

33. **Archambaud II** "the Frank," Sire de Bourbon; adherent of Hugh Capet (134-34); enemy of Laundry de Monceaux; d.1032/1034; md c1000, **Ermengarde**, d. after 1049; possibly dau of **Hubert**, Sire de Sully.

32. **Archambaud III**, Sire de Bourbon; founded the Church of le Montet-aux-Moines; d. 16 July 1079; bur at Church of le Montet-aux Moines; md (1) **Biletrude** (mother of Gen. 31); d. before 1048; md (2) Aurea, occ 1048.

31. **Archambaud IV** "the Bold," styled "the Prince," Sire de Bourbon, 1078; d. 1095; bur at Sauvigny; md **Beliarde**, occ 1078/1095.

30. **Aymon II** "Vairvache," styled "the Prince," Sire de Bourbon; d. 5 July 1116; md **Lucia** (Alsinde) **de Nevers** (61-30).

29. **Archambaud VII** "the Strong," Sire de Bourbon; built Villafranche; Crusader; went on the 2nd Crusade, 1147; b. 1110/1115; d. 1171; md 1130/1137, **Agnes**, dau of **Humbert II** (93-30), Count of Maurienne, and **Gisela of Burgundy** (93-30).

Sources: Blass, R. 1939, II:244, 245; Chezaud, A. ; Isenburg, W. 1932; Latrie, M. 1889; Moriarty, G.1985, 152–153 (Gen. 29–37); Winkhaus, E. 1953.

## LINE 60

30. **Hugh II** (377-30), Duke of Burgundy; b. c1085; md **Mathilda de Turenne**, dau of **Boson I** (156-30), Vicomte de Turenne.

29. **Eudes II** "Borel," Duke of Burgundy; b. c1118; d. 27 Sept 1162; bur at Citeaux; md 1145, **Marie de Champagne**; b. c1129; d. c1190, a nun at Fontevrault; dau of **Theobald IV** (133-30), Count of Blois and Champagne, and **Mathilda von Sponheim** (81-29, 133-30, 228-30).

Sources: Blass, R. 1939, II:238, 242; Brandenburg, E. 1935; ; Mesmay, J. de 1963, III:2227+; Isenburg, W. 1953, pt. ii, table 24; Moriarty, G.1985, 153 (Gen. 28–29); 114 (Gen. 29–30); Winkhaus, E. 1953.

## LINE 61

32. **William I** (232-32), Count of Nevers and Auxerre, md **Ermengarde** (254-32), heiress of Tonnerre.

31. **William de Nevers**, Count of Tonnerre; d. after 1090.

30. **Lucia** (Alsinde) **de Nevers** md **Aimon II** (59-30), Sire de Bourbon.

Sources: Angot, A. 1942, 713–804; ES, III 1989:716 (Gen. 31–32); Garrigues, M. 1981, nos. 13, 50, 85; Guillot, O. 1972, 351; Mirot, L. 1945; Moriarty, G.1985, 64 (Gen. 30–32);Waquet, J. 1950.

## LINE 62

37. **Eberhard II**, Count of Meinvelt and Zurichgau; b. 885/900; d. c994; prob md **N.N.**, dau of **Adalbert I 332-37**), Marquesse of Ivrea .

36. **Udon**, Count of Meinvelt, exiled 966; md N.N., dau of **Luitfried (III)**, Count of Landengau, occ 964; bro of **Walaho of Spayergau** (359-40, where line continues).

35. **Konrad**, Count of Arlon; d. 994; md **Luitgardis**.

34. **Waleran I** "the Old," Count of Arlon; d. before 1078; md **Adelaide of Upper Lorraine** (319-34).

33. **Waleran** (Udo) **II**, Count of Arlon and Limburg, Duke of Lower Lorraine. In 1064, built the Castle of Limburg; d. 1070/82; md 1060/61, **Jutta** (Judith) **of Luxemburg** (58-33,387-31).

32. **Henry I**, Count of Arlon and Limburg, Duke of Lower Lorraine, Pfalzgrave of the Rhine and of Lorraine; adherent to the Emperor Henry IV in his quarrel with his son; b. c1060; d. 1119; md **Adelaide von Botenstein**, dau of **Boto von Botenstein** (48-33) and **Judith von Schweinfurt** (47-33, 48-33), widow of Konrad of Bavaria.

31. **Waleran III** "Paganus," Count of Arlon, Wassenburg and Limburg, Duke of Lower Lorraine; made Margrave of Antwerp, 1128, by the anti-king Lothare III; md **Jutta** (Judith), heiress of the lordship of Wassenburg; b. c1090; d. 26 June 1151; dau of **Gerard II** (119-31), Count of Guelders, and wife, **Clemence of Poitou** (same as 3-31, 119-31).

30. **Henry II**, Duke (and Count) of Limburg, Count of Arlon; b. 1110/

32

1015; d. Aug 1167, Rome; md (1) 1136, **Mathilda von Saffenburg**, heiress of the lordship of Roda; d. 2 Jan 1145; dau of **Adalbert** (Adolph) **von Saffenberg** (71-28).

    29. **Margaret von Limburg**; b. c1139; d. 1172/1173; md before 1155, **Godfrey III** (68-29), Duke of Brabant, 1143–1183.

    Sources: Blass, R. 1939, II:267, 268; Brandenburg, E. 1935; Dungern, O. von 1910; Isenburg, W. 1953; Jackman, D. 1997:62,65,78-81, 227 table 2; Moriarty, G.1985, 159–160 (29–36); Northoff, L. von 1929; Winkhaus, E. 1953.

## LINE 63

    37. **Arnulf** (270-37), Duke of Bavaria, md c910, **Judith of Friuli** (272-37).

    36. **Luitpold** (Leopold) **I**, Count in the Eastmark of Bavaria, Margrave of Austria; b. c932; d. 10 July 994, Wurzburg; md **Richwara** (279-35), dau of **Ernst**, Count in Sualafeld.

    35. **Ernst I von Babenburg**, Margrave of Austria, Duke of Swabia, d. 31 May 1015; md 1003/1005, **Gisela of Swabia** (199-34), b. 11 Nov 985; d.14 Feb 1043; dau of **Hermann II** (199-35,229-34,347-32), Duke of Swabia, and **Gerberge** (201-35), Princess of Upper Burgundy.

    34. **Hermann IV**, Duke of Swabia; b. c1015; d. 28 July 1038; md c1036, (his 1st) **Adelaide von Susa** (48-32,93-32,173-33). She md (2) 1042, Henry, Margrave of Montferrat; md (3) c1046, Odo I (173-33), Count of Maurienne.

    33. **Gebhard I**, Count of Sulzbach; murdered c1080; md N.N., dau of **Berenger**, Count in the Bavarian Nordgau.

    32. **Gebhard II**, Count of Sulzbach; built the Castle of Sulzbach near Bamburg in Bavaria, b. c1058; d. c1085; md c1079, **Irmgard von Rot** (49-33), d. 14 June (1101).

    31. **Berenger II**, Count of Sulzbach, advocate of Bamburg; b. c1080; d. 3 Dec 1125 at Kastel; md (2) c1111, **Adelaide von Wolfratshausen** (64-31).

    30. **Luitgarde von Sulzbach**, d. after 1162; md **Godfrey II**, Duke of Brabant (68-30).

    Sources: Blass, R. 1939, II:277, 306; ES, I 1980:10 (Gen. 31–35); I I I 11980:39 (Gen. 35–37); Hofmeister, A 1920, 33; Isenburg, W. 1932, 41; Moriarty, G.1985, 156–158 (Gen. 31–35); 90 (Gen. 35–36); 57 (Gen. 37); Tyroller, F. 1950.

## LINE 64

    37. **Arnulf** " the Bad" (270-37), Duke of Bavaria, md **Judith of Friuli** (272-37).

    36. **Arnulf**, Pfalzgrave in Bavaria, who engaged in a revolt against Otto I; b. c913; slain in the siege of Regensburg, 22 July 954.

    35. **Berthold I**, Count in the Upper Isar, d. 26 Aug (990); md N.N., dau of **Frederick I** (319-36), Count of Bar and Duke of Upper Lorraine;

b. c912; d. 18 May 978 or 17 June 984; md **Beatrice**, b. 939/940; d. after 987, possibly 1005. Parents of Frederick I were **Wigeric** and **Kunigunde** (104-37, 353-37). Father of Beatrice was **Hugh Magnus** (134-35), Duke of France and Normandy. Berthold I was an ally of Henry "the Wrangler," of Bavaria against Otto II. He administered his brother Luitfold's countship on the Upper Isar, and in 955 the Count was in alliance with the Hungarians to aid Henry "the Wrangler."

34. **Frederick I,** Count in the Upper Isar and of Wassenburg; md **Hemma,** dau of **Kuno**, Count of Ohningen and **Richilde** (321-34).

33. **Berthold II,** Count in the Upper Isar and of Diessen; liv 1025–1060; md **N.N. von Hohenwart.**

32. **Otto II von Wolfratshausen,** Count of Diessen, Thanning, and Ambras; d. 1120; md (2) **Adelaide von Regensburg,** dau of **Henry**, Burggrave of Regensburg.

31. **Adelaide von Wolfratshausen,** b. c1084; d. 11 Jan 1126; md c1111, **Berenger II** (63-31, 68-30), Count of Sulzbach; b. c1080; d. 3 Dec 1125, Kastel, Germany.

Sources: Blass, R. 1939, II:277; Dungern, O. von 1931; ES, I 1980:36 (Gen. 31–35); I 1980:9 (Gen. 35–37); Jackman, D. 1997; Moriarty, G.1985, 156–158 (Gen. 31–37); Tyroller, F. 1950; Tyroller, F. 1951; Winkhaus, E. 1953.

## LINE 65

41. **Dietrich** (32-35,338-37), Count of the Saxon Hamalant (Ringelheim), md **Reginhilde von Friesland,** dau **Godefrid** (217-38), King of Haithabu.

40. **Amalrada** md **Eberhard I,** Count in the Lahngau, who fell 1 May 902, at Bamburg, Germany.

39. **Eberhard II,** Count in the Lahngau, md **Mathilda.**

38. **Eberhard III,** Count in the Maingau, and in the Lahngau; d. 10 May 966; md, say some authorities, **Luitgard of Chiny,** dau of **Wigeric** (316-37), Count Palatine of Aachen; and wife **Kunigunde** (104-37, 353-37).

37. **Arnold I,** a count, killed at Calabria, 982; md **Mathilde of Chiny;** d. c992.

36. **Otto I,** Count of Warcq and Chiny; d. 1013; md (2) **Ermengarde of Namur** (mother of Gen. 35), dau of **Adalbert** (Albert) **I** (403-35), Count of Namur, and **Adelaide of Lorraine** (120-34); Otto I md (1) Almaraide, dau of Mengoz, Count of Guelders; (d. 1001). For a time, Otto I was Count of Chiny, 966; dispossessed (recorded after 990) as Count of Labengau by Adalbert of Ivrea (son of King Berenger II of Italy, 974); built a castle at Warcq, 971; adherent of Charles, Duke of Lower Lorraine, and an enemy of Archbishop Adalbern of Rheims.

35. **Louis I,** Count of Ivoix in Luxemburg, and of Chiny; Governor of Verdun He was in Italy in 1013 with the Emperor Henry III; slain 28 Sept

1025 in battle with Gonzelon, Duke of Upper Lorraine; Louis I md **Adelaide,** a benefactress of St. Varne.

34. **Louis II,** Count of Ivoix and Chiny, defeated Duke Gonzelon and revenged his father's death; founded the monastery of Suxi; entertained the Emperor Henry III and King Henry I of France, 1048; d. 1068; md **Sophia of Verdun,** styled "Countess of Bricy," d. 1078; dau of **Frederick,** Count of Verdun, c988; Duke of Upper Lorraine; d. 6 Jan 1022; granddau of **Godfrey** "the Captive" (104-35), Count of Bidgau, and **Mathilda of Saxony.**

33. **Arnold** (Arnulf) **II,** Count of Warcq, Ivoix, and Chiny; founded the Abbey of Orval in Belgium, 1097; opponent of Godfrey de Bouillon; founded Paies Priory, 1068; and that of Chiny, 1097; d. 16 Apr 1106, a monk of St. Hubert; md (3) **Adela** (Agnes) of Rameru and Montdidier (66-33).

32. **Otto II,** Count of Chiny, d. a monk, 28 Mar 1125; md (1) Ermengarde; md (2) **Adelaide of Namur** (120-31).

Sources: Blass, R. 1939, II:230; Brandenburg, E. 1935; Dek, A. 1959, XIII (1959), 105–146; ES, VII 1979:42 (Gen. 33–37); Goffinet, H. 1935, VIII:155–269; IX:7+; Jackman, D. 1990; Moriarty, G.1985, 155 (who skips Gen. 37) (Gen. 33–40), Winkhaus, E. 1953.

## LINE 66

34. **Hildouin III** (56-33,266-31), Count of Rameru, etc., md **Alice de Roucy** (170-31).

33. **Adela,** of Rameru and Montdidier, d. 1068/1069; md **Arnulf II** (65-33), Count of Chiny, etc.

Sources: Blass, R. 1939, II:246; Brandenburg, E. 1935; ES, VII:42 (Gen. 33–34); Goffinet, H. 1935; Moriarty, G.1985, 49–50 (Gen. 33–34); Newman, W. 1971; Saillot, J. 1980; Sars, M. 1924, 218–228.

## LINE 67

36. **Hermann I** "Pusillus" (the Little) (97-32,208-36), Count in the Bonngau, d. 16 July 996; md **Heilwig von Dillingen.**

35. **Hermann II,** Lord of Norvenich and Count in the Keldachgau, Governor of Dentz, 1019; d after 1041.

34. **Adolph II** of Norvenich; liv 1041.

33. **Hermann IV,** Count of Norvenich, Lord of Saffenburg, Governor of Cornelimster; liv 1091; md **Gepa von Werl,** dau of **Adalbert,** Count of Werl.

32. **Adalbert von Saffenberg,** Count of Norvenich and advocate of Klosteroth; d. 16 Dec 1109; md (2) **Mechtild,** d. 4 Nov 1110; widow of Gisa II, Count of Hollenden, slain in 1073.

31. **Adolph von Saffenberg,** Count in the Kolngau and in the Ruhrgau; advocate of Merieuthal and St. Cassius of Bonn; b. c1095; d. 1152; md

1122, **Margaret von Schwartzenburg** (388-31).

30. **Matilda von Saffenberg**, heiress of the lordship of Rode; d. 2 Jan 1145; md 1136, **Henry II** (62-30), Duke of Limburg and Count of Arlon. Sources: Blass, R 1939, 267; Brandenburg, E. 1935; E.S. I: 1980:37; E.S. VI: 1978:2; Hoffmeister, A. 1920, vol. 33; Isenburg, W. 1953; Moriarty G.1985, 86,160,164; Winkhaus, E. 1953, 415.

## LINE 68

37. **Regnier I** (207-38), Count of Hainault, Lay Abbot of Echternach, Luxemburg; md (1) **Hersent** (mother of Gen. 36), dau of **Charles II** (250-39), King of France.

36. **Regnier II**, Count of Hainault; b. c890; d. c932; md **Adelaide of Burgundy** (206-37); md also Adelaide of Dagsburg.

35. **Regnier III** "Longhals," Count of Hainault; b. c920; d. 973; md **Adele of Louvain** (310-35).

34. **Lambert I** "the Bearded," Count of Louvain; b. c952; d. in battle 12 Sept 1015, near Florennes; md c990, **Gerberge of Lower Lorraine** (121-35). He and his wife were bur in the cloister of St. Gertrud, at Nivelles.

33. **Lambert II**, Count of Louvain and of Brussels; b. c990; d. about 21 Sept 1062; bur at Nivelles; md **Oda** (104-33); d. 23 Oct 1044.

32. **Henry II**, Count of Louvain; b. c1020; d. 1078/79; bur at Nivelles; md **Adelaide of the Betuwe** (138-32, 389-32), b. c1045; d. after 1086.

31. **Godfrey I** "the Bearded," Duke of Brabant and of Lower Lorraine, Count of Louvain, Margrave of Antwerp; b. c1060; d. 25 Jan 1139; bur at Efflighem; md (1) c1100, **Ida of Namur and Chiny** (120-30) (mother of Gen. 30); md (2) c1121, Clemence, dau of William II (94-31), Count of Burgundy, and sister of Pope Calixtus II.

30. **Godfrey II**, Duke of Brabant and of Lower Lorraine, Count of Louvain; b. c1108, Louvain, Brabant; d. 1142; md c1139, **Luitgarde von Sulzbach** (mother of Gen. 29); b. c1120, Sulzbach, Germany; d. after 1162; dau **Berenger II** (63-31), Count of Sulzbach, and **Adelaide von Wolfratshausen** (63-31, 64-31).

29. **Godfrey III** (62-29), Duke of Brabant and of Lower Lorraine, Count of Louvain; b. 1142, Louvain, Brabant, France; d. 10 Aug 1190; bur St. Peter's Church, Louvain; md (1) before 1155, **Margaret von Limburg** (62-29) (mother of Gen. 28); dau of **Henry II**, Count of Limburg, and **Matilda of Saffenburg** (68A-30), whose father was **Adolph**, Count of Saffenburg. Godfrey III md (2) Imagina, dau of Count Ludwig of Loos.

28. **Henry I**, Duke of Brabant and Lower Lorraine, Count of Louvain; b. 1165; d. 5 Sept 1235, Cologne, Germany; bur St. Peter's Church, Louvain; md (1) 1179, **Matilda** (Maud) **of Alsace and Flanders** (mother of Gen. 27); md (2) 1213, at Soissons, **Marie**, dau of **Philip II Augustus**, King of France (70-28, 133-28).

27. **Henry II** "the Courageous," and "the Magnanimous;" Duke of Bra-

bant and Lorraine; b. 1207; d. 1 Feb 1248, Louvain; md by 22 Aug 1215, **Maria von Hohenstaufen** (125-27) He md (2) c1240, Sophia von Hessen, dau of Ludwig IV, Landgrave of Thuringia.

Sources: Brandenburg, E. 1935, Chaume, M. 1977, I:542, 551–552; ES, I 1980:95–96 (Gen. 25–37); James, E. 1985; Moriarty, G.1985, 154 (Gen. 27–31); 125 (Gen. 31–34); 50 (Gen. 34–37); Moriarty, G. 1945; Rubincam, M. 1949, XXV:224–232 (Gen. 27–37); Saillot, J. 1980, 102; Weis, F. 1992, line 155 (Gen. 25–37).

## LINE 68A

35. **Herimann**, Lord of Norvenich, 1028; advocate of the Abbey of Deutz, 1003-1032.

34. **Hermann of Saffenberg**, Lord of Norvenich, 1041-1045; Governor of Deutz, 1045; and of Werden, 1052.

33. **Hermann**, Lord of Norvenich and Saffenberg; liv 1056-1083; md **Gepa**, liv 1108; dau of **Adalbert of Werl**.

32. **Adalbert**, Count of Saffenberg, d. 16 Dec 1109; md **Mathilde**, who d. 4 Dec 1110 at Burg, Hollende. She was the widow of Count Giso I of Hollende.

31. **Adolph**, Count of Saffenberg; md 1122, **Margaret**, dau of **Engelbert of Schwarzenburg**, by his wife **N.N. of Mullenark**.

30. **Matilda** (68-29), d. 2 Jan 1145/6; md 1136, **Heinrich**, Duke of Limburg, Count of Arlon, who d. 11 Aug 1167 at Rome.

Sources: ES I.1 1997; ES VI 1978:2; ES XVIII 1998:1; Winkhaus, E. 1950: 156.

## LINE 69

32. **Guethenoc**, Vicomte de Chateau-en-Porhoet; liv 1008-1021; md **Allarum**.

31. **Joscelin**, Count of Porhoet.

30. **Eudon** (Eudes ) I, Vicomte de Porhoet and Rohan; b. c1078; md **Emme** (Ann) **de Leon;** d. after 1092; dau of **Conan**, Duke of Brittany (167-34) and **Maud**, Princess of France, dau of of **Louis VI** (70-30, 134-30), King of France, and **Adelaide of Maurienne** (124-31)

Sources: Anselme, III:50-51;Brandenburg, E. 1935;Cokayne, G. 1959; IX:8,9,14a,15,16; VI: 528-531; X: charts 780,786,788,789;XII, pt.2: 930-932; Paz, A du, 1619.

## LINE 70

30. **Louis VI** (69-30,134-30), King of France, md **Adelaide of Maurienne** (124-31).

29. **Louis VII** "the Young," King of France, 25 Dec 1170–1180; b. 1120; d. 18 Sept 1180, Paris; bur Notre Dame de Barbeau, near Fontainebleau; md (1) 25 July 1137, **Eleanor of Aquitaine** (88-29), divorced 18 Mar 1152; md (2) Constance of Castile, dau Alfonso VII, King of Castile, and

Berengaria; md (3) **Adelaide of Blois** (Alix de Blois-Champagne) (133-29) (mother of Gen. 28).

28. **Philip II Augustus** (68-28), King of France, 1180-1223; b. 22 Aug 1165, Gonesse, France; d. 14 July 1223, Mantes; bur St. Denis; md (1) 28 Apr 1180, Bapaume, France, **Isabella of Hainault and Flanders** (132-27).

27. **Louis VIII** "the Lion," King of France, 1223–1226; b. 5 Sept 1187, Paris, France; d. 8 Nov 1226, Montpensier-en-Auvergne, France; bur St. Denis; md 23 May 1200, Abbey of Port-Mort, Bapaume, near Pont-Audemer, Normandy, France, **Blanche of Castile** (88-27), Princess of Castile.

26. **Louis IX** "St. Louis," King of France, 1226–1270; a famous Crusader; canonized 11 Aug 1297 by Pope Boniface VIII; b. 25 Apr 1215, Poissy, France; d. in battle 25 Aug 1270, near Tunis, Africa, on the Eighth Crusade; bur St. Denis; md by permission of Pope Gregory IX, 27 May 1234, Sens, France, **Margaret of Provence** (93-25).

25. **Philip III** "the Bold," King of France, 1270–1285; b. 1 May 1245, Poissy, France; d. 5 Oct 1285, Perpignan; md (1) by permission of Pope Urban IV, 28 May 1262, Clermont, Auvergne, France, **Isabella of Aragon** (51-25) (mother of Gen. 24); md (2) Marie of Brabant.

24. **Charles of Valois,** Prince of France and Count of Valois; b. 12 Mar 1270/1, Vincennes, France; d. 16 Dec 1325, Paris, France; bur St. Jacques, Paris; md 16 Aug 1290, Corbeil, France, **Marguerite** (88-24), Princess of Sicily and Naples.

23. **Jeanne de Valois**; b. c1294, Valois, France; d. 7 Mar 1342; md 19 May 1305, Chauny, **William III d'Avesnes** (50-23), Count of Hainault and Holland.

Sources: Brandenburg, E. 1935; ES II 1984:4 (Gen. 23–24); II 1984:11, 12 (Gen. 25–30); Isenberg.S (1953 ed.); Martindale, J. 1992; Moriarty, G.1985, 197 (Gen. 23–24); 116 (Gen. 24–29); 51 (Gen. 29–30); Shaw, M. 1963; Turner, R. 1988; Vambery, A.1894:120–147; Vajay, S. de 1989, 372, 374, 379 (Gen. 26–29); Vale, M. 1990; Von Redlich, M. 1941 , 267, 268.

## LINE 71

28. **Henry II** (62-30), Duke of Limburg and Count of Arlon; b. 1110/1015; d. Aug 1167, Rome; md (1) **Mathilda von Saffenburg**, d. 2 Jan 1145; dau of **Adalbert von Saffenburg** (62-30). Mathilda was heiress of Landes Rode.

27. **Henry III** "the Old," Duke of Limburg, Count of Arlon; b. c1140; d. 21 June 1221; bur at Rolduc; md **Sophia von Saarbrucken** (23-27).

26. **Waleran IV,** Duke of Monschou, Count in the Ardennesgau; d. 2 July 1226; bur Rolduc; md (2) May 1214, **Ermesinde of Namur** (mother of Gen. 25), Countess of Luxemburg; b. July 1186; d. 12 Feb 1247; dau

**Henry** "the Blind," Count of Luxemburg and Namur; son of **Godfrey** (126-30), Count of Dagsburg and Namur, and **Ermesinde of Luxemburg** (3-30). **Henry** md **Agnes**, dau of **Henry I** (304-29), Count of Guelders.

25. **Henry III** "the Blond," Count of Luxemburg; b. 1217; d. 24 Nov 1281; md 4 June 1240, **Mathilde de Bar-le-Duc** (36-25).

24. **Philippa of Luxemburg** md, 1270, **Jean II d'Avesnes** (50-24), Count of Holland and Hainault.

Sources: Blass, R. 1939, II:267, 268; Brandenburg, E. 1935; ES, VI 1978:28 (Gen. 24–25); VI 1978:26 (Gen. 25–28); Isenburg, W. 1953; Moriarty, G.1985, 191–193 (Gen. 24–27); 160 (Gen. 27–28); Northoff, L. von 1929; Vambery 120–147; Winkhaus, E. 1953.

## LINE 72

31. **Malcolm III Canmore** (165-31), King of Scotland, md St .**Margaret of Scotland** (233-32).

30. **David I** "the Saint," King of Scotland, 23 Apr 1124-1153; Earl of Huntingdon, in England; b. c1080, Scotland; d. 24 May 1153, Carlyle, Cumberland; md (her second) 1113/1114, **Matilda** (Maud) **of Huntingdon** (221-31); widow of Simon de St. Liz.

29. **Henry of Huntingdon**, Prince of Scotland, 23 Apr 1124-1153; Earl of Huntingdon and Northumberland; b. c1115, Scotland; d. 12 june 1152, bur Kelso, Roxburgh, Scotland; md 1139, **Ada** (Adelaide) **de Warenne** (77-31,135-28).

28. **Ada de Huntingdon**, b. c1146, Scotland; d. 11 Jan 1216/1222; md 28 Aug 1161/1162, **Florenz III** (390-28), Count of Holland (France) and West Sealand, Earl of Ros; Crusader; b. c1138; d. 1 Aug 1190, on the 3rd Crusade, at Antioch; a companion of the Emperor Frederick Barbarosa who also died on this Crusade.

27. **William I,** Count of Holland (France) and East Friesland; fought at Bovines in the Imperial army, 1215; went on a Crusade to Damietta, 1215–1219; b. c1174; d. 2 July 1222; md 1198, **Adelaide (Adelheid) of Guelders** (304-27).

26. **Florenz** (Florens) **IV**, Count of Holland (France), 1222; and Sealand, 1226; b. 24 June 1210; d. 19 July 1234; md **Matilda** (Mechtild) **of Brabant** (120-26).

25. **Adelaide of Holland**, heiress of the countship of Holland (France); governed Holland and Sealand, 1256–1263; b. c1225; d. 1284; md 9 Oct 1246; **Jean I d'Avesnes** (50-25), Count of Hainault.

Sources: Anderson, A. 1990, I:268; Bingham, C. 1974; Brandenburg, E. 1935; Burke, B. 1963; Cokayne, G. 1959, IV:670, chart iii; VII:646-647; Langer, W. 1948, I:56-57; Moriarty, G. 1985, 30-32,182-184; Pirie, C. 1962, I:1-4; II: 1,2; Paul, J. 1914, I:3, 4, 7; III: 142, 143; Stockvis, A. 1966, III:11; Tyre, W. 1943; Winkhaus, E. 1953.

33. **Baldwin V de Lille** (141-32), Count of Flanders, md **Adela** (140-32), Princess of France.

32. **Baldwin I,** Count of Hainault (VI of Flanders); b. c1030; d. 17 July 1070; md 1055, **Richilde von Egisheim**, d. 15 Mar 1086. *NOTE: Von Redlich, M. 1941 , p. 277, makes Regnier V, Count of Hainault, Richilde's father. ES, II:5 clarifies this. Her parentage is unknown.* Richilde was the widow of Herman, Count of Hainault (son of Regnier V); md (3) 1070, William de Crepon; d. in battle at Cassel, 22 Feb 1071.

31. **Baldwin II,** Count of Hainault; Crusader; b. c1056; d. after 8 June 1098, in the East on the 1st Crusade; md 1084, **Ida of Louvain** (138-31).

30. **Baldwin III,** Count of Hainault; b. 1088; d. 1120; md c1107 (1) **Yolande** (Jolante) **of Guelders** (119-30).

29. **Baldwin IV**, Count of Hainault; b. c1110; d. 6/8 Nov 1171; bur at St. Waldthud Abbey at Mons; md 1130, **Alice de Namur** (37-28,126-29), heiress of Namur; b. c1115; d. end of July 1169.

28. **Baldwin V,** Count of Hainault (VIII of Flanders); b. c1150; d. 17 Dec 1195, Mons; bur in St. Waldthud Abbey at Mons; md (2) Apr 1169, **Marguerite of Lorraine** (132-28), heiress of Flanders.

27. **Baldwin VI** (IX of Flanders), Count of Hainault, Latin Emperor of Constantinople, Emperor of the East (1204), and a leader of the 4th Crusade; b. July 1171, Valenciennes, France; d. 11 June 1205; md 6 June 1186, **Marie of Champagne** (137-27).

26. **Margaret,** heiress of Hainault and Flanders; b. 2 June 1202, Constantinople, Turkey; d. 10 Feb 1280; md July 1212, **Bouchard d'Avesnes** (50-26), Archdeacon of Laon and Canon of St. Pierre de Lille.

Sources: Cokayne, G. 1959, IX:18; Eggenburger, D. 1985, 112; ES, I 1980:95 (Gen. 31); II 1984:5, 6 (Gen. 26–30); Flahiff, G. 1947; Jeffrey, J. 1980; Moriarty, G.1985, 177 (Gen. 26–27); 124 (Gen. 27–32); 15 (Gen. 32–33); Pears, E. 1885; Quellan, D. 1977; Rosch, S. 1977; Tyre, W. 1943; Vambery, 120–147; Van Overstraeten, D. 1976, 33–36; Vercauteren, F. 1938, XV–XIX; Villchardouin, G. n.d.

30. **Andronikos Angelos Doukas** (215-30), Ambassador to Jerusalem; fl. 1155–1182; d. before 12 Dec 1185; md before 1155, **Euphrosyne Kastamonitissa,** d1185/1195.

29. **Alexios Angelos** (Alexius III), Emperor (Basilius) of the East, 1195–1203; imprisoned by his son-in-law Theodoros Laskaris; b. after 1155; d. in captivity in a monastery, after 1211; md **Euphrosyne Kamatera Doukaina** (394-30).

28. **Anna Angelina**, d. 1212; md (2) 1199, **Theodore Komnenos Lascaris I** (Theodore I), Despot, 1197; Emperor (Basilius) of the East, 1204; expelled by the Latins, 1204; Basileus of Nicea, 1206–1222; b. 1173;

d. cAug 1222; son of **Manuel Lascaris**, who md **Ionna.**

27. **Maria Laskarina**, b. c1206; d. 1270; md 1218, **Bela IV** (78-27), King of Hungary, 1235–1270.

Sources: Allen, J. 1985; Brook, L. 1981; ES, II 1984:182 (Gen. 27–29); II:179 (Gen. 30); Hanowelt, E. 1982; Isenburg, W. 1932; Langer, W. 1948, chart 251; Moriarty, G.1985, 174 (Gen. 27–30).

## LINE 75

34. **Mieszko II** (378-34), King of Poland; md **Richenza** (Rixa) (237-34).

33. **Rixa** (281-30), Princess of Poland; b. 1018; d. after 1052; md c1040, **Bela I** (51-33), King of Hungary.

32. **Ladislas I** "the Saint," King of Hungary, 1077; d. 27 July 1095; md 1077, **Adelaide of Rheinfelden** (97-29,381-32).

Sources: Brandenburg, E. 1935; ES I 1980:129; ES II 1984:154 (Gen. 32–33); Moncreiffe, I. 1982, 83; Moriarty, G.1985, 140–141 (Gen. 32–33); 84 (Gen. 33–34); Moriarty, G. 1947; Polemis, D. 1968.

## LINE 76

42. **Jimeno.**

41. **Inigo Jiminez** md (1) N.N.; md (2) N.N. (mother of Gen. 40), widow of Musa Ibn Fortun, Chief of the Banu Qasi family.

40. **Inigo Iniguez Arista**, King of Pamplona (822-851), a Basque leader; b. c790; d. 5 July 851 or 22 May 852; md **Oneca**.

39. **Garcia I Iniguez** (292-41,294-43), King of Pamplona (852-882); b. c810; d. 882; md (1) **Urraca** (mother of Gen. 38); md (2) **Leogundis**, Infanta of Asturia; dau of **Ordogno I** (267-41, 276-39), King of the Asturias.

38. **Jimena Garces**, d. by 912; md 869/870, **Alfonso III** (276-38), King of the Asturias.

Sources: Collins, R. 1987; ES II 1984:53 (Gen. 38–42); II 1984:49 (Gen. 38–39); Mateos, R. 1984 (Gen. 38–42); Salazar, J. de 1984 (Gen. 38–42).

## LINE 76A

34. **Rognald** (Rognwald), Prince of Polotsk, a Verangian; b. 936; d. 963.

33. **Rogneda** (Rogniede) of Polotsk, Russia, b. c956, d. 1000; was a nun in 989; md St. **Vladismir I**, "the Great", Grand Duke of Kiev and Novgorod.

32. **Premylslava**, of Kiev, Ukraine, Russia, b. c980; d. 1018; md **Ladislas I** (51-34), Prince of Hungary.

Sources: ES II 1984; Mateo, R. 1984; Salazar, J de 1984.

## LINE 77

34. **Matilda of Louvain** (121-34) md **Eustace I** (242-34), Count of Boulogne.

33. **Lambert of Boulogne** (Lambert of Lens), Count or Seigneur of Lens-Aumale; b. c1022, Lens, Normandy; slain 1054 in Battle of Lille, Phalampin, France; md 1053/1054, **Adelaide of Normandy** (131-31).

32. **Judith of Lens** (same as 131-30); b. 1054; liv after 1086; md 1070, **Waltheof II** (221-32), Earl of Huntingdon,Northampton and Northumberland. *NOTE: Her maternal parentage has come under question. See note following 131-30.*

31. **Maud of Huntingdon**, Queen of Scots; b. c1072; d. 1130/31; md 1089 (1) Simon de St. Liz (Simon de Senlis), Earl of Huntingdon and Northampton; md (2), 1113/1114, **David I** (72-30), King of Scotland.

Sources: Cokayne, G. 1959, I:350–352; IV:670, chart iv; V:472, 736; VI:638–642; VII:640–641; ES, II 1984:89 (Gen. 31–32); III 1989:621 (Gen. 32–34); Moriarty, G.1985, 183–184 (Gen. 31–32); 13 (Gen. 33); 125, 165 (Gen. 34); Paget, G. 1977 (Gen. 31–32).

## LINE 78

28. **Andrew II** (51-27), King of Hungary, 1205–1235; King of Galicia, 1214; b. 1176; d. 21 Sept 1235; md (1) before 1203, **Gertrude von Meran** (7-28, 51-27) (mother of Gen. 27); md (2) **Yolande de Courtenay** (51-27, 79-26); md (3) 14 May 1234, Beatrice von Este, d. 1245; dau of Margrave Aldobrandino I.

27. **Bela IV**, King of Hungary, 1235–1270; Duke of Styria, 1254–1269; b. 1206; d. 3 May 1270; md **Maria Laskarina** (74-27).

26. **Stephen V**, King of Hungary and Croatia, 1270; b. Dec 1239; d. 1 Aug 1272; md 1253, **Elizabeth of Bosnia** (of Kumans); d. after 1290; dau **Kuthen**, Khan (Prince) of the Kumans.

25. **Maria**, Princess of Hungary; b. c1257; assassinated 25 Mar 1323; md 1270, **Charles II** (88-25), King of Naples and Prince of Salerno.

Sources: Dworzaczek, K. 1959, tables 84, 85 (Gen. 25–28); ES, II:155 (Gen. 25–28); Moriarty, G.1985, 198 (Gen. 25–28); Rubincam, M. 1957 (Gen. 25–28); Von Redlich, M. 1941 , 267–268 (Gen. 25–28); Woegerer, H. 1866 (Gen. 25–28).

## LINE 79

29. **Louis VI** "le Gros" (134-30), King of France, md **Adelaide of Maurienne** (124-31).

28. **Peter of France**; of Courtenay, Loiret, France; Prince of France, Count of Courtenay and Montargis, Sire de Courtenay; Crusader; b. c1126; d. 10 Apr 1183; md after 1150, **Elizabeth de Courtenay** (144-28).

27. **Peter II de Courtenay**, Emperor of the East, 1217; Count of Courtenay, 1193; of Nevers, 1184; of Auxerre and Tonnerre, 1199; Mar-

quis of Namur, 1212–1216; b. c1155; d. after June 1219, Eperus, Turkey; md (2) 1 July 1193, Soissons, France, **Yolande of Flanders,** Countess and heiress of Namur; dau of **Baldwin V** (73-28), Count of Hainault, and **Marguerite of Lorraine** (132-28), heiress of Flanders.

26. **Yolande de Courtenay,** Queen of Hungary and Galicia; b. c1194; d. 1233; md (2) 1215, **Andrew II** (51-27), King of Hungary; he also md Gertrude von Meran.

Sources: Brandenburg, E. 1935; Dworzaczek, K. 1959, tables 84, 85 (Gen. 26–28); ES, II 1984:17 (26–28); Flahiff, G. 1947; Isenburg, W. 1953; Moriarty, G.1985, 148 (Gen. 26–27); 51 (Gen. 27–29); Tyre, W. 1943; Winkhaus, E. 1953.

## LINE 80

32. **Robert Guiscard d'Hauteville** (296-32), Norman Conqueror of Southern Italy; Duke of Apulia; md (1) 1054, **Albereda** (296-32) (mother of Gen. 31 below); div 1058; md (2) Sikelgaita (297-32).

31. **Bohemond I,** Prince of Antioch, Duke of Calabria; Crusader; a leader of the 1st Crusade, 1098; b. 1052, d. 3 Mar 1111, at Canossa, Italy; md (2) 1106, at Chartres, **Constance** (146-31), Princess of France.

30. **Bohemond II,** Prince of Antioch and Taranto, Duke of Calabria; b. 1107/1108; slain Feb 1130, in Sicily; md 1126, **Alice de Rethel** (145-29), Princess of Jerusalem.

29. **Constance of Antioch,** Princess and heiress of Antioch; b. 1127; d. 1163; md (1) Raymond, Prince of Antioch; md (2) 1152, **Renaud de Chatillon** (99-29), Prince of Antioch (father of Gen. 28).

28. **Agnes de Chatillon-sur-Loing;** b. 1153; d. 1184; md **Bela III** (51-28), King of Hungary.

Sources: Agiles, R. 1968; Bennenisti, M. 1972; Boase, T. 1971; ES, III 1984:154 (Gen. 28–30); II 1984:205 (30–32); Evans, C. 1976; Foucher, 1971; Gautier, P. 1971; Holt, O. 1986; Krey, A. n.d.; Moncreiffe, I. 1982, chart 22, p.83; Moriarty, G.1985, 142 (Gen. 28–31); 71 (Gen. 31–32); Phillips, J. 1996; Prawer, J. 1972; Prawer, J. 1973; Riley-Smith, J. 1973; Tibble, S. 1989.

## LINE 81

31. **William I,** the Conqueror (89-30), md **Maud** (Matilda) **of Flanders** (141-31).

30. **Adele of Normandy and England**, Princess of England; b. c1062; d. 8 Mar 1138, at Maringuy, a nun; md 1080/1081, **Stephen III of Blois** (Étienne Henri) (133-31), Count of Blois, Champagne, Brie, and Chartres; a leader of the First Crusade; son of **Thibaud III**, Count of Champagne, and wife, **Gundrada.**

29. **Thibaud IV** (II) (same as 60-29,133-30), of Blois, Loir et Cher, France; Count of Blois and Champagne; b. 1090; d. 8/10 Jan 1151/52; md

43

1123, **Mathilda von Sponheim** (Maud of Carinthia) (60-29,133-30, 228-30), d. 13 Dec 1160/1161, at Fontevrault.

28. **Henry I** "the Generous," (131-28), Count of Champagne and Brie; b. c1126; d. 17 Mar 1181, Troyes; md 1164, **Marie of France** (134-28), Princess of France.

27. **Theobald III**, Count of Briey; b. 13 Jan 1179, Troyes; d. 24 May 1201; md at Chartres, 1 July 1199, **Blanche** (86-27), Princess of Navarre.

26. **Theobald IV** "the Great," (55A-26), King of Navarre, 1234; Count of Brie and Bar-sur-Seine; Crusader 1239/40; b. 3 May 1201, Navarre,Spain; d. 8 July 1253, Pamplona; md (3) 12 Sept 1232, **Marguerite de Bourbon** (84-26).

25. **Henry I**, of Troyes, Aube, France; King of Navarre; b. c1244; d. 22 July 1274; md (2) 1269, **Blanche of Artois** (147-25) (mother of Gen. 24). She md (2) Edmund Plantagenet, son of Henry III, King of England.

24. **Jeanne of Navarre**, Princess of Navarre, Queen of France; b. Jan 1272, France; d. 2 Apr 1305, Château-de-Vincennes, France; bur Church of the Grey Friars in Paris; md 16 Aug 1284, **Philip IV** (51-24), King of France, 1285–1314.

Sources: Agiles, R. 1968; Bard, R. 1982; Blass, R. 1939, II:251; Chaume, M. 1977, 542, 551–552; Cokayne, G. 1959, I:350–352; VII:378–387; Douglas, D. 1964; ES, II 1984:12 (Gen. 24–25); II 1984:26–27 (Gen. 24–31); Foucher, 1971; Krey, A. n.d.; Moriarty, G. 1945; Moriarty, G. 1947; Pine, L. 1973; Winkhaus, E. 1953.

## LINE 82

*NOTE: This line has undergone considerable revision, since the lineage as given in customary sources is known to be incorrect. Articles by Charles Evans (1965, 1983), Fiennes (1980), and Parsons, J. (1989), help to clarify the situation, as does ES III 1989:649, 650 .*

30. **Gilbert,** Lord of Mello, d. after 25 Feb 1084.

29. **Aubrey de Mello** md **Aelis de Dammartin** (397-29).

28. **Alberic** (Aubrey) **I**, Count of Dammartin, 1122, 1125–1129; High Chamberlain of France; b. 1110; d. 1183; md (her 3rd) **Joan Basset** of Wallingford, Oxford, England (prob mother of Gen. 27); dau of **Gilbert Basset** (395-29) and **Edith d'Oilly** (396-29); Alberic also md Clemence de Dammartin, liv 1154.

27. **Alberic** (Aubrey) **II**, Count of Dammartin, Ile de France; b. c1135; d. 19 Sept 1200, London; bur Abbey of Jumieges; md **Mathilda of Ponthieu** (149-27).

26. **Simon II de Dammartin**, Count of Dammartin, Aumale, Ponthieu and Montreuil; b. c1180; d. 21 Sept, 1239, Abbeville, France; bur at Valloires; md Sept 1208, **Marie** (Jeanne) **of Ponthieu** (148-26), heiress of Ponthieu and Montreuil, 1225; she md (2) Matthew de Montgomery, Seigneur de Montmorency.

25. **Jeanne** (or Joan) **de Dammartin,** Countess and heiress of Ponthieu, 1251; b. c1208/1220; d. 16 Mar 1279, Abbeville, France; bur Abbey de Valloires; md **Fernando III** (52–25), King of Castile and Leon.

Sources: ES, III 1989:649 (Gen. 25–28); III 1989:650 (Gen. 28–30); Evans, C. 1965; Evans, C. 1983; Fagat, H. 1980; Fiennes, D. 1980; Garrigues, M. 1981; Johnson, H. 1969, 14–44; Newman, W. 1971, 73+, 81–88; Parsons, J. 1984; Parsons, J. 1988; Parsons, J. 1989.

## LINE 83

29. **Alfonso VII** (52-28,86–29), King of Castile and Leon; md **Berengaria of Barcelona** (86-29) (mother of Gen. 28); md also **Richilde of Poland** (378-29). *NOTE: Some authorities indicate Richilde of Poland as mother of Sancho III.*

28. **Sancho III,** King of Castile, 1157; b. 1134; d. 31 Aug 1158, Toledo, Spain; betrothed 25 Oct 1140, at age 5; md 30 Jan 1151, age 16, Logera or Calaharra,Spain, **Blanche** (called "Sancha") (151-28), Princess of Navarre.

27. **Alfonso IX** "the Noble," King of Castile (1158–1214), Toledo and Extramadura; the victor of Los Navas de Tolosa; b. 11 Nov 1155, Soria; d. 5 Oct 1214, near Avevalo; bur Cistercian monastery, Santa Maria la Real, called de las Huelgas, near Burgos, Spain; md 1170, Burgos, **Eleanor** (88-28), Princess of England.

26. **Berengaria of Castile,** heiress of Castile; b. 1180, Burgos, Spain; d. 8 Nov 1246, Las Huelgas, near Burgos; md (2), Valladolid, Dec 1197 (div 1204), **Alfonso IX** (52-26), King of Leon.

Sources: Banfield, A. 1990 (Gen. 26-29); Cokayne, G. 1959, II:59 note b; ES, II 1984:62 (Gen. 26–29); Evans, C. 1932 (Gen. 26–29); Moriarty, G.1985, 108–109 (Gen. 26–29); Stimmel, R. 1978.A (Gen. 26–28); Vajay, S. de 1989, 376, 378.

## LINE 84

32. **Viter** (Gauthier) **de Moeslain,** d. c1080.

31. **Thibaud de Dampierre-sur-l'Aube,** Seigneur de Dampierre and St. Dizier; d. 1106/1107; md **Elizabeth de Montlhery** (57-31).

30. **Gui I,** Seigneur de Dampierre, 1118–1150; Viscount of Troyes, 1130; In the service of the Count of Champagne, 1118–1150; b. c1100; d. 1151; md (his 2nd, her 2nd) 1120/1125, **Helvide de Baudemont,** b. c1105; d. 1165; dau of **Andre de Baudemont** (124-30), Seigneur de Baudemont and of Braine, Senechal of Champagne; b. c1060; d. a monk; who md **Agnes de Braine,** heiress of Braine, and widow of Hugh, Sire de Montreal.

29. **William I,** Seigneur de Dampierre, Constable of Champagne; d. after 1161; md **Ermengarde de Mouchy** (56-29).

28. **Gui II,** Seigneur de Dampierre, de Bourbon, St. Just and St. Dizier, Constable of Champagne, procurator of Auvergne; Crusader; loyal

fiefholder of the Seigneurie de Montlucon; d. 18 Jan 1216; bur at St. Laumesin in Blois, France; md 9 Sept 1196, **Mathilda**, Dame de Bourbon, heiress of Bourbon; b. c1165; d. 18 June 1228; bur as a nun of Fontevault at Montelaux Moines; dau of **Archambaud VIII**, Seigneur de Bourbon, and **Alice of Burgundy**.

27. **Archambaud VIII de Bourbon** (Dampierre-Bourbon) "the Great," (He took his mother's family name); Seigneur de Bourbon, procurator of Auvergne; slain 23 July 1242, in the Battle of Taillebourg near Cognac; md 1205, **Guigone of Forez** (mother of Gen. 26), d. before 1220; he md (2) Beatrice de Montlucon, dau of Archambaud V (440-28).

26. **Marguerite de Bourbon**, b. c1211; d. 12 Apr 1256, Provins, Brie, France; md 12 Sept 1232, **Theobald IV** (81-26), King of Navarre, etc.

Sources: ES, III 1984:51 (Gen. 26-32); Isenburg, W. 1932; Jubainville, M. 1869, I:318, II:491–492; Mesmay, J. de 1963; Moriarty, G.1985, 149–150 (Gen. 26–31); Winkhaus, E. 1953.

## LINE 85

36. **William**, Seigneur de Semur, 858–864.

35. **Freelan** (Froilan) **de Chamelet,** Seigneur de Semur, Count in the Brionnaise; liv 892.

34. **Joceran de Semur**, Count in the Brionnaise, d. 992/994, md **Ricoara**.

33. **Geoffrey I**, Seigneur de Semur; liv 1015; md (1) **N.N.**, dau of **Damas** (Dalmace), Vicomte de Brioude, d. c962.

*NOTE: Some sources have an additional generation (Geoffrey II) between Gen. 33 and Gen. 32 but Geoffrey II was actually brother of Helie (Gen. 31).*

32. **Damas** (Dalmace), Sire de Semur, d. after 1048 (said to have been murdered by his son-in-law, Robert, Duke of Burgundy); md **Aremburga**, formerly thought to be dau of Henry I, Duke of Burgundy, and Mahaut de Chalon, but latest work (1987) (cf. Bouchard, 356–361) says ancestry unknown.

31. **Helie de Semur** (Eleanor de Semour-en-Auxois) (154-33), b. 1016; d. 22 Apr (1055); md c1033, **Robert I** "the Old" (154-33), Duke of Burgundy, d. 21 Mar 1076.

30. **Henry**, Duke of Burgundy, heir apparent of the Duchy of Burgundy; b. c1035; d.27 Jan 1070/74; md c1056, **Sibylle** (Sybilla) **of Barcelona**,d. 6 July 1074; dau of **Raymond Berenger I** (54-33), Count of Barcelona, and **Gisela of Lluca** (245-32).

29. **Henry I of Burgundy**; Count of Portugal; Crusader in Spain; b. 1069/1070, Dijon, Burgundy, France; d. 1 Nov 1112, Astorga, Galicia, Spain; bur Braga Cathedral; md 1093, **Teresa of Castile and Leon** (430-30) who inherited the countship of Portugal; d. 1 Nov 1130; bur Braga Cathedral; dau **Alfonso VI** (248-31), King of Castile and Leon, by **Zaida**

(430-31), Princess of Dania.

28. **Alfonso I Henriques**, first King of Portugal, 1128–1185; the famous crusading king who recovered Lisbon from the Moors; Count of Portugal; b. 25 July 1110, Guimaraes, Portugal; d. 6 Dec 1185, Coimbra; bur there; md 1146, **Maud of Savoy** (182-28); d. 4 Dec 1157, Coimbra.

27. **Urraca**, Princess of Portugal; b. c1150; d. 16 Oct 1188, Bamba, near Valladolid, Spain; bur monastery of Saint Juan Bautista of the Knights of St. John; md 1165, **Fernando II** (52-27), King of Leon, 1157–1188. She separated June 1175, and became a nun at Bamba.

Sources: Blass, R. 1939, II:242; Bouchard, C. 1987, 356–361; ES, II 1984:38 (Gen. 27–29); II:69 (Gen. 30); III 1985:434 (Gen. 31–35); Evans.P Payne, S. 1973; Vajay, S. de 1962 (Gen. 30–34); Vajay, S. de 1989, 374 (Gen. 27–28); Winkhaus, E. 1953.

## LINE 86

30. **Raymond of Burgundy** (94-30) md **Urraca** (155-30), Princess of Castile and Leon.

29. **Alfonso VII** (52-28, 83-29,151-29), King of Castile and Leon, Emperor of Spain, 1126; b. 1 Mar 1105; d. 21 Aug 1157; md **Berengaria of Barcelona** (83-29), (mother of Gen. 28 below); d. Feb 1149; dau of **Raymond Berenger III** (54-30), Marquis of Barcelona, Count of Provence, and **Dulce di Gievaudun** (257-30); Alfonso md (2) July 1152, **Richilde of Poland** (378-29), d. 1166.

28. **Sancha**, Infanta of Castile; b. c1140; d. 5 Aug 1179; bur Cathedral of Santa Maria, Pamplona; md 20 July 1153, Carrion de los Condes, **Sancho VI** "el Sabio" (the Wise), King of Navarre; b. 1132; d. 27 June 1194, Pamplona; son of **Garcia VII** (151-29), King of Navarre and **Margaret de l'Aigle** (178-29).

27. **Blanche of Navarre**, Princess and heiress of Navarre; d. 12/14 Mar 1229; md **Theobald III** (81-27), Count of Brie.

Sources: Bard, R. 1982; Barton, S. 1997; Brandenburg, E. 1935; Glick, T. 1995; Mac Kay, A. 1977; Moriarty, G.1985, 148–149 (Gen. 27–28); 108–109; (Gen. 28–30); Isenburg, W. 1953; Moriarty, G. 1947; O'Callaghan, J. 1983; Vajay, S. de 1989, 374, 375 (Gen. 27–29); Winkhaus, E. 1953.

## LINE 87

37. **Wulgrim**, Count of Agen, etc. (326-38) md **Roselinde** (326-38).

36. **Auduin** (Hildouin, Alduin), Count of Angoulême; d. 27 Mar 916; bur at Saint-Cybard, Angoulême.

35. **William I** "Taillefer," Count of Angoulême, Aquitaine, France; a minor in 916; d. 6 Aug 962 (md) **N.N.** (mother of Gen. 34), a concubine.

34. **Arnaud** "Manzer," Count of Angoulême; a bastard; b. c952; d. a monk, 988/992, at Saint-Cybard, Angoulême; md (1) **Raingarde**.

33. **William II** "Taillefer," Count of Angoulême; b. c978; d. 6 Apr 1028; bur Saint-Cybard, Angoulême; md **Gerberge of Anjou** (157-33).

32. **Geoffrey I** "Taillefer," Count of Angoulême, 1032; b. c1014; d. 1048; md (1) 1020/23, **Petronel** (Petronille) **d'Archiac** (398-33), (mother of Gen. 31); liv 1048; heiress of Bonteville, France; dau **Mainard d'Archiac** "the Rich," Sire d'Archiac and de Bonteville; md (2) Asceline , liv 1038/1048.

31. **Fulk** "Taillefer," Count of Angoulême and Archiac; b. 1030; d. 1087; md **Condoha** (Condor) **Vogena** of Angoulême, Aquitaine; b. c1032; dau **Robert**, Count of Eu.

30. **William III** "Taillefer," Count of Angoulême; b. perhaps c1065; d. 6 Apr 1118; md **Vidapont de Benauges** of Benauges, France; b. 1066; dau **Amalric** (Amanieu) **de Benauges**, Sire de Benauges and St. Macaire in Angoulême, Aquitaine, France.

29. **Wulgrin II** "Taillefer," Count of Angoulême; b. c1089; d. 16 Sept 1140; md (1) **Pancia de la Marche** (Ponce de Montgomery) (mother of Gen. 28); b. c1109; dau of **Roger de Montgomery** and **Adelmode de la Marche**, heiress of la Haute Marche, who was dau of **Adalbert III**, Count de la Haute Marche who md **Poncia**, liv 1076.

28. **William IV** "Taillefer," Count of Angoulême, 1140; d. 7 Aug 1179, Messina, Sicily, Italy, on a crusade; md (1) c1138, Emma de Limoges, dau of Ademer de Limoges; md (2) (her 3rd) 1147, **Marguerite de Turenne** (156-28) (mother of Gen. 27).

27. **Aymer de Valence** (Aymer Taillefer), Count of Angoulême, Crusader; b. c1160; d. Limoges, 16 June 1202; md Apr 1186, **Alice** (Adelaide) **de Courtenay** (144-27).

26. **Isabella** (Isabel) **of Angoulême**, heiress of Angoulême, Queen of England; b. 1188; d. 31 May 1246; bur Fontevrault, Maine-et-Loire, France; md (1) (his 2nd), 24 Aug 1200, **John** "Lackland" (2-26), King of England, 1199–1216; she md (2) Hugh X de Lusignan (cf. ES, III:564).

Sources: Beauchat, E 1978, 667; Cokayne, G. 1959, V:736; X:377–382; Levillain, L. 1937, 237–263; Lievre, A. 1885; Lot, F. 1903, 388–395; Winkhaus, E. 1953.

**LINE 88**

35. **William I** (162-35,163-35), Count of Poitou, and as William III, Duke of Aquitaine; md **Gerloc** (162-35).

34. **William II** "Bras de Fer," Count of Poitou (his 3, her 2) and as William IV, Duke of Aquitaine; b. c937; d. 995; md 968, **Emma of Blois** (340-34).

33. **William III** (119-33,150-32) "the Great," Count of Poitou; as William V, Duke of Aquitaine; b. c969; d. a monk, 31 Jan 1030; md (his 3rd, her 2nd) 1019, **Agnes of Burgundy** (161-32), Princess of Lombardy.

32. **William IV** (also called Gui Geoffrey), Count of Poitou; and as

William VIII, Duke of Aquitaine; b. c1024; d. 25 Sept 1086; md (3) 1068/1069, **Hildegarde of Burgundy** (154-32).

31. **William VII**, Count of Poitou; and as William IX, Duke of Aquitaine; Crusader; b. c22 Oct 1071, France; d. 10 Feb 1126/1127; md (her 2) 1094, div 1115, **Philippa** (Mathilde) (160-29), regent of Toulouse.

30. **William VIII**, a Crusader, Count of Poitou; and as William X, Duke of Aquitaine; b. 1099; d. 9 Apr 1137, in Galicia, on a pilgrimage to St. Iago de Compostela; md late 1121, **Eleanore de Châtellerault** (159-30) (mother of Gen. 29); md (2) Emma de Limoges, dau Count Aymer III.

29. **Eleanor of Aquitaine** (134-29), heiress of Aquitaine; Queen of France and England; b. 1122, prob Bordeaux; d. 31 Mar 1204, Mirabell Castle, Poitiers, France; md (1) 25 July 1137, Bordeaux; div 18 Mar 1152, **Louis VII** (70-29), King of France, 1170–1180; md (2) 18 May 1152, **Henry II** "Curt Mantel," (2-27), King of England (and father of Gen. 28 below); Louis VII md (2) Constance of Castile, and (3) **Adelaide of Blois** (133-29).

28. **Eleanor**, Princess of England and Queen of Castile; b. 13 Oct 1162, Falaise, Calvados, France; d. 25 Oct 1214, Burgos, Spain, but Vajay, S. de 1989, 376, says Domfront, Normandy; bur with her husband; md 1170, **Alfonso IX** "the Noble" (83-27), King of Castile.

27. **Blanche of Castile**, Princess of Castile, Queen of France; b. 4 Mar 1188, Palencia, Spain; d. 27 Nov 1252, Paris; bur at Abbey of Montbuisson; md 23 May 1200, Abbey of Port-Mort, Bapaume, near Pont-Audemer, Normandy, **Louis VIII** "the Lion" (70-27), King of France, 1223–1226.

26. **Charles I**, King of Naples, Sicily and Jerusalem, Count of Anjou, Provence and Maine; b. Mar 1226; d. 7 Jan 1285, Foggia, Italy; bur Naples; md (1) 31 Jan 1246, **Beatrice of Savoy** (164-26), Countess of Provence.

25. **Charles II** "le Boiteux," (the lame), King of Naples, Sicily and Jerusalem, Prince of Salerno; b. 1254; d. 5 June 1309, Caranova (near Naples); md 1270, **Maria** (78-25), Princess of Hungary.

24. **Marguerite**, Princess of Naples & Sicily; b. c1273; d. 31 Dec 1299; md 16 Aug 1290, Corbeil, **Charles of Valois** (70-24), Count of Valois.

Sources: Agiles, R. 1968; Archern, K. 1993; Cokayne, G. 1959, VII:386; ES, II 1984:15 (Gen. 24–26); II 1984:11, 12 (Gen. 27–30); II 1984:76 (Gen. 29–35); Conder, C. 1978; Foucher, 1971; Fryde, E. 1986; Krey, A. n.d.; Martindale, J. 1992; Mayer, H. 1994; Moriarty, G.1985, 197 (Gen. 24–26); 108, 116 (Gen. 26–29); 35–37 (Gen. 29–34); 27 (Gen. 34–35); Munro, D. 1935; Poole, S. 1978; Prawler, J. 1952; Prawler, J. 1972; Prawler, J. 1980; Richard, J. 1979; Riley-Smith, J. 1973; Runciman, S. 1987; Turner, R. 1988; Vannerus, J. 1946.

## LINE 89

33. **Richard I** (166-32,222-35), Duke of Normandy; (md) **Gunnora** (Gonnor) **de Crepon** (156-32,166-33) (mother of Gen. 32).

32. **Richard II** (176-33), "the Good," Duke of Normandy; b. Normandy France; d. 28 Aug 1027, Fecamp, S-Infr, France; md c1000, **Judith of Brittany** (Rennes) (167-33).

31. **Robert I** "the Devil," Duke of Normandy; a Crusader; b. c1000, Normandy; d. 22 July 1035, Nicaea, Bithynia, Turkey, (md) **Herleve** (Harlette de Falaise), b. c1003, dau **Fulbert of Falaise**, a tanner, and **Doda** (Dode), a concubine. For **Herleve's** marriage to **Herlevin de Conteville** see 160-32.

30. **William I the Conqueror** ( 81-31,140-31), Duke of Normandy, King of England, 1066–1087; b. 1027/8, Falaise, Calvados, France; d. 9 Sept 1087, Rouen, France; bur at Caen; md 1053, **Maud (Matilda) of Flanders** (141-31).

29. **Henry I** "Beauclerc," King of England, 1100–1135; Duke of Normandy, 1100–1135; b. 1070, Selby, Yorkshire, England; d. 1 Dec 1135, Angers, Maine-et-Loire, France; bur Reading Abbey; md (1) 11 Nov 1100, **Matilda** (Edith) **of Scotland** (165-30) (mother of Gen. 28); he md (2) 29 Jan 1121, Adeliza of Louvain, b. c1103; d. 23 Apr 1151; dau Godfrey I (68-31,120-30), Duke of Lorraine and Count of Louvain; md Ida of Chiny and Namur. Henry I was the first king of England to use and grant a coat of arms.

28. **Matilda**, Princess of England, Empress of Germany; b. cFeb 1102, England; d. 10 Sept 1167, Notre Dame, France; md (2) 22 May 1127, **Geoffrey V Plantagenet** (2-28), Count of Anjou, Duke of Normandy; b. 24 Aug 1113;.d. 7 Sept 1151; she was the widow of Henry V, Emperor of Germany, who d.s.p. 22 May 1125.

Sources: Crispin, M. 1969, 186–187; Douglas, D. 1964; ES, II 1984:81–82 (Gen. 28–30); II 1984:79 (Gen. 30–33); Fryde, E. 1986; Isenburg, W. 1953 (1953 ed.); Moriarty, G.1985, 13 (Gen. 28–32); 11 (Gen. 32–34); Onslow, Earl of 1945; Paul, J. 1914, I:1–2; Williams, A. 1995.

## LINE 90

30. **Amauri de Montfort**, Seigneur of Montfort-l'Amauri, France, md **Bertrade de Gometz**, dau of **William de Gometz**.

29. **Simon I de Montfort** of Montfort l'Amauri, France; Seigneur de Montfort l'Amauri and Count of Montfort; b. c1026; d.1087; bur at Epernon; md (3) **Agnes d'Evreux** (168-31), b. c1030.

28. **Bertrade de Montfort** of Montfort l'Amauri, France; b. c1060; d. 14 Feb 1117, Fontevrault; md (his 5th) c1090, (div 15 Apr 1092); **Fulk IV** "Rechin"( 2-30), Count of Anjou; she md (2) 1092, **Philip I** (134-31), King of France, d. 24 July 1108.

Sources: Blass, R. 1939, II:251, 252; Cokayne, G. 1959, X, appendix A, p.3; XI, appendix D, 114; Crispin, M. 1969, table IV; ES II 1984:82 (Gen. 28); III 1989:642 (Gen. 28–30); Labarge, M. 1962, 51, 269, 273; Longnon, J. 1978, 113; Marot, P. 1984, 574; Moriarty, G.1985, 10 (Gen.

28–30); Prawer, J. 1970, 290; Winkhaus, E. 1953.

## LINE 91

33. **Geoffrey I** "Grisgonelle" (167-35), md(1) **Adele** (Adelaide) of Troyes and Vermanois (258-36).
32. **Fulk III** "the Black," Count of Anjou; b. by 976; d. 21 June 1040, Metz; md (2) 1000, **Hildegarde of Metz**, d. 1 Apr 1046, Jerusalem, Palestine on a pilgrimage.
31. **Ermengarde** (called Blanche) **of Anjou** (154-33); b. c1018; d. 21 Mar 1076, Fleury-sur-Ouche; md (1) 1035, **Geoffrey II** "Ferreol" (2-31) (Geoffrey de Château-Landon), Count in the Gatinais; md (2) 1055, **Robert III** (Aubrey-Geoffrey) (154-33), Prince of France.

Sources: ES II 1984:82 (Gen. 31–32); Hiestand, R. 1979, 545–553 (Gen. 31–33); Isenburg, W. 1953 (1953) (Gen. 31–33); Moriarty, G.1985, 4 (Gen. 31–33); Moriarty, G. 1945b (Gen. 31–33); Settipani, C. 1979b.

## LINE 92

41. **Bruno I**, warlord of the Saxons in Engern; Lord of Brunisberge-by-Hoxter; d. after 775; md c755, **N.N. of Asseburg**, dau of Count **Dietrich**, war leader of Eastphalia.
40. **Bruno**, Count in Saxon-Engen; b. c756; d. c813; md **Hasalda**, a dau of **Wittikind**. of the Saxons, whose parents were **Warnechin**, Count of Engern and wife **Kunhilde of Rugen**. Wittikind md **Geva**, daughter of **Eystein of Westfold** (339-42) and wife **Hild**, dau of **Eric Agnarsson**.
39. **Bruno**, Duke of Saxony; b. c786; d. before 844; md **Oda**.
38. **Ludolph** (301-39), Duke of Saxony, Count in East Saxony, Lord of Herzfeld; b. 816; d. 866; bur at Brunohausen; md **Oda**, dau of **Billung**, Count of Thuringia, and **Aeda**, a noble Frank.
37. **Otto** "the Illustrious" and "the Grand" (Otton le Grande), Duke of Saxony; Count in South Thuringia; b. c836; d. 30 Nov 912; md 869, **Hedwige** (172-38) Princess of Bavaria, d. 906.
36. **Henry I** (134-35,319-36) "the Fowler," Emperor of the West, 919–936; Emperor of Germany, 912–936; Duke of Saxony; b. 876, Germany; d. 2 July 936, Memleben, Saxony; md (2) 909, **Mathilda** (Mechtilde) **von Ringleheim** (321-37,338-36).
35. **Gerberge of Saxony** (120-36,230-36), b. 913/14, Nordhausen, Saxony; d. 5 May 984, Rheims, Marne, France; md (1) 929, **Giselbert** (207-37) (father of Gen. 34), Duke of Lorraine, 928; Lay Abbot of Echternach, 915–939; Count of Hainault, 916; b. c890, France; d. 2 Oct 934, Echternach, Rhineland, Prussia; Gerberge md (2), **Louis IV** "d'Outremer" (171-36), King of France, 936–954.
34. **Alberade of Lorraine**; of Hainault, Holland, France; b. c930; d. 15 Mar 973; md 944/947, **Ragnvald** (170-34), Count of Roucy.
33. **Ermentrude de Roucy**; Queen of Lombardy, Countess of Macon;

b. 958; d. 5 Mar 1005; md before 971, **Alberic** (Aubri) **II** (101-33) (father of Gen. 32), Count of Macon and Burgundy; md (1) **Otton I** (94-33), King of Lombardy.

32. **Beatrice of Macon,** of Burgundy France; md **Geoffrey** "Ferreol" (2-32), Count in the Gatinais.

Sources: Chaume, M. 1977, 549; Cokayne, G. 1959, XI :appendix D, 112–113; Curschmann, F. 1921; ES, I 1980:3 (Gen. 35–38); ES I.1 1997; Isenburg, W. 1953; James, E. 1985; Moriarty, G. 1945b; Moriarty, G. 1947 (Gen. 36-38) Moriarty, G.1985, 1 (Gen. 32–33); 39 (Gen. 33–36); 37 (Gen. 33); 38 (Gen. 34); ; Rubincam, M. 1949 (Gen. 34–35); Saillot, J. 1980.

## LINE 93

43. **Richbald.**

42. **Bonifacio I,** prob a Frank of Lucca, sent to Bavaria by Pepin "the Short" in c750; d. before 785.

41. **Bonifacio II,** Count in Liguria and Lucca; sent by Charlemagne from Bavaria to Italy; d. before 5 Oct 823.

40. **Bonifacio III,** Count and Duke of Lucca, 828-830; Judge of Corsica, 835; d. after 838 and before 846; md N.N (perhaps Bertha).

39. **Adalbert I,** Count and Duke of Lucca; Margrave of Tuscany (including Florence and Fiesole), c846; d. after 27 May 884; md (1) Anonsuara; md (2) before 863, **Rothielde** (Rohaut) (265-39).

38. **Adalbert II** "the Rich," Count and Duke of Lucca and Margrave of Tuscany; d. 10/19 Aug 915; bur Lucca Cathedral; md 990/998, **Bertha of Lorraine** (mother of Gen. 37); d. 8 Mar 925; bur Lucca St. Maria; dau of King **Lothar II,** "the Carolingian;" Bertha was widow of Theobold of Arles.

37. **Gui** (Guido), Count and Duke of Lucca; Margrave of Tuscany; d. imprisoned, 928/929; md 924/925, **Marozia** (Mariuccia), Senatrix and Patria of Rome; d. imprisoned, 932/937; she was dau of **Theophylactus,** and widow of Alberico, Margrave of Spoleto.

36. **Adalbert III,** Margrave of Tuscany; named in a charter; b. after 900; d. c950/960.

35. **Alberto Azzo** (106-35), Count of Lucca; made Marchese by Berenger II, 960; Pfalzgrave, 962–972; d. c975; md (2) **Guilla,** dau of **Bonifacio I,** Duke of Spoleto, d. 928.

34. **Humbert** (Oberto) **I** (43-35), Count of Genoa and Tortone, Marchese of Italy and Este in Liguria; d. 1014/1021; md **Railinda** (mother of Gen. 33), dau of Count **Wiprand of Como** (d. 999), who is said to have been the son of **Olderado** and **Railinda,** dau of the Lombard, **Auprando,** Count of Verticilio. *NOTE: The mother of Gen. 33 was formerly thought to be Auxilia von Lenzburg, dau of Arnold I of Lenzburg.*

33. **Bertha of Este,** d. 29 Dec 1037; md before 1014, **Odalrico Manfrido II** (7-33, 32-31, 315-34), Margrave of Turin; occ 1014.

52

32. **Adelaide von Susa**, heiress of Turin and Susa; b. c1015; d. 14 Dec 1091; md (3) c1036, **Odo** (Otto) **I** (173-33) (father of Gen. 31), Count of Maurienne and Margrave of Susa; d. 19 Jan 1057/1058; she md (1) **Hermann IV** (63-34), Duke of Swabia, d. 1038; md (2) 1042, Henry, Margrave of Montferrat.

31. **Amadeus** (Amadeo) **II**, Count of Savoy and Margrave of Susa; b. c1046; d. 26 Jan 1080; md c1065/1070, **Johanna of Geneva**, d. c1095; dau of **Gerold I** (175-31), Count of Geneva, and his wife **Gisela**.

30. **Humbert** (Umberto) **II** "il Gross" (same as 124-32), Count of Maurienne and Savoy, Marquis of Turin; b. c1070; d. 14 Oct 1103; md (1) 1090, **Gisela of Burgundy** (59-29), b. c1070; d. after 1133; dau of **William II** (94-31), Count of Burgundy, and **Stephanie of Longwy**.

29. **Amadeus** (Amadeo) **III**, Count of Savoy and Marquis of Maurienne; Crusader; b. c1080/1092; d. 30 Mar 1148, Nicosia, Cyprus, on the 2nd Crusade; md 1133/34, **Matilda** (Maud) **d'Albon** (182-29,192-29).

28. **Humbert** (Umberto) **III** "the Saint," Count of Savoy and Marquis of Italy; b. 4 Aug 1136, Aveillave, Savoy, France; d. 4 Mar 1189, Cyprus; md (4) 1175, **Beatrice of Macon** (187-28).

27. **Thomas I**, Count of Savoy; b. 20 May 1178, Carbonierres, Savoy, France; d. 1 Mar 1233, Aosta, Italy; bur at St. Michael de la Cluse, Aosta, Italy; md 1196, **Margaret of Geneva** (175-27).

26. **Beatrice of Savoy**, Countess of Provence; b. 1198; d. Dec. 1266; md Dec 1220, **Raymond Berenger V** (54-26), Count of Provence and Forcalquier.

25. **Margaret of Provence**, b. 1221, St. Maime, near Forcalquier; d. 20/21 Dec 1295, Paris; bur St. Denis; md 27 May 1234, **Louis IX** "St. Louis" (70-26), King of France, 1226–1270.

Sources: Clairvaux, B. 1963; Constable, G. 1953; ES, II 1984:12 (Gen. 25–26); II 1984:70 (26–27); II 1984:190 (Gen. 28–34); III 1985:590 (Gen. 37–40); Hlawitschka.F, 1960:147+ (Gen. 37–40); James, E. 1985; Shaw, M. 1963; Moriarty, G.1985, 68 (Gen. 25–26); 104 (Gen. 26–29); 59 (Gen. 29–33); 61–62 (Gen. 33–43); Rosch, S. 1977 (Gen. 37–40).

## LINE 94

35. **Berenger II** (106-36,332-36), King of Italy, md **Willa of Arles** (263-36).

34. **Adalbert II** (348-36), King of Lombardy, Joint-king of Italy, 950–961; b. c936; d. about 30 Apr 971; md (1) 956, **Gerberge** (348-36), heiress of Macon, d. 11 Dec 986/991; dau of **Othon** (says ES, II 1984:59).

33. **Otto William** (Otton I) (298-33), King of Lombardy, Count of Burgundy and Macon; b. c958/959; d. 21 Oct 1026; bur Dijon; md (1) 982, **Ermentrude de Roucy** (161-33) (mother of Gen. 32); he md (his 2nd, her 2nd) Adelaide (Blanche), dau Fulk III "the Good," Count of Anjou.

32. **Renaud** (Raymond) **I**, Count of Macon and Burgundy; b. c990; d.

3/4 Sept 1057; md before 1 Sept 1016, **Judith** (Adelaide) **of Normandy** (176-32).

31. **William II** "the Great," (149-30,245-31,364-30,377-31) Count of Burgundy and Macon; b. c1024; d. 12 Nov 1087; md 1049/1057, **Stephanie of Longwy** (same as 93-30), b. c1035; d. after 1088; dau of **Adalbert III** (105-33), Count of Longwy, and **Clemence de Foix**. *NOTE: The parentage of Stephanie is based on Szabolcs de Vajay's article in Annales de Bourgogne, XXXII:247–267 (Oct–Dec 1960).*

30. **Raymond of Burgundy and Ivrea**, Count of Castile, Galicia, Coimbra, and d'Amous; Governor of Toledo; went to Spain on a crusade against the Moors; b. c1070, Burgundy, France; d. 13/20 Sept 1107, Grajal; bur Cathedral of Santiago el Mayor, Santiago de Compostella; md c1095, Toledo, Spain, **Urraca** (155-30,248-30), heiress of Castile and Leon; dau of **Alfonso VI** (248-31), King of Castile and Leon, and **Constance of Burgundy**.

29. **Alfonso VII** (86-29,151-29), King of Castile, Leon, Galicia, Toledo, Zaragoza and the Asturias, 1126–1157; King (styled Emperor) of Spain, 1126–1157; b. 1 Mar 1105, Castile, Spain; d. 21 Aug 1157, Fresneda; bur Cathedral of Santa Maria, Toledo; md (1) Nov 1128, Saldana, **Berengeria of Barcelona**; d.Feb 1149, Palencia; bur Cathedral of Santiago el Mayor, Santiago de Compostella; dau **Ramon Berenger III**, Count of Barcelona, and **Dulce I**, Countess of Provence; md (2) July 1152, **Richilde** (Richenza) **of Poland** (378-29) (mother of Gen. 28).

28. **Sancha** (Sanchia), Princess of Castile, Leon, Galicia and the Asturias; Queen of Aragon; b. 21 Sept 1154; d. 9 Nov 1208, Sijena; bur Monastery of Nuestra Senora, Sijena; md 18 Jan 1174, **Alfonso II** (54-28), King of Aragon.

Sources: Blass, R. 1939, II:241; Brandenburg, E. 1935, ES II 1984:62 (Gen. 28–30); II 1984:59 (Gen. 31–35); Moriarty, G. 1947; Moriarty, G.1985, 81 (Gen. 28–30); 62 (Gen. 30–32); 37 (Gen. 33–35); Vajay, S. de 1960; Winkhaus, E. 1953.

## LINE 95

33. **Sancho Garcia III** "the Great" (151-33,223-36,248-33), King of Navarre, 999, Count of Castile, 1026; and Aragon, 1030; b. 990/992; murdered 18 Oct 1035; (md) **Sancha de Aybar** (223-36) (mother of Gen. 32), Dame and heiress of Aybar, a concubine; md also, **Munia Mayor** (285-33), co-heir of Castile.

32. **Ramiro I**, King of Aragon, 1035–1063 (a bastard); slain 8 May 1063, Graus; md (1) 22 Aug 1036, Jaca, **Gilberga** (Hermesenda) **de Conserans** (227-33); d. 1054; dau of **Bernard Rodger**, Count of Conserans and Bigorre, Lord of Foix and half of Carcassonne, who md **Gersende** (227-33), heiress of Bigorre. Bernard Roger was son of **Roger I de Comminges** (291-35) and **Adelaide de Rouergue**.

31. **Sancho Ramirez I**, King of Aragon, 1063–1094; and as **Ramiro IV**, King of Navarre, 1076; b. 1042/1043; d. in battle at Huesca, 6 July 1094; md (2) **Felicie de Roucy**; d. 24 Apr 1123, dau **Hildouin III** (266-31) and **Alice de Roucy** (170-31).

30. **Ramiro II** "the Monk," King of Navarre and Aragon, 1134–1137; monk 1093–1134, San Pedro el Viejo de Huesca; returned to the cloister, 1137; b. 1075; d. 16 Aug 1157, Huesca, Spain; md (2) Nov/Dec 1135, Jaca, Spain, **Matilda** (Agnes) **of Aquitaine** (177-28), widow of Amauri de Thouars.

29. **Petronilla** (Petronel) **of Aragon**, Spain; b. 1135; d. 17 Oct 1174, Barcelona; md 11 Aug 1137, **Raymond** (Ramon) **Berenger IV** (54-29), Count of Barcelona, etc.

Sources; Bard, R. 1982; Cancellos, A. 1945, I:149–192; ES, II 1984:58 (Gen. 29-32); II 1984:69 (29–30); III 1989:677 (Gen. 31); II:55 (Gen. 32–33); Isenburg, W. 1953; Langer, W. 1948, chart 236; Moriarty, G.1985, 78 (Gen. 29–33); Newman, W. 1971; Pidel, R. 1969; Saillot, J. 1980; Sars, M. 1924, 218–228; Winkhaus, E. 1953.

## LINE 96

36. **Damianus Dalassenos**, Duke of Antioch; Magister of the Armenian Lords of Delash (in Claudia); d. in battle, 19 July 998.

35. **Theophylactos Dalassenos**; Strategos of the Anatolics; revolted in 1022.

34. **Adrian**, exiled in 1038/39.

33. **N.N. Dalassene** md **Alexios Pharo** (or Charon) (111-33), the Patrician, Prefect of Italy.

Sources: Blass, R. 1939, II:263; Buckler, G. 1929; Chalendon.T; Chalandon, F. 1912b; ES, II 1984:174 (Gen. 33); Moriarty, G.1985, 137 (Gen. 33-36); Sturdza, M. 1983; Winkhaus, E. 1953.

## LINE 97

32. **Hermann I** (67-36,208-36) "Pusillus" (the Little), Count in the Bonngau, etc.; md **Heilwig von Dillingen**.

31. **Henry**, Pfalzgrave of Lorraine; Count in the Zulpichgau; d.29 Sept 1033. *NOTE: ES, I:129 calls him Konrad.*

30. **Richwara**, of Lorraine and Carinthia md (his 1) c1032, **Berthold I** (113-30), Count of Ortengen.

29. **Adelaide of Rheinfelden**, d. 1090; md 1079, **Ladislaw I**, "the Saint," King of Hungary, d, 27 July 1095 (75-32, 381-32).

Sources: ES I:1980, 129; ES VI: 1978, 1,2; Moriarty, G. 1985, p.140,141; Winkhaus, E. 1953.

## LINE 98

39. **Aethelwulf** (Adalulf), Count of Boulogne, 918-933.

38. **Hunfrid** (345-42), Count of Istria and both Rhaetias, Missus Diminicus in Corsica; founded the monastery of Scharais; liv 804-823.

37. **Adalbert I,** Count in the Hegau and both Rhaetias; liv c850.

36. **Adalbert II,** Count in the Thurgau, in the Scherregau, in the Schwarzwold-Alpgau and the Hegau; b. c835/40; d. 6 June c905; md **Judith,** dau of **Eberhard** (269-39,281A-33), Margrave of Fruili and wife **Gisela** (185-40), Princess of France.

35. **Adalbert III,** Count in the Zurichgau, b. c867; d. 911.

34. **Eberhard II,** Count in the Thurgau and Zurichgau, 903-929; b. c890; md prob **Gisela of Nullenburg.**

33. **Eberhard III** (98-33), Count in the Thurgau; b. c915; d. 995; went into a cloister about 971.

32. **Luitgard von Habsburg** md **Lanzelin von Altenburg,** Count in the Thurgau and Herr von Muri; son of **Gunthram** "the Rich," Herr von Muri, 973.

31. **Luitgard von Habsburg** md **Berthold III** (113-31), Count in the Ortengau, 1016.

Sources: ES I, 1980:12; Kruger, E. 1899:129; Moriarty, G. 1985: 205-206 (Gen. 32-38); Winkhaus, E. 1953.

## LINE 99

36. **Baldwin Balza,** Count of Cambrai.

35. **Raoul de Cambrai**; built the castle at Chatillon-sur-Marne; Vidame de Rheims under Hugh Capet (134-34) and King Robert, 981; d. c982; md **Wivette of Champagneois.**

34. **Herve,** Lord of Chatillon-sur-Marne, Viscomte of Rheims; d. c999; md **Gisele,** d. c1001, a nun; dau of **Arnaud** (400-35), Count and Bishop of Cambrai, and **Bertha of the Betuwe** (401-35). *NOTE: ES, VII 1979:17 says for Gen. 34 "N. de Chatillon, Vidame de Reims," and does not continue the line. The Authority is Andre Duchesne's Histoire de la Maison de Chatillon-sur-Marne, published in Paris in 1621, and more recent research would tend to discredit this work.*

33. **Milo,** Seigneur de Chatillon-sur-Marne and Bazoches; d. 1044; md **Avemelle**; d. 1031; dau of **Amauri,** Seigneur de Montfort.

32. **Gui I,** Seigneur de Chatillon-sur-Marne; d. after 1076; md c1034, **Ermengarde de Choisy,** dau of **Alberic,** Seigneur de Chevier.

31. **Gautier,** Seigneur de Chatillon-sur-Marne and Percy-sur-Marne; d. 1097, in the East, on the First Crusade; md **Mahaud** (Malande), b. c1046; d. c1112; dau of **Reginald of Louvain,** Count of Louvain.

30. **Henry I de Chatillon,** Seigneur de Chatillon-sur-Marne, and Montjoy; Crusader; prob went on the 1st Crusade; b. c1063; d. after 1135; md 1089/1094, **Ermengarde de Montjoy,** dau of **Alberic,** Seigneur de Montjoy and Pacy (d. 1139).

29. **Renaud de Chatillon,** res. of Chatillon-sur-Marne, went on the 2nd Crusade and remained; Lord of Krale in Moab and Prince of Antioch;

executed by Saladin with his own hands after battle of Hattin in 1187; md
1152, **Constance of Antioch** (80-29), md (2) Stephanie de Willy, heiress
of Montreal in Moab.

Sources: Agiles, R. 1968; Blass, R. 1939, II:255; Boase, T. 1971;
Chenaye, F. 1964; Chalandon, F. 1913; Charters, Cluny, vol. III; Con-
stable, G. 1963; Clairvaux, B. 1963; ES, VII 1979:17 (Gen. 29–33);
Foucher, 1971; Krey, A. n.d.; Morenas, J. 1934; Moriarty, G.1985, 272
(Gen. 29–36); Prawler, J. 1973; Riley-Smith, J. 1973; Stauffenburg, F.
von 1961; Tanner, H. 1992; Tibble, S. 1989.

## LINE 100

35. **Nevelung** (401-36), Count in the Betuwe, md **N.N.**, a dau of
**Regnier II** (68-36), Count of Hainault, and wife **Adelaide of Burgundy**
(206-37,300-38).
34. **Rudolph of the Betuwe**, Count of Hainault, liv 967; md **N.N.**, a
dau of **Immo**, Count of Vliermal, in Hasbergau.
33. **Giselbert I**, Count of Loos in the Maasgau and in the Haspengau;
advocate of St. James at Liege; liv 1015; d. 1044/1046; md **Erlende of
Jodoigne**.
32. **Immo** (Emmo) **IV**, Count of Loos; d. by 17 Jan 1078; md by 1055,
**Irmengard von Hornes**, a widow in 1078; dau of **Conrad**, Count of
Hornes.
31. **Arnulf** (320-29), Count of Loos, md **Agnes von Mainz**.

Sources: ES, VI 1978:60 (Gen. 31–35); ES XVIII 1998; Moller, W. 1950,
table XLVIII Moriarty, G.1985, 189 (Gen. 31–33); Winkhaus, E. 1953.

## LINE 101

41. **Guerin** (2-45,345-44), Count in the Thurgovie; liv 754–772; d. 20
May 772; md **Adelindis**.
40. **Milo**, Count of Narbonne, liv 782.
39. **N.N.**
38. **N.N.**
37. **Lievin**, Viscount of Narbonne, liv 878.
36. **Mayeul** (218-37), Viscount of Narbonne, d. 15 June 911; md 870,
**Raimodis** (Raymonde), d. by June 911.
35. **Aubri** (189-30), Viscount of Narbonne, Count of Macon, Sire of
Brecon and Salins; d. 945; bur Besancon St.-Étienne; md **Attelane de
Macon**, dau of **Ranulf**, Viscount of Macon, 893–915.
34. **Lietaud II**, Count of Macon; d. 17 Sept 965; md (1) Ermengarde
of Chalons, d. 931; md (2) 941, **Berta**, dau of **Garnier** (173-37), Viscount of Troyes, and **Tetberga of Arles** (174-37); md (3) **Richilde**, dau
of **Richard** "the Justiciar" (206-38), Count of Autun and Duke of Burgundy, and **Adelheid of Burgundy** (300-38). *NOTE: The mother of Alberic (Gen. 33) is uncertain. ES, III 1985:439 say she is either wife (2) or*

57

*(3). Many others say wife (1).*

33. **Alberic** (Aubri) **II**, Count of Macon and Burgundy; liv 952; d. 981/ 982; md (1) **Ermentrude de Roucy** (92-33).

Sources: Baildon, W. 1926; Blass, R. 1939; Burke P36, 34–34c; Chaume, M. 1977, I 754, 772; Chaume.R, 194–216; Cokayne, G. 1959, V:320–324 (Ferrars); ES, III 1985:439 (Gen. 33–36); Isenburg, W. 1953; Moriarty, G.1985, 1 (Gen. 33–41); Settipani, C. 1997b; Vajay, S. de 1962, 153–169.

## LINE 102

44. **Rutpert I** (169-42), Count in the Wormsgau, md **Williswint,** of the Wormsgau.

43. **Rutpert**, Count in the Thurgau, in the Breisgau and in the Zurichgau; d. after 782; md **Angila.**

42. **Heinrich**, Count in Wettergau, Oberrheingau and in Saargau; slain 5 May 795.

41. Count **Heinrich**, liv 812; md **Hadaburg.**

40. **Poppo I** (211-42), Count in the Saargau; liv 819–839.

39. **Poppo II**, Margrave of Sorbenmark; liv 903–906.

38. **Poppo III** (281-33), Count in the Grabfeld and in the Bavarian Nordgau; liv 906; d. 945.

37. **Otto I of Tullfeld**, liv 982.

36. **Otto II of Tullfeld**, liv 1008.

35. **Gerberga of Henneberg** (362-34), md c1003, **Henry von Schweinfurt** (7-34,47-35,262-34,270-35), Margrave in the Nordgau.

Sources: ES, III 1984:54 (Gen. 35–42); II 1984:10 (Gen. 42–44); Friese, A. 1979 (Gen. 35–44); Geldner, F. 1971 (Gen. 35–44); Glockel, M. 1970 (Gen. 35–44); Jackman, D. 1997; Metz, W. 1958, 295–304 (Gen. 35–44).

## LINE 103

36. **Bernard Harcourt**, b. c904, Normandy, France; md **Sprote de Bourgogne** of Normandy; b. c928.

35. **Torf de Harcourt**, of Normandy; b. c928; md **Ertemberge de Briquebec;** b. c930; dau of **Lancelot de Briquebec.**

34. **Touroude de Pont-Audemer**, Seigneur of Port-Audemer; b. c949; bur Preaux, Normandy; md **Wevia** (Eve) **de Crepon**, b. c942, Pont-Audemer, Normandy.

33. **Humphrey de Vielles**, Seigneur de Pont Audemer de la Haie, md **Aubrey de la Haye**, of Pont-Audemer, Normandy; b. c984; d. 20 Sept 1045.

32. **Roger de Beaumont**, Seigneur de Brionne and Pont-Audemer; Companion of William the Conqueror; b. c1022; d. 29 Nov 1094; md 1040, **Adelaide of Meulan** (de Mellant) (185-32).

31. **Robert I de Beaumont**, Earl of Leicester, Seigneur de Beaumont, Vatteville and Brionne; Count of Meulan in the French Vexin; Earl of

Lancaster; b. c1049, Hastings; d. June 1118; md (his 2nd, her 1st); div 1115, **Elizabeth** (Isabel) **de Vermandois** (143-29).

30. **Waleran IV**, Count of Beaumont-sur-Seine, Sire de Pont-Audemer, de Beaumont-le-Roger and de Brionne; md **Agnes de Montfort**, Dame de Gournay-sur-Marne; d 15 Dec 1181, dau of **Amaury III**, Sire de Montfort-l'Amaury and Count d'Evreux.

29. **Robert II**, Count of Meulan and d'Elbeuf, 1167; d. Poitiers, 6 Aug 1204; md 1165, **Maud**, dau of **Reginald de Dunstanville**, Earl of Cornwall; son of **Henry I**, King of England (89-29).

Sources: CP IV 670, Chart III; 672-673; CP VIII, 53-56,,,520,523-526,737;CP X 351; ES III 1984:55; ES III 1989:700; Houth, E. 1981; Sanders, I. 1960.

## LINE 104

37. **Kunigunde** (64-35,316-37,353-37); b. c870/890, md after 910, **Wigeric** (319-37), Count in the Triergau and Ardennesgau, Count Palatine of Aachen; occ 899–916.

36. **Gozelin**, Count in the Bidgau; b. c911; d. 18 Oct 943; md **Uda of Metz**, d. 7 Apr 963; widow 943–963; dau of **Gerhard**, Count in the Metzgau; killed in battle 910; and **Uda of Saxony**, dau of **Otto of Erlauchten**.

35. **Godfrey** (Gottfried) (65-34) "the Captive," Count in Bidgau in the Methingau and of Verdun, Marquis of Antwerp and Eenam; b. c930/935; d. after 3 Sept 1005; md (2) after 962, **Matilda of Saxony** (379-33); d. 25 May 1005; widow of **Baldwin III** (141-35), Count of Flanders, and dau of **Hermann Billung** (312-36), Duke of Saxony, and **Hildegarde of Westerbourg**.

34. **Gonzelon** (Gozelo) I (120-33,242-33), Margrave of Antwerp; Count of Verdun; Duke of Lower Lorraine and of Upper Lorraine; b. c967; d. 19 Apr 1044.

33. **Oda**, d. 23 Oct 1044; md **Lambert II** (68-33), Count of Louvain; d. c21 Sept 1062.

Sources: Blass, R. 1939, II:271–305; Brandenburg, E. 1935; ES VI 1978:127 (Gen. 33–37); Moriarty, G.1985, 126 (Gen. 33–37); Saillot, J. 1980, 24; Vanderkindere, L. 1902, II: table III and text; Winkhaus, E. 1953.

## LINE 105

34. **Adalbert II** (continue with 158-34), md **Judith**.

33. **Gerhard**, Count of Metz, Duke of Upper Lorraine, d. 1045; md **Gisela**.

32. **Adalbert III** (364-30), Count of Longwy, Duke of Upper Lorraine; b. c1000; slain at Thuim, 1048; md **Clemence de Foix**, dau of **Bernard Rodger**, Count of Conserans, and **Gersende**, heiress of Bigorre (227-

33).His parents were **Roger I de Comminges** and **Adelaide de Rouergue** (291-35).

31. **Ermesinde of Longwy**; d. after 1058, a widow and nun; md **William V** (called Peter) (119-31), Count of Poitou.

Sources: Blass, R. 1939, II:271; ES, VI 1978:129 (Gen. 32–34); Jackman, D. 1990; Moriarty, G.1985, 129–130 (Gen. 33–34); 37 (Gen. 32); Vannerus, J. 1946, XXV:801–858; Winkhaus, E. 1953.

## LINE 106

37. **Guglielmus**, Count of Torresana; liv 925; a Frank or Burgundian; Came to Italy in the time of the contest between the Houses of Friuli and Spoleto. He was a great lord in the Piedmont and Liguria; "lived under the Salic law" (was a pagan).

36. **Aledram**, Marchese di Liguria and of Piedmont, Count of Savona and perhaps Montferrat; founded the Abbey of Grassano; d. after 991; md (1) N.N., md (2) before July 961, **Gerberge of Ivrea** (mother of Gen. 35), b. 945; dau of **Berenger II** (332-36), Marquis of Ivrea and King of Italy.

35. **Anselm I**, Marchese di Savona (Industria); d. before 1014; md **Gisela of Vincenza,** dau of **Adalberto II,** Marchese of Este, Count of Vincenza; d. Mar 1000; granddau of **Alberto Azzo** (93-35), Count of Lucca, who md **Guilla.**

34. **Oberto I**, Lord of Savona, Marchese of Liguria; occ 1004–1014; d. c1035.

33. **Oberto II**, Marchese di Savona and Liguria; d. after 1062; md **Beatrice di Ramagnano** (107-33).

32. **Teto II**, Marchese di Savona Vasto; d. 1064; md **Berta**, liv 1065; dau of **Odalrico Manfrido II** (315-34), Marchese in Turino Albange, and **Bertha of Este** (93-33).

31. **Bonifacio I**, Marchese di Savona Vasto; b. 1060; d. 1130; md (his 3rd, her 3rd), **Agnes de Vermandois** (mother of Gen. 30); dau of **Hugh Magnus de Crepi** (143-29), and **Adelaide de Vermandois** (239-30); he md (1) 1079, N. N., widow of his brother Anselmo, a lady of the House of Braciza; md (2) Adalme, dau of Manfredo, Marchese de Romagnano.

30. **Sibel de Vasto di Savona**; d. before 1146; md Aug 1129, William VI (150-30), Seigneur de Montpellier.

Sources: Brand, C. 1968; Brandenburg. E. 1935; Carutti.D. 1884; ES, II 1984:199 (Gen. 33–37); Lognon; Moriarty, G.1985, 133 (Gen. 30–37); Settipani, C. 1994; Ureglio, L. 1893, X:385–430; Winkhaus, E. 1953.

## LINE 107

37. **Ardoino III Glabrione** (315-36), Count of Auriata and Torino, Marchese of the March of Tours, d. c975; md **N.N. di Mosezzo.**

36. **Ardoino IV**, Marchese of the March Tours; d. 1026.

35. **Guido,** Marchese of the House of Torino Alberaza, 1026.

34. **Odelrico** (Ulrich), perhaps Marchese di Ramagnano, of the House of the Marchese de Torino; occ 1040, 1064.

33. **Beatrice di Ramagnano** md **Oberto II** (106-33), Marchese di Savona.

Sources: Carutti, D. 1884b, 253; Moriarty, G.1985, 133 (Gen. 33-37); Winkhaus, E. 1953.

## LINE 108

38. **Ragnvald** (170-35), a Viking, who established the House of Roucy in Burgundy.

37. **Archard de la Ferte-sur-Aube,** of the Norman-Burgundian House of Roucy; liv 901–936; d. c950; md **N.N.**, heiress of Bar-sur-Aube and a descendant of the Counts **Gui** and **Fulk of Bar-sur-Aube** at the end of the 9th century. She may have married Nocher I, instead.

36. **Nocher I,** Count of Bar-sur-Aube; d. after 1010.

35. **Nocher II,** Count of Bar-sur-Aube and of Soissons; d. after 1019; md **Aelis of Soissons** (188-35).

34. **Nocher III,** Count of Bar-sur-Aube; d. before 1040.

33. **Adele** (Aelaide) **of Bar-sur-Aube,** d. 1053; md (4) **Raoul III** (268-33), Count of Valois, de Crepy, Amiens and Vexin.

Sources: Blass, R. 1939, II:239; Chaume, M. 1977, I:401n, 443, 446n6; Chaume, M. 1947a, 273–277; ES, III 1989:729A; Moriarty, G.1985, 136–137 (Gen. 33–38); Settipani, C. 1997b.

## LINE 109

37. **Fulk I "the Red"** (167-37), Count of Anjou, md **Roscilla**, dau of **Werner,** Seigneur de Loches, Villentrois and la Haye, who md **Tescenda.** They were probably parents of Gen. 36.

36. **Adele** md **Gautier I** (185-36), Count of Vexin, Valois and Amiens.

Sources: Chaume, M. 1977, I:533; Grierson, P. 1939, 10:81–125; Moriarty, G.1985, (Gen. 36–37); Paget, G. 1977, I; Saillot, J. 1980, 36–40; Werner, K. 1958, 264–279.

## LINE 110

40. **Sieghard I** (130-38), Count of Bavaria, d. 10 Oct 906; md **Kotini,** (130-38); dau **Rabold,** Count in the Ambergau.

39. **Sieghard II,** Count in the Lower Sulzburggau; d. 916/923; md **N.N.**, dau of **Engelbert I,** Count in the Inngau.

38. **Sieghard III,** Count in the Chiemgau; liv 940/959.

37. **Sieghard IV**, Count in the Salzburggau; d. c980; md c965, **Willa of Bavaria** (118-37).

36. **Engelbert III,** Count in the Chiemgau; liv 960/989; d. 1020; md **Adela**, d. after 1020; widow of **Aribo I** (48-35), Pfalzgrave of Bavaria.

35. **N.N.**, md **Frederick I** (129-35), Count in the Pusterthal, 990–1020.

Sources: Dopsch, H. 1970, 125–151 (Gen. 35–40); ES III 1984:28 (37–40); Heck, H. 1955, 11–29 (Gen. 35–40); Leut, R. 1954, 84 (Gen. 35–40); Moriarty, G.1985, 120–121 (Gen. 35–39); Tyroller, F. 1969, 62–70, 89–114 (Gen. 35–40); Winkhaus, E. 1953, 165 (Gen. 35–39).

## LINE 111

34. **Manuel Komnenos** "Exoticus," of Castamin in Paphlagonia; prefect of the East, 976–1025; curopalates and strategos under Basil II, d. c1025.

33. **Ioannes** (John) **Komnenos** (51-30), curopalates and grand domestic; b. c1015; d. 12 July 1067; md 1042, **Anna Dalassena**, created "Augusta" 1081; b. 1025/1030; d. 1100/1102; dau of **Alexios Pharo** (or Charon), the Patrician, Prefect of Italy; md **N.N. Dalassene** (96-33).

32. **Alexios I Komnenos**, (Alexius I, 1081–1118), Emperor (Basilius) of the East; b. c1048; d. 15 Aug 1118; bur in the monastery of Philanthropos; md (2) **Eirene** (Irene) **Doukaina** (42-31,215-32).

31. **Iohannes Komnenos**, (John II, 1118–1143), Emperor (Basilius) of the East; b. 13 Sept 1087; d. 8 Apr 1143, Cilicia; md 1104/1105, **Pyriska** (Eirene, Irene) (381-31), Princess of Hungary; b. c1088; d. 13 Aug 1134, as a nun at Bithynia.

30. **Andronikeo Komnenos**, sebastokrator; b. c1108; d. 1142, Herbst; md **Eirene**, d. 1150/1151.

29. **Alexies Komnenos**, protostrator; lover of the Empress Maria and Governor during her regency, 1180–1182; murdered 1183; md **Marie Dukaina.**

28. **Eudoxia Komnena**, b. c1168; d. a nun, after 4 Nov 1202; md 1178/1179 (div 1187), **William VIII** (150-28), Seigneur de Montpellier.

*NOTE: The parentage of Eudoxia Komnena (Gen. 28) has been the subject of much discussion over the past several decades. The late G. Andrews Moriarty claimed the Basileus Manuel Komnensos as her father (Moriarty, G.1985, 137, 138). Detlev Schwennicke, (ES, II 1984:175, 177, 178), citing sources unavailable to Moriarty, particularly one by the great scholar Szabolcs de Vajay, published in 1980 (Vajay, S. de 1980), attempts to set the matter straight. Nonetheless, the present author feels that more research is indicated.*

Sources: Allen, J. 1985; ES, II 1984:177 (Gen. 28–31); II 1984:175 (Gen. 31–32); II 1984:174 (Gen. 32–34); Hanowelt, E. 1982; Moriarty, G.1985, 137 (Gen. 31–34);Vajaay de 1980.

## LINE 112

41. **Boso III** "the Old" ( 174-40); Count of Turin; liv 826–829; an East Frank, d. before 855.

40. **Richilde of Arles** (258-39,343-40,357-37), md **Budwine** (170-

39,206-39), Count of Italy and Metz, Lay Abbot of Gorze, 842–862.

Sources: Blass, R. 1939, II:275; Chaume, M. 1977, I:254, 539, 544–545; Isenburg, W. 1953; Moriarty, G.1985, 19; Winkhaus, E. 1953 .

## LINE 113

33. **Berthold I,** Count in the Briesgau, perhaps the "Count Bezelin" who faught with Otto II agains the Saracens and was slain at Calabria, 13 July 982.

32. **Berthold II,** Count in the Briesgau and in the Thurgau; d. 1005/6; md **Bertha von Buren,** sister of Frederick von Buren, ancestors of the Hohenstauffens.

31. **Berthold III** (called Bezelin von Villengen), Count of Ortengau; adherant of Kaiser Henry II; d. 15 July 1024; md **Luitgard von Habsburg** (98-31).

30. **Berthold IV,** "the Bearded," of Zahringen, Count in the Ortengen, in the Briesgau and Fuergau; Duke of Carinthia, Marchese of Verna; d. 5/6 Nov 1078; md (1) c1032, **Richwara** (97-30). Berthold md (2) Beatrice, d. 26 Oct 1092; dau of Louis, Count of Montbeliard (d. 1071/76).

Sources: ES I 1980:129; Isenburg, W. 1953: part i, table 82; Moriarty, G. 1985:141; Winkhaus, E. 1953:197.

## LINE 114

42. **Charles Martel** (171-43,269-44), Mayor of the Palace, md **Chrotrude** (Rotrou) **of Allemania.**

41. Duke **Bernard,** d. c784; md **N.N.,** dau of **Caribert** (214-43), Count of Laon.

40. **Gondres** (or Therese) md perhaps **Pippin** (231-40), King of Italy.

Sources: Auzias, L. 1937, 525; Blass, R. 1939, II:251, 274, 313; Chaume, M. 1977, I:142,392, and IV:535; Depoin, J.1922, XI:244–258; XII 13–25, 109–112; Fortunatus, V. 1954, Bk. VII, nos. v, vi; Isenburg, W. 1953; Moriarty, G.1985, 220 (Gen. 40–42);

## LINE 115

36. **Munir Skleros,** so called in Arabic sources (possibly the same as Photeinos, fl. c921); md **Gregoria** (322-38).

35. **Bardas Skleros,** anti-Emperor in 976–979, 987, and 989, when he assumed the emperorship upon the death of his brother-in-law, the Emperor John I Tzimisces, in 976. He finally submitted to Basil II in 989.

34. **Romanos Skleros,** fl. c976–993; md **N.N.,** a dau or sister of **Abu Taglib Fad'lallah,** Hamdanid Emir of Mosel, 969–979. *NOTE: for information about the Hamdanids of Mosel, see Marius Canard's:* Histoire de la Dynastie des H'amdanides de Jazira et de Syria *(Algiers, 1951),* reptd in *Publications de la Faculte des Lettres d'Alger (Paris, 1953), especially pp. 844-849.*

33. **Basileios Skleros**, magistros, c1028; md **Pulcheria** (Argyropoulina) (382-33).

32. **N.N. Skleraina** (mother of Gen. 31); d. 1032/1034; md (his 2nd), before 1025, **Konstantinos Monomachos** (Emperor Constantine IX) (115A-32), 1042–1055; d. 11 Jan 1055; he md (3) 11 June 1042, Empress **Zoe**, the Macedonian; d. 1050.

31. **Maria Monomacha** md 1046, **Wsewolod I** (240-31), Prince of Perejaslaw, 1054; Grand Prince of Kiev, 1078; b. c1030; d. 13 Apr 1093.

Sources: Allen, J. 1985; Blankenship, K. 1993; Brook, L. 1981, nos. 34, 134, 147–148, 185–189 (Gen. 31–36); Collenburg, W. 1963; Hanawelt, E. 1992; Seibt, W. 1976.

## LINE 115A

40. **Ashot IV** "the Valiant" and "the Carniverous," Prince of Armenia, 806-820.

39. **Bagrat I**, Prince of Taron, 826-852.

38. **Tarnik.**

37. **Apoganem**, protospatherios, patrikos, d. c900; md **N.N.**, dau of **Constantin Lips**, patrikos.

36. **Tornik**, patrikos, liv 923.

35. **Constantin Tornikos.**

34. **Nikolaos Tornikios.**

33. **Maria** md **Theodosius Monomachos.**

32. **Konstantinos Monomachos** (115-32) (Emperor Constantine IX).

Sources: Toumanoff, C. 1976, 103; Willoughby, R, 1991a.

## LINE 116

35. **Rostaing** (Rostagnus), who gave Lisoc in Avignon to St. Andre in Avignon, 21 Sept 1006; md **Beletrude**, occ 1006.

34. **Emenon de Sabran**, occ 18 Dec 1029, and in 1043 at St. Andre with his son Rostaing.

33. **Rostaing de Sabran**, known in 1043 with his father at St. Andre.

32. **William de Sabran**, occ 1068–Jan 1109; Crusader; went on the 1st Crusade, 1096; md **Adalaicia.**

31. **Rostaing de Sabran**, b. c1090; d. Nov 1184; md (1) **Constance Amic** (194-31) (mother of Gen. 30 below), heiress; d. 1136; md (2) Roscie, Dame d'Uzes, and of Caylar, 1156; d. after April 1192; dau of Rainon de Cayler and Beatrix d'Ezes

30. **William de Sabran**, Constable of the Counts of Toulouse in Provence, 1152-1199; b. c1115; d. c1199.

29. **Rostaing**, Seigneur de Sabran, Constable of the Counts of Toulouse in Provence, 1199/1206; b. c1133; d. 1208/1209; md (1) **Clemencia de Montpellier**, d. before 1204; dau of **Guillem IV**; md (2) 1205 Almode de Mevouillon, d. after 1227; dau of Raymond III and Soure de Foys.

28. **Raimon de Sabran**, Seigneur de Castellar and Forcalquier, Seigneur de Costellar, Count of Forcalquier; b. c1155; d. 1224; md, c1178, **Gersinde**, heiress of Provence and Forcalquier; dau of **William IV** (195-29), Count of Forcalquier, and **Adelaide de Beziers**.

27. **Gersinde** (Gersinda II) **of Sabran**, Spain; heiress and regent of Provence and Forcalquier; d. after 1222, a nun; md **Alfonso** (54-27), Count of Provence.

Sources: Agiles, R. 1968; ES, XIV 1991:179; Foucher, 1971; Krey, A. n.d.; Mantayer., G. de, 1907, 408-414; Mantayer, G. de, 1908, 336–337, 402–414; Mateos, R. 1984; Moriarty, G.1985, 101 (Gen. 27–28); 98–99 (Gen. 28–35); Salazar, J. de 1984; Winkhaus, E. 1953.

### LINE 117

38. **Markwart I von Eppenstein** (229-36), Count in the Viehbachgau.

37. **Markwart II von Eppenstein**, Count in the Lower Isar; a Bavarian vassal, 927–940; liv 951.

36. **Richgard von Eppenstein**, d. 23 Apr 1013; md **Ulrich von Ebersberg** (130–35).

Sources: Blass, R. 1939, II:247, 274; Bollnow, H. 1930; Butler, P. 1897, vol. 22; ES, III 1984:24 (Gen. 36–38); Moriarty, G.1985, 122–123 (Gen. 36–38); Tangl, K. 1937; Winkhaus, E. 1953.

### LINE 118

41. **Aribo**, liv 871-907, Margrave in the Donaugrafschaften and Count in the Traungau, d. after 909.

40. **Ottokar**, Count in Karamantanien.

39. **Adelbert**, Archbishop of Salzburg and Euphra; d. 14 Nov 935; md **Rihni of Hungary.**

38. **Bernhard**, Count of Bavaria, md 931, **Engilrat.**

37. **Willa of Bavaria** md **Sieghard IV** (110-37), Count in the Salzburggau.

Sources: Blass, R. 1939, II 1984:274, 278; ES, III 1984:128 (37–38); Mateos, R. 1984; Moriarty, G.1985, 121 (Gen. 37–39); Salazar, J. de 1984; Winkhaus, E. 1953.

### LINE 119

33. **Gerard Flamens**, (Same as 11-34), Count of Teisterbant; a vassal of the Bishop of Utrecht; liv 1033–1053; he was prob from Lorraine.

32. **Dietrich Flamens**, Count in the Velue; liv 1058; d. 1092, a captive at Bouillon; bur in the Abbey of St. Hubert's in the Ardennes.

31. **Gerard I Flaminus**, Count of Wassenburg and Guelders, built the castle of Wassenburg, between the Rhine and the Meuse, 1085; b. c1053; d. after 1138; md **Clemence of Poitou**, (same as 3-31, 278-31), heiress of Longwy and Blieskastel; d. after 1129; widow of **Conrad I** (3-31, 30-30),

Count of Luxemburg; d. 1086; Clemence was dau of **William V** (called Peter), Count of Poitou; b. c1023; d. 1058; and (md 1051) **Ermesinde of Longwy** (105-32); d. after 1058, a nun; and granddau of **William III** (88-33), Count of Poitou (V of Aquitaine), and **Agnes of Burgundy** (161-32).

 30. **Yolande** (Jolande) **of Guelders** md **Baldwin III** (73-30), Count of Hainault, 1098.

 Sources: Blokland, W. 1948, 339; Boeren, P. 1938, XI:1–23; ; ES, VI 1978:25 (Gen. 30–33); ES XVIII 1997; Hoffman, W. 1950, 206–211; Moriarty, G.1985, 127 (Gen. 30–33); Sloet, L. 1876; Ten Hoff, 305+; Vannerus, J. 1946; Vries, W de 1947.

## LINE 120

 36. **Louis IV** "d'Outremer" (171-36), King of France; md **Gerberge of Saxony** (92-35).

 35. **Charles of Laon (121-36)**, Aisne, France; Duke of Lower Lorraine, Prince of France; set aside for the French throne by Hugh Capet (134-34); b. 953; d. 21 May 992; md before 979, **Adelaide**.

 34. **Adelaide** (Ermentrude) **of Lorraine (65-36)**; b. c970/75; d. after 1012; md 990, **Adalbert I** (158-32,403-35), Count of Namur.

 33. **Adalbert II**, Count of Namur; b. c1000; d. between July 1063 and July 1064; md **Regelinde of Lorraine**, heiress of the countship of Chatenois; b. c994; d. after 1064; dau of **Gonzelon** (Gothelo) **I** (104-34), Duke of Upper and Lower Lorraine; b. 967; d. 19 Apr 1044.

 32. **Adalbert III** (126-31), Count of Namur; b. c1030; d. 1102; md 1065/1066, **Ida of Saxony** (204-33).

 31. **Adelaide of Namur**, b. c1068; d. 1124; md **Otto II** (65-32), Count of Chiny.

 30. **Ida of Namur and Chiny** (of Alsace-Lorraine, France); b. 1083; d. after 1125; md c1100, **Godfrey I** (same as 68-31,89-29), Duke of Brabant and Lorraine, Count of Louvain.

 29. **Godfrey II** (same as 68-30), Duke of Brabant, md **Luitgarde von Sulzbach**, dau of **Berenger II** (same as 63-31), Count of Sulzbach.

 28. **Godfrey III** (same as 68-29), Count of Louvain, Duke of Brabant, md **Margaret von Limburg** (same as 62-29).

 27. **Henry I** (same as 68-28), Duke of Brabant and Lower Lorraine; b. 1165; d. 5 Sept 1235, Cologne; md (1) **Matilda of Flanders** (205-28).

 26. **Matilda** (Mechtild) **of Brabant**, d. 21 Dec 1267; bur Cistercian Abbey at Loosdunen near the Hague; md (1) Henry II, Count Palatine, d. 25/26 Apr 1214 and bur at Cistercian Monastery at Schonau; (2) **Florenz** (Florent) **IV** (72-26) (father of Gen. 25), Count of Holland, d. 1234.

 25. **Adelaide** (Alida) **of Holland**; b. c1225; d. c1284; md **Jean** (John) **I d'Avesnes** (50-25), Count of Hainault.

 Sources: Bouchard, C. 1981:268-287; Moriarty, G.1985, 178 (Gen. 25-26); 154–156 (Gen. 26–32); 128 (Gen. 33–35); Rousseau, F. 1936,

66

CXXIV–CXXV, CXXXIV; Rousseau, F. 1921, vol. 27 (1921); Rubincam, M. 1949 (Gen. 25–30); Winkhaus, E. 1953.

## LINE 121

36. **Charles of Laon** (120-35), Duke of Lower Lorraine, md **Adelaide**.

35. **Gerberge of Lower Lorraine**, b. c975; d. after 1017; md c990, **Lambert I** "the Bearded" (68-34), Count of Louvain.

34. **Matilda of Louvain**, France; md **Eustace I** (77-34,242-34), Count of Boulogne.

Sources: Cokayne, G. 1959, I:352; ES, III 1989:621 (Gen. 34–35); I 1980:95 (Gen. 35–36); Mayer, H. 1984, 10–91; Prawer, J. 1970, 152, 209; Round, J. 1971, 147–180; Saillot, J. 1980, 192; Smith, J. 1973, appendix A.

## LINE 122

36. **Bernard I de St. Valery** md **Emma**, dau **Renaud I de St. Valery**.

35. **Gulbert de St. Valery**, chieftain of Saint-Valery-en-Caux district, liv 1011; md N.N., a dau of **Richard I** "the Fearless" (156-32,166-33), and unk. concubine.

34. **Bernard II de St. Valery**.

33. **Gauthier de St. Valery**, d. c1061, md **Elizabeth de Montlhery** (241-31).

32. **Bernard III de St. Valery**, d. c1091; md **Avoris**, perhaps dau of **John St. John**.

31. **Renaud II de St. Valery**, d. 1166.

30. **Bernard IV de St. Valery**, d. 1190, md **Eleanor de Domnart**.

29. **Thomas de St. Valery** md 1178, **Adele de Ponthieu**, dau **Jean (John) I** (148-28), Count of Ponthieu, and **Beatrice of St. Pol** (242-28).

Sources: Latrie, M. 1889 (29–36); Searle, E. 1988, 100, 101, 136, 137, 218, 219, 289, 319; Turton, W. 1984, 178 (Gen. 29–36).

## LINE 123

48. **Dagobert I** (same as 303-47), King of Austrasia, md (2) **Nantilda**.

47. **Chlodovech** (Clovis) **II**, King of the Franks, c657; King of Neustria and Burgundy from 639; King of Austrasia, c656; b. 634; d. 657; md **Balthild**.

46. **Theuderic III**, King of the Franks, d. 691; md **Chlotilde**.

45. **Chrotlind** md c695, **Lambert** (Leutbertus) **II** (169-43) Comes in Neustria.

Sources: Gregory of Tours, 1974; James, E. 1988; Lasco, P. 1971; Vajay, S. de 1966a, table II; ES, II, 1984, p.10 (Gen. 45); ES, I, 1980,p.1 (Gen. 46–48).

## LINE 124

32. **Humbert** (Umberto) **II** (93-30), Count of Maurienne, Margrave of

Italy; md **Gisele of Burgundy**, dau of **William II** (94-31), Count of Burgundy, and wife, **Stephanie**.

31.  **Adelaide of Maurienne** (69-30,70-30; b. c1092; d. 18 Nov 1154; md 1115, **Louis VI** "the Fat" (79-29, 134-30), King of France.

30.  **Robert I**, Prince of France, Count of Dreux, Perche, and Braine; b. c1123; d. prob. Braine, 11 Oct 1188; bur at the monastery of St. Ived, Braine; md (1) 1139/1141, **Agnes de Garlande**, b. c1122, d. 1143 (dau of **Anselm de Garlande**, Count of Rochefort and wife, N.N. de Montmorency); md (2) 1144, Hawise, b. c1118, d. 1152 (widow of Rotrou II, Count of Perche, and dau of Walter, Count of Salisbury, and Sibylle de Chaworth); md (3) 1152, **Agnes de Baudemont** (mother of Gen. 29), Countess of Braine-sur-Vesle, Dame de Fere-en-Tardenois, de Pontarcis, de Nestle, de Longueville, and de Quincy; b. c1130; d. 1202/1218 (widow of Milon II of Bar-sur-Seine, and **N.N.**, dau of **Guy de Baudemont**, Count of Braine, and wife **Alix** (Adelaide). The parents of Guy were **Andre de Baudemont**, (see 84-30), Seigneur de Baudemont; b. c1060, d. a monk; and **Agnes de Braine**, heiress of Braine.

29.  **Robert II**, Count of Dreux and Braine; Crusader; at Acre, 1191, on 3rd Crusade; fought against the English and against the Emperor Otto at Bouives, 1215; b. c1154; d. 28 Dec 1218; bur St. Ived, Braine; md (2) 1184, **Yolande de Coucy** (37-27).

Sources: Chaume, M. 1977, I 374n, 416n2, 447n2, 544–545; Cokayne, G. 1959, V:632, 634, 736, 796 note; Flahill, G. 1947; Isenburg, W. 1953 Moriarty, G.1985, 195–196 (Gen. 29–30); 51 (Gen. 30–31), Winkhaus, E. 1953.

**LINE 125**

29.  **Frederick III Barbarosa** (40-29), Emperor of the West, md **Beatrice of Burgundy** (of Macon) (41-29).

28.  **Philip von Hohenstauffen**, King of the Romans, 6 Feb 1199; Duke of Tuscany and Swabia, 1196; Emperor of Germany, 1198; Emperor of the West (not crowned), 1198–1208; b. 1176; murdered 21 June 1208 at Bamburg, Germany; md 25 May 1197, **Eirene Angelina** (215-28), Princess of the East.

27.  **Maria von Hohenstaufen**, Princess of Germany; b. 1201; d. 1235, Louvain; md **Henry II** (68-27), Duke of Brabant.

26.  **Matilda of Brabant**, d. 29 Sept 1288; bur Chercamp, Artois; md 14 June 1237, **Robert I** (147-26), Count of Artois.

Sources: Chaume, M. 1977, 542, 551–552; ; Cokayne, G. 1959, VII:386; Moriarty, G.1985, 154 (Gen. 26); 166–167 (Gen. 27–29); Moriarty, G. 1945; Moriarty, G. 1947; Thatcher, O. 1897, 322 (Gen. 26–29); Voltaire 33:384–388.

**LINE 126**

31. **Adalbert III** (120-32), Count of Namur, md (2) **Ida of Saxony** (204-33).

30. **Godfrey**, Count of Dagsburg and Namur; b. c1067; d. 19 Aug 1139; bur at Florette; md (his 2nd, her 2nd), c1101, **Ermesinde of Luxemburg** (3-30, 30-30) (mother of Gen. 29 below), heiress of Luxemburg and Longwy; b. c1075; d. 1141; she md (1) c1092/1095, **Adalbert II von Egisheim** (30-30), Count of Dagsburg-Moka, who d. 24 Aug 1098.

29. **Alice de Namur**, heiress of Namur; b. c1115; d. end of July 1169; md **Baldwin IV** (37-28,73-29), Count of Hainault.

Sources: Blass, R. 1939, 271, 278; Cokayne, G. 1959, I:235; ES, II 1984:6 (Gen. 29); VI 1978:128 (Gen. 30); VII 1979:68 (Gen. 31); Moriarty, G.1985, 128 (Gen. 29–31); Rousseau,.F. 1936, CXXIV–CXXV, CXXXIV; Rousseau, F. 1921; Winkhaus, E. 1953.

**LINE 127**

39. **Arimannus**, Viscount; b. 898; md **Bertildis**, b. 898.

38. **Robertus I**, Viscount of Auvergne; liv 922–945; md **Eldearde** (Algardis), liv 922–945; dau of **Hucbert** and **Hildegarde**.

37. **Robertus II**, Viscount of Auvergne, appointed in 979 by William "Taillefer," Count of Toulouse; d. before 989; md **Ingelberge**, Dame de Beaumont in the Chalonais, who may have been dau of **Acfred**, Count of Auvergne, Duke of Aquitaine, d. 927.

36. **Guy I**, Princeps Arvernorum, Count of Auvergne; liv 940–969; d. 989; md **Ancelende**, liv 954–986.

35. **William IV**, Count of Auvergne; an adherent of Charles, Duke of Lower Lorraine against Hugh Capet (134-34); d. before 1016; md **Humberge**, a widow in 1017.

34. **Robert I**, Count of Auvergne; d. before 1032; md **Ermengarde**, dau of **William I**, Count of Arles and Provence, and wife **Adelaide** (Blanche) **of Anjou** (333-35), dau of **Fulk II** (167-36,298-34,347-35), Count of Anjou, and **Gerberge of the Gatinais** (167-36,298-34).

33. **Ermengarde of Auvergne**, d. c1042; md **Odo** (Eudes) **II** (133-33), Count of Blois and Champagne.

Sources: Bachelier, E. 1959, 139–159 (Gen. 33–39); Blass, R. 1939, II:245, 272; Bouchard, C. 1987, 651-658; Chaume, M. 1977, 222, 223, 235n2, 236n1, 530, 531, 550, 551; ES, III 1989:732 (33–39); Moriarty, G.1985, 117–119 (Gen. 33–39); Sanders, I. 1960, 77.

**LINE 128**

36. **Rapoto I**, Count in the Traungau, 1 Oct 977.

35. **Rapoto II**, Count in the Traungau, 1006; d. after 1013.

34. **Diepold I**, Count in the Angstgau, 1059/60.

33. **Rapoto IV** (279-32), Count of Cham; killed in battle 15 Oct 1080; md **Mathilde,** dau of **Siegfried VI** (128A-34), Count in the Chiemgau; d. 7 Aug 1046.

32. **Ulrich** "the Rich," Count of Passau, 1072; d. 14 Apr 1099, of the plague, at Regensburg, Germany; md **Adelaide von Frantenhausen** (213-32), d. 24 Feb 1110, bur at Sulzbach. Adelaide was the widow of Markwart von Markwardstein; she md (3) 1099, Berenger von Sulzbach.

31. **Uta von Passau** (Utha von Sulzbach), heiress of the lordship of Marquardstein, occ 1105–1140; bur at Sean; md by 1105, **Engelbert II von Sponheim** (228-31), Duke of Carinthia.

Sources: Binhack, 1887; Blass, R. 1939, II:243; Dungern, O. von 1931; ES III 1984:28; ES XVI:78; Moriarty, G.1985, 123 (Gen. 31–36); Winkhaus, E. 1953.

## LINE 128A

36. **Sieghard IV,** Count in the Chiemgau and the Sulzburggau; d. 26 Sept 980; md c965, **Willa of Bavaria** (110-37,118-37).

35. **Sieghard V**, Count in Chiemgau, liv 1010/1020; md **Zloubrana,** liv 1010/1020.

34. **Sieghard VI**, Count in Chiemgau, killed in battle 15 Oct 1080.

33. **Mathilde** md **Rapoto IV** (128-33), Count of Cham.

Source: ES III 1984:28.

## LINE 129

37. **Albuin von Jaun,** liv 940; md **Hildegarde.**

36. **Hartwig,** Count and Forest Ward in Carinthia, Count in the Isengau; md **Wichburg**.

35. **Frederick I**, Count in the Pusterthal; liv 990–1020; md **N.N.**, dau of **Engelbert III** (110-36), Count in the Chiemgau.

34. **Engelbert**, Count in the Pusterthal; d. 1039; md **Luitgard of Istria** (130-33).

33. **Richgard von Lavant** (228-33), heiress of the countship of Lavant; md **Siegfried von Sponheim** (228-33), Count of Sponheim, etc.

Sources: Blass, R. 1939, II:247; Dopsch, H. 1970, 125-151; ES, III 1984:28 (Gen. 33–35); Heck, H. 1955, 11-29; Moriarty, G.1985, 120 (Gen. 33–37); Tyroller, F. 1969, 60-70, 89-107 (Gen. 33–35); Winkhaus, E. 1953.

## LINE 130

39. **Sieghard** (110-40), Count in the Kraichgau; liv 858–861.

38. **Sieghard I**, Count of Bavaria, Lord of Ebersburg and Persenberg; founder of the castle of Ebersburg, c880; d. 10 Oct 906; md **Kotini** (Kottine), heiress of Ebersburg; d. 20 Dec 906; dau of **Rabold**, Count in the Ambergau.

37. **Rabold I**, Lord of Ebersburg and Persenberg, Count of Carinthia;

defeated the Hungarians, 902, being intrusted with the defense of the frontier of Carniola against them; d. 20 Jan 919; md **Engemunt.**

36. **Adalbert I** (229-35), Count of Carinthia; liv 928–934; d. c969; md **Luitgard,** dau of **Papo von Preising**; advocate, 977; granddau of **Pilgrim**, Count in the Fiero-Marle; liv 937–950.

35. **Ulrich von Ebersberg** (117-36), Count of Ebersburg, Margrave of Carniola; d. 11 Mar 1029; md c970, **Richgard von Eppenstein;** d. 23 Apr 1013; dau of **Markwart II von Eppenstein** (117-37).

34. **Wilibirg** (281-31), heiress of the countship of Ebersburg; d. 25 Nov 1064/1065, as Abbess of Grisenheim; md **Werigand** (Wezzelin) **von Friuli,** Count of Istria and Friuli; d. by 1040; an official of his wife's cousin, Adalbert, Duke of Carinthia.

33. **Luitgard of Istria,** d. after 1051; md c1030, **Engelbert** (129-34), Count in the Pusterthal.

Sources: Blass, R. 1939, II:274, 278; Dopsch, H. 1970, 125–151; ES III 1984:28 (Gen. 34–39); IV 1981:118 (Gen. 33); Historich, 1934e; Isenburg, W. 1953; Leut, R. 1954, 84; Merz, W. 1930; Moriarty, G.1985, 122 (Gen. 33–38); Trotter, K. 1937; Tyroller, F. 1969, 62–70, 89–107.

## LINE 131

32. **Robert I** (89-31), Duke of Normandy, (md) **Herleve,** dau of **Fulbert of Falaise**.

31. **Adelaide of Normandy,** Countess of Aumale; b. c1030, Falais, Calvados, France; d. 1081/1084; sister of **William the Conqueror. Md** (1) Enguerrand II, Count of Ponthieu, slain 1053, at siege of Arques; son of Hugh II (d. 20 Nov 1052), Count of Ponthieu, and Bertha of Aumale; md (2) **Lambert of Boulogne** (77-33), (father of Gen. 30), Count or Seigneur of Lens in Artois; slain 1054 at the Battle of Lille; md (3) Eudes, Count of Champagne.

30. **Judith of Lens** (77-32), dau of **Lambert of Boulogne** (not Enguerrand II); b. 1054, md 1070, **Waltheof II** (221-32), Earl of Huntingdon, Northampton and Northumberland; son of **Siward,** Earl of Northumberland, and **Aelflaed,** dau of **Alfred of Bernicea.**

*NOTE: The parentage of Judith of Lens has come under critical study since the early 1970's, when Enguerrand II was thought by some to be her father. The currently acceptable parentage among most scholars is as originally stated (see Gen. 30 above).*

Sources: Brandenburg, E. 1935; Cokayne, G. 1959, I:350–353; IV:670, chart iv; V:472, 736; VI:638–642; VII:640–641; XII, appendix K, 33–34; Searle, W. 1899, 374; Paul, J. 1914, I; Winkhaus, E. 1953.

## LINE 132

29. **Dietrich von Lothringen II** (205-30), of Lorraine  md **Sybil of Anjou** (152-30).

28. **Marguerite of Lorraine**, Flanders and Alsace; heiress of Flanders; b. c1148, prob Alsace, France; d. 15 Nov 1194; bur at Bruges; md 1169, **Baldwin V** (73-28), Count of Hainault; and as **Baldwin VIII**, Count of Flanders.

27. **Isabella of Hainault and Flanders**; b. Apr 1170, Valenciennes, Hainault, France; d. 15 Mar 1190, Paris; bur Notre Dame; md **Philip II Augustus** (70-28, 133-28), King of France, 1180–1223; a Crusader.

Sources: Brandenburg, E. 1935; Dek, A. 1955; ES, II 1984:6 (Gen. 28–29); II 1984:11 (Gen. 27); Moriarty, G.1985, 124 (Gen. 27–28); 130 (Gen. 28–29); Moriarty, G. 1945b; Rosch, S. 1977; Vercauteren, F. 1938, XV–XIX; Winkhaus, E. 1953.

**LINE 133**

38. **Charles II** "the Bald" (171-39, 250-39,367-43), King of France, md (2) 25 Nov 870, **Richeut**, dau **Budwine** (206-39), Count of Metz.

37. **Roheut** (Rothaut), b. c870; md **Hugh** (346-37), Count of Bourges.

36. **Richilde**, b. 892; md **Theobald I** (340-36), Viscount of Bourrges and Tours.

35. **Theobald II** "le Tricheur" (the Cheat), Count of Blois; b. c910; d. 16 Jan 975; md 943/944, **Liutgarde de Vermandois** (231-35).

34. **Odo** (Eudes) I, Count of Blois, Chartres, Tours, Chateaudun, Beauvais, Meaux and Provins; b. c950, Mormontier; d. 12 Mar 995, Marmontier; md **Bertha** (230-34), Princess of Burgundy.

33. **Odo** (Eudes) II, Count of Blois, 1005; Champagne, 1019; Chartres, Tours and Beauvais; b. c983/90; d. 15 Nov 1037, md (2) **Ermengarde of Auvergne** (24-34, 127-33).

32. **Theobald III**, Count of Blois and Champagne; b. before 1012; d. 29/30 Sept 1089, Epernay; md (divorced 1049) (1) Garsenda of Maine, dau of Herbert, Count of Maine. He md (2) **Gundrada** (mother of Gen. 31 below), not Alix de Crepi, as given in some sources (See ES 1984:II:46); md (3) Alix de Crepy.

31. **Stephen III** (Étienne Henri) (299-31), Count of Blois, Champagne, Brie, and Chartres; Crusader; a leader of the 1st Crusade, 1096; b. 1046; slain 19 or 27 May 1102, Battle of Ramleh, Holy Land; md 1080/81, **Adela of Normandy and England** (81-30), Princess of England.

30. **Theobald IV** "the Great," (60-29, 81-29), Count of Blois, 1125; and Champagne; b. 1090, Blois, Loir-et-Cher, France; d. 8/10 Jan 1151/52, Ligny; md 1123, **Mathilda von Sponheim** (Maud of Carinthia) (36-28,81-29, 228-30), d. 13 Dec 1160/1161, at Fontevrault.

29. **Adelaide of Blois** (Alix de Blois-Champagne) (243-28), regent of France; b. c1140; d. 4 June 1206, Paris, France; bur Abbaye de Fontigny; md 1160, **Louis VII** (70-29, 88-29,134-29,243-28), King of France; d. 18 Sept 1180.

28. **Philip II Augustus** (68-28,70-28), King of France; Crusader; md **Isabella of Hainault** (132-27).

72

Sources: Agiles, R. 1968; Chaume, M. 1977, I:558; Cokayne, G. 1959, V:156; ES, II 1984:11 (Gen. 28); II 1984:46–47 (Gen. 29–36); Evans, C. 1981 (Gen. 35–38); Foucher, 1971; Keats-Rohan, K. 1997a; Krey, A. n.d.; Moriarty, G.1985, 116–117 (Gen. 28–34); 36–37 (Gen. 36–38); Thatcher, O. 1897, 320–323; Winkhaus, E. 1953.

## LINE 134

36. **Robert I** (169-37), Count of Paris and Poitiers, anti-king of France, Duke of France, Marquis of Neustria and Orleans; b. 866, France; killed 15 June 923, Soissons; md (2) 890, **Beatrix de Vermandois** (mother of Gen. 35), and dau of **Herbert I** (231-37), Count of Vermandois, and **Beatrice of Morvois** (264-37). He also md **Adele** (Adelaide) (259-39), Princess of France.

35. **Hugh Magnus** (64-35), Count of Paris, Orleans and Vexin, Duke of France; b. c895; d. June 956, Deurdan; bur St. Denis; md (3) c938, **Hedwig of Saxony**; b. c921; d. 10 May 965; dau of **Henry I** "the Fowler" (92-36), King of Germany, Lorraine, etc., and **Mechtilde** (Matilda) **von Ringelheim** (338-36).

34. **Hugh Capet** (244-35), King of France, 987–996; Count of Paris, Poitou and Orleans; First Capetan king; b. late 941, France; d. 24 Oct 996, Les Juifs, near Chartres; bur St. Denis; md 963/968, **Adelaide** (Adela) **of Poitou** (163-34).

33. **Robert II** (140-33,154-34) "the Pious," King of France, 988–1031; b. 27 Mar 972, Orleans, France; d. 20 July 1031, Meulan; bur St. Denis; md (3), 998, **Constance of Arles** (333-34), and of Provence and Toulouse; d. 25 July 1032.

32. **Henry I**, King of France, 1031–1060; Duke of Burgundy, Count of Paris; b. 1008, Bourgogne, France; d. 4 Aug, 1060, Vitry-en-Brie; buried St. Denis; md (3) 19 May 1051, Rheims, France, **Anna Jaroslawna**, of Kiev (143-30).

31. **Philip I**, King of France, 1060–1108; b. before 23 May 1053; d. 29 July 1108, Meulan; bur Abbey of St. Benoit-sur-Loire; md (1) 1072; divorced 1091; **Bertha of Holland** (311-32).(mother of Gen. 30); md (2) 15 May 1092, Bertrade de Montfort l'Amaury.

30. **Louis VI** "le Gros" (the Fat) King of France, 1108–1137; a Crusader; b. late in 1081, Herbst; d. 1 Aug 1137, Château Bethizy in Paris, France; bur St. Denis; md 1115, **Adelaide** (Adela) **of Maurienne** (124-31).

29. **Louis VII** "the Young," King of France; b. 1120; d. 18 Sept 1180, Paris; bur Notre-Dame-de-Barbeau, near Fontainebleau; md (1) 22 July 1137, Bordeaux, **Eleanore of Aquitaine** (88-29) (mother of Gen. 28); md (2) 1153/54, Constance of Castile, d. 4 Oct 1160; bur St. Denis; dau Alfonso VII, King of Castile and Leon; md (3) 1160, **Adelaide of Blois** (Alix de Blois-Champagne) (133-29), b. c1140; d. 4 June 1206, Paris; bur Abbaye de Fontingy.

28. **Marie of France**, Princess of France; b. 1145, France; d. 11 Mar 1198; md 1164, **Henry I** (81-28, 137-28), Count of Champagne.

Sources: Agiles, R. 1968; Fisher, G. 1885, 287 (Gen. 29–36); Gardiner, S. 1899, xxxi (Gen. 29–36); Isenburg, W. 1953, II:table 11 (Gen. 28–36); Krey, A. n.d.; Martindale, J. 1992; Moriarty, G.1985, 116 (Gen. 28–29); 51 (Gen. 29–33); 24 (Gen. 33–36); Saillot, J. 1980, 5; Settipani, C. 1991; Thatcher, O. 1897, 320, 323 (Gen. 29–36); Turner, R. 1988.

## LINE 135

33. **Walter de St. Martin**, b. c925; of Normandy, France.
32. **William**, Earl of Warenne, b. c950; of Normandy, France; md **N.N. de Torta**.
31. **Rodulf de Warenne**; b. c998; liv 1074; md (her 1st), **Beatrix** (mother of Gen. 30); dau of **N.N.**, granddau of **Herbastus de Crepon** (166-33); **N.N.** d. 1059; Rodulf md (2) Emma, b. c1020, France.
30. **William de Warenne ( I)**, Seigneur de Varennes, near Dieppe; Earl of Surrey; b. c1055 of Bellencombe, S-Infr, France; d. 1088, Lewes, Surrey, England; md (1) before 1077, **Gundrada** (135A-30); b. c1063, Normandy; d. 27 May 1085, Castle Acre, Norfolk, England, sister of Gerbod, Earl of Chester, 1067; a Fleming.
29. **William de Warenne ( II)**, 2nd Earl of Surrey; fought at Tenchebray, 1106, for Henry I; b. Sussex, England; d. prob 11 May 1138; bur at Lewes; md c1118, **Elizabeth** (Isabel) **de Vermandois** (143-29), Countess of Leicester.
28. **Ada** (Adelaide) **de Warenne**, b. c1120, Surrey, England; d. 1178; md 1139, **Henry of Huntingdon** (72-29), Prince of Scotland, Earl of Huntingdon and Northumberland.

Sources: Clay, C. 1952a, VIII; Cokayne, G. 1959, IV:670, chart iv; VII:642; XII, pt. 1, 492–495; ES, III 1989:699 (Gen. 28–31); Farrar, II:295+; Loyd, L. 1933, 97–113; Moriarty, G.1985, 184 (Gen. 28–31); Paul, J. 1914, I:4; Sanders, I 1960, 101; Warlop, E. 1975, II:1024.

## LINE 135A

33. **Gerbod I**, advocate of St. Bertin, liv 986.
32. Prob. **Arnold I of Schelderwindeke**; liv 986.
31. **Gerbod of Oosterzele**, Earl of Chester; advocate of St. Bertin; liv 1070.
30. **Gundrada**, d. 27 May 1085; md before 1077, **William de Warenne (I)** (135-30).
Source: Warlop, E. 1975, II:1020.

## LINE 136

38. **Boto I**
37. **Retig I**

36. **Boto II**

35. **Retig II**, Count of Bavaria; d. before 994; md (1) **Glismode of Saxony** (356-35), founded after 994 the Benedictine monastery of Ozziach in Friuli; she md (2) before 994, Ozi I, Count of Friuli.

34. **Frideruna** md **Hardwig II** (48-34), Pfalzgrave in Bavaria.

Sources: Blass, R. 1939, II:268, 311; ES III 1984:26 (34–35); Dungern, O. von 1935 ; Hofmeister, A 1920; Isenburg, W. 1953; Moriarty, G.1985, 162 (Gen. 34–38).

## LINE 137

28. **Henry I** (81-28), Count of Champagne md **Marie of France** (134-28), Princess of France.

27. **Marie of Champagne**, Empress of Constantinople; b. 1174; d. 9 Aug 1204; md 6 June 1186, **Baldwin VI** (IX) (73-27), Emperor of Constantinople, Count of Hainault and Flanders; Crusader; a leader of the 4th Crusade.

Sources: ES, II 1984:6 (Gen. 27–28); Jeffrey, J. 1980; Jubainville, M. 1869; Latrie, M. 1889; Moriarty, G.1985, 148, 177 (Gen. 27–28); Pears, E. 1885; Queller, D. 1977; Rosch, S. 1977; Villchardouin, G. n.d..

## LINE 138

32. **Henry II** (68-32), Count of Louvain md **Adelaide** (Adele) **of the Betuwe** (68-32, 389-32).

31. **Ida of Louvain**; b. c1065; d. 1139; was a widow in 1107; md 1084, **Baldwin II** (73-31), Count of Hainault.

Sources: ES, II 1984:6 (Gen. 31–32); Moriarty, G.1985, 124–125 (Gen. 31–32); Rosch, S. 1977 (Gen. 31–32); Vanderkindere, L. 1902 (Gen. 31–32).

## LINE 139

35. **Regnier III** "Longhals" (68-35), Count of Hainault, md **Adele of Louvain** (310-35).

34. **Regnier IV**, Count of Hainault; b. c950; d. 1013; md c996, **Hedwig** (163-33), Princess of France.

Sources: Blass, R. 1939, II:246, 305; Knetsch, C. 1931; Moriarty, G.1985, 50 (Gen. 34–35); Rubincam, M. 1949; Winkhaus, E. 1953.

## LINE 140

33. **Robert II** (134-33), King of France; md **Constance of Arles** (333-34).

32. **Adela**, Princess of France, d. 8 Jan 1078/1079; md 1028, **Baldwin V de Lille** (73-33,141-32), Count of Flanders.

31. **Maud** (Matilda) **of Flanders**, (See also 81-31, 141-31), Duchess of Normandy and Queen of England; b. 1032; d. 1083; md 1053, **William the Conqueror** (89-30); Duke of Normandy, King of England, 1066-1087.

Sources: Brandenburg, E. 1935, E. 1935; Cokayne, G. 1959; Douglas, D. 1964; Fryde, E. 1986; Moriarty, G.1985, 15 (Gen. 31–33); 24 (Gen. 32–33).

## LINE 141

37. **Baldwin II** (235-37), Count of Flanders, md **Aelfthryth**, d. 929, dau of **Alfred** "the Great," (233-39), King of England, and **Eahlswith**.

36. **Arnold I** (356-37) "the Old," Count of Flanders and Artois; b. 885/890; d. 27 Mar 964; md (2) 934, **Adelaide** (Adele) **de Vermandois** (169-35).

35. **Baldwin III** (104-35), Count of Flanders; b. c940; d.1005; md 961, **Mathilda of Saxony**, d. 1005; dau **Hermann Billung** (312-36), Duke of Saxony, and **Hildegarde of Westerburg**.

34. **Arnulf** (Arnold) **II** (184-35) "the Young," Count of Flanders; b. 961/962; d. 30 Mar 987; bur Ghent; md 968, **Susanna** (Rosella) (332-35), Princess of Italy.

33. **Baldwin IV de Lille** of Flanders; Count of Valenciennes and of Flanders; b. c980, Flanders, France; d. 30 May 1035; md c1012, **Ogive** (Otgiva) **of Luxemburg** (353-34) (mother of Gen. 32); md (2) **Eleanor of Normandy**, dau of **Richard II** (89-32), Duke of Normandy, and **Judith of Rennes** (Brittany) (167-33).

32. **Baldwin V de Lille** (73-33), Count of Flanders; b. c1013, Flanders, France; d. 1 Sept 1067, Lille, France; md (her 2nd), 1028, **Adela** (Adele) (140-32), Princess of France.

31. **Maud** (Matilda) **of Flanders** (See also 81-31, 140-31), b. 1032, Flanders, France; d. 3 Nov 1083, Caen, Calvados, France; md 1053, **William the Conqueror** (81-31, 89-30), Duke of Normandy, King of England.

Sources: Blass, R. 1939, II:270, 272; Brandenburg, E. 1935; II:5 (Gen. 31–36); Cokayne, G. 1953; Dougles, D. 1964; Fryde, E.1986; Isenburg, W. 1953; Malmesbury, W. 1911, 121; Moriarty, G.1985, 14–15 (31–37); Winkhaus, E. 1953.

## LINE 142

31. **Pons III** (374-31), Count of Toulouse, Albi and Dijon; md **Almode de la Haute Marche** (327-32).

30. **Almode of Toulouse**, liv 1132; md c1065, **Pierre** ( 203-30), Count of Substantion Melgueil; liv 1085.

29. **Ermesende de Melgueil**, md **William V** (150-31), Seigneur de Montpellier.

Sources: Cokayne, G. 1953; ES, III 1985:445 (Gen. 29–30); Fryde, E. 1986; Moriarty, G.1985, 41–42 (Gen. 30–31); 131 (Gen. 31); Turton, W. 1984, 58 (Gen. 29–31).

## LINE 143

44. **Frodi Fridleifson** of Denmark (321-51).

43. **Ingialdr Starkadarfostri.**

42. **Rurick,** Skioldung (Hroehr), Prince of Lethra, "great-grandfather" of Rurick (See Gen. 39 below).

41. **Frodi Vhroerekrsson,** King of Lethra.

40. **Ivar Vidfadmi,** a Skioldung of Skane; King of Uppsala, in Sweden, and Lethra, in Denmark.

39. **Rurick** (Hroerekr), Woden-born King of Lethra, ("great-grandson of Rurick," Skioldung at Lethra); md **Auda Ivarsdotter** (240-43), dau of **Ivar** "Wide Fathom from Scane," King of Uppsala, in Sweden, and Lethra, in Denmark. She md (2) **Radbard** (240-49) of the 7th century saga line.

38. **Harold Hilditonn** (Hilditoma), King of Lethra in Stealland, Denmark; defeated by Sigurd Ring at Bravalle, 770; slain in sea battle at Bravik, 770.

37. **Halfdan,** Margrave of Frisia, d. 831, when he was exiled to the Frankish empire; he was a Christian.

*NOTE: ES, II:128; Turton, W. 1984, 26, start this genealogy with Rurick (Gen. 36); Moriarty, G.1985, 51, starts with Ivar Vidfadmi (Gen. 40); Moncreiffe, I. 1982, table 33, p. 103, starts with Gen. 42, by virtue of the statement that Rurick (Gen. 39) is "great-grandson of Rurick."*

36. **Rurick** (Hrorekr), of Frisia, Jutland, Prince of the trading town of Novgorod, d. 879; He relapsed to paganism and was expelled from Frisia after 855; md **Alfrind,** sister of Oleg.

35. **Igor** (Ingvar), Grand Prince of Novgorod and Kiev; b. c875; murdered 945, Kiev; md c903, **St. Olga** (Helga), Regent, 945/957; Princess of Izborsk; d. 969, dau of **Oleg** (Helgi II), Danish Prince of Kiev, 911; expelled, 891; slain c912.

34. **Svatoslav** (Sviatoslav, Swjatoslaw) **I Igorjewitsch,** Prince of Novgorod, Grand Duke of Kiev, Grand Prince of Perejaslaw; b. c915/927; slain 972; md (1) Predslawa, Princess of Hungary; md (2) **Maloucha** (Malfreda) (209-34) (mother of Gen. 33), a Slav, formerly a concubine.

33. St. **Vladimir I Swjatoslawitsch** "the Great," of Kiev, Ukraine, Russia; Grand Prince of Novgorod and Kiev; b. c955, Kiev, Ukraine; bapt a Christian, 988; d. 15 July 1015, Berestow, near Kiev, Ukraine; md (3) **Rognieda of Polotsk** (mother of Gen. 32); b. c956; d. 1002. He had many pagan wives and concubines of whom these are known: md (1) Adlaga; (2) Olava; (4) Malfrida, a Bohemian, d. 1002; (5) a Greek, widow of his brother, Teropolk; (6) **N.N.** (27-36), a Bulgarian; (7) 989, Anna, dau of the Eastern Emperor, the Basilius Romanos, d. 1011; (8) **N.N.** (321-33), dau of **Kuno,** Count of Ohningen; b.28 July 1016; d. 19 March 1058.

32. **Debroneiga,** dau of St. **Vladimir** by (8) **N.N.** (321-33), md 1038, **Casimir** (378-33), King of Poland, (378-33); b. 28 July 1016; d. 19 March 1058.

31. **Jaroslav I Wladimirowwitsch** (363-34), Grand Prince of Kiev; b. 978, Kiev, Ukraine; d. 20 Feb 1054, Kiev, Ukraine; md (2) Feb 1019,

Ingegerd (240-32), Princess of Sweden.

30. **Anna** (Agnes) **Jaroslawna**, of Kiev, Ukraine; b. 1036; d. 1076/1089; bur Abbaye Villiers; md, 1051, **Henry I** (134-32), King of France (father of Gen. 30); md (2) 1060, Raoul II, Count of Crecy and Valois.

29. **Hugh Magnus de Crepi** (106-31), Duke of France and Burgundy, Marquis of Orleans, Count of Amiens, Clermont, Paris, Valois and Vermandois; Crusader; a leader of the 1st Crusade; b. 1057; d. 18 Oct 1101, Tarsus, Asia Minor; md after 1067, **Adelaide de Vermandois** (4-30, 239-30).

28. **Elizabeth** (Isabel) **de Vermandois** (103-31), Countess of Leicester; b. 1081, Vermandois, Normandy; d. prob July 1147, St. Nicaise, Meulan, France; md (1) Robert I de Beaumont, Count of Meulan, Earl of Leicester; md c1118 (2) **William de Warenne II** (135-29).

Sources: Agiles, R. 1968; Cokayne, G. 1959, X:351 (Gen. 29–31); ES, II 1984:90 (Gen. 29); III 1980:55 (Gen. 29–30) II 1984:128 (Gen. 31–36); Foucher, 1971; Jacobus, D. 1933 (Gen. 31–36); Krey, A. n.d.; Moncreiffe, I. 1982, chart 33:103 (Gen. 32–42); Moriarty, G.1985, 135 (Gen. 29); 51-53 (Gen. 30–40); Nicholls (gen. 33-36); Taube, M. de 1947; Turton, W. 1984, 26.

## LINE 144

33. **N.N. Castellan** of Château Renard, perhaps descended from the Counts of Sens.

32. **Athon de Courtenay**, Sire de Courtenay in the Gatinais and of Château Renard; Built the castle at Courtenay, 1010; b. c985, of Courtenay, Loiret, France; d. c1034; md c1030, **N.N.** of Courtenay, Loiret, France; b. c1000.

31. **Joscelin de Courtenay**, Lord of Courtenay, Sire de Courtenay and Château Renard, Courtenay, Loiret, France; md (1) Hildegarde de Château-Landon; b. c1032; md (2) after 1065, **Elizabeth de Montlhery** (241-31) (mother of Gen. 30).

30. **Miles** (Milo) **de Courtenay**, Sire de Courtenay; b. c1069, Courtenay, Loiret, France; d. after 1127; md (2) c1095, **Ermengarde de Nevers** (232-30).

29. **Renaud de Courtenay** of Sutton, Berkshire, England; Sire de Courtenay; exiled 1150; b. c1100, Courtenay, Loiret, France; d. 1189/1190; md 1111, (1) **Hedwig** (Hawise) **du Donjon**, occ 1148–1155; dau of **Frederick du Donjon** of Yerre, S-O, France; Sire of the donjon at Corbeil, 1138; b. c1085; d. Donjon Castle, Corbeil, S-O, France; granddau of **Everhard** (Everard) **du Donjon**, occ 1083.

28. **Elizabeth de Courtenay** of Sutton, Berkshire, England, heiress of Courtenay; b. 1127, Courtenay; d. c1205; md after 1150, **Peter of France** (79-28), Prince of France.

27. **Alice** (Adelaide) **de Courtenay**, of Courtenay, Loiret, France; b.

c1160; d. c14 Sept 1205 (or 1218); md **Aymer de Valence** (87-27) (Aymer Taillefer), Count of Angoulême.

Sources: Blass, R. 1939, II:241; ES, II 1984:17 (Gen. 27–29); III 1989:629 (Gen. 28–31); Cokayne, G. 1959, IV:37; Isenburg, W. 1932; Mayer, H. 1988, 63–89 (Gen. 28–31); Moriarty, G.1985, 63 (Gen. 27–33); Prower, 398 (Gen. 27–31); Winkhaus, E. 1953.

## LINE 145

36. **Doon**, called nephew of Bernard, Count of Porcieu, 933–945; liv 949.

35. **Manasses**, Count in 974 and 990 (prob father of Gen. 34).

34. **Manasses I**, Count of Rethel; adherent of Charles, Duke of Lower Lorraine, against Hugh Capet (134-33), 974-990.

33. **Manasses II**, Count of Rethel; liv 1026; md **Judith**.

32. **Manasses III**, Count of Rethel and Porcieu, 1048; d. 1056; md **Yvette de Reucy** (mother of Gen. 31), dau of **Giselbert**, Count of Reucy (6-34,170-33).

31. **Hugh I**, Count of Rethel; liv 1081; d. c1118; bur at Novi; md **Melisende de Montlhery**, dau of **Guy I de Montlhery** (5-32, 241-32), Seigneur de Montlhery and Bray, and wife **Hodierne de Gometz**.

30. **Baldwin II**, Count of Rethel and Edessa, King of Jerusalem, 1118/1131; Crusader; Went with Geoffrey de Bouillon on the 1st Crusade, 1098; b. c1058; d. 21 Aug 1131; md 1101, **Malfia** (Moraphia), d. c1126/1127; dau of **Gabriel the Armenian**, Prince and Governor of Melitene on the Upper Euphrates, at first for the Eastern Emperor, then for the Sultan.

29. **Alice de Rethel**, Princess and Regent of Jerusalem; b. c1110; d. after 1136; md 1126, **Bohemond II** (80-30), Prince of Antioch.

Sources: Agiles, R. 1968; Archern, K. 1993; Benvenisti, M. 1972; Boase, T. 1971; Bresc, G. 1984, Chalandon, F. 1912; Cokayne, G. 1959, I:352; Conder, C. 1978; ES, II 1984:205 (Gen. 30–31); III 1989:625 (Gen. 30–37); III 1989:624 (Gen. 32); Foucher, 1971; Krey, A. n.d.; Mayer, H. 1994; Moriarty, G.1985, 142–143 (Gen. 30–35); Munro, D. 1935; Poole, S. 1978; Prawler, J. 1952; Prawler, J. 1972; Prawler, J. 1980; Richard, G. 1979; Riley-Smith, J. 1973; Runciman,S, 1987, II:chart 492; Speculum, Jan. 1942, p.100; Warlop, E. 1976,

## LINE 146

32. **Philip I** (134-31), King of France, 1060–1108; b. 1053; d. 29 July 1108; md (1) 1072, **Bertha of Holland** (311-32).

31. **Constance**, Princess of France; b. c1078; d. 1124/1126; md **Bohemond I** (80-31), Prince of Antioch.

Sources: Jacobus, D. 1933; Moriarty, G.1985, 51 (Gen. 31-32); Runciman, II: chart 492; Thatcher, O. 1897, 320, 323; Vambery, 120–147 (Gen. 31-32) Von Redlich, M. 1941 , 267–268 (Gen. 31-32).

## LINE 147

27. **Louis VIII** (70-27), King of France; md **Blanche of Castile** (88-27).

26. **Robert I** (125-26), Prince of France, Count of Artois; Crusader; b. Sept 1216; d. 9 Feb 1250; slain at Mansoure, Egypt, on the Crusade of St. Louis; md 14 June 1237, Compiegne, **Matilda of Brabant** (125-26); d. 29 Sept 1288.

25. **Blanche of Artois**, b. c1248; d. 2 May 1302, Paris, France; md (1) 1269, **Henry I** (81-25), King of Navarre; md about 1275, his 2nd, **Edmund Plantagenet**, Prince of England, Earl of Lancaster, son of **Henry III** (53-25), King of England.

Sources: Bard, R. 1982; Chaume, M. 1977, 542, 551–552; Cokayne, G. 1959, VII:378–387 (Gen. 25–27); ES, III 1980:70 (Gen. 25–26); Fisher, G. 1885, 287; Moriarty, G.1985, 154 (Gen. 25–26); 116 (Gen. 26–27); Moriarty, G. 1945; Moriarty, G. 1947; Voltaire 33:384–388; Winkhaus, E. 1953.

## LINE 148

30. **William I Talvas** (244-30, 245-30), Count of Ponthieu, md **Helie (Alice) of Burgundy** (245-30).

29. **Gui II de Ponthieu**, Count of Ponthieu; Crusader, 1127; d. 1147, Ephesus, Turkey, on 2nd Crusade; md c1139, **Ida**, d. c1180.

28. **Jéan** (John) I, Count of Ponthieu and Montreuil; fought in wars against the English; Crusader, 1147; b. c1140; d. 30 June 1191, Acre, Palestine, on 3rd Crusade; md (his 3rd, her 3rd) **Beatrice of St. Pol** (Beatrice de Candavene de St. Pol) (242-28).

27. **William II Talvas**, Count of Ponthieu and Montreuil; commanded the right wing for the French at Bouvines, on the Albigensian Crusade; b. 1179; d. 6 Oct 1221; md, Meudon, 20 Aug 1195, **Alice of France**, Princess of France (243-27).

26. **Marie** (Jeanne), Countess of Ponthieu and Montreuil; b. 17 Apr 1199; d. Sept 1250; md 1208, (1) **Simon II de Dammartin** (82-26).

Sources: Agiles, R. 1968; Blass, R. 1939 II:238; Cokayne, G. 1959, I:351; XI:689–697; Douglas, R. 1946; ES, III 1989:638 (Gen. 26–30); Evans, C. 1965 (Gen. 26–30); Fiennes, D. 1980; Foucher, 1971; Krey, A. n.d.; Tourtier, C. de 1960 (Gen. 26–30), 102–134.

## LINE 149

35. **Frederick**, Count of Bar, Duke of Upper Lorraine; md **Beatrice of France**.

34. **Thibaud**, Count of Bar, Duke of Mosellane, Duke of Upper Lorraine; b. c965; d. 11 Apr 1032; md **Sconehilde of Metz**, d. before 995.

33. **Louis I de Mousson**, Undercount of Bar; liv 1019–1022.

32. **Richwin** (Richuris), Count of Scarpone; liv 1019–1028; md **Hildegarde**, dau of **Hugh VI** (26-31, 30-33, 33-33), Count of Egisheim,

and **Heilwig Von Dagsburg** 26-31,(33-33, 175-32).

31. **Louis II**, Seigneur of Montbeliard, St. Mihel, Mousson and Aimance; Count of Bar and Montbeliard; adherent of the Emperor Henry II in the Burgundian wars; was at Rome in 1052 with Pope Leo IX; b. 1019; d. 1071/76; bur Notre Dame at Bar; md 1040, **Sophia of Bar le Duc** (247-31), heiress of Bar-le-Duc; b. c1025; d. end of 1092;

30. **Thierry II** (Dietrich I), Count of Bar and Montbeliard, 1093; b. c1045; d. 2 Jan 1105; md 1065, **Ermentrude of Burgundy;** b. c1060; d. after 8 Mar 1105; dau of **William II** (94-31), Count of Burgundy and Macon and **Stephanie** (not of Vienne).

29. **Renaud I**, Count of Bar-le-Duc and Mousson; opponent of the Emperor Henry V; Crusader; went with Louis VII on 2nd Crusade, 1147; founded the Priory of Moncon and the monastery at Rieval; b. c1090; d. 24 June 1150; bur at Mousson; md (2) c1108, **Gisela de Vaudemont** (246-29), d. before 1127.

28. **Clemence of Bar-le-Duc**, of Dammartin-en-Goele, Ile de France, France; d. after 20 Jan 1183; md 1140, **Renaud II** (344-28), Count of Clermont (father of Gen. 27), d. c1162; md (2) Thibaut III de Crepy, liv 1150–1182. *NOTE: Moriarty, G.1985, 112, gives an incorrect husband.*

27. **Matilda** (Mahaut, Maud) **of Ponthieu**, b. c1138; d. after Oct 1200; md **Alberic** (Aubrey) **II** (82-27), Count of Dammartin; b. c1135; d. 19 Sept 1200.

Sources: Clairvaux, B. 1963; Constable, G. 1953; Dungern, O. von 1910; ES, III 1989:649 (Gen. 27–28); VI 1978:146–147 (Gen. 28–31); Isenburg, W. 1932; Jackman, D. 1990; Jackman, D. 1997; Maton, vol. 43; Merz, W. 1914; Moriarty, G.1985, 112 (Gen. 27–28); 123, 194 (Gen. 28–34); Poull, G. 1979.

## LINE 150

34. **William II** (Bernard William), Seigneur de Montpellier; liv 1019–1025; md **Beliarde.**

33. **William III**, Seigneur de Montpellier; b. c1000/1001; d. c1068.

32. **William IV**, Seigneur de Montpellier, c1068–1076; bought the castle at Melgueil; b. c1030/1035; d. 1076; md c1060, **Ermengarde of Melgueil**, dau of **Raymond I** (203-31), Count of Melgueil, and **Beatrix of Poitou**, dau of **William III** (88-33), Count of Poitou, and **Agnes of Burgundy** (161-32); Ermengarde md (2) Ramonde de Andruze.

31. **William V**, Seigneur de Montpellier, 1076; held Melgueil, 1103; went on the 1st Crusade with Raymonde de St. Gilles; b. c1065/1069; d. c1122; md (2) c1086/1087, **Ermesende de Melgueil**, dau of **Pierre** (203-30), Count of Substantion Melgueil, and **Almode of Toulouse** (142-30).

30. **William VI**, Seigneur de Montpellier; received Tortosa, 1136; became a Cisterian monk at Grandselver; b. c1100; d. 1162; md Aug 1129, **Sibel de Vasto di Savona** (106-30), d. before 1146.

29. **William VII**, Duke of Montpellier and Montferrier, Seigneur de Tortosa; b. c1130; d. after May 1173; bur Abbey of Granselvre; will dtd 20 Sept 1172; md 25 Feb 1157, Montpellier, **Mathilda of Burgundy** (377-29), Dame de Montferrier, d. before 29 Sept 1172.

28. **William VIII**, Seigneur de Montpellier; b. c1158; d. 1218; md (1) 1178/1179 (divorced 1187), **Eudoxia** (Marie) **Komnena** (111-28), b. c1168; d. a nun, after 4 Nov 1202. *See note at end of line 111, regarding parentage of Eudoxia.*

27. **Marie**, Queen of Aragon, Dame de Montpellier, heiress of Montpellier; b. 1182; d. Rome, 21 Apr 1213; bur St. Peter's; md (3) 15 June 1204, **Pedro II** ( 51-26), King of Aragon, Count of Barcelona and Gevaudun, Marquis of Carlat; b. 1176; d. 14 Sept 1213; fell in the battle of Murat, fighting on behalf of the Albigenses. He was son of **Alfonso II** (58-28), King of Aragon and **Sancha** (94-28).

Sources: Agiles, R. 1968; Brandenburg, E.; ES, III 1985: 445–446 (Gen. 27-35); Foucher, 1971; Isenburg, W. 1953, Part ii, table 142; Krey, A. n.d.; Moriarty, G.1985, 131–132 (Gen. 27–35); Rouquette, J. 1914 (Gen. 27–35); Settipani, C. 1988.

## LINE 151

33. **Sancho Garcia III** (95-33,223-36,248-33,),, King of Navarre, Castile, and Aragon; md **Munia Mayor** (285-33), co-heir of Castile.

32. **Garcia IV**, King of Navarre, 1035; b. c1020; killed in battle 1 Sept 1054 at Atapuerca, Spain; md 1038, **Stephanie de Foix**, d. after 1066; dau Count **Bernard Rodger**, son of **Roger I de Comminges** (291-35) and **Gersende de Bigorre** (227-33).

31. **Sancho Garcia** (Sancho IV), res. of Uncastillo y Sanguesa, d. after Dec 1073; md (1) 1057, **Constanza of Moranon** (mother of Gen. 30); dau of **Sancho Fortun**, Seigneur of Moranon, and wife **Velasquita**; md (2) Audregoto.

30. **Ramiro II Sanchez**, the disinherited Infante of Navarre; Count of Moncon, Lord of Urroz and Lord Moncon; Crusader; went on the 1st Crusade with Raymond of Toulouse; b. c1070; d. Jan/Feb 1116; md after 1098, **Christina** (Elvira) **Diaz**, dau of **Rodrigo Diaz de Castro** ("el Cid") (179-31), and Dona **Jimena Diaz** (180-30).

29. **Garcia Ramirez V** (Garcias VII), King of Navarre, 1134; b. after 1110; d. 21 Nov 1150, Larca de Navarra; md 1130, **Margaret de l'Aigle** (178-29) (mother of Gen. 28); md (2) Leon, 24 June 1144, **Urraca Alfonsa of Castile**, b. after 1126; d. Palencia, 12 Oct 1189; dau of **Alfonso VII**, (86-29, 94-29), King of Castile.

28. **Blanca**, Princess of Navarre; b. c1134; d. 12 Aug 1156; betrothed 25 Oct 1140, at his age 5; md at Logera or Calaharra, Spain, 30 Jan 1151, **Sancho III** (83-28), King of Castile.

*NOTE: Stimmel (Stimmel, R. 1976) notes that many authors have an*

82

*incorrect name for Gen. 31. Bayne.K, p. 294, for instance, says Ramiro of Calaharra; Moriarty, G.1985, p. 109, says Ramiro, Count of Moncon.*

Sources: Agiles, R. 1968; Archern, K. 1993; Bard, R. 1982; Cancellos, A. 1945, I 149–192; Conder, C. 1978; ES, II 1984:56 (Gen. 28–32); II 1984:55 (Gen. 33); Evans, C. 1932 (Gen. 28–29);Mayer, H. 1994; Munro, D. 1935; Moriarty, G.1985, 109 (Gen. 29–32); 78 (Gen. 32–33); Prawler, J. 1952; Prawler, J. 1972; Prawler, J. 1980; Riley-Smith, 1973; Runcimern, S. 1987; Stimmel, R. 1976 (Gen. 28–33); Vajay, S. de 1966, 725–750 (Gen. 28–33).

## LINE 152

31. **Fulk V** (313-29), Count of Anjou, King of Jerusalem, Crusader; b. 1092; d. 10 Nov 1143; md (2) c1108, **Erembourg**, heiress of Mans (313-29).

30. **Sybil** (Sibille) **of Anjou**; b. c1112; d. 1165, Bethlehem; md **Dietrich II** (205-30), Count of Alsace and Flanders.

Sources: Agiles, R. 1968; Blass, R. 1939; Brandenburg, E. 1935; Chaume, M. 1977, I 532–533;ES, VI 1978:129 (Gen. 30–31); Foucher, 1971; Krey, A. n.d.; Moriarty, G.1985, 2 (Gen. 30–31); Poole, S. 1978.

## LINE 154

34. **Robert II** "the Pious" (134-33,140-33,333-34), King of France, md **Constance of Arles** (333-34).

33. **Robert III** (154-33), the Old," Duke of Burgundy; Prince of France; b. c1011; d. 21 Mar 1076, Fleury-sur-Ouche, France; bur Semur; md (1) c1033, **Helie de Semur** (85-31,245-33) (mother of Gen. 32); md (2) 1055, **Ermengarde of Anjou** (91-31); div for consanguinity.

32. **Hildegarde of Burgundy**, b. c1033; d. after 1104; md (3) 1068/ 1069, **William IV** ( also called Gui Geoffrey) Count of Poitou; and as Duke of Aquitaine, **William VIII** (88-32).

Sources: Blass, R. 1939, II:242, 243; Cokayne, G. 1959, X:351; Moriarty, G.1985, 40 (Gen. 32–33); 24 (Gen. 33–34); Moriarty, G. 1945; Moriarty, G. 1947; Reilly, B. 1982; Winkhaus, E. 1953.

## LINE 155

32. **Robert III** "the Old" (154-33), Prince of France, Duke of Burgundy; b. c1011; d. 21 Mar 1076; md (1) c1033, **Helie de Semur** (Eleanor of Semur-en-Auxois) (85-31).

31. **Constance of Burgundy** (248-31), b. c1046; d. Jan/Feb 1093; md (his 2nd), 8 May 1081, **Alfonso VI** (248-31), King of Castile and Leon.

30. **Urraca** (94-30,248-30), heiress of Castile and Leon; b. c1082; d. 8 Mar 1126, Saldana, Spain; bur at Leon; md **Raymond of Burgundy** (86-30), Count of Castile.

Sources: Brandenburg, E; ES, II 1984:57 (Gen. 30–32); Moriarty,

G.1985, 82–83 (Gen. 30–31); 24, 40 (Gen. 32); Petit, E. 1894 (Gen. 30–32); Reilly, B. 1982; Winkhaus, E. 1953.

**LINE 156**

34. **Hugh,** First hereditary Vicomte de Camborn; Sire de Quercy.

33. **Archambaud II** "the Stumbler," Vicomte de Camborn, Ventadour and Turenne; built the castle of Monceaux, 963–992; d. after 993; md **Sulpice** (308-33), heiress of Turenne.

32. **Ebles I,** Vicomte de Turenne; d. 1030; md 1000 (divorced before 1030) (1) **Beatrice of Normandy,** d. 18 Jan 1035; dau of **Richard I** (166-33), Duke of Normandy, and **Gunnora de Crepon** (89-33,122-35,166-32).

31. **William,** Vicomte de Turenne; liv 1000–1030; md **Matilda.**

30. **Boson I** (377-30), Vicomte de Turenne; b. c1050; d. 1092, Jerusalem, on a pilgrimage to the Holy Land; md (2) **Gerberge de Terrasson,** b. c1055; d. 1103; dau of **Pierre,** Count of Terrasson.

29. **Raymond I,** Vicomte de Turenne; b. c1080; d. c1137; a Crusader; went on Crusades in 1096, and in 1124–1127; md c1122, **Matilda de Perche** (249-29).

28. **Marguerite de Turenne,** b. c1120; md (1) Ademir IV of Limoges; md (2) c1140,(div 1150), Ebles II, Vicomte of Ventadour; md (3) **William IV** "Taillefer" (87-28), Count of Angouleme, d. Messina, 7 Aug 1179.

Sources: Agiles, R. 1968; Aubel, F. 1997:309-335; Brandenburg, E. 1935;ES, III 1989:766 (Gen. 28–30); III 1989:765 (Gen. 30–34); II:78; Foucher, 1971; Krey, A. n.d.; Moriarty, G.1985, 48 (Gen. 28–34); Winkhaus, E. 1953.

**LINE 157**

34. **Geoffrey I Grisgonelle** (167-35), Count of Anjou, Seneschal of France; md **Adele of Troyes** (167-35,258-36).

33. **Gerberge of Anjou** md **William II** "Taillefer" (87-33), Count of Angoulême (Aquitaine, France).

Sources: Blass, R. 1939, II; Brandenburg, E. 1935; Chaume, M. 1977, I:533; Curschmann, F. 1921, 57; Moriarty, G.1985, 4 (Gen. 33–34); Moriarty, G. 1945b.

**LINE 158**

39. **N.N.,** father of Matfried, Gerhard and Richar.

38. **Matfried,** Count in the Metzgau, d. in 930; md **Lantsind.**

37. **Adalbert,** Count (of Metz), killed in battle, 944; md **Luitgarde,** occ 960; dau **Wigeric** (of Luxemburg). She md (2) **Eberhard IV** (33-35, 202-37, 316-36), Count in the Nordgau; she d. 966.

36. **Matfried,** occ 960.

35. **Richard** (Berhard), Count of Metz, liv 986.

34. **Adalbert II** (same as 105-34), Count in the Saargau, of Alsace and of Metz, Duke of Lower Lorraine; liv 974; d. 1033, Bouzonville, returning from Jerusalem; md **Judith** (Jutta), liv 1032; dau of **Konrad II** of Ohningen, Duke of Swabia., d.977, and his wife **Richlint**, dau of **Liudolf**, Duke of Swabia.

33. **Gerhard**, Count of Metz, Duke of Upper Lorraine; d. 1045; md before 979, **Gisele** , dau of **Dietrich I**, Duke of Upper Lorraine (319-35).

32. **Gerhard IV** (246-30), Count of Alsace and of Chatenois, Duke of Upper Lorraine; d. 14 Apr 1070, Remiremont; md **Hedwig**; d. 1075/1080; prob dau of **Adalbert I** (120-34), Count of Namur, and **Ermengarde (Adelaide) of Lorraine**

31. **Dietrich II of Alsace**, Duke of Upper Lorraine; d. 23 Jan 1115; bur at Chetenois; md (2) c1100, **Gertrude** (205-31), heiress of Flanders, and widow of Henry III, Count of Louvain; He md (1) c1075, **Hedwig von Formbach** (41-32).

Sources: Blass, R. 1939, II:264; Brandenburg, E. 1935; Dollinger, P. 1991; ES VI 1978:129 (Gen. 31–39); Hlawitschka, E. 1969; Parisse, M. 1976; Poull, G. 1979; Putnam, R. 1971.

## LINE 159

39. **Geoffrey**, Vicomte de Thouars; occ Aug 876 (prob father of Gen. 38).

38. **Aimery** (Amauri, Amalric) I, Vicomte de Thouars; d. by 936; md **Aremburge**, a widow in 936.

37. **Aimery** (Amauri) II, Vicomte de Thouars, d. c956; bur at St. Leger; md **Alianore** (Hardovine), liv 995.

36. **Herbert I**, Vicomte de Thouars; d. 13 May 988; md before 969, **Aldegarde** (331-36).

35. **Savaric** (Savary) III, Vicomte de Thouars; d. c980/1004.

34. **Geoffrey II**, Vicomte de Thouars; d. a monk, c1055, in St. Michael in Lherm, 1055; md **Eleanor** (Aenor), liv 1055.

33. **Aimery** (Amaury) IV, Vicomte de Thouars; Companion of **William the Conqueror**; fought at Hastings, 14 Oct 1066 in Duke William's army; b. c1024; murdered 1093; bur at Saint-Nicholas-de-la-Chaise; md (1) **Aurengarde de Mauleon**, b. c1030.

32. **Eleanor de Thouars**; md before 1075, **Boso II** (305-32), Vicomte de Châtellerault, 1070–1088 and 1092.

31. **Aimery I** (Amauri, Amalric), Vicomte de Châtellerault; b. c1076; d. 7 Nov 1151, a monk at Notre Dame de Noyers; md (2) **Dangerose**, b. c1080; liv 1119; dau of **Bartholomew**, Seigneur de l'Isle Bouchard.

30. **Eleanore de Châtellerault**; b. c1105; d. after Mar 1130; md late in 1121, **William VIII** (X) (88-30), Count of Poitou.

Sources: Blass, R. 1939, II:253; ES, III 1989:810 (Gen. 32–39); Moriarty, G.1985, 45–46 (30–39); Morin, A. 1964, 18–37 (Gen. 31–39); Sugar, A. 1929, VI:127.

## LINE 160

33. **Jean de Conteville** (185-33).

32. **Herlevin de Conteville**, Vicomte de Conteville, Normandy, France; b. c1001; d. c1066; bur at Grestain; md c1028/30 **Herleve**, called Harlette de Falaise; b. c1003, dau **Fulbert of Falaise**, Calvados, France; a tanner, and **Doda** (Dode), a concubine. See 89-31 for her connection with Robert I, Duke of Normandy.

31. **Robert de Mortain**, Earl of Cornwall, Count of Mortain; was in command of the men at Cotentin; Companion of his half-brother, William the Conqueror at the Battle of Hastings, 14 Oct 1066; b. after 1040, Normandy, France; d. c1090; bur at Grestain; md **Matilda** (Maud) **de Montgomery** (335-31).

30. **Emma de Mortain**, b. c1058, Mortaigne, France; occ 1080; md about 1071, **William IV** (374-30), Count of Toulouse; b. 1040; d. 1093, in battle at Huesca.

29. **Philippa** (Mathilde), regent of Toulouse; b. c1073; d. 28 Nov 1117; md 1094; divorced 1115, **William VII** (88-31), Count of Poitou, (and IX as Duke of Aquitaine). She md (1) and div, Sancho I, King of Aragon and Navarre.

Sources: Blass, R. 1939, II:259, 269; Douglas, R. 1944, 27, 33–36; ES, II 1984:76 (Gen. 29–30); III 1989:694B (Gen. 30–32); Gastebois, V. 1934,16+; Moriarty, G.1985, 44 (Gen. 29–30); 42 (30–32); Vand Houts, E. 1986.

## LINE 161

34. **Ragnvald** (170-34) md **Alberade** (Aubree) **of Lorraine** (92-34).

33. **Ermentrude de Roucy** (298-33), Queen of Lombardy; b. 958; d. 5 Mar 1005; md **Otto William** (Otton I) (94-33), King of Lombardy, in Italy.

32. **Agnes of Burgundy**, Princess of Lombardy; b. c995; d. 10 Nov 1068; md (his 3, her 2) 1019, **William III** (88-33), Count of Poitou (V as Duke of Aquitaine), 990; b. c969; d. a monk, 31 Jan 1030.

31. **Agnes of Poitou** md (his 2nd) **Henry III** "the Black" (359-33), King of Germany, Emp. of the West, 1036–1056.

Sources: Chaume, M. 1977, I 400n, 401n, 443, 446n6;Cokayne, G. 1959, XI: appendix D, 112–113; ES, I 1984:4 (Gen. 31–32); II 1984:59 (Gen. 33–34); Moranville, 83:1–42; Moriarty, G.1985, 36–39 (Gen. 31–34); Saillot, J. 1980; Vambery, 120–147; Von Redlich, M. 1941, 267–268.

## LINE 162

36. **Rollo** (Rollon, Granger Rolf) (166-35), Duke of Normandy, md **Poppa de Bayeux**. He was a Viking.

35. **Gerloc** (Adele) **of Normandy**, b. c920; d. after 969; md 935, **William I** (88-35,163-35), Count of Poitou (William III as Duke of Aquitaine).

Sources: Cokayne, G. 1959, X: appendix A, 3; ES, II 1984:76 (Gen.

35–36); Moriarty, G.1985, 11 (Gen. 35–36); Rosch, S. 1977 (Gen. 35–36); Saillot, J. 1980 (Gen. 36); Vitalis, O. 1857, (Provost ed.) II:403–404.

## LINE 163

39. **Gerard I** (352-40), Count of Auvergne, an Aquitaine magistrate slain 25 June 841 at Battle of Fontenay; md **Hildegarde**, dau **Louis I** (171-40), Emperor of the West, and **Ermengarde of Hesbaye** (352-41).

38. **Ranulf I**, Count of Poitou and Duke of Aquitaine; b. 820; slain Oct 866 by the Normans at Brisarte; md (1) Rotrude, dau Charlemagne. md (2) c845, **N.N.of Maine** (perhaps Bilihilde); dau **Rorick II**, Count of Maine and part of Brittany; and wife **Bilihildis** (284-39). Rorick's parents were **Gauzelin,** a Neustrian nobleman, and **Aldetrude.**

37. **Ranulf II**, Count of Poitou and Duke of Aquitaine; b. 848; d. 3/5 Aug 890; (md) **Irmgard** (Ermengarde) (mother of Gen. 36), a concubine.

36. **Ebles "Manzer,"** Count of Poitou and Duke of Aquitaine; b. 890; d. 934; md (2) 911, **Emilienne.**

35. **William I "Tete d'Etoupe"** (Same as 88-35, 162-35), Count of Poitou, 955; and of Duke of Aquitaine (as William III); Count of Auvergne, 959/962; b. c915; d. a monk 3 Apr 963; md 935, **Gerloc** (Adele) **of Normandy** (88-35,162-35).

34. **Adelaide** (Adela) **of Poitou**, b. c950; d. 1004; md 963/68, **Hugh Capet** (134-34), King of France.

33. **Hedwig**, Princess of France; b. c972; d. after 1013; md c996, **Regnier IV** (139-34), Count of Hainault.

32. **Beatrice of Hainault**, b. c997; liv 1035; md (1) and divorced **Ebles I** (170-32), Count of Rheims and Roucy, 997; she md (2) c1035, Manasses "the Bold," Viscount of Rheims.

Sources: Brandenburg, E. 1935; ES, III 1989:675A (Gen. 32–33); II 1984:76 (Gen. 34–39); Luke Stevens mms, version 12, Aug. 1997; Moriarty, G.1985, 50 (Gen. 32–33); 24–27 (Gen. 33–39); Moriarty, G. 1955; Prawler, J. 1952; Prawler, J. 1972; Prawler, J. 1980; Riley-Smith, J. 1973; Saillot, J. 1980 (Gen. 34–39).

## LINE 164

27. **Raymond Berenger V** (54-26), Count of Provence and Forcalquier, md **Beatrice of Savoy** (93-26).

26. **Beatrice of Savoy**, Countess of Provence and Forcalquier; b. 1234; d. 23 Sept 1267, Nocera; bur Roque-Pymont; md **Charles I** (88-26), King of Naples, Sicily; and Jerusalem, Count of Anjou, Crusader.

Sources: Addington, A. 1976; Archern, K. 1993; Cokayne, G. 1959, IV 321; Conder, C. 1978; ES, II 1984:15 (Gen. 26–27); Mayer, H. 1994; Munro, D. 1935; Moriarty, G.1985, 68 (Gen. 26–27); Pinoteau, H. 1958b; Poole, S. 1978; Prawler, J. 1952; Prawlerr, J. 1972; Prawler, J. 1980; Richard, J. 1979; Riley-Smith, J. 1973; Runcimen, S. 1987; Vrignault, H. 1965.

## LINE 165

53. **Eochaid Munrevar** (Muinremur), King of Irish Dalriada, d. before 439; prob md **N.N.** (Erca?), dau of **Laorn**, son of **Eru**.

52. **Ercc**, King of Irish Dalriada; b. c400; d. 474; md **Misi** (Mist); d. 474.

51. **Fergus Mor Mac Ercc**, King of Dalriada, Argyle, Scotland, 498–c501; Invaded Kyntire, 496, and founded the kingdom of the Scottish Dalriada; d. 501. Sometimes confused with Ercc, a son of Laorn's dau.

50. **Domongart** (Dumngalhen), King of Scottish Dalriada, 499–504; d. c504; md **Feldelm Foltchain** (Fedelmia) (251–52).

49. **Gabran Mac Domangart** (Gavran, Goranus), King of Dalriada and of Scots, 538–560; d. 560; md **Lleian**, dau **Brachan** (Brychan) of South Wales.

48. **Aidan mac Gabran** (Aldanus) crowned King of Dalriada in Scotland by St. Columba of Iona, 574; b. 532; d. 606.

47. **Eochaid Buide**, King of Picts and of Dalriada, 608–629; educated by St. Columba; a younger son of Aidan who succeeded his father as his older brothers had all been killed; ruled 608–629; d. 629.

46. **Domnall Brec** (Donald Breck), King of Dalriada, d.c 642, in battle of Strathcarron; md **N.N.**(439-48).

45. **Domangart II** (did not rule), d. prob 673.

44. **Eochaid II** "Rianamhail" (crooked nose), King of Dalriada, c694–697; killed in battle, c697 after ruling prob 3 years (c694–c697); md **N.N.**, a Pictish princess (341-47,345-44).

43. **Eochaid III**, King of Dalriada, 721–733; Knapdale and Kintyre.

42. **Aed Find**, King of Dalriada, 748–778; liv 778.

41. **Eochaid IV** "Annuine" (the poisonous), King of Dalriada, 781–789; md **Fergusa** (355-43).

40. **Alpin mac Eochaid**, King of Kintyre, Mar 834; King of Dalriada, 834–837; b. c778, Scotland; killed in battle, Galloway, 20 July 841.

39. **Kenneth mac Alpin**, King of Scotland, 843–858, King of Picts and Scots (as Cinead); ruled in Dalriada, 844–859; b. c810, Scotland; d. 859, Forteviot, Perth, Scotland.

38. **Causantin** (Constantine), King of Scotland, 863–877; b. c836; slain in battle with the Norsemen, Inverdovat, Forgan, Fife, Scotland, 877.

37. **Domnall** (Donald), King of Scotland, 889-900; b. c862; d. 900, Forres, Moray, Scotland.

36. **Malcolm** (Mael-Coluim) I, King of Scotland, 942–954; killed 954 by the men of Moray, Fordoun, Kincardine, Scotland.

35. **Kenneth** (Cinaed), King of Scotland, 971–995; murdered 995, Fettercairn, Kincardine, by his own men; his wife or mistress was from Leinster.

34. **Malcolm** (Mael-Coluim) **II**, King of Strathclyde, 990–995; King of Scotland, 1005–1034; fought in battle in 1008 at Corham with Uchtred, son of Waltheof, Earl of Northumberland; overcame the Danes in 1017; published a code of laws; b. c954; murdered 25 Nov 1034.

33. **Bethoc** (Beatrix), heiress and Princess of Scotland; b. c984, Angus, Scotland; md 1000, **Crinan the Thane** (252-34).

32. **Duncan mac Crinan** (Duncan I), King of Strathclyde, 1018–1034, King of Scots, 1034–1040; b. c1001/1005, Scotland; d. 14 Aug 1040, near Elgin, Moray, Scotland; murdered by Macbeth; he beseiged Durham, 14 Aug 1040. (See *Macbeth*, a work of fiction, by William Shakespeare); md c1030, **Sibil**, b. c1009; a cousin of Siward, Danish Earl of Northumbria.

31. **Malcolm III Canmore** (72-31,233-32,242-32), King of Scotland, 1058–1093; Crowned at Scone, 17 Mar 1057/8; b. c1031, Scotland; d. in battle 13 Nov 1093 while besieging Alnwick Castle, Alnwick, Northumberland; md (2) 1068/1069, Saint **Margaret of Scotland** (233-32) (mother of Gen. 30 below). Malcolm III md (1) 1059, Ingeborg of Holland, dau of Jarl Finn Arnesson and Berglioth of Norway; and widow of Thorfin II, Earl of Caithness.

30. **Matilda** (Edith) **of Scotland**, Queen of England; b. 1079, Scotland; d. 1 June 1118; md (1) 11 Nov 1100, **Henry I** "Beauclerc" (89-29), King of England.

Sources: Anderson, A. 1990, I:268; Ashley, M. 1998; Barrow, G. 1981; Bingham, C. 1974; Chadwick, H. 1949; Cokayne, G. 1959, II:704; IV:504 and note G, 669 chart II; V:736; VII:641–642, 737; IX:704; Dillon, M. 1967; Ellis, P. 1990; ES, II 1984: 88–89 (Gen. 30-41); Hartwell, R. 1975 (Gen. 35-40); Hubert, H. 1992; Moriarty, G.1985, 28–30 (Gen. 30-53); O'Kelly, M. 1989; Pirie, C. 1962, I:35–40, 79–87, 143–148, 192–196; II:9–14, 92–102 (Gen. 39-52); Powell, T. 1958; Weis, F. 1992, line 170 (Gen. 30-52); Williamson, D. 1996.

## LINE 166

64. **Njord**, King of the Swedes; of Nortun, Sweden; b. c214; md **N.N.**,his sister.

63. **Yngvi-Frey of Uppsala**, Sweden, King of Sweden; b. c235; md **Gerd Gymersdotter** of Uppsala, b. c239; dau of **Gymer of Scandinavia**, b. c214; and **Orsoda of Berg**, Scandinavia; b. c218.

62. **Fjolnar Yngvi-Freysson**, of Uppsala, Sweden; b. c256; d. Hleithra, Denmark.

61. **Svegdi Fjolnarsson**, b. c277, Uppsala, Sweden; md **Vana**.

60. **Vanlandi Svegdasson**, b. c298, Uppsala, Sweden; md **Driva Snaersdotter**, Princess of Finland; b. c302, Finland; dau of **Snaer**, King of Finland.

59. **Visbur Vanlandasson**, b. c319, Uppsala, Sweden; md **N.N.**, dau of **Authi** or Audi.

58. **Domaldi Visbursson**, b. c340, Uppsala, Sweden.

57. **Domar Domaldsdotter**, b. c361, Sweden; md **Drott Danpsson**, son of **Rig**.

56. **Dyggvi Domarsson**, b. c382, Sweden.

55. **Dag Dyggvasson**, b. c403, Sweden.

54. **Agni Dagsson**, b. c424, Sweden; md **Skjalf Frostasdotter**, b. c428, Finland.

53. **Alrek Agnasson**, b. c445, Sweden; md **Dagreid Dagsdotter**.

52. **Yngvi Alreksson**, b. c466, Sweden.

51. **Jorund Yngvasson**, b. c487, Sweden.

50. **Aun Jorundsson**, of Sweden, b. c509.

49. **Egil Aunsson**, b. c530, Sweden.

48. **Ottar Egilsson**, b. c551, Sweden.

47. **Adils Ottarsson**, b. c572, Sweden; md **Yrsa Helgasdotter** (324-48).

46. **Eystein Adilsson**, b. c594, Sweden.

45. **Ingvar Eysteinsson**, b. c616, Sweden.

44. **Braut-Onund Ingvarsson**, b. c636, Sweden.

43. **Ingjald Braut-Onundson** "ill-ruler," King of Uppsala in Sweden; the last Fray-born pagan sacrol "peace king" associated with human sacrifice in his own family; b. c660; md **Gauthild**, dau of **Algout Gautreksson**.

42. **Olaf Ingjaldsson** "Trekalia" (tree-hewer); King of Vermaland in Sweden; sacrificed his own people in time of famine; the last Yngling ruler of Uppsala; settled in West Sweden; d. c710; md **Solveig Halfdansdotter**, b. c684; dau of **Halfdan** "Guldand" (gold tooth) of Sweden.

41. **Halfdan Olafsson** "Huitbein" (white leg), King of the Uplanders of Sweden, King of Salver and Vestfold; conquered Roumarike; founded the pagan temple at Skiringssal, 8th century; md **Asa Eysteinsdotter**, dau of **Eystein** "Hardrade" (the severe), King of the Uplands, and his wife **Solveig Halfdansdotter**. *See note after Gen. 33.*

40. **Gudrod Halfdansson** "Mikillati" (the magnificent), King of Vestfold and Roumarike; ruled in Norway and in Denmark; probably the "Godfrey the Proud" (and so identified by Moncreiffe, I. 1982) of the Franks who opposed the Emperor Charlemagne; b. c738, Vestfold, Norway; killed 810; md (2) **Asa** (mother of Gen. 39); dau of **Harold** "Ridskeg" (red lips), King of Agder. He md (1) Alfhilda, dau of Alfheim, ruler of Vingulmark. *See note after Gen. 33.*

39. **Olaf II Gudrodsson**, b. c770, Norway; d. 840.

38. **Rognvald Olafsson** b. c790, Jutland, Norway; d. 850.

37. **Aseda Rognvaldsdotter**, b. c812, Maer, Norway; md **Eystein Ivarsson** (Eistain Glumra) (44-39), b. 800/810; son of **Ivar**, Jarl of Uplanders of Norway.

36. **Rognvald Eysteinsson** "the Wise" (same as 295-39), Jarl of More;

a Norwegian Viking; b. c830, Maer, Norway; d. c890, Maer, Norway; md **Rognhild** (Hildir) **Hrolfsdotter**, b. c848, Norway; dau of **Hrolf** "Nefja."

35. **Rollo** (Rollon, Ganger Rolf) (162-36, 166A-35) 1st Duke of Normandy, Count of Rouen; conquered Normandy; b. c870, Maer, Norway; d. 927–932; md (2) 891, **Poppa de Bayeux** ; b. c872, Bayeux, France; dau **Berenger** (166A-36),

34. **William I** "Longsword," Duke of Normandy; b. c900, Normandy; murdered 17 Dec 943, France; md (1) **Sprote de Bretagne** "Danish Wife" (mother of Gen. 33); a Breton captive; md (2) 940, Luitgarde de Vermandois, b. c915/920; dau of Herbert II, Count of Blois and Chartres.

33. **Richard I** (122-35,156-32), "the Fearless," Duke of Normandy; b. c932, Fecamp, France; d. 20 Nov 996, Fecamp; md after 962, (1) Emma (Agnes), b. c943; d. 968, dau of Hugh le Grand, Count of Paris; md c978, **Gunnora** (Gonnor) **de Crepon** (89-33), b. c936; d. 1027 or 1031, France; dau of **Herbastus de Crepon**, Forester of Arques.

*NOTE: Unlike many other sources I have used, Moncreiffe, I. 1982 (chart 35, p. 109) adds two generations between my Gen. 40 and Gen. 41: (41B): Halfdan "the Stingy," King of Vestfold, as father of Gudrod (Guthroth), whom he calls "Godfrey the Proud;" whose father was (41A) Eystein "the Fart," King of Roumarike. Though the work carries no bibliography, Moncreiffe was an outstanding authority, and pending proof otherwise, may well be considered correct. Moncreiffe is in agreement with Sturluson, S. 1991 (pp. 47-48) but Sturluson is not highly regarded by many authorities.*

Sources: Blass, R. 1939, II:251; Cokayne, G. 1959, I:22; IV:670 chart iii; V:694–495, 737; VII:520; IX:590; X:348–357, 364 and note e; ES II:1984:79 (Gen. 33-38); Jackman, D. 1990; Keats-Rohan, K. 1997b; Moncreiffe, I. 1982, 35:109; Moriarty, G.1985, 10–11; Sturluson, S. 1991, 47-48; Winkhaus, E. 1953 (1950); Wunder, G. 1967, 19–47.

### LINE 166A

39. **Udo**, Count of Orleans, d. 834; md **Engeltrude**, dau of **Leuthard**, Count of Paris and Fezensac.

38. **Gebhard**, Count in the Lahngau, d. after 879; md **N.N.**, sister of Ernst, Duke of the Bohemians, who d. 865.

37. **Berenger**, Count of Hessengau, liv 879; prob md **N.N.**, dau of **Liutold**, Count of Berthold-Baar.

36. **Berenger**, Margrave of Neustria, d. 896; md **N.N.**, perhaps Adelheid, dau of **Heinrich**, Duke of the Austrasians (Thuringia), who d. 28 Aug 886.

35. **Poppa de Bayeux**, b. c872, Bayeux, France; md **Rollo** (166-35), Duke of Normandy.

Source: ES III 1984:54.

## LINE 167

41. **Hugh** "le Méfiant" (29-40,224-37,263-40,364-39), Count of Tours; b. c765; d. Sept/Nov 836; md **Aba** (Bava), b. c779; liv 837.

40. **Hugh,** Count of Bourges, Auxerre and Nevers, d. after 853.

39. **Tertulle** (Tertullus), Seneschal of the Gatinais, md **Petronille.**

38. **Ingelgar,** Count of Anjou; d. c888; md **Adele de Gatinais;** dau of **Geoffrey,** Count in the Gatinais.

37. **Fulk I** "the Red (109-37)," Viscount of Angers; the first real Count of Anjou, 929; b. 888; d. 941/942; md before 5 July 905, **Roscilla,** dau of **Werner** (Garnier), Seigneur de Loches, Villentrois, and de la Haye, who md **Toscanda.**

36. **Fulk II** (127-34,298-34, 333-35, 347-35) "the Good," Count of Anjou; b. c920; d. 11 Nov 958; md **Gerberge of the Gatinais;** d. after 952; dau of **Geoffrey V of Orleans.**

35. **Geoffrey I** "Grisgonelle," Count of Anjou, Seneschal of France; b. c940; d. in battle 21 July 987; md (1) **Adele of Troyes** (157-34,258-35).

34. **Ermengarde of Anjou;** md 980, **Conan I** "le Tort" (24-36,67-34,334-35), Duke of Brittany, Count of Rennes.

33. **Judith of Brittany** (Rennes); b. 982, Bretagne, France; d. 16 June 1017; md c1000, **Richard II** (43-32,89-32), Duke of Normandy.

Sources: ES II 1984:79 (Gen. 33-34); III 1980:116 (Gen. 34-38); Isenburg, W. 1953; Moriarty, G.1985, 14 (Gen. 33); 4 (Gen. 34-39); 21,37 (Gen. 40-41); Moriarty, G. 1945b; Settipani, C. 1997b; Winkhaus, E. 1953.

## LINE 168

34. **Richard I** (89-33,166-33), Duke of Normandy, (md) **Gunnora** (Gonnor) **de Crepon** (89-33).

33. **Robert,** Count of Evreux; Archbishop of Rouen; b. c964, Normandy; d. 1037; md **Herleve** (Havlive), b. 968, Normandy.

32. **Richard,** Count of Evreux; b. 986, Rouen, France; d. 1067; md **Adelaide of Barcelona,** b. c1004, d. 1051; widow of Roger de Toeni; dau of Count **Ramon Borrel I** (54-34,291-34).

31. **Agnes d'Evreux;** b. c1030; md (3) **Simon I de Montfort** (90-29), Seigneur de Montfort-l'Amauri; Count of Montfort; d. 1087.

Sources: Blass, R. 1939, II:251, 252; Cokayne, G. 1959, III:167; V:689, 692+; VII:537–547; 708–717; ; ES, II 1984:79 (Gen. 31-34); ; Labarge, M. 1962, 51, 269, 273; Longnon, J. 1978, 113 Marot, P. 1984, 574; Moriarty, G.1985, 11 (Gen. 31-34); Motey, V de 1920; Onslow, Earl of 1945; Prawler, J. 1970, 290.

## LINE 169

47. **Charibert,** nobleman in Neustria, d. after 636; md **Wulfgurd of Paris,** his cousin.

46. **Chrodobertus** (Rutpert) **I,** nobleman in Neustria, 630; a teacher of

King Dagobert I.

45. **Lambert I** (Lantbertus), a nobleman in Neustria; liv 650.

44. **Chrodobertus** (Rutpert) **II** (171-43); nobleman in Istria, major-domo of King Chlodwig II, Count Palatine, Chancelor of King Chlothar III of Neustria; liv Oct 678; md **Doda**, d. after 678.

43. **Lambert** (Lantbertus) **II**, Comes in Neustria and Austrasia, d. by 741; md **Chrotlind** (123-45).

42. **Rutpert** (Robert) **I** (69-42), Duke in the Haspengau, Count in the Upper Rhine and Wormsgau, Royal Missus in Italy; b. 689; d. by 764; md 730, **Williswint** (102-44); occ 768; heiress of lands in the Wormsgau; founded, 12 July 764, with her eldest son, Count Cancor, the Imperial Monastery at Lorsch, near Worms; Wiliswint was dau of Count **Adelheim**, a widower in 764.

41. **Thuringbert**, d.before 767.

40. **Rutpert II**, Count in the Upper Rhine and the Wormsgau; Lord of Dienheim; d. 12 July 807; md **Theodedrata** (Tiedrada) (mother of Gen. 39); d. after 789; also md Isengarde, liv 789.

39. **Rutpert III**; Count in the Wormsgau and the Upper Rhine; d. after 834; md 808, **Waldrada** (Wiltrud) **of Orleans,** dau of **Hadrian** (336-42), Count of Orleans and wife **Waldrat. Waldrat** was dau of **Lambert** (330-42), Count of Hornbach.

38. **Rutpert IV** (326-37,348-41), (called "Robert the Strong"), Count of Paris, Tours and Wormsgau, Marquis of Anjou, Blois, Auxerre, and Nevers, Lay Abbot of Tours, 836–866; slain 25 July 866, at Brissarthe; md (2) c864, **Adelaide** (Aelis) **of Alsace and Tours** (224-37) (mother of Gen. 37 below).

37. **Robert I**, Count of Paris and Poitiers, Marquis in Neustria and Orleans, anti-king of France, 922; b. 866 (posthumously), France; d. in battle 15 June 923, Soissons, France; md (1) N.N., sister of Adelheim, Count of Laon; md (2) **Aelis** (mother of Gen. 36); widow of **Conrad I** (300-40), Count in the Argenau; md (3) 890, **Beatrice de Vermandois** (134-36).

36. **Hildebrande of Neustria**, b. 887; d. 943; md **Herbert II** (188-38,231-36,235-36,239-35), Count of Vermandois and Troyes (father of Gen. 35).

35. **Adelaide** (Adela) **de Vermandois**, b.c915; d. 958/960, Bruges; md 934, **Arnold I** "the Old" (141-36,311-36), Count of Flanders and Artois.

Sources: Blass, R. 1939, II:270–272; Cokayne, G. 1959 (Gen. 38-43) ES, II 1984:10 (Gen. 35-47); Irving, E. 1973; Moriarty, G.1985 6 (Gen. 35-37); 211 (Gen. 38-41); Moriarty, G. 1945b; Rubincam, M. 1963 (Gen. 35-47).

## LINE 170

35. **Ragnvald** (Reinold) (108-38), one of the Norse invaders of Burgundy who remained there; occ 924/925. *NOTE: ES III 1989: 675A, does not accept this generation.*

34. **Ragnvald,** (161-34), Count of Roucy, Seigneur de Roucy, Viscount and Count of Rheims; b. c926; d. 10 May 967; bur Abbey of St. Remi, Rheims, Marne; md 944/47, **Alberade of Lorraine** (92-34).

33. **Giselbert** (6-34,145-32), Count of Roucy and Vicomte of Rheims; b. c956; d. 991/1000; bur at Abbey of St. Remi, Rheims, Marne, France; md **N.N. de Poitiers,** possibly dau **Aubri,** Count of Macon.

32. **Ebles I,** Count of Roucy and Rheims; Archbishop of Rheims; b. c988; d. 11 May 1033; md and divorced **Beatrice of Hainault** (163-32); she md (2) c1035, Manassas Calva Asini "the Bold," Vicomte de Rheims.

31. **Alice** (Isabelle, Adelaide) **de Roucy** (344-29), heiress of Roucy, Aisne, France; 1063; b. c1014; d. 1063; md 1031 **Hildouin III** (56-33,66-34, 95-31,266-31), 4th Count of Montdidier and Roucy; b. c1010; d. c1063.

Sources: Blass, R. 1939, II:239, 246, 251; Gregory of Tours, 1974; Irving, E. 1973, James, E. 1988; Lasco, P. 1971; Moranville, H. 1925; Moriarty, G. 1985, 6, 9, 49–50 (Gen. 31-33); 38–40 (Gen. 34-35); Newman, W. 1971; Saillot, J. 1980, 602–606 (Gen. 31-33).

## LINE 171

53. **Clovis** "the Riparian," Frankish King of Cologne; living in 420; md **N.N.,** a Merovingian, fl c420.

52. **Childebert,** King of Cologne, liv c450.

51. **Siegbert I** "the Lame," King of Cologne; murdered in 509 by his own son, Cloderic, at the instigation of Clovis I, King of Salic Franks, 481–511; md **Theodelinde of Burgundy**.

50. **Cloderic** "the Parricide," King of Cologne; murdered 509 by agents of his kinsman, Clovis I; md **N.N.,** a dau of **Agilolfinges.**

49. **Munderic,** Lord of Vitry-en-Parthois; revolted against Thierry I who killed him; b. c500; d. 532; md **Artemia** (171A-49).

48. **Gondolfus,** Bishop of Tongres, occ 599; perhaps father of Bodegeisel II. Some authors say Bodegeisel I, brother of Gondolfus, is the father. There is no proof, one way or the other, but the weight of evidence points to Gondolfus.

47. **Bodegeisel II** "Dux," d. 588, Carthage, Africa; md **Oda,** a Suevian. He appears to have been Governor of Aquitaine and was murdered at Carthage returning from an embassy at Constantinople in 588.

46. **St. Arnulf** (Arnoul) (258-47), Bishop of Metz, c613-629; Mayor of the Palace of Austrasia and tutor of Dagobert; b. 582, Austrasia; d. 16 Aug 641; md c596, **Dode** of Old Saxony; b. c586, Old Saxony; she became a nun at Treves, 612. She was dau of **Arnaold,** Bp. of Metz; gdau of **Ansbertus** (173-44,214-44,236-48), a Gallo-Roman senator and (probably) **Blithilda.**

45. **Ansgise** (Ansegisel), b. 602, Austrasia; murdered 685; md before 639, **St. Begga** (Begue) (260-45), of Landen, Liege, Belgium; d. c698.

44. **Pippin II of Heristal** (Liege, Belgium); Mayor of the Palace of

Austrasia; b. c635; d. 16 Dec 714, Jupile on the Meuse; md before 673, Plactruda, dau of Hubert; (md) **Aupais** (Alpaida) (mother of Gen. 43); b. c654, a concubine.

    43. **Charles (Karl) Martel** (114-42,269-44),"the Hammer," b. c688, of Heristol, Leige, Belgium; Mayor of the Palace of Austrasia, King of the Franks, 724; victor at the Battle of Poitiers, 732; d. 22 Oct 741, Quierzy, Aisne, France; md (1) **Chrotrude** (114-42) (mother of Gen. 42); Duchess of Austrasia; d. 724; dau St. **Lievin** (Leutwinus), Bishop of Treves, 685–704; d. 724; who md **N.N.**, a dau of **Chrodobertus** (169-46) and **Doda**; Charles Martel md (2) Swanhilde, a Bavarian.

    42. **Pippin III**"the Short," Mayor of the Palace of Austrasia, King of the Franks; b. 715. Austrasia; d. 24 Sept 768, St. Denis, France; md c740, **Bertha** "Broadfoot" (214-42,231-41,264-41), of Laon, Aisne, France; d. 12 July 783.

    41. **Charlemagne** (Charles the Great), King of France, 767–814; Emperor of the West, 25 Dec 800–814; b. 2 Apr 747, Aachen, Rhineland, Germany; d. 28 Jan 814, Aachen; md 771, Aachen, **Hildegarde** (33A-40,262-41), Countess of Vinzgau.

    40. **Louis I** (163-39,172-42,328-39,352-41)"the Fair," Emperor of the West, 814–840; King of France; b. Aug 778, d. 20 June 840; md 819, **Judith of Altdorf** (mother of Gen. 39), b. c800, Bavaria; d. 19 Apr 843, Tours, Indre-et-Loire, France; dau of **Welf** (300-41), Count in the Entgau, of Bavaria, and of Swabia, and wife, **Egilwich**, a Saxon. She became Abbess of Challes, near Paris; d. after 833. Louis I also md **Ermengarde of Hesbaye** (352-41), d. Oct 818.

    39. **Charles II "the Bald"** (133-38, 250-39), King of West Franks, Emperor of the West, 25 Dec 875; King of Burgundy, 869; King of Italy, 875; b. 13 June 823, Frankfurt-on-Main, Germany; d. 6 Oct 877, Brides-les-Bains, near Mt. Cenis in the Alps; bur St. Denis; md 13 Dec 842, **Ermentrude of Orleans** (250-39); b. 27 Sept 830; d. 6 Oct 869, St. Denis; dau of **Eudes** (Odo) (336-41), and **Engeltrude**, dau of **Leutaud**, Count of Paris, whose parents were **Begue** (269-41,350-41) and **Aupais**, dau of **Charlemagne** (171-41); Charles II also md **Richardis of Metz**, dau of **Budwine** (206-39), Count of Metz, and **Richilde of Arles** (112-40).

    38. **Louis II** (353-39) "the Stammerer," King of West Franks, King of France, 877–879, Emperor of the West, 878–879; b. 1 Sept 846; d. 10 Apr 879, Compiegne; md 868/870, **Adelaide of Paris** (350-38), b. 855/860; d. after 10 Nov 901.

    37. **Charles III "the Simple,"** King of West Franks, 893; b. 17 Sept 879; d. 7 Oct 929, Peronne, Somme, France; bur St. Fursy; md (3) 918, **Edgiva** (261-37) (mother of Gen. 36), Princess of England; md (1) Apr 907, Frederuna, d. 10 Feb 917.

    36. **Louis IV** (120-36, 230-36) "d'Outremer," of Laon, Aisne, France; King of France, 936–954; b. 10 Sept 920; d. 10 Sept 954, Rheims, Marne, France; bur St. Remy; md 940, **Gerberge of Saxony** (92-35), widow of

Giselbert, Duke of Lorraine.

35. **Matilda of France**, Princess of France; b. end of 943; d. 26/27 Jan 981/92; bur Vienne; md **Conrad I** (175-34) "the Peaceful," King of Burgundy.

Sources: Cokayne, G. 1959, X:805; Gregory of Tours, 1974; James, E. 1988; Lasco, P. 1971; Martindale, J. 1967; Martindale, J. 1980; McKitterick, R. 1983; Moriarty, G. 1985, 35 (Gen. 35–37); 16, 21 (Gen. 37–40); 5 (Gen. 40–53); Moriarty, G. 1944 (Gen. 43–53); Moriarty, G. 1947 (Gen. 43–53); Nelson, J. 1992; Rignall, J. 1972 (Gen. 39–53); Saillot, J. 1980, 192; Settipani, C. 1993; Settipani, C. 1996b; Van Dam, R. 1985.

## LINE 171A

54. **Decimus Rusticus**, proprietor in Gaul, c407; prefect of the Gauls, c409-413; md **Artemia**.

53. **N.N.**, curate, 423-448.

52. **Aquilinus**, noble of Lyons, d. after 470.

51. **Rusticus**, Bp of Lyons, c 494-501; d. 25 Apr 501; perhaps md **N.N.**, dau of **Ruricus**, Bp of Limoges, c 485-507; by his wife **Hiberia**, dau of **Omnatius**, senator from the Auvergne.

50. **Artemia**(fem.) md **Florentinus**, Bp of Geneva, 513; d. after 513.

49. **Artemia** (fem.) md **Munderic** (171-49).

Source: Settipani, C. 1989: 96-97, 111-112, 129,172.

## LINE 172

42. **Louis I** (163-39,170-40), King of France, md **Ermengarde of Hesbaye** (352-41).

41. **Louis II** "the German," King of East Franks; b. 806;d. 28 Aug 876; md **Emma of Bavaria**, d. 31 Jan 876; dau of **Welf I**, Count in Bavaria, by wife **Heilwig**.

40. **Carloman**, King of Bavaria, liv c820-880; md **Litwinde**.

39. **Arnulf**, King of Germany, Emperor, 896; md **Oda of Bavaria.**

38. **Hedwige**, Princess of Germany; d. 906; md **Otto** "the Illustrious" (92-37), Duke of Saxony.

*NOTE: There are several divergant views regarding the parentage of Hedwige (Gen. 38). The line shown here was supplied by Robert Stimmel for Weis' Ancestral Roots of Certain American Colonists, 7th edition (1992), line 141.*

Stimmel reviewed the work of Moriarty, Brandenburg, Isenburg, Saillot and others. The source cited is *Charlemagne and His World*, by Heer, p. 226. *Europaische Stammtafeln* (Vol. 1, table 3, 1980) does not give Hedwig's parentage, nor does Moriarty's *Plantagenet Ancestry*.

Sources: Brandenberg, E. 1935; Buhler, H. 1984; ES I 1980:3, (Gen. 38); ES I.1 1997; ES III 1989:736; Jackman, D. 1997; Moriarty, 25 (1985) (Gen. 38); Settipani, C. 1993:286; Weis, F. 1992, Line 141 (38-42)

44. **Ansguise,** (171-45) md **St. Begga** (260-45).

43. **Pepin of Heristol,** Mayor of the Palace in Austrasia, d. 16 Dec 714 (md) **Aupais** (a concubine).

42. **Childebrand I,** Lord of Perracy and of Bougy, Count of Autun; d. 751; md **Rolande,** dau of **Bertha,** a Merovingian.

41. **Nivelon** (Nibelung) **I** of Perracy "the Historian," Lord of Perracy, Montisan and Hesburg; d. 9 Oct 768.

40. **Childebrand II,** Lord of Perrecy; d. 826/836; md **Dunne of Autun.**

39. **Thierry I** (258-40),"the Treasurer," Count of the Autunois and Chaumois; Chamberlain of Charles "the Bald;" occ 817–879; d. by 880.

38. **Richard,** occ 883–885.

37. **Garnier** (Warinus), Viscount of Sens and Troyes; b. c868; slain in battle with the Normans, 6 Dec 925; md **Teutberga** (174-37).

36. **Hugh** (317-34), Count of Vienne, Count Palatine of Burgundy; b. c900; d. c948; md before Apr 927, **Willa,** dau of **Richard** (100-35,173-36,206-38), Duke of Burgundy, and **Adelaide of Burgundy** (300-38).

35. **Humbert** (Hubert, Umberto), b. c926/930; d. c976; md N.N., b. c930/945; occ May 976; d. before Oct 993; perhaps dau of **Amadeo of Spoleto.**

34. **Humbert** (Umberto) **I** "Bianca Mano," Count of Aosta, 1025 and of Maurienne, 1027; acquired Chablis, 1035; b. c975; d. 1048/1050; md before 1020, **Auxilia** (273-34).

33. **Odo** (Otto) **I,** Count of Maurienne, Margrave of Susa; b. c1020; d. 19 Jan 1057/1058; md c1036, **Adelaide von Susa** (63-34; 93-32,381-33), heiress of Susa and Turin.

Sources: Blass, R. 1939, II:248, 249, 250; Chaume, M. 1977, 374n, 416n, 447n2, 542, 544, 545, 551–552; Chaume.R, 228–258; Isenburg, W. 1953; Moriarty, G. 1985, 237 (Gen. 33–36); 257 (Gen. 36–44); 255.

42. **Boso I,** Count in Italy, occ 750.

41. **Boso II,** Count in Italy, occ 814–826.

40. **Boso III** (112-41), Count of Turin, an East Frank, d. c855.

39. **Herbert,** Lay Abbot of St. Maurice, Marquis of Transjuranian Burgundy, after 855; slain at Orbe, 864.

38. **Theobald** (Thibaud) (186-39), Count of Arles and Vienne; d. by 895; md c879, **Bertha** (263-38), Princess of Lorraine.

37. **Teutberga** (173-37), d. before 30 Sept 948; md **Garnier** (173-37), Viscount of Sens, 895; and Count of Troyes, 895–896; died 6 Dec 925.

Sources: ES III 1980:662A (Gen. 37–38); II 1984:186 (Gen. 37–40); Irving, E. 1973, Manteyer, M, 1904: 38–42; Moriarty, G. 1985, 19 (Gen. 37–42).

37. **Conrad II** (300-39), Count of Auxerre, 858; Margrave of Transjuranian Burgundy, Lay Abbot of St. Moritz; d. before 876; md **Waldrada** (Vaudrie) (mother of Gen. 36); prob an Alsacian Etichonid. He md, also, Ermentrude, dau of Luitfried.

36. **Rudolph I**, Count, Marquis, and King, 888; of Upper Burgundy; d. 25 Oct 912; md 888, **Willa of Vienne** (343-38).

35. **Rudolph II** (323-35), King of Burgundy and Italy, 920–932; d. 11 July 937; md 922, **Bertha of Swabia** (345-37).

34. **Conrad I** (171-35),"the Peaceful," King of both Burgundies, 936–993; b. c925; d. 19 Oct 993, Regensburg; bur Vienne; md (2) after 964, **Matilda of France** (171-35, 230-35), Princess of France.

33. **Mathilda of Burgundy** md prob **Udalrich I**, 'the Rich," Count of Schanis, d. 10 Aug 1046/50.

32. **Bertha of Burgundy**, md **Gerhard I**, of Egisheim, d. 1038; son of **Hugh VI** (33-33), Count of Nordgau and Egisheim, by his wife **Heilwig of Dagsburg** (26-31,33-33,93-31,149-32).

31. **Gerold I**, Count of Geneva, occ 1034; d. 1061/1080; md (his 2nd, her 2nd) **Tietburga of Savoy** (mother of Gen. 30); widow of **Louis I** (288-32), Seigneur and Lord of Faucigny, She was dau of **Amadeo I**, Count of Savoy, Maurienne and Aosta, who md **Auxilia** (273-34); and Adelaide of Albon. Gerold I also md (1) Gisela. **Amadeo I** was son of **Humbert I** (173-34).

30. **Aimon I**, Count of Geneva, founder of Chamonix Priory; advocate of St. Victor; b. c1050; d. 1125/1128; md **Ida of Faucigny**, prob **N.N.**, dau of **Louis I**, (288-32), Seigneur de Faucigny, d. c1060, wife unknown.

29. **Amadeo (Amadeus) I**, Count of Geneva; b. c1100; d. 26 June 1178; md (1) before 1130, **Matilda of Cuiseaux**; d. before 2 July 1137; dau of **Hugh**, Seigneur de Cuiseaux.

28. **William I**, Count of Geneva; b. 1130; d. 25/27 July 1195; md (2) c1165, **Beatrice of Faucigny** (288-28). *NOTE: Weis, F. 1992 does not carry the female line. See note after 288–28 for Moriarty's view.*

27. **Margaret of Geneva**; (also called Beatrix and Nicole); b. c1180; d. 13 Apr 1236, Pierre Chatel, Hautecombe; md **Thomas I** (93-27), Count of Savoy.

Sources: Chaume, M. 1977, I:170, 217n, 383, 552, 553; Cokayne, G. 1959, IX:805; Fausnor, H. 1981; Hayward, F. 1941; Historich, 1934; Isenburg, W. 1932; Isenburg, W. 1953, pt. ii, table 23; Jackman, D. 1990; Jori, I 1942; Moriarty, G. 1985, 107 (Gen. 27–33); 33 (Gen. 33–37); Rosch, S. 1977.

33. **Richard II** (89-32), Duke of Normandy md **Judith of Rennes** (167-33).

32. **Judith of Normandy**, b. c1003, Normandy; d. after 1 July 1037; md before 1 Sept 1016, **Renaud** (Raymond) **I** (94-32), Count of Burgundy.

Sources: Magnurson, IV (1905); Mateos, R. 1984; Moriarty, G. 1985, Motey, V de 1920; Onslow, Earl of 1945; Vitalis, O. 1857 (Provost ed.) II 403–404; Salazar, J. de 1984; Winkhaus, E. 1953.

## LINE 177

29. **Philippa** (Mathilde) (160-29), regent of Toulouse, md **William VII** (88-31,160-29), Count of Poitou (IX as Duke of Aquitaine).
28. **Matilda** (Agnes) **of Aquitaine**, b. c1100; md (his 2nd) **Ramiro II** (95-30), King of Aragon.

Sources Bard, R. 1982; ES II 1984:58 (Gen. 28–29); Moriarty, G. 1985, 36 (28–29); Salazar, J. de 1984.

## LINE 178

33. **Fulbert de Beine**, a Frenchman who went to Normandy and built the Château de l'Aigle.
32. **Engenulf**, Seigneur de l'Aigle, slain at Hastings, 14 Oct 1066; may have been a Companion of William the Conqueror; md **Richvaride**.
31. **Richer**, Seigneur de l'Aigle; b. c1045; slain 18 Nov 1085 at St. Suzanne in Maine, France; md **Judith d'Avranches**, dau of **Richard d'Avranches**, "le Goz" (295-33).
30. **Gilbert**, Seigneur de l'Aigle in Normandy; b. c1061; d. 1118; in the *Domesday Book* as a tenant in England; md 1091/1092, **Julienne of Perche**, b. c1069; liv 1109; dau of **Geoffrey II** (249-30), Count of Perche, and **Beatrice de Montdidier** (266-30).
29. **Margaret de l'Aigle**, b. c1104; d. 25 May 1141; md (his 1st), **Garcia Ramirez V** (151-29), King of Navarre.

Sources: Bard, R. 1982; Bayne, W. 1969 (Gen. 29–30); Brandenburg, E. 1935; Isenburg, W. 1953; Moriarty, G. 1985, 110–111 (Gen. 29–33); Motey, V de 1920; Winkhaus, E. 1953.

## LINE 179

37. **Lain Calvo of Castile** (same as 181-38).
36. **Fernan Lainez**.
35. **Lain Fernandez**.
34. **Nuno Lainez** md **Eilone Fernandez** (181-34).
33. **Lain Nunez**, a lord of Castile at the court of Fernando I; occ 1045–1063.
32. **Diego Lainez**, Senor de Bivar in Castile; witnessed a charter of Cardena, 29 Oct 1047; fought against the Navarrese; d. c1058; md **N.N.**, (perhaps Teresa) **Rodrigues**, dau of **Roderigo Alvarez**, Count in the Asturias; occ 1038–1066; and **Theresa Lainez**. Roderigo Alvarez' father was **Alvaro**, a nobleman of Castile.

31. **Rodrigo Diaz de Castro** (150-30), ("el Cid"); Senor de Bivar; Count of Valencia; "Muy Ciel el Compeador;" Conquered and held Valencia; b. c1043; d. July 1099; md 14 July 1074, Dona **Jimena** (Ximena) **Diaz** (180-30).

    30. **Christina** (Elvira) **Diaz**, b. 1077; md **Ramiro II** (151-30), Count of Moncon.

    Sources: Arteta, A. 1952; Moriarty, G. 1985, 110 (Gen. 30–37); Moriarty, G. 1963 (Gen. 30–37); Pidal, R. 1969, II:718–719; Pidal, R. 1971.

## LINE 180

    35. **Jimeno Jimenez,** came from Navarre to the Asturias; md the Condesa **Aragonta**.

    34. **Piniola Jimeno,** Count in the Asturias; occ 949; md **Eldonza Munez.**

    33. **Gondemaro of the Asturias,** d. 1011.

    32. **Fernando Gundemarez** md **Jimina** (Ximena) **de Leon,** dau of **Alfonso V** (276-33), King of Castile and Leon, and **Urraca Garces of Navarre,** dau of **Garcia IV Sanchez** (223-37), King of Navarre, and **Jimena Fernandez,** dau of **Fernando Vermudez** (267-38).

    31. **Christina Fernandez** md **Diego,** Count of Orviedo.

    30. Dona **Jimena** (Ximena) **Diaz,** of the Asturias, b. c1054; d. 1115; md **Rodrigo Diaz de Castro** "el Cid" (151-30,179-31), Senor de Bivar.

    Sources: Bard, R. 1982; Evans, C. 1932; Moriarty, G. 1985 110, (Gen. 32–35); Pidal, R. 1969, II:718–719; Pidal, R. 1971.

## LINE 181

    38. **Lain Calvo of Castile** (Same as 179-37).

    37. **Bermudo Lainez.**

    36. **Rodrigo Bermudez.**

    35. **Fernan Ruiz.**

    34. **Eilone Fernandez** md **Nuno Lainez** (Lain Nunez) (179-34).

    Sources: Moriarty, G. 1985, 110 (Gen. 34–38); Pidal, R. 1969, II:718–719.

## LINE 182

    29. **Amadeus** (Amadeo) **III** (93-29), Count of Savoy and Marquis of Maurienne; Crusader; b. c1088/1092; d. 30 Mar 1148, in Nicosia, Cyprus, on the 2nd Crusade; md 1133/34, **Mathilda** (Maud) **d'Albon** (192-29).

    28. **Matilda** (Maud) **of Savoy,** Queen of Portugal, d. 4 Dec 1157, Coimba; md **Alfonso I Henriques** (85-28), first King of Portugal.

    Sources: Blass, R. 1939, II:248; Brandenburg, E. 1935; Clairvaux, B. 1963; Constable, G. 1953; ES II 1984:38 (Gen. 28–29); Moriarty, G. 1985, 104 (Gen. 28–29); Winkhaus, E. 1953.

## LINE 183

32. **Roger de Montgomery** (335-33), Earl of Chichester and Montgomery, etc. md **Mabel Talvas** (de Alencon) (360-32).

31. **Robert II de Belleme** (Montgomery) "Talvas," Earl of Shrewsbury and Arundel, Seigneur de Belleme and Alencon, Count of Ponthieu, Alencon and Montreuil; exiled from England, 1102, by Henry I and lost his English lands; d. 8 May 1131, a prisoner at Wareham Castle, Dorsetshire; md before 9 Sept 1087, **Agnes de Ponthieu** (244-31), heiress of Ponthieu and Montreuil.

Sources: Blass, R. 1939, II:238; Cokayne, G. 1959, I:351; XI: 689–697; Douglas, R. 1946; Moriarty, G. 1985, 44–45 (Gen. 31–32); Peraud, E. 1900; Toutier, C. de 1960: 102–134.

## LINE 184

35. **Arnulf II** (141-34), Count of Flanders (141-34) md **Susanna** (Rosella) (332-35).

34. **Eudes** (385-35), Count of Cambrai, md **Adele of Bois Ferrand**, dau of **Thibaud**, Seigneur de Bois Ferrand.

33. **Roger**, Count of St. Pol; received St. Pol as vassal of Count Baldwin of Flanders; d. 13 June 1067; md **Hadwide** (Hedwig), heiress of "Houchin;" parentage unknown.

32. **Manasses**, liv 1031/1056; or his brother, **Robert**, liv 1031/1056, one of which was father of Gen. 31.

*NOTE: The work of the French genealogists, Pierre Feuchere (1953, 1957) and Didier-Georges Dooghe (1985) make Hugh I, Count of St. Pol, who md Clementina, formerly thought to be the father of Gen. 31, Hugh II, a possible brother instead; and make either Manasses or Robert (as shown above) the father of Gen. 31. This makes the work of Vanderkindere, L. 1902 (1:331–332) outdated for the Ternois and St. Pol lineage, and corrects Moriarty, G. 1985, 115.*

31. **Hugh II**, Count of St. Pol; a Crusader; went on the 1st Crusade with Robert of Normandy and distinguished himself at the seige of Antioch and Jerusalem; d. c1118/19; md **Helisende**, sister of **Gui**, Count of Ponthieu (244-32).

30. **Hugh III** "Candavene," Count of St. Pol; Count of Hesdin, 1136; d. 1141; md (1) **Beatrice** (mother of Gen. 29); md (2) 1128, Marguerite de Clermont-en-Beauvaisis. Hugh III destroyed the Abbey of St. Requier and was excommunicated. He was an opponent of King Louis VI.

29. **Anselme Candavene**, Count of St. Pol; d.1174; md **Eustachie de Champagne** (242-29).

Sources:Agiles, R. 1968; Blass, R. 1939,II:238; Brandenburg, E. 1935; Dooghe, D. 1985; ES, III 1989:622 (Gen. 29–33); Foucher, R,1971; Moriarty, G. 1985, 115 (Gen. 29–33); 277 (Gen. 33–35); Krey, H. n.d.; Peraud, E. 1900; Winkhaus, E. 1953.

41. **Louis I** (163-39,171-40,352-41), King of France, md **Judith of Bavaria** (171-40), dau of **Welf** (300-41), Count in Bavaria.

40. **Gisela**, Princess of France and the West; b. 818/822; d. 1 July 874; md 836, **Eberhard** (269-39,345-38,404-39), Margrave of Friuli; d. 16 Dec 862; son of **Hunroch**; grandson of **Berenger**, an East Frank, whose wife was **Engeltrude**, prob dau of **Begue** (171-39,269-41), Count of Paris.

39. **Hawise of Friuli**, d. 936; md **Hucbald** (father of Gen. 38), Count of Ostrevant, d. after 895; md (2) Roger I, Count of Laon, d. 926.

38. **Raoul I** "de Cambrai," Count of Valois d'Amiens and Vexin; d. in battle, 944; md **Liegard**, Countess of Mantes and Meulan, 985–987; d. 12 Nov 990/991.

*NOTE: Weis, F. 1992, line 250, shows a problem between Hawise of Friuli (my Gen. 39) and Raoul de Gouy (my Gen. 37), and ES III 1989:657 confirms this by adding a generation (my Gen. 38) between the two. Formerly, Gen. 39 was thought to be the father of Gen. 37. Hopefully, this settles the matter.*

37. **Raoul** (Ralph) **de Gouy**, Count of Ostrevant, Amiens, Valois and Vexin, 923; d. 926; md **Eldegarde** (or perhaps, N.N.) of Valois; d. after 965, a dau or sister of **Ermenfroi**, Count of Amiens, 901–919.

36. **Gautier I**, Count of Valois and Vexin, 952; advocate of St. Denis; b. c925; d. 992/998; md (2) **Adele** (109-36).

35. **Gautier II** "the White" (same as 268-35), Count of Vexin, Valois and Amiens; b. c944; d. c1027; md **Adele de Senlis** (268-35).

34. **N.N. de Vexin**, of Mellant, Normandy; md **Hugh I** (234-34), Count of Meulan.

33. **Galeran III**, of Mellant, Normandy, Count of Meulan; b. c990; d. 8 Dec 1069; md **Oda de Conteville**, b. c994; dau of **Jean de Conteville** (160-33).

32. **Adelaide of Meulan** (de Mellant); of Pont Audemer, France; b. c1014; d. 1081; md **Roger de Beaumont** (103-32).

Sources: ES, III 1989:700 (Gen. 32–33); III 1989:657 (Gen. 34–39 but see notes throughout); II 1984:188a (Gen. 40–41); Crispin, M. 1969, 186–187; Moriarty, G. 1985, 135 (Gen. 34–37); 228–229 (Gen. 36–39); 16, 18 (Gen. 39–41); Moriarty, G. 1945; Sanders, I. 1960, 20+, 85+.

39. **Theobald** (Thibaud) (174-38), Count of Arles and Vienne; d. before 895; md (his 1st, her 1st), **Bertha** (263-38), Princess of Lorraine.

38. **Hugh of Provence**, Count of Provence and Vienne, King of Italy; b. c880; d. 10 Apr 947; md **Wandelmodis** (perhaps mother of Gen. 37). He md four times and had issue by various mistresses.

37. **Humbert**, Margrave of Tuscany; d. 967/970, Toledo; md c945, **Willa of Camerino** (366-37), d. after 978.

36. **Berta**, Princess of Lorraine, md **Ardoino** (198-36), Marquis of Ivrea, King of Italy, 1002.

Sources: Blass, R. 1939; Brandemburg, E. 1935; Chaume, M. 1977; ES, II 1984:186 (Gen. 37–39); Moriarty, G. 1985, 104 (Gen. 36–39); Rosch, S. 1977 (Gen. 37–39).

## LINE 187

32. **William II** (94-31), Count of Burgundy, md **Stephanie of Longwy**, dau of **Adalbert III** (105-32), Count of Longwy, and **Clemence de Foix**.
   31. **Stephen**, Count of Vienne, Mâcon and Burgundy, 1096; Crusader; b. c1055; d. 27 May 1102, Rama, in Palestine, on the 1st Crusade; md **Beatrice**, d. after 1112; dau of **Gerhard III**, Duke of Upper Lorraine.
   30. **William IV**, Count of Auxerre, Mâcon and Vienne; Crusader; on 2nd Crusade, 1147; b. c1090/1095; d. 27 Sept 1155; md (2) before 1140, **Poncette** (190-30), Dame de Treves.
   29. **Gerard**, Count of Mâcon and Vienne; b. c1142; d. before 15 Sept 1184; md **Maurette** (189-29), heiress of Salins.
   28. **Beatrice of Mâcon**, b. c1160; d. 8 Apr 1230; md **Humbert III** (93-28), Count of Savoy, Marquis of Italy.

Sources: Agiles, R. 1968; Blass, R. 1939, II:251; Brandenburg, E. 1935, ES, II 1984:190 (Gen. 28–29); III 1980:122 (Gen. 28–29); Foucher, 1971; Krey, A. n.d.; Moriarty, G. 1985, 105 (Gen. 29–31); 62 (Gen. 31–32); Winkhaus, E. 1953.

## LINE 188

38. **Herbert II** (169-36,231-36,235-36,239-35), Count of Vermandois; md **Hildebrante of Neustria** (169-36).
   37. **Albert I** (239-34), Count of Vermandois; b. c920; d. 8 Sept 987/ 988; md **Gerberge of Hainault and Lorraine** (207-36).
   36. **Gui de Vermandois**, Count of Soissons; d. after 13 June 989, md **Adelaide** (mother of Gen. 35), heiress of Soissons; d. before 1042; Adelaide md (2) Nocher I, Count of Bar-sur-Aube. Adelaide was the dau of **Giselbert**, Count of Soissons.
   35. **Aelis** (Adelaide), Countess of Soissons, md **Nocher II** (108-35), Count of Bar-sur-Aube; d. after 1019.
   34. **Renaud**, Count of Soissons, Viscount of Troyes; d. 1057.
   33. **Aelis**, Countess and heiress of Troyes and Soissons; d. 18 Sept 1066; md 1058, **William d'Eu** (222-33), Count of Eu, Exemes, Soissons and Troyes.
   32. **Lithuaise**, heiress of the Vicomtes de Troyes, Dame de Bray; md **Milon I** (57-32), Seigneur de Montlheri, etc.

Sources: Blass, R. 1939, II:239; Brandenburg, E. 1935; ES, VII 1979:15 (Gen. 33–34); Moriarty, G. 1985, 267 (Gen. 32–36); 134 (Gen. 36–37); 6 (Gen. 37–38); Newman, W. 1971 (Paris ed.), I; Settipani, C. 1997b.

36. **Aubri** (101-35), Viscount of Narbonne, md **Attelane de Macon**, dau of **Ranulf**, Viscount of Mâcon, 893–915.

35. **Humbert I** (383-32), Sire de Salins; inherited a part of the vicounty of Narbonne; d. 958; md **Windelmode**, dau of **Gui**, Count of Escuens.

34. **Humbert II** (191-34), Count of Salins; during his minority, his uncle Letaud, Count of Mâcon, was his guardian; b. c950; d. before 1028; bur at St. Paul's in Berancon; md c995, **Erembourg** (191-34).

33. **Gautier I**, Sire de Salins; occ 1000–1044; benefactor of St. Paul's Abbey at Berancon, 1044; md (2) **Arembourge**.

32. **Gautier II**, Sire de Salins; d. after 1100; md **Beatrix**.

31. **Humbert III** "le Renforce," Sire de Salins; Crusader; young in 1084; d. 1149, Palestine.

30. **Gautier III**, Sire de Salins; d. 15 Aug 1175, at St. Dyan; bur at Berancon in St. Stephen's.

29. **Maurette**, heiress of Salins; b. c1140; d. 15 Sept 1184; md c1160, **Gerard** (187-29), Count of Mâcon and Vienne.

Sources: Blass, R. 1939, II:249; Brandenburg, E. 1935; Chaume, M. 1947a, Chaume, M. 1977, I:532–533; Moriarty, G. 1985, 105–106 (Gen. 29–35); 1 (Gen. 35–36); Winkhaus, E. 1953.

## LINE 190

33. **Hugh**, Seigneur de Treves, liv 1073.

32. **Stephen**, Seigneur de Treves, liv 1098.

31. **Thibaud**, Seigneur de Treves, md Alice.

30. **Poncette**, Dame de Treves, heiress of Treves; b. c1090; widow in 1156; md before 1140, **William IV** (187-30), Count of Auxerre, Mâcon and Vienne.

Sources: Blass, R. 1939, II:240; Brandenburg, E. 1935; Guillaume, J. 1757, 92–96; Moriarty, G. 1985, 105 (Gen. 30–33); Winkhaus, E. 1953.

## LINE 191

36. **Geoffrey de Semur**, Seigneur de Semur, md **Mathilda of Chalon**.

35. **Lambert** (348-35), (perhaps father of Gen. 34 below.)

34. **Erembourg**, dowered with Cando in Varsae, confirmed by Rudolph, King of Burgundy; d. a widow, 29 Oct 1028; md **Humbert II** (189-34), Count of Salins.

Sources: Blass, R. 1939, II:249; Brandenburg, E. 1935; Chaume, M. 1947a; Chaume, M. 1977, I 532, 533; Moriarty, G. 1985, 106 (Gen. 34–36); Winkhaus, E. 1953.

## LINE 192

30. **Guigues VIII** (196-32), Count d'Albon, Dauphin de Viennois.

29. **Matilda** (Maud) **d'Albon**; d. after Jan 1145; md 1133/34, **Amadeo III** (93-29, 182-29), Count of Maurienne.

Sources: Blass, R. 1939, II:242; Brandenburg, E. 1935; ES, II 1984:190 (Gen. 29–30); Hayward, F. 1941; Chevalier, R. 1947; Winkhaus, E. 1953.

## LINE 193

36. **Berenger**, a judge, liv 967, prob father of Gen. 35.

35. **Adalelme** (194-35), Judge at Avignon, md **Belielde** (194-35).

34. **Berenger**, Viscount of Avignon and Judge of Provence; confirmed a gift of his uncle Hildebert to St. Andre at Avignon; occ with his sons in Bishop Bezenet's foundation charter of St. Ruf, 1038/1039; d. before 13 July, 1065; md **Gerberge of Nice**, dau of **Miron of Nice**, liv 1041; and **Odile of Venice**, liv 1041.

33. **Raimon**, Dean of Avignon; removed to Nimes in Languedoc by 12 July 1096; d. 1096/1097; md **N.N.**, a sister of Ramon and Rostaing de Posquieres; dowered with the lands at Nimes.

32. **Raimond**, Dean of Avignon, Seigneur de Posquieres; Crusader; went on the 1st Crusade with Count Raimond de St. Gilles. Was in the East 31 Jan 1104/5, and home by 13 Jan 1111/1112; he lived in Languedoc; d. Aug 1138; md **N.N.**, prob a dau and heiress of **Eleazer**, Seigneur d'Uzes in Languedoc.

31. **Bremond**, Seigneur d'Uzes; did homage for Saye to the Bishop of Avignon, 1151; liv 1168.

30. **Raimond** (Rainou "Roscas"), Seigneur d'Uzes; b. c1115; liv 1200; did homage for Saye to the Bishop of Avignon, 1199/1200; md **Beatrice**.

29. **Rosine** (Rocie), Dame d'Uzes, d. 1206; md **Rostaing** (116-29), Seigneur de Sabran.

Sources: Agiles, R. 1968; Foucher, 1971; Krey, A. n.d.; Manteyer 1907; Moriarty, G. 1985, 99–100 (Gen. 29–36); Sabran 1897.

## LINE 194

36. **Bernier**, judge at Avignon, (prob father of Gen. 35).

35. **Adalelme** (Same as 193-35), judge at Avignon, 976–1005; md before 987, **Belielde**, liv 987/1036; d. 1036, dau of **William I**, Viscount of Marseilles, d. 1004/1008; and **Belielde**, d. 1036, his first wife.

34. **Amic of Avignon**, occ 1019–1036; d. 1050/1064; prob father of Gen. 33, says ES, III:761, but not various other sources.

33. **Peter Amic**, occ 1064, 1094; d. before 1112; md **Agnes**, liv 1094–1113.

32. **Giraud Amic**, Seigneur de Vedene; d. 1113; md **Ayelmna** (Ayalmus), liv 1101/1105.

31. **Constance Amic**, d. 1136; md (1) **Rostaing de Sabran** (116-31).

Sources: ES, III 1989:761 (Gen. 31–35); Mantayer 1907 (Gen. 31–35);

**105**

Moriarty, G. 1985, 99 (Gen. 31–35).

## LINE 195

36. **Borrel II** (54-35), Count of Barcelona, md **Liutgarde de Toulouse,** dau of **Raymond III,** Count of Toulouse, and **Gersende of Gascony.**

35. **Armengol** (Ermengaude) **I,** Count of Urgel; b. c975; d. 1 Sept 1010 at Cordoba; md before 1001, **Gerberge** (Teutberga) **of Provence,** d. after 1010, dau of **Rotbaud I,** Count of Provence (375-33), and **Eimilde de Gevaudun.**

34. **Armengol** (Ermengaude) **II,** Count of Urgel; b. 1009; d. 1038, on a pilgrimage to Jerusalem; md (2) 1030, **Constance Velasquita** of Besalu (347-34).

33. **Armengol** (Ermengaude) **III,** Count of Urgel; b. c1033; slain Feb/ Mar 1065 at Barbastro; md (2) 1055, **Clemencia de Bigorre,** d. after 1065; dau of **Bernard II,** Count of Bigorre, d. 1077; and **Clemence,** liv 1062; The parents of Bernard II were **Bernard Rodger** (227-33) and **Gersinde** (227-33), heiress of Bigorre.

32. **Armengol** (Ermengaude) **IV,** Count of Urgel; b. c1056; d. 28 Mar 1092; md 1076/80 (2) **Adelaide** (197-32), heiress of the countships of Forcalquier, Provence and Avignon.

31. **William III,** Count of Forcalquier and Marquis of Provence; d. Oct 1129, Avignon; md **Gersende of Albon** (196-31); liv 1158/1160.

30. **Bertrand II,** Count of Forcalquier; b. c1110; d. 1149/50; md Josserande de la Flotte, dau of **Arnaud de la Flotte,** Seigneur de Ravel.

29. **William IV,** Count of Forcalquier; b. 1130; d. Nov 1208; md **Adelaide de Beziers,** prob dau of **Raymond Trencavel** of Beziers (195A-30)

28. **Gersende,** heiress of Provence and Forcalquier; d. after 1193; md **Raimon de Sabran** (116-28), Seigneur de Castellar and Forcalquier, etc.

Sources: Brandenburg, E. 1935; Cheyette, F. 1988; ES II 1984:68 (Gen. 35, 36); ES, III 1980:132 (Gen. 28–35); ES III 1985:145 NEU; Latrie, M. 1889; Latour, P de 1997; Manteyer, G. de 1907; Moriarty, G. 1985, 99–101 (Gen. 28–35); 67 (Gen. 35–36); Stasser, T. 1996; Winkhaus, E. 1953.

## Line 195A

38. **Roger I,** Count of Carcassonne, vassal of William the Pious; md (her 2nd) **Adelaide of Auvergne,** widow fof Acfrid I, Count of Carcassonne, and dau of **Bernard** "Hairy Foot," Count of Auvergne, who d. 886.

37. **Roger II,** Count of Carcassonne, liv 950; bro of Arnold I, Count of Carcassonne.

36. **Arnold II,** Count of Comminges and Conserans, 944-949; d. 27 Nov

957; md **Arsinde**, Countess of Carcassonne, 945-969; dau of **Acfrid II** (291-37), Count of Carcassonne and Rasez.

35. **Roger I**, Count of Carcassonne, de Rasez, Conserans and Comminges; Seigneur de Foix, 949; d. after Apr 1010; md before 970, **Adelaide**, dau of **Bernard II**, Count of Melgueil by wife **Senegonde**, who d. after 996 (203-34).

34. **Ramon Roger I**, Count of Carcassonne, 979; d. by Apr 1011; md beforre 990 **Garsindis de Beziers**, dau of **William Beziers** and **Ermentrudis**. She md (2) 1013, Bernard, Seigneur de Auduze.

33. **Redro Ramon**, Count of Carcassonne, Viscount of Beziers and d'Agde, 1043-1054; d. c1060; md **Rangarde**, dau of **Bernard I**, Count de la Mancha, by his wife **Amelia** (327-33).

32. **Ermengarde**, liv 1054-1076; md **Raymond-Bernard Trencavel**, Vicomte d'Albi, and Nimes; d. 1074.

31. **Bernard IV**, Viscomte d'Albi, de Nimes, de Carcassonne, de Beziers and d'Agde; d. 1129; md 1083, **Cecilia of Provence**, d. 1150; dau of **Bernard II**, Count of Provence, by wife **Mathilde**.

30. **Raymond Trencavel** of Beziers, Viscomte de Beziers, d'Agde, d'Albi, Carcassonne, and Rasez; liv 1131-1167; md **Adelaide de Beziers**.

29. **Adelaide de Beziers** md **William IV** (195-29), Count of Forcalquier.

Sources: Cheyette, F. 1988; ES III 1985:145 NEU; ES III 1985:163; ES III 1989:763, 819; Latour, P. 1997:354-355; Stasser, I. 1996:185,187.

## LINE 195B

36. **Atto Trencavel**, liv c950; md **Diafronissa**.

35. **Bernard Trencavel**, liv 950s-970s; md **Gauciana**.

34. **Atto (Atton) Travencal**, d. c1032; md **Gerberga**.

33. **Bernard Travencal**, d. c1060; md **Rangarde**.

32. **Raymond-Bernard Travencal**, Vicomte d'Albi and Nimes; d. 1074; md **Ermengarde** (195A-32).

Sources: Cheyette, F. 1988: 820-830; ES III 1985:132; ES III 1985: 145 NEU.

## LINE 196

41. **Rostaing I**, Seigneur in the Southern Vienneois; b. c800; d. 844; md **Sufficia**.

40. **Rostaing II**, Seigneur d'Annonay; sold lands in St. Maurie de Vienne, 20 Apr 873; b. c838; d. before 889; md **Berthilda**, occ 20 Apr 873; survived her husband.

39. **Guigues I**, Seigneur d'Annonay; b. c860; md **Gandalmoda**.

38. **Domnus Guigues II**, Sire de Vion; occ in a charter to Cluny, Oct 934; b. c885/895; d. before 957; md **Wandelmodis de Salins**, b. c885; (she md (2) before Oct 957, Bernard, Sire de Beaujeu in the Maconnaise, 957–960; Her father was **Humbert I** (189-35) Sire de Salins, *not Hugh of Provence, King of Italy, as given by Moriarty, G. 1985.*

37. **Guigues III**, Sire de Vion; liv 942–954; d. 996; md **Fredeburga**.

36. **Guigues IV**, Count in the District of Grenoble; Sire de Vion; d. 18 Oct 996, md **Fredeburga**; prob a dau of **Richard** (25-37), Prince of Provence.

35. **Guigues V**, Count of Albon, with the territory around Grenoble; Sire de Vion; b. c970; d. before 6 June 1009; md **Gotelena**, dau of **Silvion**, Sire de Clerieu, and **Willa**, sister of William de Clerieu.

34. **Guigues VI** "the Old," Count of Albon and of Grenoble, Sire de Vion; b. c1001; d. a monk, 22 Apr 1063, at Cluny; md before 18 Oct 1013, **Adelaide** (Alix) **Beaujeu**, dau of **Guiscard I**, Sire de Beaujeu, 992/993; d. 1031/1050; who md **Adelaide**. Guiscard's parents were **Humbert I**, Sire de Beaujeu, 966/67-998; d. 1016; who md **Hermelt**, d. 997/998. Humbert's parents were **Bernard de Beaujou**, 957/960, who d. 961/966; md **Wandalmodis de Salins**, liv 957/960.

33. **Guigues VII** "le Gros," Count of Albon and Grenoble, Sire de Vion; witnessed a charter with his brother Humbert, 20 Aug 1034; occ with his father, 27 Apr 1050 and 1053; b. c1025; d. 22 Apr 1075; bur in St. Robert; md (1) 27 Apr 1050, **Petronel of Turin** (mother of Gen. 32 below), dau of **Artaud**, Seigneur d'Annonay and **Petronel of Grenoble** who d. by 1070; bur at Domene. He md (2) 10 May 1070, Agnes, dau of **Ramon Berenger I** (54-32), Count of Barcelona, by his third wife, Almada, b. c1056.

32. **Guigues VIII**, Count of Albon and Grenoble; b. c1050/60; d. 21 Dec 1125; md (2) 1106/10, **Mathilda**; b. c1075; d. 1142/1144; prob a dau of **Eadgar** "the Athling;" b. c1048; d. 1126; and his wife, **N.N.**, the dau of **Maldred,** Lord of Carlisle; b. 1005; d. 1045; who md **Ealdgyth of Northumberland**. Maldred's parents were **Crinan the Thane** (252-34), and **Bethoc** (165-33), heiress and Princess of Scotland. Eadgar's parents were **Edward** "the Exile" (233-33) and **Agatha von Braunschweig** (318-34).

31. **Gersende of Albon**, liv 1158/1160; md **William III** (195-31), Count of Forcalquier, Marquis of Provence.

*NOTE: The numbering of the Guigues (Gen. 32-39) is from Moriarty, G. 1985. ES III 1989:738 calls Gen. 33 Guigues I and leaves the earlier generations unnumbered. Also, one source, Charles Evans, says Matilde, wife of Guigues VIII (Gen. 32), was widow of King Konrad (d. 27 July 1101), and dau of Roger I, King of Sicily.*

Sources: Bachelier, E. 1959, I and II:140–145 (Gen. 31–39); ES, III 1989:738 (Gen. 31–39); Evans, C. 1981b; Manteyer,1908; Moriarty, G. 1985 258–259 (Gen. 31–41); Rudt-Collenberg, 1969.

## LINE 197

34. **Fulk Bertrand**, Count of Provence, md **N.N.**, dau of **William IV Tailefer,** Count of Toulouse, who d. Sept 1037, by his wife **Emma of**

**Provence.**

33. **William Bertrand**, Count of Provence at Avignon, Marquis of Provence; b. c1025; d. after May 1065/1067; md **Adelaide of Ivrea** (198-33); d. after 12 Oct 1113.

32. **Adelaide**, heiress of the countships of Forcalquier, Provence and Avignon, which after the partition of 1102/1105 was called the Comte de Forcalquier; d. 1129; md (his 2nd), 1076/1080, **Armengol** (Ermengaude) **IV** (195-32), Count of Urgel, 1065.

Sources: Blass, R. 1939, II:254; Brandenburg, E. 1935; ES III 1989:763; Mantayer,1908; Moriarty, G. 1985, 100–101 (Gen. 32–34);Winkhaus, E. 1953.

## LINE 198

40. **Adalbert II** (31-38, 263-38), Margrave of Tuscany, md **Bertha** (263-38), Princess of Lorraine.

39. **Ermengarde of Tuscany**, b. 901; d. 29 Feb 932; md **Adalbert**, Margrave of Ivrea (332-37).

38. **Anskar III**, Margrave of Camerino and Spoleto, d. 940.

37. **Dadone**, Count of Pombia, 973; d. 1000.

36. **Ardoino**, Marquis of Ivrea, Count of the Sacred Palace, 991; King of Italy, 1002; b. c960; d. 1015; md **Berta** (186-36), Princess of Lorraine.

35. **Ardicino**, Prince of Italy; b. c980; liv 1029; md before 1019, **Willa of Tuscany**, dau of **Hugh**, Marquis of Tuscany, d. 21 Dec 1001, Pistoja.

34. **Ardoino II of Ivrea**, Count of Ivrea.

33. **Adelaide of Ivrea**, d. after 12 Oct 1113; md **William Bertrand** (197-33), Count of Provence at Avignon, Marquis of Provence.

Sources: Brandenburg, E. 1935; Carutti, D. 1884a, 11, 65, 233, 257–283; Carutti, D. 1884b; ES, II 1984:59 (Gen. 38–40); Moriarty, G. 1985, 103–104 (Gen. 33–40); Winkhaus, E. 1953.

## LINE 199

37. **Eldo** (351-37), Count in the Wetterau; md before 918, **N.N.**, dau of **Herbert I** (231-37), Count of Vermandois.

36. **Conrad**, Count in the Rheinegau and Duke of Swabia; b. c920; d. 20 July 997; md **Jutta.**

35. **Hermann II** (63-35,229-34,247-32), Duke of Swabia, 997; d. 4 May 1003; md prob c988, **Gerberge** (201-35), Princess of Upper Burgundy.

34. **Gisela of Swabia**, b. 11 Nov 985; d. 14 Feb 1043; md (1) c1000, **Bruno von Braunschweig** (32-33); md also Ernst von Babenberg 63-35), Duke of Swabia, d. 31 May 1015; md (3) 1036, **Conrad II of Franconia** (359-34), King of Germany, Italy and Brunswick, Emperor of the West, 1024–1039.

Sources: Balde, H. 1913; Blass, R. 1939, II:274, 280, 311; Chaume, M. 1977, I:542, 551–552; Dungern, O. von 1910; Jackman, D. 1997;

Moriarty, G. 1985, 94 (Gen. 34–36); 23 (Gen. 36–37); Moriarty, G. 1945; Moriarty, G. 1947; Thatcher, O. 1897, 322.

## LINE 200

44. **Lambert** (265-44,330-42), Lord of Hornbach; liv 760–783.

43. **Werner**, Count in the Lobdengau, Lord of Hornbach; liv 783–813; slain 814 at Aachen; md **Friderun**, occ 786.

42. **Widechowo**, Count in the Lobdengau and Lord of Hornbach, 817–823; liv 823.

41. **Werner**, Count in the Lobdengau and Lord of Hornbach; liv 825–847; md **Rotlint**.

40. **N.N. von Lobdengau**, heiress of the abbotship of Hornbach; heiress of Lobdengau and Hornbach; md c860/865, **Walaho VI** (359-40), Count in the Wormsgau, etc.

Sources: Chaume, M. 1977, 535; Jackman, D. 1990; Jackman, D. 1997:135,136; Levillain, L. 1937; Moriarty, G. 1985, 93 (Gen. 40–43); 74 (Gen. 43–44); Winkhaus, E. 1953.

## LINE 201

36. **Conrad I** "the Peaceful" (175-34), King of both Burgundies; b. c925; md **Matilda** (171-35, 230-35), Princess of France.

35. **Gerberge**, Princess of Upper Burgundy; b. 965/966; d. 1017; md (1) Bernard von Werl, Count of Werl, d. 31 July 995; md (2) **Hermann II** (63-35,199-35), Duke of Swabia.

Sources: Balde, H. 1913; Blass, R. II:274, 280, 311; Brandenburg, E. 1935; Isenburg, W. 1953; Moriarty, G. 1985, 94 (Gen. 35–36); Winkhaus, E. 1953.

## LINE 202

45. **Eticho I** (same as 224-42), Duke of Alsace, d. 20 Feb 690.

44. **Eticho II,** of the Nordgau; liv c698.

43. **Alberich,** b. c698; d. 735.

42. **Eberhard I**, Count in the Nordgau and Hamalant; b. c730; d. 777.

41. **Meginhard I**, Count in the Hamalant; d. between 12 Nov. 843 and 15 June 844.

40. **Eberhard II** (Wichmann) (see also 311-37), Count in the Nordgau and Hamalant; d. 881; md **Evesna** (Evesa), a Saxon.

39. **Eberhard III**, Count in the Nordgau and Northern Hamalant; Count in the Ortengau and Argau, Duke of Friesland in Hamalant; captured by the Norsemen and ransomed by his mother, Evesna; murdered, after 898, while in pursuit of Walcher, Count of Friesland, son of Gerold de Fries.

38. **Hugh III of Hohenburg**, Count in the Alsacian Nordgau and of Hohenburg in Alsace; advocate of Luden; d. 940; md **Hildegarde**.

37. **Eberhard IV** (33-35,316-36), Count in Alsace and in the Nordgau;

110

vassal of the Archbishop of Rheims; d. 18 Dec 972/973; md **Luitgarde of Trier**, dau of **Wigeric** (33-35, 104-37, 319-37), Count in the Triergau and **Kunigunde** (353-37), Princess of West Franks.

36. **Gerhard** (Gerard), Count in Alsace; md **Eva**, d. 1006/1024; dau of **Siegfried** (316-36), Count of Luxemburg, and **Hedwig**, a Saxon.

35. **Adelaide** (Adelheid) **of Alsace** founded 1020, the monastery of Oehringen; d. 19 May 1040/46; md c986, **Henry of Franconia** (359-35), Duke of Franconia and Carinthia; Count in the Spayergau.

Sources: Blass, R. 1939 II:272; Bouchard, C. 1981; Jackman, D. 1990; Jackman, D. 1997;Kruger, E. 1899, 14; Merz, W. 1914; Moriarty, G. 1985, 93–94 (Gen. 35–38); 181–182 (Gen. 38–42); Vanderkindere, L. 1902, vol. II; Weiss, S. 1910; Winkhaus, E. 1953.

## LINE 203

40. **Aigulf**, Count of Substantion; liv c752.
39. **Amic**, Count in the Council of Narbonne, 791.
38. **Robert**, Count of Substantion, liv 819.
37. **N.N. of Substantion**, md **Guillenette**, liv 899.
36. **Bernard I**, Count of Melgueil and Substantion.
35. **Berenger of Melgueil**, md **Gisele**.
34. **Bernard II**, Count of Melgueil; d. c989; md **Senegunde**, d. 989.
33. **Berenger**, d.before 985.
32. **Bernard III**, Count of Melgueil; liv 989, d. c1055, md **Adele**, Countess of Substantion, 1066.
31. **Raymond I** (150-32), Count of Melgueil, d. c1079, md before 1055, **Beatrix of Poitou**, dau of **William III** (88-33), Count of Poitou, and **Agnes of Burgundy** (161-32).
30. **Pierre**, Count of Melgueil, liv 1085; bur Maguelone; md c1065, **Almode of Toulouse** (142-30).

Sources: Devie, A. 1872, 174–180 (Gen. 30–40); ES, III 1985:444 (Gen. 30–40); Rouquette, J. 1914 (Gen. 30–40); Settipani, C. 1988.

## LINE 204

39. **Guthroth** (Gudrod) **Halfdansson** (same as 166-40).
38. **Halfdan** "the Black," King of Vestfold, 830–870; King of Agde and Sogn, in Norway; ruled 827–860; b. 820; md Thora, dau of Harold "Gullskeggr" (Gold Beard); md (2) **Ragnhild** (mother of Gen. 37); b. c830; dau **Sigurd Hjort Helgasson**, King of Ringerike, and **Helga**, dau of **Dag Frode**.
37. **Harold I** "Haarfager" ("fair hair" meaning "thick hair") (see also 28-38, 44-38), first over-king of all Norway, 883; he conquered the separate fjord kingdoms; King of Vestfold, 853–858; b. 860; d. c936; md (6) **Ragnhild** (mother of Gen. 36), dau of **Erik**, King of Jutland.
36. **Eric I** "Blood Axe," King of Norway, 930–935, Jarl of Northum-

berland; b. c895; killed 954; md **Gunhild**, dau **Gorm** (369-39), King of Denmark.

    35. **Harold II** "Graypelt," King of Norway, 960–965; killed 970.

    34. **Bertrade**, Princess of Norway, md **Bernard II** (312-34), Duke of Saxony.

    33. **Ida of Saxony**, heiress of Laroche, 31 July 1102; md **Adalbert III** (120-32), Count of Namur.

Sources: Baumgarten, N. 1928, XXIV, 36, and table; Cokayne, G. 1959, I:235; ES I.1 1997; ES, VII 1979:68 (Gen. 33–34); II 1984:105 (Gen. 35–39); Howarth, H. 1920, vol. IX; Moncreiffe, I. 1982, chart 35:109; Sturluson, S. 1991, 6-50; Von Redlich, M. 1941, 274.

## LINE 205

    33. **Baldwin V de Lille** (141-32) md **Adela of France** (140-32).

    32. **Robert I** "the Frisian," Count of Flanders, 1071; Count of Holland, 1062–1071; b. c1035; d. 3 Oct 1093; md 1063, **Gertrude of Saxony** (312-33) (mother of Gen. 31), b. c1030; widow of Florenz I, Count of Holland; d. 4 Aug 1113.

    31. **Gertrude**, heiress of Flanders; b. c1070; d. 1115/1126; md (1) c1095/1096, Henry III, Count of Louvain; md (2), c1100, **Dietrich II of Alsace** (158-31) (father of Gen. 30); Duke of Upper Lorraine; b. 1060; d. 23 Jan 1115; bur at Chetenois.

    30. **Dietrich II** (called by some Thierry of Lorraine), Count of Alsace and Flanders, 1128; b. 1099 or 1101, Alsace, France; d. 17 Jan 1168; md (2) 1134, **Sybil** (Sibylle) **of Anjou** (152-30).

    29. **Matthew of Alsace**, of Flanders, Belgium; Count of Boulogne; b. c1137; d. in battle 25 July 1173; bur at Josse; md before 1160, **Mary of Blois** (299-29); Princess of England, Countess of Mortain.

    28. **Mathilda** (Maud) **of Flanders**, heiress of Boulogne, b. 1160/1165; d. 1211, Louvain; md (his 1st) **Henry I** (68-28, 120-27), Duke of Brabant and Lower Lorraine; d. 5 Sept. 1235.

Sources: Brandenburg, E. 1935; Dillinger, P. 1991; ES II 1984:7 (Gen. 28–30); VI 1978:129 (Gen. 30–32); Moriarty, G. 1985, 130 (Gen. 28–32); 15 (Gen. 32–33); Putnam, R. 1971.

## LINE 206

    40. **Richard**, Count of Amiens and of Meaux in the Lyonais; liv 801–825; d. 825.

    39. **Budwine** (257-37,258-39,346-37), Count of Italy and Metz, Lay Abbot of Gorze; d. 864/869; md (1) **Richilde of Arles** (112-40), d. 883.

    38. **Richard** (317-34) "the Justicier," Duke of Burgundy, Count of Autun, prob Count of Sens; Burgundian opponent of the Capets; d. Auxerre, 1 Sept 921; md before 888, **Adelaide of Burgundy** (300-38).

    37. **Adelaide** (Aelis) **of Burgundy** md **Regnier II** (68-36), Count of

Hainault.

Sources: Blass, R. 1939, 305; Chaume, M. 1977, I: 254n, 416n2,534,544,545; Isenburg, W. 1953; Knetsch, C. 1931; Moriarty, G. 1985, 51 (Gen. 37-39); Motey, V de 1920, V:304; Rubincam, M. 1949; Winkhaus, E. 1953.

## LINE 207

39. **Giselbert** (continue 303-40), Count in the Maasgau, 840-877; d.c885; md before March 846/8, **Ermengarde of Lorraine and Burgundy** (302-39), Princess of Italy.

38. **Regnier I** "Longhals," Duke of Lorraine, 900, and Count of Hainault by 886, Lay Abbot of Echternach, Luxemburg; d. after 15 Oct 915 and before 19 Jan 916. Meersen in the Palatine; md (2) Albrada of Mons, Duchess of Lorraine, who was a widow in 916; md (1) **Hersent**, Princess of France, dau of **Charles II** (250-39, 303-39), King of France, and **Ermentrude**, dau of **Eudes** (Odo) (336-31), Count of Orleans.

37. **Giselbert**, Duke of Lorraine, Lay Abbot of Echternach, Count of Hainault, b. c890, France; d. 2 Oct 934, Echternach, Rhineland, Prussia; md 929, **Gerberga of Saxony** (92-35); d. 5 May 984. She me (2) **Louis IV** "d'Outremer" (171-36), King of France.

36. **Gerberge of Hainault and Lorraine**, b. c935; md before 954, **Albert I** (239-34), Count of Vermandois and Troyes; d. 8 Sept 987/8.

Sources: Chaume, M. 1977, 548-549; ES I 1980:95 (Gen. 36-39); Isebburg, W. 1953; Knetsch, C. 1931; Moriarty, G. 1950; Moriarty, G. 1985,39 (Gen. 36-39); Round, J. 1971; Rubincam, M. 1949 (Gen. 36-39);Strickland, A. 1902, I:170; Vanderkindere, L. 1902; Winkhaus, E. 1953.

## LINE 208

38. **Eberhard** (same as 389-37), Count in the Bonngau.

37. **Ehrenfeld** (also called Ezzo, Erenfried), Count in the Zulpichgau, in the Bonngau, and in the Keldachgau; md **Richwara**, d. before 10 July 963.

36. **Hermann I** "Pusillus" (the Little) (same as 67-36,97-32), Count in the Bonngau, the Eifelgau, and Mieblgau, and the Avalgau; d.996; md (1) **Heilwig von Dillingen** (mother of Gen. 35).

35. **Ezzo** (Erenfried of the Rheinphapz) (379-34), Count Palatine of Lorraine, Pfalzgrave of Lorraine, Lord of Duisburg and Kaiserwerth; b. c955; d. 21 May 1034, Saalfeld; bur at Brauweiler; md 991, **Matilda of Saxony** (237-35).

34. **Otto**, Count Palatine of Lorraine, 1035; Duke of Swabia, 1025; Count in the Deutzgau; md **N.N.**, dau of **Hugh VI** (33-33), Count in Nordgau, by wife **Heilwig of Dagsburg**, and sister of Bruno, Bp of Toulouse, 1049-54, who became Pope Leo IX.

33. **Richenza of Swabia** (26-31), d. after 1050; md (1) Hermann III,

Count of Werl, d. 1050; md (2) **Otto, I von Northeim** (26-31), Count of Northeim and in the Rittigau, d. 1083.

Sources: Blass, R. 1939, R. 1939, II:264, 290, 311; Carutti, D. 1884a; Dungern, O. von 1910; ES, VI 1978:1 (Gen. 35–38); ES VIII 1980:132; Historich, 1934; Isenburg, W. 1953; Kruger, E. 1899; Vanderkindere, L. 1902; Winkhaus, E. 1953.

## LINE 209

37. **Askold**, Swedish chief ruler of Kiev, 855/856; slain c882.
36. **Dir**, Prince of Kiev; slain after 883.
35. **Mal**, Prince of the Drevianes.
34. **Maloucha** (Malfreda, Debrima), formerly a concubine; d. 1002; md **Svatislav** (Siratozlaw, Swjatislaw) **I** (143-34), Grand Duke of Novgorod, Kiev and Perejaslaw.

Sources: Moriarty, 221 (Gen. 34–37); Taube, M. de 1947, 141–143 (Gen. 34–37).

## LINE 210

41. **Burkhard I**, Count in the Grabfeldgau; liv 858-866.
40. **Burkhard II**, Count in the Frankish Grabfeldgau, and then in the Thuringinian Hiutsitingau, Margrave of the Sorbenmark; fell in battle with the Hungarians, 909; md **Adred of Loingau**, liv 936; dau of **Bardo**, Count of Soltau in the Loingau.
39. **Burkhard III** (359-38), of Wettin and Grabfeldgau, driven from his lands by Henry "the Fowler;" md **Mathilda of Hesse**.
38. **Dedi** ( 17-36), Count in the Hessegau; an overleader in Thuringia; adherent of Otto "the Great," at Birthen in 939; d. 14 Apr 957; md **N.N.**, dau of **Frederick II**, Count in the Herzgau.
37. **Dietrich I von Wettin**, Count in the Hessegau, slain 976, in battle with the Magayars; md **N.N.**, liv 976.
36. **Dedi I**, Count in the Northern Hessegau; opponent of Otto II, 976; first to obtain (capture) Wettin; liv 947; slain 13 Nov 1009, at Mose; md before 19 Dec 985, **Thietburga von Haldenslaben**, dau of **Dietrich** (27-37), Count of the Saxon Nordmark and Lord of Haldensleben.
35. **Dietrich II von Wettin**, (See also, 8-33), Count of Brehna and Eilenburg, Margrave of Niederlausitz; liv 1009; murdered 19 Nov 1034; md c1016, **Mathilda von Meissen** (212-35), heiress of Meissen.
34. **Dedi** (Dedo, Dedon) **II**, Margrave of the Ostmark (Niederlausitz), Count of Eilenburg and of Lausnitz; b. c1016; d. Oct 1075; md (his 1, her 2) after Apr 1039, **Oda von der Ostmark** (211-34); widow of **William III** (211-34), Count of Weimar.
33. **Adelaide von Eilenburg**, b. c1040; d. 26 Jan 1071; md **Ernst** "the Bold" (279-33), Margrave of Austria.

Sources: Blass, R. 1939,II:292; Brandenburg, E. 1935; ES, I 1984:44

(Gen. 33–41); Kotzschke, R. 1929; Moriarty, G. 1985, 95–96 (Gen. 33–41); Posse, O. 1887; Sachsischer, 173, 184, 191.

## LINE 211

42. **Poppo I** (102-40), Count in Grabfeld in the Saargau, liv 819-839.

41. **Christian I**, Count in Grabfeld; d. 871.

40. **Christian II** (281A-35), Count in Grabfeld, md **N.N.**, dau of **Thakulf**, Duke in Thuringia.

39. **N.N.** (dau.) md **Richwin**.

38. **Christian**, Margrave of the Saxon Nordmark; liv 937–945; md **Hidda**, d. 969 at Jerusalem; sister of Margrave Gero, d. 965.

37. **Dietmar** (Thietmar) **I**, Margrave of the Saxon Eastmark; d. 3 July 978; md (1) **Swanhilde**, d. 26 Nov 1014; dau of **Hermann Billung** (312-36), Duke of Saxony, and **Hildegarde of Westerbourg**.

36. **Gero**, Margrave of the Saxon Nordmark; liv 978; d. 1015; md **Adelaide**.

35. **Dietmar** (Thietmar) **II**, Margrave of Lausnitz and the Saxon Eastmark; d. 1030; md **Reinhild von Beichlingen**.

34. **Oda von der Ostmark** md (his 1st, her 2nd) **Dedi II** (210-34), Margrave of Ostmark; md (2) **William III** (210-34), Count of Weimar in the Eichsfeld; d. 16 Apr 1039; son of **William II von Weimar** (281-32), Duke of Thuringia.

Sources: Blass, R. 1939, II:292; Brandenburg, E. 1935; ES I.1 1997; Isenburg, W. 1953; Jackman, D. 1997:147-152,198-202; Kotzschke, R. 1929; Moriarty, G. 1985, 96 (Gen. 34–38); Posse, O. 1887; Winkhaus, E. 1953.

## LINE 212

43. **Thankulf,** a Thuringian, liv c800.

42. **Hadulf** (Adulph, Odi) of Thuringia, Count in Derlingau; occ 802-820+.

41. **Thankulf,** Duke of Thuringia; occ 849; d. 873.

40. **N.N.** (fem.) md **Eckard I,** Count in Thuringia; d. 2 June 871.

39. **Gunther**, Count in Thuringia, d. 17 May 925.

38. **Eckard II**, Count in Thuringia, d. 6 Sept 954.

37. **Gunter von Merseburg**, Margrave of Merseburg liv 974; removed 976/977; fell in battle, 19 July 982, Possano in Calabria; md (div by 965), **Dubrawka**, dau of **Boleslaw I** (362-37), Duke of Bohemia.

36. **Ekkehard I**, Margrave of Meissen and Thuringia; competitor for the German throne; murdered 30 Apr 1002 at Pohlde; bur at Grossjena; md after 979, **Swanhilde of Saxony**; d. 26 Nov 1014; dau of **Hermann Billung** (312-36), and **Hildegarde of Westerbourg.**

35. **Mathilda von Meissen**, heiress of Meissen; md c1016, **Dietrich II von Wettin** (8-33, 210-35), Count of Brehna in the Hessegau, and

Eilenburg.

Sources: Blass, R. 1939, II:292; Hlawitschwa, E. 1987; Isenburg, W. 1953, part i, table 42; Jackman, D. 1997:145,146,153; Moriarty, G. 1985, 95–97 (Gen. 35–40); Posse, O. 1882; Raumer, G. 1837; Winkhaus, E. 1953.

## LINE 213

35. **Henry von Schweinfurt** (7-34,47-35,270-35), Margrave of Schweinfurt and Nordgau; b. 975, d. 18 Sept 1017; md **Gerberge of Henneburg** (102-35).

34. **Henry von Schweinfurt**, Count in the Pegnitz; liv 1021–1042; md **N.N. of Altdorf**, dau of **Kuno I**, Count of Altdorf, liv 1017, whose parents were **Rudolph II** (29-35), Count in the Swabian Altdorf and **Itha von Oningen** (29-35).

33. **Kuno I von Frantenhausen**, ruler of Reichpoldesberge, Count in the Pegnitz, md **Mathilde of Achalm**, dau of **Rudolph**, Count of Achalm, liv 1030; and **Adelheid von Wulflingen**, d. by 1065, who was dau of **Liutold von Mompelgard**, d. after 1044, and **Willebirg von Wulflingen**, d. a nun, Cloister of Geisenfeld, 1044/1052.

32. **Adelaide von Frantenhausen**, d. 24 Feb 1110, bur at Sulzbach; md **Ulrich** (128-32), Count of Passau; d. of the plague 14 Apr 1099, Regensburg, Germany.

Sources: Blass, R. 1939, I:283, 296; Brandenburg, E. 1935; ES, I 1980:38 (Gen. 32–33); I 1980:9 (33–35); Jeritsch, G. 1894, 12, 13; Moriarty, G. 1985, 123 (Gen. 32–33); 57 (Gen. 34–35).

## LINE 214

46. **Theotar**, liv 682.

45. **Theoderic III**, King of Burgundy, 670; and of the Franks, 690/691; md **Clotilde** (Doda), Queen regent, 690/691.

44. **Bertrada**, a Merovingian princess, founded the Abbey of Prun, 720; md **Martin of Laon**, (father of Gen. 43 below). Martin was son of **Ansguise** (171-45), Mayor of the Palace, and **St. Begga of Landen** (260-45).

43. **Caribert** (114-41) (Cambert, Charibert), Count of Laon, liv 720–747; md **Bertrada**.

42. **Bertha** (Bertrada) "au Grand Pied" (Broad foot), of Laon, Aisne, France, b. c720; d. 12 July 783; md c740, **Pippin**"the Short" (171-42), King of the Franks.

Sources: ; ES, I 1984:2 (Gen. 42–43); Gregory of Tours, 1874; James, E. 1988; Lasco, P. 1971; Levillain, vol. 49 (1937) 337–408; vol. 50 (1938) 65–66; Moriarty, G. 1985, 232 (Gen. 42–45),Vajay, S. de 1966a.

## LINE 215

38. **Andronikos**, Dux, Domestikos ton Stoln, liv 908.

37. **Konstantinos**, Dux, Domestikos ton Stoln; Kaisar; d. June 913; md **N.N.**, dau of **Gregorias Iberitzes**.

36. **Gregoras**, d. in battle, Constantinople, June 913 (or his brother, Stephanos, liv 913).

35. **Andronikos Doukas**, liv 1020; probably protostatharios and strategos of Bulgaria.

34. **Ionnes (John) Doukas**, Caesar, pretender to the Imperial throne, 1059 and 1073; d. c1088; md before 1045, **Eirene Pegonitissa**, d. c1060; dau of General **Niketas Pegonites**, the Patrician; liv 1018–1057; d. after 1057.

33. **Andronikos Doukas** (394-34), protovestiarios; b. by 1045; d. 14 Oct 1077, as the monk Antonios; md by 1066, **Maria of Bulgaria** (309-33).

32. **Eirene Doukaina** "Augusta," b. 1066; d. 19 Feb 1127, a nun; md **Alexios I Komnenos** (111-32), (Alexius I), Emperor (Basilius) of the East, 1081–1118; b. c1048; d. 15 Aug 1118; bur in the monastery of Philantropos.

31. **Theodora Komnene**, b. c1070; d. 20 Feb 1116; md **Konstantinos Angelos**, a patrician of Philadelphia in Asia Minor; General of Byzantium in the war with the Normans, 1143–1154, fl. 1110–1166. His father was **Manuel Angelos**, liv 1081.

30. **Andronikos Angelos Doukas** (same as 74-30), kuropalates at the Court of the Emperor (Basilius) Manuel I, 1166–1185; blinded 1182/3; a General in the Civil and Moslem wars; d. by Dec 1185; md by 1155, **Euphrosyne Kastamonitissa**, d. 1185/1195.

29. **Isaakios II Angelos** (Isaac II), Emperor of the East, 1185–1195; and 1203–1204; b. c1155; executed, 1204; md **Eirene Komnena** (42-29).

28. **Eirene (Maria) Angelina**, b. c1181; murdered 27 Aug 1208, Hohenstaufen; bur at Lorsch; md (2) **Philip von Hohenstauffen** (125–28), Emperor of Germany, 1198; Emp of the West; b. c1176; d. 21 June 1208, Bamburg; bur Speyer monastery.

Sources: Allen, J. 1985; Brook, L. 1981, 13, 16–18, 55, 58–60, 91, 98, 115, 170 (Gen. 28-35); Buckler, G. 1929; Chaume, M. 1977, 542, 551–552; ES II 1984:179 (Gen. 28-32); II 1984:178 (Gen. 31-38); Hanowelt, E. 1982; Leib, B. 1950; Moncreiffe, I. 1982, chart 13, p.57 (Gen. 30-35); Moriarty, G. 1945; Moriarty, G. 1985, 166 (Gen. 28); 174 (Gen. 29-31); 137–138 (Gen. 31-35): Polemis, D. 1986, 86n10; Silverman, D. 1997; Winkhaus, E. 1953.

## LINE 216

37. **Garcia Sanchez** (289-38, 290-39), Count of Gascony, md **Amuna**.

36. **Arnaldo**, Count of Astarac; liv c920–960.

35. **Garsenda of Astarac** md **Raymund I Dato** (227-36), Count of Bigorre and founder of the monastery of St. Savin. She md (2) **Oriol**.

Sources: ES, III:119 (Gen. 35–36); Isenburg, W. 1953; Lacarra, J. 1945, I:210, table at 285; Moriarty, G. 1985, 79–80 (Gen. 35–37); Winkhaus, E. 1953.

## LINE 217

43. **Halfdan Olafsson** (Continue with 166-41).

42. **Eystein of Westfold** (92-40, 339-42).

41. **Harold**, King of Haithabu, d. c750, in the Irish sea; md **Emhild of Engern**, dau of **Warnechin** (339-41), Count of Engern, and wife **Kunhilde of Rugen**.

40. **Halfdan**, King of Haithabu; b. 775/780; d. 810 in battle at Walcheran.

39. **Harold** "Klak," King of Haithabu, King of Rustringen, 819–827; King of Jutland; b. c800; d. 844 in battle at Walcheran.

38. **Godefrid**, King of Haithabu, of Dorestad and of Rustringen; md **Gisela of Lorraine**, d. by 26 Oct 907; dau of **Lothar II** (93-38,263-39,310-37,338-37), King of Lorraine, and **Waldrada**.

Sources: ES, II 1984 1984:104 (38–41); Moriarty, 1965, 38-42), Schilling, H. 1936 (Gen. 38–41); Wallmichrath, E. 1966 (Gen. 38–41).

## LINE 218

39. **Wilfred I** (54-37,347-38), Count of Urgel and Barcelona, md **Guinidilda** (Winidilde), dau of **Baldwin I** (235-38), Count of Flanders.

38. **Wilfred II Borrel**, Count of Barcelona, Gerona and Osona; d. 26 Apr 911; md **Gersenda of Toulouse**, dau of **Eudes**, Count of Toulouse and Rouergue, and wife **Gersinda de Albi**.

37. **Richilde of Barcelona** (218A-37), d. 962; md **Odo**, Vicomte de Narbonne, d. 933; son of **Francon II** (218B-34), Vicomte de Narbonne, son of **Meyeul** (101-36), Vicomte de Narbonne, and wife **Raimondis** (Raymonde) (101-36)

36. **Matfred**, Vicomte de Narbonne; b. c933, d. 970; md **Adelheid of Toulouse**, liv 977; dau of **Raymond Pons** and **Gersende of Gascony**.

35. **Raimond I**, Comte de Narbonne, liv 1023; md **Richarda of Rodez**, liv 1023; dau **Hugh**, Count of Rodez.

34. **Berenger I** (same as 226-33), Viscount of Narbonne, d. 1067; md c1010, **Gersenda of Besalu**, dau of **Bernard I**, Count of Besalu.

33. **Rixinde**, Dame de Lodeve, md **Richard II** (226-33), Viscount of Milhaud.

Sources: ES, II 1984:68 (Gen. 37–39); Latour, P de 1997; Mateos, R. 1984; Moriarty, G. 1985, 41 (Gen. 36–38); 67 (Gen. 37–39); Salazar, J. de 1984; Stasser, T. 1993; Turton, W. 1984, 218 (Gen. 33–34); 52, (Gen. 34–37).

## LINE 218A

39. **Raimond I** md **Berthiez of Toulouse**.

38. **Arsinde de Rosillon** md **Francon II** (218B-36), Viscount of Narbonne.

37. **Odo**, Viscount of Narbonne, md **Richilde of Barcelona** (218-37).

Sources: Latour, P. 1997:337-355; Strasser, T. 1993: 489-507.

## LINE 218B

36. **Francon I**, Viscount of Narbonne, 854.

35. **Mayeul**, Viscount of Narbonne md **Raimonde**.

34. **Francon II** (218-38) Viscount of Narbonne, md**Arsinde de Rosillon**, dau of **Suniario II**, Count of Rosellon and Ampurias.

Sources Latour, P. 1997:337-355; Strasser, T. 1993:489-507.

## LINE 219

40. **Nikephoros Phokas**, an Armenian nobleman of Cappadocia; Constantinople.

39. **Bardas Phokas**, Caesar at Constantinople; b. c880; d. 969; md before 912, **N.N. Maleine**, dau of **Eudokios Maleinos**, liv 900.

38. **Leo Phokas**, Prefect of Cappadocia, Great Admiral and Curopalates; d. 976.

37. **Sophia Phokas**, b. c936; md c950, **Konstantin Skleros** (322-37), Patrician at Constantinople; b. c920; d. after 980.

Sources: Blass, R. 1939, II:264; Brook, L. 1981 (Gen. 37–40); Paul, J. 1914; Isenburg, W. 1953; Moriarty, G. 1985, 89 (Gen. 37–40); Vanislev, A. 1951, 6:234–246; Winkhaus, E. 1953.

## LINE 221

37. **Ursus of Denmark.**

36. **Shrotlingus of Denmark.**

35. **Ulfius of Denmark.**

34. **Biorn Ulfiusson** a Dane, Jarl of Denmark; b. c975, Denmark.

33. **Siward Biornsson** (called Digera), Earl of Northumbria, Northampton and Huntingdon; came to England with the Danish invaders; b. c1020, Denmark; d. 1055, York, England; md **Aelflaed II of Northumberland** (314-33).

32. **Waltheof II**, Earl of Huntingdon, Northampton and Northumberland, 1065; b. 1045; beheaded 31 May 1076, Winchester, Hampshire, England; md 1070, **Judith of Lens** (77-32, 131-30).

31. **Matilda** (Maud) **of Huntingdon**; Queen of Scotland; d. 1130/1131; md (2) 1113/1114, **David I** (72-30), King of Scotland; b. c1080; d. 24 May 1153, Carlisle, Cumberland; bur at Scone, Perths. Scotland; md (1) 1089, Simon de St. Liz (Senlis), Earl of Huntingdon and Northampton; a Crusader, d. 1111.

Sources: Cokayne, G. 1959, XI:479; Dooghe, D. 1985; Dunbar, A. 1906,

59; Moriarty, G. 1985, 183 (Gen. 31-34); Paul, J. 1914, I:1; Prawler 1970, 152, 209, 237, 263+, 299; Round, J. 1971 ,147–180; Vanderkindere, L. 1902, 333+.

## LINE 222

35. **Richard I** "the Fearless" (89-33), Duke of Normandy, md **Gunnora de Crepon** (89-33,156-32,166-33,176-33).
34. **William**, Count of Eu and Exemes, d. 26 Jan 1057/8; md **Lesceline de Turqueville**; d. a nun, 1057/1058; bur Abbey of St. Pierre-sur-Dives; dau of **Turketil**, Seigneur de Turqueville; b. c960; d. after 1024; md **Anceline de Montfort-sur-Risle**, dau of **Hugh II**, Sire de Montfort. Turketil's father was **Torf of Normandy**, Seigneur de Turqueville.
33. **William d'Eu**, Count of Exemes, Soissons, Eu and Troyes; rebelled and was deprived; went to France; d. after 1076; md 1058, **Aelis** (188-33).

Sources: Altschul, M. 1965, 18; Blass, R. 1939,II:241, 245, 255; Depoin, J.1912, vols. I, II; Douglas, R. 1946, 65; ES, VII 1979:15 (Gen. 33–35); Estournet, G. 1926; Monteforte, A. 1962; Moriarty, G. 1985, 267 (Gen. 33–35).

## LINE 223

44. **Jimeno.**
43. **Garcia Jiminez.**
42. **Jimeno Garcia.**
41. **Garcia II Jiminez** (Inigo Arista), King of Navarre (Pamplona), c880; b. c845; liv 890; md (1) 860, **Oneca Rebelle de Sanguesa** (see 292-40); md (2) 884, **Dadildis de Pallars** (mother of Gen. 40); dau **Lope I** (286-39), Count of Bigorre.
40. **Sancho I Garces** (285-36), "Optimo Imperator," King of Navarre (Pamplona), 905-925; b. c865; d. 11 Dec 925; md (1) Urraca Galindez, dau of Aznar II Galindez; md (2) **Toda** (Tota) **Aznarez de Larron** (293-40) (mother of Gen. 39.
39. **Garcia III Sanchez** (55-38), King of Navarre, 931–970; Count of Aragon; b. 913; d. 970; bur St. Mary of Pamplona; md (1) 920, **Andregota Sanchez** (Endragot Galindez) (292-39), heiress of Aragon.
38. **Sancho II Abarca**, King of Navarre (Pamplona), 970–994, and Count of Aragon; b. after 935; d. Dec 994; bur Monastery of St. John de la Pena; md 962, **Urraca Fernandez** (mother of Gen. 37); b. 935; d. after 1007; md (her 2nd) **Teresa of Leon**, dau of **Ramiro II** (276-36), King of Leon, and **Adosinda Gutierrez** (20-36); Urraca's parents were **Fernan** (Fernando) **Gonzalez** (285-36), Count of Castile; and (2) **Urraca Garces**, dau of **Garcia Sanchez I**, King of Navarre (Pamplona) and niece of Garcia Sanchez' first wife.
37. **Garcia IV Sanchez** (180-32), King of Navarre, 994–999; b. c964; d. before 8 Dec 999; bur Monastery of St. John de la Pena; md before

981, **Ximena** (Jimena, Chimene) **Fernandez** (267-37).

36. **Sancho Garcia III** (95-33,151-33,248-33) "the Great," King of Navarre (Pamplona), 999; Count of Aragon, 1030; and Castile, 1026; b. 990/992; murdered at Bureba 18 Oct 1035; bur St. Salvador of Ona; md **Munia Mayor** (285-33), Co-heir of Castile; (md) also **Sancha de Aybar** (95-33), a concubine, Dame and heiress of Aybar.

Sources: Bard, W. 1969; Bayne, W. 1969 (Gen. 36–40, but is incorrect for Gen. 41); Bayne, W. 1970; ES, II 1984:53–55 (Gen. 36–44); Mateos, R. 1984; Salazar, J. de 1984; Salazar, J. 1983, 322–323; Stimmel, R. 1976 (Gen. 36–40); Urbal, J. 1950; Vajay, S. de 1962e; Vajay, S. de 1966 (Gen. 36–40).

## LINE 224

42. **Eticho I** (same as 202-45), Duke of Alsace; head of the House of Eticonides, d. 20 Feb 690; md **Berswinde of France**, dau of **Siegbert III** (303-46), King of Austrasia.

41. **Adalbert**, Duke of Alsace, d. 722; md **Gerlinde**.

40. **Luitfride I**, Duke of Alsace, d. 767, md **Edith**.

39. **Luitfride II**, Count of Upper Alsace, d. 802; md **Hiltrude**.

38. **Hugh** "le Méfiant" (167-41, etc.), Count of Tours; d. 20 Oct 837; md **Aba** (Bava);d. 4 Sept 839.

37. **Adelaide of Alsace and Tours**, md c864, **Rutpert IV** (169-38), Count of Paris, Tours and Wormsgau. Adelaide was widow of Conrad I, Count of Aargau and Auxerre.

Sources: Dollinger, P. 1991; Minguez, F. 1945; Moriarty, G. 1985; Putnam, R. 1971; Saez, E. 1946; Saez, E. 1948; Taberner, E. 1961; Urbal, J. 1945; Vajay, S. de, 1948; Vajay S. de 1964.

## LINE 224A

37. **Gutierre Menendez** md St. **Ilduara Eriz** (same as 277-36).

36. **Froila Gutierrez** d. 934; md **Sarracina**.

35. **N.N.** md **N.N.**

34. **Tutadomna**, d. c1022; md **Menendo Gonzales** (277-34), Count of Gallicia.

Source: Saly, E. 1946.

## LINE 225

35. **Ladislas I** (also called Basil and Vasul) (51-34), King of Poland.

34. **Andrew I**, King of Hungary, 1045–1060; slain 1060, at Winsselburg; md c1039, **Anastasia**, dau of **Jaroslav I** (143-31), Grand Prince of Kiev, and **Ingegerd** (240-32), Princess of Sweden.

33. **Adelaide**, Princess of Hungary; b. c1038/40; d. 27 Jan 1062; md 1056/1058, **Wratislaw II** (362-33), King of Hungary and Bohemia.

Sources: Blass, R. 1939, II:262, 265, 292; Csuday, E. 1899; Eckhart,

F. 1928, vol. I; ES, I 1984:54 (Gen. 33–34); II 1984:153 (Gen. 35); Hofmeister, A 1920, 33; Isenburg, W. 1953; Moriarty, G. 1985 (Gen. 33–35); Von Redlich, M. 1942.

## LINE 226

39. **N.N. of Agde**, liv 897; md **Arsinde**, liv 897.

38. **Boso**, Vicomte of Beziers, liv 921; md **Adelheid of Beziers**, liv 924; dau of **Reinold I**, Viscount of Beziers, who md **Dida**.

37. **N.N. of Agde**.

36. **Reinold II**, Viscount of Beziers, liv 969.

35. **William de Agde**, Viscount of Beziers and Agde, liv 969–1013; md **Arsinde**.

34. **Senegunde de Beziers**, liv 990/1013; md **Richard I** (402-34), Vicomte de Milhaud, 1002/1023.

33. **Richard II**, Vicomte de Gievaudun and Milhaud, 1049; d. 1049/1051; md **Rixinde** (218-33), Dame de Lodeve and Montbrun, 1061/1079.

32. **Berenger II**, Vicomte de Gievaudun, Milhaud, Carlat, and Rodene; liv 1051; d. after 12 Apr 1080, md before 1050, **Adele** (257-32), heiress of the vicounts of Carlat and Lodeve.

Sources: Arrieres, J. 1921, XXI:490–504; ES, III 1989:805 (Gen. 32–34); Ourliac, P. 1985, nos. 32, 55, 68; Turton, W. 1984, 218 (Gen. 32–35).

## LINE 227

38. **Sancho I Garces** (223-40), King of Navarre, 905–925; (md) a handmaiden.

37. **Lope Sanchez of Navarre**, md **Dato II**, Count of Bigorre, c910/940; son of **Lope I** (286-39), Count of Bigorre, and a dau of **Raimonde I** (329-38), Count of Toulouse.

36. **Raimonde I Dato**, Count of Bigorre, founder of the monastery of St. Savin; liv 940-956; md **Garsenda of Astarac** (216-35).

35. **Arnold I**, Count of Bigorre.

34. **Garcia Arnaldo**, Count of Bigorre, md **Ricar d' Astarac**, dau Guillermo I, Count of Astarac. *NOTE: Moriarty, G. 1985 skips Gen. 34.*

33. **Gersende** (95-32,105-32), heiress of Bigorre, d. after 1038; md **Bernard Rodger**, Count of Conserans, Carcassonne, and Bigorre; son of **Roger I de Comminges** (151-32,291-35), Count of Carcassonne, and **Adelaide de Rouergue**.

Sources: Bard, R. 1982; ES, III 1984:119 (Gen. 33-38); Isenburg, W. 1953; Lacarra, J. 1945, I 210, table at 285; Mateo; Moriarty, G. 1985, 80 (Gen. 33-38); Salazar, J. de 1984; Winkhaus, E. 1953.

## LINE 228

33. **Siegfried von Sponheim**, Count of Sponheim, of Levanthal in the

Pusterthal, and of Carinthia zu Sonnesburg; b. Sponheim, in the Rhineland; d. 5 July 1065, Bulgaria, on his return from a pilgrimage to Jerusalem (Crusader?); md before 1023, **Richgard von Lavant** (129-33), heiress of the countship of Lavant.

32. **Engelbert I von Sponheim**, Count of Sponheim, in the Lavanthal, in the Kraichgau, of Treveso (in Italy) and Ortenburg; advocate of Salzburg; liv 1060; d. 1 Apr 1096; md **Hedwig of Flinsbach** (388-33); b. c1040; d. after 1100; dau of **Bernhard von Flinsbach and Cecilia**.

31. **Engelbert II von Sponheim**, Governor of St. Paul, Duke of Carinthia, Count of Ortenburg, Margrave of Istria and Lord of Marquardstein; d. 1141, a monk at Sean; md **Uta von Passau** (Utha de Sulzbach) (128-31) (mother of Gen. 30); dau of Count **Ulrich** and **Adelaide von Frantenhausen and Lechsgemund**. Englebert II also md Edith of Carinthia. *NOTE: Uta von Passau's parentage has long been debated. Moriarty, G. 1985 (p. 120) gives earlier views. The current thinking [ES IV 1981:118] supports the line given here.*

30. **Mathilda von Sponheim** (Maud of Carinthia); d. 13 Dec 1160/ 1161, Fontevrault; md 1123, **Theobald IV** (60-29,81-29, 133-30), Count of Blois and Champagne, d. 8/10 Jan 1152.

Sources: Blass, R. 1939, R. 1939, II:247, 272; Brandenburg, E. 1935; Dungern, O. von 1935 ; ES, IV 1981:118 (Gen. 30–33); Isenburg, W. 1953, (1953), pt. ii, table 182; Jaksch, vol. 4; Moller, W. 1950; Moriarty, G. 1985, 119–120 (Gen. 30–34); Winkhaus, E. 1953.

## LINE 229

36. **Markwart II von Eppenstein** (117-37).

35. **Markwart III von Eppenstein**, Lord of Eppenstein, Count in the Ufgau and Margrave of Upper Carinthia; b. after 930, d. c995/1000; md **Hademut**, dau of **Adalbero I** (130-36), Count of Carinthia.

34. **Adalbero**, Margrave of Carinthia, 1000; expelled 1036; exiled at Ebersburg; d. 25 Nov 1039, in the monastery of Grisenfeld; md **Beatrice,** dau **Hermann II** (199-35), Duke of Swabia,who d. 4 May 1003.

33. **Wilibirg of Eppenstein**, d. 1075, Rome; md **Ottokar VI** (12-33), Count in the Chiemgau.

Sources: Blass, R. 1939, II: tables, 247, 274; Brandenburg, E. 1935; Isenburg, W. 1953, table 181; Moriarty, G. 1985 122–123 (Gen. 33–36); 201 (Gen. 33–34).

## LINE 230

36. **Louis IV** "d'Outremer" (171-36), King of France; md **Gerberge of Saxony** (92-35).

35. **Matilda of France**, Princess of France; b. c943; d. 26/27 Jan 981/ 92; md after 964, **Conrad I** "the Peaceful" (175-34), King of Burgundy.

34. **Bertha**, Princess of Burgundy, d. c1016; md **Odo I** (Eudes) (133-

34), Count of Blois.

Sources: Brandenburg, E. 1935; Cokayne, G. 1959, IX:805; ES, II 1984:46 (Gen. 34–35); Moriarty, G. 1985, 34–35 (Gen. 34–36); Winkhaus, E. 1953 85, 95.

## LINE 231

41. **Charlemagne** (171-41) md **Hildegarde** (262-41).

40. **Pippin**, King of Lombardy, 781; b. Apr 773, Aachen, Rhineland, Prussia; d. 8 July 810, md **Chrothais** (mother of Gen. 39); md also, **Gondres or Therese** (114-40).

39. **Bernard**, King of Italy, 813–817; b. c797; d. 17 Apr 818, Milan, Italy; bur Milan; md **Cunigunde** (Kunigunde), d. 15 June 835.

38. **Pippin of Peronne**, France; Count of Senlis, Peronne, St. Quentin and Vermandois, Prince of Italy, b. 817/818; d. after 840.

37. **Herbert I**, Count of Vermandois and Soissons, Seigneur de Senlis, Peronne and St. Quentin; b. c840; murdered 900/908; md prob **Liegardis**.

36. **Herbert II** (188-38, 235-36, 239-35,258-36), Count of Vermandois, Troyes, Meaux and Soissons; b.887; d. 943, St. Quentin; md before 907, **Hildebrante** (Adela, Liegarde) **of Neustria** (169-36, 188-38).

35. **Luitgarde de Vermandois**, widow of William Longespe, b. 915/920; md (2) **Thibaud** (Theobald) **II** "le Tricheur" (133-35, 340-35), Count of Blois.

Sources: Chaume, M. 1977; Cokayne, G. 1959; ES, III 1980:49 (Gen. 36–41); Jackman, D. 1997;Jessee, W. 1990; Moriarty, G. 1945; Moriarty, G. 1955; Moriarty, G. 1985, 5–6 (Gen. 35–41); Saillot, J. 1980, 45 (Gen. 35–37); Settipani, C. 1993; Settipani, C. 1994; Stone, D. 1995; Thatcher, O. 1897; Von Redlich, M. 1941 , 120–121; Willoughby, D. 1991a; 1991b; Winter, H. 1987.

## LINE 232

34. **Robert II** (134-33), King of France, md (2) **Constance of Arles** (333-34).

33. **Hawise**, Princess of France; b. c1003; d. 8 Jan 1078/79; md **Renaud I** (255-33), Count of Nevers and Auxerre.

32. **William I**, Count of Nevers, Auxerre and Turenne; b. c1030; d. 20 June 1100, Nevers; bur Saint-Étienne, Nevers; md (1) 1045, **Ermengarde** (254-32), heiress of Tonnerre.

31. **Renaud II de Nevers**, Count of Nevers and Auxerre; b. c1046; d. 5 Aug 1089; md (1) **Ida Raimonde de Lyon** (317-31), heiress of the countship of la Forez.

30. **Ermengarde de Nevers**, of Nevers, Nievre, France; b. c1073; md **Miles** (Milo) **de Courtenay** (144-30), Sire de Courtenay.

Sources: Brandenburg, E. 1935; ES, III 1989:717 (Gen. 30–31); III 1989:716 (Gen. 30–34); Garrigues, M. 1981, nos. 13, 50, 85; McKitterick,

R. 1983;  Mirot, L. 1945; Moriarty, 64–66 (Gen. 30–33); 24 (Gen. 33–34).

## LINE 233

77. **Noe**
76. **Sceaf**
75. **Bedwig**
74. **Hwala**
73. **Hathra**
72. **Itermon**
71. **Heremod**
70. **Sceldwa**
69. **Beaw**
68. **Taetwa**
67. **Geata**
66. **Godwulf**
65. **Finn**
64. **Froethelaf**
63. **Frithuwald** (Bor), b. c190; md **Beltsea**, of Asgard, Asia; or Eastern Europe; b. c194/215.
62. **Odin** (Woden), of Asgard, Asia; b. c215; md **Frigg** (Frigida). (mother of Gen. 61). (437-58).
61. **Beldig of Scandinavia**, b. c243; md **Nanna of Scandinavia**, b. c247; dau of **Gewar**, King of Norway.
60. **Brand of Scandinavia** (See also 406-60), b. c271.
59. **Frithogar**, of ancient Saxony; b. c299.
58. **Freawine**, of ancient Saxony; b. c327.
57. **Wig**, of ancient Saxony; b. c355.
56. **Gewis**, of ancient Saxony; b. c383.
55. **Elsa** (male), of ancient Saxony; b. c411.
54. **Elesa** (Elera) (male), of ancient Saxony; b. c439.
53. **Cerdic**, of ancient Saxony, King of West Saxons, 519–534; invaded Hampshire in 496; b. c467; d. 534.
*NOTE: Moriarty, G. 1985, (p.15) starts the line with Gen. 53 saying that it is reasonably clear. Schwennicke (ES, II 1984:76) does likewise.*
52. **Creoda**, Prince of Wessex; b. c493. *NOTE: Some authorities, including ES II 1984:77 and Stone, D. 1996 omit this generation.*
51. **Cynric**, King of West Saxons, 534–560; b. c525; d. 560.
50. **Ceawlin**, King of West Saxons, 560–593; and Bretwala (King of Kings) 560–572; b. c547; d. 593.
49. **Cuthwine**, Under-ruler of Wessex, b. c560; d. 584, Battle of Barbery Hill.
48. **Cutha** (or Cuthwulf), Under-ruler of Wessex, b. Wessex.
47. **Ceolwald,** Under-ruler of Wessex, b. c622, Wessex; liv 688.
46. **Cenred**, Under-ruler of Somerset; occ. 644, Wessex; liv 694.

45. **Ingild,** b. c680, Wessex
44. **Eoppa,** of Wessex.
43. **Eafa,** b. c732, Wessex.
42. **Eahlmund,** King of Kent, 784–786; b. c758, Wessex; md **N.N.**, a dau of **Aethelbert II** (233A-42) King of Kent, 725-762.
41. **Egbert** "the Great," Under-King of Kent, 784–786; King of Wessex, 802; King of England, 827–836; b.775, Wessex; d. 4 Feb 839, Wessex; md **Redburga** (Raedburh); b. c788. *NOTE: The official male line for British royalty starts with Egbert (Gen. 41) and extends to Edward the Confessor; the female line extends to the present time.*
40. **Aethelwulf** (367-41), King of Wessex and Kent, King of England, 839–858; b. c806, Wessex; d. 13 Jan 858, England; He visited Rome in 839; md (1) **Osburh** (mother of Gen. 39 below); annulled 853; b. c810, Wessex; d. after 876; dau of **Oslac,** Royal Cup Bearer (Pincerna Regis) of England. He md (2) 1 Oct 856, **Judith** (250-38), Princess of France, dau of **Charles II** "the Bald" (171-39), Emperor of the West, King of West Franks, of Burgundy, and of Italy. Oslac is called "a descendent of **Wihtgar,** nephew of Cerdic" who ruled the Isle of Wight early in the 6th Century.
39. **Alfred** "the Great (235-37,238-39), King of England, 871–899; and Wessex; b. 849, Wantage, Berkshire, England; d. 26 Oct 899, England; md 868, **Ealhswith** (Alswitha) **of Mercia** (238-39); b. c852, Mercia, England; d. 904.
38. **Edward** "the Elder" (261-38,321-36,376-38), King of England, 901–924; King of Wessex; b. c869, Wessex; d. 26 May or Aug, Ferrington; md (2) Aelflaed, dau of Aethelhelm, Earldorman of Wiltshire, d.c919; md (3) Berkshire, England, **Eadgifu** (Edgiva) **of Kent** (mother of Gen. 37); b. c896, Kent; d. 25 Aug 968; dau **Sigehelm,** Earldorman of Kent (d. after 962). Edward was a Bretwala (King of Kings).
37. **Edmund I** "the Deed Doer," King of England, 940–946; b. c920; murdered by a robber, 26 May 946, Pucklechurch; md (1) **St. Alfgifu** (Elgiva) (mother of Gen. 36); d. 944; md (3) Helfthryth (Ethelfled) of Damerham, d. after 975; dau of Alfgar.
36. **Edgar** "the Peaceful," King of England, 959–975; b. 943, Wessex; d. 8 July 975; md (3) 965; **Elfrida,** b. 945, Devonshire; d. a nun, c1000; widow of Eathelwold, Earldorman of East Anglia; dau of **Ordgar,** Earldorman of Devonshire, and wife, **Wulfrith.**
35. **Aethelred** (Ethelred) **II,** "the Unready" (314-35) of Wessex, King of England, 979–1016; b. c968; d. 23 Apr 1016, London; md (1) **Aelfgifu** (Elgiva) (342-35).
34. **Edmund** "Ironside," of Wessex; chosen King of England, April, 1016; b. c989, Wessex; d. London; md (2) Aug 1015, **Ealdgyth,** of Northumbria (mother of Gen. 33 below); dau of **Morcar,** High Reeve of Northumbria and **Eadgyth** (22-34). Ealdgyth md (1) Siegferth, Earldorman and High Reeve of the Danes of the seven boroughs.

126

33. **Edward** "the Exile" (196-32), Prince of England; b. 1016, Wessex; d. c1057, London; exiled to Hungary; prob held lands in Berenger county, Hungary; md c1043, **Agatha von Braunschweig** (318-34), of West Friesland.

32. **St. Margaret of Scotland**, Queen of Scotland; b. c1045; d. 16 Nov 1093, Edinburgh Castle, Edinburgh, Scotland; md 1068/69, **Malcolm III Canmore** (72-31,165-31), King of Scotland, 1058–1093.

Sources: ASC (dates): 495, 519, 530, 534, 538, 552, 560, 568, 591, 593, 688, 715, 718, 722, 728, 784, 800, 823, 825, 827, 828, 836, 840, 853, 854, 871, 891, 894, 897, 901, 924, 925, 942, 946, 965, (Gen. 36–53); Brooke, C. 1969; Burke, B.1973 (Gen. 32–65); Clark, A. 1973 (Gen. 32–65); Copley, J. 1954; Cokayne, G. 1959, V:736 chart; VII:641–642 (Gen. 32–33); ES, II 1984:77–78 (Gen. 32–53); Kotzschke, R. 1929 (Gen. 34–35); Montague, P. 1986; Moriarty, G. 1985, 30–31 (Gen. 32–38); 15–16 (Gen. 38–54); Reed, T. 1947, chart 31; Smith, H. 1953 (Gen. 41–45).

## LINE 233A

53. **Whitgils** [a legendary figure; not a real person].

52. **Hengist**, King of Kent, 455-488; d. 488.

51. **Oesc**, King of Kent, 488-512.

50. **Octha**, King of Kent, 512-543; d. 543.

49. **Ermenric**, King of Kent, 543-560; d. 560.

48. **Aethelbert I**, King of Kent, 560-616, md **Bertis**, dau of **Cheribert** (233B-49), King of Paris.

47. **Eadbald**, King of Kent, 616-640; d. 664; md **Emma**, dau of **Clothaire II** (303-48), King of Neustria.

46. **Eorconbeorht**, King of Kent, 640-664; d. 664; md **Sexburga** (437-36).

45. **Egbert** (Ecbert), King of Kent, 664-673; d. 673.

44. **Wihtread**, King of Kent, 694-725; d. 725.

43. **Eadbert** (Eardwulf), King of Kent, 725-748; d. 748.

42. **Aethelbert II**, King of Kent, 725-762; d. 762. He was a king with his brothers, Eadburht I and Alric.

41. **N.N.** md **Eahlmund** (Edmund) (233-42), King of Kent, 784-78 Source: Britannia, 1997. [Also, see sources for Line 233].

## LINE 233B

50. **Clothaire I** (cont. 303-50), King of Franks; liv 501-561.

49. **Cheribert** (233A-48), King of Paris; liv 520-567.

48. **Bertha** md **Aethelbert I**, King of Kent (233A-48).

Sources: James, H. *Ancestry of Homer Beers James*; O'Hart: *Irish Pedigrees*, 5th edition, vol. I, p.42; Wagner, A. 1975

## LINE 234

36. **Galeran I,** of the House of the Vicounts of Chartres; Count of

Meulan; d. 11 Nov 985/987; md **Liegard**, Countess of Meulan and de Mantes; d. 12 Nov 990/991; widow of Raoul I (185-38), Count of Valois.

35. **Galeran II**, Count of Meulan.

34. **Hugh I**, Vicount, 990/991, then Count of Meulan, 998; d. after 25 Aug 1005; md **N.N. de Vexin** (185–34).

Sources: ES, III 1989:701A (Gen. 34–36); Houth, E. 1963, 499–543 (Gen. 34–36); Houth, E. 1981 (Gen. 34–36); Sanders, I. 1960, 72+ (Gen. 34–36).

## LINE 235

41. **Lideric**, Forester of Flanders, 792.

40. **Enguerrand** (Engleram), Count, c851.

39. **Odoacer**, Count, d. 864.

38. **Baldwin I** "Bras de Fer," Count of Flanders; d. 879, Arras; md 862, **Judith** (54-37,250-38), Princess of France, Queen of Wessex and England.

37. **Baldwin II** "the Bald" (141-37,247-38,400-38), Count and Marquis of Flanders; b. 863/865; d. 918; md 884, **Aelfthryth of Wessex**, Princess of England; b. c877, Wessex; d. 7 June 929; dau of **Alfred** "the Great" (233-39), King of England, and **Ealhswith of Mercia** (238-39).

36. **Arnulf** (Arnold) "the Old," Count of Flanders and Artois; b. 885/890; d. 27 Mar 964; md (2) 934, **Adela de Vermandois**, b. c915; d. 960; dau of **Herbert II** (169-35,188-38, 231-36, 239-35), Count of Vermandois, and **Hildebrande**, dau or sister of **Hugh**, the Great, of France

35. **Elstrude of Flanders** md **Sigefried**, Count of Guisnes.

34. **Adolphus**, Count of Guisnes, md **Mahaut** (Matildis), dau of **Baudouin** (Ernicule III), Count of Boulogne, and **Adelaide**.

33. **Raoul** (Rodelphus), Count of Guisnes, md **Rosela of St. Pol**; dau of **Hugh II** (184-31), Count of St. Pol who md **Helissende** (Elisenda) **de Ponthieu**, dau of **Enguerrand** (244-34), Count of Montreuil.

Sources: Blass, R. 1939, R. 1939, II:270, 272; Brandenburg, E. 1935; Crispin, M. 1969, 186–187; ES II 1984:5 (Gen. 35–38); Isenburg, W. 1953 (1953); Malmesbury, W. 1911, 121; Moriarty, G. 1985, 14 (Gen. 35–40); Rosch, S. 1977 (Gen. 35–38); Winkhaus, E. 1953.

## LINE 236

53. **Flavius Afranius Syagrius**, a Gallo-Roman Senator at Lyons; Consul, 381; Proconsul in Africa, Magister Officorum Praetorian, Prefect of the West.

52. **N.N.** md **N.N.**, "Clarrisima femina."

51 **Tonantius Ferreolus (I)**, Prefect of Gaul, 451/453, Gallo-Roman senator. Served in Rome at the trial of Arvandus, 469; md **Papianilla.**

50. **Tonantius Ferreolus (II)** "Vis Clarisimus,"507-511; a senator at Narbonne a Roman commander at the Battle of Chalons; at Rome in 469

and 475; md **Industria,** perhaps dau of **Omnatius, of Auvergne,** 468; whose father was perhaps **Agricola,** consul, occ 418,421; son of **Philagrius,** occ 361,362,382.

49. **Ferreolus,** senator in the Narbonne region, md **Dode,** Abbess of St. Pierre de Rheims; dau of **Cloderic,** King of Cologne, 508-509 (171-50).

48. **Ansbertus** (171-46), a Gallo-Roman Senator of Narbonne; prob md **Blithilda** (Bilhildis),

47. **Erchenaud.**

46. **Leutharius** md **Gerberge,** dau of Duke **Ricomer** of the old royal Burgundian House.

45. **N.N.** (fem.) md **Ansaud.**

44. **Sigrada** (Sigree) md **N.N.**( perhaps Bodilon) ( 2-46).

Sources: Blass, R. 1939, R. 1939, 313; Chaume, M. 1977, I 242, 546, 547, 754, 772; Kelley, D. 1947 (Gen. 48–52); Moriarty, G. 1985, 7, 8 (Gen. 44–52); Moriarty, G. 1985.Cokayne, G. 1959 (chart); Stone, D.1995, chart 50; (Gen. 48-53); Winkhaus, E. 1953.

## LINE 237

37. **Otto I** "the Great" (321-36), Emperor of the West; md **St. Adelaide of Burgundy** (323-34).

36. **Otto II,** Emperor of the West, 973–983; King of Italy, 973; b. 955; d. 7 Dec 983; md (2) 14 Apr 972, Rome, **Theophano Skleros** of Byzantium (322-36); b. 956; d. 15 Sept 991.

35. **Matilda of Saxony** (379-34), b. 981; d. 4 Nov 1025, Esch, Sauer; md **Ezzo** (208-35), Count Palatine of Lorraine.

34. **Richenza** (Rixa) **of Pfalz-Lorraine,** b. c1000; d. 21 Mar 1063, Saalfeld; bur at Cologne; md **Mieszko II** (75-34,363-33,378-34), King of Poland, 1026–1034. **Richenza** also md **Otto I von Northeim** (26-31).

Sources: Balzer, O 1971; Brandenburg, E. 1935 (Gen. 34–37); ES, II 1984:120 (34); I 1984:3 (35–37); Forssman, tables xviii–xix; JAMS, vol. II (1983); Moriarty, G. 1985, 86–87 (Gen. 34–37); Moriarty, G. 1985, G. 1945 (Gen. 34–37); Moriarty, G. 1985, G. 1947 (Gen. 34–37).

## LINE 238

40. **Eadburh** (Edburga) **of Mercia,** md **Aethelred Mucil,** Earldorman of Gainsborough.

39. **Ealhswith of Mercia,** Queen of England; b. c852, Mercia; d. 904, England; md **Alfred** "the Great" (233-39), King of England.

Sources: Brooke, C. 1969; ES, II 1984:78 (Gen. 39–40); Moriarty, G. 1985, 16 (Gen. 39–40); Paget, G. 1977 (Gen. 39-40).

## LINE 239

35. **Herbert II** (169-36,188-38, 231-36, 235-36), Count of Vermandois and Troyes md **Hildebrante of Neustria** (169-36), Princess of West

Franks.

34. **Albert I** "the Pious," Count of Vermandois and Troyes; b. c920; d. 8 Sept 987/88; md before 954, **Gerberge of Hainault and Lorraine** (207-36).

33. **Herbert III**, Count of Vermandois; b. c955; d. c1002; md (2) 997/1000, **Ermengarde** (256-34) heiress of Bar-sur-Seine, 992–1002; b. c970; d. after 1035; widow of Milo IV, Count of Tonnerre. Her father was **Renald**, Count of Bar-sur-Seine; d. c997/1018. Renald's father was **Raoul**, Count of Bar-sur-Seine; d. after 981.

32. **Otho** (Eudes, Otto), Count of Vermandois, 1010; b. c1000; d. 25 May 1045; md **Pavie**.

31. **Herbert IV** (248-37), Count of Vermandois, Vexin and Valois; b. c1032; d. c1080/1096; md **Adela de Valois** (Vexin) (268-32).

30. **Adelaide de Vermandois**, Countess of Vermandois and Valois; b. c1062; d. 1120/1124, Meulan, France; md **Hugh Magnus de Crepi** (4-30, 106-31,143-30), Duke of France and Burgundy, etc.

Sources: Brandenburg, E. 1935; Chaume, M. 1977, I 443n1, 549, 553; Cokayne, G. 1959, I:22; IV:670, 672–274; V:736; VII:520, 737; X: 351; ES III 1980:55 (Gen. 30–31); Moriarty, G. 1985, 134–135 (30–34); Von Redlich, M. 1941 , 120–121 (Gen. 30–35); Winkhaus, E. 1953.

## LINE 240

49. **Halfdan Frodasson,** of Denmark (Cont. with 324-50); b. c503, Denmark; md **Sigris**.

48. **Hroar Halfdansson**, b. c526, Denmark; md **Ogne**, b.c530, Northumberland; dau of **Norbril**, King of Northumbria.

47. **Valdar Hroarsson**, b. c547, Denmark; md **Hildis**, Princess of Vandals, d. c572. *NOTE: Some authorities give, as her father, Hilderic, King of Vandals, thus opening up the possibility of a royal Vandals line going back to Genseric, a Vandal who conquered much of Africa about 425–455 AD. This lineage may be sound but needs more work.*

46. **Harold Valdarsson**, b. c568, Jutland, Denmark.

45. **Halfdan Haroldsson**, King of Sweden; b. c590, Jutland, Denmark; md **Maolda**.

44. **Ivar Halfdansson**, ("wide fathom from Skane") Woden-born King of Uppsala in Sweden, by conquest; King of Lethra, c690; b. c612, Denmark.

43. **Aud Ivarsdotter**, of Am, Denmark; md (1) Rurick (143-39), King of Lethra; md (2) **Radbard** (143-39), (father of Gen. 42), King of Gardarike (Russia); b. c638.

42. **Randver Radbardsson**, of Denmark, slain in epic sea battle of Bravik, 770.

41. **Sigurd Randversson**, of Denmark, b. c710; d. 812; md **Alfhild Gandoldotter.**

40. **Ragnar Sigurdsson,** of Uppsala, Sweden; Danish King at Lethra said to have perished in a Northumbrian snake pit; b. c750; d. 845, England; md (2) **Aslang of Denmark,** b. c755, dau of **Sigurd** "Fofnersbane."

39. **Bjorn Ragnarsson,** Swedish King at Uppsala; led the great Viking raid around Spain into the Mediterranean, 859.

38. **Erik Bjornsson,** b. c814; Swedish King at Uppsala.

37. **Edmund Eriksson,** Swedish King at Birka; b. c832, Sweden.

36. **Erik Edmundsson,** Lord of Finland, Eastland and Kurland; and for a time, part of Norway, which he lost to Harold "the fair-haired;" King of the Swedes and Goths; b. c849; d. 906.

35. **Bjorn** (Bijorn) "a Haugi" (the Old), King at Uppsala; 900; b. 868; d. c956.

34. **Erik** "Segersall" (the Victorious), King of Sweden, c950; and Denmark, 957; b. c935, Sweden; d. Uppsala, Sweden; md **Sigrid** "Starrade" (the Proud) (mother of Gen. 33 below); b. c950; dau of **Skoglar-Toste**; she md (2) Svene Gobelbart "Turskagg," King of Denmark, who d. 3 Feb 1014.

33. **Olaf III** "Skotkonung," King of Sweden, a Christian; d. winter of 1021/22; md (2) **Astrid** (380-33) (mother of Gen. 32); md (1) Endia, dau of a Wendish magnate. *(Moriarty, G. 1985, p.54, says N.N. for mother of Gen. 32.)*

32. **Ingegerd** (363-34), Princess of Sweden; b. c1001; d. 10 Feb 1050, Kiev, Ukraine; md Feb 1019, **Jaroslav** (Yaroslav) I (143-31), Grand Prince of Kiev.

31. **Wsewolod I,** Prince of Perejaslaw, 1054; Grand Prince of Kiev, 1078; b. c1030; d. 13 Apr 1093; md (1) 1046, **Maria Monamacha** (115-31).

30. **Wladimir** (Vladimir) II "Monomachos," Prince of Smolensk, 1077; of Tschernigow, 1078; Grand Prince of Kiev, 1113; and Perejaslaw, 1094; b. 1053; d. 19 May 1125; bur at Kiev; md c1070, **Gytha of Wessex** (368-30), a bastard, Princess of England.

29. **Mystislaw I Harold** (Mstislav), Grand Prince of Kiev, 1125; Grand Prince of Novgorod, 1081; of Bjelgorod, 1117; b. 1076; d. 15 Apr 1132; md (1) 1095, Christine, dau of Inge I, King of Sweden; md (2) 1122, **Lyubawa**; d. 1168; dau of **Dimitri Zaviditsch,** Possadnik of Novgorod, and mother of Gen. 28.

28. **Euphrosyne Mstislawna,** of Kiev, Ukraine, Russia; b. 1130; d. 1175/76; md 1146, **Geza** (Gesa) II (51-29), King of Hungary.

Sources: Baumgarten, N. 1928, XXIV: 1-37; Blass, R. 1939, II:260, 264;   ES, II 1984: 114 (Gen. 32–35); Jacobus, D. 1933 (Gen. 28–32); Moncreiffe, I. 1982, chart 37, p.113 (Gen. 33–44); Moriarty, G. 1985, 144–145 (Gen. 28–31); 53–54 (Gen. 31–37); Sawyer, B. 1993.

# LINE 241

37. **Lisier,** Seigneur de Sceaux, in the Gatinais, 941;d.  a monk of Saint

Benoit-sur-Loire.

36. **Ansaud I** "le Riche;" Vicomte d'Auxerre, (md) **Raingarde de Dijon**, d. before 954; she was a concubine of Hugh le Grand; her parents were **Raoul**, Comte de Dijon, and **Raingarde** (d. 958).

35. **Ansaud II** "le Riche" of Paris, France; counselor of King Robert II; md **Reitrude**.

34. **Thibaud**, Grand Forester of King Robert II of France, Seigneur of Montlhery and Chevreuse; built the castle of Montlhery, 1015; b. c970; d. 1031.

33. **N.N.**, Dame de Montlhery and Chevreuse; md **Milon I de Monteleherico**, Seigneur de la Ferte-sur-Ourcy; liv 1034/1057.

32. **Gui I de Montlhery**, Seigneur de Montlhery and of Chevreuse, Lord of Chateaufort and Bray; founded the Abbey at Longpont; b. c1009; d. 1095, a monk at Longpont, where buried; md during the reign of Henry I (1031–1060), **Hodierne de Gometz** (5-32, 57-33), (Saint Hodierne) Dame de la Ferte; heiress and dau of **William I de Gometz**, Seigneur de Bures.

31. **Elizabeth** (or Isabel) **de Montlhery**, France; b. c1040, md after 1065, **Joscelin de Courtenay** (144-31), Sire de Courtenay and Château Renard; md also, **Gautier de St. Valery** (122-33); he md (1) c1060, Hildegarde of the Gatinais, b. c1032.

Sources: Bournazel, 32+, 46; Depoin, J.1909; J.1912, vol. I, II; ES, III 1989:624 (Gen. 31–33); III 1980:73 (Gen. 32–33); Moriarty, G. 1985, 63 (Gen. 31–32); 265–266 (Gen. 31–37); Moutie, 1960s; Settipani, C. 1994;Vivian, T. 243.

## LINE 242

39. **Baldwin II of Flanders**, liv 879-918; md Princess **Aelfthryth**, d. 7 June 929, dau of **Alfred** "the Great," King of England (235-37).

38. **Aethelwulf**, Count of Boulogne, 918-933.

37. **Ernicule**, Count of Boulogne, d. 972.

36. **Arnulf II**, Count of Boulogne; d. after 31 Jan 972.

35. **Baldwin III**, of Boulogne, Upper Lorraine, France, Count of Boulogne; b. c976; md **Aleida**, perhaps dau of **Arnulf**, Count of West Friesland and Ghent; d. 993; who md **Luitgarde of Luxemburg** (311-35).

34. **Eustace I** (58-34), Count of Boulogne, 1042; b. c1004; d. c1049; named in a charter of 1038 as Baron of Flanders; md **Matilda of Louvain** (77-34,121-34).

33. **Eustace** (Eustache) **II** "aux Gernons," Count of Boulogne and of Lens, 1054; prob a Companion of **William the Conqueror**; was present in the Norman army at Battle of Hastings, 14 Oct 1066; b. c1030, Boulogne, Lorraine, France; d. 1070/1080; md (1) 1036, **Goda**, d. 1049,

132

dau **Aethelred II** (233-35), King of England, and **Emma of Normandie;**
md (2) Dec 1057, **Ida of Bouillon** (St. Ida of Lorraine), ultimate heiress
of Bouillon (mother of Gen. 32); b. c1040, Bass, Lower Lorraine; d. 13
Aug 1113; dau of **Geoffrey** (Godfrey) **II** "the Bearded," Duke of Upper
Lorraine, 1044/1046, and Lower Lorraine, 1065-1069; Count of Verdun;
d. 24 Dec 1069. Eustace II also md **Dode** (Ida), granddau of **Gonzelon I**
(104-34,120-33), Margrave of Antwerp.

32. **Eustace III,** Count of Boulogne and of Lens; Crusader; went on
the 1st Crusade, 1125; b. c1058; d. a monk, after 1125; md 1102, **Mary,**
Princess of Scotland; d. 31 May 1116; bur Bermondsey Priory, London,
England; dau **Malcolm III Canmore** (72-31,165-31,233-32), King of Scotland, and **St. Margaret of Scotland** (233-32).

31. **Mathilda of Boulogne,** Queen of England, heiress of Boulogne; b.
c1105; d. 3 July 1151, monastery at Faversham; md, c1120, **Stephen of
Blois** (299-30), King of England, 1135–1154.

30. **Eustace IV,** Count of Boulogne, 1150; b. c1129; d. unmarried, 10
Aug 1153 (md) **N.N.,** an unknown mistress (mother of Gen. 29).

29. **Eustachie de Champagne** md (2) **Anselme Candavene** (184-29)
(father of Gen. 28 below), Count of St. Pol; d. 1174; Her 1st husband was
Geoffrey de Mandeville who d. 21 Oct 1166 w/o issue.

28. **Beatrice of St. Pol** (called Beatrice Candavane de St. Pol) (242-
28), b. c1160; liv 1204; md (3) **Jean** (John) **I** (148-28), Count of Ponthieu.

Sources: Agiles, R. 1968; Chibnall, M. 1991; Dooghe, D. 1985; ES, II
1984:46 (Gen. 28–32); ES II 1984:621 (Gen. 31–34); Foucher, 1971; Krey,
A. n.d.; Mayer, H. 1984, 10–91; Moriarty, G. 1985, 115–117 (Gen. 28–
31); Paul, J. 1914, I:1,2; Prawler, 1970, 209, 237, 263+, 299; Riley-Smith,
J. 1973, appendix A; Round, J. 1971, 147–18; Tanner, H. 1992; Thompe
son, K. 1997.

**LINE 243**

28. **Adelaide of Blois** (Alix de Blois-Champagne) (133-29) md **Louis
VII** (70-29), King of France.

27. **Alice of France,** Princess of France; b. c1170, France; d. after 18
July 1218; md 20 Aug 1195, **William II Talvas** (148-27), Count of
Ponthieu and Montreuil.

Sources: Brandenburg, E. 1935; ES, II 1984:11 (Gen. 27–28); Isenburg,
W. 1953 (1953); Montgomery, G. de 1948; Moriarty, G. 1985, 113, 116
(Gen. 27–28); Tourtier, C. de 1960, 102–134; Winkhaus, E. 1953.

**LINE 244**

44. **Charlemagne** (33A-40,171-41) md **Hildegarde** (262-41).

43. **Bertha of France,** b. 776; d. 826; md **Angilbert,** Benedictine Abbot of St. Riquier; d. 814.

42. **Nithard** "the Chronicler," d. 823.

41. **Heligaud**, Count, 831; d. c866.
40. **Herlouin**, d. c878; prob father of Gen. 39.
39. **Heligaud**, Count of Montreuil; liv 877–879.
38. **Herlouin**, Count of Ponthieu and Amiens; killed in battle, Normandy, 13 Aug 945; md (2) before 927, **N.N.** (mother of Gen. 37).
37. **Roger**, d. c957, prob father of Hugh (Gen. 36).
36. **Hugh**, d. 961.
35. **Hugh I de Montreuil**, Seigneur of Abbeville, advocate of St. Riquier, advocate of Ponthieu, 981; adherent of Hugh Capet (134-34); d. 4 July 1000; md c987; **Gisela**, Princess of France, who inherited Abbeville; dau of **Hugh Capet** (134-34), King of France, and **Adelaide of Poitou** (163-34). *NOTE: Moriarty, G. 1985, p.113, says the pedigree before Gen. 34 is unreliable. Though updated considerably from ES, III 1989:635 (there are still two breaks in the line: at Gen 41-40, and at Gen. 38-37. Of the sources for this line, only Turton includes Gen. 43-44.*
34. **Enguerrand** (Engelram) (244-34), Count of Poitou and Montreuil; advocate of St. Riquier, 1043; liv 1026; d. aged, c1045; md **Adele of Ghent,** dau of **Arnulf I** (311-35), Count of West Friesland and Ghent, who md **Luitgarde of Luxemburg** (316-35).
33. **Hugh II**, Count of Ponthieu and Montreuil; Seigneur of Abbeville; d. 20 Nov 1052; bur in St. Riquier; md **Bertha d'Aumale**, heiress of Aumale, dau of **Guenfroi**, Sire of Aumale.
32. **Guy I** (184-31), Count of Ponthieu and Montreuil; the captor of Harold; Crusader; went on 1st Crusade; Companion of William the Conqueror; d. 13 Oct 1101; md **Ada of Amiens,** d. Mar 1066.
31. **Agnes de Ponthieu**, heiress of Ponthieu and Montreuil; d. after 1103, Ponthieu, France; md before 9 Sept 1087, **Robert II de Belleme** (Montgomery) (see also 183-31), Earl of Shrewsbury; d. 8 May +1131.
30. **William I Talvas**, Count of Alencon, Montreuil and Ponthieu; b. c1090; d. 29 June 1172; md (his 2nd, her 2nd) c1115, **Alice of Burgundy** (148-30, 245-30).

*NOTE: Unlike most other authorities (for instance, Moriarty, G. 1985, 113), ES III 1989:635 inserts a generation between Gen. 32 and Gen. 33: Enguerrand II, Count of Montreuil; d. 25 Oct 1053; md Adelaide of Normandy, d. 1090; making Enguerrand II, then, the father of Guy I (Gen. 32), rather than his brother, as usually stated.*

Sources: Agiles, R. 1968; Brunel, C. 1930; Cokayne, G. 1959, I:351; IV:670, chart II; XI:277, 695–696 and notes; ES, II 1984:20 (Gen. 30); III 1989:635 (Gen. 31–41); Foucher, 1971; Krey, A. n.d.; Montgomery, G. de 1948; Moriarty, G. 1985, 113 (Gen. 30–35); Roux, G. 1966; Settipani, C. 1993; Tourtier, C. de 1960, 102–134; Turton, W. 1984, 13 (Gen. 31–44); Willoughby, R. 1991a; Winter, H. 1987.

33. **Robert III** (154-33), Prince of France; md **Helie de Semur** (Eleanor of Semur-en-Auxois) (85-31,154-33).

32. **Henry**, Duke of Burgundy; b. c1035; d. 27 Jan 1070/74; md **Sibylle of Barcelona**, b. c1035; d. 6 July 1074; bur Église St. Étienne, Besancon; dau **Raymond Berenger I** (54-33) and (3) **Gisela of Lluca** (85-30).

31. **Eudes I Borel** (377-31), Duke of Burgundy; Crusader; founded the Abbey at Citeaux, where he was buried; b. c1060; d. 23 Mar 1103, Tarsus in Asia Minor, on the 1st Crusade; md 1080, **Sibylle** (Mathilda) **of Burgundy**; b. c1065; d. after 1103; dau of **William II** (94-31,148-30), Count of Burgundy and Mâcon, and **Stephanie of Longwy**, dau of **Adalbert III** (105-32), Count of Longwy.

30. **Alice** (Helie, Ela) **of Burgundy**, b. Nov 1080; d. 28 Feb 1142; widow of Bertrand, Count of Toulouse; md (2) c1115, **William I Talvas** (William Talvas Comet) (148-30, 244-30), Count of Alencon, Ponthieu and Montreuil.

Sources: Agiles, R. 1968; Behr, K. 1854; Blass, R. 1939, R. 1939, II:242, 253; Brandenburg, E. 1935; Courty; Vajay, S. de 1960a; Dussieux; ES II 1984:20 (Gen. 30–33); Foucher, 1971; Garnier; Glockner.A, 301+; Grote; Isenburg, W. 1953 (1953); Krey, A. n.d.; Moriarty, G. 1985, 114 (Gen. 30–31); 40, 83 (Gen. 32–33); Petit, E. 1894; Pinoteau, H. 1958b; Pinoteau.A; Settipani, C. 1993; Sirjean; Winkhaus, E. 1953 (1953).

33. **Hugh V** (33-34), Count in the Nordgau.

32. **Gerhard II**, Count in the Alsacian Nordgau, d. 1038; md **Berta**, niece of Rudolph, King of Burgundy.

31. **Gerhard III**, Count of Egisheim; d. 1075; md **Petronilla of Verdun** (also called Richarda).

30. **Heilwig von Egisheim** (Edith of Egisheim), d after 1118; md before 1092 **Gerhard I** (Gerard of Lorraine), Count of Vaudemont; b. 1057; d.. c1120; bur at Belval; son of **Gerhard IV** (158-32), Count of Alsace, and wife **Hedwig.**

29. **Gisela de Vaudemont**, b. c1090; d. before 1127; md c1108, **Renaud I** (36-29,149-29), Count of Bar-le-Duc; d. 24 June 1150.

Sources: Blass, R. 1939, R. 1939, II:269, 272; Burckhardt, A. 1915; ES, VI 1978:146 (Gen. 29–30); Isenburg, W. 1953, pt. ii, table 37; Jackman, D. 1990; Kruger, E. 1899; Moriarty, G. 1985, 194–195 (Gen. 29–32); Merz, W. 1914; Schopflin, G. 1761, II; Vanderkindere, L. 1902, II:153–154, 333–336, 424–425; Weiss, S. 1910; Winkhaus, E. 1953.

33. **Dietrich I** (319-35), Count of Bar-le-Duc and Duke of Upper Lorraine; md **Richilde** (337-35).

32. **Frederick II**, Count of Bar-le-Duc and Duke of Upper Lorraine; b. c995; d. 1026/7; md 1012/13, **Matilda of Swabia**; b. c998; d. 1043/1044; dau **Hermann II** (199-35), Duke of Swabia, and **Gerberga** (201-35), Princess of Upper Burgundy.

31. **Sophia**, heiress of Bar-le-Duc; b. 1025; d. end of 1092; md **Louis II** (149-31), Count of Bar, etc.

Sources: Blass, R. 1939, R. 1939, II:268, 269, 272; Brandenburg, E. 1935; ES, VI 1978:146 (Gen. 31–32); Merz, W. 1914; Moriarty, G. 1985, 160 (Gen. 31–33); Vanderkindere, L. 1902, II:153–154, 333–336, 424–425; Winkaus.

## LINE 248

33. **Sancho Garcia III** "the Great" (95-33,151-33,223-36), King of Navarre, Castile and Aragon, 1000–1035; md (2) **Munia Mayor** (285-33), Co-heir of Castile, Spain; d. after 13 July 1066.

32. **Fernando I** "the Great," King of Castile, 1035–1065; and Leon, 1037–1065; b. 1016/1018; d. 27 Dec 1065, Leon, Spain; bur St. Isidoro of Leon; md Nov/Dec 1032, **Sancha** (Sanchia) (276-32), heiress of Leon; b. 1013; d. 7 Nov 1067, Fromista; bur St. Martin of Fromista; dau of **Alfonso V** (276-33), King of Leon, and **Elvira Menendez** (Eloisa) (277-33).

31. **Alfonso VI** "the Brave," King of Leon, 1065–1072; King of Castile, 1072–1109; and Navarre; conquered Toledo, 1085; Madrid, 1085; Lisbon, 1093; b. June 1040; d. 29 June 1109, Toledo; bur Monastery of Sahegun; md (1) 1069, (div c1077), Agnes of Aquitaine, b. 1052; d. c7 June 1078; md (2) 8 May 1081, **Constance of Burgundy** (155-31) (mother of Gen. 30 below); md (3) 1093, Bertha of Burgundy, d. 19 May 1097/1098; md (4) **Isabel** (Zaida) (430-31), d. 12 Sept 1107, widow of Prince Al Mamun of Seville; dau of **Muhammad III**, (430-32), King of Seville  md (5) 1108, Beatrice of Aquitaine, dau of Count William VI (VIII); d. 1110.

*NOTE: The parentage of Isabel, 4th wife of Alfonso VI, has been of much concern. Now, with the discovery of her tomb in the Chapel Royal of San Isidio, with its inscription stating that she was the wife of Alfonso VI, the matter rests.*

30. **Urraca** (94-30,155-30), Infanta of Castile, Countess of Galicia, 1093; Queen of Galicia, Castile, Leon and Toledo, 1 July 1109; b. c1082; d. 8 Mar 1126, Saldana; bur Monastery of St. Isidoro, Leon; md (1) Toledo, c1095, **Raymond** (Ramon) **of Burgundy** (94-30); she md (2) Monzon Castle, near Carrion, early in Oct 1109 (marriage annulled 1115), Alfonso I, King of Aragon (by whom no issue).

Sources: Bard, R. 1982; Barrau, H. 1972; Cancellos, A. 1945, I:149–192; ES, II 1984:57 (Gen. 30–32); II 1984:55 (Gen. 32–33); Mateos, R. 1974; Miller, E. 1990; Minguey,E. 1945: 321-326; Pidal, R. 1969; Reilley, B. 1982; Salazar, J. de 1983 (Gen. 31-33; Salazar, J. 1984; Saez,.E. 1946;

Saez, E 1948; Sanchez, R. 1945; Taberner, E. 1961; Urbal.J. 1945; Urbal, J. 1950; Vajay, S de 1989.

## LINE 249

35. **Geoffrey** (Gausfred), Viscount of Chartres, 939.

34. **Geoffrey I**, Vicomte de Chateaudun, d. c986; md **Hildegardis**, d. 14 Apr 1023; sister of Gerberge who md Giilduin, Seigneur de Semur.

33. **Hugh I**, Vicomte de Chateaudun and Archbishop of Tours; d. before 989; md (2) **Hildegarde**, liv 1008, widow of Ernaud de la Forte. Hildegarde's parents were prob **Thibaud II** "le Tricheur" (340-35), Count of Blois, and **Liutgarde de Vermandois** (133-35, 231-35).

32. **Geoffrey II**, Vicomte de Chateaudun; Seigneur de Nogent-le-Rotrou; d. before 1005; md **Helvise** (Elizabeth), dau of **Fulk**, Count of Corbon (later called Montagne).

31. **Rotroc I**, Count of Montagne, Vicomte de Chateaudun, Seigneur de Nogent-le-Rotrou; occ 1005; md before 1041, **Adela** (Adelaide) **de Domfront**, dau of **Warin de Belleme** (de Domfront), Seigneur de Domfront, whose parents were **William I Talvas** "Fabour" (360-34), Seigneur de Belleme, and **Mathilda**.

30. **Geoffrey II** (178-30), Count of Perche and Montagne; He fought in the Norman army at the Battle of Hastings, 11 Oct 1066; an associate, if not a Companion of William the Conqueror; md **Beatrice de Montdidier** (266-30).

29. **Matilda** (Maud) **de Perche**, b. 1105; d. 28 May 1143; bur at Arnac; md c1122, **Raymond I** (156-29), Vicomte de Turenne.

Sources: Angot, A. 1942, 158–161; Crispin, M. 1969, 25; Debuisser, J. 1981, 11, 31–41; Keats-Rohan, K. 1997a; Longnon, J. 1978, 105+; Minguez, F. 1945; Moriarty, G. 1985, 48–49 (Gen. 29–34); Saez, E. 1946; Saez, E. 1948; Saillot, J. 1980; Settipani, C. 1997b; Taberner, E. 1961.

## LINE 250

39. **Charles II** "the Bald" (133-38, 171-39,346-37,367-43), King of France and Italy, Emperor of the West; md **Ermentrude of Orleans** (171-39), dau **Eudes** (Odo) (336-41), Count of Orleans, and **Engeltrude** (Ingeltrude), dau of **Leutaud**, Count of Paris, whose parents were **Begue** (269-41) and **Aupais**, dau of **Charlemagne** (171-41); he md, also, **Richeut** (Richildis) (346-37).

38. **Judith**, Princess of France, Queen of Wessex, Queen of England, Countess of Flanders; b. c844; d. after 870; md (3) 862, **Baldwin I** "Bras de Fer" (54-37,235-38,400-38), Count of Flanders; Judith md (his 2nd) **Aethelwulf** (233-40), King of England.

Sources: Blass, R. 1939, R. 1939, II:270, 312, 313; Crispin, M. 1969, 186–187; ES, II 1984:78 (Gen. 38–39); Moriarty, G. 1985, 16 (Gen. 38–39); Rosch, S. 1977; Settipani, C. 1993; Winkhaus, E. 1953; Willoughby,

R. 1991a; Winter, H. 1987.

## LINE 251

*NOTE: Some authors, for instance William and Mary Durning in* Guide to Irish Roots *(La Mesa CA, Irish Family Names Society, 1986), with no substantial verification, extend this line into antiquity.*

54. **Eochaid Mugnedon**, King of Ireland.

53. **Brion**, King of Ireland; half brother of Niall "of the nine hostages."

52. **Feldelm Foltchain** (Fedelmia), Queen of Scottish Dalriada, md **Domangart** (165-50), King of Scottish Dalriada, 499–504.

Sources: Anderson, A. 1990, I:268; Blass, R. 1939, II:257; Borrow, G. 1928; Greenham, J. 1994; Hubert, H. 1992; Mac Lysaght, E. 1985; Moriarty, G. 1985, 28 (Gen. 52–54) Pirie, C. 1959;O'Laughlin, M. 1995; Pirie, C. 1962; Weis, F. 1992, Line 170.

## LINE 252

36. **Duncan**, Thane of Dule, Earl of Strathclyde.

35. **Duncan**, Lord of the Isles and of Atholl, Thane of Dule.

34. **Crinan the Thane** (Albanock, Grimus), of the kin of St. Columba, Lord of the Isles, Governor of Scots Island, Earl of Strathclyde, hereditary Abbot of Dunkeld; b. 978, Scotland; slain 1045; md c1000, **Bethoc** (165-33), heiress and Princess of Scotland.

Sources: Anderson, A. 1990, I:268; Chadwick.E 1949; Cokayne, G. 1959, IV:504; IX:704; ES, II 1984:88 (Gen. 34–36); Paget, G. 1977, I; Pirie, C. 1959, I:4 II 1960:1, 2; Paul, J. 1914, III:239–245; IV:135–138.

## LINE 253

42. **N.N.**, perhaps of Scandinavian origin, md **N.N.**, sibling of Anastasios Martinakios, whose parents are unknown.

41. **Inger** (Martinakios?)

40. **Eudokia Ingerina**, b. c840; d. 882/883; md **Basil I** (322-40), Byzantine Emperor; mistress of **Michael III**, Byzantine Emperor (322A-40), one of whom was father of Gen. 39.

*NOTE: For many years there have been challenges to Leo VI's male parentage. Linsay L. Brook (in* Genealogist *2:6,Spring 1981), quoting Cyril Mango, argues that the Emperor Michael III (322A-40), whose mistress was Eudocia Ingerina, wife of Basil I (322B-40) was the father of Leo VI (Gen. 39). Christian Settipani (Settipani, C. 1991), airs the same view. Both sources, and others, too, say that the male parentage can not be satisfactorily resolved, but the weight of evidence leans toward Michael III. At this juncture, I accept the Michael III parentage.*

39. **Leo VI** "the Philosopher," King of Byzantium, Emperor of the East, 886–912; b. 1 Sept 866; d. 12 May 912; md 898, **Zoe Tzautzina** (mother of Gen. 38); d. Dec 899; dau of **Stylianos Tzautzes**; d. June/July 899; granddau

of **Tzautzes**, strategos of Macedonia, c813.

38. **Anna of Byzantium,** b. 889; d. 962, md **Louis III Beronides** (25-39), Emperor of the West.

Sources: Allen, J. 1985; Bierbrier, M. 1993; Brook, L. 1981; Collins, R. 1991; Hannawelt, E. 1982; Mango, C. 1973; Oxford, 1991; Psellus, M. 1982, 383 (appendix I); Settipani., C. 1991, chart, p. 17; Settipani, C. 1997; Stone, D. 1995, chart 40; Treadgold, W. 1988; Willoughby, R. 1991a; Willoughby, R. 1991b.

## LINE 254

39. **Milo I,** Count of Tonnerre; Cadet of the Milonides, counts of Langues; liv c850; md **Atila.**

38. **Milo II,** Count of Tonnerre; founded St. Michael Abbey in Tonnerre; liv c880.

37. **Gui I,** Count of Tonnerre, liv c930–970; md **Adela of Salins,** dau of **Humbert I** (189-35), Sire de Salins, and **Windelmode,** dau of **Gui,** Count of Escuens.

36. **Milo III,** Count of Tonnerre; became a monk in 980; d. 987; md **Engeltrude of Brienne;** dau of **Engelbert I** (383-34), Count of Brienne.

35. **Gui II,** Count of Tonnerre, like his father, became a monk; b. c920; d. by 993; md **Adela** (mother of Gen. 34).

34. **Milo IV** (383-30), Count of Tonnerre, 992/993; b. c950; d. before 998; md (her 1st) c975, **Ermengarde** (256-34), heiress of Bar-sur-Seine; d. after 1035; She also md (2) 997/1000, **Herbert III** (239-33), Count of Vermandois.

33. **Renaud,** Count of Tonnerre; Seigneur of Avisoy and Polisz; b. c980; d. 16 July 1039; md **Helvise** (Erviz), sister of Ardvin, Bishop of Noyen.

32. **Ermengarde,** Countess and heiress of Tonnerre; liv 1036–1089; d. after 1090; md **William I** (61-32,232-32), Count of Nevers and Auxerre.

Sources: Blass, R. 1939: II:247; Bur, M. 1977; Chaume, M. 1977, 441n1, 470–471; 538–539; Chaume, M. 1947a, 65; ES, III 1989:716 (Gen. 32–33); III 1989:730 (Gen. 32–38); Moriarty, G. 1985, 240 (Gen. 32–39).

## LINE 255

37. **Landeric** (Laundry) **I,** Seigneur de Maers; went from Poitou to Burgundy; md, before 868, **Hildegard.**

36. **Landeric** (Laundry) **II,** Seigneur de Maers; one of the chief knights of Richard "le Justiciar" (206-38), Duke of Burgundy; liv 880–922.

35. **Bovin** (Bodo), Seigneur de Maers and de Monceau-le-Comte; built the castle at Monceaux; liv 950.

34. **Landeric** (Laundry) **III,** Seigneur de Maers, Count of Nevers and Auxerre, Senechal of France; d. 11 May 1028; md 989, **Mathilda,** Princess of Burgundy (Ivrea); d. 13 Nov 1005; bur at Auxerre Saint-Étienne; dau of **Otto William** (94-33), Count of Mâcon and Burgundy; King of Lombardy; and **Ermentrude de Roucy** (161-33).

33. **Renaud I**, Count of Nevers and Auxerre; liv 1000; slain 29 May 1040, at Sauvigny le Bourgvinon; md 1006/20, **Adela** (Adelaide) (232-33), Princess of France.

Sources: Blass, R. 1939, R. 1939, II:247; Brandenburg, E. 1935; ES, III 1989:716 (Gen 33–37); Mirot, L. 1945 (Gen. 33–37); Moriarty, G. 1985, 64 (Gen. 33–37); Petit, E. 1894; Winkhaus, E. 1953.

## LINE 256

41. **Raoul**, Count of Ponthieu, d. 866; brother of the Empress Judith von Altdorf (171-40).

40. **Raoul of Laesoie**, occ 860–866; perhaps father of Gen. 39 below.

39. **N.N.** md **Renaud**, Viscount of Auxerre, Count of Bar-sur-Seine; seized the lands of Charouce, 896; occ 890–924.

38. **N.N.**

37. **N.N.**

36. **Raoul**, Count of Bar-sur-Seine; d. after 981.

35. **Renaud** (Renald), Count of Bar-sur-Seine; liv 993–997.

34. **Ermengarde** (239-33), heiress of Bar-sur-Seine; d. after 1035; md (1) **Milo IV** (254-34), Count of Tonnerre, etc., d. before 998; md (2) **Herbert III** (239-33), Count of Vermandois.

Sources: Blass, R. 1939, II:247; Chaume, M. 1977, I 441n1, 549, 553; Chevalier R. 1947, nos. 3589, 3781, 3818; Garrigues, M. 1981, nos. 13, 50, 85; n. 35–36); Waquet, J. 1950; Winkhaus, E. 1953.

## LINE 257

37. **Bernard I**, Vicomte de Carlat; liv 932.

36. **Gerhard**, Vicomte de Carlat; liv c950.

35. **Bernard II**, Vicomte de Carlat; liv c980.

34. **Gilbert** (Giselbert) I, Vicomte de Carlat in the time of King Robert (996–1031); md **Agnes of Mels**.

33. **Gilbert II**, Vicomte de Carlat; he and his wife gave the manse of Serq to St. Guillem de Desert, in the diocese of Lodeve, Oct 1048; d. before 1071; md about 1020, **Nobilia** (282-33), heiress of Lodeve.

32. **Adele**, heiress of the Viscounts of Carlat and Lodeve; md before 1050, **Berenger II** (226-32), Vicomte of Gievaudun, Milhaud, Carlat and Lodeve; d. after 12 Apr 1080. Berenger was present 29 Feb 1051, when Hugh de Roverge, Comte de Roverge, and Hugh's mother the Countess Richarde made a gift to Conquer Abbey. Berenger was named in a letter of Pope Gregory VII, dated 12 Apr 1080, complaining that he had refused the homage which he owed to the Abbey of Curillac. (Ref: Moriarty, G. 1985.P, p. 76.)

31. **Gilbert**, Vicount of Gievaudun, Carlat, and Milhaud; b. c1071; d. 1110/1113; md 1092/1098, **Gerberga** (298-31), heiress of Provence and Arles; b. c1055; d. between 3 Feb 1112 and Jan 1113. With his father Berenger II, and his brothers Richard and Raymond, was at the foundation of the Abbey of

Monts in Auvergne.

30. **Dulce di Gievaudun** (86-29), of Provence; heiress of Provence-Arles; b. c1095; d. 1127/1130; md 3 Feb 1112, **Raymond Berenger III** (54-30, 86-29), Count of Provence and Marquis of Barcelona.

Sources: Arriers, 1921:XXI:490–504; Barrou.A; ES, II1984:69 (Gen. 30–31); III1989:805 (Gen. 30–32); Laine, P la 1928; Moriarty, G. 1985, 75 (Gen. 30–37); Ourliac, P. 1985, nos. 32, 55, 68; Poree, C. 1919; Winkhaus, E. 1953.

## LINE 258

40. **Thierry I** "the Treasurer" (173-39), Chamberlain of Charles "the Bald."

39. **Thierry II**, Count of Chaunois, 880; d. before 893; md **N.N. of Metz,** dau of **Budwine** (206-39), Count of Metz, and **Richilde of Arles** (112-40).

38. **Manassas I**, Count of Chalons-sur-Saone, of Vergy, Auxonne, Dijon, and Beaune; d. before 31 Oct 920; md **Ermengarde,** Princess of Burgundy; d. 12 Apr 935; prob dau of **Boso,** King of Burgundy.

37. **Giselbert de Vergy**, of Burgundy, Count of Chalons and Vergy; Count and Duke of Burgundy; d. 16 Apr 956; md **Ermengarde,** prob dau of **Louis,** Count in Thurgau; d. after 929.

36. **Adelaide** (Adele, Wera), of Vergy, Troyes and Vermandois; d. 959/960; md before 950, **Robert de Vermandois**, Count of Troyes and Meaux; b. c922; d. 19/29 Aug 978; son of **Herbert II** (188-38,231-36,235-36,239-35), Count of Vermandois, and wife, **Hildebrante of Neustria** (169-36).

35. **Adele** (Adelaide), of Troyes and Vermandois; b. c950; d. after 16 Mar 975 and before 978; md **Geoffrey "Grisgonelle"** (167-35), Count of Anjou.

Sources: Blass, R. 1939, II:242, 251; Chaume, M. 1977, 421–423, 445, 447n2, 464n4, 473–474, 549; ES, III 1984:49 (Gen. 36–37); III 1985:433, 439 (Gen. 38–40); Moriarty, G. 1985, 4, 6, 10 (Gen. 35–37) 10 (Gen. 38–40); Moriarty, G. 1985, G. 1945b; Settipani, C. 1994; Vajay, S. de 1962; Winkhaus, E. 1953.

## LINE 259

40. **Louis I** (171-40, 172-42), King of France, 815-840; md **Ermengarde of Hesbaye** (351-41).

39. **Adele** (Adelaide), Princess of France, md **Robert I** (169-37), Count of Paris, Marquis of Neustria.

Sources: Irving, E. 1973; Moriarty, G. 1985, p.6 (Gen.39); p.9 (gen. 40; Rubincam, M. 1963.

## LINE 260

46. **Pippin of Landen** "the Old," Mayor of the Palace of Austrasia, 623; b. c585; d. 640; md **Iduberga** (Saint Itta); d. 652; dau of **Arnoldus**, Bishop of Metz, granddau of **Ansbertus** (236-48), the Senator, who md **Blithilda**, Princess of Cologne. *NOTE: While G. Andrews Moriarty in his* Plantagenet Ancestry... *(pp. 7, 8) records the ancestry of Iduberga (Saint Itta) as you see it*

141

*here, he says that the pedigree is "by no means thoroughly established." Research is in progress which may shed new light on this interesting personage. Detlev Schwennicke (ES, I: 2), 1984 research, does not accept the traditional lineage but suggests no alternative.*

45. **St. Begga** (St. Begue) **of Landen**, Liege, Belgium; b. c613; d. c698; md **Ansguise** (171-45,173-44), Duke or Mayor of the Palace of Siegbert, 632.

Sources: Anselme, A. 1890; Chaume, M. 1977, I:530–551; ES, I 1980:2 (Gen. 45–46); Kelley, D. 1947 (Gen. 45–46); Moriarty, G. 1985, 7, 8, 224 (Gen. 45–46); Moriarty, G. 1985, G. 1944.

## LINE 261

38. **Edward I** "the Elder" (233-38), King of England; md (2) **Aelflaed,** dau of **Aethelhelm** (376-39), Earldorman of Wiltshire, d.c 919.

37. **Edgiva** (Eadgifu), Princess of England; b. c904; d. after 951; md (3) 918, **Charles III** (171-37), King of France, 893–922; md also, Heribert, Count of Meaux and Troyes, d. 980/984.

Sources: Blass, R. 1939, II:257; ES, II 1984:78 (Gen. 37, 38); Fest, A. 1938; Moriarty, G. 1985, 30,31 (Gen. 37, 38); Moriarty, G. 1985, G. 1952; Searl, E. 1988; Von Redlich, M. 1942 , XXVIII:105-109.

## LINE 262

54. **Theodon I**, Duke of Bavaria.

53. **Theodon II**, Duke of Bavaria.

52. **Theodon**, Duke of Lower Bavaria.

51. **Theodebert**, Duke of Lower Bavaria.

50. **Garibald I**, Duke of Bavaria, d. 592; md **Waldrada** (380-49).

49. **Theudelinde**, d. 625; md (1) Authari, King of the Lombards; d. 590; md (2) **Agilolf** (father of Gen. 48), King of the Lombards; d. 616.

48. **Chrodaold** "Agilolingo" (nimble-tongued); d. 624; md **N.N.**, dau of **Gisulf**.

47. **Fara**, d. 611; inherited Bavaria from her grandmother.

46. **Theodo II**, Duke of Bavaria, d. 716; md **Regintrude**, bastard dau of **Dagobert I** ( 303-47), King of Austrasia, d. 639; and **Regintrude of Austrasia**.

45. **N.N.** md **Godefried** (Godfrey, Godefroy) (262A-45), Duke of Allemania; d. 708/709; held lands in Thurgau.

44. **Nebi-Huoching** (or Theutbold), Duke of Allemania; d. 727; md **Hersuinda**.

43. **Nebi** (Huabi) "Dux," Duke of Allemania, Count in the Linzgau, 709; d. 788.

42. **Emma** (Imma) **of Allemania**, d. 798; md **Gerold** (364-41), Count in the Vinzgau.

41. **Hildegarde** (244-44), Countess in Linzgau; b. 758; d. 30 Apr 783; md 771, **Charlemagne** (171-41).

Sources: Blass, R. 1939, R. 1939, II:313; Chaume, M. 1977, I:528, 537, 543, 550–551; ES, I 1984:2 (Gen. 41–42); Levillain, vol. 49 (1937); vol. 50 (1938); Moriarty, G. 1985, 8–9 (Gen. 41–45); Settipani, C. 1993; Vajay, S. de 1966a (Gen. 41-50); Voltaire, vol. 33; Willoughby, R. 1991a, b; Winkhaus, E. 1953.; Winter, H. 1987.

## LINE 262A

47. **Liuthaire II**, Duke of Allemania, 643; md **Appa** (Acca), dau of **Gisulf II**, Duke of Frioul.

46. **N.N.** (male) md **N.N.** (fem.), dau of **Willibald**, patrician of Burgundy, who was great-great grandson of **Godomer III**, King of the Burgundians.

45. **Godefried** (Godfrey,Godefroy), Duke of Allemania; d. 708/9; held lands in the Thurgau; md **N.N.** (262-45), dau of **Theodo II**, Duke of Bavaria.

Source: Settipani, C. 1989.

## LINE 263

40. **Lothar I** (25-42, 302-40), King of Italy, md **Ermengarde of Orleans**, d. 20 Mar 851; dau of **Hugh "le Méfiant"** (same as 29-40,167-41,224-37,300-40, 302-40), Count of Tours, and wife **Aba**.

39. **Lothar II** "the Saxon," King of Lorraine; b. 827; d. 8 Aug 869, Placenza; md (1) c855, Teutberga, dau of Boso, Count of Arles and Count in Italy; d. c855; md (2), 25 Dec 862, **Waldrada** (mother of Gen. 38 below), long his concubine, who d. a nun, after 868; she prob belonged to the Alsacian family of the Etichonides.

38. **Bertha**, Princess of Lorraine; b. 863; d. 8 Mar 925; bur Lucca; md (1) c879, **Theobald** (174-38), Count of Arles, (father of Gen. 37), d. by 895; she md (2) **Adalbert II** (31-38, 198-40), Margrave of Tuscany.

37. **Boso**, Count of Arles, Margrave of Tuscany (913–936); b. c885; d. 936/940; md **Willa of Tuscany**.

36. **Willa of Arles**, d. after 966, Bamberg; md 936, **Berenger II** (106-36,332-36), King of Italy.

Sources: Blass, R. 1939, R. 1939, II:275; Brandenburg, E. 1935; Chaume, M. 1977, I:224n1; Vajay, S. de 1966a; ES, II 1984:59 (Gen. 36–37); II 1984:186 (Gen. 37–39); Isenburg, W. 1953; Moriarty, G. 1985, 19–20 (Gen. 36–40); Saillot, J. 1980, 9; Winkhaus, E. 1953.

## LINE 264

41. **Begue** (269-41 etc.), Count of Paris, d. 816; md **Aupais,** dau of **Charlemagne** (171-41,231-41), and **Himiltrude**, a concubine.

40. **Lisiard**, Count of Fezensac.

39. **Gerard of Roussillon**, Count of Paris; d. 877; md **Bertha of Tours**, dau

of **Hugh** "le Méfiant" (167-41, 346-40, etc.), Count of Tours and Bourges; and wife **Aba**.

38. **Eve of Roussillon** md **Guerri I**, Count of Morvois.

37. **Beatrice of Morvois** md **Herbert I** (231-37), Count of Vermandois, b. c840; d. 900/908 (murdered).

36. **Beatrice de Vermandois** (134-36) md **Robert I** (169-37), King of West Franks.

Sources: McKiterick, R. 1983; Moriarty, G. 1985, 6, 21, 23, 37; Settipani, C. 1993; Willoughby, R. 1991a, b; Winter, H. 1987.

## LINE 265

44. **Lambert** (200-44, 330-42), Count and Lord of Hornbach, 760–c783.

43. **Gui** (Guido), Count on the Breton March; d. 814.

42. **Lambert I**, Count of Nantes, 818-834; went with the Emperor Lothar I to Italy, 834; d. 1Sept 836; md **N.N.**, perhaps one of the four daughters of Pepin, King of Italy, viz: Athalia, Gundrada, Bertha, or Theodrada.

41. **Gui** (Guido) **I**, Margrave of Spoleto, Lay Abbot of Lettlach; d. c858; md **Itta** (Itana), dau of Duke **Sico**.

40. **Gui** (Guido) **II**, Duke of Spoleto, 888; Count of Camerino; King of Italy, 891; d. 894; md **Angiltrude** and/or perhaps Judith (Itta).

39. **Rothilda** (Rohaut) **of Spoleto**; mentioned in a charter, 25 Apr 975; d. after 27 May 884 (perhaps 889); md before 863, **Adalbert I** (31-39,93-39), Count of Lucca, Margrave of Tuscany, d. 889 or 894.

Sources: Chaume, M. 1977, 535; Chaume, M. 1947a; 322; ES, II 1984:188b (Gen. 39–41); Levillain (1934) vol. 49; (1937) 50; Moriarty, G. 1985, 74 (Gen. 39–43); Rosch (Gen. 39–41); Winkhaus, E. 1953.

## LINE 266

34. **Helpuin**, Count of Arcis-sur-Aube, md **Hersinde**, Dame de Rameru, liv in 970.

33. **Hildouin** ( 397-32), Count of Montdidier; Seigneur de Rameru; made a pilgrimage to Jerusalem, 992; d. sometime after.

32. **Hildouin II**, Count of Montdidier; Seigneur de Rameru and Montdidier; occ 1033/1037; d. c1063.; md prob **N.N.** (Adelaise ?), dau of **Nocher I,** Count of Bar-le-Aube.

31. **Hildouin III** (66-34), Count of Montdidier and Roucy, 1031; Seigneur de Rameru, 1061; Count of Rameru, 1068; b. c1010; d. c1063; md 1031, **Alice** (Isabelle, Adelaide) **de Roucy** (170-31), heiress of Roucy.

30. **Beatrice de Montdidier**, d. after 2 Sept 1129; md **Geoffrey II** (178-30,249-30), Count of Perche and Mortagne.

Sources: Bur, M. 1977; ES, III 1989:676, 677 (Gen. 30–34); II 1984:58 (Gen. 31); III 1989:676, 677 (Gen. 30–34); Guerard, B., I:125; Moriarty, G. 1985, 49–50 (Gen. 30–32); 231 (Gen. 32–34); Newman, W. 1971; Saillot, J. 1980.

41. **Ordogno I** (76-39,276-39), King of the Asturias; b. 830; md **Nuna** (Munia), sister of Gaton, Count of Viero.

40. **Nunio Ordonez**, d. after 870.

39. **Vermudo Nunez**, b. c900; d. after 958; md **Velasquita Velasquez** (mother of Gen. 38); dau of **Vela Nunez**. *Salazar, J de 1983,, p.324, says wife was Countess Argilo, d. before 949.*

38. **Fernando Vermudez**, Count of Cea; b. c930; d. 978; md before 960, **Elvira Diaz of Saldana**; b. c930; d. after 975. Elvira was dau of **Diego Munoz**, Count of Saldana, d. 951; md c920 to wife **Tigrida**, d. after 940.

37. **Ximena** (Jimena, Chimene) **Fernandez**, b. c970; d. after 1035; md before 981, **Garcia IV Sanchez** (223-37), King of Navarre; b. 964; d. before 8 Dec 999.

Sources: Bard, R. 1982; Bayne, W. 1969; Bayne, W. 1970; Burke, B.1883; ES, II 1984:55 (Gen. 37–38); Isenburg, W. 1953; Mateos, R. 1984; Salazar, J. 1983, 322–324, 326 note 5; Salazar, J. 1984.

35. **Gautier II** "the White" (185-35), Count of Vexin, Valois and Amiens; advocate of St. Germain des Pres and Jumieges; b. c944, Vexin, Normandy; d. c1027; md **Adele de Senlis** (185-35); b. c944, Ile de France.

34. **Raoul II**, of Vexin, Normandy; Seigneur de Crepy and Valois, Count of Vexin; d. 1040; md **Adelaide de Breteuil** (mother of Gen. 33); b. 980; dau of **Hildouin**, Count of Breteuil, and Vicomte de Chartres; d. a monk, 18 May 1060; Raoul II also md Emeline de Chartres, dau of Foucher, Vicomte de Chartres.

33. **Raoul III** "the Great," Count of Valois, de Crepi, Vitry, Amiens and Vexin; b. 1025; d. 8 Sept 1074; bur at Crepy; md **Adele** (108-33), heiress of Bar-sur-Aube.

32. **Adele de Valois** (de Vexin), heiress of the countship of Valois; b. by 1043; md before 1068, **Herbert IV** (239-31), Count of Vermandois.

Sources: Anselme, A. 1890; Brandenburg, E. 1935; Bur, M. 1977 92; ES, III 1989:657 (Gen. 32–35); III: 1989:59 (Gen. 34); Grierson, P. 1939, 10:81–125; Moriarty, G. 1985, 135–136 (Gen. 32–35); Sanders, I. 1960, 20+, 85+; Von Redlich, M. 1941, 120–121.

44. **Charles Martel** (114-42,171-43), victor of Poitiers, md (1) **Chrotrude** (Rotrude).

43. **Carloman,** Mayor of the Palace in Austrasia, 741–747; d. 754, a monk, at Montecassino.

42. **Rotrou** md **Girard**, Count of Paris; liv 743–755.

41. **Begue** (185-40,250-39 etc.), Count of Paris, Chamberlain of Louis of Aquitaine; liv 776; d. 816; md **Aupais** (Alpis), dau of **Charlemagne** (171-

41).

40. **Engeltrude** (289-39) md **Hunroch** (Unruoch) (185-40), Margrave of Friuli and Count of Ternois; d. after 853; son of **Berenger**, an East Frank.

39. **Eberhard** (Everard) (272-40,345-38,389-37), Marquis of Friuli, d. 16 Dec 862; bur Cysoing; md 836, **Gisela** (185-40,389-39), Princess of France.

38. **Berenger I**, King of Italy, Jan. 888–924; Emperor of the West, Dec 915–924; Marquis of Friuli; b. c840/845; murdered 7 Apr 924, Verona, Italy; md (1) 880/890, **Bertila of Spoleto** (mother of Gen 37); d. after 915; dau of **Suppo II**, Margrave of Spoleto, in Perugia, Italy; Margrave of Camerino and Count of Turin, Italy; Ambassador to Constantinople; d. 882/888; also md Berta, dau of Count Wilfred, nun, 902; d. before 921. Suppo's father was **Maurin**, Pfalzgrave; a Salic Frank who held lands in Parma, Reggio, and Piacenza, 835–844.

37. **Gisela of Friuli**, Princess of Italy; b. 880/890; d. 13 June 910; md before 900, **Adalbert** (332-37), Margrave of Ivrea in Turin, Italy; d. 923/925.

Sources: ES, II 1984:188a (Gen. 37–40); I 1984:2 (Gen. 43–44); Fortunatus, V. 1954, Bk VII, nos. V and VI; James, E. 1988; Gregory of Tours, 1974; Kelley, D. 1947; Lasco, P. 1971; Moriarty, G. 1985, 18–19 (Gen. 37–39); 229 (Gen. 39–40); 22–23 (Gen. 41–42); 5 (Gen. 43–44); Settipani, C. 1991; Willoughby, R. 1991a, 1991b; Winter. H. 1987.

## LINE 270

38. **Luitpold**, Count of Carinthia, Margrave in Nordgau; kinsman of the Emperor Arnulf; slain 4 July 907 at Pressburg; md **Kunigunde,** dau of **Berthold**, Pfalzgrave of Swabia.

37. **Arnulf** "the Bad" (63-37,64-37,279-36), Duke of Bavaria; army leader in Bavaria; d. 14 July 937, Regensburg; md c910, **Judith of Friuli** (272-37).

36. **Berthold I von Babenberg**, Margrave of the Bavarian Nordgau, Rodensgau, and Volkfeld; b. c915; d. 15 Jan 980; md **Eiliswinta von Walbeck** (271-36), d. 19 July 1015; founder of the monastery of Schweinfurt.

35. **Henry von Schweinfurt** ( 7-34, 47-35,213-35,262-34,270-35,307-31), Margrave in the Nordgau; b. 975; d. 18 Sept 1017; md c1003, **Gerberge of Henneberg** (102-35).He also md **Bertrade** (204-32), Princess of Normandy.

34. **Elica von Schweinfurt**, d. after 1055; md **Bernard II** (312-34), Duke of Saxony, d. 1059; Bernard II also md **Bertrade** (204-32), Princess of Normandy.

Sources: Blass, R. 1939,II:283, 296; ES, I 1984:9 (Gen. 35–39); VIII 1980:134 (Gen. 36); III 1989:54 (Gen. 35); Isenburg, W. 1953, pt. i, tab 8, 15; Jackman, D. 1997; Moriarty, G. 1985, 57 (Gen. 34–38); Moritz, 3–35; Winkhaus, E. 1953.

## LINE 271

39. **Bruno I**, Count of Iverfort, possibly father of Gen. 38.

38. **Bruno**, Count of Arneburg and Iverfort; d. 19 Oct 1009/1017; md

Frederika of Ringleheim.

37. **Mathilda von Arneburg**, d. 3 Dec 990; md **Lothar II** (15-37), Count of Walbeck.

36. **Eiliswinta von Walbeck** (270-36), d. 19 July1015, at monastery of Schweinfurt, which she founded, and where she is buried; md **Berthold I von Babenberg** (270-36), Margrave of the Bavarian Nordgau, etc.

Sources: Blass, R. 1939, II:283, 290; Bude, G. 1900; Dungern, O. von 1910; ES, VIII 1980:134 (Gen. 36–37); Isenburg, W. 1932; Isenburg, W. 1953; Moriarty, G. 1985, 57 (Gen. 36–39); Raumer, G. 1871; Winkhaus, E. 1953.

## LINE 272

40. **Eberhard** (269-39,345-38), Marquis of Friuli, md **Gisela** (185-40), Princess of France and of the West.

39. **Hunroch** (Unroch) **III**, Margrave of Friuli; b. c840; d. 874; md **Ava**, dau of Duke **Liutfried**. I, whose parents were **Hugh** "le Mefiant" (224-38 etc.) and his wife, **Aba**.

38. **Eberhard**, Count in the Sulichgau.

37. **Judith of Friuli**, (279-36) md **Arnulf** "the Bad" (63-37,64-37,270-37), Duke of Bavaria.

Sources: Blass, R. 1939 II:270; Buhler, H. 1984; Chaume, I:463+, 539, Curschmann, F. 1921, 27; ES, I 1984:9 (Gen. 37–38); II 1984:188A (Gen. 39–40); Grierson, P. 1938; Isenburg, W. 1953; Moriarty, G. 1985, 18 (Gen. 37–40); Rosch, S. 1977 (Gen. 39–40); Winkhaus, E. 1953.

## LINE 273

36. **Anselm**, Count of Noyen (I), liv 966.

35. **Anselm**, Count of Noyen (II); md **Adelaide**, heiress of Ortigen.

34. **Auxilia** (171-31) md before 1020, **Humbert I** (173-34), Count of Aosta and Maurienne.

Sources: Chaume, M. 1940, 113–137; ES, III 1989:731; Hayward, F. 1941; Mantayer, 1899, XIX:363–539; Moriarty, G. 1985, 237 (Gen. 34–36); Vernet, A. 1956; Winkhaus, E. 1953, 110; Wollasch, J. 1959.

## LINE 274

35. **Fouchard**, Lord of Ham, md (1) Geila "the Venerable;" md (2) by 981, **Ivo** (mother of Gen. 34), in the retinue of Hugh Capet, 978.

34. **Ivo I of Ham** md by 981, **N.N.** (prob Gisela, sister of Milon de Chevreuse), prob Ivo was father of Gen. 33.

33. **Ivo II Bellomontensis**, known in 1029 at St. Leonor-de-Beaumont; d. c1036; prob father of Gen. 32.

32. **Ivo III Bellomontensis**, d. 22 May 1059, md **Emma** liv 1039.

31. **Ivo IV**, Count of Beaumont, known 1080 at Conflans-Saint-Honorine; d. c1083; md (1) Judith; md (2) **Adelaide de Gournay** (mother of Gen. 30); d. 8 Apr 1099, dau of **Hugh**.

30. **Agnes de Beaumont** d. after 1124; md **Bouchard III** (34-30), Seigneur de Montmorency.

Sources: Coucy, A de 1981; ES, III 1984:644 (Gen. 30–35); Leblond, V. 1910, 53+; Newman, W. 1971, 80–88.

**LINE 275**

39. **N.N. Phokas,** turmarch, liv c872; md **N.N.**
38. **Nikephoros Phokas,** called "the Old;" patrikos, domestikos ton scholon, c873; d. 896/7; md **N.N.**
37. **Bardas Phokas,** Caesar; patrikios, magistros, domestikos ton scholon; d.969; md before 912, **N.N. Maleine.**
36. **N.N. Phokaina** md N.N. (Theodoros ?) **Kourkouas** (370-36).
Source: Brook, L. 1981, 110, 176–179.

**LINE 276**

44. **Ervigio,** of Spain md **Liubigotona,** of Spain.
43. **Pedro,** Duke of Cantabria; Visigothic leader said to be descended from the kings of Toledo, Leovigildo and Ricaredo.
42. **Fruela of Bardalia,** Count of Bartulio, d. c765.
41. **Vermudo** (Bermudo) **I,** King of the Asturias, 788–791; d. 797; md **Ursinda Munilona.**
40. **Ramiro I** (same as 35-41), King of the Asturias; b. c790; d. 1 Feb 850; md **Paterna of Castile.**
39. **Ordogno I** (76-39, 267-41), King of the Asturias and Galicia, 850; b. c830; d. 27 May 866; bur at Orviedo; md **Nuna** (Munia), sister of Gaton, Count of Viero.
38. **Alfonso III** "the Great," King of the Asturias, 866; dismissed c905; b. 848; d. 20 Dec 910; md 869/870, **Jimena Garces** (76-38).
37. **Ordogno II,** King of Asturia, Galicia and Leon; b. c873; d. 3 Jan 924; md (1) **Nunja Elvira Menendez,** d. Sept/Oct 921; dau of **Hermengildo Gutierrez** (277-36), of Portugal, (d. c943) and **Hermesinde Gatonez** (21-38); dau of **Gaton,** Count of Viero who md **Egilona.**
36. **Ramiro II** (223-38), King of Leon, 931; conquered Madrid; b. c900; d. 1 Jan 951; bur at St. Salvador de Leon; md (1) 925, **Adosinda Gutierrez** (20-36).
35. **Ordogno III,** King of Leon, 951/955; captured Lisbon, 955; b. c926; d. 955, Zamora; bur St. Salvador de Leon; md 952 (2) **Aragonta** (Gontroda) **Pelaez,** dau of **Pelayo Gonzalez** (277-36) and **Hermesenda Gutierrez** (277-36).
34. **Vermudo** (Bermudo) **II** "the Gouty," King of Leon, 995/999; b. c953; d. Sept 999, Villabueno del Bierzo; bur at Carrac Edo; md (2) 26/30 Nov 991, **Elvira Garcia of Castile,** b. c970; d. after 1 Mar 1028; bur at St. Isidore de Leon; dau of **Garcia I Fernandez** (285-35), Count of Castile, and **Aba Ribagorza** (286-35).
33. **Alfonso V** (180-32), King of Castile and Leon, 999; Emperor of Spain;

148

b. 994; slain 7 Aug 1028, at Viseu; bur at St. Isidore de Leon; md (1) 1015, **Elvira Menendez** (277-33).

32. **Sancha** (Sanchia) (248-32), heiress of Leon; b. 1013; d. 13 Dec 1067; md **Fernando I** (248-32), King of Castile.

Sources: Barton, S. 1997; Blade, J. 1896, 23:312+; ES, II 1984:49–50 (Gen. 32–43); Glick, J. 1995; Mac Kay, A. 1977; Mateos, R. 1984; Moriarty, G. 1985, 82 (Gen. 32–43); O'Callaghan, J. 1983; Pidal, R. 1969; Pidal, R. 1931; Salazar, J. de 1984; Sanchez, R. 1930; Sanchez, R. 1945; Urbal, J. 1950; Winkhaus, E. 1953.

## LINE 277

37. **Menendo Gonzalez**, Count of Galicia, d. c944; md **Munia Diaz**, d. c980; bur at Guimaraes; dau of **Diego Fernandez**, Count of Limia. *NOTE: This information, if it goes unchallenged, supersedes that of Moriarty, G. 1985 (p.223) wherein Gen. 37 is said to be Gonzalo Betote, Count of Orzo, d. c924; son of Alfonso Betote; md Teresa Eriz, dau of Ero Fernandez, Count of Lugo; d. 926; and wife Adosinda.*

36. **Pelayo Gonzalez** (276-35), Count of Galicia; d. c959; md **Hermensenda Gutierrez**, dau of **Gutierre Menendez** and St. **Ilduara Eriz**; son of **Hermenegildo Gutierrez** (276-37), md **Hermesinde Gatonez** (21-38,276-37).

35. **Ilduara Pelaez**, d. by 985; md **Gonzalo Menendez**, Count of Galicia; d. c985.

34. **Menendo Gonzalez**, Count of Galicia; md (1) **Totadomna** (Toda) (mother of Gen. 33); d. c1022; granddau of **Froila Gutierrez**; liv 954; d. 1025; and **N.N.** a Saracen, liv 936/944. *NOTE: Brook, L. 1989, 326 note 3, says "we are unable to determine whether this descent is through the father or the mother."* **Menendo Gonzalez** md (2) 1023, **Urraca Garces**, Princess of Navarre, dau of **Garcia IV Sanchez** (223-37), King of Navarre, whom some authorities say is father of Gen. 33.

33. **Elvira Menendez** (248-33), of Galicia, b. c996; d. Dec 1022, Leon; bur St. Isidore of Leon; md 1015, **Alfonso V** (276-33), King of Leon.

Sources: Bard, R. 1982; ES, II 1984:50 (Gen. 33–34); Mateos, R. 1984; Minguey F. 1945, 321-326; Moriarty, G. 1985, 223 (Gen. 33–38); Salazar, J. 1983, 322, 323, 326 note 3; Salazar, J. 1984; Saez, E. 1946; Saez.E. 1949; Taberner, E. 1961; Urbal.H, 1945; Vajay, S. de 1964.

## LINE 278

32. **Folmer** (45–31), Count of Metz, md **Swanhilde**.

31. **Gottfried**, Count in the Bliesgau; liv 1075–1098; md **Mathilde of Luxemburg**, dau of **Conrad I** (3-31), Count of Luxemburg, and **Clemence of Poitou** (119-31).

30. **Gottfried I**, Count of Blieskastel, d. after 1127.

**29. Hedwig of Blieskastel** md **Gerhard** (320-29), Burggrave of Rieneck and Mainz, 1090–1106; d. after 1127.

Sources: ES, VI 1978:127 (Gen. 29–32); ES XVIII 1998:152; Moriarty, G. 1985, 129 (Gen. 31); Parisse, M. 1976 (Gen. 29–32); Renn, 1941 (Gen. 29–32).

## LINE 279

**36. Arnulf** "the Bad" (64-37,63-37,270-37), Duke of Bavaria, md **Judith of Friuli** (272-37).

**35. Leopold I**, Count in the Bavarian Eastmark, and the Donagau; Margrave of Austria; b. c932; d. 10 July 994, Wurzburg; md **Richwara** (63-36), dau of **Ernst**, Count in the Sualafeld.

**34. Adelbert**, Count in the Schweinachgau; Margrave of Austria; d. 26 May 1053; md (1) **Adelaide** (mother of Gen. 33); md (2) Frowila Orseola, dau of Piers Orseolo, Doge of Venice.

**33. Ernst** "the Bold," Margrave of Austria; b. c1020/1027; slain 9 June 1075, at Homburg; bur at Melk; md **Adelaide** (Maud) **von Eilenburg** (210-33).

**32. Leopold II** "der Schone" (the Handsome) (same as 12-32), Margrave of Austria; Crusader, 1101; liv 1070; d. 12 Oct 1102; md **Ida** (Ita) **of Cham**, dau of **Rapoto IV of Cham**, d. 1080; and granddau of **Diepold I** (128-34), Count in the Angstgau; liv 1060. **Rapoto IV of Cham** md N.N., a dau of **Hermann I**, Count of Castile, whose wife was **Haziga von Diessen** (46-30). Hermann I's parents were **Hermann IV** (63-34), Duke of Swabia, and **Adelaide von Susa** (93-32). *Ida went on the 1st Crusade and some say she died there in 1101. Harold Lamb in* Iron Men and Saints, *says she did not die but was captured and placed in the harem of Sultan Kilidge-Arslan and had issue by him whom the Emperor Frederick Barbarosa met when he was on a later crusade. (Ref: Moriarty, G. 1985.P, p. 90)*

**31. Leopold III** "the Saint" (40-31,279-31), Margrave of Austria; liv 1096; d. 15 Nov 1136; md (his 2nd, her 2nd), 1106, **Agnes of Franconia** (40-31, 359-31), Princess of Franconia.

**30. Agnes of Austria** md c1126, **Wladislaw II** (378-30), King of Poland.

Sources: Blass, R. 1939, II:280; Brandenburg, E. 1935; Chaume, M. 1977, I:542, 551–552; Dungern, O. von 1935 ; ES, I 1984:39 (Gen. 31–35); I 1984:9 (Gen. 35–36); Irving, E. 1973; Isenburg, W. 1953; Jackman, D. 1990; Moriarty, G. 1985 90 (Gen. 31–35); 57 (Gen. 35–36); TAG, 9:113; 322.

## LINE 280

**42. Marinus** (Marino), a Greek ruler at Naples, md **Eupraxia** (Euprassia).

**41. Sergius** (Sergio) **I**, Duke of Naples; liv 840–864; md **Drosu**.

**40. Gregory III**, Duke of Naples; "He gave (very) little obedience to the Basileus at Constantinople;" d. 870.

**39. Athenasius** (Atanasio II), Duke and Bishop of Naples; "Magister Militius;" deposed and blinded by his brother; d. c900.

38. **Gemma of Naples** (283-38), a widow in 961, md **Landolfo I** (297-37), Prince of Benevento, Count of Capua, Patrician of Byzantium.

Sources: Blass, R. 1939; Gay, J. 1904, 56, 118, 240; Evans, C. 1976 (Gen. 38–42); Lacarra, J. 1945; Moriarty, G. 1985, 73 (Gen. 38–42); Oxford, 1991; Pidal, R. 1969; Solar, 72–73; Winkhaus, E. 1953.

## LINE 281

37. **Udo** (281A-36), Count in the Lahngau, Margrave of Neustria, d. 885; md **Judith**, dau of **Konrad I** (300-40), Count in the Argengau and Linzgau.

36. **Konrad** (the Elder), Duke of Swabia, d.906; md **Glismode**.

35 **N.N.(fem.)** md **Eberwin**, Margrave of Mersberg.

34. **Gerlint**, d. 949, md **Meinwerk (I)**, Count in Thuringia; d. 937.

33. **William I von Weimar**, Count in South Thuringia, in the Helme and Altgaus and of Weimar; fought for Otto I at Birthen in 939; but in 953 joined his rebellious son Liudorf, but later regained the Emperor's favor; d. 16 Apr 963; md **N.N.**, dau of **Poppo III** (102-38), Count in Grabfeld, who d. 945

32. **William II von Weimar**, Count in the Helmagau and Duke of Thuringia; adherent of Henry "the Wrangler," Duke of Bavaria; d. 15 Dec 1003; bur at Naumburg, md **N.N.**(281A-32), a dau of **Otto I of Grabfeld**.

31. **Poppo I von Weimar**, Margrave of Carniola and Istria; d. before 1044; md **Hadamut** (Azzela) **of Friuli**, heiress of the countship of Istria; a widow in 1044; dau of **Wirigand**, Count of Istria, and **Wilibirg** (130-34); d. 25 Nov 1064/65, an abbess of Grisenheim.

30. **Udalrich I** (same as 10-33), Margrave of Carniola and Istria; d. 6 Mar 1070; md (1) **Sophia**, Princess of Hungary, d. 18 June 1095, dau of **Bela I** (51-33), King of Hungary, and **Rixa** (75-33). **Sophia** md also **Magnus** (28-32), Duke of Saxony.

29. **Richardis of Weimar**, d. after 16 May 1120; md **Otto II von Scheyern** (307-29), Count in the Kelsgau, etc.

Sources: Blass, R. 1939, II:278, 293; ES I.1 1997:144; Isenburg, W. 1953, table 184 (1936/37 ed.); Jackman, D. 1997: charts pp. 40,70,150,152,201; Moriarty, G. 1985, 188 (Gen. 29–33); Posse, O. 1882; Posse, O. 1887; Winkhaus, E. 1953.

## LINE 281A

36. **Udo**, Count in Landgau (281-37), Margrave of Neustria; d. c885; md **Judith**, dau of **Conrad I** (300-40), Count of Auxerre, etc.

35. **Gebhard**, Duke of Lorraine; b. 860/70; d. 910; md **Idda** (Hidda), dau of **Christian II** (211-40), Count of Grabfeld.

34. **Udo I**, Count in Rheingau; d. 949; md **Kunigunde**.

33. **Otto I**, Count of Grabfeld, d. 983-985; perhaps md **N.N.**, dau of **Eberhard II** (98-34), Count of Meinfeld, Thurgau and Zurichgau.

32. **N.N.** (fem.) md **Wilhelm II von Weimar** (281-32).

Source: Jackman, D. 1997:150+.

35. **Antgarius**, Vicomte de Lodeve; md **Geriberge**.

34. **Odo**, Vicomte de Lodeve; occ 1048; md **Chimberge**.

33 **Nobilia** (Noblia), heiress of the vicomte de Lodeve; occ 1098; md **Gilbert II** (257-33) , Vicomte de Carlat.

Sources: Barrau, H. 1972; Laine P. 1928; Morriarty, G. 1985 75-76 (Gen. 33-35; Turton, W. 1984; Winkhaus, E. 1953.

## LINE 283

41. **Landolfo**, ruler of Capua; d. 842; md **N.N.**, dau of **Rofrit of Benevento**.

40. **Landolfo**, Count of Capua; liv 866-870; Bishop, 840. *Note: at this time bishops could marry.*

39. **Atenolfo I**, Prince of Benevento and Capua, Patrician of Byzantium; d.10 Apr 910; md **Sikelgaita**, a Lombard.

38. **Landolfo I**, Prince of Benevento and Capua, Patrician of Byzantium; d. 10 Apr 943; md **Gemma of Naples** (280-38).

37. **Landolfo II**, Count of Capua, md **Wanzia**.

36. **Landolfo III**, Prince of Benevento, d. 969.

35 **Pandolfo** "the Elder," Prince of Benevento and Capua, d. 1014.

34. **Gaitelgrima**, of Benevento, regent of Salerno for her minor son; d. 1027: md after 1010, **Guaimar III** (297-34), Prince of Salerno.

Sources: Blass, R. 1939, II:310;Brandenburg, E. 1935;Gay, J. 1904,358.370,404,425,441;Hofmeister, A. 1920,33;Moriarty, G. 1985, 72.

## LINE 284

41. **Bellon** (54-39,291-40), Count of Barcelona, Carcassonne, Ampurias and Urgel, liv 812.

40. **Suniare I**, Count of Barcelona and Urgel, etc., d. after 862.

39. **Suniare II**, Count of Barcelona, Urgel, etc. , d. 915; md **Ermengarde**, prob dau of **Ranulf I**, Count of Poitiers, by wife **Bilichildis of Maine** (163-38). Bilichildis was the widow of Bernard, Count of Poitiers.

38. **Gausbert I**, Count of Ampurias and Rosellon; d. 931; md **Trudegarde**, dau of **Francon of Narbonne**, occ c876-after 924; by his wife **Arsinde**, dau of **Raimond I** and wife **Bertheiz**.

37. **Gausbert II**, Count in Ampurias and Rosellon, d. 991; md (1) **Ava of Ribagorza** (mother of Gen. 36); md (2) Gisela of Melgueil. Ava may have been dau of **Bernat Unifred**, Count of Ribagorza, who d. 950/956; by his wife **Tota Gonzales** (286-37,290-37) of Aragon.

36. **Ermengarde**, of the Ampurias, d. 991; md **Oliva II** (346-36), Count of Cerdagne and Besalu, d. 990.

Sources: Aurell, M. 1997:357-380;ES III 1980:138 (Gen. 36-39); III

1980:137 (Gen. 36–37); II 1984:68 (Gen. 39–40); Mateos, R. 1984; Salazar, J. de 1984; Stasser, T. 1993.

## LINE 285

39. **Nuno Nunez of Branosera** (same as 287-39), d. after 860; md **Argilo of Branosera.**

38. **Fernando Nunez** (287-38), of Castrosiero md **Gutina** (Gutinez) **of Castile** (35-38).

37. **Gonzalo Fernandez de Lara**, Count of Burgos and Castile; vassal of the Asturian kings, 889–914; d. 932; bur at Cereso de Rio Tiron; md before 912, **Munia** (Nuna) **of Castile** (287-37), his cousin.

36. **Fernan Gonzalez**, Count of Castile, 932; Burgos and Lara; Asturian vassal; b. c912; d. June 970; bur St. Peter of Orlanza; md (1) 932, **Sancha Sanchez of Navarre** (mother of Gen. 35 below); b. c915; d. Dec 959; dau of **Sancho I Garces**, (223-40), King of Navarre (Pamplona), and **Toda Aznarez of Larron** (293-40); he md (2) 960/962, **Urraca Garces**, dau of **Garcia Sanchez I** (55-37), King of Pamplona (niece of his first wife).

35. **Garcia I Fernandez de Lara** Count of Castile, 970; b. c940; d. between 18 Apr and 19 July 995, near Cordoba; bur at St. Peter of Cerdana; md 958/961, **Aba** (Ava) **de Ribagorza** (286-35).

34. **Sancho Garcia**, Count of Castile; b. c965; d. 5 Feb 1017; bur Monastary of Saint Salvador de Ona; md 994, **Urraca Gomez** (55-34).

33. **Munia Mayor** (248-33), co-heir of Castile and of the countship of Alava; b. 995; d. after 13 July 1066, at Fromista; bur St. Salvador de Ona; md **Sancho Garcia III** (95–33, 151–33, 223–36, 248–33), King of Navarre; murdered 18 Oct 1035.

Sources: Bard, R. 1982; ES, II 1984: 51 (Gen. 33–39); Mateos, R. 1984; Minguez, F. 1945, 321-326; Moriarty, G. 1985, 79 (Gen. 33–39); Pidal, R. 1969; Saez, E. 1946; Saez, E. 1948; Salazar, J. de 1983, 322, 323; Salz, E. 1946; Salz, E, 1948; Taberner, E. 1961; Urbal, J. 1945; Urbal, J. 1945;Vajay, S. de 1964.

## LINE 286

42. **Lupus**, Duke of Gascony; d. c778; prob md **N.N.**, dau of **Fruella**, Count of Calabria.

41. **Llop Centull Gascon**, Duke of Gascony; b. c775; d. after 818.

40. **Donat Llop**, Count of Bigorre, 835; md before 835, **Facquila**, dau of **Mancio**, first Count of Bigorre.

39. **Llop I** (223-41), Count of Bigorre, 870; d. after 910; md **N.N.**, dau of **Raymond I** (329-38), Count of Toulouse.

38. **Ramon** (Raymond) **I**, Count of Pallars and Ribagorza; b. c860; d. after 920; md **Guinigenta** (Ginigenta) **Asnarez** (mother of Gen. 37); dau of **Asnar Dato**; md (2) a dau of Mutarrif-ibn-Lope, of the Banu Qasi family.

*NOTE: In 1969, Charles J. Jacobs in "A Suggested Moslem Descent from Eleanor of Provence and Eleanor of Castile" in Augustan, XII:217–222 (July–*

*Aug. 1969) makes a good case for Bernard I (Gen. 37) having as his mother,
his father's wife (cf. Gen. 38) a dau of Mutarrif-ibn-Lope of the Banu Qasi
family, and he makes Guinigenta Bernard's sister-in-law. If these findings are
sustained, this opens up a six-generation Moslem descent.*

37. **Bernard** (Bernardo) **I** (347-37), Count of Ribagorza; and of Pallars;
founded the monastery of Dourra; d. soon after 950; md **Tota Galindez,** of Aragon
(290–37).

36. **Ramon** (Raymond, Raimondo) **II,** Count of Ribagorza; d. c970; md
**Gersinde de Fezensac** (289-36).

35. **Aba** (Ava) **de Ribagorza,** d. after 995; bur St. Peter of Cerdana; md
958/961, **Garcia I Fernandez de Lara** (285-35), Count of Castile.

Sources: Aurell, M. 1997:309-335; Brandenburg, E. 1935; ES, III 1989:119
(Gen. 35–39); Isenburg, W. 1953; Jacobs, C. 1969; Latour P. de 1997; Malan,
R. 1997; Mateos, R. 1984; Minguez, F. 1945, 321-326; Moriarty, G. 1985, 80
(Gen. 35–38); 222 (Gen. 38–41); Salazar, J. 1983, 323, 234; Urbal, J. 1945;
Winkhaus, E. 1953.

## LINE 287

39. **Nuno Nunez of Branosera** ( 285-37), md **Argilo.**

38. **Nuno Nunez,** Count of Castile, liv 909; md **N.N.,** a dau of **Rodrigo** (35-
40), Count of Castile. He was bro of **Fernando Nunez** (285-38).

37. **Munia** (Muniadomna) **of Castile**; d. after 5 Aug 935; bur Santa Marie
de Lara; md before 912, her cousin **Gonzalo Fernandez de Lara** (285-37),
Count of Burgos and Castile.

Sources: ES, II 1984:51 (Gen. 37–39); Jacobs, C. 1969; Mininguez, F. 1945,
321-326; Moriarty, G. 1985, 79 (Gen. 37–39); Pidal, R. 1969; Soler, A. 1930;
Urbal, J. 1945; Winkhaus, E. 1953.

## LINE 288

33. **Aimeraud** (Ermenrad), Lord of Faucigny; md c980/1030, **Aalgut.**

32. **Louis I** (175-30), Sire de Faucigny; md (2) **Thietburga of Savoy** (mother
of Gen. 31); as a widow, she md (2) **Gerold I** (175-31), Count of Geneva.

31. **William** "the White," Sire de Faucigny, 1084-1124; md 1119, **Leticie.**

30. **Rudolph I,** Sire de Faucigny, liv 1125.

29. **Aimon I,** Sire de Faucigny; a knight; d. 1178; md **Clementia.**

28. **Beatrice of Faucigny** md **William I** (175-28), Count of Geneva. *NOTE:
Moriarty personally expressed doubt that Beatrice of Faucigny was the wife
of William I, but nonetheless (Moriarty,G. 1985, 108) he gives the line as you
see it here, without a caveat.*

Sources: Authier, M. 1988, 47-54; Blass, R. 1939, II:248, 250, 311; Bollnow,
H. 1930, table 4; Brandenburg, E. 1935; ES, XIV 1991:70; Historich, 1934;
Moriarty, 1985: 107–108 (Gen. 28–33); Schultress, 1932; Winkhaus, E. 1953.

## LINE 289

42. **Lupus** (286-42), Duke of Gascony, d. c778; prob md **N.N.**, dau of **Fruela**, Count of Calabria.

41. **Sancho Lupus,** Duke and Prince of Gascony; md perhaps **N.N.**,dau of **Aznar I Galindez** (292-43), Count of Aragon, 806.

40. **Sancho Sanchez** "Mitarra," Duke of Gascony; d. 864/866.

39. **Sancho Sanchez,** Count and Marquis of Gascony, 886-920; d. 920; md **Amuna of Agen,** dau of **Vulgrim,** Count of Perigueux and Angouleme, by his wife **N.N.,** dau of **Bernard of Septimania** and wife **Dhouda.**

38. **Garcia Sanchez** (same as 216-37, 290-39), Count of Gascony, md **Aminiana.**

37. **William I Garcis,** Count of Fezensac and d'Armagnac.

36. **Gersinde de Fezensac** md **Ramon** (Raymond) **II** (286-36), Count of Ribagorza.

Sources: Aurell, M. 1997; ES, III 1984:119 (Gen. 36–37); Lacarra, J. 1945, I: table at 185, 205; Latour, P. 1997:337-355; Malan, R. 1997; Moriarty, 79 (Gen. 36–38); Salazar, J. 1983, 324; Soler, A. 1930; Urbal, J. 1950.

## LINE 290

39. **Garcia Sanchez** (same as 216-37, 289-38), Count of Gascony, md **Amuna.**

38. **Acibella of Gascony,** md (1) **Galindo II Aznarez,** Count of Aragon; liv 893–920; d. c920/22 (father of Gen. 37); He md (2) **Sanchia Garcie,** of Navarre 292-40).

37. **Tota Galindez,** of Aragon; md 890, **Bernard** (Bernardo) **I,** (286-37), Count of Ribagorza and Pallars.

Sources: ES, III 1984:119 (Gen. 37–38); Lacarra, I: table at 185, 205; Moriarty, G. 1985:79 (Gen. 37–39).

## LINE 291

40. **Bellon** (54-39, 284-41), Count of Carcassonne, a Goth, liv 812.

39. **Oliva I,** Count of Carcassonne; d. 837; md (1) **Ermentrude** (mother of Gen. 38); md (2) **Richilda.**

38. **Oliva II,** Count of Carcassonne and Rasez; d. 879.

37. **Acfrid II,** Count of Carcassonne and Rasez; d. 934/935.

36. **Arsende,** heiress of Carcassonne and Rasez; liv 945–969; md 940, **Arnold II,** Count of Conserans and a part of Comminges, 945; d. before 957.

35. **Roger I de Comminges,** Seigneur of Comminges, Count of Carcassonne and Conserans; d. 1019; md before 970, **Adelaide de Rouergue** (105-32), of Pons, d. after 1011; dau of **Bernard II,** Count of Melgueil; d.989, and wife **Senegonde.**

34. **Ermesinde de Carcassonne,** d. 1 Mar 1057; md 990/991, **Raymond Borrel I** (54--34, 168-32), Count of Barcelona.

Sources: Abadolin, R. 1949, vol. 61, 346–357; ES, II 1984:68 (Gen. 34–

40); III 1984:145 (Gen. 35–37); Higounet, C.17-34, 69-160, 250-259, 293-295, 515-606; Mateo, 1984; Moriarty, 68–69 (Gen. 34–40); Salazar, J. de 1984; Stasser, T. 1993; Stasser, T. 1996.

## LINE 292

44. **Galindo.**

43. **Aznar I Galindez** (298-41,326A-40), Count of Aragon, Gascony and Urgel; was from upper Aragon; adherent to the Carolingians, c809–839; Captured by the Navarrese in 824; driven out of Urgel by the Moors after 825; d. c839.

42. **Galindo Aznarez I,** Count of Aragon, Fallou, Ribagorza, and perhaps Toulouse; md **Guldregut.**

41. **Aznar II Galindez,** Count of Aragon, d. before 893; md **Oneca Inigo,** dau of **Garcia I Iniguez** (294-43), King of Pamplona and wife **Urraca.**

40. **Galindo II Aznarez** (290-38), Count of Aragon; d. c920/922; md (2) **Sanchia Garces** (mother of Gen. 39); dau of **Garcia II Jiminez** (223-41), King of Navarre; who md (1) **Oneca Rebelle de Sanguesa** (see 223-41).

39. **Andregota Sanchez** (Endragot Galindez), heiress of Aragon; d. 972; md (1) 920, **Garcia III Sanchez** (55-38,223-39), King of Navarre and Count of Aragon; md (2) 943, Teresa.

Sources: Abadolin, R. 1949, vol. 61; Auzias, L. 1937, 32n, 120;Bard, R. 1982; Chaume.O, I:532; ES II 1984:52 (Gen. 39–43); Higounet, C. 1982; Isenburg, W. 1953; Moriarty, 1985, 77 (Gen. 39–43); 67 (Gen. 43–44); Pidal, R. 1969, II:718–719; Salazar, J. 1983, 323 (Gen. 39–40); Winkhaus, E. 1953.

## LINE 293

43. **Garcia I Iniguez** (294-43, 292-41), King of Pamplona, 852–882; md **Urraca.**

42. **Sancho Garcia,** of Pamplona, md **Leodegunda,** dau of **Ordogno I** (276-39), King of Asturias and Gilicia.

41. **Aznar Sanchez de Larron,** md 880, **Oneca Fortunez,** (285-36,294-41), of Pamplona.

40. **Toda Aznarez de Larron,** b. c885; d. after 970; md **Sancho I Garces** "Optimo Imperator" (223-40), King of Navarre, 905–925; d. 925.

Sources: Blade, J. 1878, vol. 23 (1886), 16–39, 308–324, 418–420; vol. 24 (1897), 34–46, 201–211, 313–329; ES, II 1994:53, 54 (Gen. 40–43); Isenburg, W. 1953, Part ii, tab 43; Lacarra, J. 1945, 207–221, table at 285.

## LINE 294

43. **Garcia I Iniguez** (76-39,292-41), King of Navarre (Pamplona), 852–882; b. c810; d. 882; md (1) **Urraca** (mother of Gen. 42); md also Leogundis of Asturia, dau of Ordono I, King of Asturias.

42. **Fortun Garces,** King of Pamplona, c880–905; md **Aria** (Aurea).

41. **Oneca Fortunez,** of Pamplona, b. c847; md 880, **Aznar Sanchez de**

156

**Larron** (293-41), Lord of Larron; md (1) Abdallah I, Sultan of Cordoba, 882–912; b. 842; d. 912.

Sources; ES, II 1984:53 (Gen. 41–43); Isenburg, W. 1953, Part ii, table 43; Lacarra, J. 1945, 207–213 and table 285; Moriarty, 70 (Gen. 41–43); Pidal, R. 1969; Stimmel, R. 1976 (Gen. 41–43); Winkhaus, E. 1953.

## LINE 295

39. **Rognvald Eysteinsson** "the Wise" (166-36) md **Ermina**.
38. **Hrollager**.
37. **Hrolf Turstan**, liv 920, md **Gerlotte of Blois**, dau of **Theobald I** (Gerlon) (340-36), Count of Chartres and Bourges.
36. **Ansfried** "the Dane," Count of Hiesmer; liv 978; said to have been a nephew of Duke Rollo.
35. **Ansfred le Goz**, Vicomte d'Hiesmer; liv 1035; exchanged Hiesmer for Tolais.
34. **Thurstan le Goz**, Vicomte d'Avranches, Vicomte d'Hiesmer; rebelled and exiled from Normandy, 1041; Chamberlain of Duke Robert and went with him to Jerusalem, c1034/1035; (Crusader ?); b. c1000; liv 1041; md **Judith de Monterolier**.
33. **Richard d'Avranches** (178-31),"le Goz;" Vicomte d'Avranches; witnessed charters, 1064, 1066; b. c1025, prob Avranches, France; d. after 1082. *NOTE: Crispin, M. 1969 (pp. 79–80) is no doubt incorrect in showing Emma de Conteville as Richard's wife. Moriarty, 1985 (p.111) says the marriage is probably unfounded.*
32. **Judith d'Avranches** md **Richer** (178-31), Seigneur de l'Aigle.

Sources: Cokayne, G. 1959, III:164; Crispin, M. 1969, 78–80; Douglas, R. 1946; ES, II 1984:79 (Gen. 39); Moriarty, 111 (Gen. 33–36); Paget, G. 1977; Winkhaus, E. 1953; Wunder, G. 1967.

## LINE 296

33. **Tancred d'Hauteville**, d. c1041; md (1) Muriella of Normandy, dau Richard I, Duke of Normandy, and N.N.; md (2) **Fredesende of Normandy**, d. 1057; dau of **Richard I** (89-33), Duke of Normandy, and **N.N.** (mother of Gen. 32). Wives were sisters.
32. **Robert Guiscard d'Hauteville** (80-32), Duke of Apulia, Calabria, and Sicily, 1058; Norman conqueror of southern Italy; a Crusader; a leader of the 1st Crusade; captured at Antioch; b. 1015, Normandy; d. 17 July 1085, Cephalonia; md (1) 1051/1052, and div 1058, **Albereda** (Alverade) (cf. 80–32); b. c1032; d. after July 1122; md (2) 1058/1059, **Sikelgaita** (297-32) (mother of Gen. 31) , heiress of Salerno, d. 27 July 1090.
31. **Mathilda of Apulia**; b. c1058; d. 1111/1112; md 1078, **Raymond Berenger II** (54-31), Count of Barcelona and Carcassonne.

Sources: Agiles, R. 1968; Benvenisti, M. 1972; Boase, T. 1971; ES, II 1984:205 (Gen. 31–33); Evans, C. 1965; Evans, C. 1976; Evans, C. 1983;

Foucher, 1971; Holt, P. 1986; Krey, A. n.d.; Prawler, J. 1972; Prawler, J. 1973; Riley-Smith, J. 1973.

## LINE 297

37. **Landolfo I** (283-38), Prince of Benevento, md **Gemma of Naples** (280-38).

36. **Landolfo II**, Prince of Benevento and Capua, d. 27 May 961; md **Wanzia**.

35. **Sikelgaita**, heiress of Salerno, md c960, **Giovanni II** (31-35), Prince of Salerno, 983; d. 999.

34. **Guaimar III**, co-regent of Salerno, 989; Prince of Salerno, 999; adherent of the Emperor Otto III, 1002; d. 1031; md after 1010 (2) **Gaitelgrima of Benevento** (283-34).

33. **Guaimar** (Waimar) **IV**, Prince of Salerno, Capua, Amalfi, Calabria and Apulia; Lost Capua, Calabria and Apulia, 1043, to the Normans; b. 1013 at the earliest; murdered 3 June 1052; md **Porpora of Tabellaria** (325-33) (Moriarty, p.72, differs).

32. **Sikelgaita**, heiress of Salerno; b. 1025; d. 27 July 1090; md **Robert Guiscard d' Hauteville** (80-32,296-32), Duke of Apulia, Calabria and Sicily.

Sources: Blass, R. 1939, II:310; ES, II 1984:205 (Gen. 32); Evans, C. 1965; Evans, C. 1976; Evans, C. 1983; Gautier, P. 1971; Hofmeister, A 1920; Moriarty, G. 1985:71–72 (Gen. 32–37); Garufi, C. 1935, vol. 7.

## LINE 298

34. **William I** (333-35), Count of Provence at Arles and Marquis of Provence; b. c955; d. 994, a monk at Avignon; md after 981, **Adelaide** (Blanche); d. 1026; dau of **Fulk II** (127-34,167-36,347-35), Count of Anjou, and **Gerberge of the Gatinais** (167-36).

33. **William II**, Count of Provence and Arles; had lands from his maternal uncle, Drozon, Bishop of Puy; b. c983/984; d. after 30 May 1018; bur at Montmajour; md c1002, **Gerberge**, b. c985; d. 1020/1023; dau of **Otto William** (Otton I) (94-33), King of Lombardy, and **Ermentrude de Roucy** (161-33).

32. **Geoffrey,** Count of Provence at Arles; d. by 1063; md **Stephanie** (Douce) (298A-32) of Marseilles; d. 11 Sept 1095.

31. **Gerberga**, heiress of Provence and Arles; d. between 3 Feb 1112 and Jan 1113; md **Gilbert** (257-31), Count of Provence, etc.

Sources: Blass, R. 1939, 254; ES, II 1984:69 (Gen. 31); II 1984:187 (Gen. 31–33); Mateo, 1983; Moriarty, G. 1985:77 (Gen. 31–33); 4, 28 (Gen. 34); Saillot, J. 1980, 114+; Salazar, J. de 1983; Winkhaus, E. 1953.

## LINE 298A

34 **William I**, Viscount of Marseilles; d. after 15 Oct 1004; md (1) **Bilichildis**, liv 984.

33. **William II,** Viscount of Marsailles, d. 14 May 1050; md (2) before 1019, **Stephanie of Baux-Rians;** d. after 1555; dau of **Pons** (the younger) of Baux-Rians and wife **"Profecta."**

158

33. **Bertrand,** liv 1035-1055.

32. **Stephanie** (Douce), d. 11 Sept 1095; md **Geoffrey**, Count of Provence at Arles (298-32).

Sources: Brandenburg, E. 1935; Moriarty, G. 1985, 77.

## LINE 299

31. **Stephen III,** Count of Blois (133-31) md **Adele of Normandy** and England (81-30).

30 **Stephen of Blois,** King of England, 1135-1154; Count of Mortain and of Boulogne; crowned king on 26 Dec 1135; b. c1095; d. 25 Oct 1154; bur at Faversham; md c1120, **Mathilda of Boulogne** (242-31).

29. **Mary of Blois,** Princess of England, heiress and Countess of Boulogne; Countess of Mortain; b. c1131, Blois, Loir-et-Cher, France; d. 25 July 1180, as Abbess of Ramsey; md before 1160 (divorced 1169/70), **Matthew of Alsace** (205-29), Count of Boulogne.

Sources: Chibnall, M. 1991; Cokayne, G. 1959, VII:641–642; ES, II 1984:46 (Gen. 29–31); Moriarty, 130 (Gen. 29); 117 (Gen. 30–31); Paul, J. 1914, I:2.

## LINE 300

44. **Richbold,** Count (in the Argengau?); b. c690; d. 15 Jan 761/762; md **Ermengarde.**

43. **Ruthard,** Count in the Argengau; b. c715; d. before 776; md (1) **Hermenlindis,** liv 757; prob dau of **Berthold.**

42. **Welf II,** b. c745; d. before 800.

41. **Welf** (171-40), Count of Entgau in Bavaria and of Swabia; d. 819; md **Eigilwich** (Heilwig) (171-40), a Saxon; Abbess of Chelles, near Paris, 826.

40. **Conrad I** (281-37,281A-36), Count in the Argengau and in the Linzgau, Count of Auxerre, Lay Abbot of St. Germain d'Auxerre; b. c800; d. 21 Sept 862; md **Aelis** (Adelaide) **of Tours** (mother of Gen. 39); dau of **Hugh** "le Méfiant" ( 224-38,302-40 etc.), Count of Tours, and wife, **Aba** (Bava).

39 **Conrad II** (175-37), Count of Auxerre and Margrave of Transjuranian Burgundy, Lay Abbot of St. Moritz; b. 825; d. before 876; md **Waldrada.**

38. **Adelaide** (Aelis) **of Burgundy** (173-36)**,** d. c929; md before 888, **Richard** (206-38), Duke of Burgundy, d. 921.

Sources: Blass, R. 1939, II:275, 313; Chaume, M. 1977, I:552+; ES, I 1984:57 (Gen. 38–41); ES, III 1989:736 (Gen. 38–41); Winkhaus, E. 1953; Wollasch, J. 1959, 20+.

## LINE 301

39. **Ludolph** (92-38), Duke of Saxony, md **Oda Billung,** dau of **Billung,** Count of Thuringia, and wife **Aeda,** a Frank.

38. **Oda of Saxony,** d. after 874, md **Lothar I** (15-39), Count of Stade, who d. in battle at Ebsdorf, Germany, 2 Feb 880.

37. **Lothar II,** Count of Stade, b. 5 Sept 929; md **Matilda von Arneburg**

(271-37).

36. **Henry von Stade** "the Bold," Count of Stade and in the Heiangau; d. 11 May 976; bur monastery at Heeringen; md (2) **Hildegarde von Rheinhausen**, dau of **Elli I**, Count of Reinhausen.

35. **Hildegarde von Stade**, b. 974/976; d. 3 Oct 1011; bur Michaeliskl in Lunenburg; md c990, **Bernard I Billung** (312-35), Duke of Saxony.

Sources: Blass, R, II:296, 301; Brandenburg, E. 1935; ES, VIII 1980:133 (Gen. 35–39); Kraus; Moriarty, 56 (Gen. 35–37); 25 (Gen. 38–39); Winkhaus, E. 1953.

## LINE 302

41. **Louis I** (171-40), King of France; md **Ermengarde of Hesbaye** (352-41, etc.).

40. **Lothar I** (25-42,263-40), King of Italy, 817–855; Emperor of the West, 840–855; b. 795; d. 29 Sept 855, Preum, Germany; md 15 Oct 821, **Ermengarde of Orleans** (same as 25-42), d. 20 Mar 851; dau of **Hugh** "le Méfiant" (same as 29-40, 300-40, etc.), Count of Tours; md **Aba** (Bava).

39. **Ermengarde** (Irmgard) **of Lorraine**, Princess of Italy; b. Italy; md 846, **Giselbert** (207-39, 303-40), Count in the Maasgau, 840–855; Count of Darnau, 840–877.

Sources: Blass, R. 1939, II:270, 275, 312, 313; Brandenburg, E. 1935; Chaume, M. 1977, I 224n1; ES I 1984:95 (Gen. 39–40): Isenburg, W. 1953 (1953); Moriarty, G. 1985, 20–21 (Gen. 39–40); 16 (Gen. 40–41); Saillot, J. 1980;Winkhaus, E. 1953.

## LINE 303

125. **Darda**.

124. **Erichthonius**.

123. **Tros**.

122. **Ilus**.

121. **Leomedon**.

120. **Priam**, King of Troy md **Strymo** ("Placia").

119. **Helenus,** King of Epirus

118. **Zeuter,** King of Troy, liv. 1149 BC.

117. **Francus,** King of Troy.

116. **Ersdron,** King of Troy.

115. **Zelius,** King of Troy.

114. **Basabelian I**, King of Troy.

113. **Plaserius I**, King of Troy.

112. **Plesron I**, King of Troy.

111. **Eliacor**, King of Troy.

110. **Zaberian**, King of Troy.

109. **Plaserius II**, King of Troy.

108. **Antenor I**, King of Troy.

107. **Priam II**, King of Troy.

106. **Helenus II**, King of Troy.
105. **Plesron II**, King of Troy.
104. **Basabelian II**, King of Troy.
103. **Alexandre**, King of Troy; d. 677 BC.
102. **Priam III**, King of Cimmerians.
101. **Gentilanor**, King of Cimmerians.
100. **Aldamius**, King of Cimmerians.
 99. **Dilulius I**, King of Cimmerians.
 98. **Helenius III**, King of Cimmerians.
 97. **Praserius III**, King of Cimmerians.
 96. **Dilulius II**, King of Cimmerians.
 95. **Marcomir**, King of Cimmerians.
 94. **Priam IV**, King of Cimmerians.
 93. **Helenus IV**, King of Cimmerians.
 92. **Antenor II**, King of Cimmerians, d. 442 BC.
 91. **Marcomir I**, King of Sicambri, d. 412 BC.
 90. **Antenor II**, King of Sicambri.
 89. **Prenus**, King of Sicambri.
 88. **Helenus I**, King of Sicambri.
 87. **Diocles**, King of Sicombri.
 86. **Bassanus**, King of Sicambri.
 85. **Clodomir I**, King of Sicombri, d. 232 BC.
 84. **Nicanor**, King of Sicombri, d. 198 BC.
 83. **Marcomir II**, King of Sicombri, d. 170 BC.
 82. **Clodius I**, King of Sicombri, d. 159 BC.
 81. **Antenor III**, King of Sicombri, d. 143 BC.
 80. **Clodomir II**, King of Sicombri, d. 123 BC.
 79. **Merodochus**, King of Sicombri, d. 95 BC.
 78. **Cassander**, King of Sicombri, d. 74 BC.
 77. **Antharius**, King of Sicombri, d. 39 BC.
 76. **Francus**, First King of the Franks, d. 11 BC. The terms "Frank" and "France" start here.
 75. **Clodius II**, King of Franks, d. 20 BC.
 74. **Marcomir III**, King of Franks, d. 50 AD.
 73. **Clodomir III**, King of Franks, b. 3 AD, d. 63 AD.
 72. **Antenor IV**, King of Franks, d. 69 AD.
 71. **Ratherius**, King of Franks, d. 90 AD.
 70. **Richimir**, King of Franks, d. 114 AD.
 69. **Odomir**, King of Franks, d. 128 AD.
 68. **Marcomir IV**, King of Franks, d. 149; md **Athildis** (438-68).
 67. **Clodomir IV**, King of Franks, b. 104; d. 166.
 66. **Farabert**, King of Franks, b. 122; d. 186.
 65. **Sunno**, King of Fanks, b. 137; d. 213.
 64. **Hilderic**, King of Franks, d. 253.
 63. **Bartherus**, King of Franks, b. 238; d. 272.

161

62. **Clodius III**, King of Franks, d. 298.

61. **Gautier**, King of East Franks, d. 306.

60. **Dagobert I**, King of East Franks, d. 317.

59. **Genebald**, Duke of East Franks, b. 262; d. 358.

58. **Dagobert II**, Duke of East Franks, b. 300; d. 379.

57. **Clodius**, Duke of East Franks, b. 324; d. 389.

56. **Marcomir**, Duke of East Franks, b. 347; d.404.

55. **Pharamond**, King of Salic Franks, b. 370; d. 427.

54. **Clodion**, (Clodius V), governed the Salic Franks, 428–448; b. c380; d. 448.

53. **Merovech**, governed the Salic Franks, 448–457; defeated Attila "the Hun" in 451; was a son or son-in-law of Clodion.

52. **Childeric, I**, King of Franks, 458–481; b. c436; d. 481; md **Basina of Thuringia.**

51. **Clovis I** "the Great," King of Salic Franks, 481–511; King of France; d. 511; md 492, **St. Clothilda** (349-51).

50. **Clothaire I**, King of Soissons, 511; King of Orleans, 524; King of France, 558-561; md (1) Guntheuca, widow of Clodomer; md (2) Chunsina; md (3) Ingunda; md (4) Aregunda, sister of Ingunda; md (5) **Rodegunda** (mother of Gen. 49); dau of **Berthar**, King of Thuringia; she became a nun at Poitiers c550; (md) (6) a concubine; md (7) Vuldetrada, widow of Theovald. He had children of record by all wives.

49. **Chilperic I,** King of Neustria, 539-584; d. 584; md (3) **Fredegunde**; b. 543; d. 597; "One of the most bloodthirsty women in history." She was the maid of Chilperic's first wife.

48. **Clothaire II** (233A-47), King of Neustria, 584; King of Franks, 613–628; Signed the "Perpetual Constitution," 614/15, an early Magna Carta; b. 584; d. 629; md **Haldetrude**, d. 604.

47. **Dagobert I**( 262-46), King of Austrasia, 622–628; King of Franks, 628–638; greatest of the Merovingian kings; b. 602; d. 639; md (1) Gometrude; (2) Nantilde; (3) Wulfegunde; (4) **Berthilde** (mother of Gen. 46).

46. **Siegbert III** (224-42), King of Austrasia, 639–654; b. 630; d. 656; md **Hymnegilde.**

45. **Dagobert II**, King of Austrasia, 678-680; King of Metz; b. 652; d. 678; md **Mechtilde.**

44. **Adela**, Princess of Austrasia.

43. **Aubri I**, Count of Blois.

42. **Aubri II**, Count of Blois.

41. **Theidlindis**, alive c795; md **Gainfroi**, a count, perhaps of Sens.

40. **Giselbert**, Count in the Maasgau, valley of the Meuse River, 840-877; md **Ermengarde of Lorraine and Burgundy** (See 207-39 and 302-39).

39. **Regnier I** md **Hersent**, dau of **Charles II** (250-39,303-39), Emp. of the West.

Sources: Bemont, C. 1891; Chaume, M. 1977, 548–549, (Gen. 41–45). ES

I 1984:1 (Gen. 44–54);  Godwin, P. 1860;Gregory of Tours, 1974; James, E. 1988; Lasco, P. 1971; Perry, W. 1857; Rubincam, M. 1949.

## LINE 304

31. **Gerard I Flaminius** (119-31), Count of Guelders and in the Teisterbant, md **Clemence of Poitou** (same as 3-31 and 278-31).

30. **Gerard II**, Count of Guelders, md **Ermengarde** (379-30), heiress of Zutphen. In a charter of between 1129 and 1138, it is noted that Gerhard, his wife, and his son Henry, donated a chapel at Ellekom to the church at Zutphen.

29. **Henry I**, Count of Guelders and Zutphen; b. 1117; d. 1182; built a castle at Zutphen; md 1135, **Agnes von Arnstein** (304A 29).

28. **Otto I**, Count of Zealand, Guelders, Zutphen, Holland and East Friesland, 1198; Crusader; went on the 3rd Crusade; fought at Bouvines in the Imperial army, July, 1214; went on a Crusade to Damietta, 1218/9; d. between 30 Apr. and 24 Sept, 1227; md **Richardis** (Richarde) **von Wittlesbach** (307-26); d. 7 Dec 1231.

27. **Adelaide** (Adelheid) **of Guelders**, b. c1186; d. 4 Feb 1218; md 1198, **William I** (72-27), Count of Holland.

Sources; Cokayne, G. 1959, VII:642; ES VI 1974:25 (Gen. 28–31); Flahiff, G. 1947; Hoffman, W. 1950, 104:206–211, citing the latest Dutch authorities at that time; Moriarty, G. 1985, 185 (Gen. 27–29); 127 (Gen. 27–31); Tyre, W. 1943; Vries, W de 1946.

## LINE 304A

32. **Arnold**, Count in Zurichgau and of Arnstein; liv 1050-1053; md **Adelheid**, dau of **Eberhard I**, Count of Nellenberg in Zurichgau.

31. **Ludwig I**, Count in the Einrichgau, Count of Arnstein, 1095.

30. **Ludwig II**, occ 1100-1117; md **Udalheid of Odenkirchen.**

29. **Agnes von Arnstein**, d. 1179; md 1135, **Henry I** (304-29), Count of Guelders and Zutphen; d. 1182.

Sources: ES VI 1974:25; Moriarty, G. 1985, 185; Vries, W. de 1946.

## LINE 305

35. **Aldradus** (Airald), Vicomte de Châtellerault, 937–976; d. before 987; md 969, **Gersende.**

34. **Boson I**, Vicomte de Châtellerault, md, 1010, **Amelie.**

33. **Hugh I**, Vicomte de Châtellerault; liv 1010–1070; md **Gerberge de la Rochefoucauld** (306-33).

32. **Boso II**, Vicomte de Châtellerault; md before 1075, **Eleanore** (Alienor) **de Thouars** (159-32).

Sources: Authier, A. 1940-88; Beauchat, E 1978; Blass, R. 1939, II:253; Duguet, J. 1981, 261-270; ES, X 1986:29 (Gen. 32); ES, III 1989:813 (Gen. 32–35); Laurent, J. 1911, 549; Moriarty, G. 1985, 45 (Gen. 32–35); Winkhaus,

E. 1953.

35. **Joscelin**, Sire de Courtenay; d. 1015; a kinsman of Hugh "the White," Sire de Lusignan.

34. **Foucauld**, Sire de la Roche in the Angoumois; liv 1019–1037; md **Gersinda**, liv 1026.

33. **Gerberge de la Rochefoucauld** md **Hugh I** (305-33), Vicomte de Châtellerault.

Sources: Authier, M. 1988, 67; Barry, F. 1957, 65–68; Blass, R. 1939, 253; Dupont; ES, X:198;629 (Gen. 34); Isenburg, W. 1932; Laurent, J. 1911, 549; Martin, G. 1975; Moriarty, G. 1985, 45 (Gen. 34–35); Winkhaus, E. 1953.

32. **Henry von Schweinfurt** (7-34,47-35,213-35,270-35), Margrave of Schweinfurt and in the Nordgau; md 1003, **Gerberge of Henneburg** (102-35).

31. **Henry von Schweinfurt**, Count in the Pegnitz, Altmuhl, and Overnaeb; liv 1021–1043; md **N.N. von Altdorf**, dau of **Kuno I** (213-34), Count of Altdorf.

30. **Otto I von Scheyern**, Count in the Middle Paar and Scheyern on the Ilm; Chief advocate of the bishopric of Freising; Crusader; d. 4 Dec 1072, on a pilgrimage to Jerusalem; md (2) 1057, **Haziga von Diessen** (46-30,279-32); d. c1104; widow of Herman von Kastl (d. 1056).

29. **Otto II von Scheyern**, Count in the Paar and in the Kelsgau, Count of Scheyern; advocate of the bishopric of Freising on the death of his half-brother Bernard (d. c1102); Otto d. c1110; md (2) 1088/1090, **Richardis of Weimar** (281-29), a widow at her death after 16 May 1120.

28. **Otto von Wittlesbach IV** (307A-28), Count of Wittlesbach, Pfalzgrave of Bavaria, 1120; re-founded the monastery of Indersdorf, founded by his father-in-law; d. 4 Aug 1156; md before 13 July 1116, **Heilika von Pettendorf** of Lengenfeld, heiress of Lengenfeld, d. 13 Sept 1170; dau of **Frederick**, Lord of Lengenfeld in the Bavarian Nordgau; d.1110; and **Sigena of Leige**, d. 24 Feb 1110; widow of Wipracht I von Groitzsch, Count in the Balranegau (d. c1150); dau of **Goswin von Leige.**

27. **Otto von Wittlesbach V**, Duke of Bavaria, the ancestor of the rulers of Bavaria to 1918; Pfalzgrave of Bavaria, 1158; made Duke of Bavaria after the fall of Henry "the Lion," 1180; Crusader; went with his father on the 2nd Crusade, 1147; and, in 1159, with the Emperor Frederick Barbarosa as Imperial Standard Bearer; fought in the Italian wars; Ambassador to Constantinople; was present in Venice at the peace between Barbarosa and the Pope, 1177; b. c1117; d. 1 July 1183, Pettendorf; bur at Scheyern; md 1159/1167, **Agnes von Loos** (320-27).

26. **Richarde von Wittlesbach**; d. 7 Dec 1231, md before 1188, **Otto I**

(304-28), Count of Guelders and Zutphen, d. between 30 Apr and 24 Sept 1207.

Sources: Agiles, R. 1968; Clairvaux, B. 1963; Constable, G. 1953; Dek, A. 1955; Dungern, O. von 1931; ES, I 1984:23 (Gen. 26–30); ES I.1 1997:14,90; ES XVII 1998; Foucher, 1971; Krey, A. n.d.; Moriarty, G. 1985, 185–186 (Gen. 26–32); Trotter, K. 1915, 12; Tyroller, F. 1950; Winkhaus, E. 1953, 423.

## LINE 307A

32. **Adalgot.**
31. **Routger,** Count of Veltheim, md N.N., dau of **Frederick I** of Burg-Lengenfeld, liv 1050; md **Sigena**, dau of **Goswin**, Count of Gross-Leinungen.
30. **Frederick III**, Duke of Swabia, md Princess **Agnes**, dau of the Salic king, Henry IV.
29. **Heilike**, d. 3 Apr 1119, md **Frederick III** of Hopfenohe-Pettendorf-Lengenfeld; d. 3 Apr 1119.
28. **Heilike**, d. 13 Sept 1170; md **Otto von Wittlebach IV** (307-28).

Sources: ES I 1980:9; ES I.1 1997: 14, 90; ES XIV:95A.

## LINE 308

39. **Rodulf,** Duke of Turenne; founded the Abbey de Saint-Geniez de Savarzac, where he was buried in 843; md **Agane**, liv 844–856; widow of Count Immo.
38. **Geoffrey I**, Count of Turenne, liv 844–865; md **Gerberge**, liv 865–878.
37. **Geoffrey II of Turenne**, liv 861–898; md **Godelinde**, liv 898.
36. **Robert II**, Count of Turenne, liv c887–932.
35. **Adhemer I**, Vicomte des Eschelles and Comte du Quercy; liv 898–941.
34. **Bernard,** created Vicomte de Turenne by Louis IV, King of France; liv 930; d. before 984; md **Deda** (308A-34), a widow in 984.
33. **Sulpice,** heiress of Turenne, occ 962–975; md before 962, **Archambaud II** (156-33), Vicomte de Camborn and Ventadour.

Sources: Aubel, F. 1997:309-335; Blass, R. 1939, II:242; Cosnac, R. (1968), vol. 49, no. 28:355–362; vol. 50 (1969), no. 29:102; no. 30:142–148; no. 32:371–376; ES, III 1989:791 (Gen. 33–39); Moriarty, G. 1985, 47–48 (Gen. 33–39, but differing from ES, III 1989:791); Winkhaus, E. 1953.

## LINE 308A

39. **Immon**, Count of Quercy.
38. **Raoul**, Count of Quercy; d. 842; md **Aiga**, from Aquitaine, d. 856/857.
37. **Robert**, d. 856/860; md **Rotrude**, liv 860.
36. **Robert**, Viscount of Turenne.

35. **Adhemer,** Viscount of Turenne, md (1) **Faucisburge** (mother of Gen. 34); md (2) Gauzla.

34. **Deda**, a widow in 984, md **Bernard** (308-34), Viscount of Turenne. Sources: Aubel, F. 1997:309-335. ES III 1989:791.

## LINE 309

41 **Krum**, 8th Khan of the Bulgars, 802–814; d. 13 Apr 814. He united with the Franks to crush Aver Khaganate.

40 **Omortag**, Khan of the Bulgars, 814–831.

39 **Enrovota**, military leader, d. 849.

38. **Boris Michael**, Khan of Bulgaria, 857–889; called "grandson of Omortag;" d. a monk, 2 May 907; md **Marija.**

37 **Nikola Kumet**, Count in West Bulgaria; md **Ripsimija**. *NOTE: Moriarty, G. 1985 (p. 139) has an additional generation, between Gen. 36 and 37, adding John of Bulgaria, as father of Aaron.*

36. **Aaron Amitopulos of Bulgaria**, liv 988.

35. **John Wladislaw**, Tsar of West Bulgaria, 1016–1018; slain 1018 at Durrachium; md **Marie of Byzantium**, a "girdled Patrician."

34. **Troianos** (Trajan), Tsar of West Bulgaria, an exile in Constantinople; md **N.N.** (perhaps Kontostephane) (370–34).

33 **Marie of Bulgaria**, d. as a nun named Xene, by 1118; md before 1066, **Andronikos Doukas** (215-33).

Sources: Adontz, N. 1938, 39:363; Adontz, N. 1938; Brook, L. 1981, 59, 114, 115, 118; ES, II 1984:167–168 (Gen. 33–41); II 1984:178, (Gen. 33–34); Leib, B. 1950; Moriarty, G. 1951; Moriarty, G. 1985, 139 (Gen. 33–41); Runciman, S. 1965; Vajay, S. de 1962; Wolff, R. 1949.

## LINE 310

37 **Dietrich** (Theoderich) (32-35,65-41,310-37,338-37), Count of the Saxon Hamalant (Ringleheim); b. c872; d. 8 Dec 917; md **Reginhilde von Friesland** (Ragnhildis Ludmilla), dau of **Godefrid** (217-38), King of Haithabu, and **Gisela of Lorraine**, dau of **Lothar II** (93-38,217-39,263-39), King of Lorraine, and **Waldrada**, a concubine.

36. **Lambert**, Count of Louvain; md **N.N.**, a dau of **Ricfrid**, Count in the Betuwe, 847; and wife **Hamesindis.**

35. **Adele of Louvain**; d. 961; md **Regnier III** (68-35, 139-35), Count of Hainault.

Sources: Blass, R. 1939, II:290, 311; Bottger, F. 1965; Brandenburg, E. 1935; ES, I 1984:95 (Gen. 35–36); II 1984:104 (Gen. 37; VI 1978:60 (Gen. 36); ES XVIII 1997; Moriarty, G. 1985, 50 (Gen. 35); 26 (Gen. 36–37); Winkhaus, E. 1953.

## LINE 311

38. **Gerulf** received lands between the Rhine and Hennemerland, from . Emperor Arnulf, 885-889

37. **Dietrich I**, Count of West Friesland; adherent of Charles "the Simple;" occ 900–928; d. after 6 Oct 929 and by 929; md **Geva** (Gerberge) (mother of Gen. 36); heiress of Friesland; dau of **Meginhard**, Count of Hamalant, Duke of Friesland; whose parents were **Eberhard II** (202-40), Count of Hamelant and **wife Evesna**.

36. **Dietrich II**, Count of West Friesland; b. c905; d. 6 May 988; md 940/945, **Hildegarde of Flanders**, d. 10 Apr 990; dau of **Arnold** (Arnulf) I (141-36), Count of Flanders, and **Adelaide de Vermandois** (169-35).

35. **Arnulf I** (244-34), Count of West Friesland and Ghent; slain 18 Sept 993; md c980, **Luitgarde of Luxemburg** (242-35,316-35).

34. **Dietrich III**, Count of West Friesland and of Holland (France); d. 27 May 1039; md **Othelendis** (Ulfrido), dau of **Bernard I** (27-36), Margrave of the Saxon Nordmark.

33. **Florenz** (Florent) **I** (38-31), Count of Holland (France) and of West Friesland; killed at Hannert, 28 June 1061; md (1) c1050, **Gertrude of Saxony** (312-33).

32. **Bertha of Holland** (France), b. c1055; d. 1094, Montreuil-sur-Mer; md 1072; div 1091; **Philip I** (134-31), King of France.

Sources: Blass, R. 1939, II:253; Chaume, M. 1977; Dek, A. 1955; ES, II 1984:11 (Gen. 32–33); II 1984:2 (Gen. 34–38); Koch, A. 1970, I; Moriarty, G. 1985, 55 (Gen. 32–38); Von Redlich, M. 1941 , 267–268; Winkhaus, E. 1953, 46, 47.

## LINE 312

37. **Billung**, Count of Saxony, b. c875; d. 26 Mar 967; md **Frederunda** (or Hildeburg).

36. **Hermann Billung** (104-35,141-35, 211-37, 212-36), Duke of Saxony and Margrave of the Billungermark, built Luneburg; b. c905; d. 27 Mar 973; md **Hildegarde of Westerbourg**.

35. **Bernard** (Benno) **I Billung**, Duke of Saxony; b. c940; d. 9 Feb 1011, at Corivey; bur at Michaeliskl in Lunenburg; md c990, **Hildegarde von Stade** (301-35); d. 3 Oct 1011.

34. **Bernard II**, Duke of Saxony; b. c995; d. 29 June 1059; md c1020, **Elica von Schweinfurt** (270-34). Bernard II also md **Bertrade** (204-34), Princess of Norway.

33. **Gertrude of Saxony**, b. c1030; d. 4 Aug 1113; md (1) c1050, **Florenz I** (311-33), Count of Holland and of West Friesland; d. 28 June 1061; She md (2) **Robert I** "the Frisian" (205-32), Count of Flanders; b. c1035; d. 3 Oct 1093.

Sources: Blass, R. 1939, II:259, 293, 301; ES, II 1984:2 (Gen. 33–34); I 1984:8 (Gen. 33–36); III 1980:133 (Gen. 35); Isenburg, W. 1953, pt. i, table 10; Mateos, R. 1984; Moriarty, G. 1985, 56 (Gen. 33–35); 17 (Gen. 35–37); Salazar, J. de 1983; Winkhaus, E. 1953.

167

## LINE 313

32. **Lancelin I** (See 4-32 and Note), Seigneur de Baugency in the Orleanais and Seigneur de la Fleche in Anjou, liv 1033; d. 1051/1060.

31. **Jean** (John) **I**, Seigneur de la Fleche, Anjou, France; d. 1097; bur Saint-Aubin-d'Angers; md **Paula du Maine** (357-31), heiress of Maine.

30. **Helie de la Fleche** (de Baugency), of Anjou, Seigneur de la Fleche, Count of Maine, and Seigneur de Ballon; d. 11 July 1110; md (1) 1090, **Matilde** (Mahaut) (354-30), Dame de Château-du-Loir.

29. **Erembourge of Mans** (Maine), France; heiress of Maine; d. 1126; md c1108, **Fulk V** (152-31), Count of Anjou, King of Jerusalem, Crusader.

Sources: Agiles, R. 1968; Archern, K. 1993; Cokayne, G. 1959, IV:670, charts I and III; V:472, 472 note f, 736; VII:640; Conder, C. 1978; ES, II 1984:82 (Gen. 29); III 1989:68 (Gen. 30); III: 1989: 692 (Gen. 29–32);Krey, A. n.d.; Latouche, R. 1959b, vol. 13; Mayer, H. 1994; Moriarty, G. 1985, 11 (Gen. 29–32); Munro, D. 1935; Poole, S. 1978; Prawler, J. 1952; Prawler, J. 1972; Prawler, J. 1980; Richard, J. 1979; Riley-Smith, J. 1973; Runcimen, S. 1987.

## LINE 314

39. **Eadwulf**, Lord of Bamborough; a favorite of King Alfred "the Great." He is perhaps descended from the kings of Northumbria; md **N.N.**, who was carried off by Edred, after slaying her husband, Eadwulf, c918.

38. **Ealdred**, Lord of Bamborough in the time of Athelstan; liv 926.

37. **Oswulf** (Uswulf), Earldorman of Northumbria, Lord of Bamborough; occ 953–c965; d. c965.

36. **Waltheof I**, Earldorman of Northumbria, occ c994.

35. **Uchtred**, Earldorman of Northumbria; b. 989, murdered, 1016 by the Dane, Thurbrand; md (1) **Ecgfrida** (mother of Gen. 34), dau of **Ealdhun**, Bishop of Durham; md (2) **Aelfgifu**, b. c997, dau of **Aethelred II** (233-35), King of England, and **Elgiva** (Aelfgifu) (342-35).

34. **Ealdred** (Aldred), Earldorman of Bernicia (Northumbria beyond Tyne), b. c1009; slew Thurebrand and was then murdered by Thurbrand's son Karl.

33. **Aelflaed II of Northumberland** (fem); md (his 1st) **Siward Biornsson** (221-33), Earl of Northumbria, Northampton and Huntingdon.

Sources: Blass, R. 1939, II: 242; Cokayne, G. 1959, IV:504; IX:704; Moriarty, G. 1985, 183 (Gen. 33–39); Searle, W. 1899, 371–374; Paul, J. 1914, III:240–241 (Gen. 35–36); Winkhaus, E. 1953 (1950).

## LINE 315

39. **Hardouin** (Arduin), Count of Neustria; a *Missus Dominicu*r of Charles "the Bald;" d. before 862.

38. **Odo**, Count of Neustria, a favorite of Louis II, King of West Franks; d. by 878.

37. **Roger of Auriate**; d. after 902; md **N.N.**, widow of Rudolph, Count of Auriate. Roger was expelled from Neustria and went to Piedmont; occ 886,

910; may have come from Auvergne.

36. **Ardoino III Glabrione** (107-37) "il Glabro," Count and Marchese of Turino and Count of Auriate; d. after 976; md **N.N. di Mosezzo,** dau of **Manfredo,** Seignore di Mosezzo, who was blinded by Lambert in 886; granddau of **Manfredo,** Count of the Sacred Palace of Lodi and Milan and Marquess of Lombardy; beheaded by Lambert, 886.

35. **Manfredo I,** Marchese di Turino; d. c1000; md before 8 Mar 991, **Prangarda di Canossa,** dau of **Adalbert** (Otto, Ottone) **II,** Count of Modena and Canossa; d. 13 Feb 988; bur Canossa; son of **Siegfried Langobarde,** a nobleman who went from Lucca to Lombardy; b. Parma; d. after 958.

34. **Odalrico Manfredo II** (7-33,32-31,47-34,93-33), Margrave of Turin and Susa; d. 23 Dec 1035; bur Turino; md before 1014, **Bertha of Este** (93-33 etc.), d. 29 Dec 1037.

Sources: Blass, R. 1939, II:249; ES, III 1989:593 (Gen. 34–39); Fumagalli, V. 1971; Glaesener, H. 1947; Grimaldi, N. 1928; Hliawitschka, E. 1969; Moriarty, G. 1985, 60 (Gen. 34–39); Overmann, A. 1895; Schumann, R. 1973; Winkhaus, E. 1953.

## LINE 316

37. **Kunigunde** (104-37, 353-37). b. c890; d. after 923; she md **(1) Wigeric** (same as 65-38, 319-37, etc.) (father of Gen. 36), Count Palatine of Aachen, d. before 919; she md (2) c920, **Richwin** (403-36), Count of Verdun; d. 923; prob son of Regnier (Rainer).

36. **Siegfried** (same as 3-34, 353-36), Count in the Moselgau and of Luxemburg, Lay Abbot of Echternach; b. c922; d. 998; md c950, **Hedwig,** a Saxon; d. 13 Dec 992, perhaps dau of **Eberhard IV,** Count of the Alsacian Nordgau (202-37, 353-36), and **Luitgarde of Trier.**

35. **Luitgarde of Luxemburg,** d. 14 May 1005; md c980, **Arnold I** (311-35), Count of West Friesland.

Sources: Cosnac, R. 1969; Dek, A. 1955; ES, II 1984:2 (Gen. 35–36); VI 1978:127 (Gen. 36–37); Moriarty, G. 1985, 21–22 (Gen. 35–37); Renn, H. 1941; Vannerus, J. 1946, vol. 25, pt. 2, pp. 801–858.

## LINE 317

38. **William I de Forez,** Seigneur de la Forez; liv 871.

37. **William II de Forez,** Seigneur de la Forez; liv 890; d. 920.

36. **Artaud I de Forez;** nobleman in the Lyonnais; liv 929; d. 960; md **Hildegarde,** occ 929.

35. **Geraldus** (Geraud) **de Forez,** nobleman in the Lyonnais, 960; d. c990; md **Gimburgia,** liv c965–993.

34. **Artaud II de Forez,** Count of Lyon and la Forez; d. 11 Feb 1000; md (1) **Theutberga,** d. after 13 Apr 1013; dau of **Hugh** (173-36), Count of Vienne, and **Willa of Burgundy,** dau of **Richard** (206-38), Duke of Burgundy.

33. **Geraud II,** Count of la Forez, Rohau and of Lyon; liv 1007; d. 1058;

md before 1032, **Adelaide.**

32. **Artaud IV de Forez,** Count of Lyon and Forez; Lost Lyon to the Archbishop of Lyon, 1058; d. by 1077; md **Ida Raimonde,** of la Forez, Provence, France, who descended from Count **Geilin** and **Raimonde.**

31. **Ida Raimonde de Lyon,** heiress of the countship of la Forez; md (1) **Renaud II** (232-31), Count of Nevers and Auxerre; md (2) Guigues Raimond d'Albon.

Sources: Blass, R. 1939, II:241, 250; Brand, C. 1968; ES, III 1989:737 (Gen. 31–35); II 1984:190 (Gen. 34); Fournial, R 1952; Fournial.R 1956; Gerner, 1968:139–145; Moriarty, G. 1985, 66 (Gen. 31–38); Winkhaus, E. 1953.

## LINE 318

35. **Ludolf** (Ludwig) **von Braunschweig** (32-32), Count in the Derlingo; Margrave of West Friesland, md **Gertrude von Egisheim** (33-32).

34. **Agatha von Braunschweig,** res. of West Friesland; b. c1025, Bavaria, Germany; d. after 1066; md c1043, **Edward** "Atheling" (233-33), Prince of England.

*NOTE: The parentage of Agatha (Gen. 34), wife of Edward "Atheling," has been under serious discussion for several decades. G. Andrews Moriarty, G. 1985, in an article in NEHGR, 106:52–60 (Jan. 1952), explains the two prevailing views—kinship with the Hungarian kings (dau of King Stephen) and kinship with the German Emperors (dau of Ludolph, Margrave of West Friesland). He opted for Stephen, and says so in his* Plantagenet Ancestry, p. 31. *The great scholar, Szabolcs de Vajay, in* Duquesne Review, 7:71–87 *(Spring, 1962), makes the very convincing case for Ludolph. I support the "German" view using Detlev Schwennicke's* Europäische Stammtafeln *(ES, II:78), 1984 research, as one of my sources.*

Sources: ES, II 1984:78 (Gen. 34–35); Paget, G. 1977 (Gen. 34–35); Vajay, S. de 1962b; Wunder, G. 1975, 81–88 (Gen. 34–35).

## LINE 319

37. **Wigeric** (see 33-35, 104-37), Count in the Triergau; md **Kunigunde** (104-37, 353-37).

36. **Frederick I** (64-34), Count of Bar and Duke of Upper Lorraine; b. c912; d. 18 May 978 or 17 June 984; md 954, **Beatrice,** dau of **Hugh Magnus** (64-35,134-35), Duke of France and Burgundy, and **Hedwig of Saxony,** dau of Henry I "the Fowler" (92-36), King of Germany; Emp. of the West.

35. **Dietrich I** (247-33), Count of Bar and Duke of Upper Lorraine; b. c965; d. 1027/1033; md **Richilde** (337-35), d. before 995.

34. **Adelaide of Upper Lorraine,** d. after 1052; md **Waleran I** "the Old" (62-34), Count of Arlon, 1052; d. before 1078.

Sources Blass, R. 1939, II:268, 272; Brandenburg, E. 1935; ES, VI 1978:127 (Gen. 35–37); Moriarty, G. 1985, 159–160 (Gen. 34–36); 126 (Gen. 37);

Parisse, M. 1976; Renn, H. 1941; Vanderkindere, L. 1902, vol. II: table IV; Winkhaus, E. 1953.

## LINE 320

29. **Arnulf** (100-31), Count of Loos and of Rieneck; Burggrave of Mainz; founded with his son Louis, the monastery of Overboden; d. 1135; md c1100, **Agnes von Mainz**, heiress of the countship of Rieneck and the burggraveship of Mainz; dau of **Gerhard**, Burggrave of Rieneck and Mainz; md **Hedwig of Blieskastel** (278-29), dau of **Gottfried I**, Graf of Blieskastel.

28. **Louis I**, Count of Loos and Rieneck, Burggrave of Mainz; advocate of Averboden and Munsterbilsen; b. c1100; d. 11 Aug 1171; md c1140, **Agnes von Metz** (45-28).

27. **Agnes von Loos**, b. c1150; d. 26 Mar 1191; md 1159/67, **Otto von Wittelsbach I** (307-27).

Sources: ES, VI 1978:60 (Gen. 27–29); I 1980:23 (Gen. 27–28); Moller, W. 1950 (but 2nd ed.), II:XLVIII (1933); Moriarty, G. 1985, 189 (Gen. 27–29); Winkhaus, E. 1953.

## LINE 321

37. **Henry I** "the Fowler" (92-36,338-36)), King of Germany, Emperor of the West, md **Mathilda** (Mechtilde) **von Ringleheim** (92-36).

36. **Otto I** (337-37,359-37) "the Great," King of Germany, 939–973; King of Italy, 951; Emperor of the West, 962–973; b. 23 Nov 912; d. 7 May 973, Memleben; md (1) **Eadgyth**, dau of **Edward** "the Elder" (233-38), King of England; and **Aelflaed** (376-38); md (2) St. **Adelaide of Burgundy** (323-34). Neither wife is mother of Gen. 35.

35. **Liudolf**, Duke of Swabia, d.957; md **Ita of Swabia** (321A-35).

34. **Richilde**, md **Kuno** (29-35,33-33), Count of Ohningen.

33. **N. N.** md (his 8th) St. **Vladimir**, Grand Prince of Kiev.

32. **Debroniega of Kiev** (361-32), b. after 1011; d. 1087; md 1035 **Casimir I** (378-33), King of Poland, b. 28 July 1016; d. 28 Nov 1058.

Sources: Decker, H. 1947, 67-85; Decker, H. 1977; ES I.1 1997; ES, II 1984:128 (Gen. 33); ES I 1984:3 (Gen. 35–36); Jackman, D. 1990; Jaclman, D. 1997; Moriarty, G. 1985, 53 (Gen. 33); 87 (Gen. 34–35); 25 (Gen. 35–36); Settipani, C. 1996a; Taube.M. 1947.

## LINE 321A

37. **Gebhard**, Duke of Lorraine, d. 910; md **Idda** (Hidda), dau of **Christian II**, Count of Grabfeld.

36. **Hermann II**, Duke of Swabia, d. 949; md **Reginlint**, widow of Burkhardt II, Duke of Swabia, and dau of **Meingaud II**, d. 892; by his wife **Gisela**.

35. **Ita of Swabia**, d. 17 May 896; md **Liudolf** (321-35), Duke of Swabia, b. 930; d. 6 Sept 957.

171

Sources: Jackman, D. 1990: 145-147,178-195; Jackman, D. 1997: 36-42; Settipani, C. 1996: 135-166.

## LINE 322

53 **Hamazasp (I)**, Prince of Mamikonids; High Constable of Armenia; b. 345 AD; d. c416; md **Sahakanoysh** (416-53), the Gregorian heiress.

52 **Hmayeak,** a Mamikonid, Ambassador of Armenia to the Eastern Roman Emperor, 449 AD; a general, 451; b. 410; d. 451 in battle; md **Dzoyk,** dau of **Vram,** prince of Artsruni.

51. **Vard,** Mamikonian patrician in Armenia; viceroy of Armenia, 505-509; b. 450; d.+509 AD.

50. **Hmayeak,** Mamikonian viceroy, c591-593.

49 **Moushegh I,** Mamikonian viceroy and sparapet of Armenia.

48. **Vahan II (III),** Mamikonian prince of Taraun, c600; b. 555; d. c600. *NOTE: Some sources question that Gen. 47 was the son of Gen. 48.*

47. **Dawith,** a Mamikonian, prob the nakharar in Taraun; prob a priest.

46. **Hamazasp III,** a Mamikonian maezpan and curopalate; b. 610; d. 658; md **N.N.**, a dau of **Theodoros Rshtouni** (Theodore I, prince of Rshtuni).

45 **Artavazd (322A-42),** a Mamikonian patrician, b. 650/655.

44. **Hamayeak,** a Mamikonian patrician. b. 700; d. c788.

43. **Artavazd,** a Mamikonian patrician who migrated from Georgia, 771 AD; strategos of the Anatalians, 778 AD; b. 740; d. c778; fought against the Arams, 774 AD.

42. **Hmayeak** (Maiactes), a Mamikonid prince; b. 755; d. 780/797; md **N.N.** of Armenia, a dau of **Leo V** "the Armenian," Emperor of the East; d. 25 Dec 820, who md **Theodocia,** dau of **Arschavier,** Prince of Kamsarakan; son of **Bardas,** strategos of Armenia, 771-780; who was b. 735; d. 791.

41. **Konstantinos,** an officer of the court of the Emperor Michael III; b. 785, md **Pancalo.**

40. **Bardas,** magistros.; b. 835; d. c867; bro of Basil I, (253-40) Byzantine Emperor.

39. **Basileos,** rector.

38. **Gregoria** (Georgia) md **Niketas Skleros,** Patrician (father of Gen. 37); b. c885; liv 921; son of **Leo Skleros.** He was at the court of the Basilius Leo VI; Gregoria also md **Munir Skleros** (cf. 115-36).

37. **Konstantin Skleros,** Patrician at Constantinople; b. c920; d. after 980; md c950, **Sophia Phokas** (219-37), b. c936.

36. **Theophano Skleros,** of Byzantium, b. 956; d. 15 Sept 991, Nymwagen; md 14 Apr 972, **Otto II** (237-36), Emperor of the West and King of Italy; b. 954/955; d. 7 Dec 983. *NOTE: Theophano Skleros was not dau of Romanus II, Eastern Roman Emperor, as stated by several sources. See Moriarty, G. 1985, G. 1950c for scholarly refutation.*

Sources: Allen, J. 1985; Bierbrier, M. 1993:200; Brook, L. 1981; Brosset, M. 1886, 387; Buckler, G. 1929; Collins, R. 1991; Geanakoplos, D. 1959,

419–420; Macler, F. 1905; Mamikonian, J. 1868, 324; Paget, G. 1977, 1:61 table IX; 70 table XVIII; 2:332, 478 table IV; Rockchow, I. 1991; Seibt, W. 1976; Settipani, C. 1991, 185-187; Stone, D. 1995, charts 80, 81; Toumanoff, C. 1966; Vajay, S. de 1962; Weis, F. 1992.

## LINE 322A

46. **Georgios**, an Armenian, b. 675; md **Anna**, b. 680.

45. **Philaretos**, consul; b. 702; d. 792; md **Theosebia**, a noble, b. 725; d. ap 782.

44. **Iohannes**, spatharios, 788/792; b. 745; d. ap c800; md **Eirene**, b. 755; d. 823; dau of **Leon**, a patrician, b. 730; and **Anna**, b. 735; dau of **Sergios**, a noble of Constantinople, b. 700, d. 745; who md **Euphemia**, b. 715; d. 747.

43. **Bardas**, b. 775; d. ap 792; prob father of Gen. 42.

42. **Theoktista Phlorina**, titled patrician, noble of Paphlogonia, b. 795; d. ap 831; md **Marinus**, b. 780; d. 815/830; toumarque and dragonaire in Paphlogonia. He was son of **Artavazd** (322-43), a Mamiconian patrician. *The joint ancestry of the emperors Michael III and Basil I begins here.*

41. Saint **Theodora**, b. c815; d. ap 24 Sept 867; regent for her son Michael III, during his minority, 842-856; md 5 June 830, **Theophilos**, Emperor of Byzantium, 820-829; d. 842; son of **Michael II**, Emperor of Byzantium, 829-842, who was son of **Leon V**, Emp of Byzantium (818-820), and gson of **Georgios**, b. 725. Michael II md (1) Thekla; md (2) **Euphrosyne**, dau of **Konstantinos** VI, Emperor of Byzantium, 780-797; b. 771; d. ap 803. Theodora, as a widow, became a nun, and later was made a saint.

40. **Michael III**, Emperor of Byzantium, 20 Jan 842- 24 Sept 867; b. 840; d. 24 Sept. 867; md (1) Eudokia Dekapolitissa (no issue); (md) (2) **Eudokia Ingarina** (253-40), his longtime mistress, whom he shared with Basil I, as Basil's wife. *Either Michael III or Basil I was the father of the emperor Leo VI (253-39).*

Sources: Karlin, P. 1991; Markropoulis, A. 1983, 249-298; Oxford, 1991; Settipani, C. 1991, chart, p. 17; Settipani, C. 1997, p. 18; Stone, D. 1985, charts 81, 82; Treadgold, W. 1988.

## LINE 322B

43. **Theoserbia**, a noble, b. 725; d. c792; md **Philaretos**, consul, 788; b. 702, d. 792.

42. **Hypatia**, b. 755; d. c788.

41. **Maria**, b. 770/775; d. c 821; md **Konstantinos VI**, Emperor of Byzantium, 780-797; b. 770/775; d. c821; son of **Leon IV** and **Eirene**.

40. **Euphrosyne** md **Michael II** (322A-41), Emperor of Byzantium.

Sources: Settipani, C. 1991, charts 30 and 31; Oxford, 1991; Treadgold, W. 1988, 421.

35. **Rudolph II** (175-35), King of Burgundy, md **Bertha of Swabia** (345-37).

34. St. **Adelaide of Burgundy**; b. 932; d. 17 Dec 999; md **Otto I** "the Great" (237-37;321-35), King of Germany; Emperor of the West.

Sources: ES, I 1984:3 (Gen. 34–35); Moriarty, G. 1985, 25, 87 (Gen. 34); 33 (Gen. 35).

## LINE 324

63. **Frithuwald** (233-63) md **Beltsea**, of Asgard.

62. **Odin**, of Asgard, Asia; b. c215; md (1) **Frigg**, b. c219.

61. **Skjold**, of Hleithra, Denmark, King of the Danes; b. c237; md **Gefion**, b. c241.

60. **Fridleif Skjoldsson**, of Hleithra, Denmark.

59. **Frodi Fridleifsson**, of Hleithra, Denmark; b. c281.

58. **Fridleif Frodasson**, of Hleithra, Denmark; b. c303.

57. **Havar Fridleifsson**, of Denmark; b. c325.

56. **Frodi Havarsson**, of Denmark; b. c347.

55. **Vermund Frodasson**, of Denmark; b. c366.

54. **Olaf Vermundsson**, of Denmark; b. c391; md **Dampi**, b. c395, Denmark (parentage unknown).

53. **Frodi Olafsson**, of Denmark; b. c433.

52. **Fridleif Frodasson** (143-44), of Denmark; b. c456.

51. **Frodi Fridleifsson**, of Denmark; b. c479.

50. **Halfdan Frodasson**, of Denmark (see also 240-49); b. c503; md **Sigris**.

49. **Helgi Halfdansdotter**, of Denmark; b. c528; md **Olaf** "the Mighty," b. c540.

48. **Yrsa Helgasdotter**, of Denmark; b. c565; md **Adils Ottarsson**, of Sweden (166-47).

*NOTE: Eric Christiansen, in Brook, L. 1989 (pp. 17–43), gives good evidence that many of the genealogies of Medieval Denmark are inaccurate or fraudulant, and that finding the true lineage of the nobility is a difficult and perhaps fruitless task. In two tables (pp. 27, 29), Christiansen summarizes four sources: Saemundr's "Aettarjaj;" the "Lejre Chronicle;" the writer Sveno; and the "Skjoldunga Saga." Two of these, Saemundr and Skjoldunga, show a relationship to RFC, line 324, though this does not improve the trustworthiness of the original RFC account, based on other sources. Saemundr covers Gen. 51–61; then continues with a different sibling (Ingialdr); Skjoldunga covers Gen. 49–61, when RFC changes to a different sibling. None of the four sources include RFC Gen. 62 and 63. Christiansen's charts include only the person's given name.*

Sources: Christiansen, E. 1989, 17–43 (Gen. 49–61); Hodgkin,.A, I:241; Searle, W. 1899, 251–255.

37. **N.N.**, md **Sergius I**, Duke of Amalfi.

36. **Leone of Amalfi.**

35. **Porpora of Amalfi**, md **Alfano**, Count of Tabellaria.

34. **Laidolfo**, Count of Tabellaria, md **Aldara** of San Massimo, dau of **Truppualdo**, Count of San Massimo.

33. **Porpora of Tabellaria** md **Guaimar** (Waimar) **IV** (297-33), Prince of Salerno, Capua, Amalfi, etc.

Sources: Brandenburg, E. 1935; Dhoudt, 119-120, 122; Evans, C. 1965; Evans, C. 1976; Evans, C. 1983; Newman, W. 1971; Provite, C. 1912, 197, 212; Sanfelice.A 1962; Vajay, S. de 1960; Vajay, S. de 1969.

## LINE 326

41. **Theuderic** (Makhir) (same as 329-41), Duke of Toulouse, Count of Autun, Exilarch of Narbonne (Septimania); liv 771-793, Septimania; md **Aude**, perhaps dau of Charles Martel (171-43). *NOTE: Some researchers feel that Theoderic and Makhir are two different persons. Line 326 follows Theuderic.*

40. **William of Gellone**, Duke of Toulouse, Margrave of Septimania (Narbonne); d. 812/813 at Gellone; md (1) Kunigunde; md (2) **Gilbour of Hornbach** (330-41) (mother of Gen, 39). *NOTE: A few serious researchers say that William of Gellone is identical with Isaac the Jew.*

39. **Bernard**, Count of Autun, Margrave of Septimania; the famous chamberlain of Louis "the Pious"; executed, 844, Aachen; md **Dhoude** (Liegard) (326A-39).

38. **Roselinde**, heiress of the countship of Agen; d. between 896 and 901; md c844, **Wulgrim**, Count of Agen, Angouleme and Perigord; Count of the Palace of King Charles "the Bald;" Vulgrim d. 3 May 886; son of Ulrich I (364-40), Count of Argengau.

37. **William**, Count of Perigord and Agen; d. 920; md **Regilinda**, dau of **Rutpert IV** (called "Robert the Strong") (169-38), Count of Paris, etc.

36. **Emma of Perigord**, md **Boso I** (327-35), Count de la Marche.

Sources: Albright, W. 1963; Beauchat, E 1978, 667; Blass, R. 1939, II:254; Bouchard, C. 1987:651-658; Boussard, J. 1957; Brady, R. 1998; Chaume, M. 1977, I:550–552; Depoin, J.1905; Enc. Jud., 1971; ES, III 1989:817 (Gen. 38–39); Goode, A., 1941; Jackman, D. 1997; Jew. Enc. 1901; Johnson, M. 1969; Levillain, L. 1937, 49:337–340, 50:5–66; Lot, F. 1908, 385, 395; Malan, R. 1997; Neusner, J. 1997; NIV 1985; Richard, A. 1903; Taylor, N. 1997; Thiele, E. 1977; Wilson, R. 1977; Winkhaus, E. 1953.

## LINE 326A

41. **Lupus**, a Gascon, md a Galician princess, perhaps **N.N.**, dau of **Fruella**, Countess of Cantabria.

40. **Sancho Lupus** of Gascony, liv c772-816; md **N.N.**, dau of **Aznar I**

Galindez (292-43,288-41).

39. **Dhoude**, b. c804; d. after 844; md **Bernard** (326-39,333A-40), Margrave of Septimania.

Source: Malan, R. 1997:116-126.

## LINE 327

37. **Geoffrey de Charroux**, Count de la Haute Marche, liv c890.

36. **Sulpice de Charroux**, Count de la Haute Marche.

35. **Boso I**, Count de la Marche and la Haute Marche, Count of Perigord and Aun; md 944, **Emma of Perigord** (326-36).

34. **Adalbert I**, Count de la Haute Marche and Perigord; was at the fall of Gencay, 997; killed 997, prob at Gencay; md c975 (her 1st, his 1st), **Almode de Limoges** (328-35), d. 1007/1011.

33. **Bernard I**, Count de la Haute Marche and Perigord; b. 986; d. 1047; md **Amelia**, dau of **Geraud de Montignac** and **Nonia de Granol**.

32. **Almode de la Haute Marche** md 1044/1045, **Pons III** (374-31), Count of Toulouse, Dijon and Albi. She was murdered 1071/1075 by her stepson Peter Raimond of Barcelona.

Sources: Blass, R. 1939, II:254; ES, III 1989:819 (Gen. 32–35); Lot, .F 1903, 351n, 396; Moriarty, G. 1985, 42 (Gen. 32–37); Thomas, G. 1928, 1–10; Winkhaus, E. 1953.

## LINE 328

40. **Raimonde I** (329-38), Count of Toulouse, md **Bertha** (Berta), dau of **Remigius** and **Arsinde of Toulouse**.

39. **Foucaud de Limoges**, d. 886; md **N.N.**, a dau of **Gerhard**, Count of Auvergne, and **Hildegarde of Francia**; dau of **Louis I** (171-40), Emperor of the West, and **Ermengarde of Hesbaye** (352-41).

38. **Hildebert** (398-39), Vicomte de Limoges, 876; b. c835; md (1) Tetburga; md (2) **Adaltrude** (mother of Gen. 37).

37. **Hildegar** (Eldegaire), Vicomte de Limoges; b. c864; d. after 26 Mar 937; md **Tietberga** (Tetrisca) **of Bourges**, dau of **Geraud**, Count of Bourges, son of **Boso of Parthois**. *NOTE: some authorities add another Hildegar between Gen. 36 and 37 (says Moriarty, G. 1985, p. 234).*

36. **Geraud** (398-35), Vicomte de Limoges; liv 960–991; md c950, **Rothilde**, heiress of her father, **Ademar**, Vicomte de Brosse and wife, **Melisendis**, widow of Archambaud.

35. **Almode de la Limoges**, d. 1007/1011; md c975 (1) **Adalbert I** (327-34), Count de la Haute Marche and Perigord.

Sources: Boussard, J. 1957; Chaume, M. 1977, 550–552; ES, III 1989:773 (Gen. 35–38); Marot, P. 1984, 574 (Gen. 35–38); Moriarty, G. 1985, 43–44 (Gen. 35–38); 41 (Gen. 40); Nadaud, J. 1974, 95–98, 580–584 (Gen. 35–38).

## LINE 329

97. **Tarakr** (Terah in Genesis 11:31) is accepted by three well-known

and trusted Sunni Arabian sources as the father of Abraham. These sources are: *al-Bidaya wan Nehaya*, by Ibn Katheer, vol. I, p. 139; *History of al Tabari*, vol. I, p. 119; and *Tafsir Tabari*, by Ibn Jarir al-Tabari, vol. 7, p. 158.

96. **Abraham** (Abram), b. in Ur of the Chaldeans; res. Caanan; d. in Caanan and bur in the cave of Machpelah near Mamre in the field of Ephrom, son of Zahar the Hittite, in a field Abraham bought from the Hittites; md **Sarah** (Serai) (mother of Gen. 95), who was b. in Ur of the Chaldeans and d. at Kiriath, Arba, in Hebron, Caanan; bur with her husband. Abraham was a wealthy livestock owner. Sources: Gen. 23:1-24; 25:7-10; 1 Chron. 1:20-27.

95. **Isaac**, son of Gen. 96, was b. in Caanan, md **Rebekah** (mother of Gen. 94) when he was 40; she was dau of **Bethuel**, the Aramean, from Paddam Aram in Northwest Mesopotamia, son of **Nahor** and wife **Micah**. They were md at Beer Lelai Roi, located in southwest Negau. Source: Gen. 21:1-3, 24:24, 25:20.

94. **Jacob** (Israel) was b. in Canaan as a twin (bro of Esau); md **Leah**, of Paddam Aram (mother of Gen. 93). They were both bur in the family cave of Machpelah. Jacob was a prosperous sheep herder and livestock owner. Sources: Gen. 25:19-26; 28:28; 29:31.

93. **Judah** (Judeh), b. in Canaan, md **Tamur** (mother of Gen. 92), a Canaanite, dau of **Shua**, and widow of Judah's elder sons Er and Onan. Source: Gen. 35:23, 1 Chron. 2:1.

92. **Perez** was a prominent clan leader in Judah. Source: 1 Chron 2:5.

91. **Hezron.** Source: 1 Chron. 2:5

90. **Aram.** Source: 1 Chron. 2:9.

89. **Amminadab.** Source: 1 Chron. 2:10.

88. **Nahshon**, a leader of the tribe of Judah. Source: 1 Chron. 2:10.

87. **Salmon.** Source: 1 Chron. 2:11.

86. **Boaz**, a wealthy Bethlehemite, md (her 2nd) **Ruth**, a Moabite (mother of Gen. 85). He was a prominent member of the clan of Elimelech. Source: 1 Chron. 2:11.

85. **Obed.** Source: 1 Chron. 2:12.

84. **Jesse.** Source: 1 Chron. 2:13.

83. **David**, King of Judah, and, later, King of Israel; md **Bathsheba** (Bathshua), (mother of Gen. 82); dau of **Ammiel** (or Eliam) and widow of Uriah, whom David sent to his death on a dangerous mission. Source: 1 Chron. 2:13-15. Mentioned on the Tel Dan stela (9th c. BCE), also mentioned on the stela of the Moabite king Mesha (c849-820 BCE).

82. **Solomon**, King of Israel, 965-928; md **Naamah** (mother of Gen. 81), an Ammorite princess. Source: 1 Chron. 3:5.

81. **Rehoboam**, King of Judah, 928-911; md **Maacah** (mother of Gen. 80), dau of **Talmai** (2 Sam. 3:3), King of Gosher, a small Aramean city-kingdom, Northeast of the Sea of Galilee. Source: 1 Chron. 3:10.

80. **Abijah** (Abijam), King of Judah, 911-908. Source: 1 Chron. 3:10.

79. **Asa**, King of Judah, 908-867; md **Azubah**, dau of **Shilhi**. Sources: 1 Chron. 3:10; 1 Kings 22:42.

78. **Jehosaphat**, King of Judah, 867-846. Source: 1 Chron. 3:10.

77. **Jehoram**, King of Judah, 846-843; introduced Baal worship; md **Athaliah**, dau of **Ahab**, King of Israel, 871-852, by unk. wife. Athaliah reigned 842-836, after her son's death. Sources: 1 Chron. 3:11; 2 Kings 8:18; mentioned on the Tel Dan stela (9th c. BCE).

76. **Ahaziah**, King of Judah, 843-842; md **Zibiah**, of Beersheba. Sources: 1 Chron. 3:11; 2 Kings 12:1; mentioned on the Tel Dan stela (9th c. BCE)

75. **Joash**, King of Judah, 836-798; md **Jehoaddin**, of Jerusalem. Sources: 1 Chron. 3:11; 2 Kings 14:2.

74. **Amaziah**, King of Judah, 798-769; md **Jecoliah**, of Jerusalem. Sources: 1 Chron. 3:12; 2 Kings 15:2.

73. **Azariah** (Uzziah), King of Judah, 769-733; md **Jerusha**, dau of **Zadok**. Mentioned in the Annals of the Assyrian king Tilglath-Pilesar III (c724-727 BCE).

72. **Jotham**, King of Judah, 740-732.Co-regent with his father from 750 (2 Chron 26:1).

71. **Ahaz**, King of Judah, 733-727; md **Abijah** (or Abi), dau of **Zechariah**. Sources: 1 Chron. 3:12; 2 Kings 18:12. *NOTE: In the July/ August, 1996*, Biblical Archaeology Review, *it was noted that recently was found a bulla [seal impression in clay] reading, in two lines, " Ahaz (son of) Jotham, King of Judah."* Also Ahaz is mentioned in the Annals of the Assyrian king Tiglath-Pilesar II (c 744-727 BCE.)

70. **Hezekiah**, King of Judah, 727-698. He reopened the Temple and for a time gained some independence from Assyria; md **Hephzibah**. Sources: 1 Chron. 3:13; 2 Kings 21:1. Hezekiah is mentioned on the Taylor prism of the Assyrian King Sennacherib (c704-681 BCE) and mentioned in the bull inscription of Sennacherib.

69. **Manassah**, King of Judah, 698-642; md **Meshullemeth**, dau of **Haroz**, of Jotbah. Sources: 1 Chron. 3:13: 2 Kings 21:1.

68. **Amon**, King of Judah, 641-640; md **Jedidah**, dau of **Adaiah**, of Bozkath. Sources: 1 Chron. 3:14; 2 Kings 21:3.

67. **Josiah**, King of Judah, 640-609; initiated many religious reforms; slain by the Egyptians at Megiddo. His body was taken by chariot to his tomb in Jerusalem; md **Zebidah**, dau of **Pedaiah**, of Rumah. Sources: 1 Chron. 3:15; 2 Kings 23:36.

66. **Jehoiakim** (Jehohaz), King of Judah, 609-598, after his brother served as king briefly in 609; appointed king by Egyptian Pharaoh Neco; md **Nehushta**, dau of **Elnathan**, of Jerusalem. Sources: 1 Chron. 3:15; 2 Kings 24:8; mentioned in the Rotation document of the Babylonian King Nebuchadnezzar II (c605-562 BCE).

65. **Jehoiachin** (or Jeconiah), King of Judah, 597-596; taken captive to

Babylon by Nebuchadnezzar II as noted on tablets found in Babylon dating from the reign of Nebuchadnezzar II, 595-570, where is listed the deliveries of rations of oil and barley to the captive Jehoiachim and five of his sons, among others. Sources: 1 Chron. 3:16; NIV Bible notes for 1 Chron. 3:17-20 and 2 Kings 25:27.

64. **Pediah**, son of Gen. 65. Source: 1 Chron. 3:17. *NOTE: Some sources give Shealtiel as father of Gen. 63.*

63. **Zerubbabel** (father of Gen. 62), a Jewish tribal leader who returned to Judah in 538 BC after Cyrus, King of Persia, captured Babylon. Source: 1 Chron. 3:19.

62. **Hananiah** (son of Gen. 63 and descendant of Gen. 61). Source: 1 Chron. 3: 19-21.

61. **Shecaniah**, descendant of Gen. 62. Source: 1 Chron. 3:22.

60. **Neariah**, a descendant of Gen. 61. Source: 1 Chron. 3:22.

59. **Hizkiah** (son of Gen. 60) and bro of Elioenai. Source: 1 Chron. 3:23.

58. **Johanan**, descendant of Gen. 59, Exilarch at Babylon.

57. **Shephat**, (son of Gen. 58); Exilarch at Babylon.

56. **Hanan** (Anan), Exilarch at Babylon, ca. 260-ca. 275 AD; md **N.N.**, a dau of **Abba ben Aivu** (or Abba Arikha), founder of the Academy at Sura and co-founder of the Babylonian Talmud.

55. **Nathan I** (Ukna), Exilarch at Babylon, ca. 318-ca. 290.

54. **Nehemiah**, Exilarch at Babylon, ca. 290-ca. 318.

53. **Nathan** (or Ukba II (III)), Exilarch at Babylon, ca. 318-ca. 337.

52. **Abba** (or Abra Mar), Exilarch at Babylon, ca. 350-ca. 370, Perhaps father of King Yezdegtrd's wife.

51. **Kahani I**, Exilarch at Babylon.

50. **Zutra I**, Exilarch at Babylon, d. 413 AD.

*NOTE: Perhaps one or more generations missing at this point.*

49. **Huna** (or Ahunai), prob an exilarch, ca. 550-ca.560.

48. **Kafnai** (or Hofnai), Exilarch at Babylon, ca. 560-ca. 581; was persecuted by Hormisdas IV.

47. **Haninai**, Exilarch at Babylon, md N.N., dau of **Hananiah**, Geon (rector of the academy) of Sura.

46. **Bostani ben Haninai,** Exilarch at Babylon; d. ca. 670; a powerful Jewish leader; md (1) **N.N.**, a Jewish wife (mother of Gen. 45); md, also, **Princess Izdundad** (or Izdadwar), dau of **Yazdagerd III** (408-45), King of Persia and last of the Sassanian dynasty.

45. **Haninai bar 'Adol,** Exilarch at Babylon succeeding his father.

44. **Nehemiah,** son of Gen. 45.

43. **Natroni ben Nehemiah,** Gaon of Pumbedia, 719-730; md N.N. (408-42), dau of **Hisdai Shahrijar,** Exilarch at Babylon, 660-665.

42. **Habibai** (or Haninai), son of Gen. 43.

41. **Theuderic** (Thierry, Makhir) (same as 326-41), Duke of Toulouse; Count of Autun, Exilarch of Narbonne (Septimania); liv 771–793, Septimania, md

**Aude**, perhaps dau of **Charles Martel** (171-43). *NOTE: Some researchers feel that Theuderic and Makhir are two different persons.*

40. **Bertha** (Auda) of Autun, md **Fredelon**.

39. **Senegonde**, b. c785, md **Fulgaud** (Foucaud), Count of Rouergue; liv 837.

38. **Raimond I** (328-40), Count of Rouergue and Toulouse, having succeeded his brother Fredelon, c852; a kinsman of Archbishop Hincmer of Rheims; d. 863; md **Bertha** (Berta), occ 833; dau of **Remigius** and **Arsinde.**

37. **Eudes** (Odon), Count of Toulouse and Rouergue, Marquis of Gothie; d. 919; md c855, **Gersinde**, heiress of Albi; dau of **Armengol**, Count of Albi, 862; d. 878.

36. **Raimond II**, Count of Toulouse and Albi, Marquis of Gothie; occ 895–961; md **Gunhilde**, dau of **Wilfred I** (54-37), Count of Urgel, and **Guinidilda**, dau of **Baldwin I** (235-38), Count of Flanders.

35. **Raimond III** (Raymond Pons), Count of Toulouse and Albi, Duke of Aquitaine, Marquis of Gothie; md (1) **Gersende of Gascony** (same as 54-35) (mother of Gen. 34), a widow in 972; dau of **Garcia Sanchez**, Count of Gascony; occ 893–920; md (2) Aimerudis d'Auvergne, dau Count Raymond.

34. **William III Taillefer** (374-32), Count of Toulouse, b. 947; d. 1037; md **Emma of Provence**, (375-32).

Sources: Aurell, M. 1997:357-380; Auzias, L. 1937; Blass, R. 1939, II:253, 259, 269, 280, 284; Bouchard, C. 1987: 651-658; Bruel, A. 1888; Calmette.J. 1963, 225-235; Collenburg, W. 1963 (Gen. 35-40; Debax, H. 1988; ES, III 1989:763 (Gen. 36–38); Fornery, J. 1982, 366; Framond, M. 1993; Guerard, B.; Latour, P. de 1997; NIV, 1995; Pirie, R. 1962; Settipani, C. 1997b; Taylor, N. 1997; Vannerus, J. 1946, vol. 25, 851–858; Winkhaus, E. 1953.

## LINE 330

45. **Warinus** (Guerin, Warin) (2-45,358-45) md **Gunza** (Kunza).

44. Saint **Lievin**, Count and Bishop of Treves; d. 724; bur at Mettlach.

43. **Count Gui**, occ 706–722.

42. **Lambert** (same as 169-39, 200-44, 265-44, 336-42), Count and Lord of Hornbach.

41. **Guibour of Hornbach** md **William of Gellone** (326-40), Margrave of Septimania; liv 790–806.

Sourcres: *Bible Review*, XI:6, Dec 1995, page 30; Chaume, M. 1977, 535; Chaume, M. 1947a; Levillain, L. 1937, vol. 49, 50; Moriarty, G. 1985, 74 (Gen. 41–45); Moriarty, G. 1985, G. 1953; Settipani, C. 1990; Winkhaus, E. 1953.

## LINE 331

39. **Cadelon I**, Vicomte d'Aunay; b. 928/937; md **Geila**, b. Dec. 928.

38. **Cadelon II**, Vicomte d'Aunay; liv 941–950; md **Gisela of Melle**, perhaps dau of **Atton**, Vicomte of Melle.

37. **Cadelon III**, Vicomte d'Aunay; liv 937; d. 967; md (1) 964, **Senegunde de Marcillac**, d. before 992; dau of **Remi** and wife **Odulgarde**.

36. **Aldegarde**, d. 1020; md **Herbert I** (159-36), Vicomte de Thouars; She md (her 2nd. his 2nd) **Arnaud "Manzier"** (87-34), Count of Angoulême, d. 989/991.

Sources: Blass, R. 1939, II 1984:253; ES, III 1989:810 (Gen. 36–37); III 1989:814 (Gen. 36–39); Geraurd, P. 1961; Moriarty, G. 1985, 46 (Gen. 36–37); 271 (Gen. 36–39); Morin, A. 1964, 18-37; Stauffenburg, F. von 1961; Winkhaus, E. 1953.

## LINE 332

40. **Hunroch** (404-40), Margrave of Friuli, md **Engeltrude** (185-40,269-40).

39. **Amadeus**, Count of Burgundy, d. after 827.

38. **Anscar II** (Anchier) "the Burgundian," Count of Orcheret, Marquis of Ivrea, d. 891/898. Went to Italy with Gui of Spoleto against Berenger I, 879–881; md **Giselle**.

37. **Adalbert I** (62-37), Marquis of Ivrea; b. 880/885; d. 923/925; md before 900, **Gisela of Friuli** (269-37) (mother of Gen. 36), Princess of Italy; md **Ermengarde of Tuscany** (198-39).

36. **Berenger** (Berengarius) **II** (94-35,106-36), King of Italy, Marquis of Ivrea; d. 6 July 966, Bamberg; md 936, **Willa of Arles** (263-36).

35. **Susanna** (Rosella), Princess of Italy, heiress of Montreuil-sur-Mer; b. c950; d. 7 Feb or 13 Dec 1003; md 968, **Arnulf** (Arnold) **II** "the Young" (141-34, 184-35), Count of Flanders.

Sources: Blass, R. 1939, II:270; Chaume, M. 1977, I 463, 539, 542, 543; Curschmann, F. 1921; ES, II 1984:59 (Gen. 35–39); Grierson, P. 1938, 24:241; Isenburg, W. 1953; Moriarty, G. 1985, 18 (Gen. 35–40); Winkhaus, E. 1953.

## LINE 333

37. **Rotbaude I d'Angelca**, a Burgundian, Seigneur d'Angelca; prob from the Maconnaise; d. c949; md **N.N. of Aquitaine**, heiress of the countship of Arles; dau of **William I le Pieux** (333A-38).

36. **Boson II** (374-34), Count of Provence at Arles and of Avignon; d. 965/967; md **Constance of Provence**, Arles and Toulouse; d. c961/965, dau of **Charles Constantine**, (25-38); Count of Vienne, and **Teutberge de Troyes** (Theibergh de Sens).

35. **William I** (298-34), Count of Provence and Arles, Marquis of Provence, 979-983; b.c 955; d. 993/994, a monk at Avignon; md after 981, **Adelaide** (Blanche) **of Anjou** (127-34); b. c942; d. 1026; dau of **Fulk II** (167-36), Count of Anjou, Mâcon and Nevers; and **Gerberge of the Gatinais**.

34. **Constance** (Constantina) **of Arles**, Provence and Toulouse; b. 986; d. 25 July 1032, Meulan; md 998, **Robert II** (134-33, 154-34), King of France. *NOTE: The identity of Constance of Arles has caused much concern.*

*Ferdinand Lot (Lott, F. 1891), pp. 366-369, showed definitely the Angevin relation of Constance and the identity of her mother, Adelaide of Anjou (333-35).*

Sources: Blass, R. 1939, II:254, 269, 272; Chaume, M. 1977, I:394n2, 447n2, 485n7, 537, 576; ES II 1984:187 (Gen. 34-35); ES, III 1984:187 (Gen. 34–37); Hartwell.R, 1991:32 (Gen. 34-36); Isenburg, W. 1932; Lot, F. 1891, appendix IX, pp. 358-369; Mantayer. G. de 1907; Moriarty, G. 1985, 24 (Gen. 34–35); 27–28 (Gen. 35–37); Saillot, J. 1980, 114+; Settipani, C. 1991, VIII (Gen. 34-36); Winkhaus, E. 1953.

## LINE 333A

40. **Bernard,** Count of Autun; Margrave of Septimania; d. 24 June 824; md **Dhouda** (326A-39), d. 2 Feb 843.

39. **Bernard,** Count of Autun, Rodez, and Auvergne; Margrave of Gothie; b. 22 Mar 841, at Uzes; d. 20 June 885 (or Aug 886); md **Ermengarde**, d. after 841; dau of **Warin** (who d. 856), Count of Auvergne, who md **Ava** (Albana).

38. **William I le Pieux (333-37),** ("the Pious"), Duke of Aquitaine, Count of Bourges and Macon; lay abbot of Brioude; founder of Cluny; d. 28 June or 6 July, 918; md before 898, **Ingelburga**; d. after Jan 917; dau of **Boso II,** (343-39), King of Lower Burgundy, Count of Vienne.

37. **N.N.,** of Aquitaine, heiress of the countship of Arles, md **Rotbaude I d'Angelica** (333-37).

Sources: Bouchard, C. 1989a: 651-658; ES III 1989:731.

## LINE 334

39. **Ridoredh,** Count of Nantes and Vannes, (md) **N.N** (a concubine).

38. **Alain I** "le Grand" (a bastard); Duke, then King of Brittany; Count of Nantes and Vannes; d. 907; md Oreguen.

37. **Paskwitan II** (405-37), Count of Rennes. 895–903; md **N.N.** (405-37), heiress of Rennes.

36. **Juhel Berenger**, Count of Rennes, a leader against the Norsemen; liv 931; d. 970; md **Gerberga**.

35. **Conan I** "le Tort," Count of Rennes and Duke of Brittany; killed 27 June 992, Conquereuil; md **Ermengarde of Anjou** (167-34).

Sources: Blass, R. 1939, 251; ES, II 1984:75 (Gen. 35–39); Keats-Rohan, K. 1997b; Moriarty, G. 1985, 13–14 (Gen. 35–39); Saillot, J. 1980, 36, 284 (Gen. 35–38); Stockvis, A. 1966, II:77 (Gen. 35–38); Winkhaus, E. 1953.

## LINE 335

38. **Rogerus Magnus,** who refounded the Abbey of St. Opportuna in 911; accompanied Rollo at the conquest of Normandy.

37. **Roger,** father of Gen. 36 below.

36. **Rogerus Magnus**

35. **Roger I de Montgomery**, Vicomte d'Hiemois (Exemes), 1031–1032;

founder of Troarn Abbey, 1022; exiled to Paris, 1037, where he died c1040.

34. **Hugh de Montgomery**, Vicomte d'Hiemes, Seigneur de Montgomery, advocate of Troarn Abbey, 1023; md **Josceline,** occ. 1067; dau of **Senfrie,** sister of **Herbastus de Crepon**( cf. 166-33), forester of Arques; and the Duchess **Gunnor,** "Danish wife" of **Richard I,** Duke of Normandy.

33. **Roger de Montgomery** (183-32), Seigneur de Montgomery, Vicomte d' Hiemois; Earl of Arundel and Shrewsbury, Regent of Normandy and England; b. c1005; d. before 1056. md **Mabel Talvas** (360-32).

32. **Roger II,** Vicomte, d'Hiemois, Sire d'Alencon, Sees, Belleme and Trun; obtained Arundel and Chichester, 25 Dec 1067; and became Earl of Shropshire and Shrewsbury, 1066; Regent of Normandy; founded the Abbey of Shrewsbury, 1053; Abbaye de Troarn; d. 27 July 1094, a monk at Shrerwsbury; md 1048, **Mabel Talvas** (360-32), de Belleme, Dame d'Alencon and Sees; bur Abbaye de Traorn.

31. **Maud** (Matilda) **de Montgomery**; d. c1085; bur at Abbey of Grestain; md before 1066, **Robert de Mortain** (160-31), Earl of Cornwall and Count of Mortain.

Sources: Cokayne, G. 1959, XI:682–697; ES, III 1989:637 (Gen. 31–35); III 1989:694B (Gen. 31–32); III 1989:636 (Gen. 33); Montgomery, G. de 1948; Moriarty, G. 1985, 44–45 (Gen. 32–33); Motey, V de 1920; Provite. D; Tourtier, C. de 1960, 102–134; Winkhaus, E. 1953.

## LINE 336

43. **Gerold I** (same as 262-42, 364-41), Duke of Allemania and Count in the Vinzgau; liv 779; md **Imma**; d.798; dau of **Nebi** (262-43), Duke of Allemania and Count in the Linzgau; liv 709–724.

42. **Hadrian** (169-39,348-41), held lands in the Wormsgau, 793–815; d. by 15 Feb 824; md **Waldrat,** heiress of lands in Orleans; alive 15 Feb 824; dau of **Lambert** (330-42), Count and Lord of Hornbach, 760–c783.

41. **Eudes** (Odo), Count of Orleans; b. 798; d. 834; md **Engeltrude** (Ingeltrude) (250-39).

Sources: Levillain, L. 1934, 287+; Levillain, L. 1937, 49:337–408, 50: 5–66; Moriarty, G. 1985, 233 (Gen. 41–43).

## LINE 337

36. **Folmar** (45-34), Count of Metz and in the Bliesgau; d. 995/996; md **Berta,** liv 996; prob. parents of Gen. 35.

35. **Richilde,** d. before 995; md **Dietrich I** (319-35), Count of Bar.

Sources: ES, VI 1978:156 (Gen. 35, 36); Moriarty, G. 1985, 190 (Gen. 35, 36); Parisse, M. 1976 (Gen. 35, 36).

## LINE 338

39. **Echbert** "the Loyal," a Saxon nobleman conquered by Charlemagne, 783; a count in the Ittergau; d. after 834; md **Ida,** d. after 21 Nov 838; dau of

Count **Dietrich** "the Riparian."

38. **Mathilda**, alive in 909, as a widow and Abbess of Horford; md **N.N. of the Threkwitigau** (339-38) (father of Gen. 37 below).

37. **Dietrich**, (32-35,65-41,310-37), Count of Saxony, and of the Saxon Hamalant; b. c872; d. 8 Dec 917; md 900, **Reginhilde von Friesland**, dau of **Godefrid** (217-38), King of Haithabu; and md 882, **Gisela of Lorraine**, (mother of Gen. 36), b. 860/865; d. by 26 Oct 907; dau of **Lothar II** (263-39 etc.), King of Lorraine, and **Waldrada**, a concubine.

36. **Mathilda von Ringleheim**, b. c890/900, Memleben, Saxony, Germany; d. 14 Mar 968; md (his 2nd) 909, **Henry I** "the Fowler" (92-36), Emperor of Germany, 912–936. Saint **Matilda** founded several monasteries and was buried at her foundation of Quedinburg. She was canonized.

Sources: Bottger, F. 1965; Blass, R. 1939, 290, 311; Brandenburg, E. 1935; Carutti, D. 1884a; ES, II 1984:104; Isenburg, W. 1932; Moriarty, G. 1985, 26 (Gen. 36–39); Winkhaus, E. 1953.

## LINE 339

43. **Halfdan Olaffson** "Huitbein" (Continue 166-41).

42. **Eystein of Westfold** (92-40,217-42), a Norwegian knight, ruled in the Uplands, md **Hild**, dau of **Eric Agnarsson**, of Westfold, a Siklinger; gdau of **Agnir**, King of Westfold; ggdau of **Sigtrygg**, King of Vandel.

41. **Geva** md **Widukind**, Duke of Westphalian Saxons; opponent of Charlemagne; d. after 807, bur at Engern; liv 778–803; son of **Warnechin** (217-41), Duke of Engern; and wife **Kunhilde of Rugen**.

40. **Wicibert**, Count in Westphalia; d. 843/851; md **Ordrad**.

39. **Walbert**, Count in the Threkwitigau; founder of Alexanderstift; occ in charters, 834–872; d. by 891; md **Altburg**, dau of **Immed I**, Count of Savoy.

38. **N.N. of the Threkwitigau**, md **Mathilda** (338-38).

Sources: Baumgarten, N. 1928, XXIV 36 table; Blass, R. 1939, II:260; Brandenburg, E. 1935; Howarth, H. 1920, vol. IX; Isenburg, W. 1953 (1953); Moriarty, G. 1985, 25–26 (Gen. 38–42); Munch, P. 1864; Sturluson, 1991, pp, 45, 46.

## LINE 340

39. **Harduin**, Count of Caux, d. before 857; md **Warinburge**, sister of Warin, Count of Macon.

38. **Eudes** (Odo) **I**, Count of Troyes and Macon; d. 10 Aug, 870; md **Wandilmodis** (348A-41).

37. **Eudes II**, Count of Chartres, liv 856; md **N.N.** *[Note: some major sources say his wife was N.N., dau of Theobald I "'le Tricheur" (the Cheat)" . If so, then he seems to have married his granddaughter!]* This needs considerable clarification.

36. **Theobald** (Gerlon) **I** (246-36,295-37), Count of Chartres and Bourges; d. c950, md **Richilde** (133-36).

184

35. **Theobald** (Thibaud) **II** (133-35,249-33) Count of Blois, Chartres and Tours; b. c910; d. 16 Jan 975/977; md 942/945, **Lieutgarde de Vermandois** (231-35).

34. **Emma of Blois**, b. c950; d. after 1004; md 968, **William II** (88-34), Count of Poitou and (as William IV), Duke of Aquitaine; d. 995.

Sources: Brandenburg, E. 1935; Depoin, J.1909, 553–609; ES, II 1984:46 (Gen. 34–36); Jackman, D. 1997:118-124,229 (table 4); Jubainville, M. 1869; Moriarty, G. 1985, 36 (Gen. 34–37); Paget, G. 1977; Pirie, C. 1962; Settipani, C. 1994; Warren, A.; Winkhaus, E. 1953.

## LINE 341

58. **Cinhil** (Quintillian).
57. **Cynloup.**
56. **Coroticus**, King of Strathclyde; removed by St. Patrick, 459.
55. **Cinuit**, Lord of Annandale.
54. **Dyfnal Hen**, Lord of Annandale.
53. **Garwynwyn Gervinion.**
52. **Cawrdar.**
51. **Gwyddno Garuntur** md N.N., a sister of Drust, King of the Picts.
50. **Nectan**, King of Picts, 599-621. He was a Christian and his home territories were on the east coast, round the Tay, mainly in what is Fortarshire, Scotland.
49. **Beli**, King of Strathclyde, d. by 641; md N.N., a sister of **Talorcan** (406-49), King of the Picts, 653-657; killed 657.
48 N.N., A dau of Beli, md **Entfidach**, possibly an Irish chieftain; d. 693.
47. **Spondana**, A Pictish princess md **Eochaid II** (165-44) "Crooked Nose," King of Dalriada.
46. **Flan**, captured and imprisoned by Vaugus I, 736; md **Foredach Wroid** (355-45), fl. 736.

Sources: Ashley, M. 1998:176,177; Firth, P. 1998; Hartwell, R. 1975. (Gen. 46–58) Jackman, D, 1997; Moriarty, G. 1985, 279 (Gen. 46–56); Pirie, C. 1962; Williamson, D. 1996.

## LINE 342

37. **Gunnor**, an Earldorman, 979.
36. **Thorod of Northumbria.**
35. **Elgiva** (Aelfgifu), Queen of England; b. c968; md **Aethelred II** (233-35), King of England.

Sources: Blass, R. 1939, 257; ES II 1984:78 (Gen. 35–36); Fest, A. 1938; Moriarty, G. 1952; Moriarty, G. 1985, 31 (Gen. 35–37); Searle, W. 1899; Von Redlich, M. 1942 , XXVIII:105–109.

## LINE 343

40. **Budwine** (Bouin) (206-39), Count in Italy, Count of Metz, Lay Abbot

of Gorze; liv 842-862; md **Richilde of Arles** (112-40,258-39).

39. **Boso II** (343A-38), Count of Vienne, King of Lower Burgundy; d. 897; md **Ermengarde** (25-40,366-38); Princess of the West.

38. **Willa of Vienne**, Queen of Upper Burgundy; d. 14 June 929, md **Rudolph I** (175-36), King of Upper Burgundy.

Sources: Blass, R. 1939, II:305; Chaume, M. 1977, I 254n2, 416n2, 539, 544, 545; ES, I 1980:57 (Gen. 38–39); Isenburg, W. 1953; Knetsch, C. 1931; Moriarty, G. 1985, 51 (Gen. 38–40).

## LINE 344

32. **Renaud de Creil, b. 970;** d. after 1047.

31. **Hugh,** Butler of France, b. 990; d. 1060.

30. **Renaud de Clermont**, Great Chamberlain of France, 1049–1098; md **Ermengardis,** (said to be parents of Gen. 29); dau of **Baldwin II,** Count of Clermont; granddau of **Baldwin I**, Count of Clermont.

29. **Hugh de Creil** (56-33), Count of Clermont, Mouchy and Creil; b. c1030, of Clermont, Beauvais, France; d. 1101; md **Margaret de Roucy,** dau of **Hildouin III** (66-34,266-31), Count of Montdidier and Rameru, and wife **Alice de Roucy** (170-31).

28. **Renaud II**, Count of Clermont-en-Beauvaisis; Crusader, 1152; d. 1162; md 1140, **Clemence of Bar-le-Duc** (149-28).

Sources: Brandenburg, E. 1935; Denis, J. 1982, 146–165, 476–516 (Gen. 28–32; ES III 1989:653 (Gen. 28–32); Longnon, J. 1978, 452+, app. II; Poull, G. 1977, I:99+ (Gen. 28–32); Rodiere, R. 1925, 577–580 (Gen. 28–32).

## LINE 345

44. **Guerin** (2-45,101-41), Count in the Thurgovie, md **Adelindis**.

43. **N.N.**, Master of the Palace.

42. **Hunfrid** (98-39), Count of Istria, Count of both Rhaetias, Missus Dominicus in Corsica; founder of the monastery of Schannis; liv 807-823; d. c830.

41. **Adalbert I**, Count of both Rhaetias and in the Thurgau; lived c850.

40. **Adalbert** "the Illustrious," Count in the Thurgau and the Scherragau; b. c837; d. c905; md **Judith**, dau of **Eberhard** (269-39), Marquis of Friuli, and **Gisela** (185-40), Princess of France.

39. **Burkhard**, Count in the Baar, Marquis in Rhaetia, Count in the Berthold-Baer: b. c865; slain 911.

38. **Burkhard II** (41A-37), Duke of Swabia; b. c885; slain in battle 29 Apr 926 at Ivrea; md **Reginlint** who, as a widow, was abbess in Zurich; Her father was **Eberhard** (269-39,404-39), Margrave of Friuli; b. c890; who md **Gisela** (185-40).

37. **Bertha of Swabia** (323-35); d. 2 Jan 966; md (her 1st), **Rudolph II** (175-35), King of Burgundy and of Italy, 920–932; d. 11 July 937.

Sources: Blass, R. 1939, II:281, 311; Brandenburg, E. 1935; Chaume, M.

1977, I 204n, 530–533; Dungern, O. von 1910; ES I: 1980:57 (Gen. 37–38);
ES I.1 1997; Fickler, C. 1859; Jackman, D. 1990; Jackman, D. 1997; Knapp,
E. 1910; Moriarty, G. 1985, 34–35 (Gen. 37–42); 1 (Gen. 42–44); Winkhaus,
E. 1953.

## LINE 346

40. **Hugh** "le Méfiant" (same as 167-41, 228-38), Count of Tours; was of
the House of Eticho; d. Sept/Nov 836; md **Aba.**
39. **Hugh,** Count of Bourges, Auxerre and Nevers; d. after 853.
38. **Stephen,** Count of Bourges; d. 864; md **N.N.**, a dau of Count **Rainard.**
37. **Hugh,** Count of Bourges; b. c862; slain 892; md **Roheut** (133-37),
(mother of Gen. 36); dau of **Charles II** (250-39), King of France, and (2)
**Richeut** (Richardis); md. **N.N.**,dau of **Budwine** (206-39), Count of Metz, and
**Richilde of Arles** (112-40).
36. **Richilde** md **Theobald** (Gerlon) **I** (340-36), Count of Chartres and
Bourges.

Sources: Blass, R. 1939, II:280; Brandenburg, E. 1935; Isenburg, W. 1953;
Moriarty 1985: 37 (Gen. 36–40); Winkhaus, E. 1953.

## LINE 347

38. **Wilfred I** (54-37,218-39), Count of Urgel and Barcelona, md **Guinidilda**
(Winidilde); dau of **Baldwin I** (235-38), Count of Flanders.
37. **Miron II,** Count of Cerdagne and Besalu; d. Oct 927; md **Ava de
Ribagorza,** dau of **Bernard** (Bernardo) **I** (286-37), Count of Pallars, and **Tota
Galindez of Aragon** (290-37).
36. **Oliva II,** Count of Cerdagne and Besalu; d. 990; md **Ermengarde of
the Ampurias** (284-36).
35. **Bernard I Tallaferro,** Count of Besalu, d. 1020; md 992, **Toda of
Provence,** dau of **William I** (333-35), Count of Provence, and **Adelaide of
Anjou**; dau of **Fulk II** (127-34,167-36,298-34), Count of Anjou, and **Gerberge
of the Gatinais** (167-36).
34. **Constance Velasquita of Besalu,** d. 1038; md **Armengol II** (195-34),
Count of Urgel; b. 1009; died on a pilgrimage to Jerusalem in 1038.

Sources: Aurell, M. 1997:357-380; ES, III 1989:132 (Gen. 34–35); III
1989:137 (Gen. 34–37); II 1984:68 (Gen. 37–38); Mateos, R. 1984; Moriarty,
G. 1985, 100 (Gen. 34); 67 (Gen. 38); Salazar; Settipani, C. 1988; Turton, W.
1984, 52 (Gen. 35–38).

## LINE 348

41. **Guiguin,** Count of Soissons; liv 835–844; md **N.N.**, dau of **Hadrian**
(169-39,336-42), Lord of Wormsgau, and wife **Waldrat of Hornbach.**
40. **Eudes,** Count of Troyes; liv 870; md **Wandilmode,** dau of **Aleran I,**
Count of Worms.
39. **Raoul,** Count of Dijon, liv 873.

38. **Robert**, Viscount of Dijon and Autun; liv 901–959; md **Ingeltrude**; liv 940–960.

37. **Lambert**, Count of Chalons, Viscount of Dijon and Autun; d. 22 Feb 979; md 945/950, **Adelaide de Vermandois**, dau of **Herbert IV** (239-31), Count of Vermandois.

36. **Gerberge** (348A-36), d. 11 Dec 986/991; md 956, **Adalbert II** (94-34), King of Lombardy.

35. **Lambert** (191-35).

Sources: Blass, R. 1939, II:251, 280; Brandenburg, E. 1935; Chaume, M. 1977, I 314n, 421n, 422, 447n2, 463n, 464n3, 537; ES, III 1985:433 (Gen. 36–39); Isenburg, W. 1953; Jackman, D. 1997; Moriarty, G. 1985: 38.

## LINE 348A

41. **Wandalmodis**, prob dau of **Adelram** Count of Troyes, Margrave of Gothie, 837-853; who md prob **Wialdruit**, sister of **Rutpert IV** (called Robert the Strong) (169-38,326-37). Wandalmodis md **Eudes** (Odo) **I** (340-38), Count of Troyes and Macon, missus in Dijonnaise; d. 10 Aug 870.

40. **N.N.** (fem.) md **N.N.** "ex senatoribus."

39. **Robert**, d. after 901.

38. **Robert**, Viscount of Dijon and Autun, 926; md **Engeltrudis**, d. after 960; dau of **Eberhard**, Duke of Franconia, and wife **Odo**, widow (1) of King Zwentibold.She md (2) Gerhard, who d. 910. Eberhard was son of **Konrad**, the elder (d. 906) by his wife **Glismode** (281-36).

37. **Lambert**, Count of Chalons, Viscount of Dijon and Autun, d. 978; md **Adelais**, d. after 9812; prob dau of **Hugh**, Count of Burgundy, d. after 936; by his wife **Willa**

36. **Gerberge** (348-36), d, 11 Dec 986/991; md 956, **Adalbert II** (94-34), King of Lombardy.

Source: Settipani, C. 1994:30.

## LINE 349

56. **Athanaric,** Visagothic chief, 368-381; d. 25 Jan 381, at Constantinople.

55. **N.N.**, md **Gebica,** King of the Burgundians, c407.

54. **Gundichar,** King of the Burgundians, 411-436.

53 .**Gundioc,** King of the Burgundians and master of the military, 456-463 (or 437-473); md **N.N.** (349A-53).

52. **Chilperic II**, King of the Burgundians, 473-492; md **Caretana**.

51. **St. Clothilde,** Queen of the Franks, 492/3-545; d. 544; md **Clovis I** "the Great" (301-51,303-51), King of the Franks, 481/2–511; b. 466; d. 27 Nov 511, at Paris.

Sources: ES I, 1984, I:1 ; Jones, A. 1971 II:1334 (stemma 42); ES I 1984:1; Martindale, J. 1980; Settipani, C. 1996b.

## LINE 349A

56. **Ricomer**, consul, 384; d. 393; md **Ascyla.**

188

55. **N.N.** (fem) md **Valis**, King of the Visagoths.

54. **N.N.** (fem) md **Ermengaire**, King of the Suavians.

53. **N.N.** (fem) md **Gundioc**, King of the Burgundians and master of the military (349-53).

Sources: *Ge* magazine, no. 153, Oct. 1996, 31; Settipani, C. 1996a.

## LINE 350

41. **Begue** (171-39,269-41), Count of Paris, md **Aupais**, an abbess of St. Peter's at Rheims; dau of **Charlemagne** (171-41, etc.).

40. **Eberhard**, Count of Paris.

39. **Begue II**, Count of Paris; d. after 23 Apr 861.

38. **Adelaide of Paris**, d. after 10 Nov 901; md 868/870, **Louis II** "the Stammerer" (171-38), King of West Franks.

Sources: Chaume, M. 1977: I 176, 177, 189n3, 218n1, 242–243, 256, 314n, 537, 551; Depoin, J. 1915, XXX:83, 117; Moriarty, G. 1985, 23 (Gen. 38–41); Settipani, C. 1993; Willoughby, R. 1991a, b; Winter. H. 1987.

## LINE 351

40. **Udo,** Count in the Nieder-Lahngau; liv 821–824.

39. **Gebhard** (359-39), Count in the Nieder-Lahngau; liv 832–879; kinsman of Adelheid, Count in the Moselgau.

38. **Gebhard,** Count in the Wetterau and Rheingau; Duke of Lorraine; slain 29 June 910.

37. **Konrad (I)** Count in Ufgau and Ortengau, Duke of Alsace; b. 915/925; d. 25 Aug 982.

36. **Herbert,** Count Palatine of Lorraine, Count in Kinziggau; d. 992; md **Ermentrude of Avalgau,** dau of **Manegold** (18-34,379-33), Count in the Avalgau, by his wife, **Gerberge of Lorraine,** dau of **Godfrey,** Count Palatine of Lorraine.

35. **N.N.** (perhaps Ermentrude) **von Gleisburg** (351-35). md after 985, **Frederick I** (58-35), Count in the Moselgau, etc.

Sources: Blass, R. 1939, II:271, 274; Brandenburg, E. 1935; Chaume, M. 1977, 542, 543, 551, 552; ES I.1 1997; ES, VI:128 (Gen. 35–36; I:1 (36–39); Moriarty, G. 1985, 23–24 (Gen. 35–40); Saillot, J. 1980, 5, 6, 51; Winkhaus, E. 1953.

## LINE 352

45. **Charles Martel** (171-43, etc.), King of Franks, md **Chrotrude** (171-43).

44. **Landree of Hesbaye** md **Sigrand** (Sigramus), Count of Hesbaye, son of **Lambert of Hesbaye**, occ 706–725; grandson of **Warinus** (53-45) and **Kunza.**

43. **N.N.** (male), perhaps **Gunderland**; liv 778.

42. **Ingram,** Count of Hesbaye.

41. **Ermengarde of Hesbaye** (163-39,171-40,259-40); d. 3 or 30 Oct 818; md c794, **Louis I** (171-40, 302-41), Emperor of the West.

40. **Hildegarde** md **Gerhard** (163-39), Count of Auvergne.

Sources: Blass, R. 1939, 275; Brandenburg, E. 1935; Chaume, M. 1977, I:336, 337, 754, 772; Moriarty, G. 1985, 20 (Gen. 41–44); 5 (Gen. 44–45); Settipani, C. 1993:253; Winkhaus, E. 1953.

## LINE 353

39. **Louis II** "the Stammerer" (171-38), King of West Franks md (2) **Adelaide of Paris** (350-38).

38. **Ermentrude,** Princess of West Franks; b. c870; md **N.N.**

37. **Kunigunde** (see also 64-35, 65-38, etc.), b. c870/890; d. after 923; she md (1) c910, **Wigeric** (319-37) (father of Gen. 36), Pfalzgrave in Trier, the Bidgau, and Aachen; md (2) c920, Richwin, Count of Verdun; d. 923; perhaps son of Rainier (Regnier).

36. **Siegfried** (3-34), Count in the Moselgau and of Luxemburg; b. c922; d. 998; md c950, **Hedwig;** d. 13 Dec 992.

35. **Frederick I** (same as 3-33,58-35), Count in the Moselgau and of Luxemburg; b. c965; d. 6 Oct 1019; md after 985, **Ermentrude von Gleiberg** (351-35), heiress of Gleiberg.

34. **Ogive** (Otgiva) **of Luxemburg,** b. c995, Luxemburg; d. 21 Feb 1030; md c1012 **Baldwin IV de Lille** (141-33), Count of Flanders; d. 1035.

*NOTE: This Charlemagne line is in dispute. The line as recorded here is substantially based on pages 21 and 22 of Moriarty's* Plantagenet Ancestry, *modified by ES, VI 1987: tables 127 and 128, with the other sources supporting. For a learned discussion of this problem, the reader is referred to "Inconsistencies in the Pedigrees of the Counts of Luxembourg," by Charles Recker, in TAG, 58:14–17 (Jan 1982).*

Sources: Blass, R. 1939, II:270, 312, 313; Brandenburg, E. 1935; ES, VI 1978:127–128 (Gen. 34–37); Isenburg, W. 1932; Moriarty, G. 1985, 249 (Gen. 34); 247 (Gen. 35); 21–22 (Gen. 35–39); Parisse, M. 1976; Renn, H. 1941; Saillot, J. 1980, 201 (Gen. 37–39); 5, 6, 51 (Gen. 35); Winkhaus, E. 1953, 103.

## LINE 354

34. **Hamon aux Dents,** Lord of Creully and of Thorigny; d. 1045.

33. **Hamon** (Hamelin), Seigneur de Château-du-Loir, in Mans (Maine), Sheriff of Kent, Companion of William the Conqueror; md **Godhaut** (Hildeburge), dau of **Yves de Creil** (360-36), Seigneur de Belleme, and wife **Godehaut** (Gohilda) (360-36).

32. **Robert,** Seigneur de Château-du-Loir, md **Elizabeth,** liv 1067.

31. **Gervase,** Seigneur de Château-du-Loir; d. c1095; md **Eremburge,** occ 1067-1095; dau of **N.N.** and **Mathildis.**

30. **Matilda**, Dame de Château-du-Loir, d. 1099; md **Helie de la Fleiche** (Helias de Baugency) (313-30), of Anjou, France; Seigneur de la Fleiche, etc.

Sources: Blass, R. 1939; ES, II 1984:82 (Gen. 30); XIII 1990:68:30–33; (Gen. 30–33); Hiestand, R. 1979; Latouche, R. 1959b, vol. 13; Mateo, R. 1984; Moriarty, G. 1985, 12 (Gen. 30–33); Motey, V de 1920; Salazar, J de 1984; Winkhaus, E. 1953.

## LINE 355

47. **Ferchar Fota**, King of Loarn and Argyll., 7th in descent from Laorn.

46. **Selbach**, King of Loarn and Argyll, 701–723; invaded Kyntyre in 712; defeated Duncan Brec in a sea fight; abdicated and became a monk, 723; d. 730.

45. **Foredach Wrold**, captured and imprisoned by Vaugus I, 736; md **Flan** (341-46).

44. **N.N.** md **Fergus**, King of Dalriada, 778–781; son of **Eochaid II** (165-44, 341-47), King of Dalriada, and **Spondana**, a Pictish princess.

43. **Fergusa**, md **Eochaid IV** "the Poisonous" (165-41), King of Dalriada, 781–789.

Sources: ES, II 1984:88 (Gen. 43–44); Gordon, P. 1962; Hartwell, R. 1975; Moriarty, G. 1985, 278 (Gen. 43–47); Pirie.S 1959, I:1–7 ; II 1960:1, 2.

## LINE 356

38. **Dietrich I** (311-37), Count of West Friesland, md **Geva** (Gerberge) heiress of Friesland.

37. **Wickmann II**, Count of Ghent and Hamalant; occ 962; d. 983; md 950, **Liutgarde**, dau of **Arnold** (Arnulf) **I** (141-36), Count of Flanders, and **Adele** (Adelaide, Aenis) **de Vermandois** (169-35).

36. **Adela**, heiress of the countship of Hamalant, md **Immed II**, Count of Saxony, d. 29 Jan 983, at Imbshausen, son of Immed I, a Saxon noble slain 953 in the army of Otto I.

35. **Glismode of Saxony**, founded after 994, the Benedictine monastery of Ozziach in Friuli; md (his first, her first), **Retig II** (136-35), Count of Bavaria; she md (2) before 994, Ozi I, Count of Friuli.

34. **Frideruna** md **Hartwig II** (48-34), Pfalzgrave in Bavaria.

Sources: Blass, R. 1939, II:268, 311; Brandenburg, E. 1935, 33; Dungern, O. von 1935; Hofmeister, A. 1920; Jackman, D. 1997; Moriarty, G. 1985, 162–163 (Gen. 34–37); 55 (Gen. 37–38); Simson, B. von.

## LINE 357

37. **Charles II** (171-39), King of West Franks, md (2) **Richardis of Metz**, dau of **Budwine** (206-39), Count of Metz, and **Richilde of Arles** (112-40).

36. **Rothilde of Neustria**, b. c871; d. c22 Mar 928; md 890, **Roger**, Count of Maine; d. after 31 Oct 900.

35. **Hugh I,** Count of Maine; occ 900–931; d. 931/939; md prob **Bilichildis,**

dau of **Gauzlin**, Count of Maine

34. **Hugh II**, Count of Maine, occ 939–942, d. c992; perhaps md **N.N.**, dau of **Herbert II**, Count of Vermandois.

33. **Hugh III**, Count of Maine, occ 967–1015, d. c1015; md **N.N.**, dau of **Conrad I** "le Tort," of Rennes, Duke of Brittany, who d. 27 June 992, by his wife **Ermengarde of Anjou.**

32. **Herbert**, Count of Maine; d. 13 Apr 1036.

31. **Paula du Maine**, heiress of Maine (Mans); md (1) **Jean** (John) **I** (313-31), Seigneur de la Fleche.

Sources: Blass, R. 1939, II:252; Douglas.D. 1964: table B; ES, III1989:692 (Gen. 31–37); II 1984:1 (Gen. 36–37); Freeman, E. 1901; Guerard, B.; Keats-Rohan, K. 1997; Keats-Rohan, K. 1997a; Latouche, R. 1959a; Latouche, R. 1959b, ch. 13, appendix III; Moriarty, G. 1985, 11 (Gen. 31–36); 16, 51, 234 (Gen. 37); Rosch, S. 1977; TAG 72 1997:194; Winkhaus, E. 1953.

## LINE 358

47. **St. Arnulf** (171-46), Bishop of Metz; b. 582; d. 16 Aug 641; md c596, **Dode** ( Clothilde,Oda) who became a nun at Treves, 612.

46. **St. Clodoule**, Bishop of Metz; b. 596; d. 690.

45. **Kunza** (Gunza) md **Warinus** (Warin) (2-45,330-45), Count of the Palace of Poitiers.

Sources: Chaume, M. 1977, I:754, 772; Moriarty, G. 1985, 5 (Gen. 45–47).

## LINE 359

45. **Wala**, who witnessed a charter to the monastery of Fulda, 24 Jan 751.

44. **Waluram I**, b. 725/730; d. 802; md c750, **Waldrada**, a kinswoman of Megingaud, Lord of Dromersheim (liv 806).

43. **Guntram I**, Lord in Mainz; md (2) a lower Frankish noblewoman.

42. **Luitfried I**, Lord at Dienheim, Count in the Niddagau and in the Enzgau; d. 826.

41. **Luitfried II**, Count in the Niddagau and Enzgau; liv 838–876; md N.N., dau of Count Burchard; md (2) **N.N.** (mother of Gen. 40 below); dau of the Matfriedinger **Stephen.**

40. **Walaho VI**, Count in the Wormsgau, the Niddegau, the Spayergau and in the Enzgau, Lay Abbot of Hornbach; occ 881–900; md c860/865, **N.N. von Lobdengau** (200-40), heiress of Lobdengau, Hornbach and the abbotship of Hornbach.

39. **Burchard**, Count in the Wormsgau and in the Mainfeldgau; Lord of Kusel and Hornbach; slain 27 Feb 906 in war with Adalbert of Babenburg; md c893, **Gisela**, widow of Megingaud, Count in the Wormgau, murdered at Retal on orders from Count Alberich, 892; Gisela was a dau of **Gebhard** (351-39), Count in the Nieder-Lahngau.

*NOTE: Gen. 38–45, given here, is undoubtedly the most authoritative of the several versions available. Those who do not wish to accept this, may terminate the line at Gen. 38 which is accepted by Europäische Stammtafeln, giving neither the ancestry of Werner nor his wife, N.N.*

38. **Werner**, Count in the Speyergau and the Wormsgau, Lord of Hornbach and Kusel, ancestor of the Salic Kaisars; d. 917; md **N.N.**, dau of **Burkhard III** of Wettin (210-39), and **Mathilda of Hesse**.

37. **Conrad** "the Wise," Count in the Wormsgau, the Spayergau and the Nahegau, Lord of Kusel and of Hornbach, Duke of Lorraine and Franconia; slain 10 Aug 955 at Lachfeld; md 947, **Luitgarde**, dau of **Otto I** (321-36), Emperor of the West, and **Eadgyth** (376-37), Princess of England.

36. **Otto of Franconia**, Duke of Carinthia and Marquis of Verona, Count in the Nahegau, Enzgau, Speyergau and Mainfeldgau; Lord of Hornbach; b. 947/948; d. 4 Nov 1006; md **Judith of Bavaria**; occ 977/978; dau of **Henry**, Count of Verdun, whose parents were **Gozelin** (104-36), Count in the Bidgau, and **Uda of Metz**.

35. **Henry of Franconia**, Count in the Speyergau, Duke of Franconia and Carinthia; brother of Pope Gregory V who was Bruno of Carinthia; b. by 970; d. 28 Mar 989; md c986, **Adelaide** (Adelheid) **of Alsace** (202-35); founded 1020, the monastery of Oehringen; d. 19 May 1040/46.

34. **Conrad II** "the Salic," King of Germany, 1026; King of Italy, 1027; King of Burgundy, 1034; b. 990; d. 4 June 1039, Utrecht, Holland; bur at Speyer; md 1016 (his 3rd, her 3rd), **Gisele of Swabia** (199-34); b. 11 Nov 985; d. 14 Feb 1043. She md after 1000, **Bruno von Braunschweig** (32-33), d. c1003; she md c1003/5, **Ernst von Babenberg** (63-35), Duke of Swabia, d. 31 May 1015.

33. **Henry III** (161-31) "the Black," Duke of Bavaria and of Swabia, King of Burgundy, 1039; King of Germany, 25 Dec 1046; Emperor, of the West, 1046; b. 28 Oct 1017; d. 5 Oct 1056, Bodfeld Hartz; bur at Speyer; md (2) 21 Nov 1043, **Agnes of Poitou** (161-31).

32. **Henry IV of Franconia**; Emperor of the West, 31 Mar 1084; b. 11 Nov 1050, Goslar; d. 7 Aug 1106, Louvain; bur Liege, Belgium; md 13 July 1066, **Bertha of Maurienne**, dau of **Odo I** (173-33), Count of Maurienne, and **Adelaide von Susa** (93-32), b. 21 Sept 1051; d. 27 Dec 1087; bur at Speyer.

31. **Agnes of Franconia**, Princess of Germany, "Last of the Salic House," b. 1072/73; d. 24 Sept 1143; bur at Klosten-Neuburg; md (his 2nd, her 2nd) **Leopold III** (279-31), Margrave of Austria, 1096; d. 1136. She also md **Frederick I**, Count von Hohenstaufen (cf. 40–31).

Sources: Balde, H. 1913; Blass, R. 1939, II: 280; Chaume, M. 1977, I:542, 551–552 (Gen. 31–34); Dungern, O. von 1935 ; ES, I 1984:4 (Gen. 31–38); 1984 I:39 (Gen. 31–32); ES I.1 1997; Fisher, G. 1885, 259 (Gen. 31–34); Moriarty, G. 1985, 91-9 (Gen. 31–45); Vanderkindere, L. 1902, II:177, 360; Winkhaus, E. 1953

**LINE 360**

37. **Yves de Creil**, Seigneur de Creil in the Baauvoisie, Regis Bolistarius;

liv 945; d. c983; md **Geile**, occ 961.

36. **Yves** (Ives) **de Creil and Belleme**, (354-33) Count of Alencon and Domfront; had Alencon and Bellesme as a gift of Richard II, Duke of Normandy; and Balistarius as a gift from Louis IV, King of France; alive in 1005; md **Godehaut** (Gohilda), alive in 1005; bur Notre-Dame-de-Belleme; sister of Seinfroi, Bishop of Mans.

35. **William de Belleme**, Seigneur de Saonnois; liv 1023–1026; md **Mathilde**, Dame de Conde-sur-Noirau, d. c1024. *This Gen. added by ES, III:636, 1989 research, and not in some other sources.*

34. **William I Talvas**, Seigneur de Belleme; Sire d'Alencon; d. c1031, Domfront; bur Notre-Dame-sur-l'Eau; md **Mathilda**.

33. **William II Talvas de Belleme** (de Alencon); Seigneur de Belleme and Count of Alencon; d. 1060/70; md (1) **Hildeburge** (mother of Gen. 32), dau of **Arnulf** md (2) N. N., dau of Rolf de Beaumont.

32. **Mabel Talvas** (de Alencon), heiress of Belleme and Alencon; b. c1015, Alencon; murdered 2 Dec 1079, Château de Bures-sur-Dives; bur Abbey of Troarn; md **Roger de Montgomery** (335-33).

Sources: ES, III 1989:636 (Gen. 32–37); XIII 1990:68 (Gen. 35); Guillot, O. 1972 (Gen. 32–37); Moriarty, G. 1985, 12 (Gen. 32–37 but lacking Gen. 35).

## LINE 361

33. **St. Vladimir I** (143-33), Grand Prince of Kiev, md **N. N.**, dau of **Kuno**, Count of Ohningen, and **Richilde** (321–34), Princess of Germany.

32. **Debronega Marie of Kiev**, b. after, 1012; d. 1087; md 1041/1042, **Casimir I** (321-32,378-32), King of Poland, 1040–1058.

Sources: Brandenburg, E. 1935; Dworzaczek, K. 1959; ES, II 1984:120 (Gen. 32); II 1984:128, 153 (Gen. 33); Hertel, J. 1980; Jasinski, K. 1977; Moriarty, G. 1947; Moriarty, G. 1985, 53 (Gen. 32–33).

## LINE 362

40. **Gostivit**, Prince of Prague.

39. **Borziwoj I**, last pagan Duke of Bohemia, Prince of Prague and, by marriage, of Psow (Psov); converted to Christianity, 871, by Methodius; d. 894; md **Ludmilla** "the Saint," heiress to the principality of Psow (Psov); murdered by pagans 16 Sept 921; dau of **Slawibov**, Princeling of Psow (Psov).

38. **Wratislaw** (Vratislav) **I**, Chief Duke of Bohemia; d. 13 Feb 921; md before 910, **Drahomir of Stodar**, a pagan who massacred Christians, dau of a lord of Luticz, a Slavic state near Pomerania and Mecklenburg.

37. **Boleslaw I** (212-37,378-36) "the Cruel," Prince of Altbunzlau, Duke of Bohemia; d. 15 July 972; md **Biagota of Stockow.**

36. **Boleslaw II** "the Pious," Duke of Bohemia; founded the bishopric of Prague, 976; captured Crakow from the Poles; d. 7 Feb 999; md **Hemma**; d. c1005.

35. **Udalrich**, Duke of Bohemia, 1012-1034; d. 9 Nov 1034, (md) **Bozena**, a concubine; d. 1055; dau of **Kresina** (male), a peasant.

34. **Bretislaw I** "the Warrier," Duke of Moravia, of Bohemia and Silesia; b. c1005; d. 10 Jan 1055; md c1021, **Judith von Schweinfurt**; d. 2 Aug 1058, Hungary; dau of **Henry von Schweinfurt** (270-35), Margrave of Nordgau; and **Gerberge of Henneberg** (102-35).

33. **Wratislaw II**, Lord of Olmutz, Duke of Bohemia, King of Bohemia and Hungary, 1086; b. c1035; d. 14 Jan 1092; md (2) 1056/58, **Adelaide** (225-33), Princess of Hungary.

32. **Judith of Bohemia**, b. c1058; d. 25 Dec 1086; md c1080, **Wladislaw I** (378-32), King of Poland; b. c1040; d. 4 June 1102.

Sources: Blass, R. 1939, II:261, 264, 265, 267; ES I 1984:54–55 (Gen. 32–39); II 1984 20 (Gen. 32–33); Isenburg, W. 1953 Krone, F. von 1902, table 3; Moncreiffe, I. 1982, 15 (Gen. 33-39); Moriarty, G. 1985, 85 (Gen. 32–40).

## LINE 363

34. **Jaroslaw I Wladimirowitsch** (143-31), Grand Prince of Kiev; md **Ingegard** (240-32), Princess of Sweden.

33. **Isjarlaw** (Isiaslaw) **I**, Grand Prince of Kiev; b. 1025; slain 3 Oct 1078 at Tchernigov; md c1043, **Gertrude**, dau of **Mieszko** (Mieszyslaw) **II** (378-34), King of Poland, and **Richenza of Pfalz-Lorraine** (237-34).

32. **Sviatpolk** (Swjatopolk Michael) **II**, Grand Prince of Kiev, Prince of Novgorod and of Turow; b. 1050; d. 16 Apr 1113; (md) **N. N.**, a former concubine, d. before 1094.

31. **Zbyslava** (Sbislawa) **of Kiev**, d. 1110/1111; md 1103, **Boleslaw III** (378-31), King of Poland; b. 1086; d. 28 Oct 1138.

Sources: Balzer, O 1971; Baumgarten, N. 1927b, I: tables I and II; Blass, R. 1939, II:table 261; Dworzaczek, K. 1959, tables 1-4; ES, II 1984:120 (Gen. 33); Hertel, J. 1980; Jasinski, K. 1977; Moriarty, G. 1985 87 (Gen. 31–33); 53 (Gen. 33–34); Winkhaus, E. 1953.

## LINE 364

41. **Gerold**, Count in the Vinzgau and Duke of Allemania; liv 779; md **Emma**, dau of **Nebi** (262-43), Duke of Allemania.

40. **Ulrich I** (same as 326-38), Count in the Argengau and in the Linzgau; liv 808.

39. **Ulrich II**, Count in the Argengau and in the Vinzgau; liv 815–818.

38. **Ulrich III**, Count in the Argengau and in the Vinzgau; liv 860–885; md **Berta**, who held lands in Alsace; occ 877–886.

37. **Ulrich IV**, Count in the Argengau and in the Vinzgau; liv 893.

36. **Ulrich V**, Count in the Argengau; liv 894–909; md **Wendelgarde**, niece of Henry (92-36)"the Fowler," King of Germany.

35. **Ulrich VI**, Count in the Upper Hatien and Lower Hatien; fell at Lechfeld, 10 Aug 955; md **Dietburga**.

34. **Luitfried I**, Count of Winterthur; built Kyburg.

33. **Adalbert I**, Count of Winterthur and Kyburg; liv 957; d. 9 Sept 980.

32. **Luitfried II**, Lord of Burgelm, d. 1040.

31. **Adalbert**, Lord of Burgelm; md **N.N. von Nellenburg**, dau of **Eberhard V** "the Saint" (18-32), Count of Zurichgau (Nullenburg). and **Ida von Alshausen.**

30. **Adalbert**, Count of Morsberg, Kyburg and Winterthur; advocate of the Heiligau monastery; d. 1124/1125; md **Mechtild of Bar**, dau of **Thibaud** (Thierry) II(149-30), Count of Bar, in Alsace, and **Ermentrude of Burgundy**, dau of **William II** (94-31), Count of Burgundy, and **Stephanie of Longwy**, dau of **Adalbert III** (105-33), Count of Longwy.

29. **Mechtilde von Morsberg**; md before 1124, **Meginhard I** (365-29), Count of Sponheim.

Sources: Levillain, L. 1937, 50:7n2; Moriarty, G. 1985, 212–213 (Gen. 29–41); 233; Settipani, C. 1990; Winkhaus, E. 1953, (1953) 408, 411.

## LINE 365

31. **Stephen**, Count of Sponheim; liv 1052; d. c1080.

30. **Stephen von Sponheim**, Count of Sponheim, advocate of the Abbey of Sponheim; d. c25 Feb 1118; md **Sophia von Hamm**, liv 1118, dau of **Berthold I of Hamm.**

29. **Meginhard I**, Count of Sponheim and Morsburg; d. 1136/1145; md before 1124, **Mechtilde von Morsburg** (364-29).

28. **Mathilda von Sponheim**, b. c1127; md **Simon I** (23-28), Count of Saarbrucken.

Sources: Brandenburg, E. 1935; ES, VI 1978:152 (Gen. 28); IV 1981:118 (Gen. 29–31); Moller, W. 1950, tables I–III; Moriarty, G. 1985, 212 (Gen. 28–30); Parisse, M. 1976; : Winkhaus, E. 1953; Witte, H. 1900.

## LINE 366

40. **Hucbald**, d. by 893, md **Andaberta.**

39. **Hubaldus**, Count of Bologna; liv 888–893.

38. **Boniface**, Count of Bologna, Prince and Margrave of Spoleto and Camerino; d. 953, md 921/923, **Waldrada of Burgundy**, dau of **Rudolph I** (175-36), King of Upper Burgundy, and **Willa of Vienne** (343-38).

37. **Willa of Camerino**, d. after 978, md c945, **Humbert** (186-37), Duke and Margrave of Tuscany, Duke of Spoleto, d. 967/970.

Sources: ES, II 1984:186 (Gen. 37–38); III 1989:592 (Gen. 37–40); Hliawitschka, E. 1960; Hlawitschka, 1969.

## LINE 367

43. **Aethelwulf** (233-40), King of Wessex and Kent, King of England, 839–858; d. 13 Jan 858; md (1) **Osburh** (mother of Gen. 42); dau of **Oslac**; who md (2) **Judith**, dau of **Charles II** "the Bald" (133-38, 171-39, 250-39)

42. **Aethelred I**, King of Wessex, 866–871; b. before 843; d. 872; md **Wulfthryth**.

41. **Aethelhelm**, Earldorman of Wiltshire; secured Compton and Crondoll, prob from King Alfred; held Aldingbourn; b. c859; d. prob 898; md **Aethelgyth** (mother of Gen. 40 below); heiress of Risborough, which was later, in 903/904, granted to Aethelfryth (Gen. 40 below), by King Edward, because the charter had been destroyed by fire. Aethelgyth was dau of **Aethelwulf**, Earldorman of Mercia, who held Risborough in Buckinghamshire, England; d. prob 903; granddau of **Aethelred**, Earldorman of Mercia who md **Eadburh of Mercia**. Eadburh descends from **Wigmund of Mercia**, son of **Wiglaf**, King of Mercia; liv 821.

40. **Aethelfrith**, Earldorman of Wessex and Mercia; first holder of Alfred's gift of Risborough and Wrington.

39. **Eadric**, Earldorman of Wessex; held Ogburn and Wrington; d. c949; md **Aethelgifu**.

38. **Aethelwerd I** "the Historian," Theign of Surrey, 973; Earldorman in Wessex, 974; liv 998; md **Aethelflaed**.

37. **Aethelmaer Cild** "the Great," Theign of Sussex, Earldorman in Devonshire, 1005; d. c1016; md **Aethelthrith**.

36. **Wulfnoth Cild**, Theign of Sussex; who held Compton; d. 1015.

35. **Godwin**, Earldorman of Wessex, 1018; Theign of Sussex; favorite of Knut; he was a great statesman of the reign of Edward "the Confessor;" d. 15 Apr 1053; md (2) 1019/1020, **Gytha** (368-32), dau of Jarl **Thorkill**.

Sources: Anscombe, A. 1913; Balderston, M. 1930; Barlow, L. 1958; Bierbrier, M. 1992; ES, II 1984:78 (Gen. 35); II 1984:98 (Gen. 35); Isenburg, II, table 70 (1976); Kelley, D. 1989, 63–93, and chart II; Moriarty, G. 1955a(Gen. 35-42); Moriarty, G. 1985, 252 (Gen. 35–42); 16 (Gen. 42–43); Williamson, D. 1996.

## LINE 368

36. **Bjorn** (Bijorn) "a Haugi" (240-35), King at Uppsala.

35. **Olaf Edmundsson**, King of Uppsala, King of Sweden; divided the ruling of Sweden with his brother, Eric, in 950; d. 964; md **Ingelberg**, dau of Jarl **Thraud of Sula**.

34. **Styrbiorn Olafsson**, leader of the Jomsborg Vikings; b. 956; slain 985, at the battle of Blackfeld; md (1) **Thyra of Denmark** (369-37); d. 18 Sept 1000.

33. Jarl **Thorkill** (Thorgils) Sprakalaeg," a follower of Knut, King of England. *NOTE: Recent research questions the relationship of Jarl Thorkill to Gytha.*

32. **Gytha** md 1019/1020, **Godwin** (367-35), Earldorman of Wessex, d. 15 Apr 1053. *NOTE: Her great-great-grandfather was Gorm (369-39), King of Denmark (says Rubincam, M. 1949 and 1957), which then gives several generations of those ancestors.*

31. **Harold II Godwinsson**, King of England, 1066; Earldorman of East Anglia and Wessex; b. c1022; d. 14 Oct 1066 at Battle of Hastings fighting against William I, the Conqueror, who became king of England in his stead; md **Ealdgyth of Mercia**, widow of Griffith I (Gruffydd), Prince of North Wales; dau of **Alfgar**, Earldorman of East Anglia; (md) also, **Ealdgyth** "Swanneshals" (Swan neck) (mother of Gen. 30); a concubine, through whom are the only known descendents of Harold II.

30. **Gytha of Wessex**, a bastard, md c1070 (his 1st) **Wladimir** (Vladimir) **II** "Monamachos" (240-30), Prince of Smolensk and Tchernigov, Grand Prince of Kiev.

Sources: Balderston, M. 1930; Baumgarten, N. 1928, XXIV:7; Blass, R. 1939, II: table 258; ES, II 1984 :78 (Gen. 30–33); II 1984:98 (Gen. 32–33); Langer, W. 1948, 168; Moriarty, G. 1985, 145–146 (Gen. 30–36); Rubincam, M. 1957 (Gen. 30–35); Winkhaus, E. 1953.

## LINE 369

44. **Ragnar Sigurdsson** (240-40), King of Lethra.

43. **Sigurd II** "dragon eye," King of Denmark, invaded England; said to have avenged his father (who is said to have perished in a Northumbrian snake pit) by making "blood eagle" of his foe; d. 873.

42. **Horda-Canute** (Knutr I), King of Staelland; d. 884.

41. **Frotho**, King of Staelland in Denmark; d. 885.

40. **Harold II**, King of Staelland in Denmark; d. 899; md **Bertrade**, princess of Norway.

39. **Gorm** "the Old" (same as 368-32), King of Denmark, 883–941; King of East Anglia, in England, 905–918; King of Seeland by conquest; and by marriage, of Jutland, c880; d. after 950; bur at Jellinge; opponent of Christianity; md **Thyra Danebord**, d. c935; dau of Jarl **Harold** "Klak," ruler of Jutland; built Danewiak, 936/940.

38. **Harold III** "Blaatand" (Bluetooth), King of Denmark, King of Norway, 936; founder of the Jomsborg Viking colony; established Christianity in Denmark; surnamed "the Old" because of the length of his reign—52 years; b. c910; murdered 1 Nov 988; md (2) **Gunhilda** (mother of Gen. 37 below); perhaps dau of **Olaf**, King of Sweden. Harold III md (1) Tofa (Tove), dau of Mistawri, Prince of Obotrides; md (3) Gyrith, dau of Olaf, King of Sweden and perhaps identical with Gunhilda, above.

37. **Thyra of Denmark** (368-34), d. 18 Sept (1000); md (1) **Styrbiorn Olafsson** (368-34), leader of the Jomsborg Vikings, killed 985.

*NOTE: Some sources do not have generations 41 and 42 as listed here, thus making Harold II (Gen. 40) the son of Sigurd II (Gen. 43).*

Sources: Blass, R. 1939, 258; Brenner, S. 1978; ES, II 1984:97 (Gen. 37–39); Moncreiffe, I. 1982, table 36, p. 110 (Gen. 38–44); Moriarty, G. 1985, 146 (Gen. 37–39, 42, 43); Rubincam, M. 1957 (Gen. 37–39, but does not give Thyra's name); Christiansen, E. 1980.

## LINE 370

38. **Ioannes Kourkouas**, protovestiarios, c. 879.

37. **Theophilos Kourkouas**, magistros, c923–940.

36. **N.N.** (perhaps Theodoros) **Kourkouas**, domestikos ton scholon; md before 925, **N.N. Prokaina** (275-36).

35. **N.N. Kourkouaina** (a sister of the Emperor John I Tzimisces); md prob. **Romanos Aballantes.**

34. **N.N.** (Kontostephane ?) md **Troianos** (Trajan) (309-34), Tsar of West Bulgaria.

Sources: Brook, L. 1981, nos.108–115; Charanis, P. 1961; Collenburg, W. 1963, note 15, table B3, p. 53.

## LINE 371

50. **Magnus "vir Clarissimus"** lived near Briord, Ain, France in the 6th century.

49. **Gallus Magnus**, a Gallo-Roman Senator, elected Bishop of Treves, 562; his grave at Briord is known and has an inscription identifying him.

48. **Palatina** md **Bodegeisel I** "Dux", bro of Gondolfus. (171-48).

Sources: Chaume, M. 1977, 142; Moriarty, G. 1985, 6 (Gen. 48–50); Strohaker, K. 1948.

## LINE 372

39 **Arnulf I** (270-37), Duke of Bavaria, md **Judith of Friuli** (272-37),

38. **Judith of Bavaria**, heiress of Bavaria, d. after 973; md **Henry I of Saxony**, Duke of Lorraine (deposed), Duke of Bavaria, 948; Marquis of Verona and Aquilea, son of **Henry** "the Fowler" (92-36) and **Matilda of Ringleheim** (338-36).

37. **Henry II**, "the Wrangler," Duke of Bavaria and Carinthia, Marquis of Verona; b. 951; d. 28 Sept 995, Gaudersheim; md **Gisela of Burgundy**, dau of **Conrad I** (175-34), King of Burgundy, and **Matilda of France**.

Sources: ES I: 1984; Moriarty, G. 1985, 57.

## LINE 374

32. **William III** "Taillefer" (329-34), Count of Toulouse; b. c947; d. Oct 1037; md (2) **Emma de Mortain,** of Provence (375-32) (mother of Gen. 31 below); md, also, Arsinde d'Anjou, dau of Count Foulques la Roux and Roscilla de Loches.

31. **Pons III** (143-41), Count of Toulouse, Albi and Dijon; b. c990; d. 1060; bur St. Sernin, Toulouse; md 1044/1045; later divorced; **Almode de la Haute Marche** (327-32).

30. **William IV** (160-30), Count of Toulouse, Albi, Perigord, Carcassonne, Rodez and Dijon; Duke of Narbonne; Crusader and poet; b. c1040; d. in battle at Huesca, 1093; md (2) c1071, **Emma de Mortain** (160-30).

Sources: Auzias, L. 1937; Blass, R. 1939, II:253, 259, 269, 280, 284; ES,

III 1989:763 (Gen. 30–32); Moriarty, G. 1985, 41–42 (Gen. 30–32); Richard, A. 1903; Vannerus, J. 1946, XXV:851–858 (1946); Winkhaus, E. 1953.

## LINE 375

34. **Boson II** (333-36), Count of Provence md **Constance of Arles,** Toulouse and Vienne, dau of **Charles Constantine** (25-38), Count of Vienne. *(ES II 1984:189 does not show Charles Constantine as father of Constance.)*

33 **Rotbaud,** Count of Provence at Avignon, 961–1005; d. before 22 Apr 1015; md c1005, **Ermengarde,** d. 22 Aug 1057.

32.**Emma de Mortain** (329-34), of Provence, md **William III** "Taillefer" (374-32), Count of Toulouse.

Sources: Blass, R. 1939, II:254; Brandenburg, E. 1935; Chaume, M. 1977, I:447n2, 485n7; ES, II 1984:189; Moriarty, G. 1985, 27–28 (Gen. 32–34); Winkhaus, E. 1953.

## LINE 376

41. **Aethelwulf** (233-40), King of Wessex, md **Osburh** (233-40).

40. **Aethelred I,** King of Wessex, 866–871; b. before 843; d. 872.

39. **Aethelhelm,** Earldorman of Wiltshire; b. c859; d. prob 898; md **Aethelglyth of Mercia.**

38. **Aelflaed,** (261-38) Queen of England; b. c878, Wessex; d. c919; md **Edward** "the Elder" (233-38), King of England.

37. **Eadgyth** (Edith), Princess of England; d. 26 Jan 946; md Kaiser **Otto I** "the Great" (321-36), Emperor of the West; who md (2) St. **Adelaide of Burgundy** (323-34).

Sources: Anderson.R, 738; Blass, R. 1939; Chadwick, H. 1924, ch. 2: Copley, J. 1954; ES, I 1984:3 (Gen. 37–38); Hodgkin.R 1952, II, table 3; Moriarty, G. 1985, 30–31 (Gen. 37–39); 16, 254 (Gen. 39–41); Reed, T. 1947; Searle, W. 1899, 330–343; Sisam, K. 1939, 39:287–348; Winkhaus, E. 1953.

## LINE 377

31. **Eudes I Borel** (245-31), Duke of Burgundy, md **Sibylle** (Mathilda) of Burgundy, dau of **William II** (94-31), Count of Burgundy and Mâcon.

30. **Hugh II** (60-30) "the Peaceful" Duke of Burgundy; b. c1085; d. 1143; bur at Citeaux; md c1115, **Mathilda de Turenne,** dau **Boson I** (156-30), Vicomte de Turenne, and **Gerberge de Terrasson.** *NOTE: ES, II 1984:20 says Hugh II md Mathida de Mayenne, not Turenne, but is, we suppose, a typographical error as it is not developed elsewhere in ES and is not in agreement with the usual sources.*

29. **Mathilda of Burgundy,** b. c1130; d. before 29 Sept 1172; md 25 Feb 1157, Montpellier, **William VII** (150-29), Duke of Montpellier.

Sources: Brandenburg, E. 1935; Blass, R. 1939, II: tables 238, 242; ES, II:20 (Gen. 29–31); Isenburg, W. 1953, pt. ii, table 24; Latrie; Moriarty, G. 1985, 48, 114 (Gen. 29–31); Petit, E. 1894, I:515; Winkhaus, E. 1953 (1950).

40. **Piast** (Chroscieszko), Prince of the Polanians, liv c840.

39. **Siemowit** (Siemouit), Duke of Polanie.

38. **Leszek** (Lestek, Lestko), Duke of Polanie, d. 921.

37. **Ziemomysl**, Duke of Polanie, liv 964.

36. **Mieszko I**, Grand Duke of Poland; founder of the Polish state, about 960; a Danish Viking; first Christian king of Poland, 962–992; b. c922; d. 25 May 992; md (2) c965, **Dubrawa**, dau of **Boleslaw I** (362-37), Duke of Bohemia, and wife **Biagota of Stockau.**

35. **Boleslaw I** "Chrobry" (Boleslas the Brave), Grand Prince and King of Poland, 992–1025; b. 967; d. 17 July 1025; md (3) **Emnilde of Silicia**, d. 1017; dau **Dobromir**, Prince of West Silicia.

34. **Mieszko** (Mieszyslaw) **II** (363-33), King of Poland, 1026-34; but after 1032 under German overlordship; b. c990; d. 10 May 1034; md 1013, **Richenza** (Rixa) **of Pfalz-Lorraine** (237-34).

33. **Casimir** (Kazimierz) "the Restorer," "the Great," King of Poland, 1040–1058; b. 25 July 1016; d. 19 Mar 1058; md 1041/1042, **Dobronega Maria of Kiev** (361-32).

32. **Wladislaw I Hermann** (Ladislas I); King of Poland, 1081–1102; b. c1040; d. 4 June 1102, Plotzk; md c1080, Plotsk, **Judith of Bohemia** (362-32).

31. **Boleslas III**, King of Poland, Lord of Breslau, Cracow and Sentomir, 1093; b. 20 Aug 1086; d. 28 Oct 1138; md (1) 1103, **Zbyslava** (Sbyslawa) **of Kiev** (363-31); d. 1010/1011, dau Count **Swjatopolk II Isjaslawitsch** (md) **N.N.**, a former concubine.

30. **Wladislaw** (Vladislas) **II**, King of Poland, 1139–1142; Duke of Breslau, Lord of Cracau and Silicia; b. 1105, Poland; d. 30 May 1159; md c1126 (1) **Agnes of Austria** (Babenberg), dau of **St. Leopold III** (279-31), Margrave of Austria.

29. **Richilde of Poland** (86-29,94-29) , Queen of Castile and Leon; b. 1130/1140; d. 1166; md July 1152, **Alfonso VII** (89-29,94-29), King of Castile and Leon; b. 1 Mar 1105; d. 21 Aug 1157.

Sources: Balzer, O. 1971; Dworzaczek, K. 1959, tables 1–4; ES, II 1984:120 (Gen. 29–37); ES III 1980:9 (Gen. 29–30); ES VI 1978:23b,26; ES XVIII 1998:24b; Moncreiffe, I. 1982, chart 28:94; Moriarty, G. 1985, 84 (Gen. 29–37); Moriarty, G. 1947 (Gen. 31–34); Pogonowski, I. 1989, 56-57; Ross, M. 1978, 434, 435.

34. **Ezzo** (208-35), Count Palatine of Lorraine, md **Matilda of Saxony** (237-35).

33. **Ludolf**, Governor of Brauweiler, d. 10 Apr 1031; md **Mathilde of Zutphen,** dau of **Otto I,** of Hammerstein, Count in Wetterau, and wife **Irmingard of Verdun.** Otto's parents were **Herbert**, Count in Kinziggau, who d. 992; and **Ermintrude**, dau of **Meingaud** (351-36), Count in the

Avalgau. Irmingarde's parents were **Godfrey** "the Captive," Count of Verdun by his second wife, **Matilda of Saxony** (104-35).

32. **Adelheid of Zutphen** md **Gottschalk von Zutphen**, Count of Zutphen, 1059; d. in battle, 1083/1084., whose father was **Hermann**, Count in the Nifterlake, 1036.

31. **Otto II**, Count of Zutphen, d. 1113, md **Judith**, d. 1118. Judith may have been dau of **Waleran II**, Count of Limburg, by wife **Jetta of Luxemburg**.

30. **Ermengarde**, heiress of Zutphen, md **Gerard II**, of Guelders (304-30).

Sources: ES I.1 1997; ES, VI 1978:23b (Gen. 30–32); VI 1978:1 (Gen. 32–34); ES XVIII 1998:24B; Hoffman (Gen. 30–33); Jackman, D. 1990; Vries, W de 1947.

## LINE 380

55. **Walia**, King of the Visagoths, 415-419.

54. **N.N.** (dau.) md a Suevic chieftain.

53. **N. N.** (dau.) md **Gundiok,** King of the Burgundians, c437-473

52. **Gundobad,** King of the Burgundians, 473-516.

51. **Sigusmund,** King of the Burgundians, 516-523, md **Theodogotho**, bastard dau of **Theodoric I**, of the Ostragoths, son of **Theodoric II**, of the Ostagoths, 493-526; who was son of **Theudemir**, King; d. 474; md **Erelica**.

50. **Wacho**, King of the Lombards, md **Austigusa**, princess of Gepidae; dau of **N.N.**, the king of Gepidae.

49. **Waldrada** md **Garibald I** (262-50), Duke of Bavaria, 553-591/2.

48. **Gundwald**, Duke of Asti, d. c614.

47. **Aripert I**, King of Lombards, 653-661.

46. **Godepert**, Prince of Lombards, fl. 662.

45. **Reginpert**, Duke of Turin.

44. **Aripert II**, fl. 712.

43. **Petrussa**, of the Lombards, md **Vislas I**, King of the Obotrites, fl. 700.

42. **Aribert I**, of the Obotrites, fl. 724, md **Mandana**.

41. **Billung I**, of the Obotrites, md **Hildegarde**.

40. **Billung (II)**, of the Obotrites, md **Jutta**.

39. **Mieceslas (I)**, of the Obotrites, md **Antonia**.

38. **Rodigastus**, of the Obotrites, fl. 840.

37. **Mistui I**, of the Obotrites, fl. 869.

36. **Mieceslas (II)**, of the Obotrites, fl. 885.

35. **Mistui II**, Prince of the Obotrites, 919–999.

34. **Mieceslas (III)**, Prince of the Obotrites.

33. **Astrid**, an Obotritian princess; b. c979; md **Olaf III** "Skotkonung" (240-33), King of Sweden.

Sources: Behr, K. 1854; (Gen. 33–53); Blass, R. 1939, 2: tables 260 and 264); *Moriarty, G. 1985, 54, says N.N. instead of Astrid, for Gen. 33*; Turton, 27, (Gen. 33–53); Wagner, A. 1975:186; Winkhaus, E. 1953.

202

## LINE 381

36. **Konrad II**, of Ohningen, Duke of Swabia; d. 20 Aug 997; md **Richlint,** dau of **Liudorf,** Duke of Swabia, d. 958; by his wife **Ita of Swabia.**

35. **Konrad III**, Count of Ortengau; d. c1005; md **Beatrix**, prob dau of **Friedrich I,** Duke of Lorraine, by wife Princess **Beatrix,** sister of **Hugh Capet,** King of France (134-34, etc.).

34. **Kuno,** of Rheinfelden, d. c1024; prob md **Gisela**, dau of Count **Rudolf** who d. 1019.

33. **Rudolph of Rheinfelden,** Duke of Swabia; King of Germany; b. 1020/1024; d. 15 Oct 1080; md (1) Mathilde, d. 12 May 1060; dau of Heinrich III, b. 1017; d. 1056; md (2) **Adelaide von Susa,** (mother of Gen. 32) dau of **Otto I,** Count of Maurienne (173-33).

32. **Adelaide of Rheinfelden,** Queen of Hungary, md **Ladislas I** (75-32,97-29), King of Hungary, d. 27 July 1095.

31. **Pyriska** (Eirene), Princess of Hungary; b. c1088; d. 13 Aug 1134, Bithyna; md **Iohannes** (John) **Komnenos** (111-31), Emperor of the East.

Sources: Dworzaczek, K. 1959, tables 84, 85; ES, II 1984:154; Jackman, D. 1990; Jackman, D. 1997; Moriarty, G. 1985, 140 (Gen. 32); Vajay, S. de 1962.

## LINE 382

39. **Leon Argyros I**, fl. 843-844.

38. **Eustathios Argyros**, patrikios, c866; d. c910.

37. **Leon Argyros II**, strategos, protospatharios, magistros, c910; d. after 922.

36. **Romanos Argyros**, b. c905; d. after 921; md Feb 921, **Agatha Lekapena** (399-36).

35. **N.N. Argyros** md N.N.

34. **N N. Argyropoulos**, patrikos, c965; d. after 985.

33. **Pulcheria** (Argyropoulina), b. c965; d. before Apr 1034, (sister of the Emperor Romanus III Argyros), md **Basileios Skleros** (115-33).

Sources: Brook, L. 1981, nos. 28–34, 188 (Gen. 33–39); Collenburg, W. 1963.W; Toumanoff, C. 1976, 344–346 note, table 72b; Vanislev, A. 1951.

## LINE 383

35. **Eudes**, Count of Cambrai, md **Adele of Bois Ferrand** (184-34).

34. **Engelbert I**, Count of Brienne, liv 968.

33. **Engelbert II**, Count of Brienne, d. c980.

32. **Engelbert III**, Count of Brienne, d. before 1035; md **Windesmode of Salins**, dau of **Adela**, Countess of Salins, whose parents were **Humbert I** (189-35), Sire de Salins, and **Windelmode of Escuens.**

31. **Engelbert IV**, Count of Brienne, md 1048/1050, **Petronille,** d. after 6 June 1050.

30. **Walter I**, Count of Brienne, d. c1089/1090; md **Eustache de Bar-sur-**

**Seine**, dau of **Milo (I)**, Count of Bar-sur-Seine and Tonnerre; (d. 1046) and **Azeka**; granddau of **Milo IV** (254-34), Count of Tonnerre, and (prob) **Ermengarde of Bar-sur-Seine**.

29. **Milo (Miles) II**, Count of Bar-sur-Seine; liv 1100; d. 1125/1126; md **Mathilde of Noyers**, liv 1116; dau of **Milo II of Noyers**, liv 1104; and **Anna**; granddau of **Milo (Miles) I of Noyers**, liv 1078.

28. **Gui**, Count of Bar-sur-Seine, d. 1145; md **Petronille of Chacenay** (384-28), d. 1161.

27. **Ermesinde of Bar-sur-Seine**, d. 1211; md 1189, **Theobald I** (36-27), Count of Briey, 1170; and of Bar, 1191.

26. **Henry II** (36-26), Count of Bar, md **Philippa de Dreux** (37-26).

Sources: Briollet, M. 1971; Chaume.R, 281+; Collenburg, W. 1963; Didion, L. 1964, 149–167); ES, VI 1978:147 (Gen. 26–28); III 1989:681 (Gen. 27–34); Longnon, J. 1978, 87; Moriarty, G. 1985, 277; Parisse, M. 1976.

## LINE 384

31, **Anseric I**, Sire de Chacenay; d. 1104; md **Gersinde of Chacenay**, liv 1075.

30. **Milon**, Sire de Chacenay; md 1102/1107, **Adelaide**.

29. **Anseric II**, Sire de Chacenay; d. 1137; md **Humbeline de Troyes** (385-29).

28. **Petronille** (Elizabeth) **of Chacenay**, liv 1135–1161, md **Gui** (383-28), Count of Bar-sur-Seine; d. 1145.

Sources: Bouchard, C. 1987, 331, 336 (Gen. 28–31); ES, XIII:63 (Gen 28–31); Parisse, M. 1976 (Gen. 28–31); Poull, G. 1979 (Gen. 28–31).

## LINE 385

30. **Tescelin Sorus**, Lord of Fontaines, md **Aleth of Montbard**; dau of **Bernard**, Lord of Montbard, liv 1065; and **Humberge**, liv 1065.

29. **Humbeline de Troyes** md **Anseric II** (384-29), Sire of Chacenay. She md (2) 1137, Gautier II, Count of Brienne, 1113–1158; d. before 1161.

Sources: Bouchard, C. 1987, C. 1987, 331, 336 (Gen. 29–30); ES, XIII:63 (Gen. 29); Laurent, J. 1911; Petit, E. 1894, 496+.

## LINE 386

43. **Thrond**.

42. **Eystein**, Earl of Throndheim, c710.

41. **Hogne**, Earl of Throndheim.

40. **N.N. of Throndheim** (dau) md **Ivar Oplaendinge** (44-40), Jarl of the Uplands in Norway, c790.

Sources: Stokvis, A. 1966, (Gen. 40–43); Turton, 6 (Gen. 40–43).

## LINE 387

31. **Waleran II**, Count of Limburg, md 1060/1061, **Jutta of Luxemburg**

30. **Henry I**, Count of Limburg, d. 1119; md **Adelaide** dau **Boto von**

Botenstein (48-33) and **Judith von Schweinfurt** (47-33).

29. **Mathilde of Limburg,** md **Henry I** (50-28), Lord de la Roche, d. 1126/38.

Sources: Blass, R. 1939, II:tables 267, 268; Brandenburg, E. 1935; ES, III 1989:26 (Gen. 30); Moriarty, G. 1985, 159, 160 (Gen. 29–31); Tyroller, F. 1968, 53-68, 85+; Vanderkindere, L. 1902, II:363–366; Winkhaus, E. 1953. .

## LINE 388

34. **Frederick II von Diessen,** Count of Diessen, md **Ermengarde von Gilching** (46-31, 49-34).

33. **Berthold I von Schwartzenburg,** d. c1090; md (2) **Richgard von Sponheim,** d. 11 Apr 1130; dau of **Engelbert I von Sponheim** and **Hedwig of Flinsbach** (228-32).

32. **Engelbert,** Count of Schwartzenburg, md **N.N. von Mullenark.**

31. **Margaret von Schwartzenburg,** b. c11; liv 1134; md c1120, **Adolph von Saffenburg** (67-31).

Sources: ES VI 1978:2 (33-34); I 1984:36–37 (Gen. 33–34).

## LINE 389

39. **Konrad II,** Margrave of Burgundy, md **Judith of Friuli,** d. after 902; dau **Eberhard** (269-39), Marquis of Friuli, and **Gisela** (185-40), Princess of France.

38. **Adalgunde of Burgundy,** d. c902; md **Erenfried I,** Count in the Bliesgau, 877; Count in the Charmois.

37. **Eberhard** (same as 208-38), Count in the Keldachgau, 913; Count in the Bonngau; prob father of Gen. 36.

36. **Dietrich,** Count in the Drenthe and in Salland; d. after 964; md **Amalrada of Hamalant,** dau of **Dietrich,** Count of Hamalant

35. **Hunroch** (Unrouch), Count in the Tristerbant, d. after 1026.

34 **Godizo** Count in the Betuwe, d. 1018; md **Bertha** (Bave).

33. **Eberhard von der Betuwe und Tristerbaut,** Count in the Betuwe.

32. **Adelaide of the Betuwe** (or Orlamunda), d. after 1086; md **Henry II** (68-32), Count of Louvain.

Sources: Aders, G. 1976 I:1–58 (1976) (Gen. 32–39); Brandenburg, E. 1935; ES, VI 1978 1978:1 1984 (Gen. 32–39); Moriarty, G. 1985, 125.

## LINE 390

30. **Florenz II** (38-29), Count of Holland, md **Gertrude** (Petronel) **of Alsace,** dau of **Dietrich II of Alsace** (158-31), Duke of Upper Lorraine, and **Hedwig von Formbach** (41-32).

29. **Dietrich VI,** Count of Holland, Crusader, d. 6 Aug 1157; md before 1139, **Sophia of Rheineck** (391-29), d. 26 Sept 1176, Jerusalem.

28. **Florenz III,** Count of Holland and West Sealand, and Earl of Ros; Crusader; b. c1138; d. 1 Aug 1190 on the 3rd Crusade at Antioch; md 28 Aug 1162, **Ada of Huntingdon** (72-28), b. c1146, Scotland; d. 11 Jan 1216/22.

205

Sources: Brandenburg, E. 1935; Dek, A. 1955; ES, II 1984:90 (Gen. 28); Flahiff, G. 1947; Moriarty, G. 1985, 178 (Gen. 28–30); Paget, G. 1977.

## LINE 391

32. **Giselbert I** (3-32), Count of Salm, Longwy and Luxemburg; b. c1005; d. 14 Aug 1059.

31. **Hermann,** Count of Salm and Luxemburg, d. 28 Sept 1088, Metz; md **Sophie.**

30. **Otto I of Luxemburg,** Lord of Rheineck, 1131; b. c1080; d. after 1154; md 1115, **Gertrude von Northeim** (392-30).

29. **Sophia of Rheineck,** d. 26 Sept 1176, Jerusalem; md before 1139, **Dietrich VI** (390-29), Count of Holland, 1121.

Sources: Blass, R. 1939, II: table 271; Brandenburg, E. 1935; ES, IV 1981:92 (Gen. 30–31); VI 1978:128 (Gen. 31–32); Moriarty, G. 1985, 179 (Gen. 29–31); 129 (Gen. 31–32); Vannerus, J. 1946, 25, 901-958 (1947); Winkhaus, E. 1953.

## LINE 392

31. **Henry,** Count of Northeim, d. in battle 1101; md **Gertrude von Braunschweig** (393-31); b. c1065; d. 9 Dec 1117.

30. **Gertrude von Northeim,** b. c1088/89; md (2) 1115, **Otto I of Luxemburg** (391-30), Count of Rheineck, d. 1150.

Sources: ES, VIII 1980:132 (Gen. 30–31); Lange, K. 1969 (Gen. 30–31); Moriarty, G. 1985, 179 (Gen. 30–31); Vogt, H. 1959 (Gen. 30–31).

## LINE 393

33. **Ludwig von Braunschweig** (32-32), Count in the Derlingau, md **Gertrude von Egisheim** (33-32).

32. **Ekbert I,** Count of Braunschweig and Margrave of Meissen; b. c1036; d. 11 Jan 1068; md **Ermengarde of Susa,** d. 1078; dau of **Meginwerd** (Meginfred). *NOTE: Moriarty, G. 1985, p.180, gives Ermengarde's parents as Odelerico Manfredo and Bertha of Este.*

31. **Gertrude von Braunschweig,** b. c1065; d. 9 Dec 1117; md **Henry** (392-31), Count of Northeim, d. 1101 in battle. She also md (1) Dietrich II, Count of Katlenburg (d. 1085); md (3) Henry, Count of Eilenburg (Wettin) (d. 1103).

Sources: Blass, R. 1939 II:290; ES, VIII 1980:131a (Gen. 31–33); Moriarty, G. 1985, 180 (Gen. 31–33); Vanderkindere, L. 1902, I:66, II:288–291, 294, 304, 395; Vogt, H. 1959 ; Winkhaus, E. 1953.

## LINE 394

34. **Andronikos Doukas** (215-33) md **Maria of Bulgaria** (309-33). *NOTE: Brook, L. 1981, who covers only Byzantine lines, says only "Marie" for wife of Gen. 34, but numerous authorities (cf. Line 309), identify her as "of Bulgaria" and extend the lineage.*

33. **Michael Doukas**, protostrator; b. c1061; d. 1100–1116.

32. **Eirene Doukaina**, liv c1093–1123; md c1100, **Gregorios Kamateros**, d. after 1176; son of the Basileios **Kamateros**.

31. **Andronikos Kamateros Doukas**, d. after 1176.

30. **Euphrosyne Kamateros Doukaina**, d. c1212; md before 1195, **Alexios Angelos** (Emperor Alexius III) (74-29).

Sources: Allen, J. 1985; Brook, L. 1981, nos. 59, 62, 63, 76-79; Hanovelt, E. 1982; Polemis, D. 1986, 85n2.

## LINE 395

32. **Thurston Basset**, liv 1080.

31. **Ralph Basset.**

30. **Thomas Basset.**

29. **Gilbert Basset,** of Wallingford, Berkshire, liv 1165; md **Edith d'Oilly** (82-28, 396-29), of Hook Norton, Oxford, England.

28. **Joan Basset** md **Alberic I** (82-28), Count of Dammartin.

Sources: Boarstall; Evans, C. 1963; Evans, C. 1983; Frideswide; Goring; Kennett; Missenden; Sanford; Turton, 127 (Gen. 28–32).

## LINE 396

34. **Sigulf** (prob father of Gen. 33), liv c1030.

33. **Forne** "the King's Theign," of Nunburholme, Yorkshire, liv 1086.

32. **Sigulf fitz Forne**, of Nunburnholme, Yorkshire.

31. **Forne fitz Sigulf**, of Greystoke, Cumberland, d. 1129/1130.

30. **Edith fitz Forne**, of Greystoke, Cumberland, a mistress of Henry I; md **Robert II d'Oilly** of Hook Norton, Oxford; d. 1142; whose father was **Nigel d'Oilly**, d. c1115, who md **Agnes**; and Nigel's father was **N.N.**, le Sire d'Ouillie.

29. **Edith d'Oilly** (82-28,395-29), of Hook Norton, Oxford, England; md **Gilbert Basset** (395-29), liv 1165.

Sources: Washington, S.1942, (Gen. 29–34); Sanders, I. 1960, 50, 54 (Gen. 29–34).

## LINE 397

32. **Hildouin** (266-33), Count of Montdidier, Seigneur de Rameru.

31. **Manasses**, Count of Dammartin, of Dampmartin, Ile de France, France; b. c1010; d. 15 Nov 1037, Battle of Bar; md **Constance of France,** dau of **Robert II** (134-33,154-34), King of France, and **Constance of Arles** (333-34).

30. **Hugh**, Count of Dammartin, c1071; of Dampmartin, Ile de France,

France; d. 1103; md **Roaide** (Rohais) **de Bulles,** Countess of Bulles; b. c1046.

29. **Aelis** (Adelaide) **de Dammartin** md (1) c1104, **Aubry de Mello** (82-

29); md (2) Lancelin II de Beauvais, regent of the countship of Dammartin-en-Goele.

Sources: Evans, C. 1965 (Gen. 29–32); Evans, C. 1983 (Gen. 29–32); ES, III 1989:650 (Gen. 29–30); Fiennes, D. 1980.

## LINE 398

39. **Hildebert** (Adalbert) I (328-38), Vicomte de Limoges, md **Adaltrude**.
38. **Foucher (I)**, Seigneur of Segur, d. c930; md **Christine**.
37. **Foucher (II)**, Count of Segur.
36. **Ademar**, Viscount de Segur, md **Milisendis**, d. 11 July (1001).
35. **Emma of Segur**, d. shortly after 1025; md **Gui I**, Viscount de Limoges; son of **Geraud** (328-36), Viscount de Limoges and wife **Rothilda**.
34. **Ademar I**, Viscount de Limoges and of Segur, 998/1036; md **Senegundis d'Aunay**, dau of **Cadelon VI**, Viscount d'Aunay.
33. **Ademar II**, Viscount de Limoges, 1030-1090; md (1) 1030, **Humberge d'Angouleme**, dau of Count **Geoffrey I** and **Petronille d'Archaic** (87-32).
Sources: Briollet, M. 1965, chart p. 102; ES III:773.

## LINE 399

38. **Theophylaktos**, an Armenian called Abastaktos, liv c871; md **N.N.**
37. **Romanos Lekapenos** (Emperor Romanus I Lecapenus, 920–944); b.
36. **Agatha Lekapena**, b. c908, md Feb 921, **Romanus Argyros** (382-36).

Sources: Allen, J. 1985; Brook, L. 1981, nos. 31, 119, 120, 122 (Gen. 36-38; Collins, R. 1991; Gregoire, H. 1932; Runcimen, S. 1921; Runcimen, S. 1963

## LINE 400

38. **Baldwin I** (235-38), Count of Flanders; md **Judith** (250-38), Princess of France.
37. **Rudolph**, Count of Cambrai, d. 17 June 896.
36. **N.N.**, md **Isaac**, Count of Cambrai, 916–940; d. after 30 Apr 948.
35. **Arnaud** (99-34,401-35), Count and Bishop of Cambrai d. 967; md **Bertha of the Betuwe** (401-35).
34. **Gisele of Cambrai** (same as 401-34); md **Herve** (99-34), Lord of Chatillon-sur-Marne.

Sources: Brandenburg, E. 1935; Dek, A. 1955; ES II 1984:5 (Gen. 36-38); Moriarty, G. 1985, 272 (Gen. 34–35); Rosch, S. 1977; Van Overstraeten, D. 1976, nos. 33, 35, 36; Vercauteren, F. 1938, XV–XIX; Winkhaus, E. 1953 .

## LINE 401

37. **Ricfrid** (same as 310-36), Count in the Betuwe, 847; md **Hamesindis**.

36. **Nevelung** (same as 100-35), Count in the Betuwe, md before 943, **N.N.**, a dau of **Regnier II** (68-36), Count of Hainault, and **Adelaide of Burgundy** (206-37).

35. **Bertha of the Betuwe** md **Arnaud** (99-34,400-35), Count and Bishop of Cambrai.

34. **Gisele of Cambrai** (same as 400-34) md **Herve** (99-34), Lord of Chatillon.

Sources: ES VI 1978:60 (35–37); Moller, W. 1933, table XLVIII (Gen. 34–37); Moriarty, G. 1985, 272 (Gen. 34–35).

## LINE 402

37. **Richard I de Milhaud**, liv c910.

36. **Bernard I**, Vicomte de Milhaud, liv 914–952; md **Adelaide**.

35. **Berenger I**, Vicomte de Milhaud, liv 1000.

34. **Richard I**, Vicomte de Milhaud, 1002/23; md **Senegunde de Beziers** (226-34), liv. 990/1013.

Sources: Arrieres, J. 1921, XXI:490–504; ES, III 1989:805 (Gen. 34–36); Laine, P. la 1928; Ourliac, P. 1985, nos. 32, 55, 68; Turton, 218 (Gen. 34–37).

## LINE 403

38. **Regnier I** (207-38) "Longhals," Count of Hainault and Duke of Lorraine; liv 886–900; md **Alberade of Mons**.

37. **N.N. of Hainault**, md **Berenger**, Count of Namur, 907–933; d. 946.

36. **Robert I**, Count of Lomme and of Namur; liv 946; d. 981; md **Ermengarde of Lorraine**, dau of **Otto of Lorraine**, 955, who was son of **Richwin** (316-37), Count of Verdun.

35. **Adalbert (Albert) I**, Count of Namur; d. shortly before 1011; md **Ermentrude of Lorraine** (120-34); b. c970/975; d. after 1012.

Sources: ES, VII 1979:68 (Gen. 35–38); Moriarty, G. 1985, 128 (Gen. 35–38); Rousseau, F. 1936 (Gen. 35–38).

## LINE 404

41. **Berenger**, an East Frank.

40. **Hunroch** (Unroch), Count of Ternois, 839; d. after 853; md **Engeltrude**, prob dau of **Begue** (269-41), Count of Paris.

39. **Eberhard** (185-40,269-39, 345-38,404-39), Margrave of Friuli, d. 16 Dec 862, Italy; bur Cysoing; md **Gisela** (185-40), Princess of France.

Sources: Moriarty, G. 1985, 18 (Gen. 39–41); Rosch, S. 1977 (Gen. 39–40).

## LINE 405

59. **Einydd ap Gwrddwfu.**

58. **Caradoc**, Lord of Meriadoc.

57. **Cynan Meriadoc**, King of Brittany and Dumnonia; liv 450; md

**Darara.**

56. **Gradlonus**, King of Brittany; liv 480.

55. **Salamon I**, King of Brittany, liv 500.

54. **Audren** (Alain), King of Brittany.

53. **Budic I**, King of Brittany, liv 516-566; md **N.N.** (405A-53).

52. **Hoel I**, King of Brittany.

51. **Hoel II**, K. of Brittany, murdered 547; md **Rimo**.

50. **Alain I** (Judicael), King of Brittany, b. 535.

49. **Hoel III**, King of Brittany, d. 612.

48. **Judicael**, King of Brittany, 632-640; d. 658 [but some sources say his brother Salamon II].

47. **Alain II le Long**, King of Brittany, d. 690.

46. **Ivor** (never ruled); d. before his father.

45. **Daniel Dremrost**, "the Red Eyed," King of Brittany, d. 703.

44. **Budic II**, King of Brittany, liv in 700s.

43.**N.N.**,( perhaps Melieu) (never ruled).

42. **Erispoe**.

41. **Nominoe**, Duke of Brittany, 826-851; Governor under Louis "the Pious," 826; d. 8 JUne or 22 Aug 851; md **Argentael**.

40. **Erispoe**, Duke of Brittany, 851-857; d. Nov 857.

39. **N.N.** heiress of Brittany, md **Gurwand**, Count of Rennes, 851; d. 876/877.

38. **Berenger**, Count of Rennes, 887-890; defeated the Norsemen at Coesnon, 890.

37. **N.N.**, heiress of Rennes, md **Paskwitan II** (334-37), Count of Rennes.

Sources: Ashley, M. 1998:122,728; Blass II: table 251; Brandenburg; ES II 1984:75; Moriarty, G. 1985, 13 (Gen. 37-41); Williamson, D. 1996; Winkhaus, E. 1953.

## LINE 405A

57. **Coel Hen**, "Old King Cole," ruler of Northern Britain, c410-c430. Some researchers say he and his son-in-law **Cunneda** (405A-56) were descended from **Bali Mawr**, prob King of Silurians of North Britain, c100BC. Bali Mawr was descended from **Adminius**, son of **Cunobelin**. (Cymbelin), rular of the Trinovantes from 1 AD; and **Catevallauni**, 40 AD. Coel Hen md **Ystradwal** (405B-57)

56. **Gwawl** (fem.) md **Cunneda Wledig**.

55. **Ceredig**.

54. **Corun** md **Teithfallt**, dau of **Nynnian** of Gwent who was son of **N.N.**, whose father was **Eudaf Hen** (405C-59).

53. **N.N.** md **Budic I** (405-53), King of Brittany.

Sources: Ashley, M. 1998: 122 (chart 3);123,728; ES III 1984:75 NEU; Williamson, D. 1996:357.

## LINE 405B

70. **Cassivellaunos**, King of Catuvellauni, liv 55-54BC.

69. **Andocomius.**

68. **Tasciovanus** (Tehvant), d. c13AD.

67. **Cumobelin** (Cymbelin), ruler of Trinovantes (from 1 AD) and Catevallauni , c10-41 AD.

66. **Arviragus.**

65. **Marius** md **N.N.** (405C-65), dau of **Prasutagus**, King of the Iceni. Source: Bertram, P. 1966.

## LINE 405C

66. **Prasutagus**, King of the Iceni, 47-59AD, md **Boudicca**, Queen 59-61AD.

65. **N.N.** (fem.) md **Marius** (405B-65).

64. **Cadfan** md **Gwladys.**

63. **Coel.**

62. **Llyrllediaith.**

61. **Bran.**

60. **Caradoc.**

59. **Eudaf Hen** (called Octavius the Old).

58. **N.N.** (male)

57. **Ystradwal** md **Coel Hen** (405C-57).

Sources: Ashley, M. 1998:122,123,728; ES III 1984:75 NEU; Williamson, D. 1996:357.

## LINE 406

60. **Brand of Scandinavia,** (same as 233-60).

59. **Benoc** (or Bernic).

58. **Aloc.**

57. **Angenwit.**

56. **Hengist.**

55. **Esa.**, perhaps same as Oisc, King of Kent, 488-c516.

54. **Eoppa**, perhaps same as Ebissa.

53. **Ida** "the Flamebearer," King of Bernicea, c 547-c559 (or c557-c569); liv 547-559; md **Beornoch**.

52. **Aethelric**, King of Bernicea, c587-c593; liv 562-572;

51. **Aethelfrith**, King of Bernicea, 593-604; and of Northumbria, 604-616; md (1) **Bebba** (mother of Gen. 50); md (2) Acha, dau of Aella, King of Northumbria.

50. **Eanfrith**, King of Bernicea,12 Oct 633/34 to April, 635/36; killed in battle after ruling for only 18 months; md **N.N.**, dau of **Gwid,** of the Picts, son of **Brude**, son of **Maelgwyn Gwynedd**. The wife of Gwid may have been a sister of **Nechtan II** (341-50), King of the Picts, 602-621, and of Strathclyde, 612-621.

211

49. **N.N.**, a sister of **Talorcam (I)**, King of the Picts ,653-655; md **Beli** (341-49), King of Strathclyde, 621-633.
Source: Ashley, M. 1998; Searl, W. 1899, 254, 255; Pirie, C. 1959; Williamson, D. 1986, appendix B, Gen. table, pp. 212, 215

## LINE 407

49. **Tiberius II Constantinus**, Eastern Roman Emperor, 578-582; md prob **Anastasia**. His reign was troubled by conflicts with the Persians and Avars, and was marked with great inundation of Slavs who advanced into Thrace and Greece and settled in great numbers.
48. **Constantina** md **Flavius Tiberius Mauricus** (Maurice), Eastern Roman Emperor, 582-602; b. Cappadocia, c539; faced by mutiny of the Danube army and forced to abdicate (602); murdered by Procas, 602.
47. **Miriam** (Maria) md **Chosroes II Perez** (Abarvez) King of Persia, (same as 408-47) 590-638; murdered 638.
Sources: Settipani, C. 1991, 63, 83; Stark, F. 1967, 354, 379, 387, 389; Webster, 1988, 819, 992, 1469.

## LINE 408

70. **Phrates III** (417-71), King of Parthia; md his sister **Piritana**.
71. **Mithradates III**, King of Parthia, 56-55 BC; of Media Athropatene, 67 BC; deposed and killed 57 BC; md (2) Princess **N.N.** (410-71); dau of **Tigranus II**, King of Armenia.
70. **Ariobarzanes I**, King of Media Athropatene, 36 BC.
69. **Artavasdes I**, King of Media Athropatene and Lesser Armenia; md **N.N.**, dau of **Artiochus I** (412-70), King of Commagene.
68. **Darius** (412-69), Prince of Media Athropatene, 66-65 BC; md Princess **N.N.** (417-68), dau of **Phraates IV**, Great King of Parthia. *NOTE: Settipani, C. 1991 (p.94) doubts the lineage beyond Gen. 67.*
67. **Vonones II**, King of Media Athropatene, c11-51 AD; King of Parthia, 51 AD; b. 10 BC; d. 51 AD; md **N.N.**, his sister.
66. **Vologaesus I**, King of Parthia, 51-77; b. 25 AD; d. 77 AD. *NOTE: after the reign of Vologaesus I, the utmost confusion prevailed in Parthia, with two or more kings (all of them little known) ruling at the same time and certainly challenged by other claimants. [Source: Langer, W. 1948]*
65. **Mithradates**, King of Armenia, 72-76 AD b. 45/50 AD; d. prob 76.
64. **Sanatroukes** (Sanstruk), King of Armenia, c80-110; b. 65; d. 110.
63. **Vologaesus I**, King of Armenia, c116-137; b. 95; d. 137.
62. **Vologaesus II**, King of Armenia, 180-191; as Vologaesus V Great King of Parthia, 190-207; b. 130; d. 207; md Princess **N.N.** (416-62). of Iberia. He lost most of his domain to the Arcasid king.
61. **Artabanus IV**, Great King of Parthia, 213-224; King of Media, 207-213; b. 160/165; d. 224; last of the Arcasids; defeated and killed in battle of Hormuz, by Ardashir, King of Persia, founder of the Sassisinae dynasty, his son-on-law.

60. **N.N.** (fem) (perhaps Ziyanak or Mirud); md **Ardashir I**, King of Persia, c222-241; King of Kings, 222; son of **Papak,** King of Persia, c208-222, and wife **Rodak.**

59. **Sapor I**, King of Persia, 241-272; md **Gurdzag** (mother of Gen. 58). He invaded Syria; waged war against Rome; defeated Romans and made prisoner of Emperor Valerian in battle near Edessa in 222, The emperor died in captivity.

58. **Nerseh** (Narses) I, King of Armenia, c273-293; King of Persia, 293-302. He seized the throne from his grand-nephew, Bahram III; made war on Rome; was badly beaten in Armenia; concluded peace with Rome.

57. **Hormisdas II**, King of Persia, 302-309; md **N.N.**, a dau of the king of Kabul (now in Afghanistan).

56. **Sapor II**, King of Persia, 309-379; one of the greatest Persian kings. In a long war (337-363) with the Romans, defeated the Emperor Constantinus II. In 363, attacked a hugh Roman army, in which the Emperor Julian was killed. He made peace with the Roman Empire which was disgraceful to the Romans; conquered Armenia.

55. **Sapor III**, King of Persia, 383-388; prob murdered.

54. **Yazdegerd** , King of Persia, 399-421; murdered; md **Sashandukht,** dau of the rash galutha, Exilarch of Jews of the Empire. He tried to keep peace with the Roman Empire; stopped persecution of Christians.

53. **Baranes V**, King of Persia, 420-439; called the "wild ass." Began persecution of Christians which led to war with Rome. Defeated 422; finally granted the same toleration of Christians as Zoroasterians received in the Roman Empire; mentioned in Omer Khayyam's *Rubaiyat* (xviii).

52. **Yazdegerd II**, King of Persia, 439-457; persecuted Christians and Jews; at war with Rome (441 AD); Battle of Avarair, 451; md **Dinak.** *NOTE: in 457-458 Hormisdad III was king.*

51. **Firoz** (Peroz) V, King of Persia, 459-484; captured at Hephthalites, 469; overcome in war with Ephthalites.

50. **Kavadh I**, King of Persia, 485-531; deposed and imprisoned by his brother; escaped and restored to throne, 485-531; made war against the Romans (503-504 and 524-531); invaded Syria, 531.

49. **Chosroes I** (Khosros, Anushiruan) "the Just," King of Persia, 531-579; d. 579; md (1) a Turkish princess. At war with Justinian, the Byzantine emperor (531, 532, 540-545); sacked Antioch (540 AD) and forced Justinian to pay tribute; one of the greatest Persian kings; reformd imperial taxation; restored Zoroastrianism.

48. **Hermisdas IV**, King of Persia, 579-590; carried on war against the Eastern Roman Empire but was defeated, deposed, blinded and assassinated.

47. **Chosroes II**, "the Victorious," King of Persia, 590-628; fled to the Byzantine emperor, 590, and regained the throne with the help of the Byzantines; imprisoned and murdered, 638; md (1) Sirin; md (2) **Miriam** (same as 407-47), (mother of Gen. 46).

213

46. **Shahrijar of Persia**.

45. **Yazdegerd III** (329-46), King of Persia, 632-641; the last of the Sassanid dynasty; too young to actually rule; country torn by civil war; Arab invasion began 633 and Persians overwhelmed by Arabs in battle of Kadisiya (637) and Neharend (c641); fled to Media; murdered at Marv (651). His assention date, June 16, 632, marks the beginning of the Jalalean era and is still used in the calendar of Parsis.

44. Princess **Izdundad** md **Bustanai ben Haninai** (329-46), Exilarch of Jews at Babylon.

43. **Hisdai Shahrijar**, Exilarch of Jews at Babylon, 660-665.

42. **N.N.** (fem.) md **Natroni ben Nehemiah** (same as 329-43), Gaon of Pumbeditha, 719-739.

Sources: Bedrosian, R. 1985; Boardman, J. 1988; Bury J. 1969;Castro, M. 1995; Chahin, M. 1987; Chamich, M. 1990; Curtis, J. 1990; Debevoise, N. 1970; Dunster, M. 1979; Grousset, R. 1984; Guerney, G. 1992; Hovannisian, R. 1997; Hunt, C. 1972; Langer, W. 1948; Moncreiffe, I. 1982, 48; Olmstead, A. 1959; Rogers, R. 1983; Settipani, C. 1991, 75, 83, 88, 91; Stark, F. 1967, 175, 179, 185, 205; etc. Taggei, B. 1989; Thomson, R. 1976; Webster, 1988, 67, 1087, 1350, 1606.

## LINE 409

76. **Pharnabazes I**, King of Iberia, 299-234 BC; b. c326 BC.

75. **Sauromaces I**, King of Iberia, 243-159 BC

74. Princess **N.N.** md **Meribanes I**, King of Iberia, 159-109 BC.

73. Princess **N.N.** md **Artavades**, King of Armenia, 125-95 BC.

72. **Artaxias I**, King of Iberia, 90-78 BC; md Princess **N.N.**, dau of **Meribanes I**, King of Iberia, 159-109 BC.

71. **Artaces I**, King of Iberia, 78-63 BC.

70. **Pharnabazes II**, King of Iberia, 63-30 BC; d. in battle, 30 BC; md (1) **N.N.**, prob dau of **Tigranus II** (410-72,411-72,416-20), King of Armenia, and wife **Cleopatra**.

Sources: Brossett, M. 1876; Castro, M. 1995; Chamich, M. 1990; Grousett, R. 1984; Taggie, B. 1989; Theroff, P. 1994; Thomson, R. 1976; Toumanoff, C. 1969.

## LINE 410

84. **Artaxerxes I** (same as 414-86), King of Persia, 464-424, d. 425 BC; (md) **Andria**, dau of **Nebuchadrezzar IV**, King of Babylon. Artaxerxes I appointed Nehemiah as Governor of Judea, 445 BC.

83. **Darius II** (same as 414-85), King of Persia, d. 404 BC.

82. **Aroandes I** (bro of **Artaxerxes II** (414-84), King of Persia); md **Rodogune of Persia**, dau of **Artaxerxes II**.

81. **Aroandes II**.

80. **Mithradanes I**.

79. **Araondes III**.

78. **Samos I.**

77. **Arsames I.**

76. **Xerxes I** md **Antiochus of Syria**, dau of **Antiochus III**, King of Syria, 223-187 BC

75. **Zariadres I**, strategos, then King of Sophene, c200-190 BC.

74. **Artaxias I**, strategos of Armenia, 200/190 BC; then King of Armenia, 190-159. He was founder of the third and greatest Armenian monarchy; at the peace of Apamea (188 BC), which sealed the Roman victory over Armenia, the kings of Armenia were given the status of independent rulers. Pursuing a lively expansionist policy, Artaxias took Media Arthrpatene (modern Azerbaijan) and seized much territory in other areas. An important result of this expansion was the cultural and linguistic consolidation of the Armenian people with Armenian becoming the dominant language.

73. **Tigranes I**, King of Armenia, 159-123 BC.

72. **Tigranes II** "the Great," King of Armenia, 95-55 BC; b. c140; d. 55; md (2) **Cleopatra** (411-72). Extendes territories by conquest, to northern Mesopotamia, Syria and Cappadocia; attacked and defeated the Romans; surrendered to Pompay (66 BC) and thereafter ruled as a harmless vassel of the Romans.

71. Princess **N.N.** md **Mithradates III** (408-71), King of Parthia, 57-55 BC; King of Media Athropatene, 67 BC.

Sources: Bedrosian, R. 1985; Brosset, M. 1876; Chamich, M. 1990; Grousset, R. 1984; Hovannisian, R. 1997; Jones, A. 1971; Manandian, H. 1963, 45; Settipani, C. 1991, 93; Seyrig, H. 1955; Thomson, R. 1976.

## LINE 411

*NOTE: This line is very confusing and somewhat conjectural beyond Gen. 79. What seems to be certain is that Gen 79 is in direct descent from Gen. 82.*

88. **Arshama.**

87. **Pharmaces**, Governor of Persopolis, 499-497 BC; b. 560; d. 497.

86. **Artabazus I**, general, 480-479; setrap of Daskyleion, 477-449; b. 525 BC; d. after 499 BC; prob father of Gen. 85.

85. **Pharnabazus**, setrap of Daskyleion, 449-414; b. 470.

84. **Pharnaces**, setrap of Daskyleion, 414-BC.

83. **Mithradates**, setrap of Phrygia (Pontus); b. 440; d. 387/367.

82. **Artiobarzanes I**, setrap of Phrygia (Pontus); b. 415; d. 362; prob father of Gen. 81.

81. **Artiobazanes II**, setrap of Chios (Cius), 362-337; father of three sons by 352; b. 395/390; d. 337; bro of Mithradates, b. 390; d. c362.

80. **Artiobarzanes**, noble Persian, b. 365; d. c339/337; bro of Mithradates II, setrap of Chios (Cius), 337-302; b. 360; d. 302.

79. **Mithradates I**, setrap of Chios (Cius), 302; King of Pontus, 281-266; was perhaps adopted by his uncle, Mithradates II, setrap of Chios

(Cius), 337-302.

78. **Ariobarzares**, King of Pontus, 266-c250 BC; b. 300; d. 250.

77. **Mithradates II**, King of Pontus, 250-220; b. c260; d. 220; md **Laodice**, his cousin, b. 260; dau of **Antiochus II Theos** (415-78), King of Syria, 261-146; b. 286; d. 246.

76. **Mithradates III** (418-77), King of Pontus, 220-190; b. c220/185; md **Loadice II**.

75. **Pharnaces I**, King of Pontus, 190-169; md **Nysa**, dau of **Laodice** (**III**), who md her brother **Artioches**. They were children of **Antiochus III Megas** (418-76), King of Syria, and **Laodice** (414-76;418-76).

74. **Mithradates V Eurugates**, King of Pontus, 151-120; assassinated; md **Laodice**, dau of **Antiochus IV Epiphanes**, King of Persia, 223-187; and **Laodice**.

73. **Mithradates VI Europator** '"the Great" (409-70,410-72), King of Pontus, 120-63 BC; annexed the kingdom of the Bosporus and became king c100 BC; d. by suicide; had many wives and concubines.

72. **Cleopatra** md **Tigranes II** "the Great," (409-70.410-72), King of Armenia, 95-55 BC.

Sources: Chamich, M. 1990; Garsoian, N. 1982; Grousset, R. 1984; Hansen, E. 1971; Luckenbill, D. 1926; Roux, G. 1966; Settipani, C. 1991, 121, 126, 127; Sherman, E. 1982; Stark, F. 1967, 4, 24, 36, 38, 45, 47, 103, 198, 288; Thomson, R. 1976; Webster, 1988, 1031.

## LINE 412

85. **Bagabigna**, liv 590/580 BC.

84. **Hydranes I** "Chief of the seven," 531 BC.

83. **Hydranes II**, liv. 480-428 BC; chiliarch of Persia.

82. **Orontes**.

81. **Artasyras**, setrap of Hyrcania, 425 BC.

80. **Orontes I** setrap of Armenia, 401-344; of Mysia, 362 BC; b. 420; d. c.362; md c401, **Rodegunde**, dau of **Artaxerxes II** (414-84), King of Parthia, and wife (2) **Stateira** (426-80), his half-sister.

79. **Orontes II**, setrap of Armenia, 344-331; King of Armenia, 331 BC; b. 400; d. 331; led the Armenian auxiliaries of Darius III in the battle of Gaugamelia, 1 Oct. 331 BC.

78. **Mithranes I**, Governor of Sardis, 334 BC; setrap of Armenia for Alexander the Great; King of Armenia, 331-317; b. 370.

77. **Orontes III**, King of Armenia, 317-260; b. 340; d. c260.

76. **Samos**, King of Armenia, 260 BC; d. 305.

75. **Arsames**, King of Armenia, 260-228.

74. **Orontes IV**, King of Armenia, 212-200; b. 235; d. 212/189.

73. **Ptolemy I**, setrap of Commagene; revolted and deposed the king of Commagene; d. 163-130.

72. **Samus**, King of Commagene, c130/96; md **Pythodoris**, prob a princess of Pont; b. 150 BC.

216

71. **Mithradates I Kallinikos**, King of Commagene, c100-c70; b. 120; d. . 63; md **Laodice Thea Philadelphos** (414-71).

70. **Artiochus I Theo Dikaios Ephipanes Philoraamos Philhellen**, King of Commagene, c69-31; md **Isias Philostorgos**, possibly his sister.

69. **N.N.** md **Artavasdes** (408-69), King of Media Atropatene and Lesser Armenia.

Sources: Bedrosian, R. 1985; Brossett, M. 1876; Bury, J. 1969; Chahin, M. 1987; Chamich, M. 1990; Grousset, R. 1984; Hovannisian, R. 1997; Stark, F. 1967, 15, 19, 25, 169, 228; Thomson, R. 1976; Toumanoff, C. 1966, 293, 294.

## LINE 413

93. **Karanos** (c. late 9th/early 8th century, BC) whose descendant was
92. **Koinos** (c mid-8th century, BC), whose descendant was
91. **Tyrimmas** (c late 8th/early 9th century, BC) whose descendant was
90. **Perdiccas**, King of Macedonia, c670-652 BC, whose son was
89. **Argaios I**, King of Macedonia, 652-621.
88. **Phillipos**, King of Macedonia, 621-588.
87. **Aeropos**, King of Macedonia.
86. **Alketas**, King of Macedonia.
85. **Amyntas I**, King of Macedonia, d. 498 BC; tributary vassal to the Persian sovereign, Darius Hystaspis.
84. **Alexander I**, King of Macedonia, c495-450; served with the Persian force under Xerxes.
83. **Amyntas**, Persian sovereign.
82. **Balakros.**
81. **Meleagros.**
80. **Lagos**, a Macedonian noble md **Antigona** (428-80).
79. **Ptolemy I Soter**, King (Pharaoh) of Egypt, 306-285 BC; md **Eurodike** (mother of Gen. 78). The father of Eurodike was **Antipatros**, regent of Macedonia, whose father was **Ioiaos**, prince of Macedonia.
78. **Ptolemy II Philadelpios**, King (Pharaoh) of Egypt, 285-247; deified 272/271; b. Island of Cos, 308 BC; md (2) his sister **Arsinoe II** Philadelphius; deified 271/272; she also md a half-bro, Ptolemy Ceraunus, who was disinherited. Ptolemy II enjoyed a relatively peaceful reigh; he encouraged commerce, gained meritime supremacy of the Mediterranean; built a canal from the Red Sea to the Nile; encouraged literature and the arts.
77. **Ptolemy III Euergates**, King (Pharaoh) of Egypt, 246-221; md **Bernice II**, dau of **Megas**, King of Cyrene (428-78), and **Apama**, dau of **Antiochus I Sotor** (415-79) of Syria. Fought war (246-245 BC) with Selucus II of Syria, and invaded the Seleucid domain; captured Babylon and Susa; recalled (243 BC) to Egypt to put down a revolt; next 20 years were peaceful; patron of the arts; added many books to the library at Alexandria.

217

76. **Ptolemy IV Philopator**, King (Pharaoh) of Egypt, 221-205; md **Arsinoe III**, his sister. He was a weak ruler, under the influence of court favorites; his army was defeated by Antiochus III of Syria (218 BC), but won a decisive victory over Antiochus at Rafah (212 BC).

75. **Ptolemy V. Epiphanes**, King (Pharaoh) of Egypt, 205-181; b. c210; md **Cleopatra I**, dau of **Antiochus III Megas** ( 414-76,418-76) King of Syria; d. 176 BC. During Ptolemy's reign, Palestine was seized by **Antiochus III** of Syria (418-76) and Egypt was threatened but saved by the intervention of Rome. His bethrothal to Cleopatra is inscribed on the *Rosetta Stone*. He was poisoned my a member of his court.

74. **Ptolemy VI Philometor**, King (Pharaoh) of Egypt (181-145 BC); md (1) **Cleopatra II**, his sister, liv c175/115. During his minority, the country was ruled by his mother. He was crowned in 173 BC; defeated and made prisoner by Antiochus IV (170 BC); restored by Rome as joint-ruler (170-164) with his brother Ptolemy VII; killed in battle.

73. **Cleopatra Theo** md **Demetrius II Nicator** (414-73), King of Syria, 146-125.

Sources: Aldred, C. 1984; Austin, M. 1970; Beckerath, J. 1971; Borza, E. 1990; Bowman, A. 1986; Callender, G. 1993; Casson, L. 1988; Charlton, N. 1974; Chavalas, M. 1993; Daumas, F. 1965; David, A. 1996; Dodson, A. 1995; Ermen, A. 1952; Garsoian, N. 1982; Grandet, P. 1993; Hammond, N. 1989; Hobson, C. 1987; MacDonald, F. 1993; O'Connor, D. 1995; Redford, D. 1986; Romer, J. 1984; Rosalie, D. 1988; Roux, G. 1966; Settipani, C. 1991, 107; Silverman, D. 1997; Stark, F. 1967, 228.

## LINE 414

93. **Archaemenes**, liv c700-675 BC.

92. **Teispes** (Chishpish), liv 675-640 BC.

91. **Ariyaramna**, liv 640-615 BC.

90. **Arshama**, liv c615-522 BC.

89. **Hystaspes** (Vishtaspa) setrap of Parthia and Hycania; b. 550 BC; d. after 521; md **Rhodogune** (414A-89),

88. **Darius I** "the Great," King of Persia, 521-486; Pharaoh of Egypt as Seteture'Antaryuash, 522-486; b. 558; d. 486; md (1) a dau of Gobryas; (2) **Atossa** (419-88) (mother of Gen. 87); (3) Artystone; (4) Parmys; (5) Phaiddyme, dau of Otames; (6) Phratagune; (7) Apame. He restored order to his troubled empire; reorganized administration; divided land into 20 setrapies; introduced reform in taxation; built roads; established a postal system; had liberal policy toward the Jews; annexed a province of India; began the great struggle with Greece; his deeds are recorded on numerous inscriptions.

87. **Xerxes I**, Great King of Persia, 486-465; b. 521 BC; d. 465; was at battles of Thermopylae and Salamis , 480 BC; and Plataea and Mykale, 479 BC; md **Amestris** (429-87). Suppressed a revolt in Egypt (485-484); carried on Darius I's task of punishing the Greeks; bridged the Hellispont;

marched through Thrace, Macedonia and Thessaly; his army checked Leonidas at Thermopylae whence he won the victory (480 BC); burned Athens; fleet defeated at Salamis (480 BC); his army beaten by the Greeks (479 BC), and his fleet at the same time; murdered by a captain of the guard.

86. **Artaxerxes I**, Great King of Partha, 465-425; King (Pharaoh) of Egypt, 465-425/423; b. 500 BC; d. 425/423; (md) (3) **Kosmartydene**, a concubine (mother of Gen. 85); also md (1) Damaspia; (md) (2) Ologune, a concubine and (md) (4) Andria, a concubine. Put down a rebellion in Bactria and a more serious one in Egypt (460-454 BC); kept Persia neutral during the Samian and Peloponnesian wars; sanctioned practice of the Jewish religion in Jerusalem (458 BC); appointed Nehemiah Governor of Judea (445 BC).

85. **Darius II** (410-83), Great King of Persia, 424-404; King (Pharaoh) of Egypt as Mery.Amen.Re', 424-404; b. 475; d. 404; md **Parysatis**, his half-sister, who dominated him. He was a weak sovereign and his reign was marked by revolts in Asia Minor and Egypt.

84. **Artaxerxes II**, King of Persia, 404-359; d. 359/358; md (1) Stratera; (2) Amestris; (3) Atossa; (4) Aspasia, one of whom (or someone else) was mother of Gen. 83. Near the beginning of his reign, faced a revolt by his brother, Cyrus, whom he defeated and killed at Cunoxa (401 BC); reign marked by many rebellions; his expedtions against Egypt (385-383; 375-374) were failures; effected changes in the Persian religion, restoring worship of the early gods.

83. **Apame** md **Pharnabazus**, setrap of Daskyleion on the Hellispont, 414-387 BC.

82. **Artabazus II**, setrap of western Asia and Bithynia under Artaxerxes III, and Baktria under Alexander the Great; retired 328 BC; d. 325.

81. **N.N.** md **Spitamenes**, setrap of Baktria, 329-328; b. 365; d. 328.

80. **Apama of Baktria** md, at Susa, 324 BC, **Seleucus I Nicator** (415-80), setrap of Babylon, 321 BC; son of **Antiochus** (who md **Laodice**); grandson of **Seleucius.**

79. **Achaeus** ((415-78), prince of Syria, md. **N.N.,** perhaps dau of **Alexander the Great**, King of Macedonia, 336-323.

78. **Andromachus**, a general, liv 245-224 BC.

77. **Laodice II** md **Seleucus II Callinius** (415-77), King of Syria, 246-226; b. 265; d. 226 BC.

76. **Antiochus III Megas** "the Great," King of Syria, 223-187; b. 242; murdered 187 BC; md **Laodice III** (418-76),"Queen and sister," dau of **Mithradates II** (411-77), King of Pontus, and wife (1) **Laodice** (mother of Gen. 75); md (2) Eubeoa of Chalsis. He suppressed revolts in Media and Persia (220 BC); recovered Armenia; made successful invasion of Parthia, Media and Bactria (210-205 BC); defeated by Romans at battle of Magnesia (189 BC).

75. **Seleucus IV Philopator,** King of Syria, 187-175; b. 220 BC; d. 175;

md **Laodice IV**, perhaps dau of **Philip V,** King of Macedonia, 220-187 BC. He was left helpless by the defeat of his father; assassinated and the throne seized by his brother Ariochus IV.

74. **Demetrius I Soter** "the Preserver," King of Syria, 162-150; b. 186; d. 150; lived as a hostage in Rome (c187-163); escaped and overthrew his cousin Artiochus V (162 BC); delivered Babylonia from tyranny (c160 BC); fought with the Maccabbes; fell in battle against Alexander Balas.

73. **Demetrius II Nicator**, King of Syria, 145-139; and 129-125; b. 165 BC; d. c125 BC; md (1) **Cleopatra Theo** (413-73) (mother of Gen. 72); md (2) Rhodogunde, dau of Mithradates I of Parthia. Aided by Ptolemy VI, he secured the throne,defeating and killing Alexander Bales (145 BC), whereupon he md the widow, Cleopatra Theo; in an expedition against Parthians, defeated and held prisoner; regained the throne and was killed in the civil war that followed.

72. **Antiochus VIII Philometer,** "Grypus" (hook-nose), King of Syria; joint ruler with his mother (124-121 BC); sole ruler (121-115 BC); divided realm with his brother, Antiochus IX (115-96 BC); b. 143; assassinated, 96 BC; md **Cleopatra Tryphaena** (mother of Gen. 71), dau of **Eurogates II,** King (Pharaoh) of Egypt, and wife **Cleopatra III**; md (2) Cleopatra V (Selene).

71. **Laodice Theo Philadelphos** md **Mithradates I Kallinikos** (412-71), King of Commagene, c. 100-c70 BC; b. 120 BC; d. 63BC.

Sources: Abu Bakr, A.; Aldred, C. 1984; Austin, M. 1970; Beckerath, J. 1971; Bennett, C. 1995;Boardman, J. 1988; Bowman, A. 1986; Bury, J. 1969; Casson, L. 1988; Charlton, N. 1974; Curtis, J. 1990; Daumas, F. 1965; Dodson, A. 1995; Editors, 1992; Ermen, A. 1952; Hammond, N. 1989; Hobson, C. 1987; Hunt, C. 1972; Redford, D. 1986; Rogers, R. 1983; Romer, J. 1984; Rosalie, D. 1988; Settipani, C. 1991, 107, 139; Stark, F. 1967, 11, 14-26, 46, 94-96; 103, 109-110, 117, 119, 211; Waterman, L. 1936.

## LINE 414A

101. **Marduk-zera-uballit.**

100. **Marduk-shakin-shumi.**

99. **Eriba-marduk,** King of Babylon, c775-c765.

98. **N.N.** md **N.N.**, dau of **Nabu-shum-ishkun,** King of Babylon, c765-748 BC.

97. **N.N.** (male).

96. **N.N.** (male), d. 703.

95. **N.N.** (male) md **N.N.** (fem.).

94. **Nebuchadnezzar,** King of Babylon.

93. **Bel-ibni,** Governor of Sealand, c650-c626, and a general of Assyrian forces.

92. **Nabopolassar** (Nabu-apla-usur), King of Babylon, 626-605; md **Shamish-iddina**, his sister, liv in 653 BC.

91. **N.N.** (fem.) md **N.N.** (male).

90. **Ugbaru,** Governor of Gutiom, a province of Persia, c600-539 BC.

89. **Rodogune** md **Hystaspes** (414-89), setrap of Parthia and Hycania.

Sources: Bennett, C. 1995; Olmstead, A. 1923; Wagner, A. 1975, 50-77; 1262-203.

## LINE 415

80. **Seleucus I Nicator,** King of Syria, 306-381 BC.; a general in Alexander the Great's army; md **Apame of Bakria** (414-80).

79. **Antiochus I Soter** "the Preserver," King of Syria, 281-261; b. 324; killed in battle, 261 BC; md **Stratonice I** (427-79), a step-mother; won great victory overthe Gauls in Asia Minor, 275 BC.

78. **Antiochus II Theos** (411-78,418-78), King of Syria, 261-247; b. 286 BC; d. 247 at Ephasus; md (1) **Laodice I** (mother of Gen. 77 and dau of **Achaeus** (414-79), prince of Syria; md (2) Bernice, dau of Ptlolemy II; lost Bactria (c250 BC) to Diodatus, and Parthia to the Arcasids.

77. **Seleucus II Callinicus,** King of Syria, 246-226; b. 265 BC; d. 226; md **Laodice II** (414-77) Raised to the throne by his mother; at war (246-245) with Ptolemy III Euergates of Egypt; defeated in war (241-236) with his brother Antiochus Hierax to whom he was forced to give Asia Minor; lost Parthia to the Arcasid dynasty.

Sources: Cambridge, 1989, 517 (genealogy chart), 520; Chavalas, M. 1993; Garsoian, N. 1982; Guerney, G. 1982; Luckenbill, D. 1926; Roux, G. 1966; Stark, F. 1967, 103; Webster, 1988.

## LINE 416

70. **N.N.,** prob dau of **Tigranus II** (410-72), King of Armenia, and wife **Cleopatra** (411-72); md **Pharnabazus II** (409-70), King of Iberia; d. in battle 30 BC.

69. **N.N.** md **K'art'am,** Prince of Kaudjide; d. 33 BC; adopted by **Pharnabazus II** (see 416-70 above).

68. **Pharasmenes I,** King of Iberia, 1-58 AD; md **N.N.,** a dau of **Mithradates I,** his brother, King of Armenia, 24-37 AD and 41-51 AD, who md a dau of Pharasmrenes I, his brother. The brothers swapped daughters as wives!

67. **Mithradates I,** King of Iberia, 58-107.

66. **Amazaspus I,** King of Iberia, 106-115.

65. **Pharasmenes II,** King of Iberia, 116-132; md Ghadama.

64. **Rhadamiste I,** King of Iberia, 132-135.

63. **Pharasmenes III,** King of Iberia, 135-185.

62. Princess **N.N.** md **Vologaesus V** (408-62) "the Great," Great King of Parthia, 190-207 AD; King of Armenia; b. 130 AD; d. 207.

61. **Khosrow** (Chosroes) **II** "the Brave," King of Armenia, 191-206; b. 165; d. 216/217 AD.

60. **Tiridates II,** King of Armenia, 217-238; b. 194; d. c253.

221

59. **Khosrow** (Chosroes) **II** "the Valiant," King of Western Armenia, 280-287; b. c236; d. 287.

58. **Tiridates IV** "the Great," first Christian king of Armenia, 298-330; b. c280; assassinated 330; educated in the Roman Empire; md **Ashken**, dau of **Ashkhadar**, King of Alania.

57. **Khosrow** (Chosroes) **(III)**, called "Kotak," King of Armenia, 330-339; b. 280; d. 338.

56. **Bambishu** (fem.), b. 315 AD; md **Athenagenes**, son of **Yusik I**, primate of Armenia, and **N.N.**, dau of **Tiridates III**, King of Armenia, who was son of **Tiridates II** (416-60), King of Armenia.

55. **Narcses** (Nersch) **I** "the Great," primate of Armenia, prince of the Gregorid domain, 355-359 and 367-373; b. 335; d. 373; md **Samdukht**, dau of **Vardan I**, prince of the Mamikonids.

54. **Sahak I** "the Great," primate of Armenia, prince of the Gregorid domain, 387-428; b. 352; d. 439.

53. **Sahakanoysh** (Sourenpahlav) (322-53), the Gregorian heiress, md **Hamazasp** (322-53), prince of the Mamikonids, 387-c416/432; High Constible of Armenia; b. 345; d. 416/432.

Sources: Bedrosian, R. 1985; Brosset, M. 1876;Castro, M. 1995; Chahin, M. 1987; Chamick, M. 1990; Dunster, M. 1979; Grosset, R. 1984; Hovannisian, R. 1997; Mamikonian, J. 1869; Mk III, 55:163; Settipani, C. 1991, 38, 39, 58, 66, 191; Stark, F. 1967, 259, 262; Taggie, B. 1989; Theroff, P. 1994; Thompson, R. 1976; Toumanoff, C. 1963.

## LINE 417

76. **Tiridates**, prince of Parthia, 247-210 BC; b. 285; established independence of Parthia; defeated Seeucus Callinus of Syria.

75. **N.N.**, prince of Parthia.

74. **Phriapatius**, King of Parthia, c191-176; b. 215; d. 176 BC.

73. **Artabanus I**, King of Parthia, 127-124; b. 185; d. 124 BC.

72. **Sinatruces**, King of Parthia, 77-70; b. 157; d. 70 BC.

71. **Phraates III** (408-70), King of Parthia, 70-57BC; b. 120; d. 57; restored order to his kingdom; desired salliance with Rome; md his sister **Piritana**.

70. **Orodes I**, Great King of Parthia, 57-39 BC; b. 80; d. 39; md **N.N.**, dau of **Antiochus I**, King of Commagene, 70-36; b. 100; d. 36 BC.

69. **Phraates IV**, Great King of Parthia, 39-32; defeated Antony (36 BC), but lost Armenia (34 BC); lost influence as Roman power increased; murdered.

68. **N.N.**, princess of Parthia, b. 30 BC; md **Darius** (408-68), prince of Media Athropatene.

Sources: Debevoise, N. 1970; Dunster, M. 1979; Settipani, C. 1991; Webster, 1988, 1181, 1473.

**LINE 418**

78. **Antiochus II Theos** (415-78), King of Syria, md **Laodice I** (mother of Gen. 77).

77. **Laodice II** md **Mithradates III** (411-76), King of Pontus,220-190 BC.

76. **Laodice III** "queen and sister" md **Antiochus III Megas** (414-76), King of Syria.

Sources: Cambridge, 328; Chavalas, M. 1993; Frye, R. 1984, 209f, 360; Garsoian, N. 1982; Luckinbill, D. 1926; Roux, G. 1966; Sellwood, D. 1980; Settipani, C. 1991; Webster, 1988, 52.

**LINE 419**

91. **Cyrus I** (Kurush II). (420-88), "the Great," Great King of Persia, 550-530; King of Anshan from 559 BC; conquered Babylonia and freed the Jews; respectied the customs, institutions and religion of those he defeated; d. 530; md prob **Kassandane.**

90. **Cambyses I** (Kambujiya), King of Ashan (Persia), liv c600-559 BC; md **Mandane**, dau of **Astyages**, King of Media.

89. **Cyrus II**, the Great," King of Persia; conquered Babylon, 539 BC; b. 570 BC; d. 540 BC; King of the World, Great King, Legimitate King, King of the Four Rims of the World; King of Babylon, Summar and Akkid; md (4) 546/545 BC, **Neithiyti** (420-88); b. c570, (mother of Gen. 88). His other wives, about which something is known, are (1) Kassadane, dau of Pharnaspes, (2) Amytis, (3) N.N.

88. **Atossa** (Hutautha, Hattuosa), b. c545 BC; md (his 2nd, her 3rd) **Darius I** "the Great," (429-88), King of Persia. She also md Cambysses II and (2) Gaumat.

Sources: Bury, J. 1969; Roux, G. 1966; Settipani, C. 1991, 144.

**LINE 420**

103. **Maat,'ka.re** (fem.) md **Osorkon (I)** (Sekhem.Kheper.re', Setep en re' (422-105), Pharaoh, fl 924-889 BC.

102. **Takelot I** (User.ma'(at).re', Takeloti, Takeloth), Pharaoh, 889-874 BC; b. 935; d. 873; md **Kapes.**

101. **Osorkon II** (User.ma(at).re, Setep.en.amun) (421-102); Pharaoh , 874-850; b. 905/900; md **Istemkheb** (mother of Gen. 100); b. 905/900; md also Karamama. Under Osorkin II, because of family feuds, Egypt declined.

100. **Takelot II** (Hejd.kheper.re'Setep.en.re') Pharaoh, 850-825; b. 875; d. 825; md **Karoma**, b. 865; dau of **Nimlot,** Grand Priest of Amon at Thebes, whose father was **Osorkon II** (421-101).

99. **Sheshonq III** (User.ma(at).re'Setep.en.amun), Pharaoh, 825-773; at Tanis; b. 860/855 BC; d. 773; md **Djed.bast.es.ankh** ( 421-99).

98. **Pimay** (User.ma(at).re'Setep.en.amun, prince of Sais, Pharaoh, 773-

767.

97. **Osorkon**, Great Chief of Ma, Prince of Sais (c.773-740?); prophet of the Neith ( at Sais) , of Edjo (at Buto), and held other offices.

96. **Tefnakhte (I)** (Shepses.re'), Great Chief of Ma; prince of Sais, 740-727; Prophet of Neith; commander; Pharaoh, 727-716.

95. **Bakenranef** (Bocchoris, Wah.ke.re'); Pharaoh, c720/719 for about eight years; in Sais and Memphis; killed by Shabaka of the XXV dynasty.

94. **Irib.re'Nakau.ba**, prince of Sais, 688-c672 BC.

93. **Necho (I)** (Mren.kheper.re'), prince of Sais and Memphis, 688-664 BC. He was "king of Sais and Memphis" as Assyrian vassal, c671 and c667/666; b. 710; d. 664; md **Istemabat.**

92. **Psammetichus (I)** (Wahib.re'Psamtek (I), Pharaoh, 656-610 BC; b. 685; d. 610; vassal.of Assyria; expelled the Assyrians, reunited the country and established the capitol at Sais; md **Mehetenweskhet**, dau of **Harsiese**, Grand Priest of Heliopolis. Psammetichus also md Shepenapt.

91. **Necho (II)** (Wehen.ib.re'), Pharaoh, 610-595; b. 660BC; d. 595; md **Chedebnitjerbone I** (fem.); defeated Josiah, King of Judea, at Megiddo (cf. 2 Kings 23:29-30 and 2 Chron. 35:20-24), in the battle of Carchemish, 605 BC; defeated by Nebuchadressar, however, in 601 BC defeated Nebuchadressar, on the Egyptian border; began construction of the Red Sea canal; his fleet successfully circumnavigated Africa after a three-year voyage.

90. **Psammetichus (II)** (Nefer.ib.re'Psamtek (II), Pharaoh, 595-585; md **Tak.huat**, princess of Athribis, b. 625 BC; d. c589 BC.

89. **Apries**, Pharaoh, 589-570 BC; defeated the Phoenicians in a great sea battle; went to rescue Jerusalem, c588 BC (cf. Jeremiah 44:30); b. 605; d. 568 BC.

88. **Neithiyti** (fem.) md **Cyrus** "the Great" (419-89), King of Persia.

Sources: Abu Bakr, A.; Aldred, C. 1984; Bowman, A. 1986; Buttery, A. 1971; Caminos, R. 1958; Casson, L. 1988; Charlton, N. 1974; Daumas, F. 1965; Dodson, A. 1995; Ermen, A. 1952; Grimal, N. 1992, charts 340, 393 and 394; Hobson, C. 1987; Kelley, D. 1995; Mac Donald, F. 1993; Redford, D. 1986; Romer, J. 1984; Rosalie, D. 1988; Roux, G. 1966; Silverman, D. 1997.

## LINE 421

101. **Osorkon (II)** (User.ma(at).re'Setep.en.amun) (420-101), Pharaoh, 873-850; b. 905; d. 850 BC; md **Karomama** , dau of **Harsiese**, High Priest of Amun at Thebes, 874 BC; son of **Sheshonq II**, High Priest of Amun at Thebes, 924-895; son of **Osorkon I** (422-105).

100. **Sheshonq**, High Priest of Ptah at Memphis, c870-851; Great Chief of Ma; b. 885 BC; d. c851.

99 **Djed.bast.es.ankh** (420-99) md **Shosenq III** (User. ma.(at).re' Setep.en.re'Amun) (420-99), Pharaoh, 825-773 BC, at Tanis.

Sources: Abu Bakr, A.; Aldred, C. 1984; Buttery, A. 1971; Caminos, R.

1958; Casson, L. 1988; Charlton, N. 1974; Daumas, F. 1965; Ermen, A. 1952; Grimal, N. 1992; Hobson, C. 1984; Redford, D. 1986; Romer, J. 1984; Rosalie, D. 1988; Settipani, C. 1991, 166.

## LINE 422

112. **Buyuwawa**, liv c1080 BC

111. **Mawasen** (Mawasta)

110. **Nabnasi** (Nabnechi)

109. **Paihut** (Paihuti), Grand Chief of Ma, 1055 BC.

108. **Sheshonq (I)**, Chief of Ma (Mashwash Libyans); liv 1030 BC; md **Mehtenouskhet** "the Royal Mother," b. 1025 BC.

107. **Nimlot**, Great Chief of Ma (Mashwash Libyans); Chief of Chiefs; b. 1005 BC; md **Tentsepeh** (his sister); b. 1005/1000 BC.

106. **Sheshonq (II)**, Chief of Ma (Mashwash Lybians) at Bubasti; Pharaoh, 945-925; b. 980 BC; d. 924 BC; md **Karomet**.

105. **Osorkon (I)** (Sekhem.kheper.re'Setep.en.re') (420-103), Pharaoh, 924-889 BC; md **Maat,'ka.re'** (423-105).

Sources: Abu Bakr, A; Aldred, C. 1984; Buttery, A. 1971; Caminos, R. 1958; Casson, L. 1988; Charlton, N. 1974; Daumas, F. 1965; Dodson, A. 1995; Ermen, A. 1952; Grimal, N. 1992; Hobson, C. 1984; Redford, D. 1986; Romer, J. 1984; Rosalie, D. 1988; Settipani, C. 1991, 166.

## LINE 423

110. **Pinudjem I**, Great Priest of Amun, 1070-1055 BC; Pharaoh, 1054-1032; md **Hent.tawy** (425-110), royal daughter and worshiper of Hethor; dau of **Rameses XI**, Pharaoh, 1098-1070.

109. **Psusennes I** (A'kheper.re'Setep.en.amun.Psib.kha'emme (I) (Ra.messe Psusennes), Pharaoh at Tanis, 1039-993 BC; md **Wiay**.

108. **Istemkbeb** (fem.) md **Men.kheper.re'** (424-107), High Priest of Amun at Thebes, 1045-992 BC.

107. **Pinudjem II**, High Priest of Amun at Thebes, 990-969; md **Istemkheb**, first chief of the Harim of Amun; viceroy at Nubia; dau of **Smendis II** (Nesu.ba.nebhjed), High Priest of Amun and wife **Tabent-Thuty**.

106. **Psusennes II** (Tit.kheper.re'Setep.en.re'Amun Har-PsibKha'emne), High Priest of Amun, Pharaoh, 959-945 BC.

105. **Maat.ka.re'** (fem.) (420-103), b. 955 BC; md **Osorkon I** (Sekhem. kheper.re' Setep.en.re') (422-105), Pharaoh, 924-889.

Sources: Abu Bakr, A.; Aldred, C. 1984; Arkill, A. 1975; Buttery, A. 1971; Casson, L. 1988; Charlton, N. 1974; Daumas, F. 1965; Dodson, A. 1995; Grimal, N. 1992, chart 393; Dodson, A. 1987; Ermen, A. 1952; Hobson, C. 1987; Redford, D. 1986; Romer, J. 1984; Rosalie, D. 1988; Settipani, C. 1991, 166.

**LINE 424**

110. **Hrihor** (Herihor) High Priest of Amun; a greatmilitary commander; md **Nodjmet**, dau of **Hrere** (fem.)

109. **Piankh** (Painkh), Great Priest of Amun at Thebes; a great commander of the army of Upper and Lower Egypt.

108. **Pinudjem (I)**, High Priest of Amun at Thebes, 1069-945; commander of the army of Upper and Lower Egypt; Pharaoh as Kheper.khare'Setep.en.amun; md **Hent.tawy**; dau of **Smendis**, Pharaoh, 1069-1043, and (1) **Tent.amun**, dau of a judge named **Nebseny**.

107. **Men.kheper.re'**, High Priest of Amun at Thebes, 1045-992 (432-108) md **Istemkbeb** (423-108).

Sources: Abu Bakr, A.; Aldred, C. 1984; Arkill, A. 1975; Buttery, A. 1971; Casson, L. 1988; Charlton, N. 1974; Daumas, F. 1965; Editors, 1992; Ermen, A. 1952; Grimal, N. 1992, chart 393; Hobson, C. 1987; Redford, D. 1986; Romer, J. 1984; Rosalie, D. 1988; Settipani, C. 1991, 168.

**LINE 425**

120. **Sety**, a commandant of troops.

119. **Rameses I**, (Men.kheper.re'Ramesse (I)), commondant of troops; visar; superintendant of horse; king's charioteer; general; primate of all Egypt; Pharaoh, 1295-1294; b. c1350 BC; md **Sit.re'** (Sat.re'); dau of **N.N.** and granddau of **Neb.ma(at)re'Amenhotep III**, Pharaoh, 1386-1349, and wife **Tiy-nefertari**.

118. **Seti** (I) (Men.ma(at).re'Sety (I) mer.en.ptah), chief of archers, High Priest of Set, Pharaoh, 1294-1279 BC; b. c1327; md **Tuya**, heiress of the XVIIIth dynasty, whose parents were **Reya**, lieutenant of chariotry, and wife **Touy** (Tuya).

117. **Rameses II** (Usir.ma(at).re'Setep.en.re'Ramesse (II)) "the Great Pharaoh," 1279-1213 or 1290-1224; b. 1314 BC; d. 1224 BC. In the early years of his reign, engaged in important campaign against the Hittites; arranged treaty of peace (1272 BC); md **N.N.**, dau of the Hittite king; remainder of his reigh peaceful; added to the temples of Karnak and Luxor; built the rock-cut temple at Abu-Simbel. Most Egyptologists hold this pharaoh to be the pharaoh of the Hebrew oppression (see Genesis and Exedus in the O.T.).

116. **Merneptah** (Usir.kha,'ure.Setep.en.Mery.amun., Pharaoh, 1186-1184 BC; md **Tiye.mer.en.esse**. Settipani, C. 1991, p. 175, gives a possible lineage for Tiyi.(See line 425A, below).

115. **Rameses III** (Usir.ma(at)'ure Mery.amun Ra.messe (III) "the Grezat," Pharaoh, 1186-1154 BC; md **N.N**, a princess of the XIX dynasty (wife "A" below); and **Isista.Hamadjilat** (wife "B" below). Engaged in war with Libya and Syria; later in his reign, built many important buildings and temples.

114A. **Rameses VIII** (Set.hir.khopshef (II) Usir.ma(at).re'Akh.en.amun

226

R.amesse (VIII), Pharaoh, 1140-1138 BC. His mother was Gen. 115, **wife "A."** He or his brother (Gen. 114B) was father of Gen. 113.

114B. **Rameses VII** (Amen.hir.hkopshef II Neb.ma(at)re' Mery amun Ra.messe (VI), Pharaoh, 1143-1140 BC, who md **Nub.khes.bed.** His mother was Gen. 115, wife "B." He or his brother was father of Gen. 113.

113. **Rameses IX** (Khaem.waset.Nefer.ka.re' Setep.en.re' Ramesse (IX)) Pharaoh, 111138-1108 BC; son of either Gen. 114A or Gen. 114 B. above, and grandson of Gen. 115.

112. **Rameses X** (Amen.hir.khops Kheper.ma(ai)re' Setep.en.re' Ra.messe X)), Pharaoh, 1108-1098 BC.

111. **Rameses XI** (Khaem.wasetmen.ma(ai).re' Setep.en. ptah Ra.messe XI) Pharaoh, 1098-1070 BC.

110. **Hent.tawy** (fem.) md **Pinudjem** (423-110), Great Priest of Amun.

Sources: Abd el Rejik, M. 1974; Arkill, A. 1975; Blankenberg, C. 1982; Christophe, L. 1953; Clayton, P. 1994;David, A. 1996; Daumas, F. 1965; Desroches, C. 1979; Desroches, C. 1985; Dodson, A. 1995; Ermen, A. 1952; Fevre, F. 1992; Grandet, P. 1993; Grimal, N. 1952, chart 393; Hobson, C. 1987; Kitchen, K. 1982; Kitchen, K. 1986;Mac Donald, F . 1993; Parker, R. 1987; Reynolds, M. 1992; Robbins, G. 1987; Seele, K. 1940; Silverman, D. 1997; Spalinger, A. 1979a; Spalinger, A. 1979b; Spalinger, A. 1979c; Stradelmann, R. 1981; Thomas, E. 1959.

## LINE 425A

The probable incestuous lineage of Tiye (425-116), wife of the pharaoh Sethnakht (425-116).

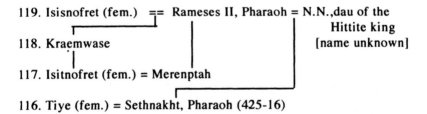

119. Isisnofret (fem.)  ==  Rameses II, Pharaoh = N.N.,dau of the
                                                   Hittite king
118. Kraemwase                         [name unknown]
117. Isitnofret (fem.) = Merenptah
116. Tiye (fem.) = Sethnakht, Pharaoh (425-16)

Source: Modified chart, Settipani, C. 1991, p. 175.

## LINE 426

84. **Megabignes.**

83. **Hydranes I,** liv 555 BC; d. after 522 BC.

82. **Hydranes II,** Governor of Sardis, 494 BC; b. c440 BC; d. c400.

81. **Hydranes III,** Setrap of Armenia.

80. **Strateira** md her half-brother **Artaxerxes II** (412-80, 414-84), King of Parthia.

Sources: Abu Bakr, A.; Aldred, C. 1984; Austin, M. 1970; Beckerath, J. 1971; Bury, J. 1969; Casson, L. 1988; Charlton, N. 1974; Daumas, F. 1965;

Editors, 1992; Ermen, A. 1952; Hobson, C. 1987; Redford, D. 1986; Romer, J. 1984; Rosalie, D. 1988; Settipani, C. 1991, 107, 139; Stark, F.

## LINE 427

82. **Philippus.**
81. **Antigonus I**, King of Macedonia, 306-301 BC; b. 382; defeated and killed at Ipsus in Phrygia (301 BC); md **Stratonice**, dau of **Korrhagos**, King of Thrace.
80. **Demetrius I** (Poliorcertes), King of Macedonia, 307-283; md **Phila I**, dau of **Antipator**.
79. **Stratonice** md (1) Selucue I; md (2) **Antiochus I Sater** (415-79), King of Syria.
Sources: Abranowski, L. 1927; Borza, E. 1990; Bradford, A. 1992; Cambridge, 1989, 319 (genealogy chart); Chavalas, M. 1993; Errington, R, 1990; Garsoian, N. 1982; Hammond, N. 1978; Hammond, N. 1981; Hammond, N. 1988; Roux, G. 1966, 382; Settipani, C. 1991, 106.

## LINE 428

81. **Kassandros.**
80. **Antigona** md **Lagos** (same as 413-80)
79. **Bernice** (mother of Gen. 78) sister of **Ptolemy I Soter** (413-79), King (Pharaoh) of Egypt, 306-283.
78. **Megas**, King of Cyrene (413-77).
77. **Bernice II** md **Ptolemy III Euergates** (413-77), King (Pharaoh) of Egypt, 247-222 BC.
Sources: Abu Bakr, A.; Aldred, C. 1984; Beckerath, J. 1971; Casson, L. 1988; Charlton, N. 1974; Dodson, A. 1995; Editors, 1992; Eren, A. 1952; Hobson, C. 1987; Mac Donald, F. 1993; Redford, D. 1986; Romer, J. 1984; Rosalie, D. 1988.

## LINE 429

90. **Pharnaspes** (Sakhres), a prince, b. 605 BC.
89. **Otones**, b. 575 BC; d. after 499; md **N.N.**, dau of **Hystaspes**, setrap of Parthia, a bro of **Darius I** (414-88). Pharaoh, King of Persia.
88. **Otones**, Chief of Persia, 480 BC.
87. **Amestris**, b. 505 BC; d. c425 BC; md **Xerxes I** (414-87), Great King of Persia.
Sources: Abu Bakr, A.; Aldred, C. 1984; Beckerath, J. !984; Bierbier, M. 1975; Buty, J. 1974; Buttery, A. 1974; Charlton, N. 1974; Kitchen, K. 1986; Romer. J. 1984; Rosalie, D. 1988; Roux, G. 1966, chart 7; Settipani, C. 1991, 114.

## LINE 430

78. **Qahtan**, liv c827 BC.

77. **Ya'rab**, b. 794 BC; founded the kingdom of Yemen.

76. **Yashub**, b. 761 BC.

75. **Abd Shams Saba** "the Great" of al-Hira, b. 728 BC.

74. **Kahlan** of Al-Hira.

73. **Zayd** of al-Hira (same as 433-72).

72. **Yashjub**, bro of **Malik** of Al-Hira (433-71).

71. **Arib**.

70. **Amr**.

69. **Humaysa**.

68. **Zayd**.

67. **Udad**.

66. **Murra**.

65. **Harith**.

64. **Adiyy**.

63. **Lakhm al- Lakhmi**.

62. **Numera**.

61. **Anamu**.

60. **Malik**.

59. **Masud**.

58. **Harith**.

57. **Amr**.

56. **Rabi'a al-Lakhmi**, King of Yemen, b. 195 AD; He migrated to Iraq.

55. **Adi** of al-Hira md **Raquash** of al-Hira (433-54).

54. **Amr al-Lakhmi**, first King of Hira.

53. **Imru'ul-Qays I**, King of Hira, d. 7 Dec 328 (as incribed on his tomb, as translated from the Arabic); bur at al-Namara, Syria. His tomb has one of the oldest Nabatean inscriptions.

52. **Amr**, King of Hira.

51. **Nu'man I**, King of Hira, d. 418.

50. **Imru'ul-Qays II**, King of Hira.

49. **Nu'man II**, King of Hira, d. 502 of battle wounds received at Circesium.

48. **Imru'ul-Qays III**, King of Hira, md **Mariyah ma as-Sama**, a famous beauty, whom he carried off during a raid into Arabia.

47. **Mundhir III**, King of Hira, b. c505; killed in battle at Qinnasrin, 554; md **N.N.**, the dau of a goldsmith. She was active in religious circles having founded a Christiam monastery. He was the most powerful king of Hira up to that time and his reign was long and prosperous.

46. **Mundhir IV**, King of Hira, d. 580; md **Salma bint al-Sa'igh**, dau of **al-Sa'igh**.

45. **Nu'man III abu-Qabus**, King of Hira, d. 602, a prisoner of the Persians.

44. **Qabus** of al-Hira.

43. **Abu 'abed** of al-Hira.

42. **Abu Farisi** of al-Hira md **Zohra** (432-41).

229

41. **Na'im** of al-Lakhmi, b.in Arabia.

40. **Itaf ibn Na'im**, b.in Arabia.

39. **'Amr ibn Itaf**, b. 834; res of Seville, Seville, Spain.

38. **Aslan ibn 'Amr**, res of Seville, Seville, Spain.

37. **Abbad ibn Aslan**, b. 894; res of Seville, Seville, Spain.

36. **Qara'is ibn Abbad**, b. 924; res of Seville, Seville, Spain.

35. **Isma'il ibn Qara'is**, Iman of Seville, b. 954; res of Seville, Seville, Spain. He was a Muslim jurist.

34. **Muhammad I** Kadi abu'l-Kasim ibn Isma'il, King of Seville, b. 984; d. c1042, Seville. He was a prosperous landowner and local judge.

33. **Muhammad II** al-Mu'tadid abu ' Amr' Abbad, King of Seville, Jan. 1042-May 1069; b. 1014; d. 1082; res of Seville, Seville, Spain; md **N.N. of Balearic Isles** (431-32). Seville reached its highest power at this time.

32. **Muhammad III** al-Mu'tamid abu'l-Qasim, King of Seville, 1069-1091; b. 1040; d. 1095, Aghmat, Morocco. He conquered Murcia in 1078.

31. **Zaida** (Maria, Isabel, Ximena), Princess of Seville; b. c1071; d. 12Sept 1107, Spain; res of Dania, Alcante, Spain; md 1096 (his 4th), **Alfonso VI** (248-31), King of Castile and Leon. *NOTE: Some sources say Zaida was not married to Alfonso VI but the inscription on her tomb in the Chapel Royal of San Isidio of Leon clearly states that she was Alfonso's wife (Source:* Chronico General, *XI:314;* Marina, *Book IX, Ch XX).*

30. **Teresa** of Castile and Leon, who inherited the countship of Portugal; d. 1 Nov 1130; bur at Braga Cathedral; md **Henry I of Burgundy** (85-29).

Sources: Barber, F. 1977, 119; Caskell, W. 1966, 206; Ceram, C. 1973; Enc. Islam I, 1987, vols. 6 and 7; Enc. Islam 2, 1996, vols. 1,5,6,7; Fletcher, R. 1989, 100-121; Fletcher, R. 1992; Gayangos, P. 1843, 2:lxxxvi; Guerney, O. 1991; Hitti, P. 1970, 70-85; Hogarth, D. 1926; Marby, J. 1989, 112; Tilisam, A. 1843; Wusterfeld, F. 1852, 349; Whitshaw, B. 1912.

## LINE 431

34. **Yasub**, b. 959, AD; res of Dania, Alicante, Spain.

33. **Mujahid** of Dania and Balearic Isles, b. 989, d. 1044, Dania; res of Dania, Alcante, Spain.

32. **N.N.** of Balearic Isles, b. 1019; res of Balearic Isles, Spain; md **Muhammad II** (430-33), King of Saville.

Sources: Barber, F. 1977; Caskell, W. 1966; Fletcher, R. 1989; Hitti, P. 1970; Marby, J. 1989; Westerfeld, F. 1852; Whitshaw, B. 1912.

## LINE 432

69. **Nahur**.

68. **Mugawwam**.

67. **Udad**.

66. **Adnam**. *NOTE: According to the prophet Muhammad, "Beyond*

230

*Adnam, none but the Lord knows, and the genealogists lie."*
   65. **Ma'add.**
   64. **Nizar.**
   63. **Mudar** md **al-Riyab** (fem.)
   62. **Ilyas** md **Layla bani Khindif**, the Codhaite.
   61. **Amr Mudrika** md **Salma.**
   60. **Khuzayma**, b. c68 AD; md **Hind 'Uwan**a.
   59. **Kinana**, b. c101 AD; md **Barra.**
   58. **Qays al-Nadr**, b. c134; md **Ikrisha.**
   57. **Malik** md **Jandala.**
   56. **Fihr Quraysh** md **Layla.**
   55. **Ghalil** md **Atika.**
   54. **Lu'ayy** md **Mawiya.**
   53. **Ka'b** md **Makhshiya.**
   52. **Murra** md **Hind.**
   51. **Kilab**, b. c365; d. c400; md **Fatima.**
   50. **Qusayy** ( Zaid )"Munjammi," b c400; md the Princess **Hubba** (434-
50). *NOTE: After the death of his father, when Zaid was an infant, his
mother married a man from the highlands of south Syria and she took
Zaid there. In adulthood, Zaid returned to Mecca and reunited with his
family. By about 440, the government of Mecca passed into his family.*
   49. **'Abd al-Manaf** al Mujira, b. c 430; md **Atika** of bani Qays Aylan.
   48. **Hashim** 'al Muttalib, Amr [a title], b. c464; d. n.d. at Ghazza; md
**Selma** bint Adi ibn Najjar Khazraji.
   47. **Abd al-Mattalib Shayba** al Hamd, md **Fatima** bint 'Amr of
Makhzum.
   46. **'Abd Manaf** abu Talib, d. before 582; md **Fatima** bint Asad ibn
Hashim, dau of **'Amr of bani Hashim** of Quraysh. He was brother of
**Abdallah** ibn Abd Mutalib (435-46).
   45. **Ali ben Abu Talib**, Caliph, b. 597; d. 661; md **Fatima** (435-44).
   44. **Al- Hasan al- Sibt**, b. 624/625; d. c670; md **Jada bint al-Ash'ath.**
He had upwards to 90 wives and 300-400 concubines. *NOTE: He died
after a long illness and is said by some sources to have been poisoned by
his wife, Jada.*
   43. **Husayn.**
   42. **Zahra** md **Abu Farisi** of al-Hira (430-42).
Sources: Barber, F. 1977; Enc. Islam 2, 1996, vol. 1, pp. 42,80,152,153;
vol. 5, pp. 434, 435; Wusterfeld, F. 1852, tables D, J. M through P, R, S,
U through Z.

## LINE 433

   72. **Zayd** of Al-Hira (same as 430-73).
   71. **Malik** of al-Hira.
   70. **Nabt** of al-Hira.
   69. **al-Ghauth** of al-Hira.

68. **al-Azd** of al-Hira (435-65), md Zaynab.
67. **Nasr** of al-Hira.
66. **Malik** of al-Hira.
65. **'Abdallah.**
64. **Ka'b** of al-Hira.
63. **al-Harith** of al-Hira.
62. **Ka'b Azd Shanuwwa** of al-Hira.
61. **Zuhran** of al-Hira.
60. **'Abdallah** of al-Hira.
59. **'Odthan** of Al-Hira.
58. **Dous** of al-Hira.
57. **Ghanm** of al-Hira.
56. **Fahn** of al-Hira.
55. **Malik** of al-Hira, d. 215 AD. He was accidentally killed with an arrow at night by his son who thought was an enemy.
54. **Raquash** of al-Hira, b. c200 AD; md **Adi** of al-Hira (430-55).
Sources: Barber, F. 1977; Beyce, T. 1997; Ceram, C. 1973; Enc. Islam 2, 1996, vol. 1, p. 450; Guerney, O. 1991; Hogarth, D. 1926; Mac Queen, J. 1966; Wusterfeld, F. 1852, table 10.

## LINE 434

65. **al-Azd** of Al-Hira (same as 433-68) md **Zaunab.**
64. **Mazin Ghassan.**
63. **Tha'laba al-Bahlul.**
62. **Imru'l Qays** al-Batriq.
61. **Tha'laba.**
60. **Harith al-Ghitrif.**
59. **Amir ma' al-Sama**
58. **Amr Muzayqiya Tarifa.**
57. **Haritha.**
56. **Rabi'a Luhayy.**
55. **Amr.**
54. **Ka'b.**
53. **Salul.**
52. **Habashiua** md **Atika.**
51. **Hulayl** (Holeil), King of the Khozaite.
50. **Hobba**, Princess of the Khozaite, md **Qusayy Zaid** (432-50).
Sources: Barber, F. 1977, 122; Ceram, C. 1973; Enc. Islam 2, 1996; Guerney, O. 1991; Hogarth, D. 1926; Wusterfelf, F. 1952, tables 10, 11.

## LINE 435

47. **Abd al-Muttalib Shayba** al Hamd (Same as 432-47), md **Fatima.**
46. **Abdallah** ibn Abd Muttalib, b. 554; d. 579; bur at Dar al Nabigha (bro of Abd Manaf abu Talib (432-46)); md **Amina** bint Wahb, d. c576; dau of **Wahb** ibn 'Abd Manaf, whose father was **'Abd Manaf.** Wahb ibn

232

''abd Manaf md **Barra** bint 'Abdul 'Uzza, whose father was '**abd al-Uzza.**

45. **Muhammad**, the Prophet, b. 25 March 570, Arabia; d. 8 June 632, Medina, Arabia; md **Khadija Qarayshi** (436-45)

44. **Fatima** md '**Ali ibn Abi Talif** (432-45).

Sources: Duckworth, J. 1980; Enc. Islam I, 1987, vol. 1, p. 438; Enc. Islam 2, 1996, vol. 1, p. 42; Guerney, O. 1991; Hitti, P. 1970, 111-114; Wusterfeld, F. 1852, tables W, Z.

## LINE 436

49. **Qusayy** (Zaid) "Mujammi," (432-50,434-50), Gov. of Mecca, md **Hobba** (434-50).

48. '**Abd al-Uzza**

47. **Asad**

46. **Khuwailid**

45. **Khadija Qarayshi** , b. c555; d. 620; md **Muhammad**, the Prophet (435-45). She also md/div Hala al-Taminia, by whom two chidren; md/div "Otayyik, by whom one child. She had five children of record by **Muhammad** (435-45).

Sources: Enc. Islam, 1987, v. 1, p. 438; Enc. Islam,2, 1996, v. 1, p. 42; Hitti, P. 1970, 111-114; Wusterfeld, F. 1852, tables W, Z.

## LINE 437

58. **Odin** (Woden) of Asgard, Asia, md **Frigg** (Frigida) (233-62).

57. **Casere.**

56. **Tytmon.**

55. **Trygils.**

54. **Hrothmund.**

53. **Hryp.**

52. **Wilhelm.**

51. **Wehha.**

50. **Wuffa**, King of East Anglia, d. 578 AD.

49. **Tytila**, King of East Anglia, d. 593 AD.

48. **Eni.**

47. **Anna** (male), King of East Anglia.

46. **Sexburga** md **Eakenberht**, King of Kent (233A-46)

Sources: Bede, V. 1903; Tompsett, N.: *Directory of Royal Genealogical Data;* Wagner, A. 1975.

## LINE 438

71. **Arvigarus Gwenivyth** md **Genuissa Venus Julia.**

70. **Marius of Siluria** md **Penardun**, dau of **Bran Fendig** "the Blessed" and **Anna of Enygeus.**

69. **Coel I Godebog**, d. 170 AD.

**68. Athildis** md **Marcomir IV** (303-68), King of Franks, who d, 49 AD
Sources: See Sources for Line 303.

## LINE 439

51. **Waelgush,** a sister of **Drust III**, King of Picts (see 341-51).
50. **Brude**, King of the Picts, md **Peithar**, sister of Aneirin.
49. **Widfroith** md N.N., a dau of **Irv** and wife **Gwyddno Garapur.**
48. **N.N.** md **Domnall Brec** (165-46), King of Dalriada.
Sources: See sources for Line 165.

## LINE 440

31. **Archambaud I**, Seigneur de St. Geran, fl. 1111-c1150.
30. **William I**, Seigneur de St. Geran and de Montculon after the death of his uncle, William de Barbo.
29. **William II**, Seigneur de St. Geran and Montculon, 1174-1197.
28. **Archambaud V**, Seigneur de Montculon in the Barbonais, 1203.
27. **Beatrice de Montculon**, occ 1212, 1216; md **Archambaud IX de Bourbon** (84-27).
Sources: Brandenburg, E. 1935; Winkhaus, E. 1953.

# Bibliography

To save space, the items in this bibliography are coded when they appear as sources for each line. The code usually calls for the last name of the author, followed by the first initial of his/her first name, and then followed by the year of publication. As an example: ABADEL, L. 1912.

## -A-

**ABADAL, L. 1912** = Abadal, Luis: "Pervet de Ribagorza la Clegenda de Bernardo des Capio," in *Estudios,* vol. III (1912).

**ABADOLIN , R. 1949** = Abadolin, Ramon d': *Annales du Médiévale* (Toulouse, 1948/49).

**ABD el RAJIK, M. 1975** = Abd-el-Rajik, Mahmond: "Dedicatory and Building Texts of Ramesses II in Luxor Temple," I The Texts, in *Journal of Egyptian Genealogy,* 60:142-160 (London, 1974).

**ABRAMOWSKI, L. 1927** = Abramowski, L.: *Macedon, 401-301 B.C.* (Cambridge Ancient History Series, Vol. 9) (1927)

**ABU BAKR, A** = Abu Bakr, A: "Pharaonic Egypt" in G. Mokhtar (ed) *General History of Africa,* II (Paris, London, Berkeley, pp. 84-111.

**ACHAU** = *Achau Brenhinoldd a Thywysogion Cymru.* (Welsh ms. of the Middle Ages, on microfilm.)

**ADERS, G. 1976** = Aders, Gunter, et al.: *Die Grafen von Limburg Stirum* (Amsterdam, Van Gorcum, 1962–1976).

**ADHEMER, J. 1974** = Adhemer, Jean: "Les Tombeaux de la Collection Gaignieres I, Nr. 835," *Gazette de Beaux-Arts,* vol. 116 (1974).

**ADLER, E. 1921** = Adler, Ekan Nathan: *Catalog of Hebrew Manuscripts in the Collection of Elkan Nathan Adler,* Ms. No. 2237 (Cambridge, 1921), p.81.

**ADONTZ, N. 1938** = Adontz, Nikolai: "Samuel l'Armenien, Roi des Bulgers," *Memoires de Académie Royal de Belgique,* 2nd Series, vol. 39 (1938).

**AELSCHKER, E. 1885** = Aelschker, Edmund: *Geschichte Karntens* (Aachen, 1885).

**AGILES, R. 1968** = Agiles, Raimundus de: *Historia Francorum qui Ceperunt Iherusalem*, trans. by John Hugh Hill and Laurita L. Hill (Philadelphia, American Philosophical Society, 1968).

**ALBRIGHT, W. 1960** = Albright, William F.: "Abram the Hebrew, " *Bulletin of the American School of Oriental Reseasrch* (October 1960).

**ALBRIGHT, W. 1963** = Albright, William F.: *The Biblical Period from Abraham to Ezra* (New York, Harper & Row, 1963).

**ALCOCK, L. 1971** = Alcock, Leslie: *Arthur's Britain* (London, 1971).

**ALDRED, C. 1984** = Aldred, Cyril: The Egyptians (London, Thames & Hudson, rev. 1984).

**ALLEN, J. 1985** = Allen, Jelisaveta Stanojevich, ed.: *Author Index of Byzantine Studies* (microfilm catalog) (Washington, DC, Dumbarton Oaks Center of Byzantine Studies, 1985)

**ALLSTROM, C. 1904** = Allstrom, C. M.: *Dictionary of Royal Lineage of Europe and Other Countries*, 2 vols. (Vienna, 1904).

**AL-MAKKARI, A. 1840** = Al-Makkari, Almed ibn Muhammad: *History of the Mohammedan Dynasties in Spain*, trans. by Pascual de Cyangos, vol. 1 (London, 1840).

**ALTSCHUL, M. 1965** = Altschul, Michael: *A Baronial Family in Medieval England: The Clares, 1217–1314* (Baltimore, 1965).

**AMARDEL, G. 1901** = Amardel, G.: "Les Derniers Chefs des Goths de Septimania," in *Bulletin de la Commission Archeologique de Narbonne*, VI (1900-1901).

**ANDERSON, A. 1990** = Anderson, Alan Orr: *Early Sources of Scottish History: A.D 500 to 1286*, Collected and translated by the author. Corrections and a new compilation by Marjorie Anderson, 2 vols. (Stamford, Lincs., Paul Watkins, 1990). *This is the definitive guide to Scottish sources for the period it covers.*

**ANGOT, A. 1942** = Angot, A.: *Généalogies Féodales Mayenneaises* (Laval, 1942).

**ANSCOMBE, A. 1913** = Anscombe, Alfred: "The Pedigree of Earl Godwin," *English Historical Society Transactions*, 3rd Series, vol. VII (1913).

**ANSELME, A. 1890** = Anselme, Père Augustin Dechausse: *Histoire Généalogique et Chronologique de la Maison Royale de France, et des Grands Officiers de la Couronne et de la Maison du Roi*, 9 volumes (Paris, 1726–1733; reptd 1879–1890).

**ARCHERM, K. 1993** = Archerm, Kingsford: *Crusades: the Story of the Latin Kingdom of Jerusalem* (1993).

**ARKILL, A. 1975** = Arkill, A. J.:"Prehistory of the Nile Valley, " in *Handbuch der Orientalistek* (Leiden, 1975).

**ARRIERES, J. 1921** = Arrieres, Jules: "Les Vicomtes de Millau, 916–1272," *Memoires de la Société des Lettres, Sciences et Arts de l'Auvergne*, XXI:490–504 (1921).

**ARTETA, A. 1952** = Arteta, A. Ubieto: "Los Reyes de Vigurra," *España*, no. 38 (Buenos Aires, 1952).

**ASC** = *Anglo-Saxon Chronicle*. There are at least three versions in print, but since citations are by date, not page, it is probably unimportant which edition is used.

I used Everyman's edition, text by Ingram; and the two-volume set by Charles Plummer (1892–1899). There is also a translation edited by G.N.Garmonsway (London, 1953).

**ASHLEY, M. 1998** = Ashley, Mike: *British Monarchs* (London, 1998).

**ASHTON, E.: 1993** = Ashton, Eliyahu: *Jews of Moslem Spain*, 2 vols. (1993).

**ASSER, W. 1904** = Asser, W. H.: *Life of King Alfred* (Oxford, 1904).

**AUBEL, F. 1997** = Aubel, F.: "Les Comtes de Quercy (Fin VIIIe - Debut Xe Siecle" *Annales du Midi*, 109 (1997).

**AURELL, M. 1997** = "Du Nouveau sur les Comtesses Catalanes (IXe - XIIe Siecles)" *Annales du Midi*, 109 (1997).

**AUTHIER, M. 1988** = Authier, Michel, et al.: *État de la Noblesse Française Subsistante*, 17 vols. (Paris, 1940–1988). This is an ongoing publication.

**AUZIAS, L. 1934** = Auzias, Leonce: "Origine Carolingienne des Ducs Féodaux d'Aquitaine et des Rois Capetiene," *Revue Historique*, vol. 175 (1934).

**AUZIAS, L. 1937** = Auzias, Leonce: *Aquitaine Carolingienne, 776–987* (Toulouse, 1937).

## -B-

**BACHELIER, E. 1959** = Bachelier, E.: ""Les Dauphins de Viennois et d'Auvergne, les Comtes de Forez, et l'Origine Première du 'Dauphin" *Bulletin de l'Académie Delphinale*, 7th Series, vol. 1 (1956); vol. 2 (1957) (Grenoble, 1959).

**BACHMANN, A. 1899** = Bachmann, Arnold: *Geschichte Bohmeus* (Gotha, 1899).

**BAER, Y. 1993** = Baer, Yitzhak: *A History of the Jews in Christian Spain* (1993).

**BAGNALL, R. 1987** = Bagnall, R. S., A. Cameron, et al: *Consuls of the Later Roman Empire*, a monograph of the American Philological Association, No. 36 (Atlanta, Scholars Press, 1987).

**BAGNALL, R. 1993** = BAGNALL, ROGER S.: *Egypt in Late Antiquity* (Princedon, Princedon University Press, 1993).

**BAIKIE, J. 1929** = *A History of Egypt From the Earliest Times to the End of the XVIIIth Dynasty* (London, 1929).

**BAILDON, W. 1926** = Baildon, William Paley: *Baildon and the Baildons...* 3 vols. (London, St. Catherine Press, 1912–1926).

**BALCER, J. 1993** = Balcer, Jack Martin: *A Prosopographical Study of the Ancient Persian Royal and Noble, ca. 550-450 B.C.* (Lewiston, Edwin Mellen Press, 1993).

**BALDE, H. 1913** = Balde, H.: *Die Salier und Threr Untergrafen in der Gaven der Mittlesheins* (Marburg, 1913).

**BALDERSTON, M. 1930** = Balderston, Marion: "The Shrine of the Last Saxon King," *Travel*, 54:44–45, 71, 73 (Apr. 1930).

**BALLYMOTE 1380** = *Book of Ballymote*. A 1380 ms. in the library of the Royal Irish Academy, Dublin. (Available on microfilm.)

**BALZER, O. 1971** = Balzer, Oswald: *Genealogia Piastow* (Krakou, 1895; reptd on microfilm, Washington, DC, Library of Congress, 1971).

237

**BANFIELD, A. 1990** = Banfield, Alan and Neal Priestland: "The family of Eleanor of Castile (d.1290)" Augustan Society *Omnibus*, Book 12 (Torrance, CA, the Society, 1990) pp. 101-109.

**BANKS, T. 1844** = Banks, T. C.: *Baronia Anglica Concentrata; or a Concenrated Account of all the Baronies Commonly Called Baronies in Fee*, 2 vols. (1843–1844).

**BANNERMAN, J. 1974** = Bannerman, John: Studies in the History of Dalriada (Scottish Academic Press, 1974). *[The definitive work on the Dalriada kingdom.]*

**BARBER, F. 1977** = Barber, Forest E.: "Arab Blood Royal," *Augustan*, vol. 18, No. 4, p.115 (Torrance, CA, Augustan Society, 1977)

**BARD, R. 1982** = Bard, Rachael: *Navarra, the Durable Kingdom* (Reno, NV, University of Nevada Press, 1982).

**BARLOW, L. 1957** = Barlow, Lundie W.: "The Antecedents of Earl Godwine of Wessex," *NEHGR*, 111:30–38 (Jan. 1957).

**BARLOW, L. 1958** = Barlow, Lundie W.: "Ancestry of Saher de Quincy, Earl of Winchester," *NEHGR*, 112:61–65 (Jan. 1958).

**BARRACLOUGH, G. 1966** = Barraclough, Geoffrey: *The Origin of Modern Germany* (New York, Putnam, 1966).

**BARRAU, H. 1860** = Barrau, Hippolyte de: *Documents des Rouergue* (1853-1860).

**BARRAU, H. 1972** = Barrau, Hippolyte de: *Documents Historiques et Généalogiques sur les Familles et les Hommes Remar quelle les de Rouergue*, vol. I (Rodez, 1853; reptd Paris, 1972).

**BARROW, C. 1995** = Barrow, C. and N. Saul, editors: *England and the Low Countries in the Middle Ages* (Allen Sutton Publishing Co. 1995).

**BARROW, G. 1981** = Barrow, G. W. S.: *Kingship and Unity: Scotland 1000-1306* (London, 1981).

**BARRY, F. 1957** = Barry, F.: *Essai d'Une Généalogie des Rochebaron, Dachtylographique* (1957), pp. 65–68.

**BARTON, S. 1997** = Barton, Simon: *The Aristocracy of Twelfth-Century Leon and Castile* (1997).

**BARTRUM, P. 1966** = Bartrum, Peter C., ed.: *Early Welsh Genealogical Tracts* (Cardiff, Wales, U. of Wales Press, 1966). Facsimile edition.

**BAUMGARTEN, N. 1927a** = Baumgarten, Nicholas Pierre de: "Dernies Mariage la St. Vladimir," *Orientalia Christiana* (Rome, 1927).

**BAUMGARTEN, N. 1927b** = Baumgarten, Nicholas Pierre de: "Généalogies et Mariages Occident aux des Rurikides Russes du Xe au XIIIe Siècle," *Orienalia Christiana* (Rome, 1927).

**BAUMGARTEN, N. 1928** = Baumgarten, Nicholas Pierre de: "Olaf Tryggurisson, Roi de Norvege," *Orientalia Christiana* (Rome, 1928).

**BAUMGARTEN, N. 1932** = Baumgarten, Nicholas Pierre de: "St. Vladimir et la Conversion de la Ruesie," *Orientalia Christiana* (Rome, 1932).

**BAYNE, W. 1969** = Bayne, William Wilfrid: "The Kings of Navarre," *Augustan*, XII:289–296 (Sept–Oct 1969).

**BAYNE, W. 1970** = Bayne, William Wilfrid: "De Ayala of Castile," *Augustan*, XIII:289–291 (Nov–Dec 1970).

**BEAUCHAT, E. 1978** = Beauchat-Filleau, Eugene Henri Edmond: *Dictionnaire Historique et Généalogique des Familles du Poitou*, volume VI, 5th edition, (Fortenay-le-Comte, Lussaud, 1978).

**BECKERATH, J. 1971** = Beckerath, Jurgrn von: "Ein Deukwal zur Genealogie der XX Dynastie" in *Zeitschrift fur Agyptische Sprache und Altertumskunde*, 97:7-12, 1971.

**BECKERATH, J. 1984** = Beckerath, Jurgrn von: "Handbuch der Agyptischen Konigsnamen," in *Munchner Agyptologische Atudien*, vol. 20, 1984 (Munich & Berlin, 1984).

**BEDE, V. 1903** = Bede, The Venerable: *Ecclesiastical History of the English Nation*, ed. by J. A. Giles (London, George Bell, 1903).

**BEDROSIAN, R. 1985** = Bedrosian, Robert: *Armenia in Ancient and Modern Times* (1985).

**BEHR, K. 1854** = Behr, Kamille von: *Généalogie der in Europa Furstenhauser...* (Leipzig, Tauchnitz, 1854). (microfilm copy, Salt Lake City, UT, 1978.)

**BELAIEV, N. 1927** = Belaiev, N. J.: "Rorik of Jutland and Rurick of the Russian Chronicles," *The Saga Book of the Viking Club, Proceedings*, vol. 10 (1925–1927).

**BEMONT, C. 1891** = Bemont, Claude, and G. Monod: *Histoire de l'Europe et en Particular de France de 395 a 1270* (Paris, F. Alcan, 1891).

**BENJAMIN OF TUDELA, 1907** = Benjamin of Tudella: *The Itiniary of Rabbi Benjamin of Tudella*, ed. and trans. by M. N. Adler (London, 1907).

**BENNETT, C. 1995** = Bennett, Chris: "A Babylonian Ancestry for King Darius," *Journal of Ancient and Medieval Studies*, XII (Torrance, CA., Octavian Society, 1995).

**BENVENISTI, M. 1972** = Benvenisti, Meron: *The Crusaders in the Holy Land*, first American edition (New York, Macmillan, 1972).

**BERNARDI, W. 1874** = Bernardi, Wilhelm: "Lothar von Supplinburg," *Jahrbrucher der Deutschen Gerchichte, 1125–1137* (Liepsic, 1874).

**BETHAM, W. 1795** = Betham, Rev. William: *Genealogical Tables of the Sovereigns of the World...* (London, W. Bennett, 1795).

**BETHANCOURT, D. 1897** = Bethancourt, D. Francisco Fernandez de: *Historia Genealogica y Heraldica de la Monarquia Espñola, Casa Réal y Grandés de Spaña*, 10 vols. (Madrid, 1897).

**BEVAN, B. 1992** = Bevan, Bryan: Edward III, *The Monarchy and Chivalry* (1992)

**BEYCE, T 1997** = Beyce, Trevor: *The Kingdom of the Hittites* (1997)

**BIERBRIER, M. 1975a** = Bierbrier, Morris L.: "The Length of the Reign of Ramesses X" in *Journal of Egyptian Archaeology*, 61:251 (1975).

**BIERBRIER, M. 1975b** = Bierbrier, Morris L.: *The Late New Kingdom of Egypt (c.1300-664 B.C.) A Genealogical and Chronological Investigation* (Warmingster, 1975).

**BIERBRIER, M. 1980** = Bierbrier, Morris L.: "Modern Descendants of Byzantine Families" in *Genealogists' Magazine*, 20:85-96 (Sept. 1980).

239

**BIERBRIER, M. 1992** = Bierbrier. Morris L.: "Medieval and Royal Genealogy Update, Genealogists' Magazine, 24, no. 1 (London, Society of Genealogists, March 1992)

**BIERBRIER, M. 1993** = Bierbrier, Morris L.: "Medieval and Royal Genealogy Update" *Genealogists' Magazine*, 24, no. 5 (London, Society of Genealogists, March 1993)

**BIERBRIER, M. 1994** = Bierbrier, Morris L.: "Medieval and Royal Genealogy Update," in *Genealogists'Magazine*, 24:510-511 (Sept. 1994).

**BINGHAM, C. 1974** = Bingham, Caroline: *The Stewart Kingdom of Scotland, 1171-1603* (Weidenfeld & Nicholson, 1974).

**BINHACK, 1887** = Binhack, 1887, F.: "Die Markgrafen Nordgau...," *Historisch Verhal Oberpfalz,* vol. 41 (Regensburg, 1887).

**BISSON, T. 1991** = Bisson, T. N.: *The Medieval Crown of Aragon*, a *Short History* (Oxford, Clarendon Press, 1986, 1991).

**BLADE, J. 1878** = Blade, J. F.: "Comtes Carolingiens de Bigorre et les Premiers Rois de Navarre," *Revue de l'Ageneis,* vol. 5 (1878).

**BLADE, J. 1896** = Blade, J. F.: Revue de l'Agenais, vol. 23 (1896).

**BLAIR, P. 1963** = Blair, Peter Hunter: *Roman Britain and Early England 55 B.C. to A.D. 871* , vol. 1 (London, Norton History of England, 1963).

**BLANKENBERG, C. 1982** = Blankenberg van Delden, C.: " A Genealogical Reconstruction of the Kings and Queens of the Late 17th and Early 18th Dynasties" in *Gottinger Miszelleu*, 54:31-46 (1982).

**BLANKINSHIP, K. 1993** = Blankinship, K. Y.: "On the Alleged Marriage of a Muslim Princess to a Byzantine Rebel," *Genealogists' Magazine*, 24, no. 5 (London, Society of Genealogists, March 1993).

**BLASS, R. 1939** = Rubel, Edward: *Ahnentafel Rubel-Blass, R. 1939*, vol. II (Zurich, 1939). NOTE: Chart numbers, not page numbers, are cited.

**BLOKLAND, W. 1948** = Blokland, W. 1948, W. A. von: *Niederlandsch Luuw* (1948).

**BOARDMAN, J. 1988** = Boardman, John: *Cambridge Ancient History: Persia, Greece and the Western Mediterranean,525-479 B.C.*, Volume IV (1988).

**BOASE, T. 1971** = Boase, Thomas S. R.: *Kingdoms and Strongholds of the Crusaders* (London, Thomas and Hudson, 1971)

**BODE, G. 1937** = Bode, G.: *Zeitschrift der Herzverciner* (1937)

**BOEREN, P. 1938** = Boeren, P. C.: *Bydragen en Mededulingen Gelre*, vol. XI (1938).

**BOFARULL, P. 1836** = Bofarull y Bascaro, Prospero de: *The Counts of Barcelona Vindicated: Chronology and Genealogy of the Kings of Spain.* Originally in Spanish under the name: *Los Condes de Barcelona Vindicados: y Cronologie y Genealogia de Los Reyes de España...*2 vols. (Barcelona, J. Oliveres y Monmany, 1836).

**BOLLNOW, H. 1930** = Bollnow, H.: *Die Grafen von Werl, Genealogische Untersuchungen zur Geschichte der 10 bis 12 Jahrhundeits* (Greifswold, 1930).

**BONDURAND, E. 1887** = Bondurand, Edouard, ed.: *Le Manuel de Dauoda (843)* (Paris, 1887).

**BORMAN, C. 1931** = Borman, C. de and E. Poncelet: *Ouvres de Jacques de Hemricourt*, II:126, 193 (1925); III:166 (1931).

**BORROW, G. 1928** = *Celtic Bards, Chiefs and Kings* (London, 1928).

**BORZA, E. 1990** = Borza, Eugene N.: *In the Shadow of Olympus. The Emergence of Macedon* (Princeton, Princeton University Press, 1990).

**BOSWORTH, C. 1967** = Bosworth, Clifford E.: *Islamic Surveys 5: The Islamic Dynasties. A Chronological and Genealogical Handbook* (Edinburgh, Edinburgh University Press, 1967).

**BOTTGER, F. 1965** = Bottger, Franz: *Die Brunonen* (Hanover, 1865).

**BOUCHARD, C. 1981** = Bouchard, Constance B.: "Consanguinity and Noble Marriages in the Tenth and Eleventh Centuries" *Spectrum* (1981).

**BOUCHARD, C. 1987** = "Family Structure and Family Consciousness Among the Aristocracy in the Ninth to Eleventh Centuries," *Francia*, 14 (1987).

**BOURNAZEL, E. 1975** = Bournazel, Eric: *Le Gouvernement Capetien au XIIe Siecle, 1108-1180* (Paris, 1975).

**BOUCHARD, C. 1987** = Bouchard, Constance B.: *Sword, Miter and Cloister* (1987).

**BOUCHARD, C. 1987a** = Bouchard, Constance B.""The Problem of the Three Bernards and the Dukes of Aquitaine" *Francia*, 14 (1987).

**BOUSSARD, J. 1957** = Boussard, Jacques: "Historia Pontificum et Comitum Englishmensium," *Bibliothèque Elzevirienne*, New Series (Paris, 1957).

**BOWMAN, A. 1986** = Bowman, Alan K.: *Egypt After the Pharaohs, 332 BC - AD 642: From Alexander to the Arab Conquest* (Berkeley, University of California Press, 1986).

**BRAND, C. 1968** = Brand, Charles: *Byzantium Confronts the West, 1180–1204* (Cambridge, MA, 1968).

**BRANDENBURG, E. 1935** = Brandenburg, Erich von: *Die Nachkommenen Karl des Grossen* (Leipzig, 1935). Folio size, very awkward to use.

**BREASTED, J. 1988** = Breasted, James H.: *Ancient Records of Egypt*, 4 vols (Chicago, 1906; reptd in 2 vols., Portland, OR, 1988).

**BRENNER, S. 1978** = Brenner, S. Otto: *Nachkomen Gorms des Alten*, 2nd edition (Lyngby, 1978).

**BRESC, G. 1984** = Bresc-Bautier, Genevieve: "Le Cartulaire du Chapitre du Saint-Sepulcre de Jerusalem," *Documents Relatifs a l'Histoire de Crusades* (Paris, l'Académie des Inscriptions et Belle-Lettres, vol. XV, no. 30, 1984).

**BRESSLAU, H. 1879** = Bresslau, H.: *Jahrbucker des Deutschen Reiches unter Konrad II*, vol. I (1879).

**BRETHOLTZ, B. 1912** = Bretholz, Berthold: *Geschichte Bohmeus und Marhens bis zum Aussterben der Premysliden (1306)* (Munich, Verlag von Dunker und Humbolt, 1912).

**BRIOLLET, M., 1965** = Briollet, Maurice: *Une Descendance des Seconds Rois d'Austrasie les Vicomtes de Limoges…*(1965).

**BRIOLLET, M. 1971** = Briollet, Maurice: *Contribution a l'Histoire Féodal de Château-Goutier* (1971).

241

**BRITANNIA, 1997** = " Monarchs of Britain" *Brittannia Internet Magazine* (Hillier, Ontario, Canada, Britannia Internet Magazine, 1997).

**BRODY, R. 1998** = Brody, R.: *Geonim of Babylonia and the Shaping of Medieval Jewish Culture* (1998)

**BROGAN, O. 1953** = Brogan, Olwen: *Roman Gaul* (London, G. Bell & Sons, 1953).

**BROMWITZ, R. 1961** = Bromwitz, Rachael, ed.: *Welsh Triads* (1961).

**BRONDSTED, J. 1960** = Brondsted, Johannes: *The Vikings* (Harmondsworth, Penguin Books, 1960).

**BROOK, L. 1981** = Brook, Lindsay L.: "The Byzantine Ancestry of H.R.H. Prince Charles, Prince of Wales," *Genealogist,* 2:3–51 (Spring, 1981). This is a complex and authoritative work containing but a few errors, from which was extracted the John of Gaunt lineage.

**BROOK, L. 1989** = Brook, Lindsay L, editor: *Studies in Genealogy and Family History in Tribute to Charles Evans on the Occasion of His Eightieth Birthday.* (Salt Lake City, UT, Occasional Pub. no. 2 of the Association for the Promotion of Scholarship in Genealogy, Ltd., 1989). This work contains, among other items, two dozen signed essays, some of which are appropriate to RFC.

**BROOKE, C. 1969** = Brooke, Christopher: From Alfred to Henry III (New York, W. W. Norton, 1969).

**BROSSET, M. 1876** = Brosset, Marie-Felicite: *Collection d'Historiens Armeniens,* tables I and II (St. Petersburg,1874-1876). Microfilm

**BRUEL, A. 1988** = Bruel, Alexandre: *Recueil des Chartes de l'Abbaye de Cluny,* vol. IV (1027-1090 AD) (Paris, 1988), No. 3499.

**BRUGSCH, H. 1879** = Brugsch, Henry: *History of Egypt Under the Pharaohs Derived Entirely from the Monuments.,* 2 vols. (London, J. Murray, 1879).

**BRUNEL, C. 1930** = Brunel, Clovis: *Recueil des Actes des Comtes de Ponthieu* (Paris, 1930).

**BUCH, H. 1961** = Buck, Heinrich and Szabolcs de Vajay: "Bourbon," *Genealogishe Handbuch der Adels Furstliche Hauser* (1961).

**BUCKLER, G. 1929** = Buckler, Georgina G.: *Anna Comnena, a Study* (London, 1929).

**BUDE, G. 1900** = Bude, G.: *Entwurf Lines Stammbaumes der Grafen von Walbeck und Verwandter Geschlechter* (1900).

**BUHLER, H. 1984** = Buhler, H.: "Studien zur Geschichte des Grafen von Achalm und Ihrer Verwandter," *Zeitschrift fur Wurttembergische Landesgeschichte,* 43 (1984).

**BULLETIN 1957** = *Bulletin de la Société des Sciences Historiques et Naturelles de l'Yonne,* vol. 96 (1953–1956) (Auxerre, 1957).

**BUR, M. 1977** = Bur, Michel: *La Formation du Comtes de Champagne vers 950– vers 1150* (Nancy, 1977).

**BUR, M. 1997** = Bur, Michael: "De Quelques Champenois dans l'Entourage Frasncais des Rois d'Angleterre aux XIe et XIIe Siecles," *Family Trees and Roots of Politics,* (Woodbridge, Suffolk, 1997).

**BURCKHARDT, A. 1915** = Burckhardt, August: *Herkunft der Grafen von Saugern (Basler Zeitschrift,* 1915).

**BURKE, B.1883** = Burke, Bernard: *Genealogical History of the Dormant, Abayant, Forfeited and Extinct Peerage of the British Empire.* (London, Burke's Peerage, 1883).

**BURKE, B.1905** = Burke, Bernard: *Genealogical and Heraldic Dictionary of the Peerage and Baronetage,* 67th edition (London, Burke's Peerage, 1905).

**BURKE, B.1963** = Burke, Bernard: Peerage, *Baronetage and Knightage.* (London, Burke's Peerage, 1963)

**BURKE, B.1973** = Burke, Bernard: *Burke's Guide to the Royal Family (London, Burke's Peerage,* 1973).

**BURKE, J. 1978** = Burke, John Bernard: *Roll of Battle Abbey,* annotated (London, 1848; reptd. Baltimore, 1978).

**BURNS, R. 1985** = Burns, Robert I: *The Worlds of Alfonso the Learned and James the Conqueror* (Princeton, Princeton University Press, 1985).

**BURNS, R. 1990** = Burns, Robert I.: *Emperor of Culture: Alfonso X the Learned of Castile...* (1990).

**BURNS, T. 1980** = Burns, Thomas S.: *The Ostragoths: Kingship and Society* (Wiesbaden, F. Steiner, 1980).

**BURNS, T. 1984** = Burns, Thomas S.: A *History of the Ostragoths* (Bloomington, Indiana University Press, 1984).

**BUTLER, P. 1897** = Butler, P.: "Ulrich von Eppenstein," *Jahrbuch Schweiz. Geschichte,* vol. 22 (1897).

**BUTTERY, A. 1974** = Buttery, A.: *Armies and Enemies of Ancient Egypt and Assyria, 3200 B.C. to 612 B.C.* (Goring by Sea, 1989)

## -C-

**CALMETTE, J. 1963** = Calmette, Joseph: The Golden Age of Burgundy, trans. by Doreen Weightsman (Weidenfeld & Nicholson, 1963) [The French version is titles: *Les Grands Ducs de Bourgogne.*]

**CALLANDER, G. 1993** = Callander, Gae: The Eye of Horus. A History of Ancient Egypt (Melbourne, Longman Cheshire, 1993).

**CAMBRIDGE, 1989** = *Cambridge Ancient History,* 2nd edition, edited by A. E. Austin, et al (Cambridge, Cambridge University Press, 1989).

**CAMERON, A. 1993** = Cameron, Averil: *The Later Roman Empire, AD 284-430* (Cambridge, Harvard University Press, 1993)

**CAMINOS, R. 1958** = Caminos, Richard A.: "The Chronicle of Prince Usorkon" in *Analecta Orientalia* (Rome, 1958).

**CAMPBELL, J. 1986** = Campbell, James: *Essays in Anglo-Saxon History* (Ronceverte, WV, Hambledon Press, 1986)

**CANCELLOS, A. 1945** = Cancellos, Angel: *Estudios de Edad Media de la Corona de Aragon* (Barcelona, 1945).

**CANDEIRA, A. 1950** = Candeira, Alfonso Sanchez: "La Reina Velasquita de Leon y su Descendencia," *Hisania,* 10:449–505 (1950).

**CANDEIRA, A. 1951** = Candeira, Alfonso Sanchez: *Regnum Imperium Leono Hasta, 1037* (1951).

**CANDEIRA, A. 1952** = Candeira, Alfonso Sanchez: *Reine Velesqueta de Leon y su Descendencia* (1952).

**CARTULAIRE, 1858** = *Cartulaire l'Abbaye de Notre Dame des Vaux de Cernay* (Paris, 1857–1858). (Original monastery record on microfilm.)

**CARTULAIRE CDY** = *Cartulaire de Yvonne*, no. 94. (Original monastery record on microfilm.

**CARTULARY CSM** = *Cartulary of St. Michael* (in Bibliothèque de Tonnerre). (Original monastery record on microfilm.)

**CARTULARY 1053** = *Cartulary of St. Bernard*, dated 13 Oct. 1053. (Original monastery record on microfilm.)

**CARUTTI, D. 1884a** = Carutti, Domenico: *Il Conte Bianca Mano Humberto Primo Edil Re Ardoino* (Rome, 1884).

**CARUTTI, D. 1884b** = Carutti, Domenico: *Il Conte Umberto Primo edil Re Ardoino* (Rome, 1884).

**CARUTTI, D. 1889** = Carutti, Domenico: *Regesta Comitum Sabindise* (Turin, 1889).

**CASKELL, W. 1966** = Caskell, Werner: *Das Genealogisches Werk des Hisam ben Muhammad al-Kalbi* (Leyden, E. J. Brill, 1966).

**CASSON, L. 1988** = Casson, Lionel: *Die Pharaoen* (Munich, 1988).

**CASTRO, A. 1954** = Castro, Americo: *The Structure of Spanish History* (Princeton University Press, 1954).

**CASTRO, M. 1995** = Castro, Maria Cruz Fernandez: *Iberia in Prehistory* (A History of Spain) (1995)

**CERAM, C. 1993** = Ceram, C. W.: *Secret of the Hittites. The Discovery of an Ancient Empire* (1973).

**CHADWICK, H. 1924** = Chadwick, H. M.: *Origin of the English Nation* (Cambridge, 1924).

**CHADWICK, H. 1949** = Chadwick, H. M.: *Early Scotland* (Cambridge, 1949)

**CHADWICK, N. 1964** = Chadwick, Nora, ed.: *Celts & Saxons: Studies in the Early British Border* (Cambridge, 1964).

**CHADWICK, N. 1971** = Chadwick, Nora K: *The Celts* (Harmondsworth, Penguin, 1971).

**CHAHIN, M. 1987** = Chahin, M.: *The Kingdom of Armenia* (1987).

**CHALANDON, F. 1907** = Chalendon, Ferdinand: *Histoire de la Domination Normand en Italia et Sicile*, 2 vols. (Paris, 1907).

**CHALANDON, F. 1912a** = Chalendon, Ferdinand: *Jean II Comnene et Manuel I Comnene* (Paris, 1912).

**CHALANDON, F. 1912b** = Chalendon, Ferdinand: *Les Comnenes* (Paris, 1912).

**CHALANDON, F. 1913** = Chalendon, Ferdinand: *Les Comnenes—Jean et Alexius* (Paris, 1913).

**CHAMCHEAU, M. 1786** = Chamcheau, Michael: *Histoire d'Armenie des Origines a 1783*, 3 vols. (Venice, 1784-1786). Microfilm.

**CHAMICK, M. 1990** = Chamick, M.: *History of Armenia*, 2 vols. ( N.Y., 1990).

244

**CHAMPEVAL, J. 1889** = Champeval, Jean-Baptiste: "Généalogie de la Maison de Combom en Bas-Limousin," *Bulletin de la Société Scientifique, Historique, et Archéologique de la Correze*, vol. XI (1889); vol. XII (1890).

**CHARNARD, F. 1870** = Charnard, F.: "Chronologie Historiques des Vicomtes de Châtellerault avant la Fin du XIIIe Siècle d'Apres les Documents Inedits," *Mémoires de la Société des Antiquaries de l'Ouest*, 25:79–122 (1870–1871). Also published as a separate article (Poitiers, 1872). Except for a few dates, the two works are substantially the same.

**CHARNIS, P. 1961** = Charnis, Pter: "The Armenians in the Byzantine Empire," *Byzantinoslavica*, 22:196-240 (1961)

**CHARLTON, N. 1974** = Charlton, Nial: "Some Reflections on the History of Pharaoic Egypt" in *Journal of Egyptian Archaeology*, 60:200-205 (1974).

**CHARTERS, CLUNY** = *Charters of Cluny*, vol. III. (Original records on microfilm.)

**CHATILAIN, V. 1901** = Chatilain, V.: "Le Comte de Metz," *Jahrbucke Lotharingen Geschichte*, vol. 15 (1901).

**CHAUME, M. 1930** = Chaume, Abbe Maurice: "Les Anciens Sires de Bourbon," *Annales de Bourgogne*, VIII:105 (1930).

**CHAUME, M. 1940** = Chaume, Abbe Maurice: "Onfroi, Marquis de Gothie ses Origines ses Attaches Familliales," *Annales du Midi*, 52:113–117 (Toulouse, 1940)

**CHAUME, M. 1947a** = Chaume, Abbe Maurice: "Comtes de Bar-sur-Seine et Tonnerre," *Notes sur Quelles Familles Comtes Champanoise* (Dijon, 1947).

**CHAUME, M. 1947b** = Chaume, Abbe Maurice: *Recherches d'Histoire Christienne et Médiévale (Dijon, 1947)*.

**CHAUME, M. 1947c**= Chaume, Abbe Maurice: *Recherches d'Histoire Oretienne et Médiévale* (Dijon, 1947).

**CHAUME, M. 1977** = Chaume, Abbe Maurice: *Les Origins du Duche de Bourgogne*, 2 vols. (Dijon, 1925–1931). (Facsimile edition, Aalen, Germany, Scientia Verlag, 1977, 2 vols. in 4 bindings.)

**CHAVALAS, M. 1993** = Chavalas, Mark, and John L. Hayes, editors: *New Horizons in the Study of Ancient Syria* (Biblioteca Mesopotamia, vol. 25) (1993).

**CHEINE, A. 1974** = Cheine, Anwar G.: *Muslim Spain* (University of Minnesota Press, 1974).

**CHENAYE, F. 1964** = Chenaye-Desbois, Francois Alexandre Aubert de: *Dictionnaire de la Noblese, Contenant les Généalogies, l'Histoire et la Chronologie des Familles Nobles de la France...* 3rd ed., 19 vols. (Paris, Schlessinger, 1863–1877; microfilm, Salt Lake City, UT, 1964.)

**CHEVALIER, R. 1947** = *Regesta Dauphinois*, ed. by Robert Chevalier (1913).

**CHEYETTE, F. 1988** = Cheyette, Frederick L.: "The 'Sale' of Carcassonne to the Counts of Barcelona (1066-1070) and the Rise of the Trencavels, " *Spectrum*, 63 (1988).

**CHEZAUD, A.** = Chezaud, A.: *Étude sur la Chronologie des Sires de Bourbo* 2nd edition, ed. by M. Max Fazy.

**CHIBNALL, M. 1991** = Chibnall, M.: *The Empress Matilda* (1991).

**CHRISTIANSEN, E. 1980** = Christiansen, E., editor: *Saxo Grammaticus*, 3 vols. (Oxford, 1980/81).

**CHRISTIANSEN, E. 1989** = Christiansen, Eric: "Royal Genealogies in Medieval Denmark," *Occasional Publication* no. 2 (Salt Lake City, UT, Association for the Promotion of Scholarship in Genealogy, Ltd., 1989), pp. 17–43.

**CHRISTOPHE, L. 1953** = Christophe, Loyis A.: "Les Fondations de Ramses III Entre Memphis et Thebes," in Cahiers d' Histoire Egyptienne, 5:227-249 (1953).

**CHRONICLE, CD** = *Chronicle of Dalriada*, Version E. (Original ms. of the Middle Ages on microfilm.)

**CHRONICLE, M** = *Chronicle of Melrose.* (Original ms. of the Middle Ages on microfilm.)

**CIBRARIO, L. 1840** = Cibrario, Luigi: *Storia della Monarchia di Savola* (Turin, 1840).

**CLAIRVAUX, B. 1963** = Clairvaux, Bernard of: *The Letters of Saint Bernard,* trans. by B. Scott James, (1963).

**CLARK, A. 1973** = Clark, Arthur Melville: "A Royal Descent: The Kings of Wessex," *Forebears,* XVI:198–202 (Spring, 1973).

**CLAY, C. 1952a** = Clay, Charles Travis: "Honour of Warenne," *Early Yorkshire Charters,* vol. VIII (1952).

**CLAY, C. 1952b** = Clay, Charles Travis: *Early Yorkshire Charters* (1952). First three volumes by W. Farrer.

**CLAY, J. 1913** = Clay, John William: *Extinct and Dormant Peerage of the Northern Counties of England* (London, James Nisbet, 1913).

**CLAYTON, P. 1994** = Clayton, Peter A.: *Chronicle of the Pharaohs* (1994).

**CLEVELAND, D. 1889** = Cleveland, Duchess of: *Battle Abbey Roll With Some Account of the Norman Lineages,* 3 vols. (1889).

**COHEN, G. 1967** = Cohen Gerson D.: *The Book of Traditions* (Sefer Ha-Qabbalah) by Abraham ibn Daud (Philadelphia, 1967).

**COIFFIES, D. 1816** = *Demoret, de Coiffies: Histoire de Bourbonnais et des Bourbons* (Paris, 1816).

**COKAYNE, G. 1953** = Cokayne, George Edward: [rev. by G. H. White]: *The Complete Peerage or the History of the House of Lords and All of Its Members From the Earliest Times* (London, 1953).

**COKAYNE, G. 1959** = Cokayne, George Edward: *Complete Peerage* (new edition, revised by Vicary Gibb, et al.), vols. I–XII, pt. 2; did not use vol. XIII. (1910–1959).

**COLLENBURG, W. 1963** = Collenburg, Weyprecht Hugo Rudt von: *Les Rupenides, Hethumides et Lusignans* (Paris, Imprimerie A. Pignie, 1963).

**COLLENBURG, W. 1964** = Collenburg, Weyprecht Hugo Rudt von: "Wer War Theophano?" *Genealogisches Jahrbuch,* 4:49–71 (1964).

**COLLINS, R. 1983** = Collins, Roger: *Early Medieval Spain, Unity and Diversity, 400-1000* (New York, Str. Martin Press, 1983, 1995).

**COLLINS, R. 1987** = Collins, Roger: *The Basques.* People of Europe Series (New York, Basil Blackwell, 1987).

COLLINS, R. 1991 = Collins, Roger: *Medieval Europe 300-1000* (New York, St. Martin's Press, 1991). [also Bassingstroke, Macmillan, 1991].

CONDER, C. 1978 = Conder, Claude R.: *The Latin Kingdom of Jerusalem* (1978).

CONSTABLE, G. 1953 = Constable, Giles: "The Second Crusade as Seen by Contemporaries" *Traditio*, vol. 9 (1953).

COOK, J. 1986 = Cook, J. M.: *The Persian Empire* (New York, Schocken, 1986).

COPE, C. 1987 = Cope, Christopher: *Phoenix Frustrated, the Lost Kingdom of Burgundy* (London, 1987).

COPLEY, J. 1954 = Copley, J. Gordon: *The Conquest of Wessex in the Sixth Century* (London, 1954).

COSNAC, R. 1969 = Cosnac, Réné de: "Étude sur Origines des Comtes de Turenne et des Vicomtes de Turenne, Comborn, Ventadour, qui Descendent, et Essai Généalogique." *Lemouzi*, 49th year (Tulle, 1968); 50th year (Tulle, 1969).

COUCY, A de 1981 = Coucy, Aubri de: *Bibliothèque de l'École de Chartes*, CXXXIX:155 (1981).

CREMER, A. 1873 = Cremer, A. J. C.: *De Graven in Hameland* (Arnheim, 1873).

CRISPIN, M. 1969 = Crispin, M. Jackson, and Leonce Macary: *Falaise Roll Recording Some of the Prominent Companions of William Duke of Normandy at the Conquest of England* (1938; reptd Baltimore, Gen. Pub. Co., 1969). Did not receive good reviews.

CRONICO, CDO = *Cronico de Origine Antiquarian Pictorium.* (Original record on microfilm.)

CROW, J. 1985 = Crow, John A.: *The Roots and the Flower* (Berkeley, U. of California Press, 1985).

CSUDAY, E. 1899 = Csuday, Eugene: *Die Geschichte der Ungarn* (Berlin, 1899).

CUMMINGS, B. 1984 = Cummings, Barbara: *Egyptian Historical Records of the Later Eighteenth Dynasty* (Westminster, 1982-1984).

CURSCHMANN, F. 1921 = Curschmann, Fritz: "Zwei Ahnentafeln," *Zeutralstelle fur Deutsche Familiengeschichte*, vol. 27 (Leipzig, 1921).

CURTIS, J. 1990 = Curtis, John: *Ancient Persia* (1990).

## -D-

DAFTARY, F. 1990 = Daftary, Farhad: *The Isma'ilis: Their History and Doctrines* (New York, Cambridge University Press, 1990).

DAMBERGER, J. 1831 = Damberger, J. F.: *Furstenbuch zur Furstentafel der Europäischen Staatengerschichte*, 2nd edition (Regensburg, 1831).

DAUMAS, F. 1965 = Daumas, Francois: *La Civilisation de l'Ehypte Pharaonique* (Paris-Grenoble, 1965).

DAVID, A. 1996 = David, A. Rosalie: *A Biographical Dictionary of Ancient Egypt* (1996).

DEBAX, H. 1988 = Debax, Helen: "Strategies Matrimoniales des Comtes de Toulouse," *Annales du Midi*, 100 (1988).

DEBEVOISE, N. 1970 = Debevoise, Neilson C.: *Political History of Parthia* (1970).

**DEBUISSIER, J. 1981** = Debuissier, J. P.: *Histoire de Pont-de-Gennes, Montfort-le-Rotrou et Saussay* (Pont-de-Gennes, 1981).

**DECKER, H. 1947** = Decker-Houff, Hansmartin, and Alexandra von Litauen: "Die Grossmutter Kaisar Friedrichs III," *Adler* I (XV) 1947.

**DECKER, H. 1977** = Decker-Houff, Hansmartin, and Alexandra von Litauen: "Konrad III und die Komburg," *Wurtemburgisch Franken,* v. 62 (1977), pp. 3-12.

**DEK, A. 1955** = Dek, Adrian William Eliza: *Généalogie der Graven van Holland* (1955).

**DEK, A. 1959** = Dek, Adrian William Eliza: "Genealogie der Heren van Broderode," *Jaarboek van het Centraal Bureau voor Genealogie,* XIII (1959).

**DELAINE, J. 1911** = Delaine, J.: *Les Comtes de Dammartin en Goele* (Liege, 1911).

**DEMANDT, A. 1971** = Demandt, A.: "Die Konsular de Jahr 381 und 382 Namens Syagrius, : *Byzantinisch Zeitschrift,* 64:38-45 (1971).

**DENIS, J. 1982** = Denis, Jean-Marie: *Les Seigneurs de Montbron et Leur Alliees du XIe au XVIIIe Siècle* (Troyes, 1982).

**DEPOIN, J. 1901** = Depoin, Joseph: Cartulaire de l'Abbaye de Saint-Martin de Pontoise 3 vols. (Pontoise, 1901).

**DEPOIN, J. 1903** = Depoin, Joseph: "Comtes d'Angoulême," *Bulletin et Memoire de la Société Archéologique de la Charente,* vol. 190 (1903/04)

**DEPOIN, J. 1905** = Depoin, Joseph: "Comtes Héréditaire d'Angoulême de Vougrim I a Audoin II," Mémoires de la Société Archéologique de la Charente, 1903–1904 (Angoulême, 1905).

**DEPOIN, J.1908a** = Depoin, Joseph: *La Legends des Première Bouchard de Montmorency* (Pontues, 1908).

**DEPOIN, J. 1908b** = Depoin, Joseph: "Thibaud le Tricheur," *Revue des Études Historique* (1908).

**DEPOIN, J. 1909a** = Depoin, Joseph: *Cartulaire de St. Martin de Pontevre* (Paris, 1909).

**DEPOIN, J.1909b** = Depoin, Joseph: "Études Préparatoires a l'Histoire de Familles Palatines Première Fascicule," *Revue des Études Historiques* (1909).

**DEPOIN, J.1912a** = Depoin, Joseph: *Recueil des Chartes et Documents de Saint-Martin-des-Champs,* 2 vols. (Paris, 1912–1913).

**DEPOIN, J. 1912b** = Depoin, Joseph: *Cartulaire de l'Abbaye de St. Martin de Pontvial* (Paris, 1912).

**DEPOIN, J. 1913** = Depoin, Joseph: *Recueil des Chartes de Abbaye de Lingue* (Paris, 1913).

**DEPOIN, J. 1915** = Depoin, Joseph: "Comtes de Paris sous la Dynastie Carolingienne," *Memoirs de la Société Historique et Archéologique de Pontoise et du Vexin,* vol. XXX (1915).

**DEPOIN, J. 1922** = Depoin, Joseph: "Les Grands Figures Monoceles du Temps Merovingiens," *Revue Mobillon,* vols. XI (1921) and XII (1922).

**DESAGE, M. 1907** = Desage M.: "Chronologie et Généalogie des Comtes d'Angoulême du Milieu du IXe a la Fin du XI Siècle," *Positions de Thèses de l'École de Chartes* (1907).

**DESROCHES, C 1979** = Desroches-Noblecourt, Christine: "Touy, Mere de Rameses II, la Reine Tanadjmy et les Reliques de l'Experience Amarnienne" in *L'Egyptogie en 1979*, II:227-244 (1979).

**DESROCHES, C. 1985** = Desroches-Noblecourt, Christine: *The Grand Pharaoh Ramses II and His Time* (Montreal, 1985).

**DEVIE, A. 1872** = Devie, A. and L. Vaissette: *Histoire Générale de Longuedoc*, vol. IV (Toulouse, 1872).

**DIDION, L. 1964** = Didion, Lucien: "Les Seigneurs de Fresnay," *La Province du Maine* (1974).

**DIE, 1929** = *Die Grafen von Ebersburg und die Ahnenden Grafen von Gortz* (Gratz, 1929).

**DIEDERICH, A. 1967** = Diederich, Anton: *Das Stift St. Florin zu Koblenz* (Gottingen, 1967).

**DILLON, M. 1967** = Dillon, Miles and Nora Chadwick: *The Celtic Realms* (1967).

**DNB, 1992** = Stephen, Leslie and Sidney Lee: *Dictionary of National Biography* (Oxford, Oxford University Press, 1992).

**DODSON, A. 1995** = Dodson, Aidan: *Monarchs of the Nile* (London, Rubicon Press, 1995).

**DOLLINGER, P. 1991** = Dollinger, Philippe, ed.: *Histoire de l'Alsace* (Toulouse, Privat, 1991).

**DOOGHE, D. 1985** = Dooghe, Didier-Georges: *Histoire Généalogique de la Francie* (Lille, 1985).

**DOPSCH, H. 1970** = Dopsch, Heinz: "Der Bayrische Adels und die Besetzung des Erzbistums Salzburg im 10 und 11 Jahrhundert," *Mitteilungen der Gesellschaft fur Salzburger Landeskunde*, vol. 110/111 (1970–1971).

**DOUGLAS, D. 1964** = Douglas, David C.: *William the Conqueror. The Norman Impact Upon England* (Berkeley and Los Angeles, CA, University of California Press, 1964), pp. x-xii, 3-476.

**DOUGLAS, D. 1944** = Douglas, David C.: *The Domesday Monachorum of Christ Church, Canterbury* (London, 1944).

**DOUGLAS, R. 1946** = Douglas, Robert: "The Earliest Norman Counts," *English Historical Review* (May, 1946), pp. 147, 148.

**DOUKAS, A. 1982** = Doukas (Ducas) Andronikos: *Praktikon*, trans. by M. J. Arnold (pub by the translator, 1982).

**DRIVER, G. 1956** = Driver, G. R.: *Caananite Myths and Legends* (Edinburgh, T. & T. Clark, 1956).

**DUCKWORTH, J. 1980** = Duckworth, John: *Muhammad and the Arab Empire* (1980).

**DUGDALE, W. 1675** = Dugdale, William: *Baronage of England*, 2 vols. (London, 1675–1676).

**DUGUET, J. 1981** = Duguet, Jacques: "Notes Sur quelque Vicomtes de Châtellerault," *Bulletin de la Société des Antiquiares de l'Ouest*, Series 4, XVI:261–270 (1981).

**DUNBAR, A. 1906** = Dunbar, Archibald H.: *Scottish Kings*, 2nd edition (Edinburgh, 1906).

**DUNCKER, M. 1882** = Dunker, Max: *History of Antiquity*, trans. by Evelyn Abbott, 2 vols. (London, 1877-1882) [microfilm].

**DUNGERN, O. von 1910** = Dungern, O. von: *Thronfolgerecht und Blutsverwandtschaft der Deutchen Kaiser, seit Karl dem Grossen*, 2nd edition (Gratz, 1910).

**DUNGERN, O. von 1931** = Dungern, O. von, editor: *Genealogishe Handbuch zur Bairisch- Oesterreichischen Geschichte* (Gratz, 1931).

**DUNGERN, O. von 1935** = Dungern, O. von: *Aus dem Brute Widukinds* (Gotha, 1935).

**DUNSTER, M. 1979** = Dunster, Mark: *Parthia* (1979).

**DUPARE, P. 1954** = Dupare, Pierre: *La Conde de Genevre, IXe au XVe Siècle* (Geneva, 1954). (Contains an extensive bibliography).

**DWORZACZEK, K. 1959** = Dworzaczek, Kazimierz: Genealogia (Warsaw, 195

## -E-

**EASTON, S. 1961** = Easton, Stewart C. and Helen Wieruszowski: *The Era of Charlemagne. Frankish State and Society* (Princeton, 1961).

**ECKHART, F. 1928** = Eckhart, F: "Introduction a l'Histoire Hongroise," *Bibliothèque d'État Hongroise*, vol. I (Paris, 1928).

**EDITORS, 1992** = Editors of Time-Life Books: *Egypt:Land of the Pharaohs* (Alexandria, VA, Time-Life Books, 1992)

**EGGENBERGER, D. 1985** = Eggenberger, David: *An Encyclopedia of Battles. Accounts of Over 1,560 Battles from 1479 B.C. to the Present* (New York, Dover, 1985).

**ELLIS, P. 1990** = Ellis, Peter Barresford: *The Celtic Empire* (London, 1990).

**ENC. ISLAM 1 , 1987** = *Encyclopedia of Islam*, original series, vols. 1-8; edited by C. E. Bosworth, et al (New York and Leiden, E. J. Brill, 1916-1938, reptd 1987).

**ENC. ISLAM 2, 1996** = *Encyclopedia of Islam*, revised series, vols. 1-7; edited by C. E. Bosworth, et al (New York and Leiden, E. J. Brill, 1960-1996).

**ENCY JUD 1971** = *Encyclopedia of Judaica* (New York, Macmillan, 1971).

**ENGLISH, B. 1991** = English, Barbara: *The Lords of Holderness, 1086-1260. A Study in Feudal Society* (Hull, Hull University Press, 1991).

**ERNST, S. 1837** = Ernst, S. P.: *Histoire de Limbourg* (Limbourg, 1837).

**ERRINGTON, R. 1990** = Errington, Robert Malcolm: *A History of Macedonia* (Hellinistic Culture and Society series, No. 5) (1990).

**ES** = Schwennicke, Detlev: *Europäische Stammtafeln*, new series (Marburg, Germany, 1978–1999). This monumental multi-volume effort supersedes the past work of Wilhelm Karl von Isenburg (See Isenburg, W. 1953). An ongoing series, it will eventually cover all of the major noble houses in Europe and many dynasties. Each page (10" x 14" ) contains one or more pedigree charts, called tables. Each volume has its own index by family name, authorities, and corrections, and several volumes have cumulative indexes. You can't seriously study European royalty without using this set.

250

**ESTOURNET, G. 1925** = Estournet, G: *Les Montmorency—Saint Denis* (Pontoise, 1925).

**ESTOURNET, G. 1926** = Estournet, G: "Origines des Seigneurs des Nemour," *Annales de la Société Historique et Archéologique de Gatinais*, vol. 30.

**EVANS, C. 1932** = Evans, Charles: "Descent from the Cid," *TAG*, 9:99–100 (Oct. 1932).

**EVANS, C. 1963** = Evans, Charles: "The Princess Zaida," *American Genealogist*, 39:157-160 (1963).

**EVANS, C. 1965** = Evans, Charles: "Dammartin," *Genealogists' Magazine*, 15:53–63 (June 1965).

**EVANS, C. 1976** = Evans, Charles: "The Hauteville Ancestry," *TAG*, 52:23–26 (Jan 1976).

**EVANS, C. 1981** = Evans, Charles: "Thibaud, le Tricheur, Count of Blois," *TAG*, 57:95–96 (Apr. 1981).

**EVANS, C. 1981b** = Letter in Coat of Arms, New Series, 4 (1981)

**EVANS, C. 1983** = Evans, Charles: "Correspondence. Dammartin," *Genealogists' Magazine*, 21:94 (Sept 1983).

## -F-

**FAGAT, H. 1980** = Fagat, Henri de, de Casteljau: "La Maison de Mello en Bourgogne, Une Revision a Partir des Archives de Chalon," *Annales de Bourgogne*, LII:4–42 (Dijon, 1980)

**FARRAR, C. 1946** = Farrar, Clarissa P. and A. P. Evans: *English Translations from Medieval Sources* (New York, Columbia University Press, 1946).

**FAUSSNER, H. 1981** = Faussner, H. C.: "Kuno von Ohningen und Seine Sippe" *Deutsches Archiv fur Erforschung des Middelalters*, 37 (1981).

**FEST, A. 1938** = Fest, Alexander: *The Sons of Edmund Ironside, Anglo-Saxon King at the Court of St. Stephen* (Budapest, 1938).

**FEUCHERE, P. 1953** = Feuchere, Pierre: "Les Origines des Comte de Saint-Pol," *Revue du Nord*, XXXV:125–149 (1953).

**FEUCHERE, P. 1957** = Feuchere, Pierre: "Registres des Comtes de Saint-Pol (1023–1205)," Part I for 1023–1145; *Revue du Nord*, XXXIX:43–48 (Lille, 1957).

**FEVRE, F. 1992** = Fevre, Francis: *Le Dernier Pharaon Ramses III on le Crepuscule d'Une Civilisation* (Paris, Presse de la France, 1992) [contains chronological tables, bibliography, glossary].

**FAWTIER, R. 1960** = Fawtier, Robert: *The Capetian Kings of France* (London, Macmillan, 1960).

**FICHTENAU, H. 1957** = Fichtenau, Heinrich: *The Carolingian Empire* (Oxford, 1957).

**FICKLER, C. 1859** = Fickler, C. A.: *Quellen und Forschungen* (Mannheim, 1859).

**FIENNES, D. 1980** = Fiennes, David: "Dammartin, Further Notes and Queries": *Genealogists' Magazine*, 21:190–191 (June 1980).

**FINE, J. 1983** = Fine, John A., Jr.: *Early Medieval Balkans* (1983).

**FIRTH, P. 1998** = Firth, Paul D.: Some Pictish High Kings (The author, 1998).

**FISHER, G. 1885** = Fisher, G. P.: *Outline of Universal History* (1885).

**FLETCHER, R. 1989** = Fletcher, Richard: *The Quest for El Cid* (New York, Alfred A. Knopf, 1989).

**FLETCHER, R. 1992** = Fletcher, Richard: *Moorish Spain* (Berkeley, University of California Press, 1992).

**FLORIVAL, R. 1907** = Florival, Roussem de "Les Comtes de Roucy," *Positions de Theses del Ecole des Chartes* (1907)

**FORNERY, J. 1982** = Fornery, Joseph: *Histoire du Comte Vanaissin et de la Ville d'Avignon*, vol. II (reptd Marsailles, 1982).

**FORTUNATUS, V. 1954** = Fortunatus, Vanantius: *Carmina*, Book VII, nos. 5, 6 (1954).

**FOUCHER, 1971** = Foucher of Chartres: *The First Crusade, The Chronicle of Foucher of Chartres*... edited by Edward Peters (Philadelphia, University of Pennsylvania Press, 1971).

**FOURNIAL, E. 1952** = Fournial, Étienne: "Recherches sur les Comtes de Lyon au IXe et Xe Siècles," *Le Moyen Age*, LVIII:221–249 (Brussels, 1952).

**FOURNIAL, E. 1956** = Fournival, Etienne: "La Souverainite du Lyonnaise au Xe Siecle," *Le Moyen Age*, LXII:413-452 (Brussels, 1956).

**FRAMOND, M. de 1993** = Framond, Martin de: "La Succession des Comtes de Toulouse, Autours de l'An Mil (940-1030: Reconsiderations," *Annales du Midi*, 105 (1993).

**FREDERICK, T. 1879** = Frederick, T.: *A Closer Look at the Ancestry of Hugues de Lusignan and His Immediate Descendents*, 6 vols. (London, 1868–1879).

**FREEMAN, E. 1879** = Freeman, Edward A.: *History of the Norman Conquest of England*, 6 vols. (London, 1868–1879).

**FREEMAN, E. 1901** = Freeman, Edward A.: *William Rufus* (London, 1901).

**FREEMAN, E. 1904** = Freeman, Edward A.: *History of the Norman Conquest. Western Europe in the Eighth Century and Onward*, 5 vols. and index vol. (London, 1867, 1904).

**FRIESE, A. 1979** = Friese, Alfred: *Studien zur Herrschaftsgesewichte des Frankischen Adels* (Stuttgart, 1979).

**FRYDE, E. 1986** = Fryde, E. B., D. E. Greenway, et al, editors: *Handbook of British Chronology* (London, Royal Historical Society, 1986).

**FRYE, R. 1984** = Frye, Richard N.: *History of Ancient Iran* (1984).

**FUMAGALLI, V. 1971** = Fumagalli, Vito: *Le Origini de Una Granda Dinastia Fendale, Alberto-Atto di Canossa* (1971

# -G-

**GARDINER, A. 1961** = Gardiner, Alan H.: *Egypt of the Pharaohs* (Oxford, 1961).

**GARDINER, S. 1899** = Gardiner, Samuel R.: *Student's History of England* (London, 1899). Contains genealogical tables.

**GARRIGUES, M. 1981** = Garrigues, Martine: *Le Premier Cartulaire de l'Abbaye Cistercienne de Pomtigny*, nos. 193, 342 (Paris, 1981).

**GARSOIAN, N. 1982** = Garsoian, Nina G.: *Syria and Armenia in the Formative Period* (1982).

**GARSOIAN, N. 1985** = Garsoian, Nina G.: *Armenia Between Byzantine and the Sasians* (London, Variorum Reprints, 1985).

**GARUFI, C. 1935** = Romualdi: "Salernitani Chronicon," ed. by C. A. Garufi, *Muratori Rerum Italiae*, new ed., vol. 7 (Belogna, 1935).

**GASTEBOIS, V. 1934** = Gastebois, Victor: *Les Comtes de Mortain, 995–1789* (Mortain, 1934).

**GAUTIER, P. 1971** = Gautier, Paul: "Le Synode de Blachernes (Fin, 1094)" *Revue de Études Byzantines*, XXIX (1971).

**GAY, J. 1904** = Gay, Julio: *L'Italie Maridionale et l'Empire Byzantine* (Paris, 1904).

**GAYANGOS, P. 1843** = Gayangos, Pascual de: *The History of Mohammedan Dynasties in Spain*, 2 vols. (London, 1843). A work in English translated from the Arabic.

**GAYANGOS, P. 1921** = Gayangos, Pascual de: *Dynasties in Spain* (reptd 1921). A work in English translated from the Arabic.

**GEANAKOPLOS, D. 1959** = Geanakoplos, D. J.: *Emperor Michael Palaeologus and the West, 1258–1282* (Cambridge, MA, 1959).

**GELDNER, F. 1971** = Geldner, Ferdinand: *Neue Beitrage zur Geschichte dur Alteren Babenberger* (Bamburg, 1971).

**GERARD, P. 1961** = Gerard, Pierre: *Cartulaire de St. Père de Chartres* (Paris, 1961).

**GERBERDING, R. 1987** = Gerberding, Richard: *The Rise of the Carolingians and the Liber Historiai Francorum* (Oxford, Clarendon Press, 1987).

**GHIRSHMAN, R. 1962** = Ghirshman, R.: *Iran, Parthians and Sassanians* (London, Thomas and Hudson, 1962).

**GIBB, H. 1992** = Gibb, H. A. R. et al, editors: *The Cambridge Encyclopaedia of Islam*, new edition (Leiden, Brill, and London, Luzac, International Union of Academics, 160-1992).

**GLASSE, C. 1989** = Glasse, Cyril: *The Concise Encyclopedia of Islam* (San Francisco, Harper & Row, 1989).

**GLICK, T. 1995** = Glick, Thomas F.: *From Muslim Fortress to Christian Castle* (1995).

**GLOCKEL, M. 1970** = Gockel, Michael: *Karoliner Konigshofe am Mittelrheim* (Gottingen, 1970).

**GODWIN, P. 1860** = Godwin, Parke: *History of France* (New York, Harper, 1860).

**GOFFART, W. 1988** = Goffart, Walter: *The Narrators of Barbarian History, AD 550-860* (Princeton, Princeton University Press, 1988).

**GOFFINET, H. 1935** = Goffinet, Hippolyte: "Les Comtes de Chiny," *Institut Archaeologique du Luxembourge*, 8:255–369; 9:7+ (Arlon, 1935).

**GOLDBLATT, D.** = Goldblatt, David: *The Monarchic Principal: Studies in Jewish Self-Government in Antiquity.* (Tubignen, J. C. B. Mohr, n.d.)

**GOODE, A. 1941** = Goode, Alexander D.: The Exilarchate in the Eastern Califate,

637-1258," *Jewish Quarterly Review*: 31:149-169 (1940-1941).

**GOODMAN, A. 1992** = Goodman, Anthony: *The Exercise of Princely Power in Fourteenth Century Europe* (1992).

**GRANDET, P. 1993** = Grandet, Pierre: *Ramses III. Histoire d'un Regne* (Paris, Pygmalion Gerard Watelet, 1993).

**GREGOIRE, H. 1932** = Gregoire, Henri: "L'Oraison Funedre de Basil I" Byzantion, 7:626-633 (1932).

**GREGORY OF TOURS, 1974** = Gregory of Tours: *The History of the Franks*, trans. by Lewis Thorpe (Harmondsworth, Penguin, 1974).

**GRENHAM, J. 1994** = Grenham, John: *Clans and Families of Ireland: The Heritage and Heraldry of Irish Clans and Families* (1994)

**GRIERSON, P. 1938** = Grierson, Philip: "Maison d'Everard de Frioul et les Origines du Comte de Flandre," *Revue de Moyen Age*, vol. 24 (1938).

**GRIERSON, P. 1939** = Grierson, Philip: "Origins des Comtes d'Amiens, Valois et Vexin," *Moyen Age*, 3rd series, vol. 10 (1939).

**GRIMAL, N. 1992** = Grimal, Nicholas: *A History of Ancient Egypt*, trans. by Ian Shaw (Oxford, UK, and Cambridge, MA, Blackwell, 1992)

**GRIMALDI, N. 1928** = Grimaldi, Natale: *La Contessa Matilde e la Sua Stirpe Fendale* (Rome, 1928).

**GROUSSET, R. 1984** = Grousset, R.: *Histoire de l'Armenie* (reptd. Paris, 1984).

**GUERARD, B.** = Guerard, B., translator: *Cartulaire de Saint-Père de Chartres*, vol. I. (Original records on microfilm.)

**GUERNEY, G. 1982** = Guerney, Gene: *Kingdoms of Europe*, an *Illustrated Encyclopedia of Ruling Monarchs from Ancient Times to the Present* (New York, 1982).

**GUERNEY, G 1986** = Guerney, Gene: *Kingdoms of Asia and Middle East and Africa...* (New York, Crown Publishers, 1986).

**GUERNEY, O. 199**1 = Guerney, Oliver Robert: *The Hittites* (1991).

**GUILLAUME, J. 1757** = Guillaume, J. B.: *Histoire Généalogique des Sires de Sabins* (Besancon, 1757).

**GUILLOT, O. 1972** = Guillot, Oliver: *Le Comte d'Anjou et son Entourage au XIe Siècle*, vol. II (Paris, 1972).

## -H-

**HALL, H. 1960 = Hall, H. R.**: *Ancient History of the Near East...*(London, Methuen, 1913; reptd 1960).

**HALPHEN, L. 1906** = Halphen, Louis: *Compte d'Anjou au XIe Siècle* (Anjou, 1906).

**HALPHEN, L. 1919** = Halphen, Louis, and R. Poupardin: *Chronique des Comtes d'Anjou* (Paris, 1913, 1919).

**HAMILTON, J. 1988** = Hamilton, J. S.: *Piers Gaveston, Earl of Cornwall 1307-1312. Politics and Patronage in the Reign of Edward II* (Wayne State University Press, 1988).

**HAMMOND, N. 1978** = Hammond, Nicholas G. L.: *A History of Macedonia, 550-336 B.C.*, 2 vols (1978).

**HAMMOND, N. 1981** = Hammond, Nicholas G. L.: *History of Macedonai* (1981).

**HAMMOND, N. 1988** = Hammond, Nicholas G. L.: and F. W. Walbank: *A History of Macedonia, 336-167 B. C.* (1988).

**HAMMOND, N. 1989** = Hammond, Nicholas G. L.: *The Macedonian State* (Oxford, 1989).

**HANAWELT, E. 1982** = Hanawelt, E.: "An Annotated Bibliography of Byzantine Sources in English Translation," *Byzantine Studies/Etudes Byzantines*, 9:1:68-87 (1982)

**HANSEN, E. 1971** = Hansen, E. V.: *The Attalids of Pergammun*, 2nd edition (Ithaca, 1971).

**HARRIES, J. 1994** = Harries, Jill: *Sidonius Apollinaris and the Fall of Rome AD 407-485* (Oxford, Clarendon Press, 1994).

**HARRIS, J. 1971** = Harris, J. R.: *The Legacy of Egypt*, 2nd edition (London, 1971).

**HART, G. 1990** = Hart, George: *Ancient Egypt* (New York, Alfred A. Knopf, 1990)

**HARTWELL, R. 1975** = Hartwell, Rodney: "Brythonic & Cymric Celts," (Long Beach CA, *English Genealogist*, no. 1, 1975). Extensively documented.

**HARTWELL, R. 1991** = Hartwell, Rodney: "Review" *Journal of Ancient and Medieval Studies*, vol. X (Torrance, CA Octavian Society, 1991), pp. 31, 32.

**HAYWARD, F. 1941** = Hayward, Ferdinand: *Histoire de la Maison de Savoie, 1000–1553*, vol. I (Paris, 1941).

**HAZARD, H. 1951** = Hazard, Harry W.: *Atlas of Islamic History* (Princeton, Oriental Studies, XII (Princeton, Princeton University Press, 1951).

**HECK, H. 1955** = Heck, Hermann: "Altleiningischer Besitz im Lahngebiet und Dessen Erben," *Nassauische Annalen*, vol. 66 (1955).

**HEINEMANN, O. 1865** = Heinemann, Otto von: "Zu Genealogie und Gerschichte der Billungischen Herzoghauses," *Ztschr. Historisch Verein Niedersachsen* (Geneva, 1865).

**HEINRICH, G. 1872** = Heinrich, G: *Gerchichte der Grafen von Rotig-Rottersburg und Moorburg...* (1872).

**HELDON, J. 1990** = Heldon, J. A.: *Byzantium in the Seventh Century...* (Cambridge, Cambridge University Press, 1990).

**HENDERSON, I. 1967** = Henserson, Isabel: *The Picts* (Thames & Hudson, 1967).

**HERTEL, J. 1980** = Hertel, J.: *Imiennictwo Dynastii Piastowskiej we Wczesniejszym Sredniowieczu* (Warsaw, 1980).

**HIESTAND, R. 1979** = Hiestand, R.: "Chronologisches zur Geschichte des Konigreiches Jerusalem im 12 Jahrhundert," *Deutsches Archiv fur Erforschung des Mittelalters*, 35 Jahrbuch (1979).

**HIGOUNET, C.** = Higounet, Charles: "Les Aznan, une Tentative Groupement de Comptes Garçons et Pyreneena au IXe Siècle," *Annales du Midi*, vol. 61.

**HISTOIRE, 1622** = *Histoire d' Harcourt* (Paris, 1622).

**HISTORICH, 1934** = *Historich-Biographisches Lexikon der Schweig*, 8 vols. (Neuenburg, 1921–1934).

**HITTI, P. 1970** = Hitti, Philip Khuri: *History of the Arabs*, 10th edition (New York, St. Martin's Press, 1970).

**HLAWITSCHKA, E. 1960** = Hlawitschka, Eduard; "Franken, Allemanen, Bayern und Burgunder," *Oberitaien* (Lothringen, 1960).

**HLAWITSCHKA, E. 1969** = Hlawitschka, Eduard: *Die Aufange des Hauses Habsburg-Lothringen* (Lothringen, 1969).

**HLAWITSCHKA, E. 1987** = Hlawitschka, Eduard: *Untersuchungen zu den Thronwechseln der Ersten Halfte des 11 Jahrhunderts...*(Sigmeringen, 1987).

**HOBSON, C. 1987** = Hobson, Christine: *The World of the Pharaohs* (New York, Thames & Hudson, 1987).

**HODGES, J. 1854** = Hodges, John O., translator: *Analia Rioghacta Eireann* (Annals of the Kingdom of Ireland by the Four Masters (commonly called "annals of the Four Masters," (Dublin, 1854).

**HODGKIN, R. 1952**= Hodgkin, R. H.: *History of the Anglo-Saxons*, 2 vols. (Oxford, 1935; third edition, London, 1952).

**HOFFMAN, W. 1950** = Hoffman, W. J.: "The Counts of Gelre and Zutphen," *NEHGR*, 104:206–211 (July 1950).

**HOFMEISTER, A 1920** = Hofmeister, A.: "Die Ahnentafeln der Markgrafen von Brandenburg, E. 1935...," *Forschung zu Brandenburg, E. 1935 und Preuss Geschichte*, vol. 33 (1920).

**HOGARTH, D. 1926** = Hogarth, D. G.: *Kings of the Hittites, Lectures on Bible Archeology* (1926).

**HOGARTH, D. 1950** = Hogarth, D. G.: *The Ancient Near East* (London, 1950).

**HOLSTEIN, L. 1874** = Holstein, L.: "Beitrage zur Genealogie des Dynasten von Tuerfurt," *Ztshr. Harz-Vereins*, 5 and 7 (1872–1874).

**HOLT, P. 1986** = Holt, P. M.: *The Age of the Crusades. The Near East From the Eleventh Century to 1517* (Longmans, 1986).

**HOPPSTADTER, K. 1977** = Hoppstadter, K.: "Die Grafschaft Saarbrucken," *Geschichtliche Landeskunde des Saarlandes*, vol. II (1977).

**HOURANI, A. 1991** = Hourani, Albert Habib: *A History of the Arab Peoples* (Cambridge, MA, Belknap Press of Harvard University, 1991).

**HOUTH, E. 1963** = Houth, Emile: Catalogue des Actes de Robert II de Meulan," *Bulletin Philogique et Historique du Comite des Travaux Historiques et Scientifiques Année 1961* (Paris, 1963).

**HOUTH, E. 1981** = Houth, Emile: *Les Comtes de Meulan* (Paris, 1981).

**HOVANNISIAN, R. 1997** = Hovannisian, Richard G., Editor: *The Armenian People from Ancient to Modern Times...*, 2 vols. (1997).

**HOWARTH, H. 1920** = Howarth, Henry H.: "Harold Fairhair and His Ancestors," *Saga Book*, Viking Society, vol. 9 (London, 1920).

**HOYT, R. 1967** = Holt, R. S. and P. H. Sawyer: *International Medieval Bibliography* (Leeds and Minneapolis, 1967-date).

**HUBERT, H. 1992** = Hubert, Henri: *History of the Celtic People* (Brachen Books, 1992).

**HUNT, C. 1972** = Hunt, Clement: *Ancient Persia and Iranian Civilization* (1972).

**HUSSEY, J. 1961** = Hussey, Joan Mervyn: *The Byzantine World* (New York, Harper & Row, 1961).

# -I-

**IMBERT, M. 1865** = Imbert, M. Hugues: "Notes sur Vicomtes de Poitou," *Memoirs de la Société des Antiquaires de l'Ouest*, vol. XXIX, 1864 (Poitiers, 1865).

**IMBERT, M. 1866** = Imbert, M. Hugues: "Notice sur les Vicomtes de Thouars," *Mémoires de la Société des Antiquaires de l'Ouest*, XXX:321–429, 1865 (Poitiers, 1866).

**IRVING, E. 1973** = Irving, Edward James Bruges: "A Scot Descent from Charlemagne: Four Interconnecting Charts," *Forebears*, XVI:50–52 (Winter 1973).

**ISENBURG, W. 1932** = Isenburg, Prince Wilhelm Karl von: *Die Ahnen der Deutschen Kaiser, Konige, und Ihrer Gemahlinnen* (Gorlitz, 1932).

**ISENBURG, W. 1953** = Isenburg, Prince Wilhelm Karl von: *Stammtafeln zur Geschichte der Europäischen Staaten*, 2 vols. (Berlin, 1936/37; Marburg, 1953). If no edition is indicated, the 1953 edition is presumed.

# -J-

**JACKMAN, D. 1990** = Jackman, Donald C.: *The Konradiner, a Study in Genealogical Methodology* (Frankfurt am Main, 1990).

**JACKMAN, D. 1997** = Jackman, Donald C.: *Criticism and Critique: Sidelights on the Konradiner* (Oxford, Unit for Prosopographical Research, 1997.)

**JACKSON, G. 1972** = Jackson, Gabriel: *The Making of Medieval Spain* (New York, 1971).

**JACOBS, C. 1969** = Jacobs, Charles J.: "A Suggested Moslem Descent for Eleanor of Provence and Eleanor of Castile," *Augustan*, XII:217-223 (July-August 1969).

**JACOBUS, D. 1932** = Jacobus, Donald Lines: "The House of Rurick," *TAG*, IX:13–15 (July 1932).

**JACOBUS, D. 1933** = Jacobus, Donald Lines, "Queries and Answers, no. 31," *TAG*, X:262–263 (April 1933).

**JAKSCH, N. VON 1928** = von Jaksch, Dr. N.: *Geschichte Karntene* (Klagenfurt, 1928/29).

**JAMES, E. 1980** = James, Edward: *Visagothic Spain*. New Approaches (Oxford, Clarendon Press, 1980.)

**JAMES, E. 1985** = James , Edward: *The Origin of France:From Clovis to the Capetians, 500-1000* (Berkelet, University of California Press, 1985).

**JAMES, E. 1988** = James, Edward: *The Franks* (New York, Basil Blackwell, 1988).

**JAMES, T. 1988** = James, T. G. H.: *Ancient Egypt: The Land and Its Legacy* (London, British Museum Publications, 1988).

**JARNUT, J. 1986** = Jarnet, Jorg: *Agilolfingerstudien: Untersuchunden zur Geschichte Einen Adlingen Familie im 6 und 7 Jahrhundert* (Stuttgart, Anton Hiersemann, 1986).

**JASINSKI, K. 1977** = Jasinski, Kazimierz: *Redworod Piastow Slaskich*, 3 vols. (Breslaw, 1973–1977).

**JAYYUSI, S. 1992** = Jayyusi, Selma Khadra: *Legacy of Muslim Spain* (Brill, 1992).

**JEFFREY, J. 1980** = Jeffrey, John: *The Unholy Crusade* (Oxford and New York, Oxford University Press, 1980).

**JERITSCH, G. 1894** = Jeritsch, Georg: *Geschichte des Babenberger und Ihrer Landen* (Innesbruk, 1894).

**JESSEE, W. 1990** = Jessee, W. Scott: "A Missing Capetian Princess:Advisa, Daughter of King Robert II of France," *Medieval Prosopography* 11/2 (1990)

**JEWISH ENC 1901** = *Jewish Encyclopedia* (New York and London, Funk and Wagnalls, 1901).

**JOHNSON, H. 1969** = Johnson, Hilda: "Le Comte de Ponthieu, 1279–1307," *Le Ponthieu et la Dynastie Anglaise au XIIIe Siècle...* (Abbeville, Somme, France, 1969).

**JOHNSON, M. 1969** = Johnson, Marshall D.: *The Purpose of the Biblical Genealogies With Special Reference to the Setting of the Genealogies for Jesus* (Cambridge, Cambridge University Press, 1969).

**JONES, A. 1910** = Jones, Arthur: *History of Gruffydd ap Conan* (Cardiff, 1910).

**JONES, A. 1971** = Jones, Arthur, et al: *The Prosopogrephy of the Later Roman Empire*, Vol. I (Cambridge, Cambridge University Press, 1971).

**JONES, G. 1968** = Jones, Gwyn: *A History of the Vikings* (Oxford University Press, 1968).

**JONES, H.** = Jones, H. L. translator: *The Geography of Strabo* (Loeb Classical Library, XI:xiv.5)

**JORDAN, D 1979** = Jordan, David Starr and Sarah Louise Kimball: *Your Family Tree* (reptd Baltimore, MD, Genealogical Publishing Co., 1979) Use with caution. Not well documented.

**JORI, I 1942** = Jori, Ilio: *Genealogia Sabauda* (Bologne, 1942).

**JUBAINVILLE, M. 1869** = Jubainville, M.H. Arbois de: *Histoire des Ducs et des Comtes de Champagne*, 2 vols. (Paris, 1859–1869).

## -K-

**KATHEER, I** = Katheer, Ibu: *al-Bidaya wan Nehaya* (n.d.)

**KAEGI, W 1992** = Kaegi, W. E.: *Byzantium and the Early Islamic Conquests* (Cambridge, Canbridge University Press, 1992).

**KARTBL, R. 1979** = Kartbl, Raimund: *Byzantinische Prinzessinnen Ungarn Zwischen, 1050–1200* (Vienna, 1979).

**KAUL, T. 1970** = Kaul, Theodor: "Das Verhaltnis de Grafen von Leiningen zum Reich," *Mitteilungen des Historischen Vereins der Pfalz*, LXVIII:222–292 (1970).

**KEATS-ROHAN, K. 1997** = Keats-Rohan, K. S. B., editor: *Family Trees and the Roots of Politics* (Woodbridge, Suffolk, 1997)

**KEATS-ROHAN, K. 1997a** = Keats-Rohan, K. S. B.: "On Vassal sans Histoire? Count Hugh II (c. 940/955-992) and the Origins of the Angevin Overlordship in Maine" *Family Trees and the Roots of Politics* (Woodbridge, Suffolk, 1997).

**KEATS-ROHAN, K. 1997b** = Keats-Rohan, K. S. B.:"Poppa of Bayeux and Her Family," *The American Genealogist*, 72 (1997).

**KELLER, J. 1984** = Keller, John Esten: *Alfonso X, el Sabio* (Lexington, KY, 1984).

**KELLEY, D. 1947** = Kelley, David H.: "Genealogical Research in England, a New Consideration Of the Carolingians," *NEHGR*, 101:108–112 (Apr 1947).

**KELLEY, D. 1982** = Kelley, David H.: and Robert C. Anderson: "Holy Blood, Holy Grail:Two Reviews" *Genealogist*, 3:249-258.

**KELLEY, D. 1989** = Kelley, David H.: "The House of Aethelred," *Studies in Genealogy and Family History in Tribute to Charles Evans,* editrd by L. L. Brook (Salt Lake City, UT, Occassional Publication, no. 2, Association for the Promotion of Scholarsdhip in Genealogy, Ltd., 1989), pp. 63–93.

**KELLEY, D. 1995** = Kelley, David H.: "A Priestly Family of Memphis," *Journal of Ancient and Medieval Studies*, XII (Torrance, CA., Octovan Society, 1995.).

**KEMP, B. 1989** = Kemp, Barry J.: *Ancient Egypt* (New York, Routledge, Chapman and Hall, 1989)

**KIMPEN, E. 1933** = Kimpen, E.: *Ezonen und Hezeliniden in der Rheinischen Pfalzgrafschaft...* (Innesbruk, 1880, reptd 1933).

**KING, P. 1972** = King, P. D.: *Law and Society in the Visagothic Kingdom* (Cambridge, 1972).

**KIRBY, L. 1962** = Kirby, L. F.: "Strathclyde and Cambria," *Transactions of the Cumberland and Westmorland Antiquarian and Archeological Society*, new series, vol. XLII (1962).

**KITCHEN, K. 1982** = Kitchen, Kenneth A.: *Pharaoh Triumphant: The Life and Times of Ramesses II King of Egypt* (Westminster, 1982).

**KITCHEN, K. 1986** = Kitchen, Kenneth A.: *The Third Intermediate Period in Egypt (1100-650 BC)* (Westminster, 1986).

**KNAPP, E. 1910** = Knapp, E.: *Die Alteste Buckhorner Urkund* (Wurttemburg, 1910).

**KNETSCH, C. 1931** = Knetsch, Carl: *Das Haus Brabant* (Marburg, 1931). He was Director of State Archives at Marburg, Germany.

**KOCH, A. 1970** = Koch, A. C. F.: *Oorkondenboek van Holland und Seeland tot 1299*, vol. I (1970).

**KOTZSCHKE, R. 1929** = Kotzschke, R.: "Die Aufange der Markgrafschaft Meissen," *Meissen-Sachs Forscher*, ed. by W. Lippert (Dresden, 1929).

**KREBEL, E. 1880** = Krebel, E.: *Die Grafen von Sulzbach...* (Innesbruk, 1880).

**KREY, A.** = Krey, A. C. : *The First Crusade. The Accounts of Eye Witnesses and Partisipants* (n.d.).

**KRONE, F. VON 1897** = Krone, Franz von: "Die Markgrafen von Steier," *Archivalien fur Oestereische Geschichte*, vol. 84/85 (Vienna, 1897).

**KRONE, F. VON 1902** = Krone, Franz von: *Osterreichische Geschichte*, 2nd edition, 2 vols. (Leipsic, 1902).

**KRUGER, E. 1899** = Kruger, Emil: *Der Ursprung der Welfenhauses und Seine Verzmeigunden in Suddeutchland* (Wolfenbutt, 1899).

259

# -L-

**LABARGE, M. 1962** = Labarge, Margaret Wade: *Simon de Montfort* (London, 1962).

**LACARRA, J. 1945** = Lacarra, José M.: *Estudios de Edad Media de la Corona de Aragon* (Zaragosa, 1945).

**LAINE, P LA 1928** = Laine, P. la: *Archives Généalogiques* (1928).

**LAMONTE, J. 1940/41** = Lamonte, John L.: "The Significance of the Crusaders' States in Medieval History" *Byzantium*, vol. 18 (1940/41).

**LANE, S. 1964** = Lane-Poole, Stanley: *Saladin and the Fall of the Kingdom of Jerusalem* (Beirut, Khayats, 1964). [reprint].

**LANE, S. 1978** = Lane-Poole, Stanley: *Saladin and the Fall of the Kingdom of Jerusalem* (1978).

**LANGE, K. 1969** = Lange, Karl Heinz: *Der Herrschaftsbereich der Grafen von Northeim, 950 bis 1144* (Gottingen, 1969).

**LANGER, W. 1948** = Langer, William L.: *An Encyclopedia of World History* (Boston, Houghton Mifflin, 1948) (contains dozens of genealogical charts.)

**LASCO, P. 1971** = Lasco, P.: *The Kingdom of the Franks: North-West Europe Before Charlemagne* (London, 1971).

**LASTEYER, R. de 1874** = Lasteyer, R. de: *Étude sur les Comtes et Vicomtes de Limoges* (Paris, 1874).

**LATOUCHE, R. 1959a** = Latouche, Robert: "Les Premières Comtes Héréditaires du Maine," *Revue Historique et Archéologique du Maine*, 2nd Series, vol. XXXIX (Lemans, 1959).

**LATOUCHE, R. 1959b** = Latouche, Robert: "Histoire du Comte de Maine Pendant le Xe et le XIe Siècle," *Bibliothèque de l'École des Hautes Études*, vol. 183 (Paris, 1910).

**LATOUR, P. de 1997** = Latour, Patrick de: "A Propos de la Comtesse Garsinde, Nouvelles Propositions pour l'Histoire de la Dynastie Toulousane au Xe Siecle," *Annales du Midi*, 109 (1997)

**LATRIE, M. 1889** = Latrie, Mas: *Tresor de Chronologie, d'Histoire, et de Géographie* (Paris, 1889).

**LAURENT, J. 1911** = Laurent, Jacques: *Cartulaire de l'Abbaye de Molesne*, 2 vols. (Paris, 1911).

**LEBLOND, V. 1910** = Leblond, V.: *Notes Pour le Nobiliaire de Beauvaisis*, vol. I (Paris, 1910).

**LEE, M. 1995** = Lee, M and M. Kelley, editors: *Larousse Pocked Guide to Kings and Queens of Great Britain and Europe* (Larousse, 1995).

**LEIB, B. 1950** = Leib, B.: "Jean Doukas, César et Moine, son Jeu Politique a Byzance de 1067 a 1081," *Analecta Ballandina*, 68:163–180 (1950).

**LEUT, R. 1954** = Leut, Robert: "Die Herrschaft Limburg und ihr Ubergang von der Konradinern Uber die Hausen Gleiberg-Luxemburg, Peilstein und Leiningen an Isenburg," *Nassauische Annalen 65* (1954).

**LEVI, E. 1934** = Levi Provencal, E. "Hispano-Aribica: la "Mora Zaida," Femme d' Alfonse VI de Castille et Leur Fils l'Infant D. Sancho," *Hesparis Archives*

*Berberes et Bulletin de l'Institute des Hautes-Etudes Merocaines,* 18: 1-8, 200 (1934)

**LEVILLAIN, L. 1934** = Levillain, Leon: "Ademer de Chabannes, Généalogiste," *Bulletin de la Société des Antiquaires de l'Ouest,* Series 3, 10:237–263 (Poitiers, 1934).

**LEVILLAIN, L. 1937** = Levillain, Leon: "Les Nibelungen Historiques," *Annals du Midivale,* vols. 49, 50 (1937/1938).

**LEWIS, A. 1967** = Lewis, Archibald R.: *Emerging Medieval Europe, A.D. 400-1000* (New York, Knopf, 1967).

**LEWIS, A. 1981** = Lewis, Archibald R.: *Royal Succession in Capatian France* (Cambridge, MA and London, 1981)

**LEWIS, A. 1988** = Lewis, Archibald R.: *Nomads and Crusaders, A.D.* 1000-1368 (Bloomington, University of Indiana, 1988)

**LEX, L 1894** = Lex, L: "Études, Comte de Blois," *Mémoires de la Société Académique de l'Aube,* no. 37 (1894).

**LIEVRE, A. 1885** = Lievre, A. F.: *Angoulême* (1885).

**LIVERMORE, H. 1971** = Livermore, Harold V.: *The Origins of Spain and Portugal* (London, Allen & Unwin, 1971).

**LIZARRA, A. de 1945** = Lizarra, A. de: *Los Vascos y as Cruzades* (Buenos Aires, 1945).

**LLOYD, J. 1954** = Lloyd, John E.: *A History of Wales from the Earliest Times to the Edwardian Conquest* (Cardiff, 1954).

**LOMAX, D. 1978** = Lomax, Derek W.: *The Reconquest of Spain* (London, Longmans, 1978).

**LONGNON, J. 1978** = Longnon, Jean: *Les Compagnons de Villehardouin* (Geneva, 1978).

**LOT, F. 1891** = Lot, Ferdinand: *Les Derniers Carolinens, Lothaire, Louis V, Charles de Lorraine* (954-991), Appendix IX, pp. 358-369.

**LOT, F. 1903** = Lot, Ferdinand: "Études sur le Règne de Hughes Capet et la Fin du Xe Siècle", *Bibliothèque de l'École de Hautes Études* (Paris, 1903).

**LOT, F. 1908** = Lot, Ferdinand: *Hugues Capet* (Paris, 1908).

**LOURIE, E. 1990** = Lourie, Elena: *Crusade and Colonisation: Moslems, Christians and Jews in Medieval Aragon* (Variorum, 1990).

**LOYD, L. 1933** = Loyd, Lewis: "Origin of the Family of Warenne," *Yorkshire Archaeological Journal,* XXXI:97–113 (1933).

**LUCKENBILL, D. 1926** = Luckenbill, D. D.: *Ancient Records of Assyria andBabylon, I: Historical Records of Assyria* (Chicago, 1926).

## -M-

**MAC DONALD, F. 1993** = Mac Donald, Fiona: *Ancient Egyptian Insights* (1993).

**MAC FINBIS, G. 1416** = Mac Finbis, Gilla-Isa: *Book of Lecain* (or Lacan), [A 1416 ms. in the library of the Royal Irish Academy, Dublin.] (Available on microfilm.)

**MAC KAY, A. 1977** = Mac Kay, A*ngus: Spain in the Middle Ages:From Frontier to Empire, 1000-1500* (New York, St. Martin's Press, 1977).

**MAC KENSIE, A. 1937** = Mac Kensie, Agnes Mure: *The Foundations of Scotland* (Oliver & Boyd, 1937).

**MAC KENZIE, D. 1930** = Mac Kenzie, David: *Scotland the Ancient Kingdom* (Glasgow, 1930).

**MAC LYSAGHT, E. 1985** = Mac Lysaght, Edward: *Irish Families: Their Names, Arms and Origins* (1985).

**MAC QUEEN, J. (1996)** = Mac Queen: J. G.: *The Hittites and Their Contemporaries in Asia Minor* (1996).

**MACLER, F. 1905** = Macler, Frederick: "Pseudo-Sebeos, Texte Armenien Tradoit en Annote" Journal Asiatique, 10th series, table VI (July-August, 1905), pp. 121-155.

**MAGNUSSON, H. 1905** = Magnusson, H., editor: *Heimskrimgla*, 4 vols. (London, 1905).

**MALAN, R. 1997** = Malan, Ronald F.: "The Ancestry of Dhouda, Duchess of Septimania," *The Genealogist*, vol. 11 (Rockport, Maine, USA, 1997)

**MALMESBURY, W. 1911** = Malmesbury, William of: *Chronicle of the Kings of England From the Earliest Period to the Reign of King Stephen*, ed. by J. A. Giles (1911). The 1904 edition, edited by J. A. Giles, is called *Historia Anglorum.*

**MAMIKONIAN, J. 1869** = Mamikonian, Jean: "Histoire du Taron" in *Collectios des Historiens Anciens et Modernes le l'Armenie*, trans. by Victor Langlois (Paris, 1869) Microfilm.

**MANGO, C. 1973** = Mango, Cyril: *Eudocia Ingerina, the Normans and the Macedonian Dynasty* (Zbornik Radova Vizantoloskog Instituta, 1973).

**MANTEYER, G. de 1901** = Manteyer, Georges de: Ibid., Notes and additions, *Moyen Age*, 2nd Series, vol. 5 (Paris, 1901).

**MANTEYER, G. de 1904** = Manteyer, Georges de: *Origins de la Maison de Savoie* (Grenoble, 1904).

**MANTEYER, G. de 1907** = Manteyer, Georges de: *Provence du Première au Vingtième Siècle* (Paris, 1907).

**MANTEYER, G. de 1908** = Manteyer, Georges de: *Provence au Douzième Siècle* (Paris, 1908).

**MANTAYER, G. de 1925** = Mantayer, Georges de: Manasses, Comte de Chaunois et Garnier, Comte de Troies," *Bulletin de la Etudes Historiques, Scientifiques, et Litteraires des Hautes-Aples*, 5th series (1925).

**MARBY, J. 1989** = Marby, John E.: *Dynasties of the World, a Chronological and Genealogical Handbook* (Oxford, Oxford University Press, 1989).

**MARCHEGAY, P. 1871** = Marchegay, Paul A.: *Chronique de Comtes d'Anjou* (Paris, 1856–1871).

**MAROT, P. 1984** = Marot, Pierre and Jean-Loup Lamaitrie: *Les Documents Necrologiques de l'Abbaye de Saint-Pierre de Solignac* (Paris, 1984).

**MARQUINA, J. 1971** = Marquina, Javier Rodriguez: "La Familis de la Madre de Sancho el Mayor," *Revista de Archivor Leonesese*, 94:143-150 (1971).

**MARSTON, E. 1996** = Marston, Elsa: *The Ancient Egyptians. Cultures of the Past* (1996).

**MARTIN, G. 1975** = Martin, Georges: *Histoire de Genealogie de la Maison de la Rochefoucould* (1975)

**MARTINDALE, J. 1967** = Martindale, J. R.: "Note on the Consuls of 381 and 382" *Historia*, 16:254-256, 1967.

**MARTINDALE, J. 1980** = Martindale, J. R.: *The Prosopography of the Later Roman Empire*, Vol. II (Cambridge, Cambridge University Press, 1980).

**MARTINDALE, J. 1992** = Martindale, Jane R.: "Eleanor of Aquitaine" in *Richard Coeur de Leon in History and Myth* (London, Kings College London Center for Late Antique and Medieval Studies, 1992.)

**MARVAUD, F. 1873** = Marvaud, F.: *Histoire des Vicomtes et la Vicomtes de Limoges*, vol. I (Paris, 1873).

**MATEOS, R. 1984** = Mateos, Ricardo, y Sainz de Madrano (Barcelona, 1984). A ms in the possession of J. A. Stargardt, Marburg, Germany.

**MAYER, H. 1984** = Mayer, Hans Eberhard: "Études sur l'Histoire de Baudouin Ier Roi de Jerusalem," *Mélanges sur l'Historie du Royaume Latin de Jerusalem* (Paris, 1984).

**MAYER, H. 1988** = Mayer, Hans Eberhard: "Die Legitimat Balduins IV von Jerusalem und das Testament der Agnes von Courtenay," *Historisches Jahrbuck* 108: 63–89 (Freiburg, 1988).

**MAYER, H. 1994** = Mayer, Haus Eberhard: *Kings and Lords in the Latin Kingdom of Jerusalem* (Collected Studies, No. 437) (1978)

**MC KITTERICK, R. 1983** = Mc Kitterick, R.: *The Frankish Kingdom Under the Carolingians, 751-987* (Longmans, 1983).

**MENENDEZ, R. 1931** = Menendez Pidal, Ramon: *Imperio Hispanico* (Barcelona, 1931).

**MENENDEZ, R. 1947** = Menendez Pidal, Ramon: "La Mora Zaida" *La Espana del Cid*, 9th edition, vol. 2 (1947), pp.760-764.

**MENENDEZ, R. 1969** = Menendez Pidal, Ramon: *España del Cid*, 2 vols. (Barcelona, 1929; reptd. Madrid,1969).

**MENENDEZ, R. 1971** = Menendez Pidal, Ramon: *The Cid and His Spain*, trans. by Harold Sunderland (London, F. Cass, 1971).

**MERZ, W. 1914** = Merz, W. (editor): *Die Burgen der Sisgaus* (Aargau, 1909/ 1914).

**MERZ, W. 1930** = Merz, W. and F. Helgi, editors: *Die Weppenrolle von Zurich* (Zurich, 1930).

**MESMAY, J. de 1963** = de Mesmay, Jean-Triburse: *Dictionnaire Historique, Biographique, et Généalogique des Anciennes Familles de Franche-Comte* (1958–1963).

**METZ, W. 1958** = Metz, Wolfgang: "Babenburger und Rupertiner in Ostfranken," *Jahrbuck fur Frankische Landesforschung*, 18:295–304 (1958)..

**MEYER, T. 1933** = Meyer, T.: "Zur Genealogie der Grafen von Formbach," *Familiengeschichte*, folio 31 (1933).

**MEYER, T. 1935** = Meyer, T.: *Ibid* with additions by K. Trotter, folio 33 (1935).

**MILLER, E. 1990** = Miller, Edmund: "The Names of Queens: With Particular Reference to the Matrimonial Entanglements of Alfonso VI of Castile," *Augustan Society Omnibus,* Book 12 (Torrance, CA, the Society, 1990), pp. 10-16.

**MINGUEZ, F. 1945** = Minguez, Fernandezo: Diplomatica de Sahagun" *Jose Maria Coleccion* (Leon, 1945).

**MIROT, L. 1945** = Mirot, Leon: "Les Origines des Premiers Comtes Héréditaires de Nevers," *Annales de Bourgogne,* XVII:7–15 (1945).

**MOLLER, A. 1936** = Moller, A.: "Die Genealogischen Zusatze," *Chronik der Albericus* (Karlsruke, 1936).

**MOLLER, W. 1933** = Moller, W.: *Stammtafeln Westdeutscher Adels Geschichter im Mittelalter,* II: table XLVIII (Darmstadt, 1933).

**MOLLER, W. 1950** = Moller, W.: *Stammtafeln Westdeutscher Adels Geschichter im Mittelalter* (Darmstadt, 1922–1926; reptd 1950).

**MOLTMANN, T. 1878** = Moltmann, T.: *Thesis at Gottingen* (Schweren, 1878).

**MONCREIFFE, I. 1982** = Moncreiffe, Iain: *Royal Highness. Ancestry of a Royal Child* (William of Wales) (London, Hamish Hamilton, 1982).

**MONTAGUE, P. 1986** = Montague-Smith, Patrick W.: The Royal Line of Succession- *The British Monarchy from Cerdic AD 534 to Queen Elizabeth II)* (Pitkin Pictorials, 1986).

**MONTGOMERY, G. de 1948** = Montgomery, Gabriel de: *Origin and History of the Montgomeries* (Edinburgh, 1948).

**MOODY, A. 1984** = Moody, A., et al, editors: *A New History of Ireland,* vol. IX: Maps, Genealogies, Lists (Oxford, Oxford university Press, 1984).

**MOOR, C. 1933** = Moor, C.: *Knights of Edward I,* 5 vols. (London, Harleian Society, vols. 80–84, 1923–1933).

**MORANVILLE, H. 1925** = Moranville, Henri: "Origine de la Maison de Roucy," *Bibliothèque de l'École des Chartes,* vols. 83, 84, and 86 (Nogent-le-Rotrou, 1921, 1922, and 1925).

**MORENAS, J. 1934** = Morenas, Jongla de: *Grand Armorial de France* (Paris, 1934 and later years).

**MORET, A. 1925** = Moret, Alexander: "La Compagne de Seti Ier au Nord du Carmel d'Apres les Forielles de M. Fisher" in *Revue de l'Egypte Ancienne,* I:18-20 (1925).

**MORETA, C de 1816** = Moreta, Coffier de: *Histoire de Bourbonnaise et des Bourbond* (Paris, 1816).

**MORIARTY, G. 1944** = Moriarty, G. Andrews: "Origin of the Carolingians," *NEHGR,* 98:303–310 (Oct 1944).

**MORIARTY, G. 1945a** = Moriarty, G. Andrews: "The Origin of the Capets," *NEHGR,* 99:130–131 and chart (Apr 1945).

**MORIARTY, G. 1945b** = Moriarty, G. Andrews: "The Origin of the Conradins," *NEHGR,* 99:242–243 and chart (Oct 1945).

**MORIARTY, G. 1945c** = Moriarty, G. Andrews: "Origin of the Plantagenets," *NEHGR,* 99:34–37 (Jan 1945).

**MORIARTY, G. 1947** = Moriarty, G. Andrews: "The Descent of the Plantagenet Kings From the Holy Roman Emperors," *NEHGR*, 101:37–41 (Jan 1947).

**MORIARTY, G. 1950a** = Moriarty, G. Andrews: "Some Notes Upon the House of Brabant," *The American Genealogist*, 26:188–189 (July 1950).

**MORIARTY, G. 1950b**= Moriarty, G. Andrews: "Who was the Empress Theophano?" Part I, *The American Genealogist*, 26:186–188 (July 1950); Part II, *TAG*, 26:233–234 (Oct 1950).

**MORIARTY, G. 1951** = Moriarty, G. Andrews: "Aaron of Bulgaria and his Son Tsar John Vladislav," *The American Genealogist*, 27 (1951).

**MORIARTY, G. 1952** = Moriarty, G. Andrews: "Agatha, wife of the Atheling Eadward," *NEHGR*, 106:52–60 (Jan 1952).

**MORIARTY, G. 1953** = Moriarty, G. Andrews: "The Origin of Capet and Plantagenet," *NEHGR*, 107:276–288 (Oct 1953).

**MORIARTY, G. 1955a** = Moriarty, G. Andrews: "Descent from Harold Godwinson," *TAG*, 33:188 (July 1957).

**MORIARTY, G. 1955b** = Moriarty, G. Andrews: "Genealogical Research in Europe," *NEHGR*, 109:174–182 (July 1955).

**MORIARTY, G. 1956** = Moriarty, G. Andrews" "Genealogical Research in Europe: the Syagrii," *NEHGR*, 110:38-40 (1956).

**MORIARTY, G. 1963** = Moriarty, G. Andrews: "The Plantagenet Descent From the Cid," *NEHGR*, 117:94–96 (Apr 1963).

**MORIARTY, G.1985** = Moriarty, G. Andrews: *Plantagenet Ancestry of King Edward III and Queen Phillippa* (Salt Lake City, Mormon Pioneer Genealogical Society, 1985). A hardbound unedited ms in the author's hand, by one of the great American genealogists. The original of the work is in the *NEHGS*, Boston, MA.

**MORIN, A. 1964** = Morin, Adrien: *Histoire de Thouars et du Pays Thouarsais* (1964).

**MORITZ, J. 1833** = Moritz Joseph: in *Abhandlung der Historiche Classe der Konigliche Bayerischen Akademie der Wissenshaft* (Munich, 1833).

**MORITZ, J. 1883** = Moritz, Joseph: Die Grafen von Sulzbach... (Munich, 1883).

**MOSES, C. 1978** = Moses, Chorene: *History of the Armenians* (1978).

**MOTEY, V de 1920** = Motey, Vicomte de: *Origins de la Normandie et du Duche d'Alencon* (Paris, 1920).

**MOUTIE, A. 1960'S** = Moutie, Auguste: "Chevreuse, Recherches Historiques, Archéologiques et Généalogiques," *Mémoires et Documents Publies par la Société de Rambouillet*, vol. III (Rambouillet, 1876), with corrections made by scholars in the 1960's), pp.11–99.

**MUNCH, P. 1864** = Munch, P. A.: *Chronica Regnum Manniae* (Has notes in English) (1864).

**MUNRO, D. 1935** = Munro, Dana C.: *The Kingdom of the Crusaders* (1935).

**MUNZ, P. 1960** = Munz, Peter: *The Origin of the Carolingian Empire* (Dunedin, New Zealand, University of Otago Press, 1960).

265

# -N-

**NADAUD, J. 1974** = Nadaud, Joseph: *Nobiliaire du Diocèse et la Générosité de Limoges*, vol. III (1878) (Limoges, reptd 1974).

**NEHGR** = *New England Historical and Genealogical Register*. One of the world's oldest genealogical journals (founded 1847) still in print.

**NELSON, J. 1992** = Nelson, Janet L.: *Charles the Bald* (Longmans, 1992)

**NEUSNER, J. 1997** = Neusner, J.: *A History of the Jews in Babylon from Shapur I to Shapur II...* (1997).

**NEWMAN, W. 1971** = Newman, William Mendel: *Las Seigneures de Nestle en Picardie...Memoirs of the American Philosophical Society*, vol. 90, Part I (Philadelphia, The Society, 1971). Also printed in Paris (1971), 2 vols.

**NICHOLSON, H. 1962** = Nicholson, Harold: *Kings, Courts and Monarchy* (New York, Simon and Schuster, 1962).

**NORGATE, K. 1887** = Norgate, Kate: *England Under the Angevin Kings* (London, 1887).

**NORTHOFF, L. von 1929** = Northoff, Levold von: *Die Chronik der Grafen von der Mark*, ed. by F. Zschaeck; *Monumenta Germania Historica* (Berlin, 1929).

**NOTES** = *Notes and Queries* (England). This series is so voluminous and disorganized that I haven't much used it, but there are important discoveries to be made here. The Family History Library, Salt Lake City, has dozens of the bound volumes, most of them needing indexing and abstracting.

# -O-

**O'CALLAGHAN, J. 1975** = O'Callaghan, Joseph F.: A *History of Medieval Spain* (Ithaca, NY, Cornell University Press, 1975)

**O'CALLAGHAN, J. 1993** = O'Callaghan, Joseph F.: *The Learned King. The Reign of Alfonso X of Castile* (Philadelphia, U. of Pennsylvania Press, 1993).

**O'CONNOR, D. 1990** = O'Connor, David: *A Short History of Ancient Egypt* (Pittsburg, Carnegie Museum of Natural History, 1990.

**O'CONNOR, D. 1995** = O'Connor, David and David P. Silverman : *Ancient Egyptian Kingship* (Leiden, E. J. Brill, 1995).

**O'DONOVAN, J. 1990** = *Annals of the Kingdom of Ireland...* 3rd edition (ed. by John O'Donovan, 1851), 7 vols. (reptd Dublin, de Burea, 1990). Probably the best translation; vol. VII is a magnificent index.

**O'KELLY, M. 1989** = O'Kelly, Michael J.: *Early Ireland* (Cambridge, Cambridge University Press, 1989).

**O'LAUGHLIN, M. 1995** = O'Laughlin, Michael C.: *The Book of Irish Families Great and Small* (1995).

**OLMSTEAD, A. 1923** = Olmsted, Arthur T.: History of Assyria (Chicago, 1923).

**OLMSTEAD, A. 1959** = Olmsted, Arthur T.: *History of the Persian Empire* (1959).

**ONSLOW, EARL OF 1945** = Onslow, Earl of: *Dukes of Normandy* (London, 1945).

**O'RAHILLY, T. 1946** = O'Rahilly, T. F.: *Early Irish History and Mythology* (Dublin, 1946).

**OURLIAC, P. 1985** = Ourliac, Paul, and Anne-Marie Magnou: *Le Cartulaire de la Selve*, nos. 32, 55A1, 68 (Paris, 1985).

**OVERMANN, A. 1895** = Overmann, A.: *Grafin Mathilde von Tuscien* (1895).

**OXFORD, 1991** = *Oxford Dictionary of Byzantium*, ed. by A. P. Kazhdan, et al (Oxford, 1991).

## -P-

**PAGET, G. 1977** = Paget, Gerald: *The Lineage and Ancestry of H.R.H. Prince Charles, Prince of Wales* (Edinburgh and London, 1977).

**PARISSE, M. 1976** = Parisse, M.: *La Noblesse Lorraine, XIe–XIIIe Siècles* (1976).

**PARKER, R. 1957** = Parker, Richard A.: "The Length of the Reign of Ramesses X," in *Revue d' Egyptologie*, II:163-164 (1957).

**PARSONS, J. 1984** = Parsons, John Carmi: "The Year of Eleanor of Castile's Birth, and Her Children by Edward I," *Mediaeval Studies*, 46:245–265 (1984).

**PARSONS, J. 1988** = Parsons, John Carmi: The Beginning of English Administration of Ponthieu: an Unnoticed Document of 1280," *Mediaeval Studies*, 50:371–403 (1988).

**PARSONS, J. 1989** = Parsons, John Carmi: "Eleanor of Castile and the Viscountess Jeanne of Châtelleraut," *Genealogists' Magazine*, 23:141–144 (Dec 1989).

**PARSONS, J. 1991** = Parsons John Carmi, ed.: "Eleanor of Castile (1241-1290): Legends and Reality Through Seven Centuries," *Eleanor of Castile, 1290-1990: Essays to Commemorate the 700th Anniversary of Her Death, 28 November 1290* (Stamford, Paul Watkins, 1991).

**PAUL, J. 1914** = Paul, John Balfour: *Scots Peerage*, 9 vols. (Edinburgh, David Douglas, 1904–1914).

**PAULER, G. 1899** = Pauler, Gyala: *A Magyars Nemzet Tortenete az Arpad haze Kiralyokalatt* (Budapest, 1899).

**PAYLING, S. 1991** = Simon Payling: *Political Society in Lancastrian England: The Greater Gentry of Nottingham* (Oxford, 1991).

**PAYNE, S. 1973** = Payne, Stanley G.: *A History of Spain and Portugal* (Madison, University of Wisconsin Press, 1973).

**PAZ, A. du 1619** = Paz, du, A.: *Histoire Générale de Pleuseurs Maisons Illustrées de Bretagne* (1619).

**PEARS, E. 1985** = Pears, E.: *The Fall of Constantinople, Being a Story of the First Crusade* (1885).

**PERAUD, E. 1900** = Peraud, Ernest: *Gui, Comte de Ponthiu* (Paris, 1900).

**PERRY, W. 1857** = Perry, Walter C.: *The Franks* (London, Longmans, Green, 1857).

**PETIT, E. 1894** = Petit, E.: *Histoire des Ducs de Bourgogne de la Race Capetienne*, vol. 5 (Paris, 1894).

**PETRIE, W. 1925** = Petrie, W. M. F.: *A History of Egypt*, vol. III (London, 1925).

**PHILLIPS, J. 1996** = Phillips, J.: *Defenders of the Holy Land. Relations Between the Latin East and West, 1119-1187* (Oxford, Oxfrd University Press, 1996.

**PIDAL, R. 1971** = Pidal, Ramon Menendez, *The Cid and His Spain*, translated by Harold Sunderland (London, F. Cass, 1971).

**PINE, L. 1973** = Pine, Leslie G.: *Sons of the Conqueror. Descendants of Norman Ancestry* (Rutland, VT, Charles E. Tuttle, 1973), pp. 5-289.

**PINOTEAU, H. 1958b** = Pinoteau, Herve: *Heraldique Capietenne*, II (Brussels, 1958).

**PIRIE, C. 1962** = Pirie-Gordon, C.: "Succession in the Kingdom of Strathclyde," *Armorial*, vol. I, nos. 1–4 (1959); II, nos. 1, 2 (Edinburgh, 1960).

**POGONOWSKI, I. 1989** = Pogonowski, Iwo Cyprian: *Poland, a Historical Atlas*, revided edition (New York:Dorset Press, 1989), pp.56, 57.

**POLEMIS, D. 1986** = Polemis, Demetrios I.: *The Doukai: a Contribution to Byzantine Prosopography* (1968).

**POREE, C. 1919** = Poree, Charles: *Archiviste de Lozer: Études Historique sur la Gievaudun* (1919).

**POSNER, G. 1962** = Posner, G., et al: *Dictionary of Egyptian Civilization* (London, 1962).

**POSSE, O. 1882** = Posse, O.: *Urkunden der Markgrafen von Meissen und der Landgrafen von Thuringen* (Liepsic, 1882).

**POSSE, O. 1887** = Posse, O.: *Die Markgrafen von Meissen und das Haus Wettin bis Konrad dem Grossen* (Leipsic, 1881 and 1887 editions).

**POSSE, O. 1897** = Posse, O., editor: *Die Wettiner* (Liepsic, 1897).

**POULL, G. 1977** = Poull, Georges: *La Maison de Bar*, vol. I (Rupt-sur-Moselle, 1977).

**POULL, G. 1979** = Poull, Georges: *La Maison Ducale de Lorraine* (Rupt-sur-Moselle, 1979).

**POWELL, T. 1958** = Powell, T. G. E.: *The Celts* (Thames & Hudson, 1958).

**POWICKE, M. 1953** = Powicke, Sir M.: *The Thirteenth Century* (1990).

**PRAROND, E. 1900** = Prarond, Ernest: *Les Comtes de Ponthieu, Gui Premier, 1053–1100* (Paris, 1900).

**PRAWER, J. 1952** = Prawer, Joshus: "The Settlement of the Latins in Jerusalem" *Speculum*, vol. 27 (1952).

**PRAWER, J. 1970** = Prawer, Joshua: *Histoire du Royaume Jerusalem*, vol. I (Paris, 1970).

**PRAWER, J. 1972a** = Prawer, Joshua: *The Crusaders' Kingdom: European Colonialism in the Middle Ages* (New York, Praeger, 1972.

**PRAWER, J. 1972b** = Prawer, Joshua: *The World of the Crusaders* (New York, Quadrangle Books, 1972).

**PRAWER, J. 1973** = Prawrer, Joshua: *The World of the Crusaders* (New York, Quadrangle Books, 1973).

**PRAWLR, J. 1980** = Prawer, Joshua: *Crusader Institutions* (Oxford University Press, 1980).

**PRESTWICK, M. 1981** = Prestwick, M.: *The Three Edwards* (1981).

**PRESTWICK, M. 1990** = Prestwick, M.: *English Politics in the Thirteenth Cen-*

*tury* (1990).

**PREVITE, C. 1912** = Previte-Orton, C. W.: *Early History of the House of Savoy* (Cambridge, England, 1912).

**PREVITE, C. 1914** = Previte-Orton, C. W.: "Charles Constantine of Vienne," *English Historical Review*, 29:703–706 (1914).

**PRIBICHEVICH, S. 1982** = Pribichevich, Stoye: *Macedonia Its People and History* (1982).

**PROSOP, 1981** = *Prosopographisches Lexikon der Palaiologenzeit*, 5 vols. (reptd, Marburg, 1974–1981).

**PSELLUS, M. 1982** = Psellus, Michael: *Fourteen Byzantine Rulers: The Chronographia of Michael Psellus*, translated from the Greek by E. R. A. Sewter (New York, Penguin, reptd 1982). Psellus lived from 1018 to 1096 and was a contemporary or near-contemporary of those about whom he wrote.

**PUTNAM, R. 1971** = Putnam, Ruth: *Alsace and Lorraine from Caesar to Kaisar: 58 B.C. - 1871 A.D.* (New York and London, Putnam & Sons (1915, reptd. 1971, Freeport, NY, Books for Libraries.).

## -Q-

**QUELLER, D. 1977** = Queller, Donald E.: *The Fouth Crusade. The Conquest of Constantinople* (Philadelphia, University of Pennsylvania Press, 1977)

## -R-

**RAMIRO, D. 1955** = Ramiro, D'Abadel y de Venejula: "Catalunga Carolingia," *Barcelona Institut d'Estudias Catalena* (1955). (*NOTE:* vol. I: Text; vol. II: Charters; vol. III: Account of the Counts of Pullars of Ribagorza).

**RASON, S. 1914** = Rason, S.: *Saga Book*, vol. VIII (London, 1914).

**RAUMER, G. 1837** = Raumer, G. W.: *Historische Cherten und Stammtafeln zu dem Regesta Historiae Brandenburgensis*, (Berlin, 1837).

**RAUMER, G. 1871** = Raumer, G. W.: *Karlan und Stammtafeln* (Berlin, 1871).

**RECKER, C. 1982** = Recker, Charles: *Inconsistencies in the Pedigrees of the Counts of Luxembourg* (TAG, 58:14–17 (Jan 1982).

**REED, T. 1947** = Reed, Trelawney Dayrell: *The Rise of Wessex* (London, 1947).

**REDFORD, D. 1986** = Redford, Donald B.: *Pharaonic King-lists, Annals and Day Books. A Contribution to the Study of Egyptian Sense of History* (Toronto, 1986).

**REILLEY, B. 1982** = Reilley, Bernard F.: *The Kingdom of Leon-Castilla Under Queen Urraca 1109-1126* (Princeton, NJ, Princeton University Press, 1982).

**REILLEY, B. 1988** = *The Kingdom of Leon-Castilla Under King Alfonso VI*, 1065-1109 (Princeton, NJ, Princeton University Press, 1988.

**RENN** = Renn, Heinz: "Das Erste Luxemburger Grafenhaus, 963–1136," *Historisches Archiv...* no. 39 (1941).

**RICHARD, J. 1979** = Richard, Jean: The Latin Kingdom of Jerusalem (Europe in the Middle Ages), Vol. 11 (1979).

269

**RIGNALL, J. 1972** = Rignall, Joel McFall, Jr.: "An Imperial Descent: Charlemagne," *Forebears*, XV:112–115 (Paul, J. 1914ring, 1972).

**RILEY-SMITH, J. 1973** = Riley-Smith, Jonathan: *The Feudal Nobility in the Kingdom of Jerusalem, 1174-1277* (London, Macmillan, 1973).

**RITSON, P. 1828** = Ritson, P.: *Annals of the Caledonians, Picts and Scots, and of Strathclyde, Cumberland, Galloway, and Morray*, 2 vols. (Edinburgh, 1828).

**ROBBINS, G. 1987** = Robbins, Gay: "The Role of the Royal Family in the 18th Dynasty Op to the Reign of Amenhotep, Part II: Royal Children" in *Wepwawet*, 3:15-17 (1987).

**ROBERTSON, E. 1872** = Robertson, Eban W.: *Historical Essays* (Edinburgh, 1872).

**ROBILLARD, T. 1852** = Robillard, Theodor: *Histoire de Crecy en Brie* (Crecy, 1852).

**ROCHOW, I, 1991** = Rochow, Ilse: *Byzant im 8 Jahrhundert n der Sicht des Theopanes* (Berlin, 1991).

**ROCKROHR, P. 1885** = Rockrohr, P.: *Die Letze Brunonen* (Kelle, 1885).

**RODIERE, R. 1925** = Rodiere, Roger: *Epitaphier du Picardie* (Paris, 1925).

**ROGERS, R. 1983** = Rogers, Robert W.: A *History of Ancient Persia From Its Earliest Beginnings to the Death of Alercxander the Great* (1983).

**ROLLNOW, H. 1930** = Rollnow, H.: "Die Grafen von Werl," *Genealogische Untersuchen zur Geschichte der 10 bis 12 Jahrunderts* (Greifwold, 1930)

**RONAY, G. 1989** = Ronay, Gabriel: *The Lost King of England* (Woodrigge, Eng., 1989).

**ROQUE, G.1662** = Roque, Giles de la: *Histoire de la Maison d'Harcourt* (Paris, 1662).

**ROSALIE, D. 1988** = Rosalie, David A.: *The Egyptian Kingdoms* (New York, Peter Bedrick Books, 1988).

**ROSCH, S. 1977** = Rosch, Siegfried: *Caroli Magni Progenies*, I (Neustadt/Aisch, Verlag Degener, 1977).

**ROSS, M. 1978** = Ross, Martha, comp.: *Rulers and Governments of the World*, vol. I (London, New York, Bowker, 1978), pp. 434, 435.

**ROUDIERE, P. 1942** = Roudiere, Pierre de la: *Las Anciens Seigneurs de Villebon et de Gatine* (Chartres, 1942).

**ROUND, J. 1971** = Round, J. Horace: *Studies in Peerage and Family History* (Westminster, 1901; reptd, London, 1971).

**ROUQUETTE, J. 1914** = Rouquette, J. and A. Villemagne: *Cartulaire de Maguelone*, 2 vols. (Montpellier, 1912–1914).

**ROUSSEAU, F. 1921** = Rousseau, Felix: "Henri l'Avengle, Comte de Namur et de Luxembourg, 1136–1196," *Bibliothèque Faculté Philosophie Lettre*, Univ. of Liege, vol. 27 (1921).

**ROUSSEAU, F. 1936** = Rousseau, Felix: *Actes des Comtes de Namur, de la Première Race, 946–1096* (Brussels, 1936).

**ROUX, G. 1966** = Roux, George: *Ancient Iraq*, 2nd edition (New York, Penguin Books, 1966.

**RUBINCAM, M. 1949** = Rubincam, Milton: "The House of Brabant," *American Genealogist*, 25:224–232 (Oct. 1949).

**RUBINCAM, M. 1957** = Rubincam, Milton: "The Family of Harold II, Last Saxon

King of England," *TAG*, 33:87–94 (Jan. 1957).

**RUBINCAM, M. 1963** = Rubincam, Milton: "Ancestry of Robert the Strong, Count of Anjou and Blois," *NEHGR*, 117:268–271 (Oct 1963).

**RUDT-COLLENBERG, Count 1969** = Rudt-Collenberg, Count: "Maximilla et Mathilda Reginae," (Palermo, 1969).

**RUNCIMAN, S. 1921** = Runciman, Steven: *The Emperor Romanus Lekapenus and His Reign* (Cambridge, MA, 1921).

**RUNCIMAN, S. 1965** = Runciman, Steven: *History of the Crusades*, 2 vols. (Cambridge, England, Cambridge University Press, 1952; reptd New York, Harper & Row, 1965). Has genealogy charts.

**RUNCIMAN, S. 1987** = Runciman, Steven: *A History of the Crusades: The Kingdom of Jerusalem and the Frankish East, 1100-1187* (A History of the Crusades, Vol. 2), (1987).

# -S-

**SABRAN-P 1897** = Sabran-Ponteves: *Histoire Généalogique de Sabran* (1897).

**SAEZ, E. 1946** = Saez, Emilio: *"Notas al Episcopologio Minduniense"* Hispania, 6:3-79 (1946).

**SAEZ, E. 1948** = Saez, Emilio: "Los Ascendientes de San Rosendo," *Hispania*, 8:3-76, 179-233 (1948)

**SAILLOT, J. 1980** = Saillot, Jacques: *La Sang de Charlemagne* (Augers, 1980). This work was published in a paperback series, in a limited edition. Vol. I (all I have seen), was in 6 parts (202 pp.).

**ST. ALLAIS, M. de 1838** = St. Allais, M. de: *Art de Verifier les Dates des Faits Historiques, des Chartres les Chroniques, en Autres Anciens,* 3rd edition, 8 vols. (1820-1838). Somewhat outdated but still useful.

**SALWAY, P. 1981** = Salway, Peter: *Roman Britain* (Oxford, 1981).

**SALAZAR, J. de 1983** = Salazar, Jaime de: "The Pedigree of King Alfonso VI of Castile in the Light of Recent Research," *Occasional Publications, no. 2* (Salt Lake City, UT, Association for the Promotion of Scholarship in Genealogy, Ltd., 1989), pp. 321–326. *NOTE: This article was completed in August 1983 (says p.325) and errors were not corrected against ES, vol. II, a 1984 publication.*

**SALAZAR, J. de 1984** = Salazar, Jaime de, y Acha (Madrid, 1984). A ms in the possession of J. A. Stargardt, Marburg Germany.

**SALY, E. 1946** = Saly, Emilio: *España*, no. 22 (1946).

**SALY, E. 1949** = Saly, Emilio: "Notes y Documentos Sabre Sancho Ordonez, Rey de Galicia," *Culdernes de Historia de España* (Buenos Aires, 1949).

**SANCHEZ, R. 1930** = Sanchez-Albornez, R.: *La Radaccion Original de la Cronica de Alfonso III* (Buenos Aires, 1930).

**SANCHEZ, R. 1945** = Sanchez-Albornez, R.: *La Succesion al Trono* (Buenos Aires, 1945).

**SANDERS, I. 1960** = Sanders, I. J.: *English Baronies, a Study of Their Origin and Descent, 1086–1327* (Oxford, 1960).

**SANFELICE, A. 1962** = Sanfelice de Monteforte, A.: *Ricerche Storico-Chitico-Genealogiche*, vol. II (Naples, 1962).

**SARS, M. 1924** = Sars, Maxine: *Le Laonnois Féodal*, vol. I (Paris, 1924).

**SAWYER, B. 1993** = Sawyer, Birgit and Peter Sawyer: *Medieval Scandinavia From Conversion to Reformation, circa 800-1500* (University of Minnesota Preess, 1993)

**SAWYER, P. 1978** = Sawyer, Peter: *From Roman Britain to Norman England* (London, 1978).

**SAXON WORLD** = *Saxon Worldchronicle*. Based on the *Chronicle of St. Michael of Lunenburg* (a medieval ms. on microfilm.)

**SCHILLING, H. 1936** = Schilling, Heiner: *Haithabu* (Leipzig, 1936).

**SCHLAGENHAUF, P. 1967** = Schlagenhauf, Paul: "Die Grafen von Lauffen," *Zeitschrift des Zabergauvereins* (1967).

**SCHLUMBERGER, M. 1898** = Schlumberger, M.: *Life of Renaud de Chatillon* (Paris, 1898).

**SCHOPFLIN, G. 1761** = Schopflin, G. D.: *Alsatia Illustrata*, 2 vols. (Kolmar, 1761). The 1851 edition of this work is called *L'Alsace Illustree..*

**SCHUMANN, R. 1973** = Schumann, Reinold: *Authority and the Commune-Parma, 833–1133* (Cambridge, England, 1973).

**SCHWARZMAIER** = Schwarzmaier, Hansmartin: "Die Reginswindis–Tradition von Laufen..." *Zeitschrift fur die Geschichte des Oberrheins*, 131:183–191 (1983).

**SCHWENNICKE, Detlev**: *Europäische Stammtafeln*. See coded entry under "ES" for details of this important work.

**SEARLE, E. 1988** = Searle, Eleanor: *Predatory Kinship and the Creation of Norman Power, 840–1066* (Berkeley, U. of California Press, 1988).

**SEARLE, W. 1899** = Searle, William George: *Anglo-Saxon Bishops, Kings and Nobles (Cambridge, England, 1899).*

**SEELE, K. 1940** = Seele, K. C.: *The Coregency of Ramses II With Seti I and the Great Hypostyle Hall at Karnek* (Chicago, 1940).

**SEIBT, W. 1976** = Seibt, Werner :*Die Skleroi: eine Prosopographisch-Sigillogeaphtsche* Studie no. 8 (Vienna, 1976).

**SELLWOOD, D. 1980** = Sellwood, David: *An Introduction to the Coinage of Parthia*, 2nd edition (London, Spink, 1980).

**SETTIPANI, C. 1988** = Settipani, Christian: "Les Origins des Seigneurs de Montpellier," *Haraldique et Genealogie*, 16 (1988)

**SETTIPANI, C. 1989** = Settipani, Christian: *Les Ancetres de Charlemagne* (Paris, Editions Christian, 1989).

**SETTIPANI, C. 199-** = Settipani, Christian: "RuricusI Eveque de Limoges et ses Relations Familiales" *Francia* 19/1: 195-222.

**SETTIPANI, C. 1990** = Settipani, Christian: Les Ancetres de Charlemagne, addenda and Corridenda" *Histoire et Genealogie*, 28:19-36 (Paris, Editions Christian, 1990).

**SETTIPANI, C. 1991** = Settipani, Christian: *Nos Ancetres de l'Antiquiete* (Paris, Editions Christian, 1991).

**SETTIPANI, C. 1993** = Settipani, Christian and Patrick van Kerrebrouck: *La Prehistoire des Capetiens 481-987. Premiere Partie: Merovingiens, Carolingiens et Robertiens* (Villeneuve d'Ascq, France, P. van Kerrebrouck, 1993).

**SETTIPANI, C. 1994** = Settipani, Christian, "Les Origins Maternalles du Comte de Bourgogne Otte-Guillaume," *Annales de Bourgogne*, 66 (1994).

**SETTIPANI, C. 1996a** = Settipani, Christian and Jean-Paul Poly" "Les Conradins "Un Debat Toujours Ouvert," *Francia* 23/1 (1996).

**SETTIPANT, C. 1996b** = Settipani, Christian: "Clovis, un Roi sans Ancetre?," *Ge Magazine*, no. 153 (October 1996) pp. 24-32 .

**SETTIPANI, C. 1997** = Settipani, Christian: *Our Ancestors from Antiquity. Studies on the Possibility of Genealogical Lines Between Families of Antiquity and Those of the European High Middle Ages*. Trans. from the French by Grant Michael Menzies (Torrance, CA, Augustan Society, 1997).

**SETTIPANI, C. 1997b** = Settipani, Christian: Les Comtes d'Anjou et Leurs Alliances aux Xe et XIe Siecles," *Family Trees and the Roots of Politics (1997)*.

**SEWARD, D. 1988** = Seward, Desmond and Susan Mountgarret: *Byzantium* (London, Harrap, 1988).

**SHAW, M. 1963** = Jonville, Jean de: *Chronicles ofthe Crusades (*a contemporary account) trans. by Margaret R. B. Shaw (Harmondsworth, 1963).

**SHEPARD, C. 1923** = Shepard, Charles: *Lineage of the Counts of Anjou* (1923).

**SHERMAN, E. 1982** = Sherman, E. J.: "Ancient Egyptian Biographies ofthe Late Period (380 BCE Through 246 BCE," in *Newsletter of the American Resesarch Center in Egypt*, 119:38-41 (1982).

**SILVERMAN, D. 1997** = Silverman, David P.: *Ancient Egypt* (1997).

**SIMSON, B. von**= Simson B. von: "Widukind der Sachsenfuhrer," *Allegemeine Deutsch Biographie*.

**SIRAM, T. 1939** = Siram, T.: "Anglo-Saxon Royal Genealogies," *Proceedings of the British Academy*, vol. 39 (1939).

**SLOET, L. 1876** = Sloet, Baron L. A. J. W.: *Von Kondenbach der Graefschofpen Gelre en Zutphen* (1872–1876).

**SMITH, H. 1953** = Smith, Harold R.: *Saxon England* (London, 1953).

**SMITH, J. 1973** = Smith, Jonathan Riley: *The Feudal Nobility and the Kingdom of Jerusalem*, 1174–1277 (London, 1973).

**SMITH, S. 1964** = Smith, S. Armitage: *John of Gaunt* (reptd 1964).

**SOLER, A. 1930** = Soler, Andres Gimenez: *Estudios de Edad Media en la Corona de Aragon* (Barcelona, 1930).

**SPALINGER, A. 1979a** = Spalinger, Anthony J.: "The Northern Wars of Seti I:an Intergrative Study," in *Journal ofthe American Research Center*, 16:29-47 (1979).

**SPALINGER, A. 1979b** = Spalinger, Anthony J.: "Traces of the Early Career of Seti I," in *Journal of the Study of Egyptian Antiquities*, 9:227-240 (1979).

**STARK, F. 1967** = Stark, Freya: *Rome on the Euphrates, the Story of a Frontier* (New York, Harcourt, Brace & World, 1967).

**STASSER, T. 1993** = Stasser, Thierry: "La Maison de Narbonne aux Xe et XIe Siecles," *Annales du Midi*, 105 (1993).

**STASSER, T. 1996** = Stasser, Thierry: "Autour de Roger le Vieuz: les Alliances Matrimoniales des Comtes de Carcassonne," *Annales du Midi*, 108 (1996).

**STAUFFENBURG, F. 1961** = Stauffenburg, Friedrich von: "A Closer Look at the Ancestry of Hughes de Lusignan and His Immediate Descendents," (a paper) (1961). He was Assistant Librarian of Congress and used primary source documents such as original letters and documents from the Middle Ages.

**STEVENS, C. 1933** = Stevens, C. E.: *Sidonius Apollinaris and His Age* (Oxford, Clarendon Press, 1933)

**STIMMEL, R. 1976** = Stimmel, Robert L.: "Descent of Alfonso X of Castile from the Earliest Kings of Pamplona (Navarre)" *Augustan*, XIII:83 (July 1976).

**STIMMEL, R. 1978** = Stimmel, Robert L.: "Ancestors of the Kings and Queens of Spain," *Augustan*, XIX, no. 3, pp. 109–120 (1978)

**STOKVIS, A. 1966** Stokvis, A. M. H. J.: *Manuel d'Histoire de Généalogie et de Chronologie de Tous les États du Globe*, 3 vols. 1888–1893. (reptd. Leiden, and edited by B. M. Israel, 1966). These volumes include extensive genealogical tables of African, American, Arabic, Indian and Oriental rulers, as well as the usual British and European houses. Usually included are only the direct male lines, omitting wives and children unless they are heirs or heads of other dynasties. Reasonably accurate. Available on microfilm.

**STONE, D. 1995** = Stone, Don Charles: *Some Ancient and Medieval Descents of Edward I of England* (Philadelphia, 1995).

**STRADELMANN, R. 1981** = Stradelmann, Rainier: "Die Lange Regierung Ramses II," in *Mitteilungen des Deutschen Archalogischen Institute*, 37:457-464 (1981).

**STRICKLAND, A. 1902** = Strickland, Agnes: *Lives of the Queens of England* (New York, 1902).

**STROHAKER, K. 1948** = Strohaker, Karl Friederich: "Der Senatorische Adel," *Paul, J. 1914itantiken Gallien* (Tubingen, 1948).

**STURDZA, M. 1983** = Sturdza, Mihail Dimitri: *Dictionnaire Historique et Généalogique de Grandes Familles de Grace, d'Albanie, et de Constantinopel* (Paris, 1983).

**STURLUSON, S. 1991** = Sturluson, Snorri: Heimskringla, *History of the Kings of Norway*, translated by Lee M. Hollander (Austin, TX, University of Texas Press, 1964, 1991). Use with care as generally unreliable.

**SUGAR, A. 1929** = Sugar, Abbott: *Vie de Louis VI le Gros*, ed. and trans. by Henri Waquet (Paris, 1929).

**SUGAR, P. 1994** = Sugar, Peter F., et al, editors: *A History of Hungary* (Bloomington, IN, University of Indiana Press, 1994).

**SURTEES SOC.** = Surtees Society: *Durham publications* (periodical).

**SYNCH. FLENN** = *Synchronisms of Flenn Mainistreach*. (Original record of the Middle Ages on microfilm).

# -T-

**TABERNER, F. 1961** = Taberner, Fernando Valls: "El Comtats de Palars: Ribacorca a Partir del Segles XI" Estudios de Historia Medieval, 4:125-205 (1961).

**TAG** = *The American Genealogist* (a periodical), vol. 9 (1932) through vol.74 (1999). Originally published by Donald Lines Jacobus, the articles are usually authoritative and well documented. The first eight volumes contain, largely, his "Families of Ancient New Haven."

**TAGGIE, B. 1989** = Taggie, Benjamin F. and Richard W. Clement: *Iberia and the Mediterranean* (1989).

**TALLON, M. 1955** = Tallon, Maurice: "Livre de Lettres, "First Group, in Malanges de l'Universite de St. Joseph, 32:1 (1955), pp. 1-146.

**TANGL, K. 1937** = Tangl K.: "Die Grafen, Markgrafen und Herzage aus dem Hause Eppenstein," *Archivalien Osterreichische Gerchichtsquellen* (1937).

**TANNER, H. 1992** = Tanner, Heather J.: "The Expansion of the Power and Imfluence of the Counts of Boulogne Under Eustace II," *Anglo-Norman Studies XIX* (Woodbridge, Suffolkm 1992).

**TARDIF, V. 1918** = Tardif, Viktor: "Procés d'Enguerran de Coucy," *Bibliothèque de l'École des Chartes*, vol. 79 (1918).

**TAUBE, M. de 1947** = Taube, Michael de: *Roma et la Russie Avant l'Invasion des Tarters* (IX–XIII Siècles) (Paris, 1947).

**TAYLOR, N. 1997** = Taylor, Nathaniel L.: "Saint William, King David and Makhir," *The American Genealogist*, 72 (1997).

**TEN HAEFF, A. 1923** = Ten Haeff, A.: *Fruin in Nederlandsche Luuw* (1923).

**THATCHER, O. 1897** = Thatcher, Oliver J.: *A Short History of Mediaeval Europe* (New York, 1897).

**THEROFF, P. 1994** = Theroff, Paul: *Kings of Iberia*, 1994).

**THIELE, E. 1954** = Thiele, Edwin R.: A Comparison of the Chronological Data of Israel and Judah," *Vetus Testamentum*, IV (1954).

**THIELE, E, 1977** = Thiele, Edwin R. : A Chronology of the Hebrew Kings (Grand Rapids, Mich., Zondervan Publishing House, 1977).

**THOMAS, E. 1959** = Thomas, Elizabeth: "Ramesses III: Notes and Queries," in *Journal of Egyptian Archaeology*, 45:101-102 (1959).

**THOMAS, G. 1928** = Thomas, Georges: *Les Comtes de la Marche de la Maison de Charroux* (Paris, 1928).

**THOMPSON, K. 1997** = Thompson, Kathleen: "The Formation of the County of Perche," *Family Trees and the Roots of Politics* (1997).

**THOMSON, R. 1976** = Thomson, Robert W.: *The Armenians* (Albany, State University of New York Press, 1976).

**THORPE, L. 1979** = Einhard the Frank: *Life of Charlemagne* (Trans. by Lewis Thorpe (London, 1970; Harmondsworth, 1979).

**TIBBLE, S. 1989** = Tibble, Stephen: *Monarchy and Lordships in the Latin Kingdom of Jerusalem, 1099-1291* (Oxford, Oxford University Press, 1989).

**TOUMANOFF, C. 1963** = Toumanoff, Prince Cyril L.: Studies in Christian Caucasian History (Georgetown, 1963).

**TOUMANOFF, C. 1966** = Toumanoff, Prince Cyril L.: "Armenia and Georgia," in *Congres des Sciences Genealogique et Heraldiques*, XIV:989-1009 (1966).

**TOUMANOFF, C. 1969** = Toumanoff, Prince Cyril L.: *Chronology of the Early Kings of Iberia* (Traditio, 25, 1969), pp. 1-33.

**TOUMANOFF, C. 1976** = Toumanoff, Prince Cyril L.: *Manuel de Généalogie et de Chronologie pour l'Histoire de la Caucasie Chrétienne* (Rome, 1976).

**TOUMANOFF, C. 1986** = Toumanoff, Prince Cyril L."More on the Mamikonids and the Liparatids,: in *Milanges Berberian*, 1986), pp. 859-860.

**TOURTIER, C. de 1960** = Tourtier, Chantl de: "Les Comtes de Ponthieu Avoues de Saint-Riquier aux Crusades, l'Histoire et la Légende," *Bulletin de la Société des Antiquaires de Picardie* (Amiens, 1960).

**TRAUTZ, F. 1953** = Trautz, Fritz: *Das Untere Neckarland im Fruheren Mittelalter* (Heidelberg, 1953).

**TREADGOLD, W. 1988** = Treadgold, Warren T.: *The Byzantine Revival, 780-842* (Stamford, 1988).

**TROTTER, K. 1915** = Trotter, K: "Zur Herkunft das Alteren Grafen von Tirol," *Forschung und Mittelalterlichen Geschichtetirols und Voralsburgs*, vol. 12 (1915).

**TROTTER, K. 1933** = Trotter, K: *Familien Gerchichte* (Berlin, 1933).

**TROTTER, K. 1937** = Trotter, K: *Beitrage zur Mittelalterlichen Geschichte Innerosterreichs* (Berlin, 1937).

**TURNER, R. 1988** = Turner, Ralph V.: "Eleanor of Aquitaine and Her Children..." *Journal of Medieval History*, 14:321-335 (1988).

**TURNER, R. 1994** = Turner, Ralph V.: *King John* (Longman, 1994).

**TURTON, W. 1984** = Turton, W. H.: *Plantagenet Ancestry* (London, 1928; reptd Baltimore, 1984). This work has never been revised and thus contains errors, but it is useful in supporting other works with which it is in agreement. Many lines are completely correct.

**TYRE, W. 1943** = Tyre, William of: Chronicles. Trans. by E. A. Blalock (1943)

**TYROLLER, F. 1950** = Tyroller, Franz: "Die Ahnen des Wittesbacher," *Supplement to Jahsesbericht des Wittesbacher Gymnasiums* (Munich, 1950/51).

**TYROLLER, F. 1951** = Tyroller, Franz: "Die Altere Genalogie der Andechser," *Supplement to Jahresbericht der Wittlesbacher Gymnasiums* (Munich, 1951/52).

**TYROLLER, F. 1968** = Tyroller, Franz: in Wilhelm Wegener, *Genealogische Tefeln zur Mitteleuropaischen Geschichte* (Gottengen, 1962/1968).

**TYROLLER, F. 1969** = Tyroller, Franz: "Genealogische Tafeln zur Mitteleuropäischen Geschichte," pp. 108–114 (Gottingen, 1962/1969).

## -U-

**URBAL, J. 1945** = Urbal, Justo Perez de: *Historia de Condado de Castilla*, 3 vols. (Madrid, 1945). Contains some errors and is somewhat confused.

**URBAL, J. 1950** = Urbal, Justo Perez de: *Sancho el Mayor de Navora* (Madrid, 1950).

**UREGLIO, L. 1893** = Ureglio, L.: "I Marchese del Vasto," *Revista Storia Italiano*, vol. 10 (Torino, 1893).

# -V-

**VAJAY, S. de 1960a** = de Vajay, Szabolcs: *Annales de Bourgogne*, XXXII:158–161 (July–Sept 1960).

**VAJAY, S de 1960b** = de Vajay, Szabolcs: "Étienne, Dite de Vienne, Comtesse de Bourgogne," *Annales de Bourgogne*, XXXII:233–267 (Oct–Dec 1960).

**VAJAY, S. de 1962a** = de Vajay, Szabolcs: "A Propos de la Guerre de Bourgogne," Note sur les Successions de Bourgogne et de Mâcon aux Xe et XIe Siècles," *Annales de Bourgogne*, XXXIV:153–169 (July–Sept 1962).

**VAJAY, S. de 1962b** = de Vajay, Szabolcs: "Agatha, Mother of St. Margaret, Queen of Scotland," *Duquesne Review*, 7:71–87 (Spring 1962).

**VAJAY, S. de 1962c** = de Vajay, Szabolcs: "Grossfurst Geza von Ungarn," *Sudostforschungen*, XXI:67–71 (1962).

**VAJAY , S. de 1964** = de Vajay, Szabolcs: "La Sintesis Europea en el Abolengo y la Politica Mzatrimonial de Alfonso el Castro" *VII Congreso de Historia de la Corona de Arazon* (Barcelona, 1964), pp. 269, 299.

**VAJAY, S. de 1966a** = de Vajay, Szabolcs: "Ramiero II le Moine, Roi d'Argon, et Agnes de Poitou dans l'Histoire et dans le Légende," *Mélanges Offerts a Réné Crozet*, vol. II (Poitiers, Société d'Études Médiévales, 1966).

**VAJAY, S. de 1966b** = de Vajay, Szabolcs: "A Propos de l'Ascendance Carolingienne," *Revista de Historia, Heraldica, Genealogia e de Artes*, 7:288–294 and Tables I–III (1966).

**VAJAY, S. de 1980** = de Vajay, Szabolcs: "Eudocie Comnene, l'Imperatrice des Troubadours," *Genealogica et Heraldica* (Copenhagen, 1980).

**VAJAY, S. de 1989** = de Vajay, Szabolcs: "From Alfonso VII to Alfonso X. The First Two Centuries of the Burgundian Dynasty in Castile and Leon—a Prosopographical Catalog in Social Genealogy, 1100–1300," *Occasional Publication* no. 2 (Salt Lake City, UT, Association for the Promotion of Scholarship in Genealogy, Ltd., 1989), pp. 366–417.

**VALE, M. 1990** = Vale, Malcolm: *The Angevin Legacy and the Hundred Years War, 1250-1340* (Blackwell, 1990).

**VAMBERY, A. 1894** = Vambery, Arminius: *Story of Hungary* (Budapest, 1894).

**VAN DAM, R. 1985** = Van Dam, Raymond: *Leadership and Community in Late Antique Gaul* (Berkeley, University of California Press, 1985).

**VANDERKINDERE, L. 1902** = Vanderkindere, Leon: *La Formation Territoriale des Principautes Belges au Moyen Age*, 2nd edition, 2 vols. (Brussels, 1902).

**VANDERKINDERE, L. 1904** = Vanderkindere, Leon: *Chronique de Gislebert de Mons*, 2nd edition (Brussels, 1904).

**VAN HOUTS, E. 1986** = van Houts, Elizabeth M. C.: "The Origins of Herleva, Mother of William the Conqueror," *English Historical Review*, CI:399–404 (London, 1986).

**VANISLEV, A. 1951** = Vanislev, Alexander A.: "Hugh Capet of France and Byzantium," *Dumbarton Oaks Papers*, 6:229–251 (1951).

**VANNERUS, J. 1946** = Vannerus, J.: "La Première Dynastie Luxembourgeois," *Revue Belge de Philologie et Histoire*, 25:801–858 (1946).

**VAN OVERSTRAETEN, D. 1976** = van Overstraeten, Daniel: *Inventaire des Archives de l'Abbaye de Ghislenghien* (Brussels, 1976).

**VERCAUTEREN, F. 1938** = Vercauteren, Fernand: *Actes des Comtes de Flandre, 1071–1128* (Brussels, Commission Royal d'Histoire, 1938).

**VERMES, G. 1973** = Vermes, G., and F. Miller, editors: *A History of the Jewish People in the Age of Jesus Christ* (Edinburgh, 1972).

**VERNET, A. 1956** = Vernet, A.: "Un Nouveau Manuscript du 'Manuel de Dhouda'," *Bibliothèque d'École des Chartes*, CXIV:18+ (Paris, 1956).

**VIENNA ARCH. 1886** = *Vienna Archivalien Geographisch* (publications) (1886).

**VILLACHARDOUIN, G.** = Villachardouin, Geoffrey de: *The Conquest of Constantinople*, trans. by M. R. B. Shaw (n.d.).

**VITALIS, O. 1857** = Ordericus Vitalis: *The Ecclesiastical History of England and Normandy.* English translation by Thomas Forester, 4 vols. (1853–1857). *NOTE: There is also an edition in French, edited by Auguste le Provost, 1835–1855.*

**VIVIAN, T.** = Vivian, T.L.: *Visitations of Devonshire.* (Original record on microfilm.)

**VOGT, H. 1959** = Vogt, Herbert W.: *Das Herzogtum Lothar's von Supplingenburg, 1106–1125* (Hildesheim, 1959).

**VOIGT, K. 1902** = Voigt, Karl: *Beitrage zur Diplomatik der Langobardischen Fursten* (Gottingen, 1902).

**VON REDLICH, M. 1941** = von Redlich Marcellus: *Pedigrees of Some of the Emperor Charlemagne's Descendents*, vol. I (n.p., Order of the Crown of Charlemagne, 1941).

**VON REDLICH, M. 1942** = von REDLICH, Marcellus: "The Descent of Queen Philippa, Wife of King Edward III of England, From the Royal Hungarian House of Arpad," *NEHGR*, 96:138–143 (Apr 1942).

**VRIES, W. de 1947** = Vries, W. de: *Bydragon en Mededulingen der Verunigen in Gelre*, vol. LVIII (1947).

**VRIES, W de 1960** = de Vries, W.: *De Opkomst van Zutphen* (1960).

**VRIGNAULT, H. 1965** = Vrignault, H.: *Légitimes de France de la Maison de Bourbon* (Paris, 1965).

## -W-

**WAGNER, A. 1975** = Wagner, Anthony: *Pedigree and Progress* (London, Phillimore, 1975).

**WALLMICHRATH, E. 1966** = Wallmichrath, Erich: "Die Sippe der Geva," *Mitteilungen der Westdeutschen Gesellschaft fur Familienkunde*, XXI:509–518 (1963–1964); XXII:39–56 (1965–1966).

**WAQUET, J. 1950** = Waquet, Jean: Recueil des Chartes de l'Abbaye de Clairvaux, no. XI (facsimile, Troyes, 1950).

**WARLOP, E. 1975** = Warlop, E.: *The Flemish Nobility Before 1300*, 2 vols in 4 (Kortrijk, Belgium, 1975/1976).

**WASHINGTON, S. 1942** = Washington, S. H. Lee: "The Early History of the Stricklands of Sizergh..." *NEHGR*, 96:98–126 (Apr 1942).

**WASHINGTON, S.1943** = Washington, S. H. Lee: "The Origin of the Families of Greystoke and Dunbar," *NEHGR*, 97: 239–252 (June 1943).

**WATERMAN, L. 1936** = Waterman, Leroy: *Royal Correspondence of the Assyrian Empire* (Ann Arbor, MI, 1930-1936).

**WAUGH, S. 1991** = Waugh, Scott L.: *England in the Reign of Edward III* (Cambridge Medieval Textbooks) (1991).

**WEBSTER, 1988** = *Webster's Biographical Dictionary* (Springfield, MA, Meriam, 1988).

**WEEVER, W. 1631** = Weever, W.: *Ancient Funerall Monuments...*(1631).

**WEIR, A. 1996** = Weir, Alison: *Britain's Royal Families, the Complete Genealogy* (Pimlico, 1996).

**WEIS, F. 1992** = Weis, Frederick Lewis: *Ancestral Roots of Certain American Colonists Who Came to America Before 1700...*, 7th edition, with additions and corrections by Walter Lee Sheppard, Jr., assisted by David Faris (Baltimore, MD, Genealogical Publishing Co., 1992). Formerly called *Ancestral Roots of Sixty Colonists Who Came to New England Between 1623 and 1650.*

**WEISS, S. 1910** = Weiss, S: *Tableaux Généalogique de la Maison de Bar* (Bar-sur-Seine, 1910).

**WERNER** = Werner, Karl Ferdinand: *Die Welt als Geschichte*, 18:264–279 (Stuttgart, 1958).

**WHITLOCK, R. 1991** = Whitlock, Ralph: *The Warrier Kings of Saxon England* (New York, Dorset Press, 1991).

**WHITSHAW, B. 1912** = Whitshaw, Bernard, and Ellen M. Whitshaw: *Arabic Spain: Sidelights on Her History and Art* (London, Smith, Elder & Co., 1912).

**WILLIAMS, A. 1995** = Williams, Ann: *The English and Norman Conquest* (Boydell Press, 1995).

**WILLIAMS, J. 1860** = *Brut y Twysogion, or the Chronicle of the Princes*, ed. by John Williams (London, Longman, Green, Longman and Roberts, 1860). A definitive work on Welsh history. (also, on microfilm, Salt Lake City, UT, 1976).

**WILLIAMSON, D. 1986** = Williamson, David, ed.: Debrett's Kings & Queens of Britain (Topsfierld, MS, Salem House, 1986; reptd 1991).

**WILLIAMSON, D. 1996** = Williamson, David: *Brewer's British Royalty* (London, 1996).

**WILLOUGHBY, R. 1991a** = Willoughby, Rupert: "The Golden Line -Byzantine, Arab, and Armenian Ancestry of the Russian Ruricks," Part I. *Genealogists' Magazine*, 23:321-327 (March, 1991)

**WILLOUGHBY, R. 1991b** = Willoughby, Rupert; Ibid, Part II, *Genealogists' Magazine*, 23:369-372 (June 1991).

**WILLOUGHBY, R. 1992** = Willoughby, Rupert: Ibid, Part III, *Genealogists' Magazine*, 24:66-67, June 1992.

**WILSDORF, C. 1964** = Wilsdorf, Charles: "Les Etichonides aux Temps Carolingiens et Ottoniens," *Bulletin Philologique et Historique* (1964).

**WILSON, R. 1977** = Wilson, Robert R.: *Genealogy and History of the Biblical World* (New Haven and London, Yale University Press, 1977).

**WINKHAUS, E. 1953** = Winkhaus, Eberhard: *Ahnen zu Karl dem Grossen und Widukind* (1950). (Additions and corrections, 1953).

**WINSTONE, F. 1986** = Winstone, F. V. F.: *Uncovering the Ancient World* (New York and Oxford, Facts on File Publications, 1986).

**WINTER, H. 1987** = Winter, H. M. West: *The Descendants of Charlemagne (800-1400)*, 4 vols. (Charlemont, MA, the author, 1987). Printed but never published, the " working copy" was distributed to reviewers and a few remainders were sold to the public. *It was never proofed and contains hundreds of errors.*

**WISE, L. 1967** = Wise, L. F. and E. W. Egan: *Kings, Rulers and Statesmen* (New York, Sterling, 1967).

**WITTE, H. 1900** = Witte-Hagenau, H.: *Burggraf Frederick von Nurnburg und Zollernsche Besitz* (Innesbruk, 1900).

**WITTE, H. 1903** = Witte-Hagenau, H.: *Genealogische Untersuchsungen zur Reichsgeschichte Unter den Salischen Kaisern...* (Innesbruk, 1896–1903).

**WOEGERER, H. 1866** = Woegerer, H: *Geschichte Ungarns* (1866).

**WOLFRAN, H. 1979** = Wolfran, Herwig: *History of the Goths* (Berkeley, University of California Press, 1979).

**WOLFF, R. 1949** = Wolff, Robert Lee: "The Second Bulgarian Empire, Its Origin and History to 1204," *Paul, J. 1914eculum*, vol. 24 (1949).

**WOLLASCH, J. 1959** = Wollasch, Jaochim: "Koningtum, Adel und Kloster im Berry Wahrend des 10 Jarhrhunderts," *Neue Forschungen Uber Cluny und die Cluniacenser* (Freiburg, 1959).

**WORDSWORTH, 1994** = *Wordsworth Handbook of Kings and Queens* (Wordsworth, 1994).

**WUNDER, G. 1967** = Wunder, Gerd: "Wilhelm der Eroberer und Seine Verwandten in der Sicht der Kontinentalen Dynastengengenealogie," *Genealogisches Jahrbuck 6/7* (Neurstadt /Aisch, 1966/67, pp. 19-47.

**WUNDER, G. 1975** = Wunder, Gerd: "Die Letzen Prinzen des Angelsachsichen Koningshauses," *Genealogisches Jahrbuck 15* (Neustadt/Aisch, 1975).

**WUSTERFELD, F. 1852** = Wusterfeld, Ferdinand: *Genealogisches Tabellem der Arabischen Stamme und Familien* (Gottingen, Dieterischen Buchhandlunger, 1852.

- Y -

**YARSHATER, E. 1983** = Yarshater, Ehsan: *Cambridge History of Iran, vol. 3(1). The Selucid , Parthian and Sassanian Periods* (Cambridge, Cambridge University Press, 1983).

**YEATMAN, J. 1882** = Yeatman, John Pym: *Early Genrealogical History of the House of Arundel...* (London, Mitchell & Hughes, 1882).

**YORKE, B. 1990** = Yorke, Barbara: *Kings and Kingdoms of Early Anglo-Saxon England* (London, Seaby, 1990)

## -Z-

**ZACUTO,A 1925** = Zacuto, Abraham ben Samuel: *Sepher Yuhasin ha Shalem, Liber Juhassen Sine* ... edited by Hershel Filipowski, 2nd edi tion (Frankfort, 1925), p. 84. [A book of lineage].

**ZIELINSKI,H.1982** = Zielinski, Herbert, editor: *Tancredi et Eilelmi III Regnum Diplomatica* (Kohl-Wien, 1982).

**ZUCKERMAN, A. 1972** = Zuckerman, Arthur J.: *A Jewish Princedom in Feudal France, 768-900* (New York and London, Columbia University Press, 1972).

# Title Index

Carcassonne, Vicomte de, 195A
Cardagne, Count of, 54
Cardena, Count of, 54
Carinthia zu Sonnesburg, Count of, 228
Carinthia, Count of, 12,41A,48,129, 130,229,270
Carinthia, Duke of, 113,128,202,359, 372
Carinthia, Margrave of, 10,229
Carinthian Mark, Margrave of, 13
Carlat, Marquis of, 150
Carlat, Viscount of, 226,257,262,282
Carlyle, Lord of, 196
Carniola, Margrave of, 30,281
Castellar, Seigneur de, 116,195
Castile, Count of, 35,54,55,94,95,155, 185,223,276,279,285,286,287
Castile, Infanta of, 86,248
Castile, King of, 52,82,83,85,88,94, 151,155,180,248,276,378
Castile, Princess of, 54,86,94
Castile, Queen of, 248,378
Castile, Titular King of, 1
Catuvellauni, King of, 405B
Caux, Count of, 340
Cea, Count of, 267
Cerdagne, Count of, 284,347
Chacenay, Sire de, 384,385
Chalons, Count of, 348,348A,358
Chalons-sur-Seine, Count of, 258
Cham, Count of, 128,128A
Champagne, Constable of, 84
Champagne, Count of, 24,36,60,81, 127,133,134,137,228
Champagne, Senechal of, 84
Charmois, Count in, 389
Chartres, Count of, 81,133,295,340, 346
Chartres, Viscount of, 249,268
Chateau Renard, Count of, 144
Chateau Renard, Sire de, 144,241

Chateau-Bassett, ,Dame de, 34
Chateau-du-Loire, Dame de, 354
Chateau-du-Loire, Seigneur de, 354
Chateau-en-Porhoet, Vicomte de, 69
Chateau-London, Count in, 2
Chateau-London, Sire de, 144
Chateaudun, Count of, 133,249
Chateaufort, Lord of, 241
Chatellerault, Vicomte de, 305,306
Chatenois, Count of, 158
Chatillon, Lord of, 5,401
Chatillon-sur-Marne, Lord of, 99,400
Chatillon-sur-Marne, Seigneur de, 99
Chaumois, Count of, 173,258
Chester, Earl of, 56,135,135A
Chevier, Seigneur de, 99
Chevreuse, Dame de, 241
Chevreuse, Seigneur de, 241
Chichester, Earl of, 183
Chiemgau, Count in, 12,48,110,128, 128A,129,229
Chiny, Count of, 65,66,120
Chios, Setrap of, 411
Cimmerians, King of, 303
Clerieu, Sire de, 196
Clermont, Count of, 56,149,344
Clermont-en-Beauvaisis, 344
Coast, Meran, Duke of, 7
Coimbra, Count of, 94
Cologne, King of, 171
Cologne, Princess of, 260
Commagene, King of, 408,412,414, 417
Commagene, Setrap of, 412
Comminges, Count of, 195A,291
Comminges, Seigneur de, 291
Conde, Lord of, 50
Conde, Seigneur de, 50
Conserans, Count of, 95,105, 195A, 227,291
Constantinople, Ambassador to, 307
Constantinople, Caesar at, 219

286

287

Eastern Roman Emperor, 407
Eastland, Lord of, 240
Eastmark, Count in, 63
Ebersburg, Count of, 130
Ebersburg, Lord of, 130
Echternach, Lay Abbot of, 68,92,207, 316
Edessa, Count of, 145
Eenam, Marquis of, 104
Egisheim, Count of 26,30,33,40,149, 175,246
Egypt, King of,SEE Egypt, Pharaoh of
Egypt, Pharaoh of, 413,420,421,423, 425,428
Egypt, Primate of, 425
Eichsfeld, Count of, 27
Eifelgau, Count in, 208
Eilenburg, Count of, 8,210,212
Einrichgau, Count in, 304A
Engadin, Count of, 41A
Engern, Count of, 217
Engern, Duke of, 339
England, King of, 1,2,22,29,51,54, 87, 88,89,103,140,141,147,165,233, 235,238,242,250,261,299,314,321, 342,367,368,376
England, Prince of, 1,2,83,147,233, 240,318
England, Princess of,81, 83,88,89,133, 171,235,242,261,299,359
England, Queen of, 52,54,87,88,140,165,235,237,238,242, 342,250,376
England, Regent of, 335
Ennsthal, Count of, 13
Enzgau, Count in, 359
Epirus, King of 303
Eppenstein, Ld of 229
Eschelles, Vicomte de, 308
Erscuens, Count of, 189,254
Este, Marchese d', 29,93,106
Etroen, Seigneur d', 50

Eu, Count of, 57,222
Euphra, Archbishop of, 118
Evreux, Count of, 103,168,188
Exemes, Count of, 222
Exemes: SEE ALSO Hiemois
Extramadura, King of, 52,83

**F**

Falkenburg, Count of, 11,14
Fallou, Count of, 292
Faucigny, Lord of, 175,288
Faucigny, Sire de, 175,288
Fere, Seigneur de, 37
Fere-en-Tardenois, Dame de, 124
Ferte, Dame de la, 241
Ferte-sur-Ourcy, Seigneur de la, 241
Fezensac, Count of, 166A, 264,289
Fiero-Marle, Count in, 130
Filsgau, Count in, 40
Finland, King of, 166
Finland, Lord of, 240
Finland, Princess of, 166
Flanders, Constable of, 50
Flanders, Count of, 43,50,54,73,104, 132,137,140,141,152,169,184,205 ,218,235,311,312,329,332347,353, 356,400
Flanders, Countess of, 250
Flanders, Forester of, 235
Flanders, Marquis of, 235
Fleche, Seigneur de la, 313,354
Foix, Lord of, 95
Foix, Seigneur de, 195A
Fontaines, Lord of, 385
Forcalquier, Count of, 54,93,164,196
Forcalquier, Lord of, 116,195
Forcalquier, Marquis of, 195
Forcalquier, Seigneur de, 116,195
Forez, Count de la, 317
Forez, Seigneur de la, 317

Ittergau, Count in, 338
Ivesfort, Count of, 271
Ivoix, Count of, 65
Ivrea, Margrave of, 198,332
Ivrea, Marquesse of, 62
Ivrea, Marquis of, 106,186,332
Izborsk, Princess of, 143

-J-
Jerusalem, Prince of, 145
Jerusalem, Regent of, 145
Jerusalem, King of, 2,88,145,152,164,
    313
Jerusalem, Princess of, 80,145
Jewish Khazars, Khagan of, 51
Jomsburg Vikings, leader of, 368,369
Judah, Governor of, 410
Judah, King of, 329
Jutland, King of, 204,217,369

-K-
Kabul, King of, 408
Kaiserwerth, Lord of, 208
Kamsarakan, Prince of, 322
Karamantanieu, Count in, 118
Kaudjide, Prince of, 416
Kelachgau, Count in, 67,208,389
Kelsgau, Count in, 281,307
Kent, Earldorman of, 233
Kent, King of, 233,233A,233B,267,
    406
Kent, Underking of, 233
Khazars, Khagan of Jewish, 51,209
Kiev, Grand Duke of, 76A,143
Kiev, Grand Prince of, 27,115,143,
    225,240,321,361,363,368
Kiev, Prince of, 143,209
Kintyre, King of, 165
Kinziggau, Count in, 351
Knapdale, King of, 165
Kolngau, Count in, 67

Kostritz, Count of, 8,26
Kraichgau, Count in, 130,228
Kurland, Lord of, 240
Kusel, Lord of, 359
Kyburg, Count of, 364

-L-
Lahngau, Count in, 65,166A,281
Lancaster, Duke of, 1
Landgau, Count in, 281A
Laon, Archdeacon of, 50,73
Laon, Count of, 114,214
Laorn, King of, 355
Lara, Count of, 55,285
Larron, Lord of, 294
Laufen, Count of, 16,19
Laurino, Count of, 31
Lausnitz, Count of, 210
Lausnitz, Margrave of, 8,211
Lechrain, Count in, 29
Leicester, Countess of, 135,143
Leicester, Earl of, 143
Lengernfeld, Lord of, 307
Lens, Count of, 131,242
Lens, Seigneur de, 131
Lens-Aumele, Count of, 77
Lens-Aumale, Seigneur de, 77
Leon, Count of, 55
Leon, King of, 20,52,82,83,85,86,94,
    155,180,223,248,276,277,378
Leon, Princess of, 84,94
Leon, Queen of, 248,378
Lerida, Marquis of, 54
Lesser Armenia, King of, 408
Lethra, King of, 143,240,369
Lethra, Prince of, 143
Leuze, Lord of, 50
Leuze, Seigneur de, 50
Leventhal, Count of, 10,228
Liguria, Count in, 93
Liguria, Marchese di, 43,106

291

Villentrois, Seigneur de, 109,167
Vincenzia, Count of, 106
Vinzgau, Count in, 262,336,364
Vion, Sire de, 196
Visagoths, King of, 349A,380
Vitry, Count of, 268
Vitry-en-Parthois, Lord of, 171
Vliermal, Count of, 100
Volkfeld, Margrave of, 270

- W-

Walbach, Count of, 14,15,271
Wales, Prince of, 1
Warq, Count of, 65
Warenne, Earl of, 135
Wassenburg, Count of, 62,64,
Weimar, Count of, 27,210,211,281
Wels-Lambach, Count of, 1
Werl, Count of, 19,67
Wessex, Count of, 376
Wessex Earldorman of, 368
Wessex, King of, 233,367,376
Wessex, Prince of, 233
Wessex, Queen of, 235,250
Wessex, Underruler of, 233
West Bulgaria, Count in, 309
West Bulgaria, Tsar of, 309
West Franks, Count of, 264
West Franks, King of, 171,233,350,
353, 357
West Franks, Princess of, 202,239,353
West Friesland, Count of, 38,244,311,
312,316,356
West Friesland, Margrave of, 32,318
West Saxons, King of, 233
West Sealand, Count of, 390
West Silicia, Prince of, 378
West, Emperor of,25,32,34A,40,41,92,
115,115A,125,161,163,171,199
269, 302,303, 319,321,322,323,
328,233,237,250,352,253,359,376,
399

West, Prefect of, 236
West, Princess of, 185,272,343
Western Armenia, King of, 416
Western Asia, Setrap of, 414,424
Westfold, King of, 339
Westphalia, Count of, 19,339
Westphalian Saxons, Duke of, 339
Wetterau, Count in, 3,102199,261
Wettin, Count of, 8
Wiltshire, Earldorman of, 233,262,
367,376
Winterthur, Count of, 364
Wittesbach, Count of, 307
Wolfratschausen, Count of, 7
Wormsgau, Count in, 102,169,348,
359
Wormsgau, Lord of, 348

-Y-

Yemen, founder of, 430
Yemen, King of, 430

-Z-

Zaragoza, King of, 94
Zealand, Count of, 304
Zulpichgau, Count in, 18,62,97, 98,
102, 208,281A,304,304A,307,364
Zutphen, Count of, 304,304A,307,379

301

# General Index

Adalbert I, C of Perigord, 327,328
Adalbert I, C of Winterburg, 364
Adalbert I, D of Lucca, 93
Adalbert I, Mg of Ivrea, 62,332
Adalbert I, Mg of Tuscany, 93, 265
Adalbert II, C in Hegau, 98
Adalbert II, C in Saargau, 105,158
Adalbert II, C in Schwarzwold, 98
Adalbert II, C in Thurgau, 98
Adalbert II, C of Alsace, 105
Adalbert II, C of Canossa, 315
Adalbert II, C of Lucca, 93
Adalbert II, C of Metz, 105,158
Adalbert II, C of Modena, 315
Adalbert II, C of Namur, 120
Adalbert II, C of Vincenza, 106
Adalbert II, D of Low. Lorraine, 158
Adalbert II, D of Lucca, 93
Adalbert II, D of Upper Lorraine, 105
Adalbert II, K of Burgundy, 348A
Adalbert II, K of Italy, 94
Adalbert II, K of Lombardy, 94, 348
Adalbert, Mch of Este, 106
Adalbert II, Mg of Tuscany, 31,93, 198,263
Adalbert III, C de la Haute Marche, 87
Adalbert III, C in Zurichgau, 98
Adalbert III, C of Longwy, 94,105, 245,364
Adalbert III, C of Namur, 120, 126, 204
Adalbert III, D of Upper Lorraine, 105
Adalbert III, Mg of Tuscany, 93
Adalbert V, C of Alsace, 158
Adalbert of Werl, 68A
Adalbert von Egisheim II, 30, 126
Adalbert von Saffenburg, 62,67,71

Adalbert von Sommerschengburg, 14, 17
Adalbert, Abp of Euphra, 118
Adalbert, Abp of Salzburg, 118
Adalbert, C in Scherragau, 345
Adalbert, C in Schweinachgau, 279
Adalbert, C in Thurgau, 345
Adalbert, C of Kyburg, 364
Adalbert, C of Longwy, 187
Adalbert, C of Lucca, 31
Adalbert, C of Metz, 158
Adalbert, C of Morsburg, 364
Adalbert, C of Saffenburg, 68A,345
Adalbert, C of Werl, 67
Adalbert, C of Winterthur, 364
Adalbert, D of Alsace, 224
Adalbert, Ld of Burgelm, 18, 364
Adalbert, Mg of Austria, 279
Adalbert, Mg of Ivrea, 198,269
Adalbert, Mg of Tuscany, 31
Adalbert II, C in Scherregau, 98
Adalgot, fath of Routger, 307A
Adalgunde of Burgundy, 389
Adalheid von Wulfingen, 213
Adaltrude md Hildebart, 238,398
Adela md Alberto Azzo I, 43
Adela md Aribo I, 48,110
Adela md Engelbert III, 48,110
Adela md Gui II, 254
Adela md Immed II, 356
Adela of France, 205
Adela of Normandy, 132
Adela of Vermandois, 167,235
Adela, C of Salins, 254,383
Adela, Pr of Austrasia, 303
Adela, Pr of England, 132
Adela, Pr of France, 73,140,141,205
Adelaicia md William de Sabran, 116
Adelaide Beaujou, 196
Adelaide de Beziers, 116,195,195A
Adelaide de Bretueil, 268

Aethelred II, K of England, 233, 342
Aethelric, K of Bernicea, 406
Aethelwerd I, Theign of Surrey, 367
Aethelwerd, E of Wessex, 367
Aethelwulf, C of Boulogne, 98,242
Aethelwulf, E of Mercia, 367
Aethelwulf, K of England, 29,233, 250,367
Aethelwulf, K of Kent, 233,267
Aethelwulf, K of Wessex, 233,267, 376
Agane md Rodulf, 308
Agatha Lekapena, 382,399
Agatha of Alsace, 41
Agatha von Braunchweig, 196,233, 318
Agilolf, K of Lombards, 262
Agilofinges, 171
Agnes d'Evreux, 90,168
Agnes de Baudemont, 124
Agnes de Baugency, 4,37
Agnes de Beaumont, 34,274
Agnes de Braine, 84,123
Agnes de Chatillon-sur-Loing, 51, 80
Agnes de Ponthieu, 183,244
Agnes de Vermandois, 106
Agnes md Archambaud VII, 59
Agnes md Frederick III, 307A
Agnes md Henry, 71
Agnes md Herve, 34
Agnes md Nigiel d'Oily, 396
Agnes md Peter Amic, 194
Agnes of Austria, 279,378
Agnes of Blois, 36
Agnes of Burgundy, 88,119, 150, 161, 203
Agnes of Franconia, 40,279,359
Agnes of Hainault, 37
Agnes of Mels, 257
Agnes of Poitou, 161,359

Agnes von Arnstein, 304,304A
Agnes von Groitzsch-Rochlitz, 7,8
Agnes von Loos,307,320
Agnes von Mainz, 100, 320
Agnes von Metz, 45,320
Agnes von Weimer, 17
Agni Dagsson, 166
Agnir, K of Westfold, 339
Agricola, Consul, 236
Ahab, K of Israel, 329
Ahaz, K of Judah, 329
Ahaziah, K of Judah, 329
Aidan mac Gabran, K of Dalriada, 165
Aiga md Raoul, C of Quercy, 308A
Aigulf, C of Substantion, 203
Aimard, Sr de Sauvigny, 59
Aimeraud, Ld of Faucigny, 288
Aimery I, Vct de Chatellerault, 159
Aimery II, Vct of Thouars, 159
Aimery IV, Vct of Thouars, 159
Aimon I, C of Geneva, 175
Aimon I, Sr de Faucigny, 288
Aimon II, Sr de Bourbon, 61
al-Azd md Zaunob, 434
al-Azd, s of al-Ghauth, 433
al-Ghauth, s of Nabt, 433
al-Harith, s of Ka'b, 433
al-Hasan al-Sibt, 432
al-Royab md Mudar, 432
al-Sa'igh, fath of Selma,430
Alain I, C of Nantes, 334
Alain I, C of Vannes, 334
Alain I, D of Brittany, 334
Alain II, K of Brittany, 405
Alan III, D of Brittany, 24
Alared I, of Peterhem, 50A
Alberada md Robert Guiscard, 80
Alberade of Lorraine, 92,161,170
Alberade of Mons, 403
Alberga md Lancelin II, 4
Alberic I, C of Dammartin, 82,395

307

Alberic II, C of Burgundy, 92,101
Alberic II, C of Macon, 92,102
Alberic, Sr de Chavier, 99
Alberic, Sr de Montjoy, 99
Alberic, Sr de Pacy, 99
Alberich, s of Eticho II, 202
Albert, Ld of Moha, 30
Albert I, C of Troyes, 207,239
Albert I, C of Vermandois, 188,
  207,239
Albert von Ravenstein, 8
Alberto Azzo I, Mch in Liguria, 43
Alberto Azzo II, Mch d'Este, 29,43
Alberto Azzo, C of Lucca, 93,106
Alberto Azzo, Mch of Lucca, 93
Alberto Azzo, Pf of Lucca, 93
Albreda md Robert Guiscard, 296
Albuin von Jaun, 129
Alda md Billung of Thuringia, 92
Aldamius, K of Cimmenians, 303
Aldara, of San Massimo, 325
Aldegarde md Herbert I, 159,331
Aldetrude md Gauzelin, 163
Aldradus, Vct de Chatellerault, 305
Aldred, K of England, 238
Aledram, C of Montferrat, 106
Aledram, C of Savona, 106
Aledram, Mch di Liguria, 106
Aledram, Mch of Piedmont, 106
Aleida md Baldwin III, 242
Aleidis Sommerschenburg, 11
Aleran I, C of Worms, 248
Aleth of Montbard, 385
Alexander I, K of Macedonia, 413,
  414
Alexandre, K of Troy, 303
Alexies Komnenos, 111
Alexios Angelos, Emp of East,
  74,394
Alexios Komnenos I, Emp of East,
  42,111,215
Alexios, Pharo, 96,111

Alexius I, Emp of East, 42,111,215
Alexius III, Emp of East, 74
Alfano, C of Tabellaria, 325
Alfgar, E of East Anglia, 368
Alfonso Henriques I, K of Portugal,
  85,182
Alfonso II, C of Barcelona, 54
Alfonso II, C of Cerdagne, 54
Alfonso, II, C of Gerona, 54
Alfonso II, C of Lerida, 54
Alfonso II, C of Terrogona, 54
Alfonso II, C of Tortosa, 54
Alfonso II, K of Aragon, 54,94,150
Alfonso II, Mq of Barcelona, 54
Alfonso II, Mq of Larida, 54
Alfonso II, Mq of Provence, 54
Alfonso III, K of Asturias, 76,276
Alfonso V, Emp of Spain, 276
Alfonso V, K of Castile,180,276
Alfonso V, K of Leon, 180,248,276,
  277
Alfonso VI, K of Castile, 85,94,155,
  248,430
Alfonso VI, K of Leon, 85,94,155,
  248,430
Alfonso VI, K of Navarre, 248
Alfonso VI, K of Seville, 430
Alfonso VI md Zaida, 430
Alfonso VII, Emp of Spain, 86
Alfonso VII, K of Asturias, 94
Alfonso VII, K of Castile, 52,83,
  86,94,151,378
Alfonso VII, K of Galicia, 94
Alfonso VII, K of Leon,
  52,83,86,94,378
Alfonso VII, K of Toledo, 94
Alfonso VII, K of Zaragoza, 94
Alfonso IX, K of Castile, 52,83,88
Alfonso IX, K of Extramadura, 83
Alfonso IX, K of Leon, 52, 83
Alfonso IX, K of Toledo, 83
Alfonso, C of Provence, 116

Alfonso of Aragon, C of Provence, 54
Alfonso of Aragon, Pr of Aragon, 54
Alfred of Bernicea, 131
Alfred, K of England, 141,233,235, 242
Alfred, K of Wessex, 233
Alfrind md Rurick, 143
Alfthryth md Baldwin II, 141
Algifu md Edmund I, 233
Algout Gautreksson, 166
Ali ben Abu Talib, Caliph, 432
Ali ibn Abi Talif, 435
Alianore md Aimery II, 159
Alice de Courtenau, 87,144
Alice de Namur, 37,73,126
Alice de Rethel, Pr of Jerusalem, 80, 145
Alice de Roucy, 56,66,95, 170,266, 344
Alice md William d'Eu, 222
Alice of Burgundy, 84,244,245
Alice of France, Pr of France, 148,243
Alix de Bois-Champagne,132 134, 243
Alice md Guy de Baudemont, 123
Alketas, K of Macedonia, 413
Allarum md Guethenoc, 69
Alleaume, fath of Williswinda, 2
Almode de la Haute Marche, 54,142, 327,374
Almode de Limoges, 328
Almode of Toulouse, 142,150,203
Almos, D of Croatia, 51
Almos, D of Hungary, 51
Almos, K of Croatia, 51
Almos, Magyr prince, 51
Aloc, s of Benoc, 406
Alpin mac Eochaid, K of Dalriada, 165

Alpin mac Eochaid, K of Kintyre, 165
Alrek Agnasson, 166
Altberg md Walbert, 339
Alvaro, noble of Castile, 179
Amadea I, C of Aosta, 175
Amadeo I, C of Geneva, 175
Amadeo I, C of Maurienne, 175
Amadeo I, C of Savoy, 175
Amadeo III, C of Maurienne, 192
Amadeo of Spolito, 173
Amadeus II, C of Savoy, 93
Amadeus II, Mg of Susa, 93
Amadeus III, C of Savoy, 93,182
Amadeus III, Mg of Maurienne, 93,182
Amadeus, C of Burgundy, 332
Amalrada md Eberhard I, 65
Amalrada of Hamalant, 389
Amalric de Benaugus, 87
Amauri, Sr de Montfort, 90,99
Amazaspus I, K of Iberia, 416
Amaziah, K of Judah, 329
Amelia md Bernard I, 54,195A,327
Amelie md Boson I, 305
Amestris md Xerxes I, 414,429
Amic of Avignon, 194
Amic, C in Council of Narbonne, 203
Amina bint Wahl, 435
Amina md Abdallah, 435
Aminiana md Garcia Sanchez, 289
Amir ma 'al-Sama, 434
Amir-al Lakhmi, K of Hira, 430
Ammiel, fath of Bathsheba, 329
Amminadab, s of Aram, 329
Amon, K of Judah, 329
Amourey III, C d'Evreux, 103
Amr ibn Itaf, 430
Amr ma' al-Sama,434
Amr Mudrika md Salma, 432
Amr Muzayqiva Tarifa, 434

Amr, K of Hira, 430
Amr, son of Arib, 430
Amr, s of Rabia Luhayy, 434
Amuna md Garcia Sanchez,
216,290
Amuna of Agen, 289
Amyntas I, K of Macedonia, 413
Amyntas, Persian sovereign, 413
Ana of Cardayna, 284
Anamu, son of Numera, 430
Anastasia md Andrew I, 225
Anastasia md Tiberius, 407
Anb al-Uzza, fath of Barra, 435
Ancelende md Guy I, 126
Anceline de Montfort, 222
Andabarta md Hucbold, 316
Andcar III, Mg of Camerino, 198
Andecar III, Mg of Spoleto, 198
Andelme de Candavene, 242
Andre de Baudemont, 84
Andregota Sanchez, 55,223,292
Andrew I, K of Hungary, 225
Andrew II, K of Galicia, 78
Andrew II, K of Hungary,
7,51,78,79
Andria md Artaxerxes I, 410
Androcomius, fath of Tasciovanus,
405B
Andromachus, general, 414
Andronikeo Kamateros, 111
Andronikos Angelos Doukas, 215,
309,394
Andronikos Kamateros Doukas, 394
Andronikos Komnenos I, Emp of
East, 42
Andronicos, Dux, 215
Angrenwit, s of Aloc, 406
Angier, C of Prun, 12
Angila md Rutpert, 102
Angibert md Bertha of France, 244
Angiltrude md Gui II, 265
Anna Angelina, 74

Anna Delassena, 51,111
Anna de Ribagorza, 347
Anna Diagenissa, 51
Anna Jaroslawna of Kiev,134,143
Anna, K of E. Anglia, 437
Anna md Georgios, 322A
Anna md Leon, 322A
Anna md Milo of Noyes II, 383
Anna of Byzantium, 25,253
Anna of Enygeus, 438
Ansaud I, Vct of Auxerre, 241
Ansaud II md Reitrude, 241
Ansaud, fath of Sigrada, 236
Ansbertus, Gallo-Rom. Senator,
171,236
Ansbertus, Senator, 260
Anscar II C of Orchert, 332
Anscar II, Mq of Ivrea, 332
Anselm I, C of Noyen, 273
Anselm II, C of Noyen, 273
Anselme Candavene,184, 242
Anselme de Garlande, 123
Anselme I, Mch de Davona, 106
Anseric I, Sire de Chacenay, 384
Anseric II, Sire de Chacenay,
384,385
Ansfred le Goz, Vct d'Hiesmer, 295
Ansfried, C of Hiesmer, 295
Ansguise md Begga of Landen,
171,173, 214
Ansguise, Mayor of the Palace,
214,260
Anskar III, Mg of Camarino, 198
Anskar III, Mg of Spoleto, 198
Antenor, I, K of Troy, 303
Antenor II, K of Sicambi, 303
Antenor II, K of Vimmonians, 303
Antenor III, K of Scambi, 303
Antenor IV, K of Franks, 303
Antharius, K of Sicambi, 303
Antigona md Lagos, 413
Antiochus Epiphanes IV, 411

Antiochus Magnas III, 411,413,418
Antiochus md Laodice, 414
Antiochus of Syria IV, 413
Antiochus Philometer VIII, 414
Antiochus Sater I, K of Syria, 413, 415,427
Antiochus Theo II, 411,415,418
Antiochus I, K of Commagene, 417
Antipator, fath of Philo I, 427
Antipatros, regent of Macedonia, 413
Apama md Megas, 413
Apama of Baktria, 414,415
Apame md Pharnabazus, 414
Apoganem, patrikos, 115A
Appa md Liuthaire II, 262A
Apries, Pharaoh, 420
Aquilinus, noble of Lyons, 171A
Aragonta md Jimeno Jimenez, 180
Aragonta Pelaez, 276
Aram, s of Hezron, 329
Archaemenes, fath of Teispes, 414
Archaeus, Pr of Syria, 414
Archambaud I, Sr de Bourbon, 59
Archambaud I, Sr de St Geran, 55A,440
Archambaud II, Sr de Bourbon, 59
Archambaud II, Vct de Camborn, 156, 308
Archambaud II, Vct de Turenne, 156
Archambaud II, Vct de Ventadour, 156,308
Archambaud III, Sr de Boutbon, 59
Archambaud IV, Sr de Bourbon, 59
Archambaud V, Sr de Montculon, 55A, 440
Archambaud VII, Sr de Bourbon, 59
Archambaud VIII, Sr de Bourbon, 84
Archambaud IX de Bourbon, 55A, 440

Archard de la Forte-sur-Aube, 108
Ardashir I, K of Persia, 408
Ardicino, Pr of Italy, 198
Ardcino Glabrione III, C of Asturia, 107,315
Ardoino Glabrione III, C of Torino, 107,315
Ardoino II, C of Ivrea, 198
Ardoino IV, Mch of Tours, 107
Ardoino, K of Italy, 186,198
Ardoino, Mg of Ivria 186,198
Ardoino of Ivrea II, 198
Arembourg md Gautier I, 189
Aremburga md Damas, 85
Aremburge md Aimery, 159
Argaios I, K of Macedonia, 413
Argentael md Nominae, 405
Argilo md Nuno Nunez, 287
Argilo of Branosera, 285
Aria md Fortun Garces, 294
Ariabarazanes I, K of Media Athropatene, 408
Arib, son of Malik, 430
Aribo I, Pz of Bavaria, 48,110
Aribo, C in Traungau, 12,48
Aribo, Mg of Donaugraftscaften, 48,118
Arimmanns md Berthilindis, 127
Ariobarzares, K of Pontus, 411
Ariochus I , K of Commagene, 408
Aripert I, K of Lombards, 380
Aripert I, of the Obotrites, 380
Aripert II, son of Reginpert, 380
Aristoabazanes II, setrap of Dask-ayeion, 411
Arivargus Gwenivyth, 438
Ariyaramna, s of Teispes, 414
Armand de la Flotte, 195
Armengol de Toulouse, 54
Armengol I, C of Urgel, 195
Armengol II, C of Urgel, 195,347
Armengol III, C of Urgel, 195

311

Armengol IV, C of Urgel, 195,197
Armengol, C of Albi, 326
Arnaold, Bp of Metz, 171
Arnaud de la Flotte, 195
Arnaud Manzer, C of Angouleme, 87
Arnaud, Bp of Cambrai, 99,331, 400,401
Arnaud, C of Angouleme, 87
Arnaud, C of Cambrai, 99,400, 401
Arnold I md Matihlda of Chiny, 65
Arnold I, C in Ratagau, 13
Arnold I, C in Traungau, 12,13
Arnold I, C of Artois, 141,169
Arnold I, C of Bigorre, 227
Arnold I, C of Flanders, 141,169,311, 356
Arnold I, C of Ghent, 311
Arnold I, C of W Friesland, 311,316
Arnold I, D of Bavaria, 372
Arnold II, C in Chiemgau, 12
Arnold II, C in Upper Austria, 13
Arnold II, C of Bigorre, 227
Arnold II, C of Carinthian Mark, 13
Arnold II, C of Chiny, 65
Arnold II, C of Comminges, 195A
Arnold II, C of Concerans, 195A,291
Arnold II, C of Ivoix, 65
Arnold II, C of Warcq, 65
Arnold II, C of Wels-Lambach, 12
Arnold Scheldewindeke I, 135A
Arnold von Gilching, 46
Arnold, C of Arnstein, 304A
Arnold, C of Zurichgau, 304A
Arnoldo, C of Astarac, 216
Arnoldus, Bp of Metz, 260
Arnulf I, C of Ghent, 311,244
Arnulf I, C of W Friesland, 311,244
Arnulf II, C of Boulogne, 242
Arnulf II, C of Chiny, 66
Arnulf II, C of Flanders, 141,184,332
Arnulf, Bg of Mainz, 320
Arnulf, Bp of Metz, 2,171,358
Arnulf, C in Chiemgau, 12
Arnulf, C of Artois, 235

Arnulf, C of Flanders, 184,235
Arnulf, C of Loos, 100,320
Arnulf, C of Rienick, 320
Arnulf, C of W. Friesland, 242
Arnulf, D of Bavaria, 63,64, 270,272, 279
Arnulf, Emp of West, 172
Arnulf, fath of Hildeburge, 360
Arnulf, Holy Roman Emp, 33A
Arnulf, K of Germany, 172
Arnulf, Pf in Bavaria, 64
Aroandes, s of Darius IV, 410
Aroandes I md Rodogunde, 410
Aroandes II, s of Aroandes I, 410
Aroandes III, s of Mithradanes I, 410
Arpad, D of Hungary, 51
Arpad, Pr of Magyars, 51
Arpo md N.N. von Chadalhoch, 48
Arsames, K of Armenia, 412
Arsames I, s of Samos I, 410
Arschavier, Pr of Kamsarakan, 322
Arsead of Bergh, 166
Arshama, fath of Pharnaces, 411
Arshama, s of Arijaramna, 414
Arsinde de Rossilon, 218,218A
Arsinde md Arnold II, 291
Arsinde md Francon II, 218A
Arsinde md Francon of Narbonne, 284
Arsinde md N.N. of Agde, 226
Arsinde md Remigius, 329
Arsinde md William d'Agde, 226
Arsinde of Toulouse, 328
Arsinde, C of Carcassonne, 195A
Arsinoe II md Ptolemy Philadelphos, 413
Arsinoe III md Ptolemy Philopator IV, 413
Artabanus I, general, 410
Artabanus I, K of Parthia, 417
Artabanus IV, K of Media, 408
Artabanus IV, K of Parthia, 408
Artabazus I, setrap of W Asia, 414
Artabazus II, setrap of Bithynia, 414

Bartholomew, Sr de l'Isle Bouchard, 159
Basabelian I, K of Troy, 303
Basebilian II, K of Troy, 303
Basil I, Emp of Byzantium, 253
Basil, K of Poland, 225
Basileios Skleros, 115,382
Basileos, rector, 322
Basina of Thuringia, 303
Bassinus, K of Scambi, 303
Bathsheba md David, 329
Baudouin, C of Boulogne, 235
Beata von Hohenwart, 29
Beatrice Candavane, 242
Beatrice de Beziers, 116
Beatrice de Montculon, 55A, 440
Beatrice de Montdidier, 177,249,266
Beatrice de Ramagnano, 106,107
Beatrice de Saint Pol, 122
Beatrice de Vermandois, 169,264
Beatrice md Adalbero I, 229
Beatrice md Frederick I, 64,319
Beatrice md Hugh III, 184
Beatrice md Raimond, 193
Beatrice md Rodulf de Warenne, 135
Beatrice md Stephen, 41, 187
Beatrice of Burgundy, 40,41,125
Beatrice of Faucigny, 175,288
Beatrice of France, 149
Beatrice of Hainault, 163,170
Beatrice of Macon, 2,92,93,125,187
Beatrice of Morvois, 134,264
Beatrice of Normandy, 156
Beatrice of Saint Pol, 148,242
Beatrice of Savoy, 54,88,93,164
Beatrice of Vermandois, 264
Beatrix de Vermandois, 134
Beatrix md Konrad III, 381
Beatrix of Poitou, 150,203
Beatrix, Pr of France, 381
Beaw, s of Sceldwa, 233
Bebba md Aethelfrith, 406
Bedwig, s of Scaef, 233
Begga md Ansguise, 171,173

Begga of Landen, 214,260
Begue, C of Paris, 171,185,264,269, 350, 404
Begue II, C of Paris, 350
Begue md Aupais, 250
Bel-ibni, Gov of Sealand, 414A
Bela I, K of Hungary, 10,28,51,281
Bela II, K of Hungary, 51
Bela III, K of Hungary, 51,80
Bela IV, D of Styria, 78
Bela IV, K of Hungary, 78
Bela V, K of Hungary, 74
Beldig of Scandinavia, 233
Beletrude md Rostaing, 116
Beli, K of Strathclyde, 341,406
Beliarde md Archambaud IV, 59
Belielde md Adelme, 193,194
Belielde md William I, 194
Beliarde md William II, 150
Bellon, C of Ampurias, 284
Bellon, C of Barcelona 284
Bellon, C of Carcassonne, 54,284,291
Bellon, C of Urgel, 284
Beltsea md Frithuwald, 233,324
Benno von Northeim, 26
Benno, s of Bernard, 27
Benoc, s of Brand, 406
Beornoch md Ida, 406
Berengaria of Barcelona, 52,83,86, 94
Berengaria of Castile, 52,83
Berengarius II, K of Italy, 332
Berengarius II, Mg of Ivrea, 332
Berenger de Bayeux, 166
Berenger I, Emp of West, 269
Berenger I, K of Italy, 269
Berenger I, Mg of Friuli, 269
Berenger I, Vct de Milhaud, 402
Berenger I, Vct de Narbonne, 218,
Berenger II, C of Sulzbach, 63,64,120
Berenger II, K of Italy, 94,263, 332
Berenger II, Mq of Ivrea, 106,332
Berenger II, Vct de Carlat, 226,257

Berenger II, Vct of Gievaudun, 226, 257
Berenger II, Vct of Milhaud, 226,257
Berenger II, Vct of Rodeve, 226,257
Berenger of Bayeaux, 166
Berenger of Melgueil, 203
Berenger, an East Frank, 185,269,404
Berenger, C in Bavarian Nordgau, 63
Berenger, C in Hessegau, 166A
Berenger, C of Namur, 403
Berenger, C of Rennes, 405
Berenger, fath of Adelme, 193
Berenger, judge of Provence, 193
Berenger, Mg of Neustria, 166A
Berenger, s of Bernard II, 203
Berenger, Vct of Avignon, 193
Berkhard II md Reginlink, 41A
Berkhard III of Wettin, 210
Berkhard of Wettin, 17
Berlinda md Henry V, 33A
Berlinda md Hugh V, 33
Bermudo Lainez, 181
Bernard Billung I, D of Saxony, 301, 312
Bernard de Beaujou, 196
Bernard de Ribagoza I, C of Pallars, 290
Bernard de St. Valery I, 122
Bernard de St. Valery II, 122
Bernard de St. Valery III, 122
Bernard de St. Valery IV, 122
Bernard Harcourt, 103
Barnard I, C de la Haute Marche, 54,327
Bernard I, C de la Mancha, 195A
Bernard I, C in N. Thuringia, 27
Bernard I, C of Besalu, 218
Bernard I, C of Melgueil, 203
Bernard I, C of Pallars, 286,290
Bernard I, C of Perigord, 54,327
Bernard I, C of Ribagoza, 286,290
Bernard I, C of Substantion,303
Bernard I, Mg of Saxon Nordmark, 27,311

Bernard I, Vct de Carlat, 257
Bernard I, Vct de Milhaud, 402
Bernard II, C of Bigorra, 195
Bernard II, C of Melguiel, 195A,203,291
Bernard II, C of Provence, 195A
Bernard II, D of Saxony, 27,28,41, 270,312
Bernard II, Ld of Haldenslaben, 27
Bernard II, Mg of Saxon Nordmark, 27
Bernard II, Vct of Carlat, 257
Bernard III, C of Melgueil, 203
Bernard IV, Vct d'Agde, 195A
Bernard IV, Vct d'Albi, 195A
Bernard IV, Vct de Beziers, 195A
Bernard IV, Vct de Carcassonne, 195A
Bernard IV, Vct de Nimes, 195,195A
Bernard of Septimania, 289
Bernard Rodger, C of Bigorre, 95, 105,151,227
Bernard Rodger, C of Carcassonne, 95,105,151,227
Bernard Rodger, C of Conserans, 95,105,151,207
Bernard Tallaferro I, C of Besalu, 347
Bernard Trencavel md Rangarde, 195B
Bernard von Flinsbach, 10,228
Bernard von Northeim, 26
Bernard von Werl I, 19
Bernard von Werl III, 19
Bernard, C of Autun, 326
Bernard, C of Auvergne, 195A
Bernard, C of Bavaria, 118
Bernard, K of Italy, 23
Bernard, Ld of Montbard, 385
Bernard, Mg of Septimania, 326,326A
Bernard, s of Dietrich, 27
Bernard, Vct of Turenne, 308
Bernice md Ptolemy Euergates III, 413,428
Bernice md Ptolemy Sater I, 428

316

Bernier, judge at Avignon, 194
Bernot Unifred, C of Ribagorza, 284
Berswinde of France, 224
Berta md Folmer, 337
Berta md Lietaud II, 101
Berta md Raimonde I, 328
Berta md Teto II, 106
Bertha d'Aumale, 244
Bertha md Aethelbert I, 233A, 233B
Bertha md Folmer, 45
Bertha md Fredelon, 329
Bertha md Gerhard II, 246
Bertha md Godizo, 389
Bertha md Peregrin 18A
Bertha md Pippin, K of Franks, 214
Bertha md Raimonde I, 329
Bertha md Ulrich III, 364
Bertha md Wolfrad, 18A
Bertha of Betuwe, 99,400,401
Bertha of Blois, 24
Bertha of Burgundy, 175
Bertha of Este, 7,32,47,93,106,315
Bertha of France, 244
Bertha of Holland, 134,146,311
Bertha of Laon, 214
Bertha of Lorraine, 93
Bertha of Maurienne, 359
Bertha of Swabia, 175,323,345
Bertha of Tours, 264
Bertha van Buren, 113
Bertha, d of Remingus, 326
Bertha, moth of Rolande, 173
Bertha, Pr of Burgundy, 133,230
Bertha, Pr of Lorraine, 30,174,
    186,198,263
Berthar, K of Thuringia, 303
Berthiez of Toulouse, 218A
Berthilda md Rostaing II, 196
Berthilde md Dagobert I, 303
Berthildis md Arimanus, 127
Berthold I, C in Bridgau, 113
Berthold I, C in Lurngau, 41

Berhold I, C in Upper Isar, 64
Berthold I, C of Ortengen, 97
Berthold II, C in Bridgau, 113
Berthold II, C in Thurgau, 113
Berthold II, C in Upper Isar, 7,64
Berthold II, C of Diessen, 64
Berthold III, C in Upper Isar, 7
Berthold III, C of Andechs, 7
Berthold III, C of Ortengen, 98,113
Berthold IV, C in Fuergau, 113
Berthold IV, C in Ortengau, 113
Berthold IV, C of Diessen, 7,10
Berthold IV, C of Plassenburg, 7
Berthold IV, C of Strain, 7
Berthold IV, D of Carinthia, 113
Berthold IV, Mch of Viera 113
Berthold V, C of Andrechs, 7
Berthold V, C of Diessen, 9
Berthold V, C of Innesbruch, 7
Berthold V, C of Wolfratschausen, 7
Berthold V, Mg of Istria, 7
Berthold VI, C of Antioch, 7,8
Berthond VI, D of Coast Meran, 7
Berthold VI, D of Croatia, 7
Berthold VI, D of Dalmatia, 7
Berthold VI, Mg of Istria, 7
Berthold von Babenburg I, 270,271
Berthold von Hamm I, 365
Berthold von Schwarzenburg I, 388
Berthold, C in Eugadin, 41A
Berthold, C in Swabia, 41A
Berthold, D of Bavaria, 41A
Berthold, fath of Hermenlindis, 300
Berthold, Pf of Swabia, 270
Bertila of Spoleto, 269
Bertrada md Caribert, 214
Bertrade de Gometz, 90
Bertrade de Montfort, 2,90
Bertrade, Pr of Normandy, 270
Bertrade, Pr of Norway,
    204,312,369
Bertrand II, C of Forcalquier, 195

Bertrar, K of Thuringia, 303  
Bertrada md Martin of Laon, 214  
Bertswinda, moth of Giselbert, 207  
Bethoc md Crinan the Thane, 196,252  
Bethoc, Pr of Scotland, 165,252  
Bethuel, fath of Rebekah, 329  
Bezelin von Villingau, 113  
Biagoto of Stockow, 362,378  
Bijorn, Underking of Vestfold, 28  
Biletrude md Berthold, 41A  
Biletrude md Archambaud III, 59  
Bilichildis md Hugh I, 357  
Bilichildis md William I, 298,298A  
Bilichildis of Maine, 284  
Billung of Obotrites I, 380  
Billung of Obotrites II, 380  
Billung of Thuringia, 92  
Billung, C of Saxony, 312  
Billung, C of Thuringia, 301  
Biogoto of Stockow, 362,378  
Bijorn, Underking of Vestfold, 28  
Billung, C of Saxony, 312  
Biorn Ulfiusson, 221  
Biorn 'a Haugi, K of Uppsala, 240  
Bjorn Ragnarsson, K of Uppsala, 240  
Bjorn, K of Uppsala, 240,368  
Blanca, Pr of Navarre, 151  
Blanche of Anjou, 91  
Blanche of Artois, 147  
Blanche of Castile, 70, 88  
Blanche, Pr of Navarre, 81,83,86  
Blithilda md Ansbertus, 171,236  
Blithilda, Pr of Cologne, 260  
Boaz md Ruth, 329  
Bodegisel I md Palatina, 37  
Bodegisel II, Gov of Aquitaine, 171  
Bodegisel II md Oda, 171  
Bohemond I, D of Calabria, 80  
Bohemond I, Pr of Antioch, 80,146  
Bohemond II, D of Calabria, 80  

Bohemond II, Pr of Antioch, 80,145  
Bohemond II, Pr of Taranto, 80  
Bokenranef, Pharaoh, 420  
Boleslas III, K of Poland, 378  
Boleslaw I, D of Bohemia, 212,362, 378  
Boleslaw I, Gr Pr of Poland, 378  
Boleslaw I, K of Poland, 378  
Boleslaw I, Pr of Albunzlau, 362  
Boleslaw II, D of Bohemia, 362  
Boleslaw III, K of Poland, 363,378  
Boniface, C of Bologna, 366  
Boniface, Mg of Camerino 366  
Boniface, Mg ofSpoleto, 366  
Boniface, Pr of Spoleto, 366  
Boniface II, C in Liguria, 93  
Boniface II, C of Lucca, 93  
Boniface III, C of Lucca, 93  
Boniface III, D of Lucca, 93  
Bonifacio I, D of Spoleto, 93  
Bonifacio I, Mch di Savona Vasto, 106  
Bonifacio I, of Lucca, 93  
Bonifacio II, C in Liguria, 93  
Bonifacio II, C of Lucca, 93  
Bonifacio III, D of Lucca, 93  
Boris Michael, Khan of Bulgars, 309  
Borrel II, C of Barcelona, 54,195  
Borrel II, C of Gerona, 54,195  
Borrel II, C of Odona, 54,195  
Borrel II, Mq of Barcelona, 54,195  
Borziwoj, D of Bohemia, 362  
Borziwoj, Pr of Prague, 362  
Borziwoj, Pr of Psow, 362  
Boso I, C de la Haute Marche, 326,327  
Boso I, C in Italy, 174  
Boso I, C of Aun, 327  
Boso I, C of Perigord, 327  
Boso II, C in Italy, 174  
Boso II, C of Vienne, 343

Boso II, K of Lower Burgundy, 25,343

Boso II, Vct de Chatellerault, 159, 305

Boso III, C of Turin, 112,174

Boso of Parthois, 328

Boso, C of Arles, 263

Boso, K of Burgundy, 258

Boso, Mg of Tuscany, 263

Boso, Vct of Beziers, 226

Boson I, Vct de Chatellerault, 305

Boson I, Vct de Turenne, 60,156,377

Boson II, C of Avignon, 333

Boson II, C of Provence, 333,375

Bostenai ben Haninai, 329

Boto I, fath of Retig I, 136

Boto II, s of Retig I, 136

Boto von Botenstein, 47,48,62,387

Bouchard d'Avesnes, 50

Bouchard de Bray-sur-Seine, 34

Bouchard I, Sr de Morency, 34

Bouchard II, Sr de Morency, 34

Bouchard III, Sr d'Herouville, 34

Bouchard III, Sr de Merle, 34

Bouchard III, Sr de Montmorency, 34,274

Bouchard, fath of Bouchard, 34

Bouchard, minur dominicur, 2

Bouchard, prefect of royal hunt, 2

Bouchard, Sr de Montmorency, 34

Boudicia md Prasutagus, 405C

Bovin, Sr de Maers, 255

Bovin, Sr de Monceau-le-Comte, 255

Bozena md Udalrich, 362

Bracen of S. Walia, 165

Bran Fendig, 438

Bran, s of Liryllediath, 405C

Brand of Scandinavia, 233,406

Braut-Onund Ingvarson, 166

Bremond, Sr d'Uzes, 193

Bretislaw I, D of Bohemia, 362

Bretislaw I, D of Moravia, 362

Bretislaw I, D of Silicia, 362

Brion, K of Ireland, 251

Brude, fath of Gwid, 406

Brude, K of Picts, 439

Bruno, C in Saxon Engen, 92

Bruno, C of Saxony, 92

Bruno I, C of Iverfort, 271

Bruno I, Ld of Brunisberge, 92

Bruno I, Saxon warlord, 92

Bruno II, C of Arneburg, 271

Bruno II, C of Iverfort, 271

Bruno von Braunchweig, 32,199, 359

Budic I, K of Brittany, 405,405A

Budic II, K of Brittany, 405

Budwine, C of Italy, 112,206,343

Budwine, C of Metz, 112,133,171, 206,258,343,346,357

Burchard, C in Meinfeldgau, 359

Buchard, C in Wormsgau, 359

Burkhard I, C in Grabfeldgau, 210

Burkhard II, C in Frankish Grab-feldgau, 210

Burkhard II, C in Thuringian Hiut-sitingau, 210

Burkhard II, D of Swabia, 345

Burkhard II, Mg of Sarbenhark, 210

Burkhard III of Grabfeldgau, 210

Burkhard III of Wettin, 210,359

Burkhard, C in Baar, 345

Burkhard, C in Bertoldbar, 345

Burkhard, Mq of Rhaetia, 345

Bustani ben Haninai, 408

Buyawawa, fath of Mawasen, 422

-C-

Cadelon I, Vct d'Aunay, 331

Cadelon II, Vct d'Aunay, 331

Cadelon III, Vct d'Aunay, 331

Cadelon VI, Vct d'Aunay, 398

Conrad II, C of Auxerre, 175,300
Conrad II, C of Luxemburg, 119
Conrad II, Emp of West, 32,199
Conrad II, K of Brunswick, 199
Conrad II, K of Burgundy,359
Conrad II, K of Germany, 199,359
Conrad II, K of Italy, 199,359
Conrad II, Mg of Transjuranian
   Burgundy, 175,300
Conrad of Franconia II,199,359
Conrad, C in Nehegau, 359
Conrad, C in Rhinegau, 199
Conrad, C in Spayergau, 359
Conrad, C in Wormsgau, 359
Conrad, C of Hornes, 100
Conrad, D of Franconia, 359
Conrad,D of Lorraine, 359
Conrad, D of Swabia, 199
Constance Amic, 116,194
Constance of Antioch, 99
Constance of Arles, 134,140,154,
   232,333,375,397
Constance of Burgundy, 94,155,248
Constance of France, 397
Constance of Provence,134,333
Constance of Toulouse, 134
Constance Valasquita, 195
Constance, Pr of Antioch, 80
Constance, Pr of France, 80,146
Constantin Tarnikos, 115A
Constantina md Flavius, 407
Constantine IX, Emp of Byzantium,
   115
Constantine Lips, 115A
Corotius, K of Strathclyde, 341
Corun md Teithfalit, 405A
Creoda, Pr of Wessex, 233
Crinan the Thane, E of Strathclyde,
   165,196,252
Crinan the Thane, Gov of Scots
   Island, 165,196,252

Cumobelin, ruler of Catevalaccvi,
   405A,405B
Cumobelin, ruler of Trinovantes,
   405A,405B
Cunigunde md Bernard, 231
Cunneda Wledig md Gwawl, 405A
Cunneda, s-in-law of Coel Hen,
   405A
Cutha, Underruler of Wessex, 233
Cuthwine, Underruler of Wessex,
   233
Cynan Meriadoc, K of Brittany, 405
Cynan Meriadoc, K of Dumnonia,
   405
Cynloup, s of Cinhil, 341
Cynric, K of West Saxons, 233
Cyrus I, K of Anshan, 419
Cyrus I, K of Persia, 419,420
Cyrus II, K of Akkad, 419
Cyrus II, K of Babylon, 419
Cyrus II, K of Persia, 419
Cyrus II, K of Summar, 419

## -D-

Dada md Bernard, 308
Dadilis de Pallars, 223
Dadone, C of Pombia, 198
Dag Dyggvasson, 166
Dag Frode, 204
Dagobert I, K of Austrasia,
   123,262,303
Dagobert I, K of East Franks, 303
Dagobert I, K of Franks, 303
Dagobert II, D of East Franks, 303
Dagobert II, K of Austrasia, 303
Dagreid Dagsdotter, 166
Damas, Sr de Semur, 95
Damas, Vct de Brioude, 85
Damianus Delassenus, D of Anti-
   och, 96
Damon, Vct de Briode, 85
Dampi md Olaf Vermundsson, 324

322

Dangerose md Aimery I, 159
Daniel Dremrost, K of Brittany, 405
Darara md Cynab Meridoc, 405
Darda, fath of Ericthonius, 303
Darius I, K of Persia, 414,419,428
Darius I, Pharaoh, 414,429
Darius II, K of Persia, 410,413
Darius II, K of Egypt, 414,429
Darius, Pr of Media Athropatene,
  408, 417
Dato II, C of Bigorre, 227
David I, E of Huntingdon, 72
David I, K of Scotland, 72,77,221
David, K of Israel, 329
David, K of Judah, 329
Dawith of Taraun, 322
Debronega Marie of Kiev, 361,378
Debroneiga md Casimir I, 143,321
Debroniega of Kiev, 321
Decimus Rusticus, 171A
Deda md Bernard, 308A
Dedi I, C in N Hessegau, 210
Dedi II, E of Eilenburg, 210
Dedi II, C of Lausnitz, 210
Dedi II, Mg of Ostermark, 210,211
Dedi, C in Hessegau, 17,210
Dedo V, C in Groitzsch-Rochlitz,
  8, 11
Dedo V, Mg of Eilenburg, 8
Dedo V, Mg of Niederlausitz, 8
Demetrius Nicator II, 413,414
Demetrius Soter I, 414
Demetrius, K of Macedonia, 427
Dhoude md Bernard, 326,326A
Diafronissa md Atto Trencavel,
  195B
Dida md Reinold I, 226
Diego Fernandez, C of Limia, 277
Diego Lainez, Sr de Bibar, 79
Diego Munoz, C of Saldina, 267
Diego Rodriguez Porcelos, 35
Diego, C of Orviedo, 180

Diepold I, C in Angstgau, 128,279
Dietmar I, Mg of Saxon Eastmark,
  211
Dietmar II, Mg of Lausnitz, 211

Dietmar II, Mg of Saxon Eastmark,
  211
Dietmar, C in Quinzgau, 41
Dietrich I, C of Bar, 247,318,319,
  337
Dietrich I, C of W Friesland, 310,
  356
Dietrich I, D of Upper Lorraine,
  158,247,319
Dietrich II, C of Alsace,152
Dietrich II, C of Ellenburg, 212
Dietrich II, C of Flanders, 152
Dietrich II, C of W Friesland, 311
Dietrich II, D of Upper Lorraine,
  23,290
Dietrich III, C of Holland, 311
Dietrich III, C of W. Friesland, 311
Dietrich V, C of W Friesland, 38
Dietrich VI, C of Holland, 390,391
Dietrich Flamens, C of Velue,
  11,119
Dietrich md Huchbald, 18A
Dietrich of Alsace I, 41,158
Dietrich of Alsace II, 38,41,158,205
Dietrich von Lothringen II, 132
Dietrich von Wettin I, 8,210
Dietrich von Wettin II, C of Brehna,
  8,210
Dietrich von Wettin II, C of Ellen-
  burg, 8,210
Dietrich von Wettin II, Mg of
  Niederlausitz, 210
Dietrich, C in Drenthe, 389
Dietrich, C in Durlingau, 27
Dietrich, C in Salland, 389
Dietrich, C in Saxon Nordmark, 27,
  210

323

Eberhard I, C in Lahngau, 65
Eberhard I, C in Nordgau, 202
Eberhard I, C in Zurichgau, 304A
Eberhard I, C of Nullenburg, 304A
Eberhard II, C in Hamelant, 202,311
Eberhard II, C in Meinfeld, 62,281A
Eberhard II, C in Nordgau, 202
Eberhard II, C in Thurgau, 98,281A, 345
Eberhard II, C in Zurichgau, 62,98, 281A
Eberhard II, C of Hamelant, 311
Eberhard II, C of Meinvelt, 62
Eberhard III, C in Argau, 202
Eberhard III, C in Lahngau, 65
Eberhard III, C in Meingau, 65
Eberhard III, C in N Hamelant, 202
Eberhard III, C in Nordgau, 202
Eberhard III, C in Ortengau, 202
Eberhaed III, C in Thurgau, 18
Eberhard III, D of Friesland, 202
Eberhard IV C in Alsacian Nordgau, 33,158,202
Eberhard IV, C in Thurgau, 18
Eberhard IV, C of Alsace, 3,202
Eberhard V md Ida von Altshausen, 18A
Eberhard V, C in Zurichgau, 18,364
Eberhard V, C of Nullenburg, 18
Eberhard von der Betuwe, 389
Eberhard von der Tristerbant, 389
Eberhard, C in Bonngau, 208,389
Eberhard, C in Keldachgau, 389
Eberhard, C in Rheingau, 351
Eberhard, C in Sulichgau, 272
Eberhard, C of Paris, 350
Eberhard, D of Franconia, 348A
Eberhard, Mg of Friuli, 98,185,269, 272,345,389,404
Eberwin, Mg of Merberg, 381
Ebles "Mancer, C of Poitou, 163
Ebles I, Abp of Rheims, 170

Ebles I, C of Rheims, 163,170
Ebles I, C of Roucy, 163,170
Ebles I, Vct de Turenne, 156
Ecgfrida md Uchtred, 314
Eckard I, C in Thurgau, 212
Eckard II, C in Thurgau, 212
Eckbert, C in Ambergau, 32
Eckbert, Ld of Alaberg, 32
Eckbert, Saxon noble, 338
Eckbert von Braunchweig, Mg of Meissen, 32
Eckbert I, C in Quinziggau, 9
Eckbert I, C of Formbach-Puttin, 9,12
Eckbert II, C of Newburg, 9
Eckhard I, C in Thuringia, 212
Eckhard I, Mg of Meissen, 213
Eckhard I, Mg of Thuringia, 212
Eckhard, C of Hesbaye, 303
Edgar, K of England, 233
Edgiva, Pr of England, 171,261
Edith d'Oilly, 82,395,396
Edith fitz Forne, 396
Edith md Dreux III, 56
Edith md Luitfried I, 224
Edith of Norway, 176
Edith of Scotland, 89
Edmund "Ironside," K of England, 22
Edmund "the Elder," King of England, 233
EDmund "the Elder," K of Wessex, 233
Edmund Eriksson, K of Birka, 240
Edmund I, K of England, 233
Edmund Plantagenet, E of Lancaster, 147
Edmund Plantagenet, Pr of England, 147
Edward "Atheling," Pr of England, 318

326

Emma md Bernard St. Hillary I, 122
Emma md Eadbald, 233A
Emma md Gerard, 364
Emma md Ivo Bellomontensis III, 274
Emma md Louis, K of Bavaria, 33A
Emma of Allemania, 262
Emma of Bavaria, 172
Emma of Blois, 88,340
Emma of Normandy, 242
Emma of Perigord, 327
Emma of Provence, 197,329, 374,375
Emma of Segur, 398
Emnilde of Silicia, 378
Emse md Ogyek, Magyar leader, 51
Endia md Olaf III, K of Sweden, 28
Englebert I, C of Brienne, 254,383
Engelbert I, C of Ortenburg, 228
Engelbert I, C of Sponheim, 228
Engelbert I, C of Trevasco, 228
Engelbert I, C of Chiemgau, 110
Engelbert II, C of Brienne, 383
Engelbert III, C in Chiemgau, 48, 110
Engelbert III, C of Brienne, 383
Engelbert IV, C of Brienne, 383
Engelbert of Schwartzenburg, 68A
Engelbert von Sponheim I, 10,388
Engelbert von Sponheim II, 128,228
Engelbert, C in Pusterthal, 129,130
Engelbert, C of Schwartzenburg, 388
Engeltrude md Berenger, 185
Engleltrude md Eudes, 250,336
Engleltrude md Hunroch, 269, 332,404
Engletrude md Uno, 166A
Engleltrude of Brienne, 254
Engeltrudis md Robert, 348A
Engenulf, Sr d'Aigle, 177

Engilrat md Bernard, 118
Engleberge, Emp of West, 25
Englebert I, C in Inngau, 110
Engleram, Sr de Coucy, 6,37
Engelram, Sr de Boves, 6
Engleram II, Sire de Coucy, 4,37
Engleram de Coucy, C of Amiens, 6,37
Enguerrand, C of Montreuil, 235, 244
Enguerrand, C of Poitou, 244
Enguerrand, s of Lideric, 235
Eni, s of Tytila, 437
Entifidach md N.N., dau of Beli, 341
Eochaid Buide, K of Dalriada, 165
Eochaid Buide, K of Picts, 165
Eochaid Monrever, K of Irish Dalriada, 165
Eochaid Mugnedon, K of Ireland, 251
Eochaid II, K of Dalriada, 165,341, 355
Eochaid III, K of Dalriada, 165
Eochaid III, K of Kintyre, 165
Eochaid III, K of Knapdale, 165
Eochaid IV, K of Dalriada, 165,355
Eofa, son of Eoppa, 233
Eoppa, son of Esa, 406
Eoppa, son of Ingild, 233
Eorconbeorht, K of Kent, 233A
Ercc, K of Irish Dalriada, 165
Erchanger I, C of Alsace, 25
Erchenaud, s of Ansbertus, 236
Erembourg md Fulk V, 2, 152
Erembourg md Humbert II, 189,191
Erembourg of Mans, 313
Eremburg md Gervase, 354
Eriba-marduk, K of Babylon, 414A
Eric Agnarsson, 92,339
Eric I, K of Norway, 204
Erichthronius, s of Darda, 303

Fasted d'Oisy II, 50
Fatima, dau of Muhammad, 435
Fatima md Abd al-Manaf, 432
Fatima md Abd al-Mattalib, 432
Fatima md Abu al-Muttalib Shayba, 435
Fatima md Ali ben Abu Talib, 432
Fatima md Ali ben Abi Talif, 435
Fatima md Kilab, 430,432
Faucisburge md Adhemer, 308A
Feldelm Foltchain, Q of Delriada, 165,251
Felicie de Roucy, 95
Fercher Foto, K of Argyle, 355
Fercher Foto, K of Laorn, 355
Fergus Mor mac Ercc, 165
Fergus, K of Dalriada, 355
Fergusa md Eochaid IV, 355
Fergusa of Dalriada, 165
Fernan Gonzalez, C of Burgos, 55, 223,285
Fernan Gonzalez, C of Castile, 55, 223,285
Fernan Gonzalez, C of Lara, 55,223, 285
Fernan Ruiz, 181
Fernando Gundemarez, 180
Fernando I, K of Castile, 248,276
Fernando I, K of Leon, 248
Fernando II, K of Extremedura, 52
Fernando II, K of Galicia, 52
Fernando II, K of Leon, 52,85
Fernando III, K of Castile, 52,82
Fernando III, K of Cordoba, 52
Fernando III, K of Extremedura, 52
Fernando III, K of Galicia, 52
Fernando III, K of Leon, 52,82
Fernando III, K of Toledo, 52
Fernando Nunez, 35, 285,287
Fernando Vermudez, 180,267
Ferreolus, senator of Narbonne, 236
Fihr Qaraysh md Layla, 432
Finn, s of Godwulf, 233

Firoz V, K of Persia, 408
Fjolmer Yngvi-freysson, 166
Flan md Foredash Wroid, 341
Flavius Afranius Syagrious, 236
Flavius Tiberius Mauricus, Emp of East, 407
Florentius md Artemia, 171A
Florenz I, C of Holland, 311,312
Florenz I, C of W. Friesland, 38, 311,312
Florenz II, C of Holland, 38,390
Florenz III, C of Holland, 38,72,390
Florenz III, C of W Sealand, 72,390
Florenz III, E of Ross, 72
Florenz IV, C of Holland, 72,120
Folmar, C in Bliesgau, 45
Folmar md Richilde, 45
Folmar, C of Homburg, 30,45
Folmer, C of Amance, 45
Folmer, C of Metz, 30,45,278,337
Foredach Wroid, 341
Fornan Lainez, 179
Forne fitz Sigulf, 396
Forne, king's theign, 396
Fortun Garces, K of Pamplona, 294
Foucauld, Sire de la Roche, 306
Fouchard, Ld of Ham, 274
Fouchaud de Limoges, 328
Fouchier I, Sr de Segur, 398
Fouchier II, C of Segur, 308
Francon I, Vct de Narbonne, 218B
Francon II, Vct de Narbonne, 218,218A,218B
Francon of Narbonne, 284
Francuc, K of Troy, 303
Francus, K of Franks, 303
Freawine. of ancient Saxony, 233
Fredeburga md Guigues III, 196
Fredeburga md Guigues IV, 196
Fredegunde md Chilperic I, 303
Fredelon md Bertha, 329
Frederick du Donjon, 144
Frederick Hohenstauffen II, 43

331

Fulgaud, C of Rouergue, 329
Fulk Bertrand, C of Provence, 197
Fulk I, C of Anjou, 109
Fulk I, Vct of Angers, 167
Fulk II, C of Anjou, 127,167, 298, 333,347
Fulk II, C of Macon, 333
Fulk II, C of Nevers, 333
Fulk III, C of Anjou, 91
Fulk IV, C of Anjou, 2,91
Fulk V, C of Anjou, 2,152,313
Fulk V, K of Jerusalem, 2,52,313
Fulk, C d'Archaic, 87
Fulk, C of Angouleme, 87
Fulk, C of Carbon, 249
Fulk, C of Montague, 249

### -G-

Gabran mac Domangart, 165
Gabriel the Armenian, 145
Gainfroi md Theidlindis, 303
Gaitelgrima md Giovanni, 31
Gaitelgrima of Benevento,283, 297
Galeran I, C of Meulan, 234
Galeran II, C of Meulan, 234
Galeran III, C of Meulan, 185
Galindo Agnaraz II, 290,292
Galindo, fath of Aznar Galindez I, 292
Gallus Magnus, 370
Garcia Arnaldo, 227
Garcia Fernandez de Lara I, 285,286
Garcia Fernandex I, 276
Garcia Iniguez I, 76,276,292
Garcia IV, K of Navarre, 151
Garcia Jiminez II, 223,292
Garcia Ramirez II, 177
Garcia Ramirez V, 151
Garcia Sanchez I, 223,285
Garcia Sanchez II, 292
Garcia Sanchez III, 55,223,292
Garcia Sanchez IV, 180,223,267,277

Garcia Sanchez, 289,290,329
Garcia VI, K of Navarre, 151
Garcia VII, K of Navarre, 86
Garnier, Vct of Sens, 173,174
Garnier, Vct of Troyes, 25,173
Garnier md Teutberga, 25
Garsenda of Astarac, 227
Gersinde de Fezensac, 289
Garwynwyn Garvinion, 341
Gaton, C of Viero, 21,276
Gaton md Egiloma, 21
Gaudalmoda md Guigues I, 196
Gausbert I, C of Ampurias, 284
Gausbert I, C of Rosellon, 284
Gausbert II, C of Ampurias, 284
Gausbert II, C of Rosillon, 284
Gauthild md Ingjald, 166
Gautier de Saint Valery, 122,241
Gautier I, C of Amiens, 109
Gautier I, C of Valois, 109,185
Gautier I, C of Vexin, 109,185
Gautier I, Sr de Salins, 189
Gautier II, C of Amiens, 185,268
Gautier II, C of Valois, 185,268
Gautier II, C of Vexin, 185,268
Gautier II, Sr de Salins, 189
Gautier III, Sr de SDalins, 189
Gautier, K of E Franks, 303
Gautier, Sr de Chatillon-sur-Marne, 99
Gautier, Sr de Percy-sur-Marne, 99
Gauzelin, C of Mans, 357
Gauzelin md Andetrude, 163
Geota, s of Taetwa, 233
Gebhard I, C of Sulzbach, 63
Gebhard II, C of Sulzbach, 49,63
Gebhard, C in Lahngau, 166A
Gebhard C in Nieder-Lahngau, 351,359
Gebhard, C in Wetterau, 351
Gebhard, D of Lorraine, 281A, 321A,350

Gebica, K of Burgundians, 349
Geffon md Skjold, K of Danes, 324
Geila md Catalon I, 331
Geilin md Raimonde, 317
Gemma of Naples, 280,283,297
Gentilanor, K of Cimmenians, 303
Genuissa Venus Julia, 438
Geoffrey de Charroux, 327
Geoffrey de Chateau-Landon, 91
Geoffrey de Semur, 191
Geoffrey Grisgonelle I, 91,157,258
Geoffrey I md Petronille d'Archaic, 398
Geoffrey I, C of Angouleme, 87
Geoffrey I, C of Anjou, 167
Geoffrey I, C of Turenne, 308
Geoffrey I, Senechal of France, 167
Geoffrey I, Sr de Semur, 85
Geoffrey I, Vct de Chateaudun, 249
Geoffrey II, C in Gatinais, 2,91
Geoffrey II, C of Montague, 249,266
Geoffrey II, C of Perche, 177,249, 266
Geoffrey II, D of Lower Lorraine, 242
Geoffrey II, Vct de Chateaudun, 249
Geoffrey II, Vct of Thouars, 159
Geoffrey of Orleans V, 167
Geoffrey of Turenne II, 308
Geoffrey Plantagenet V, C of Anjou, 2,89
Geoffrey Plantagenet V, D of Normandy, 2, 89
Geoffrey, C in Gatinais, 2,92,167
Geoffrey, C of Anjou, 258
Geoffrey, C of Chateau-Landon, 2
Geoffrey, C of Provence, 298
Geoffrey, C Palatine, md Gerberge, 351
Geoffrey, D of Brittany, 24
Geoffrey, Vct d' Orleans, 2

Geoffrey, Vct de Thouars, 159
Geoffrey, Vct de Chartres, 249
Georgios, an Armenian, 322A
Georgios md Leon V, 322A
Georgios, of Byzantium, 322A
Geovanni II, Pr of Salerno, 31
Gepa md Hermann, 68A
Gepa von Werl md Hermann IV, 67
Geraldus de Forez, 317
Gerald I, C of Geneva, 93
Gerald II, C de la Forez, 317
Gerard Flamens, C in Teisterbant, 11,119
Gerard Flaminus I, C of Guelders, 119,304
Gerard Flaminus I, C of Wassenburg, 119
Gerard, C of Macon, 187,189
Gerard, C of Vienne, 187-189
Gerard I, C of Auvergne, 163
Gerard I, C of Genoa, 288
Gerard II, C of Guelders, 62,304
Gerard II, C of Lyon, 317
Gerard II, C of Rohan, 317
Gerard of Rousillon, 264
Geraud de Montignos, 327
Geraud, C of Bourges, 328
Geraud, Vct de Limoges, 328,398
Geraud I, C of Geneva, 288
Geraud II, C of Lyon, 317
Geraud II, C of Rohan, 317
Gerberga de Terrasson, 156
Gerberga md Atto Trencavel, 195B
Gerberga md Gilbert, 257,298
Gerberga md Juhel Berenger, 334
Gerberga md William II, 157
Gerberga of Henneburg, 7,102
Gerberga of Saxony, 207
Gerberga of Upper Burgundy, 247
Gerberge de la Rochefoucauld, 305, 306
Gerberge de Terrasson, 377

334

Goswin, C of Gross-Lenungen, 307A
Gotelena md Guigues V, 196
Gottfried I, C of Blieskastel, 278
Gottfried I, Graf of Blieskastel, 320
Gottfried, C in Bleisgau, 278
Gottfried, C of Metz, 45
Gottschalk von Zulphen, 379
Gozelin, C in Bidgau, 104,359
Gradionus, K of Brittany, 405
Gregoria md N.N. Skleros, 115
Gregoria md Niketas Skleros, 322
Gregorias, s of Konstantinos, 215
Gregorias Iberitzes, 215
Gregorios Kameteros, 394
Gregory III, D of Naples, 280
Guaimar III, Pr of Salerno, 283,297
Guaimar IV, Pr of Amalfi, 297,325
Guaimar IV, Pr of Apulia, 297
Guaimar IV, Pr of Calabria, 297
Guaimar IV, Pr of Capua, 297,325
Guaimar IV, Pr of Salana, 297
Guaimar IV, Pr of Salerno, 325
Gud de Montlhery, 57
Gudbrand Kule, 28
Gudrod Bjornsson, 28
Gudrod Halfdansson, K of Roumar-ike, 166
Gudrod Halfdansson, K of Vestfold, 166
Guenfroi, Sr de Aumale, 244
Guerin, C in Thurgovie, 2,101,345
Guerin, C of Poitiers, 2
Guerri I, C of Morvois, 264
Guethenoc, Vct de Chateau-en-Porhoet, 69
Guglielmus, C of Terrasana, 106
Gui de Montlhery, 57
Gui de Ponthieu II, 148
Gui de Vermandois, 188
Gui I, C of Montreuil, 244
Gui I, C of Ponthieu, 244

Gui I, C of Tonnerre, 254
Gui I, Mg of Spoleto, 265
Gui I, Sr de Chatillon-sur-Marne, 99
Gui I, Sr de Dampierre, 84
Gui I, Vct de Limoges, 398
Gui I, Vct of Troyes, 84
Gui II, C of Camerino, 265
Gui II, C of Tonnerre, 254
Gui II, D of Spoleto, 265
Gui II, K of Italy, 265
Gui, C of Bar-sur-Seine, 383,384
Gui, C of Escuens, 189,254
Gui, C of Lucca, 93
Gui, C of Ponthieu, 184
Gui, C on Breton March, 265
Gui, D of Lucca, 93
Gui, Mg of Tuscany, 93
Gui, s of Lievin, 330
Gui, Sr de Guise, 34
Guibour of Hornbach, 330
Guido, Mch of Torino Alberaza, 107
Guigone of Forez, 84
Guigues I, Sr d'Aunonay, 196
Guigues III, Sr de Vion, 196
Guigues IV, C of Grenoble, 196
Guigues V, C of Albon, 196
Guigues VI, C of Albon, 196
Guigues VI, C of Grenoble, 196
Guigues VI, Sr de Vion, 196
Guigues VII, C of Albon, 196
Guignes VII, C of Grenoble, 196
Guigues VIII, C of Albon, 196
Guigues VIII, C of Grenoble, 196
Guigues, C d'Albon,192
Guigues, Dauphin de Vermandois, 192
Guiguin, C of Soissons, 348
Guilla md Alberto Azzo, 93,106
Guillaire md N.N. of Ogiers, 12
Guillenette md N.N. of Substantion, 203
Guillermo I, C of Astarac, 227

337

Guinidilda md Wilfred I,
218,329,347
Guinigenta Asnarez, 286
Guiscard I, Sire de Beaujou, 196
Gulbert de St. Valery, 122
Guldregut md Galindo, 292
Gundabad, K of Burgundians, 380
Gunderland, s of Landree, 352
Gundicahar, K of Burgundians, 349
Gundioc, K of Burgundians, 349,
349A,380
Gundrada md Theobald III, 81,132
Gundrada md William de Warenne,
56,135,135A
Gundwald, D of Asti, 380
Gunhild md Eric I, 204
Gunhilda md Harold III, 369
Gunhilde md Raimond II, 329
Gunnor de Crepon, 24,89,156,166,
168,222,335
Gunnor, fath of Thorod, 342
Gunnor md Herbastus de Crepon,
335
Gunter von Merseburg, 212
Gunther, C in Thuringia, 212
Gunthram, herr von Muri, 98
Gunthram I, Ld of Mainz, 359
Gutdzag md Sopor I, 408
Gurina of Castile, 285
Gunwand, C of Rennes, 405
Guthroth Halfdansson, 204
Gutiar md Elvira, 20,21
Gutierre Menendez, 224A,277
Gutierre Osoriz, 20,21
Gutina of Castile, 35,285
Guy de Baudemont, C of Braine,
124
Guy de Montlhery I, 145
Guy I, C of Auvergne, 127
Guy I, Sr de Montlhery, 5
Guy II, C of Rochefort-en-Yvelines,
5

Guy II, Ld of Chateaufort, 5
Guy II, Senechal of France, 5
Guy II, Sire de Montlhery, 5
Guy II, Sr de Dampierre, 84
Guy II, Sr de Formay, 5
Guy II, Sr de Gomez, 5
Guy II, Sr de Saint Dizier, 84
Guy II, Sr de Saint Just, 84
Gwawl md Cunneda Wlegig, 405A
Gwid md Eanfrth, 406
Gwladys md Cadfan, 405C
Gwyddno Garunter, 341
Gwynnedd Garhpur, 439
Gymer of Scandinavia, 166
Gytha md Godwin, 367,368
Gytha of Wessex, 240,368

### -H-
Habashiua md Atika, 434
Habibai, s of Hisdai, 329
Hadaburg md Heinrich, 102
Hadamut md Markwasrt, 229
Hadamut of Friuli, 281
Hadrian md Waldrat, 336
Hadrian, C of Orleans, 169
Hadrian, Ld of Wormsgau, 348
Hadulf, C in Durlingau, 212
Hadwide md Roger, 184
Haldetrude md Clothaire II, 303
Halfdan "Guldand," 166
Halfdan Frodasson, 240, 324
Halfdan Haroldsson, K of Sweden,
240
Halfdan Olafsson, K of Salver, 166,
217,339
Halfdan Olafsson, K of Uplanders
of Sweden, 166,217,339
Halfdan Olafsson, K of Vestfold,
166,217,339
Halfdan, fath of Ivar Oplaendinge,
44
Halfdan, K of Agde, 204

338

Henry I of Burgundy, 85,430
Henry I. Pf of Lorraine, 62
Henry I, Pf of the Rhine, 62
Henry I, Pz of Rhine, 62
Henry II, C of Anjou, 2
Henry II, C of Arlon, 62,71
Henry II, C of Bar,-le-Duc, 36,37,
 383
Henry II, C of Limburg, 67
Henry II, C of Louvain, 68,138,389
Henry II, C of Luxemburg, 36
Henry II, C of Maine, 2
Henry II, C of Namur, 36
Henry II, D of Brabant, 68,125
Henry II, D of Limburg, 62,67,71
Henry II, D of Lorraine, 68
Henry II, D of Normandy, 2
Henry II, K of England, 2,88
Henry III, C of Arlon, 36,71
Henry III, C of Luxemburg, 36,71
Henry III, Dof Bavaria, 359
Henry III, D of Limberg, 23,71
Henry III, D of Swabia, 359
Henry III, Emp of West, 161,359
Henry III, K of Burgundy, 359
Henry III, K of England, 2,54,147
Henry III, K of Germany, 161,359
Henry IV of Franconia, 359
Henry IV, D of Bavaria, 359
Henry IV, Emp of West, 359
Henry IV, Salic king, 307A
Henry of Franconia, 202,359
Henry of Huntingdon, , 72,135
Henry von Egisheim I, 30
Henry von Schweinfurt, 7,47,102,
 213, 270, 307, 362
Henry von Stade, 301
Henry von Werl II, 19
Henry, Bg of Regensburg, 64
Henry, C in Ammergau, 29
Henry, C in Zulpishgau, 97
Henry, C of Altdorf, 29

Henry, C of Carinthia, 202,359
Henry, C of Francobnia, 202,359
Henry, C of Laufen, 16,19
Henry, C of Luxemburg, 71
Henry, C of Naimur, 71
Henry, C of Northeim, 392,393
Henry, C of Portugal, 85,430
Henry, C of Verdun, 359
Henry, D of Burgundy, 85,245
Henry, D of Carinthia, 202
Henry, D of Franconia, 202,359
Henry, Pf of Lorraine, 97
Henry, Sr de la Roche, 50
Hent.tawy md Pinudjem I, 424
Henr.tawy md Pinudjem II, 425
Henwig du Donjon, 144
Hephzibad md Hezekiah, 329
Herbastus de Crepon, 135,166,335
Herbert I, C of Soissons, 231
Herbert I, C of Vermandois, 134,
 199, 231,350
Herbert I, Vct de Thouars, 159,331
Herbert II, C of Meaux, 231
Herbert II, C of Soissons, 231
Herbert II, C of Troyes, 169,231,239
Herbert II, C of Vermandois, 169,188,
 231,235,239,258
Herbert III, C of Vermandois, 239,
 256
Herbert IV, C of Valois, 239
Herbert IV, C of Vermandois, 239,
 268, 348
Herbert IV, C of Vexin, 239
Herbert, C in Kinziggau, 379
Herbert, C of Maine, 357
Herbery, C Palatine, 351
Herbert, Mg of Trans. Burgundy, 174
Heremod, s of Itermon, 233
Heribert, C in Wetterau, 3,351
Heribert, C of Gleiburg, 351
Heribert, Mg of Schweinfurt, 351
Herimann of Saffenburg, 68A

342

Jutta of Luxemburg, 58,62,379,387

**-K-**

Ka'b Azd Shanuwwa, 433
K'ab md Makhshiya, 432
Ka'b, s of Abdallah, 433
Ka'b, s of Amr, 434
Ka'b of al-Hira, 433
Kafnai, Exilarch at Babylon, 329
Kahani, Exilarxh at Babylon, 329
Kahlan of al-Hira, 430
Kamateros, basileos, 394
Kapes md Takelot I, 420
Kar,am,at md Shoshenq II, 422
Karanos, ancestor of Koinos, 413
Kafnai, Exilarch of Babylon, 329
Kahani, Exilarch of Babylon, 329
Karoma md Takeloth, 420
Karomat md Sheshonq, 420
Karomamma md Osorkin II, 422
Karrhagos, K of Thrace, 427
Kassandane md Cyrus I, 419
Kassandros, fath of Antigona, 428
Katherine Roet md John of Gaunt, 1
Kavadh I, K of Persia, 408
Kazimirez I, K of Poland, 361,378
Kenneth mac Alpin, K of Picts, 165
Kenneth mac Alpin, K of Scotland,
    165
Kenneth, K of Scotland, 165
Khadija Qarayshi, md Muhammad,
    the Prophet, 435
Khosrow II, K of Armenia, 416
Khosrow II, K of Western Armenia,
    416
Khosrow III, K of Armenia, 416
Khun, Khan of Bulgars, 309
Khuwalid, fath of Khadija, 436
Khuzayma md Hind'Uwana, 432
Kilab md Fatima, 432
Kilab, son of Murra, 431
Kinana md Barra, 432

Koinos, ancestor of Tyrammas, 413
Konrad I, C in Argenau, 29,281,
    281A,300
Konrad I, C in Linzgau, 29,281,
    281A,300
Konrad I, C of Auxerre, 29,281A,
    300
Konrad I, D of Franks, 41A
Konrad I, K of Germany, 41A
Konrad II, C of Auxerre, 300
Konrad II, D of Swabia,
    105,158,381
Konrad II, Mg of Burgundy, 389
Konrad II, Mg of Trans. Burgundy,
    300
Konrad III, C of Ortengen, 381
Konrad md Glismode, 348A
Konrad, C in Groitzsch-Rochlitz, 8
Konrad, C of Arlon, 62
Konrad, C of Brehna, 8
Konrad, C of Camburg, 8
Konrad, C of Haldenslaben, 27
Konrad, D of Swabia, 281
Konrad, Mg of Lausitz, 8
Konrad, Mg of Meissen, 8
Konstantin Skleros, 219,322
Konstantinos Angelos, 215
Konstantinos Diogenes, 51
Konstantinos Monomachos, 115
Konstantinos VI, Emp of Byzant-
    ium, 322A,322B
Konstantinos, court officer, 322
Konstantinos, Dux, 215
Kosmartydene md Artaxerxes I, 414
Kotini md Sieghard I, 130
Koustantinos Monomachos, 115A
Kraemwase, s of Ramses II, 425A
Kresina, a peasant, 362
Kresina, fath of Bozena, 362
Kresina, f of Bozena, 362
Kunhilde of Rugen, 92,217,339
Kunigunde md  Luitpold,  270

353

Matilda, Pr of France, 19,201
Matthew of Alsace, 205-299
Maud de Montgomery, 335
Maud md Robert II, 103
Maud of Carinthia, 81
Maud of Flanders, 81,89,141
Maud of Huntingdon, 77
Maud of Savoy, Q of Portugal, 85
Maud, Pr of France, 69
Maurette md Gerard,187,189
Maurice, Emp of East, 407
Maurin, s of Suppo II, 269
Mawasen, s of Buyuwawa, 422
Mawiya md Lu'ayy, 432
Mayeul, Vct of Narbonne, 101,218,
218B
Mazin Ghassan, 434
Mechtild md Adalbert von Saffen-
burg, 67
Mechtild of Bar, 364
Mechtilde md Dagobert II, 303
Mechtilde von Morsburg, 364,365
Mechtilde von Ringelheim,134
Megabignes, fath of Hydranes I,
426
Megas, K of Cyrene, 413,428
Meginhard I, C in Hamelant, 202
Meginhard I, C in Traungau, 13,41
Meginhard I, C of Morsburg, 365
Meginhard I, C of Sponheim, 364,
365
Meginhard II, C in Traungau, 13
Meginhard III, C in Traungau, 13
Meginhard, C of Hamalant, 311
Meginhard, D of Friesland, 311
Meginwerd md Ermengarde of
Susa, 393
Mehtenweskhet md Psammetichus
I, 420
Mehetenweskhet md Shoshenq, 422
Meingaud II md Gisela, 321A
Meingaud, C in Avangau, 379

Meinwerk I, C in Thuringia, 281
Meleagros, s of Balakros, 413
Milisenda de Rethel, 2
Melisende de Crecy, 5,37
Melisende de Montlhery, 145
Men.kheper.re', High Priest of
Amun, 424
Menendo Gonzalez, C of Galicia,
224A,277
Meribanes I, K of Iberia, 409
Merneptah, Pharaoh, 425
Merodochus, K of Sicambi, 303
Meronech, Governed East Franks,
303
Meshullemeth md Manassah, 329
Meyeul, Vct of Narbonne, 2188
Micah md Nabor, 329
Michael Botaneiates, 51
Michael Doukas, 394
Michael, Kuman of Samogy, 51
Michael, Magyar prince, 51
Michael, regent of Poland, 51
Michael II, Emp of Byzantium,
322A,322B
Michael III, Emp of Byzantium,
253,322A
Mieceslas I, of the Obotrites, 380
Mieceslas II, of the Obotrites, 380
Miecesias III, Pr of Obortrites, 380
Mieszko I, f of Adelaide of Poland,
51
Mieszko I, Gr D of Poland, 378
Mieszko I, K of Poland, 378
Mieszko II, K of Poland, 75,237,
363,378
Miles de Courtenay, 144,232
Milesendis md Ademer, 328,398
Milo I, C of Bar-sur-Seine, 383
Milo I, C of Tonnerre, 254
Milo II, C of Bar-sur-Seine, 383
Mistui I of the Obotrites,380
Mistui II, Pr of Obotrites, 380

Plaserius I, K of Troy, 303
Plaserius II, K of Troy, 303
Plesron I, K of Troy, 303
Ponce de Montgomery, 87
Poncette, Dame de Treves, 187,190
Poncia de la Marche, 87
Pocia md Adalbert III, 87
Pons III, C of Albi, 142,327,374
Pons III, C of Dijon, 142,327,374
Pons III, C of Toulouse,142,327,
Poppa de Bayeux, 162,166,166A
Poppa II, Mg of Istria, 10
Poppo I C in Grabfeld, 211
Poppo I, C in Saalgau, 102,211
Poppo II, Mg of Sarbenmark, 102
Poppo III, C in Bavarian Nordgau, 102
Poppo III, C in Grabfed, 102,281
Poppo von Rot II, C in Isergau, 49
Poppo von Rot III, C in Isergau, 49
Poppo von Rot III, C of Rot, 49
Poppo von Weimar I, Mg of Istria, 281
Poppo von Weimar I, Mg of Carni-ola, 281
Porpora of Amalfi, 325
Porpora of Tabellaria, 297,325
Prangarda di Canossa, 315
Praserius, K of Cimmenians, 303
Prasutagus, K of the Iceni, 405B,405C
Predslawa Swjatopolkowna, 51
Premylslava md Ladislas I, 51,76A
Prenus, K of Sicambi, 303
Priam II, K of Troy, 303
Priam III, K of Cimmenians, 303
Priam, K of Troy, 303
Profecta md Pons, 298
Psammetichus I, Pharaoh, 420
Psammetichus II, Pharaoh, 420
Psusennes I, Pharaoh, 423

Psusennes II, High Priest of Amun, 423
Psusennes II, Pharaoh, 423
Ptolemy I Soter, Pharaoh, 413,428
Ptolemy I, setrap of Commagene, 412
Ptolemy II Philadelphos, Pharaoh, 413
Ptolemy III Euergates , Pharaoh, 413, 428
Ptolemy IV Philopator, Pharaoh, 413
Ptolemy V Epiphanes, Pharaoh, 413
Ptolemy VI Philometor, Pharaoh, 413
Pulcherina md Basileios Skleros, 115,382
Pyriska, Pr of Hungary, 111,381
Pythodoris md Samus, 412

**-Q-**
Qabus of al'Hira, 430
Qahtan, fath of Ya'rob, 430
Qara'is ibn Abbad, 430
Qasayy Zaid, md Hubba, 432
Qays al-Madr md Ikrisha, 432,434

**-R-**
Rabi'a al Lakhmi, K of Yemen, 430
Rabi'a Luhayy, s of Haritha, 434
Rabold I, C in Carinthia, 130
Rabold, C in Ambergau, 110,130
Radbard md Auda Ivarsdotter, 143, 240
Radbard, K of Gardarike, 240
Ragnar Sigurdsson, K of Lethra, 240, 369
Ragnhild Hrolfsdotter, 166
Ragnhild md Halfdan, 204
Ragnhildis Ludmilla, 310
Ragnvald md Alberade, 161
Ragnvald, C of Roucy, 92
Rainilda md Humbert I, 43,93
Rainilda md Olderado, 93
Raimon de Sabran, C of Forcal-quier, 116,195

Raimond, Dean of Avignon, 193
Raimond I md Berthiez of Tou-
    louse, 218A
Raimond I, C of Narbonne, 218
Raimond I, C of Rouergue, 329
Raimond II, C of Albi, 329
Raimond II, C of Toulouse, 326,328
Raimond II, Mq of Gothie, 329
Raimond III, C of Albi, 329
Raimond III, C of Toulouse, 54,329
Raimond III, D of Aquitaine, 329
Raimond III, Mq of Gothie, 329
Raimond, Sr d'Uzes, 193
Raimonde md Mayeul, 218,218B
Raingarde de Dijon, 241
Raingarde md Artaud, 87
Raingarde md Raoul, 241
Ralph Basset, 395
Rameses I, general, 425
Rameses II, Pharaoh, 425,425A
Rameses III, Pharaoh, 425
Rameses VI, Pharaoh, 423
Rameses VIII, Pharaoh, 425
Rameses IX, Pharaoh, 425
Rameses X, Pharaoh, 425
Rameses XI, 423,425
Ramiro I, K of Aragon, 95
Ramiro I, K of Asturias, 35,276
Ramiro II, C of Moncon, 179
Ramiro II, K of Aragon, 95,177
Ramiro II, K of Leon, 223,276
Ramiro II, K of Navarre, 95
Ramiro Sanchez II, C of Monzon, 151
Ramon Borrel I, 168
Ramon I, C of Pallars, 286
Ramon I, C of Ribagorza, 286,289,
    296
Ramon II, C of Ribagorza, 286,289
Ramon Roger I, C of Carcassonne,
    195A
Randvar Radbarsson, 240

Rangarde md Bernard Trencavel,
    195B
Rangarde md Redro Ramon, 195A
Ranulf I, C of Poitou, 163
Ranulf I, D of Aquitaine, 163
Ranulf II, C of Poitou, 163
Ranulf II, D of Aquitaine, 163
Ranulf, Vct de Macon, 101,189
Raoul de Cambrai, 99
Raoul de Coucy I, 37
Raoul de Gouy, C of Amiens, 185
Raoul de Gouy, C of Ostrevant, 185
Raoul de Gouy, C of Valois, 185
Raoul de Gouy, C of Vexin, 185
Raoul I, C of Valois, 185
Raoul II, C of Vexin, 268
Raoul II, Sr de Crepy, 268
Raoul II, Sr de Valois, 268
Raoul III, C de Crepy, 108,268
Raoul III, C of Amiens, 108,268
Raoul III, C of Valois, 108,268
Raoul III, C of Vexin, 108,268
Raoul III, C of Vitry, 108,268
Raoul of Laesole, 256
Raoul, C of Bar-sur-Seine, 239,256
Raoul, C of Dijon, 241,348
Raoul, C of Guisnes, 235
Raoul, C of Ponthieu, 256
Raoul, C of Quersy, 308A
Raoul, Sr de Baugency, 4
Rapoto I, C in Traungau, 128
Rapoto II, C in Traungau, 128
Rapoto IV, C of Cham, 128,128A,
    279
Raquash md Adi, 430
Raquash of al-Hira, 430,433
Ratherius, K of Franks, 303
Ratpot I, fath of Beata, 29
Ratpot I, C of Montagne, 249
Ratroc, Vct de Chateaudun, 249
Raymond Berenger I, C of Barcel-
    ona, 54,85,245

Robert I, C of Dreux, 124
Robert I, C of Flanders, 205,312
Robert I, C of Holland, 205
Robert I, C of Lomme, 403
Robert I, C of Namur, 403
Robert I, C of Paris, 134,169,259
Robert I, C of Perche, 124
Robert I, C of Poitiers, 134,169
Robert I, D of Burgundy, 85
Robert I, D of France, 134
Robert I, D of Normandy, 89,131
Robert I, K of W Franks, 264
Robert I, Mq of Neustria, 134,169,
   259
Robert I, Mq of Orleans, 134,169
Robert I, Pr of France, 91,123,147
Robert II, C of Braine, 37,124
Robert II, C of Dreux, 37,123
Robert II, C of Meulan, 103
Robert II, C of Turenne, 308
Robert II, K of France, 134,140,
   154, 232,297,333
Robert III, D of Burgundy, 154,155
Robert III, Pr of France, 154,155
Robert md Rotrude, 308A
Robert the Strong, 169
Robert, Abp of Rouen, 168
Robert, C of Eu, 87
Robert, C of Evreaux, 168
Robert, C of Hesbaye, 2
Robert, C of Substantion, 203
Robert, fath of Hugh II, 184
Robert, Sr de Chateua-du-Loire, 354
Robert, Vct de Turenne, 308A
Robert, Vct of Autun, 348,348A
Robert, Vct of Dijon, 348,348A
Robertus I, Vct of Auvergne, 127
Robertus II, Vct of Auvergne, 127
Robi'a al-Lakhi, K of Hira, 430
Rodak md Papak, 408
Rudegunda md Clothaire I, 303
Rodegunde md Orontes I, 412

Roderigo Alvarez,179
Rodigustus, of the Obotrites, 380
Rodogune md Hystaspes, 414A
Rodogune of Persia, 410
Rodrigo Alvarez, C in Asturias, 179
Rodrigo Bermudez, 180
Rodrigo Diaz de Castro, C of
   Valencia, 179
Rodrigo Diaz de Castro, Sr de
   Bivar, 151,179,180
Rodrigo, C of Castile, 35,287
Rodulf de Warenne, 135
Rodulf, D of Turenne, 308
Rofrit of Benevento, 283
Roger de Beaumont, 103,185
Roger de Comminges I, C of Car-
   cassonne, 95,105,151,227,291
Roger de Montgomery I, Vct d'Hie-
   moi, 335
Roger de Montgomery, E of Chich-
   ester, 183
Roger de Montgomery, E of Mont -
   gomery, 183
Roger de Montgomery, E of
   Shrewsbury, 335
Robert de Montgomery, regent of
   England, 335
Roger de Montgomery, regent of
   Norm andy, 335
Roger de Montgomery, Vct
   d'Hiemois, 335
Roger I, C of Conserans, 195A
Roger I, Sr de Foix, 195A
Roger II, C of Carcassonne, 195A
Roger II, E of Shrewsbury, 335
Roger II, E of Shropshire, 335
Roger II, regent of Normandy, 335
Roger II, Vct d'Hiemois, 335
Roger of Auriate, 315
Roger, C of Maine, 357
Roger, C of Saint Pol, 184
Roger, s of Herlouin, 244

Roger, s of Rogerus Magnus, 335
Rogerus Magnus, fath of Roger, 335
Rogerus Magnus, s of Roger, 335
Rognald, Pr of Polotsk, 76A
Rogneida of Polotsk, 76A
Rogneida md Vladimir I, 51
Rognhild md Harold I, 204
Regnieda de Polotsk, 143
Rognvald Eysteinsson, 166,295
Rognvald Olafsson, 166
Rognvald, C of Rheims, 170
Rognvald, C of Roucy, 92,170
Rognvald, Norse invader, 170
Rognvald, Sr de Roucy, 170
Rognvald, Vct of Rheims, 170
Rognvald, Viking, 108
Rohaut md Hugh, C of Bourges,
    133,346
Rohaut, Pr of France, 346
Rolande md Childebrande I, 173
Rollo, D of Normandy,
    162,166,166A
RomanosAballantes, 370
Romanos Argyros, 382,399
Romanos Lekapenos, Emp of West,
    399
Romanos Skleros, 115
Romanus Argyros, 399
Romanus II, Emperor, 382
Roquash md Adi, of al-Rira, 430
Roredach Wrold, 355
Rorick II, C of Maine, 163
Roscilla md Fulk I, 109,167
Rosela of Saint Pol, 235
Roselinde md Wulgrim, 86,87,326
Rosella, Pr of Italy, 141
Rosine, Dame d'Uzes, 193
Rostaing de Sabran md Constance
    Amic, 116,194,323,345
Rudolph II, K of Italy, 175-345
Rudolph of the Betuwe, 100

Rostaing de Sabran, s of Emernon,
    116
Rostaing md Beletrude, 116
Rostaing, Sr de Sabran, 116,194
Rostaing I, Sr in S. Vienneois, 196
Rostaing II, Sr d'Annonay, 196,375
Rotbaude s'Angelea I, 333
Rothilda md Geraud, 398
Rothilda of Spoleto, 31,265
Rothilde de Limoges, 59
Rothilde md Adalbert I, 93
Rothilde md Geraud, 269
Rothilde of Neustria, 357
Rotlint md Werner, 200
Rotrou md Girard, 269
Rotrude md Robert, 308A
Rotrudis, f of Eschanger I, 25
Routger, C of Veltheim, 307A
Rudolph I, C of Altdorf, 29
Rudolph I, K of Upper Burgundy,
    175,343,366
Rudolph I, Mg of Upper Burgundy,
    175
Rudolph I, Sr de Faucigny,  288
Rudolph II, C in Swabian Altdorf,
    29,213
Rudolph II, K of Burgundy, 175,
Rudolph of Rheinfelden, 381
Rudolph, C of Achalm 213
Rudolph, C of Cambrai, 400
Rudolph, fath of Gisela, 381
Rupert, C in Breisgau, 102
Rupert, C in Thurgau, 102
Rupert, C in Zurichgau, 102
Rurick, K of Lethra, 143
Rurick, Pr of Lethra, 143
Rurick, Pr of Novgorod, 143
Ruricus, Bp of Limoges, 171A
Ruth md Boaz, 329
Ruthard, C in Argengau, 300
Rutpert, C in Upper Rhine, 169
Rutpert I, C in Wormsgau, 102,169

Seimowit, D of Polania, 378
Selback, K of Argyle, 355
Selback, K of Laorn, 355
Seleucus Calliinicus II, K of Syria, 414
Seleucus Nicator I, K of Syria, 414,415
Seleucus Philopator IV, K of Syria, 414
Seleucus I, setrap of Babylon, 414
Selma md Hashim, 432
Senegonde md Bernard II, 195B, 291
Senegonde md Fylgaud, 329
Senegunde de Beziers, 226,402
Senegunde de Marcillac, 331
Senegunde md Bernard II, 203
Senegundis d'Aunay, 398
Senfrie, fath of Josceline, 335
Sergios, nobleman, 322A
Sergius I, D of Amalfi, 325
Sergius I, D of Naples, 280
Sethnakht, Pharaoh, 425A
Seti I, High Priest of Set, 425
Seti I, Pharaoh, 425
Seti, commandant of troops, 425
Sexburga md Eakenberht, 437
Sexburga md Eorconbeorht, 233A
Shahrijar of Persia, 408
Shgamish-iddina md Nabopolasser, 414A
Shecaniah, des of Hananiah, 329
Shephat, Exilarch of Babylon, 329
Shephat, s of Johanan, 329
Shilhi, fath of Azubah, 329
Sheshonq I, Chief of Ma 422
Sheshonq I, Pharaoh, 422
Sheshonq II, Chief of Ma, 422
Sheshonq II, High Priest of Amun, 422

Sheshonq II, Pharaoh, 422
Sheshonq III, Pharaoh, 420,421,422
Sheshonq, Gr Chief of Ma, 421,422
Sheshonq, High Priest of Phah, 421
Shrotingus of Denmark, 221
Shua, son of Tamur, 329
Sibil md Duncan I, 165
Sibil de Vasco di Savona, 106,150
Siburgis md Rudolph I, 29
Sibyl of Anjou, 132,152,205
Sibylle md Eudes Borel I, 377
Sibylle of Barcelona, 85,245
Sibylle of Burgundy, 245
Sico, Duke, 265
Siegbert I, C in Saagau, 23
Segbert I, K of Cologne, 171
Siegbert III, K of Austasia, 224,303
Siegfried VI, C in Chemgau, 128, 128A
Siegfried md Mathilda, 26
Siegfried von Sponheim, C of Loventhal, 228
Siegfried von Sponheim, C of Sponheim, 129,228
Siegfried von Walbeck II, C in Derlingau, 15
Siegfried von Walbeck II, C in Siegfried, C in Moselgau, 3,316,353
Siegfried, C in Northeim, 26
Siegfried, C in Rittegau, 26
Siegfried, C of Guisnes, 235
Siegfried, C of Luxemburg, 3, 202, 316,353
Sieghard I, C of Bavaria, 110,130
Sieghard II, C in Low. Salzburggau, 110
Sieghard III, C in Chiemgau, 110,128A
Sieghard IV, C in Salzburggau, 110, 118,128A
Sieghard V, C in Chiemgau, 128A

Stephen of Blois, C of Boulogne, 299
Stephen of Blois, C of Mortain, 299
Stephen of Blois, K of Eng. 242,299
Stephen V, K of Croatia, 78
Stephen V, K of Hungary, 78
Stephen von Sponheim, 365
Stephen, C of Bourges, 346
Stephen, C of Burgundy, 187
Stephen, C of Macon, 187
Stephen, C of Sponheim, 365
Stephen, C of Vienne, 41,187
Stephen Matfriedinger, 359
Stephen, Sr de Treves, 190
Strateira md Artaxerxes II, 426
Stratonice I md Antiochus Soter I,
    415,427
Stratonice md Philippus, 427
Strymo md Priam, K of Troy, 303
Stylinos Tzautzes, 253
Styrbiorn Olafsson, 368,369
Sufficia md Rostaing I, 196
Sulprice de Charroux, 327
Sulpice md Archambaud II, 156,308
Suniare I, C of Barcelona, 284
Sunaire I, C of Urgel, 284
Suniare II, C of Barcelona, 284
Sunaire II, C of Urgel, 284
Suniario II, C of Ampurias,
    218,218B
Suniario II, C of Rosellon,
    218,218B
Sunifred, C of Barcelona, 54
Sunifred, C of Besalu, 54
Sunifred, C of Genoa, 54
Sunifred, C of Osona, 54
Sunifred, C of Urgel, 54
Sunifred, Mg of Gothie, 54
Sunno, K of Franks, 303
Suppo II, C of Turin, 269
Suppo II, Mg of Camerino, 269
Suppo II, Mg of Spoleto, 269
Susanna md Arnulf II, 184

Susanna, Pr of Italy, 141,332
Svatislav I, Gr D of Kiev, 209
Svatislav I, Gr D of Perejaslaw, 209
Svatislaw I, Gr Pr of Novgorod, 209
Svatislav Igorjewitsch I, 143
Svatispolk II, Gr Pr of Kiev, 363
Svatispolk II, Pr of Novgorod, 363
Svatispolk II, Pr of Turow, 363
Svegdi Fjolnarsson, 166
Swanhild md Dietmar I, 211
Swanhilde md Folmar, 45,278
Swanhilde of Saxony, 212
Swjatopolk II, Pr of Novgorod, 51
Swjatopolk Isjaslawitsch II, 378
Sybil of Anjou, 152

-T-
Tabent-Thuty md Smendis II, 423
Taetwa, s of Beaw, 233
Taetwa, K of Kent, 233
Tafnakhte I, Gr Chief of Ma, 420
Tafnakhte I, Pharaoh, 420
Tafnakhte I, Pr of Sais, 420
Tak.huat, Pr of Athribes, 420
Takelot I, Pharaoh, 420
Takelot II, Pharaoh, 420
Taksony, Pr of Hungary, 51
Talorcam I, K of Picts, 341,406
Tamur, son of Judah, 329
Tancred d'Hauteville, 296
Tarakr, fath f Abraham, 329
Tarnik, s of Bagrat I, 115A
Tascivanus, s of Androcomius,
    405B
Teispes, s of Archaemenes, 414
Teithfalit md Corun, 405A
Tent.amun md Smendis, 424
Tentsepeh md Nimlot, 422
Teresa Lainez, 179
Teresa of Castile, 85,223,430
Teresa of Leon, 85,223,430

374

Theutberga md Artaud II, 317

Thibaud de Dampierre-sur-l'Aube, 57,84

Thibaud I, C of Bourges, 340,346

Thibaud I, C of Chartres, 340,346

Thibaud II, C of Bar, 364

Thibaud II, C of Blois, 231,249

Thibaud III, C of Champagne, 81,133

Thibaud IV, C of Blois, 81

Thibaud IV, C of Champagne, 36,81

Thibaud IV, K of Navarre, 84

Thibaud, C of Bar, 149,364

Thibaud, C of Bourges, 346

Thibaud, C of Chartres, 346

Thibaud, D of Mosellane, 149

Thibaud, D of Upper Lorraine, 149

Thibaud, Sr de Bois Ferrand, 184

Thibaud, Sr de Chevreuse, 241

Thibaud, Sr de Montlhery, 241

Thibaud, Sr de Treves, 190

Thiemo I, C of Brehna, 8

Thiemo I, C of Kostritz, 8

Tiiemo I, C of Schweinachgau, 9

Thiemo I, C of Wettin, 8

Thiemo II, C in Quinziggau, 9

Thierry, Chamberlain of Charles, 258

Thierry I, C of Chaunois, 173

Thierry II, C of Bar, 149

Thierry II, C of Chaunois, 258

Thierry II, C of Montbeliard, 149

Thierry of Lorraine, C of Alsace, 205

Thietburga of Savoy, 288

Thietburga von Haldenslaben, 210

Thomas Basset, 395

Thomas de Coucy, C of Amiens, 5,37

Thomas de Coucy, Sr ce Coucy, 5, 37

Thomas de Coucy, Sr de Merle, 5,37

Thomas de Saint Valery, 122

Thomas I, C of Savoy, 93,175

Thorkill, Jarl, 367,368

Thorod Gunnarsson of Northumbria, 342

Throud of Sula, Jarl, 368

Thrond, fath of Eystein, 386

Thurinbert, s of Rutpert I, 169

Thurstan le Goz, Vct d'Avranches, 295

Thurstan le Goz, Vct d'Hiesmer, 295

Thurston Basset, 395

Thyra Danebord, 369

Thyra of Denmark, 368,369

Tiberius Constantinus II, Emp of East, 407

Tietbutga md Gerold I, 175

Tietburga md Louis I of Savoy, 175, 288

Tietberga of Bourges, 328

Tigranus I, K of Armenia, 410

Tigranus II, K of Armenia, 409,416

Tigrida md Diego Munoz, 267

Tije md Sethnakht, 425A

Tiridates II, K of Armenia, 416

Tiridates III, K of Armenia, 416

Tiridates IV, K of Armenia, 416

Tiridates, Pr of Parthia, 417

Tiy.nefertari md Amenhoyep III, 425

Tiye md Sethnakht, 425A

Tiye.mer.en.esse md Merneptah, 425

Toda Agnarez de Larron, 223,285, 293

Toda of Provence, 347

Tonantius Ferreolus I, Gallo-Roman Senator, 236

Tonantius Ferreolus II, Senator at Narbonne, 236

Torf de Harcourt, 103
Torf of Normandy, 222
Toscanda md Werner, 167
Tota Galindez of Aragon, 286,290, 327
Tota of Aragon, 284
Totadomna md Menendo, 277
Touroude de Pont-Audemer, 103
Touy md Reya, 425
Trancon I, Vct of Narbonne, 218
Troianos, Tsar of West Bulgaria, 309,370
Tros, s of Erichthonius, 303
Trungarde md Gausbert I, 284
Truppualdo, C of San Massimo, 325
Trygils, s of Tytmon, 437
Tutadomna md Menendo Gonzales, 224A,277
Tuya md Seti, Pharaoh, 425
Tyrimmas, ancestor of Perdiccas, 413
Tytila, K of East Anglia, 437
Tymon, s of Casere, 437
Tzantzes, strstego of Macedonia, 253

-U-

Uchtred, E. of Northumbria, 314
Uda of Metz, 359
Uda of Saxony, 104
Udad, son of Mugawwam, 432
Udad, son of Zayd, 430
Udalheid of Odenkirchen, 304A
Udalrich I, C of Schanis, 175
Udalrich I, Mg of Carniola, 10,281
Udalrich I, Mg of Istria, 10,281
Udalrich, D of Bohemia, 362
Udo I, C in Rheingau, 281A
Udo I, C of Grabfeld, 281A
Udo, C in Landgau, 281,281A
Udo, C in Nieder-Lahngau, 351
Udo, C of Meinvelt, 62
Udo, Mg of Neustria, 281,281A

Ugbaru, Gov of Gutium, 414A
Ulfhild of Norway, 28
Ulfhild of Saxony, 43
Ulfhilde md Dietrich V, 38
Ulfius of Denmark, 221
Ulfrida md Gudbrand Kule, 28
Ulrich I md Kunigunde, 41A
Ulrich I, C in Argengau, 364
Ulrich I, C in Linzgau, 364
Ulrich II, C in Argengau, 364
Ulrich II, C in Linzgau, 364
Ulrich III, C in Argengau, 364
Ulrich III, C in Vinzgau, 364
Ulrich IV, C in Argengau, 364
Ulrich IV C in Vinzgau, 364
Ulrich V, C in Argengau, 364
Ulrich V, C inVinzgau, 364
Ulrich VI, C in Lower Hatien, 364
Ulrich VI, C in Upper Hatien, 364
Ulrich md Adelaide, 228
Ulrich von Ebersburg, C of Ebersburg, 117,130
Ulrich von Ebersburg, Mg of Carniola, 117,130
Ulrich, C in Schweinachgau, 41
Ulrich, C of Passau, 128,213
Uno, C of Orleans, 166A
Urdina Munulona, 276
Uros I, Pr of Serbia, 51
Urraca Alfonsa, Pr of Castile, 151
Urraca Garces of Navarre, 55,180, 223,277,2855
Urraca md Garcia Iniguez I, 76, 293,294
Urraca Salvadores, 55
Urrace, C of Galicia, 248
Urraca, Pr of Castile, 86,94,155
Urraca, Pr of Leon, 86,94,155
Urraca, Pr of Portugal, 52,85
Urraca Fernandez, 223
Urraca Gomez, 285
Ursus of Denmark, 221

377

378

Wilfred Borrel II, C of Barcelona, 218
Wilfred Borrel II, C of Geneva, 218
Wilfred Borrel II, C of Barcelona, 218
Wilfred Borrel II, C of Osona, 218
Wilfred I, C of Barcelona, 218
Wilfred I, C of Besalu, 54
Wilfred I, C of Gerona, 54
Wilfred I, C of Urgel, 218,329,347
Wilfred, fath of Berta, 369
Wilhelm, s of Hryp, 437
Wilhelm von Weimar II, 281A
Wilibirg md Werigand, 130,281
Wilibirg von Eppenstein, 12,229
Wilibirg von Steirmark,12
Wilifred I, C of Cardena, 54
Wilifred I, C of Osona, 54
Wilifred I, C of Urgel, 54
Wiliswint md Roupert I, 169
Willa md Hugh, C of Vienne, 173
Willa md Silvion, 196
Willa of Arles, 94,263,332
Willa of Bavaria, 110,118,128A
Willa of Burgundy, 317
Willa of Camarino, 186,366
Willa of Tuscany, 198,263
Willa of Vienne, 175,343,366
Willebirg von Wulfingen, 213
William Bertrand, 197,198
William Berziers, 195A
William d'Agde, 226
William d'Avesnes III, C of Hainault, 50,70
William d'Avesnes III, C of Holland, 50,70
William d'Eu, C of Eu, 188,222
William d'Eu, C of Exemes, 188, 222
William d'Eu, C of Soissons, 188, 222
William d'Eu, C of Troyes, 188,222
William de Belleme, 360
William de Forez I, 317

William de Forez II, 317
William de Gometz, 89
William de Nevers, 61
William de Sabran, 116
William de Warenne md Gundrada, 135A
William de Warenne, E of Surrey, 56, 135,
William de Warenne II, 135A
William Garces I, C d'Armagnac, 289
William Garces I, C of Fezensac, 289
William I, C of Angouleme, 87
William I, C of Arles, 127
William I, C of Auxerre, 232,254
William I, C of Besalu, 347
William I, C of East Friesland, 72
William I, C of Geneva, 175,288
William I, C of Holland, 72,304
William I, C of Nevers, 232,254
William I, C of Poitou, 88,162,163
William I, C of Provence, 127,298, 333
William I, C of Turenne, 232
William I, D of Normandy, 89,140, 166
William I, K of England, 81,89, 140,141
William I, Mq of Provence, 298,333
William I, Sr de Dampierre, 56,84
William I, Sr de Montculon, 55A, 440
William I, Sr de Saint Geran, 55A, 440
William I, Vct of Marsaills, 194,298A
William von Weimar II, 211
William II, C of Angouleme, 87,157
William II, C of Arles, 298,
William II, C of Burgundy, 93,94,123, 149, 187,245,364,377
William II, C of Macon, 94,149,377
William II, C of Poitou, 88,340
William II, C of Provence, 298
William II, Sr de Montculon, 440
William II, Sr de Montpellier, 150

William II, Sr de Saint Geran, 440
William II, Vct of Marsailles, 298A
William III, Bg of Meissen, 27
William III, C in Eichsfeld, 27
William III, C of Angouleme, 87
William III, C of Forcalquier, 195,196
William III, C of Poitou, 88,119,150,
 161,203
William III, C of Toulouse,374, 375
William III, C of Weimar, 27,210,211
William III, D of Aquitaine, 88,162
William III, Mq of Provence, 195, 196
William III, Sr de Montpellier, 150
William IV, C of Albi, 374
William IV, C of Angouleme,
 187,87,
William IV, C of Auvergne, 127
William IV, C of Auxerre, 187,190
William IV, C of Carcassonne, 374
William IV, C of Dijon, 374
William IV, C of Forcalquier, 116,
 195
William IV, C of Macon, 187, 190
William IV, C of Perigord, 374
William IV, C of Poitou, 88,154
William IV, C of Rodez, 374
William IV, C of Toulouse, 160,374
William IV, C of Vienne, 187,190
William IV, D of Aquitaine, 88,340
William IV, D of Narbonne, 374
William V, C of Aquitaine, 119
William V, C of Poitou, 88,119
William V, D of Aqiitaine, 161
William V, Sr de Montpellier,
 142,150
William VI, C of Poitou, 88,160
William VI, Sr de Pontpellier, 150
William VII, C of Poitou, 160,177
William VII, D of Montferrier, 150
William VII, D of Montpellier, 150,
 377
William VII, Sr de Tortosa, 150

William VIII, C of Poitou, 88,159
William VIII, D of Aquitaine,
 88,154
William VIII, Sr de Montpellier,111,
 150
William IX, D of Aquitaine,88, 160,
 177
William le Pieux, 333
William of Gellone, 326,330
William Talvas de Belleme II, C of
 Alencon, 360
William Talvas I, C of Alencon,
 244, 245
William Talvas I, C of Montreuil, 244
William Talvas I, C of Ponthieu,
 244,245
William Talvas II, C of Montreuil,
 148,243
William Talvas II, C of Ponthieu,
 148,243
William the Conqueror, D of Norm-
 andy, 89,140,141
William the Conqueror, K of Eng-
 land, 89,140,141
William von Weimar I, C in Algaus,
 281
William von Weimar I, C in Helma-
 gau, 281
William von Weimar I, C in South
 Thur ingia, 281
William von Weimar I, C of
 Weimar, 281
William von Weimar II, C in
 Helmagau, 281
William von Weimar II, D of
 Thuringia, 281
William C of Agen, 329
William, C of Auxerre, 61
William, C of Eu, 57,222
William, C of Exemes, 222
William, C of Nevers, 61
William, C of Perigord, 326

380

## -Z-

CPSIA information can be obtained at www.ICGtesting.com
Printed in the USA
267569BV00008B/12/P